PRINTREADING

Part 2

For RESIDENTIAL AND LIGHT COMMERCIAL CONSTRUCTION

Fourth Edition

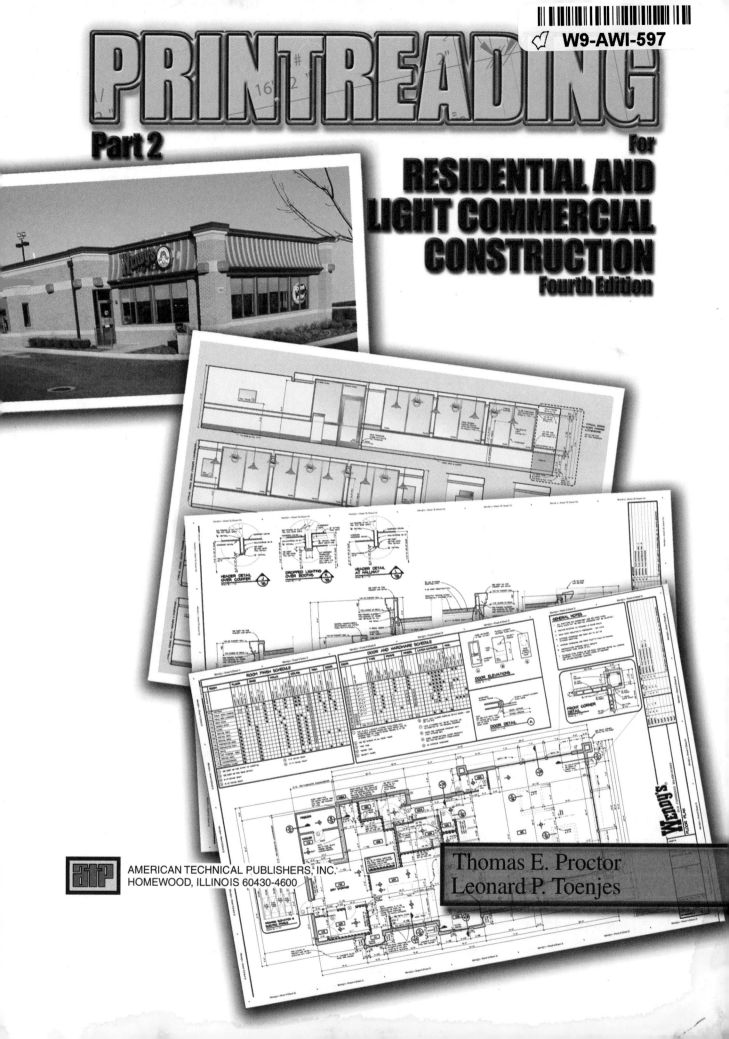

AMERICAN TECHNICAL PUBLISHERS, INC.
HOMEWOOD, ILLINOIS 60430-4600

Thomas E. Proctor
Leonard P. Toenjes

Printreading for Residential and Light Commercial Construction—Part 2, 4th Edition, and CD-ROM contain procedures commonly practiced in industry and the trade. Specific procedures vary with each task and must be performed by a qualified person. For maximum safety, always refer to specific manufacturer recommendations, insurance regulations, specific job site and plant procedures, applicable federal, state, and local regulations, and any authority having jurisdiction. The material contained is intended to be an educational resource for the user. American Technical Publishers, Inc. assumes no responsibility or liability in connection with this material or its use by any individual or organization.

American Technical Publishers, Inc. Editorial Staff

Editor in Chief:
    Jonathan F. Gosse
Production Manager:
    Peter A. Zurlis
Technical Editor:
    Michael B. Kopf
Copy Editor:
    Richard S. Stein
Cover Design:
    James M. Clarke
Illustration/Layout:
    James M. Clarke
    Erin E. Clifford
    Maria R. Aviles
    Thomas E. Zabinski
    William J. Sinclair
CD-ROM Development:
    Carl R. Hansen
    Sarah E. Kaducak
    Gianna C. Butterfield

4 5 6 7 8 9 – 05 – 9 8 7 6 5 4 3 2

Printed in the United States of America

ISBN 0-8269-0425-4

Acknowledgments

The authors and publisher are grateful to the following companies and organizations for providing plans, technical information, and assistance:

American Hardwood Export Council
APA—The Engineered Wood Association
ATAS International, Inc.
Autodesk, Inc.
Barclay and Associates
Barry R. Nelson & Associates Inc., Architects
Carrier Corporation
CertainTeed Corporation
Compass Consulting Group, LTD.
David White Instruments
Design Concepts Associates
Ductsox
ECO-Block, LLC
Ekroth, Martorano, & Ekroth, Architects
Elkay Mfg. Co.
Emory L. Jackson, Architect
The Garlinghouse Company
Harold L. LePere and Assoc. Inc., Architects, Planners, and Interior Designers
John Deere Construction & Forestry Company
JonesMayer Architecture, Inc.
Kohler Co.

Leica Geosystems
Mansfield Plumbing Products LLC
Marvin Windows and Doors
Merillat Industries
Metropolis Architecture and Interior Design
National Gypsum Company
National Wood Flooring Association
NIBCO, Inc.
Pella Corporation
Portland Cement Association
Rock Island Millwork
Rodger A. Brooks, Architect
Senco Products, Inc.
Simpson Strong-Tie Company, Inc.
Sioux Chief Manufacturing Company, Inc.
Southern Forest Products Association
Structural Insulated Panel Association
Tremco Barrier Solutions
Trus Joist, A Weyerhaeuser Business
United States Gypsum Company
Wendy's International, Inc.

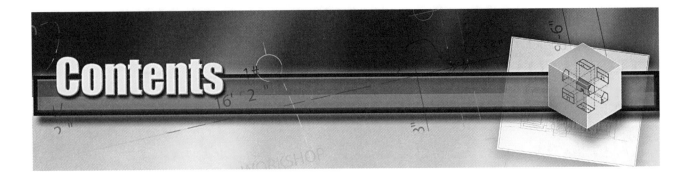

Contents

11   Quantity Takeoff   415

Quantity takeoff is the process of determining the quantities of materials to be included in a bid for a construction project, and is the initial step in preparing an estimate. Quantity takeoff totals are combined with labor, equipment, overhead costs, and other factors when preparing an estimate.

12   Final Exam   447

Chapter 12 is a comprehensive examination based on Chapters 1 to 11. Construction materials and techniques and general printreading concepts are addressed in the final exam.

A   Appendix   455

G   Glossary   487

I   Index   495

C   CD-ROM Contents

- Using This CD-ROM
- Quick Quizzes™
- Illustrated Glossary
- Wendy's Restaurant

- Printreading Tests
- Master Math™ Problems
- Media Clips
- Reference Material

Introduction

About Printreading for Residential and Light Commercial Construction—Part 2, *4th Edition*

Printreading for Residential and Light Commercial Construction—Part 2, 4th Edition, provides printreading experience in residential and light commercial construction. Printreading fundamentals, construction materials, and light frame construction utilized in residential and light commercial buildings are covered in detail. Heavy emphasis is placed on residential and commercial building code requirements and Americans with Disabilities Act (ADA) requirements. Expanded coverage is provided for construction materials including engineered wood products, exterior insulation and finish systems (EIFS), and electrical and mechanical systems. Chapter 11—Quantity Takeoff—provides an introduction to quantity takeoff principles and techniques for calculating quantities of structural components, finish materials, and mechanical and electrical systems.

Five sets of plans are included in the storage folder that accompanies the *Printreading for Residential and Light Commercial Construction—Part 2* book. These plans are discussed in detail in the associated chapters of the book and include the Brick-Veneer Residence, Multifamily Dwelling, Commercial Building, Branch Bank, and Wendy's Restaurant prints. The Multifamily Dwelling plans feature a modern light frame condominium unit. The Wendy's Restaurant plans and specifications are also included on the CD-ROM in the back of the book. Three trade plans provide an opportunity to develop additional printreading skills. A list of the plans is included in the storage folder.

The CD-ROM in the back of the book contains a wealth of information to supplement the book, including the following:

- Quick Quizzes™ provide an interactive review of topics covered in the chapters of the book. Each chapter Quick Quiz™ includes 10 questions. Each question screen includes textbook reference and glossary icons for obtaining related information about the question. A video icon appears on selected question screens and provides access to a media clip related to the question.
- An Illustrated Glossary provides a helpful reference to key terms included in the text. Selected terms are linked to illustrations and media clips that augment the definition provided.
- The Wendy's Restaurant Prints allow interactive navigation of the electronic version of the Prints. The electronic prints can be viewed on-screen for easy reference. The Wendy's Restaurant Specifications allow interactive navigation of the electronic version of the Specifications. Keywords can be located using the search feature.
- The Printreading Tests reinforce the ability to identify and interpret abbreviations and symbols commonly included on prints and provide an opportunity to apply critical thinking skills when reading prints.

- Media Clips provide a convenient link to selected video and animation clips.
- Master Math™ Problems provide formulas for interactive calculation and application of math-related concepts.
- The Reference Material button accesses links to web sites that contain useful related manufacturer and reference information.

Information about using the *Printreading for Residential and Light Commercial Construction—Part 2* CD-ROM is included on the last page of the book. Information about related training products is available on the American Tech web site at www.go2atp.com.

Using Printreading for Residential and Light Commercial Construction—Part 2, *4th Edition*

To obtain maximum benefit from *Printreading for Residential and Light Commercial Construction—Part 2*, 4th Edition, read each chapter carefully, noting the new terms introduced, elements detailed in the illustrations, and related information provided in the factoids and photographs. Identify and review the key concepts presented in the chapter before completing the Review Questions and Trade Competency Test included at the end of the chapter and the Quick Quiz™ included on the CD-ROM. Review Questions are based directly on the content included in the chapter. Trade Competency Tests are based on prints associated with particular chapters and other reference material such as the Appendix. Chapter 12—Final Exam comprehensively assesses mastery of information covered throughout the book. The Review Questions and Quick Quizzes should be reviewed prior to completing the Final Exam. Each of these learning activities provides an opportunity to reinforce and apply concepts presented in the chapter.

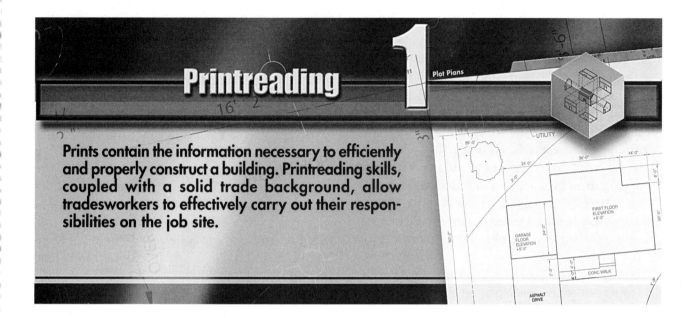

Printreading

Plot Plans

Prints contain the information necessary to efficiently and properly construct a building. Printreading skills, coupled with a solid trade background, allow tradesworkers to effectively carry out their responsibilities on the job site.

PRINTS

An architect works closely with a client or owner to determine building requirements, often developing sketches of the building or details to convey ideas to the client or owner. The sketches are developed into working drawings that contain the information necessary to complete the construction project. Working drawings are reproduced as prints and distributed to the contractors and subcontractors working on the project. The original working drawings are retained by the architect for safekeeping.

Print Processes

Prior to 1840 when the blueprint process was developed, architects drew working drawings in ink on heavy, durable paper. Each original drawing was the only one available during construction unless additional copies were made by tracing them on translucent (allowing light to pass through) paper or by making an exact duplicate on heavy paper.

When the blueprint process was developed, original working drawings were drawn on translucent paper using pencil or ink. Each original drawing sheet was placed over a sheet of paper that was treated with light-sensitive chemicals and placed in a glass frame to hold the sheets

together. The sheets were then exposed to a light source. Wherever lines, dimensions, or notations appeared on the original drawing, the areas on the sensitized paper were shielded from the light.

When the sensitized paper was washed with water, these shielded areas remained white and the light-exposed background turned a deep blue—thus the term "blueprint." One advantage of the blueprint process was that numerous blueprints could be made from the same original drawing. The blueprints were distributed to estimators, builders, and owners and the original drawings were stored in the architect's office to be used for additional blueprints as needed. Today, the blueprint process is rarely used as other, more efficient processes have been developed.

Xerox Engineering Systems
Electrostatic prints are produced using an engineering copier.

1

Many prints used today have blue or black lines on a white background and are made using the diazo or electrostatic process. Diazo prints, with their white background, are easier to read than blueprints. In addition, the white background provides a convenient area for writing field notes or noting required changes. Electrostatic prints are produced using the same process as used by office photocopiers. Full-size working drawings are exposed to light and projected directly through a lens onto a negatively charged drum, which transfers the image to positively charged copy paper. Many prints from large reprographic centers are produced from digital files using a laser printer process. The advantages of the laser printer process include easy enlargement and reduction of drawings, small storage size of the digital files, quick retrieval and duplication of the files, and reduced shipping costs.

Conventional Drafting

Working drawings are created using conventional drafting methods or computer-aided design. Conventional drafting tools include T-squares, triangles, compasses, scales, and pencils. Conventional drafting methods are utilized for small construction projects such as a garage or storage building.

Conventional drafting tools may be used to develop drawings for small buildings such as a garage.

Computer-Aided Design

Computer-aided design (CAD), also known as computer-aided drafting or computer-aided drafting and design (CADD), utilizes computers to produce architectural drawings. CAD systems are common in architectural and engineering firms because of their efficiency and the quality of drawings produced. Architects benefit from increased drafting productivity achieved in the planning, design, drafting, and reproduction of prints. CAD-generated prints provide consistent linework, symbol representation, and lettering. See Figure 1-1. CAD systems offer many advantages for architects when developing drawings, including the following:

- Consistency—uniform line width, symbol depiction, and representation of drawing components
- Changeability—revisions, additions, and deletions are easily made to the electronic file
- Layering—a method, similar to using overlays on conventional drawings, in which trade-specific information is added to a base drawing to generate trade-specific drawings such as mechanical plans
- Modeling—viewing a building in pictorial form and subjecting the model to engineering tests such as a stress test. See Figure 1-2.
- Storage—drawings stored on electronic media such as compact discs consume less physical storage space than paper drawings
- Duplication—an unlimited number of prints may be reproduced, each with original quality
- Information Management—information about the materials used in drawings is stored and updated as drawings are generated or changed, allowing the drafter to extract information for takeoff purposes

Virtual walkthroughs can be created from CAD files, allowing a potential owner to realistically view a building before it is constructed.

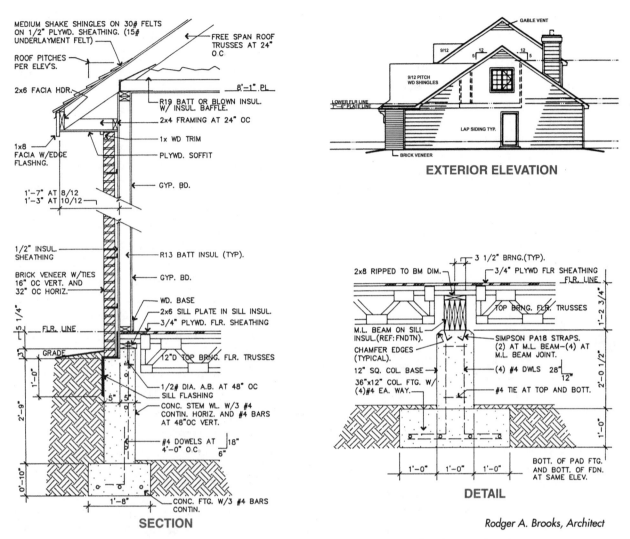

MEDIUM SHAKE SHINGLES ON 30# FELTS ON 1/2" PLYWD. SHEATHING. (15# UNDERLAYMENT FELT)

ROOF PITCHES PER ELEV'S.

FREE SPAN ROOF TRUSSES AT 24" O.C.

2x6 FACIA HDR.

8'-1" PL

R19 BATT OR BLOWN INSUL. W/ INSUL. BAFFLE.

2x4 FRAMING AT 24" OC

1x WD TRIM

1x8 FACIA W/EDGE FLASHNG.

PLYWD. SOFFIT

GYP. BD.

1'-7" AT 8/12
1'-3" AT 10/12

1/2" INSUL. SHEATHING

R13 BATT INSUL (TYP).

BRICK VENEER W/TIES 16" OC VERT. AND 32" OC HORIZ.

GYP. BD.

WD. BASE

2x6 SILL PLATE IN SILL INSUL.

3/4" PLYWD. FLR. SHEATHING

5 1/4"

FLR. LINE

12"D TOP BRNG. FLR. TRUSSES

GRADE

1/2# DIA. A.B. AT 48" OC SILL FLASHING

1'-0"

CONC. STEM WL. W/3 #4 CONTIN. HORIZ. AND #4 BARS AT 48"OC VERT.

2'-9"

#4 DOWELS AT 4'-0" O.C.

18"
6"

0'-10"

1'-8"

CONC. FTG. W/3 #4 BARS CONTIN.

SECTION

GABLE VENT

9/12

5   12   12   5

9/12 PITCH WD SHINGLES

LOWER FLR LINE
7'-6" PLATE LINE

LAP SIDING TYP.

BRICK VENEER

EXTERIOR ELEVATION

3 1/2" BRNG.(TYP).

2x8 RIPPED TO BM DIM.

3/4" PLYWD FLR SHEATHING
FLR. LINE

TOP BRNG. FLR. TRUSSES

1'-2 3/4"

M.L. BEAM ON SILL INSUL.(REF:FNDTN).

CHAMFER EDGES (TYPICAL).

12" SQ. COL. BASE
36"x12" COL. FTG. W/ (4)#4 EA. WAY.

SIMPSON PA18 STRAPS. (2) AT M.L. BEAM—(4) AT M.L. BEAM JOINT.

(4) #4 DWLS 28"
12"

#4 TIE AT TOP AND BOTT.

2'-0 1/2"

1'-0"

1'-0"   1'-0"   1'-0"

BOTT. OF PAD FTG. AND BOTT. OF FDN. AT SAME ELEV.

DETAIL

Rodger A. Brooks, Architect

Figure 1-1. Computer-aided design (CAD) systems are used for a wide variety of architectural applications.

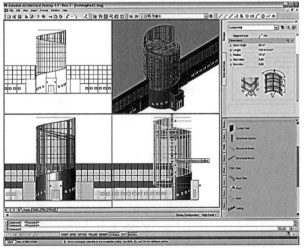

Autodesk, Inc.

Figure 1-2. Modeling allows a building design to be subjected to stress tests prior to construction.

CAD systems utilize hardware (computer equipment) and software (computer programs) to generate drawings. Hardware is the physical components of a computer system, including the input devices (mouse or trackball, keyboard, and scanner), central processing unit (CPU), and output devices (printer, plotter, and monitor). A variety of hardware is commercially available. Software allows the hardware to properly interact in the generation of CAD drawings, and captures information provided by input devices.

TYPES OF DRAWINGS

Pictorial drawings, such as isometric and perspective drawings, provide a sense of realism to the object being viewed. Pictorial drawings show the three principal measurements of height, length, and depth on one drawing. An orthographic projection shows the faces of an object projected onto a flat plan. A minimum of three orthographic views are typically used to describe most objects. Information regarding sketching pictorial and orthographic projections (multiview drawings) is included in the Appendix.

Orthographic projections are the most common type of drawing in a set of prints.

Isometric Drawings

An *isometric drawing* is a drawing in which the three principal axes are 120° apart. Since the principal axes are at an angle, the three principal faces are skewed. However, isometric drawings provide a realistic-looking view of the object. Isometric drawings are commonly used for piping diagrams to depict the arrangement of piping in a building. See Figure 1-3.

Perspective Drawings

Perspective drawings are the most realistic type of pictorial drawing. A *perspective drawing* is a pictorial drawing showing an object as it appears when viewed from a given point. Perspective drawings are commonly used as artist's renderings of a proposed building. The rendering allows a potential owner to visualize the overall appearance of the completed building and may be used for presentations to various zoning boards. See Figure 1-4.

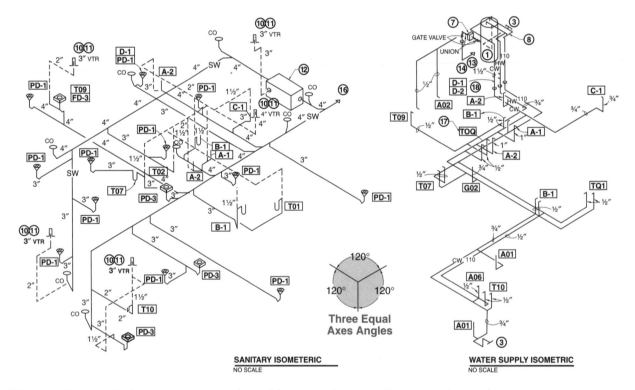

Figure 1-3. Isometric drawings are commonly used for piping diagrams. The principal axes of isometric drawings are 120° apart.

Figure 1-4. An artist's rendering utilizes perspective drawing techniques.

Orthographic Projection

An *orthographic projection,* or multiview drawing, is a drawing in which all the faces of an object are projected onto flat planes, generally at 90° to one another. The front, top, and right side views are most commonly shown. The top view is always directly above the front view, and the right side view is always directly to the right of the front view. See Figure 1-5. In orthographic projection, each view is shown two-dimensionally.

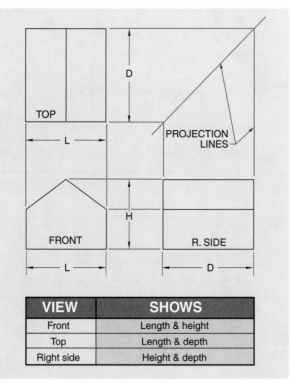

VIEW	SHOWS
Front	Length & height
Top	Length & depth
Right side	Height & depth

Figure 1-5. Each view of a multiview drawing shows only two dimensions.

Victaulic Company of America
Prints provide the information necessary to efficiently and properly construct a building.

Working drawings are drawn using orthographic projection techniques. The front, back, and right and left side views of a building are drawn as elevations. Top views are drawn as plan views on working drawings.

ALPHABET OF LINES

Lines should be properly presented on prints and used properly when creating working drawings. Line type guidelines are specified in ANSI Y14.2M—*Line Conventions and Lettering.* The American National Standards Institute (ANSI) is a private, nonprofit organization that coordinates national and international standards for U.S. companies, including many building trades standards. By drawing lines according to ANSI standards, an alphabet of lines is established and is easily read and interpreted. For example, a line that is always drawn with a series of equal-length dashes is immediately identified as a hidden line.

Line types used on drawings include object lines, hidden lines, centerlines, dimension lines, extension lines, leaders, break lines, cutting planes, and section lines. See Figure 1-6. Other line types may also be used on drawings. Refer to ANSI Y14.2M. All lines on working drawings must be sharp and dark so good-quality reproductions can be made.

Object lines are the most common line type used on prints. Edges or shapes that create visible lines are shown with object lines on prints. For example, object lines are used on elevations to show edges of doors and windows and the profile of the building.

Cutting planes for longitudinal and transverse sections are shown on floor plans.

ALPHABET OF LINES		
Line Type	**Conventional Representation**	**Use**
OBJECT LINE	*Most Common used* THICK *on prints*	Define shape.
HIDDEN LINE	⅛″ ⅟32″ THIN	Show hidden features.
CENTERLINE	¾″ TO 1½″ THIN ⅛″ ⅟16″	Locate centerpoints of arcs and circles.
DIMENSION LINE	DIMENSION LINE ⌐ ⌐ DIMENSION THIN 3'-0"	Show size or location.
EXTENSION LINE	EXTENSION LINE	Define size or location.
LEADER	THIN OPEN ARROWHEAD OR CLOSED ARROWHEAD x 3x	Call out specific features.
BREAK LINE	¾″ TO 1½″ THIN	Show long breaks.
BREAK LINE	FREEHAND THICK	Show short breaks.
CUTTING PLANE	¾″ TO 1½″ ⅛″ THICK ⅟16″ A A	Show internal features.
SECTION LINE	⅟16″	Identify internal features.

Figure 1-6. The alphabet of lines is specified in ANSI Y14.2M—*Line Conventions and Lettering.*

Lines that are not visible, such as those below a surface or behind an object, are represented with hidden lines. Lines above or behind a cutting plane are drawn as hidden lines in plan views. For example, wall cabinets are represented with hidden lines on plan views. Hidden lines are typically included on working drawings where they are necessary to provide information. Centerlines indicate the centers of symmetrical objects and are used to locate the centers of columns, windows, doors, and other openings.

Sections may be taken through walls or parts of buildings, such as windows or cabinets, to show greater detail. The location of each section, as well as the direction in which each section is viewed, is indicated by cutting planes, arrows, and identifying letters or numbers. Various building materials are represented by different section lines and material symbols.

Dimension lines are terminated by extension lines projecting from the feature being dimensioned. Dimensions are added above a continuous dimension line or centered along the dimension line. Break lines are used where an architect wishes to terminate a feature or show that the feature continues but is not drawn. See Figure 1-7.

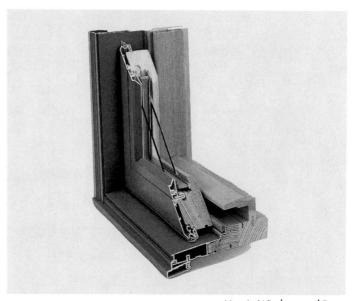

Marvin Windows and Doors

Sections are created by passing a cutting plane through a building component or portion of a building to show greater detail.

SIZE DESCRIPTION

Prints are drawn to scale and dimensioned to give a complete and accurate size description of the building. While different working drawings of a set of prints may be drawn to different scales, all parts of a single drawing are drawn to the same scale to clearly show size relationships. In addition, dimensions applied to the drawings establish particular sizes and locations of the features shown.

In Figure 1-8, the Shelf Detail is drawn to the scale of 1½″ = 1′-0″. The larger scale allows small features to be shown more clearly. The ¾″ oak varnished shelf is 5′-8″ above the finished floor. Oak braces, at 32″ on center (OC), support the 30° inclined shelf which projects 1′-4″ from the ⅝″ gypsum board wall. The note (N.I.C. BY OWNER) indicates that the shelf is not included in the contract and is to be supplied by the owner.

Scale

Scale is the relative size to which an object is drawn. It is impractical to create working drawings at actual or half size. Working drawings must be drawn large enough to clearly show all necessary information, yet must fit the drawing sheet specified for the project.

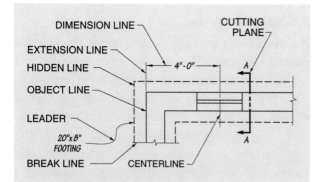

Figure 1-7. Each line on a drawing has a specific function.

While dimensioning and line type guidelines are published by ANSI, slight variations in dimensioning styles and line types may exist on working drawings.

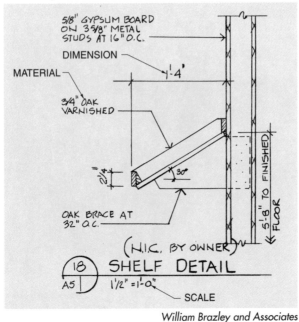

Figure 1-8. Prints are drawn to scale and clearly dimensioned to give a complete size description.

An appropriate scale must be selected to clearly show elements of the working drawings. The most common scale for working drawings is ¼″ = 1′-0″ (read "one-quarter of an inch equals one foot"). For most situations, a ¼″ = 1′-0″ scale provides an architect with enough space to draw working drawings on a reasonably large sheet and also permits the various parts of a building, dimensions, and notes to be clearly shown. The layout, size, and unique features of most buildings can be formed with a set of prints drawn to a scale of ¼″ = 1′-0″.

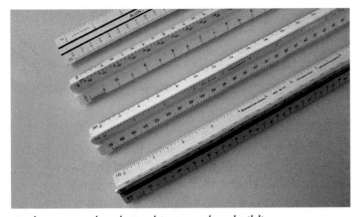

Scales are used to draw objects, such as building components, to a specific size and reduce or enlarge them proportionately.

When reading a print, first identify the scale of the working drawing(s) on the sheet. The scale is located in the title block or below the title of the working drawing. The scale provides a frame of reference when envisioning the size of a building or building component.

Other scales are used when necessary. For example, ½″ = 1′-0″ or ¾″ = 1′-0″ scales are often used to show room elevations and sections through walls. Details are often used to show small features at a larger scale. The 1″= 1′-0″, 1½″ = 1′-0″, and 3″ = 1′-0″ scales are often used for details. Conversely, floor plans of large buildings and large plot plans are drawn at smaller scales. Commercial building drawings may utilize a scale of ⅛″= 1′-0″. Plot plans are scaled with one inch on prints equal to many feet of actual length—for example, 1″ = 50′-0″.

Complex features may be drawn to a scale of 6″ = 1′-0″ (half size) or 12″ = 1′-0″ (full size). Large scales such as these are often required when molding or other trim pieces have special profiles that must be shown.

Architect's Scales

An architect's scale is used to draw objects to a particular size. Common architect's scales are triangular in cross section and have six faces. Five faces have two scales each and one face is divided into inches and fractional parts of an inch.

To use an architect's scale, place the 0 of the appropriate scale on one end of the line and read the largest increment falling on the other end of the line. Inches are read between the 0 designation and the scale size shown near the end of the architect's scale. The various scales can be read right or left—not both. See Figure 1-9. Scales that are multiples of one another are shown on the same edge to conserve space. For example, the ⅛″ = 1′-0 ″ and ¼″ = 1′-0″ scales are located on the same edge, with the ⅛″ scale read from left to right and the ¼″ scale read from right to left.

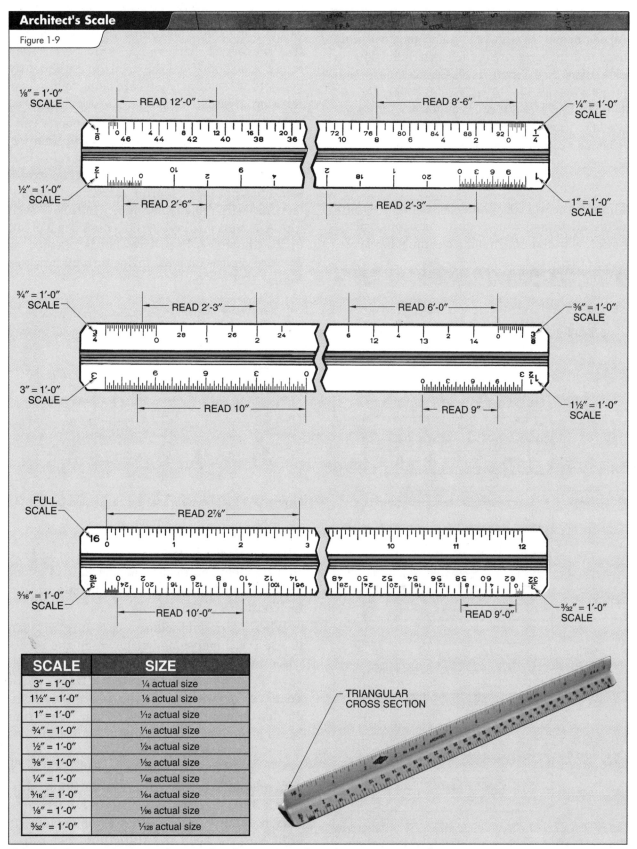

Figure 1-9. An architect's scale is used to draw most working drawings in a set of prints.

Engineer's Scales

An engineer's scale is a triangular, six-sided scale used to draw large areas such as building lots on plot plans. See Figure 1-10. Scales on an engineer's scale are 1″ = 10′, 1″ = 20′, 1″ = 30′, 1″= 40′, 1″ = 50′, and 1″ = 60′. Since engineer's scales are used for drawing large areas, the inch divisions of a foot on an engineer's scale are omitted.

Dimensions

Through the working drawings, an architect provides all dimensions required to construct a building. Individual dimensions must be correct so they total overall dimensions. All size and location dimensions should be verified to ensure they are correct. Tradesworkers must accurately read dimensions from the prints and frequently verify that the dimensions are being followed as work progresses.

Dimensions are shown to locate points from other points on the prints. Extension lines extend from a surface or other point of reference. Dimension lines terminate (end) on the extension lines and are generally drawn as continuous lines with dimensions appearing above each line. A dimension may also be centered in a break in the dimension line. Arrowheads, slashes, or dots are used as dimension line terminators. See Figure 1-11.

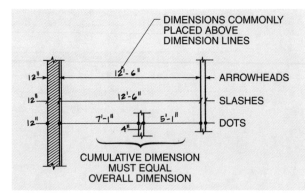

Figure 1-11. Dimension lines are terminated by arrowheads, slashes, or dots.

Dimensions on plan views and elevations are shown in feet and inches (such as 3′-0″, 4′-8″, or 28′-3″). A dash is placed between the feet and inch portions of the dimensions.

When laying out buildings, care must be taken to use the dimensions as shown on the prints while making slight adjustments for material variations. For example, interior frame partitions finished with gypsum board are usually indicated on prints as 4″ thick. When ½″ gypsum board is applied to both sides of 2 × 4 studs, the actual partition thickness is 4½″ (½″ + 3½″ + ½″ = 4½″). When ⅝″ gypsum board is applied to each side of 2 × 4 studs, the actual partition thickness is 4¾″ (⅝″ + 3½″ + ⅝″ = 4¾″). Adjustments must be made during layout to accommodate the difference between the stated dimension and actual dimension. A tradesworker responsible for

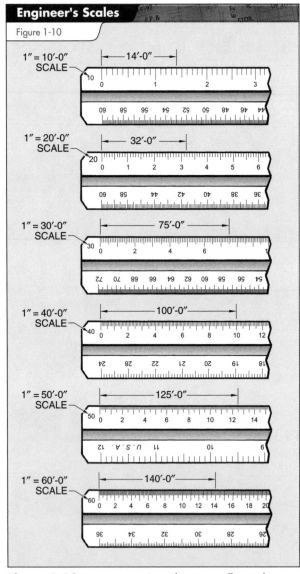

Figure 1-10. An engineer's scale is typically used to draw plot plans.

the partition layout lays out all partitions on the floor according to the dimensions of the floor plan and then centers each partition on these marks. Window or door openings near room corners must also be accurately laid out. Precise dimensioning is difficult in concrete work since it is difficult to erect rough formwork so precisely that dimensions will not vary slightly from the plans.

Dimensions should be positioned on working drawings to avoid confusion. The same dimension should not be shown twice, unless marked REF (reference). Eliminating redundant dimensions avoids cluttering the drawing with unnecessary dimensions and prevents the possibility of two dimensions referring to the same measurement not being the same.

SHAPE DESCRIPTION

Each working drawing in a set of prints represents a part of a building as an orthographic projection. Orthographic projection allows the individual parts of a building to be shown in their true shape and not distorted for perspective allowances as they would be on pictorial drawings.

Several working drawings may be required to clearly describe the shape and size of all components. In general, an architect draws only those working drawings required to completely show and describe the building. The most essential working drawings required include plot plans, floor plans, elevations, sections, and details.

Plot Plans

A *plot plan* is a scaled working drawing that shows the shape and size of a building lot; location, shape, and overall size of a building on the lot; and the finished floor elevation of the building. Other information, such as setbacks, may also be included on a plot plan as required by local ordinances.

Prior to the start of construction, a legal survey of the property must be performed by a licensed surveyor, who establishes the lot corners relative to official points of measurement in the vicinity. A survey drawing is provided to the architect, indicating the north compass direction, angles at the lot corners, locations of existing buildings and large trees, land contour, and other physical features of the lot. Utilities, including water, sewer, and electrical power may also be indicated.

When designing a building, an architect must comply with zoning ordinances and local building codes. Zoning ordinances restrict the use of land in each area of a town or city to single-family dwellings, multifamily dwellings, commercial buildings, or other designated building types. The front setback (minimum distance from street or front sidewalk to the building), side setbacks (minimum distances from the sides of the building to the property lines), and area covered by the building in relation to the area of the lot are some provisions of zoning ordinances. For example, zoning ordinances may stipulate that a commercial building can occupy no more than 40% of the lot size and that the minimum front setback is 65'-0" from the centerline of the street. Building codes may specify materials and methods of construction. For example, all-masonry buildings may be required in a commercial business development to ensure continuity of exterior appearances.

An architect must observe all zoning ordinances and building codes when drawing plot plans. Information provided in the survey drawing is shown and the new structure is located on the lot. A point of beginning is established on the lot. The *point of beginning (POB)* is a fixed location on a building site used as a reference for horizontal and vertical dimensions. The POB, in turn, is related to a benchmark or city datum point. A benchmark or datum point may be a concrete marker within sighting distance of the lot, a mark on a fire hydrant, the top of a sewer grate or access cover in the street, or another point established by the city as a local point of reference.

Benchmarks are also basic points of reference for vertical measurements. For example, a benchmark and the POB for a particular building are both at a height of 220′ above sea level. The finished first floor is at +224′ elevation and the basement floor is at +215′ elevation. The "+" designation indicates the number of feet above sea level. The finished first floor is 4′-0″ above the POB and the basement is 5′-0″ below the POB. A POB may be set at zero (+0′-0″) elevation. The finished first floor is then at +4′-0″ elevation and the basement floor is at –5′-0″ elevation.

The POB is used in excavation work in which the excavation must be at the proper location and depth. Concrete forms must also be set at the proper location and depth to ensure that the foundation and building walls are the proper distance from the property lines and that the first floor and basement elevations are correct.

When buildings are to be erected on sloping ground, information about the slope is shown on plot plans using contour lines. A *contour line* is a dashed or solid line on a plot plan that passes through points with the same elevation. Solid contour lines, commonly marked with "FG" (finished grade), represent the finished grade of the lot. Dashed contour lines represent the natural or existing grade. The lines are spaced at graduated intervals, such as 2′-0″ or 4′-0″ elevations, depending on the amount of slope. Contour lines are spaced closer together if there are significant changes in the lot grades. Contour lines spaced farther apart indicate less slope.

Figure 1-12 shows a typical plot plan. The POB, shown at the intersection of the existing sidewalks, is +0′-0″. Other information about grading and location of water, sewer, utilities, large trees, walkways, and driveways is also shown on the plot plan. The lot shown on this plot plan is 90′-2″ × 126′-4″ and contains approximately 11,300 sq ft. The opposite property lines on the plot plan are not the same lengths, and therefore the area obtained is an approximate value.

Existing sidewalks are located on the south and east sides of the lot. The sidewalks are 4′-0″ wide and are bordered by an 8′-0″ parkway. The sidewalks extend to the curbs of Green and Oak Streets. A utility pole is located on the north side of the lot. A utility pole indicates that electrical service will be installed overhead. Water and sewer lines extend under Green Street in front of the house.

The front and side setbacks are 30′-0″ from the existing sidewalks. The first floor elevation is +6′-0″ above the POB. Overall dimensions of finished floor space are 38′-0″ × 50′-0″ (less 8′-0″ × 14′-0″ on the northeast corner of the building). There are 1788 sq ft of finished floor space (38′-0″ × 50′-0″ = 1900 sq ft; 8′-0″ × 14′-0″ = 112 sq ft; 1900 sq ft – 112 sq ft = 1788 sq ft). The garage, which is 5′-0″ above the POB, contains an additional 576 sq ft (24′-0″ × 24′-0″ = 576 sq ft). The front porch length is not indicated on the plot plan, and no indication is made as to whether the front porch is open or enclosed. The front entrance of the house is reached by a 4′-0″ concrete walkway from the asphalt driveway, which exits into Green Street.

Total station instruments are used by tradesworkers to perform a variety of traditional leveling and plumbing functions. In addition, total stations are used to electronically measure distances and record and store data using an integral computer.

Floor Plans

A *floor plan* is a plan view of a building that shows the arrangement of walls and partitions as they appear in an imaginary horizontal section taken approximately 5′-0″ above floor level. Floor plans are views of a building as though cutting planes were made through it horizontally. A one-story building requires one floor plan. Buildings with more than one story generally require a floor plan for each level. Floor plans are considered to be one of the most used working drawings in a set of prints.

Exterior wall and interior partition locations are shown and dimensioned on floor plans. Door and window openings are indicated and dimensioned. Reference letters or numbers refer to door and window schedules, which show the type and size of door or window required at each opening.

Plot Plans

Figure 1-12

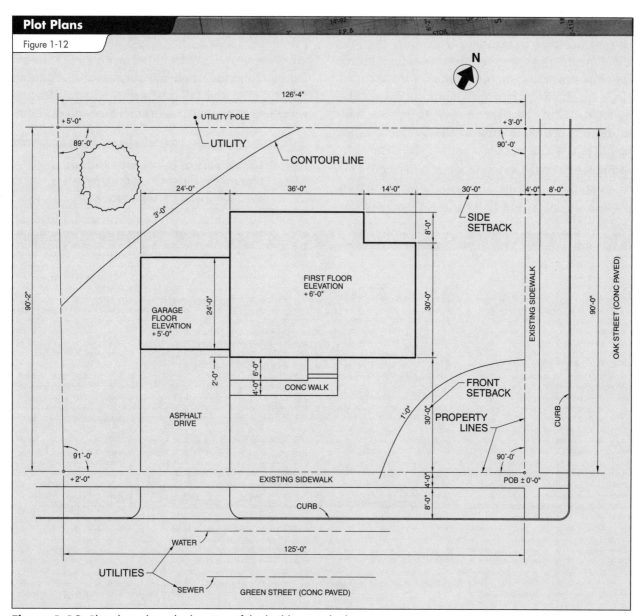

Figure 1-12. Plot plans show the location of the building on the lot.

Plumbing fixtures such as water closets, lavatories, shower stalls, and bathtubs are shown on residential floor plans. On smaller sets of prints, electrical information is included on floor plans. The general locations of receptacles, lights, and switches are indicated. On larger sets of residential prints and on commercial prints, electrical information is usually shown on electrical plans. Information pertaining to heating, ventilating, and air conditioning (HVAC) systems may also be shown on floor plans. Registers and grilles connecting to the system are located on floor plans. On larger sets of prints, HVAC information is usually included on mechanical plans.

When designing floor plans, an architect must consider the overall room relationships and their functions. For example, a dining room is placed adjacent to a kitchen in residential buildings. For multistory buildings, load-bearing walls and stairway openings must be provided. Wall and stairway openings must be placed so as not to compromise the structural integrity of the building.

Room volume in relation to floor space must be considered as an architect determines the ventilation and glass area requirements for a building. For example, the *International Residential Code* specifies the glass area for a room must be at least 8% of the floor area of the room. The minimum openable area to the outdoors must be at least 4% of the floor area of the room.

Figure 1-13 shows a portion of a floor plan for a commercial building. Dimensions are shown on dimension lines terminated by extension lines leading from the building. Slashes are used to terminate dimension lines. The loading dock area is 40′-0″ wide and is designated as Room 147. Doors leading from the loading dock area are designated 147-1, 147-2, and 147-3. The door schedule for this set of prints provides additional door information.

Larger sets of prints may include a legend that identifies the various symbols used on the drawings.

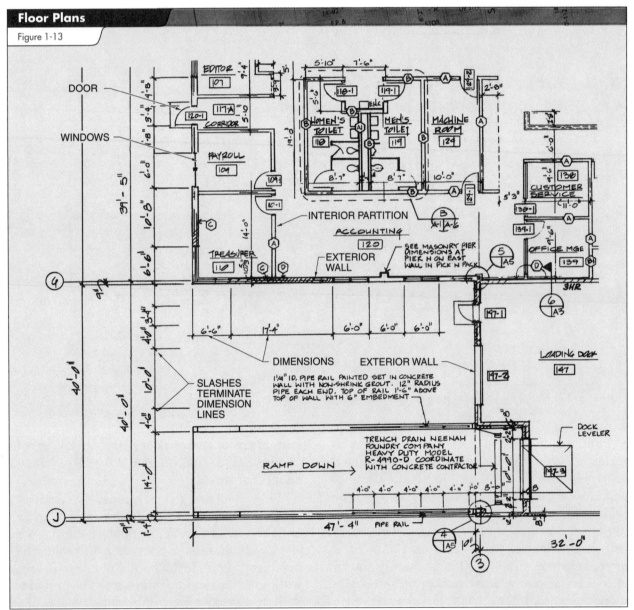

William Brazley and Associates

Figure 1-13. Floor plans show locations of exterior walls, interior partitions, doors, windows, and other components. The cutting plane is taken 5′-0″ above the floor.

Door 147-1 swings out from the loading dock area onto a floor-level landing (stoop) as required by the local building code. An outswinging door allows the door to swing outward and eliminates the hazard of a large group of people crushing others against an inswinging door. Doors 147-2 and 147-3 are overhead doors allowing for delivery or shipment of goods. Door 147-2 is at floor level.

The ramp leading to the overhead door (147-3) at the dock leveler has a 1¼″ inside diameter (ID) pipe rail on both sides. The pipe rails are set 1′-6″ above cast-in-place concrete walls. The masonry wall between the loading dock area and office portion of the building has a 3-hour fire rating.

Room 109 is the payroll office and has two windows. Room 110, belonging to the treasurer of the company, is a larger office and has four windows arranged in a corner unit. The letters in the hexagons indicate wall treatment. Wall treatment information is included in a schedule and details elsewhere on the set of prints.

The accounting area (Room 120) has four windows and serves as a common area to the payroll office, treasurer's office, office manager's office, customer service office, and the machine room. The 5/A5 reference refers to a steel column detail found on Sheet A5. The B/A-1—A-6 reference refers to a separate toilet detail found on Sheet A-6. Partitions around the water closets are handicapped accessible.

Elevations

An *elevation* is a scaled view looking directly at a vertical surface. Depending on building size, shape, and complexity, four or more elevations may be required to clearly show the exterior walls. Generally, however, four exterior elevations are sufficient—the Front, Rear, Right Side, and Left Side, or North, South, East, and West. The North Elevation of a building is the elevation facing north, not the direction a person faces to see that side of the building. Elevations are identified and the scale is provided.

The exterior elevation in Figure 1-14 is a portion of the Revised West Elevation of a commercial building. Masonry control joints (MCJ) are shown on both sides of the window units. Three of the masonry control joints extend the full height of the wall and two extend from the tops of the windows to the top of the wall.

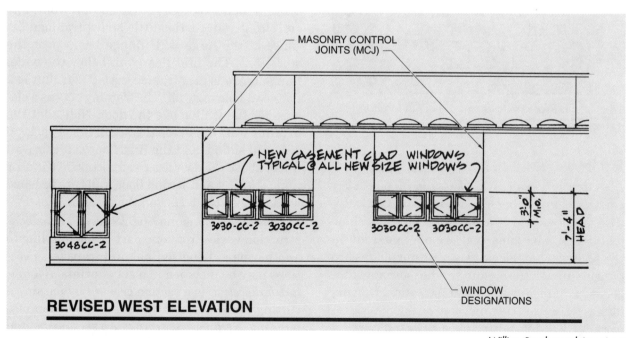

REVISED WEST ELEVATION

Figure 1-14. An exterior elevation is an orthographic projection of an exterior wall.

The head jambs for the casement clad windows are 7'-4" above the finished floor. The two corner windows are designated 3048 CC-2 and measure 30" × 48". The remaining windows are designated 3030 CC-2 and measure 30" × 30". The hinged sides of the windows are indicated by the apex of the hidden lines. Skylights shown on the lower roof are not called out in this elevation.

Interior elevations clarify size dimensions and locations of items such as appliances, fixtures, cabinets, mantels, and bookcases. The interior elevations in Figure 1-15 show a master bath. The floor-to-ceiling height in the bathroom is 8'-0". The walls are finished with gypsum board. A water closet (WC) is installed between the shower and vanity. The shower has a glass door and the vanity has two lavatories separated by an all-drawer unit. The countertop and backsplash are marble. Medicine cabinets, on each side of the mirror, are hinged along the outside edge.

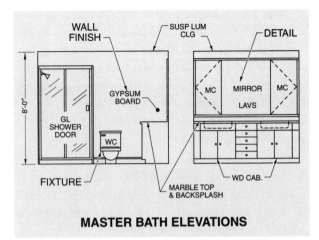

MASTER BATH ELEVATIONS

Figure 1-15. Interior elevations are orthographic projections of interior walls and partitions.

Interior elevations indicate the locations of built-in furniture, appliances, and lighting fixtures.

Sections

A *section* is a scaled view created by passing a cutting plane either horizontally or vertically through a portion of a building. Sections show features of a building that are not apparent on the plan views or elevations. Cutting planes are passed through the building at the most advantageous point to provide clear information. Cutting planes for sections are included on many types of working drawings. Direction arrows indicate the line of sight and a reference indicates the sheet on which the identified section is located.

The most common section is taken through an exterior wall. Exterior wall sections show foundation wall and footing details, wall and floor framing details, height of windows above the floor, eaves construction, and roof construction. The wall section in Figure 1-16 is a section taken through the storefront of a commercial building with a slab-on-grade foundation. The wall of the second floor portion of the building is a typical wood-framed wall using 2 × 4s. The wall is supported by a steel plate welded to the wide-flange beam, which is located above the storefront. The storefront wall carries little structural load because of the large wide-flange beam over the storefront. The first floor wall below the wide-flange beam is also framed with 2 × 4s, but is a non-load-bearing wall. The framing acts as a closure for the wall above the door. Note that the exterior wall finish for the second floor is 1 × 6 redwood siding, and the first floor exterior wall finish above the door is a fixed section of the door unit. The first and second floor walls are finished with ½" gypsum board on the interior.

Several sections may be required if the construction varies from one part of the building to another part. Longitudinal and transverse sections may be included in a set of prints. A *longitudinal section* is a section created by passing a cutting plane through the long dimension of a building. A *transverse section* is a section created by passing a cutting plane through the short dimension of a building.

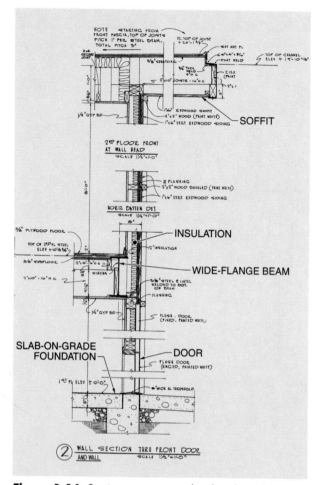

Figure 1-16. Sections are commonly taken through exterior walls and provide information about wall construction.

An offset section may be shown on a set of prints when an architect shows features such as windows or doors that are not in a straight line. The cutting plane for an offset section is bent or "offset" to allow the cutting plane to intersect the desired feature.

Details

A *detail* is a scaled plan view, elevation, or section drawn at a larger scale to show special features. Standard working drawings in a set of prints are generally drawn at a small scale and do not always show small details clearly. When this occurs, an architect draws a small part of a building at a larger scale or full size, if possible.

See Figure 1-17. Details are drawn of any part of a building that cannot be shown clearly and conveniently on working drawings.

WRITTEN DESCRIPTIONS

Working drawings show exterior walls, interior partitions, and other features of a building using lines, symbols, and conventional representations. Specifications and notations provide additional clarity and reinforce information presented on the working drawings. Specifications may consist of a few printed sheets or a book of several hundred pages, depending on the complexity of the project. A variety of notations may be included on a set of prints. This information is shown in one or more of the following four ways:

- Information is included in the title block.
- Descriptive information is placed near a specific item and connected with a leader terminated by an arrowhead or a dot.
- Specific information that refers to one building condition is noted near its location on the prints.
- General information applying to several sheets in the prints is placed in a convenient space.

American Hardwood Export Council
Details may be provided to show special features such as the construction of an elaborate handrail.

Details

Figure 1-17

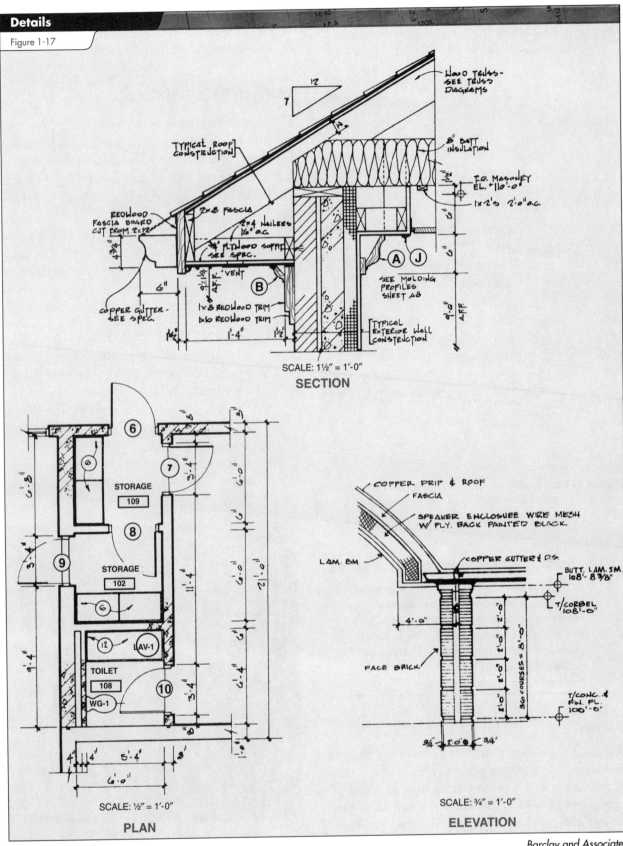

Barclay and Associates

Figure 1-17. Details are sections, plans, or elevations drawn to a larger scale.

Title Block

The title block is the best place to begin reading a set of prints. The title block includes the project name and location, architect's name and office location, architect seal, plan completion date, drafter initials, sheet number and number of sheets in the set of prints, name of the sheet, and other information as determined by the architect. See Figure 1-18.

CONVENTIONS

Depiction and description of relatively complex building parts is simplified using conventions such as abbreviations and symbols. An *abbreviation* is a letter or series of letters denoting a complete word. Standard abbreviations prevent clutter on working drawings and allow the drawing to be more clearly presented. A *symbol* is a pictorial representation of a structural or material component used on a print. Standard symbols allow common objects to be shown at a scale to fit the sheets on which plans are drawn and provide a consistent appearance for similar objects. Building components such as windows, doors, masonry, plumbing, and electrical parts are easily shown with symbols.

The American National Standards Institute (ANSI) is a national organization that helps to identify industrial and public needs for national standards. ANSI standards are commonly produced and co-published with ANSI and member technical societies, trade associations, and governmental agencies. Trade associations such as the American Welding Society (AWS), ASME International, and ASTM International are actively involved in standards development.

Abbreviations

Abbreviations are used throughout a set of prints to describe materials and processes while conserving space on the sheets. Abbreviations also save drafting time while presenting information in a standard manner.

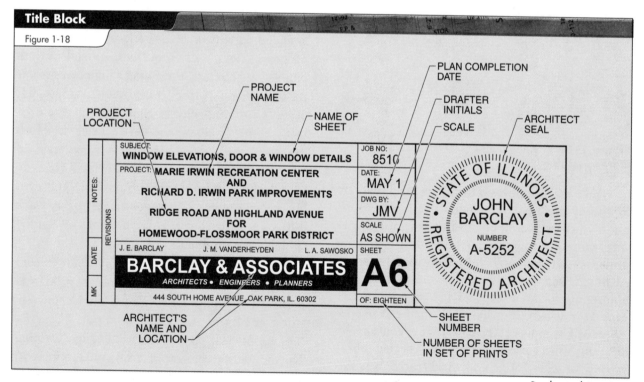

Barclay and Associates

Figure 1-18. Title blocks provide basic information for the complete set of prints.

Only uppercase letters are used for abbreviations. All abbreviations that make an actual word end in a period in order to distinguish the abbreviation from the actual word. For example, IN. is the abbreviation for inch and CAB. is the abbreviation for cabinet. See Figure 1-19.

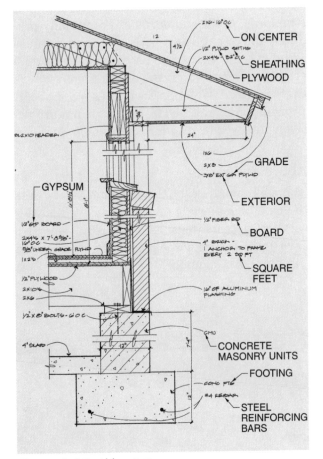

Figure 1-19. Abbreviations conserve space on drawing sheets.

While many abbreviations are accepted by virtue of their common usage, only standard abbreviations should be used on working drawings. Standard abbreviations eliminate confusion and misinterpretation of the working drawings. Although some words use the same standard abbreviations, an interpretation based upon the context in which they are used clarifies the specific use. Examples of the same abbreviations for different words are WF and R. WF is the abbreviation for wide flange and wood frame. R is the abbreviation for riser and room. A table of abbreviations is included in the Appendix.

Symbols

Prints use a variety of symbols to represent various building materials and components. Symbols are shown on plan views, elevations, sections, and details. Publications available from standards organizations such as ANSI include standard symbols used to represent the building materials and components. For example, ANSI Y32.9—*Graphic Symbols for Electrical Wiring and Layout Diagrams Used in Architecture and Building Construction* includes standard symbols representing various electrical devices and components. While standard symbols are recommended for use, symbols may vary depending on the architect.

Symbol appearance and consistency have improved with the use of computer-aided design (CAD) symbol libraries. Individual symbols are selected from symbols libraries and inserted into the working drawings in the proper position. All symbols representing the same objects will be shown with the same symbols.

Symbols represent structural or material components and commonly eliminate the need for descriptive notations. Electrical symbols represent components such as general outlets, convenience outlets, switch outlets, special outlets, panels, and circuits. Plumbing symbols represent fixtures, drains, piping, pipe fittings, valves, and other plumbing-related components. Architectural symbols represent earth, brick, concrete masonry units, stone, tile, glass, wood, gypsum board, and other building materials. Heating, ventilating, and air conditioning (HVAC) symbols represent valves, gauges, heaters, ductwork, diffusers, and other HVAC components. Symbol tables are included in the Appendix.

Figure 1-20 is a detail of the wall of a light commercial building. Standard symbols are used to depict building materials. The 2 × 6s below the storefront frame are shown using an "X" across the end of each piece, indicating rough framing. The foundation consists of a concrete footing with a CMU foundation wall. Insulation is shown in the 2 × 6 lower wall and above the header and top plate.

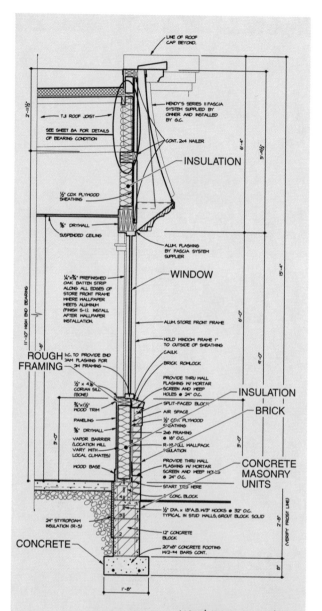

Wendy's International, Inc.

Figure 1-20. Symbols are used on details to clearly show different materials and components.

Windows

Windows are shown on plan views and elevations with symbols. Basic information such as rough opening size is included on plan views, elevations, and window schedules. Three classifications of windows are fixed-sash, sliding-sash, and swinging-sash. See Figure 1-21.

A *fixed-sash window* is a window in which the sash is inoperable. Fixed-sash windows are usually large and often fitted with insulating glass. A *sliding-sash window* is a window in which the sashes slide vertically or horizontally past one another. Sliding-sash windows include double-hung and horizontal sliding windows. A *double-hung window* is a sliding-sash window in which the two sashes slide vertically past each other. A *horizontal sliding window* is a sliding-sash window with sashes that slide horizontally past each other. A *swinging-sash window* is a window in which the sashes pivot to provide ventilation. Swinging-sash windows include casement, awning, and hopper windows. A *casement window* is a swinging-sash window with a vertically hinged sash that swings outward. Casement windows are available as singles, in pairs, or in multiples. The apex of hidden lines included on casement windows in elevations indicates the hinged side of the window. An *awning window* is a swinging-sash window that is hinged on the top rail of the sash with the lower rail swinging outward. A *hopper window* is a swinging-sash window that is hinged along the bottom rail of the sash with the upper rail swinging inward. Outswinging windows have screens toward the room side and are closed by roto-operators or lever mechanisms.

The Window and Door Manufacturers Association (WDMA) is a trade association that represents approximately 150 manufacturers of sashes, frames, window units, flush doors, panel doors, skylights, and patio door units for domestic and export markets.

Window Types

Figure 1-21

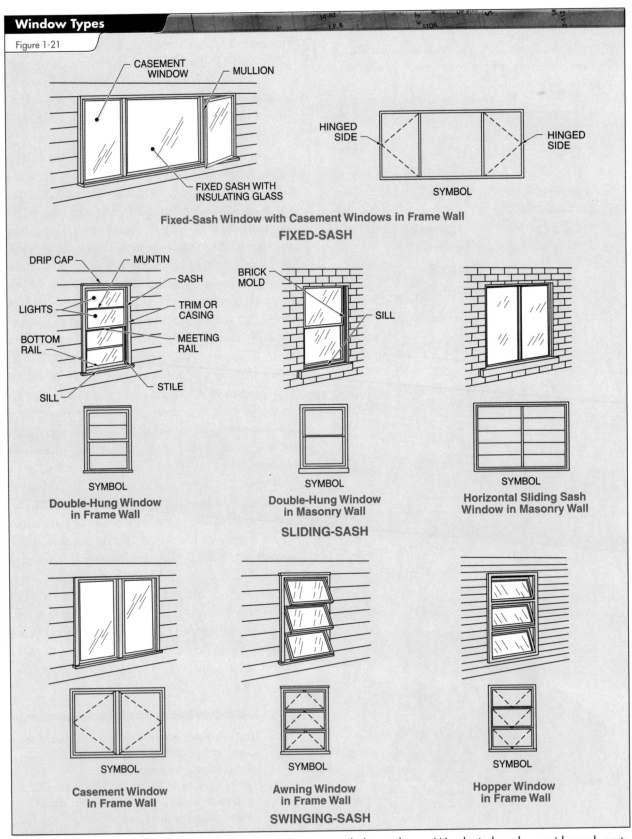

CASEMENT WINDOW

MULLION

FIXED SASH WITH INSULATING GLASS

HINGED SIDE

HINGED SIDE

SYMBOL

Fixed-Sash Window with Casement Windows in Frame Wall

FIXED-SASH

DRIP CAP

MUNTIN

SASH

LIGHTS

TRIM OR CASING

BOTTOM RAIL

MEETING RAIL

SILL

STILE

SYMBOL

Double-Hung Window in Frame Wall

BRICK MOLD

SILL

SYMBOL

Double-Hung Window in Masonry Wall

SLIDING-SASH

SYMBOL

Horizontal Sliding Sash Window in Masonry Wall

SYMBOL

Casement Window in Frame Wall

SYMBOL

Awning Window in Frame Wall

SWINGING-SASH

SYMBOL

Hopper Window in Frame Wall

Figure 1-21. Many lines are omitted when window elevation symbols are drawn. Wood windows have wider sash parts than metal windows. Windows in wood-framed walls have wood trim. Windows in masonry walls have a narrow brick mold. The hinged side of swinging-sash windows is indicated by the apex of a triangle made with hidden lines.

Since dimensions and notations are not generally repeated on a set of prints, it is often necessary to refer to a plan view, elevation, section, and a schedule to obtain all the information about a window. A plan view indicates the location of the windows from the corner of the building, from other openings, or both. Dimensions locating windows in frame walls or masonry-veneer walls are usually given to the centers of the windows. Dimensions for windows in solid masonry walls are usually given to the edge of the opening. See Figure 1-22.

Elevations provide information about the window type and its light (glass) size. See Figure 1-23. The light size is described using two numbers, such as 24/60, 24–60, 24 × 60, or 2460, unless there is a window schedule included in the working drawings. The first digits in the number represent the light width and the last digits represent the light height. For example, the light width of a 24/60 window is 24″ and the light height is 60″. Additional letters and numbers are often used to provide more information. When several windows are the same type and size, dimensions and light sizes are not shown for each window. Rather, this information is indicated for one window with a notation indicating that the window type and size are typical.

Windows are commonly combined in the same frame with other types of windows. Swinging-sash and fixed-sash windows are commonly combined in the same frame. Elevations show the arrangement of mullions. A *mullion* is a vertical member of the frame between the sashes. Hidden lines typically identify the swinging-sash window. When lines are not shown on one sash of a multiple casement window, one sash is fixed and the others open.

> The American Architectural Manufacturers Association (AAMA) and Window and Door Manufacturers Association (WDMA) identify the five classes of windows and glass doors as Residential, Light Commercial, Commercial, Heavy Commercial, and Architectural.

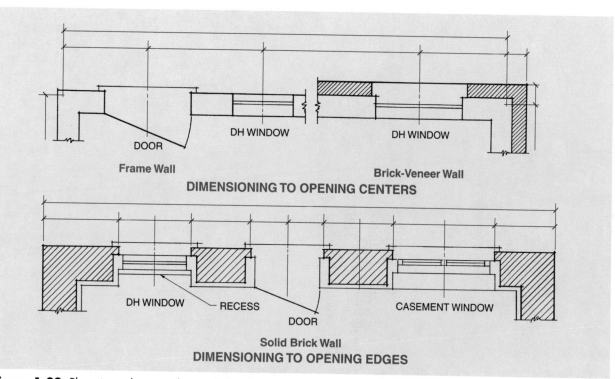

Figure 1-22. Plan views show window and door locations.

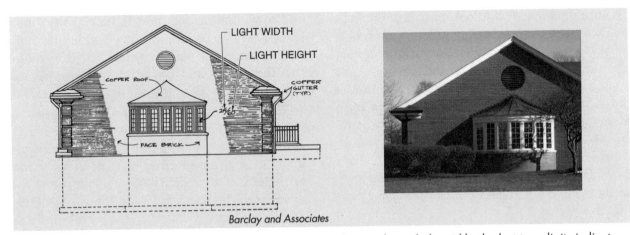

Barclay and Associates

Figure 1-23. Light size is shown on elevations. The first two digits indicate light width; the last two digits indicate light height.

The vertical location of the window in the wall can be shown in many places including sections taken through exterior walls and elevations. Window height may be indicated from the finished floor level to the top of the window stool (inside windowsill) or to the bottom of the top window jamb. See Figure 1-24. Dimensioning window heights to the bottom of the top window jamb is preferred since the top members of windows usually align horizontally.

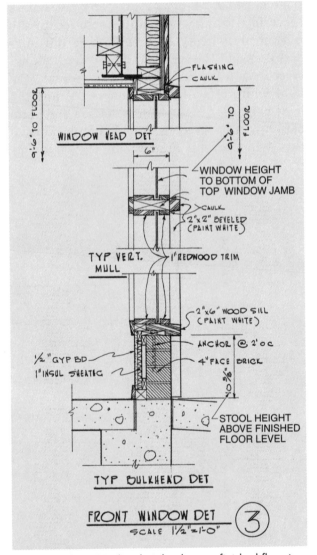

Figure 1-24. Window height above a finished floor is usually given to the bottom of the top window jamb.

Elevations and window schedules provide information about windows to be installed.

Most windows and frames are prefabricated in a manufacturing facility and are ready to install. Tradesworkers prepare exterior walls by erecting structural members on each side and above and below the opening. Prints provide dimensions locating the rough opening from the building corner or adjacent opening. After determining the window height above the finished floor, tradesworkers make allowances in the rough opening to allow the window to be adjusted to level.

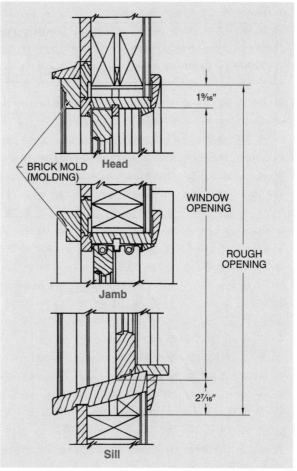

The National Fenestration Rating Council (NFRC) has developed a window energy rating system based on the performance of the entire window, including the frame, light, sashes, and other components. An NFRC label includes information about visible light transmittance, solar heat gain coefficient, and air leakage.

When windows differ from stock windows in trim or installation, a large-scale detail is shown on the prints. Figure 1-25 shows a detailed section through a double-hung window taken from a manufacturer catalog. The portion of the section labeled "Jamb" is a section of the window side jamb looking down that has been revolved into place. When reading the section, cover the portion labeled "Jamb." Note how the top and bottom sashes slide vertically in grooves formed by the window frame members. Rough framing members are shown as rectangles with diagonal lines.

Window schedules are typically included on a set of prints. A *schedule* is a detailed list on a print that provides information about building components such as windows, doors, and mechanical equipment. See Figure 1-26. A window schedule describes each window by type, size, and special features, such as insulated or tinted glass, and factory number. A letter or number code on the elevation or floor plan and on the schedule identifies each window. Often, window schedules are combined with door information as a door and window schedule.

Rock Island Millwork

Figure 1-25. A vertical cutting plane passing through the window head jamb and sill and a horizontal cutting plane passing through the jamb provide a detailed section of a window.

Wood Truss Council of America
Prefabricated building components, such as trusses, are constructed in a manufacturing facility and are ready to install.

WINDOW SCHEDULE						
Code	Quantity	Number of Lights	Glass Size	Sash Size	Rough Opening	Remarks
E	3	2	39" x 51" 39" x 19"	3'-6" x 6'-6"	3'-8¾" x 6'-8¾"	No. 4456 Fix Over 4424 Pella Multipurpose Windows
F	2	1	35" x 43"	3'-2" x 3'-10"	3'-4¾" x 4'-0¾"	No. 4048 Fix Pella Multipurpose Windows
G	1	1	15" x 35"	1'-6" x 3'-2"	1'-8¾" x 3'-4¾"	No. 4020 Pella Multi-purpose Window
H	2	1	15" x 27"	1'-6" x 2'-6"	1'-8¾" x 2'-8¾"	No. 3220 Pella Multi-purpose Windows

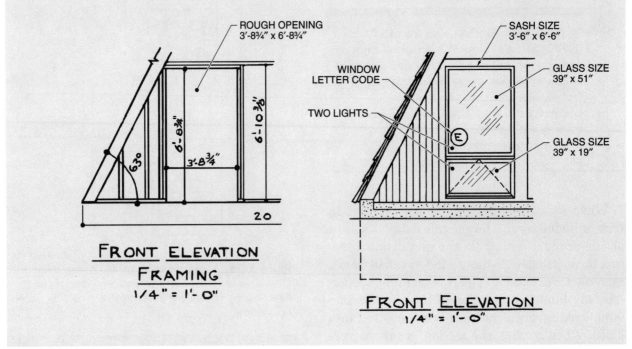

The Garlinghouse Company

Figure 1-26. Window schedules describe each window by type, size, and special features. The window manufacturer's product number is often included in a window schedule.

Doors

Door classifications include swinging, accordion, pocket, sliding, and bifold doors. The symbol for swinging doors on plan views is a single line with an arc to show the direction of swing. See Figure 1-27. Other symbols are used for other door classifications. *Door hand* is the direction in which a door swings. When determining door hand, the viewer always stands on the outside of the door. The outside may be a hallway or the street side of an entrance door. For doors that open between rooms, the keyed side of the lock is considered the outside.

Reference letters, which are keyed to a door schedule, are commonly placed on floor plans. The door schedule provides information such as the size, type, description, and the manufacturer number. Doors may also be described by notations at each door and descriptions in the specifications. The designation 2'-8" × 6'-8" × 1¾" indicates the door width, height, and thickness, respectively.

Door Symbols and Hands
Figure 1-27

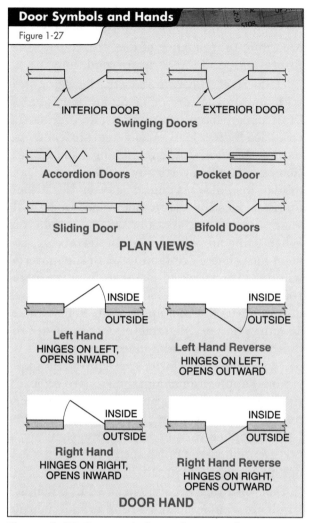

PLAN VIEWS

DOOR HAND

Figure 1-27. Door symbols are shown on plan views. Door hand is the direction in which a door swings.

Door Types
Figure 1-28

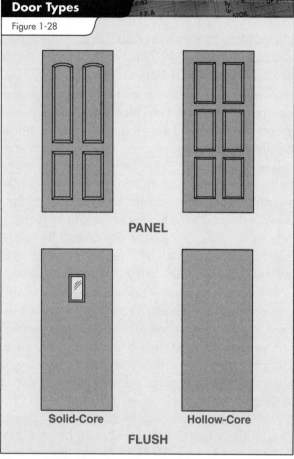

PANEL

Solid-Core Hollow-Core

FLUSH

Figure 1-28. Two general types of doors are panel doors and flush doors.

Two general types of doors are panel and flush doors. See Figure 1-28. A *panel door* is a door with individual panels between the stiles and rails. A *flush door* is a door with flat surfaces on each side; the stiles and rails are concealed within the door.

Some doors are also designated as fire doors. A *fire door* is a fire-resistant door and assembly, including the frame and hardware, commonly equipped with an automatic door closer. The five classifications of door openings for fire door installation are Class A, B, C, D, and E. The classifications are based on the time that a door opening withstands penetration by fire. See Figure 1-29.

Class	Time	Application
A	3	Walls separating buildings or dividing one building into separate fire areas
B	1 to 1½	Enclosures of vertical egress in a structure, such as stairways and elevators
C	¾	Hallways and room partitions
E	1½	Exterior walls subject to fire exposure from outside the structure
F	¾	Exterior walls subject to moderate to light fire exposure

FIRE DOOR OPENING CLASSIFICATIONS

* in hr

Figure 1-29. Fire door classifications are based on the time that a door opening withstands failure and penetration by fire.

Both leaves of a pair of hinged swinging fire doors must have latch bolts to secure the door when it is closed.

Wood Doors. Stiles and rails of flush wood doors are covered with veneer plies with adjacent plies placed at right angles to minimize movement and warpage of the door. Two types of wood doors are solid-core and hollow-core.

A *solid-core door* is a wood door with a core constructed of solid wood blocks or particleboard glued together and covered with veneer plies. Solid-core doors are heavier, resist sound transmission better, and have less tendency to warp than hollow-core doors. Solid-core doors are weather-resistant and commonly used for exterior openings. Three hinges are required to properly hang solid-core doors. Solid-core doors are also manufactured with a fire-resistant mineral core and are available with various fire ratings.

A *hollow-core door* is a wood door with a core constructed of corrugated wood or fiber and covered with veneer plies. The edges are banded with wood stiles and rails for securing hardware. Hollow-core doors are not permitted for use in exterior openings, as they do not have sufficient strength or fire resistance. Building codes require that interior doors be at least 1⅜″ thick. Due to their light weight, only two hinges may be required to properly hang hollow-core doors.

Panel doors are constructed of solid wood strips or wood planks arranged in various patterns and rabbeted (grooved) to hold thin panels. Panel doors are used for both exterior and interior doors in buildings with traditional architecture.

Flush or panel prehung (package) doors may be specified for residential or light commercial construction. A *prehung door* is a wood or metal door which is hung in the frame with hardware installed. Prehung doors are delivered to the job site ready for installation.

Metal Doors. Metal doors are utilized in heavy traffic areas and where fire resistance is required. Metal frames and doors are commonly referred to as hollow metal frames and doors. The National Association of Architectural Metal Manufacturers (NAAMM) is a trade association that represents manufacturers of architectural metal products such as metal doors and frames. NAAMM publishes a variety of specifications and standards related to hollow metal frames and doors. Metal frames and doors are installed for commercial and residential applications according to frequency of use, traffic patterns, fire ratings, and temperature conditions.

Hollow metal doors are constructed using steel stiffeners in the core or using an impregnated kraft paper, foam, or mineral blocking as the core. See Figure 1-30. When steel stiffeners are used in the core, steel channels or Z-shaped sections are installed vertically in the core and foam or fiber insulation is placed between the stiffeners. Steel face sheets are spot welded to the stiffeners to enclose the stiffeners and insulation. When using an impregnated-material core, the steel face sheets are laminated to the material using a structural adhesive. Minimum metal thicknesses are specified for metal door faces depending on the door application. For example, 16 gauge (ga) or 18 ga metal door faces are required for commercial applications while 12 ga or 14 ga metal door faces are required for institutional applications. Metal doors are typically finished with a primer at the factory. The doors may also be finished with a baked enamel finish, an applied finish such as vinyl cladding, a textured, embossed finish such as stainless steel, or a polished metal finish.

Door openings are dimensioned in a manner similar to window openings. Centerlines indicate the center of each door opening. Dimension lines from corners or adjacent building members provide horizontal location information.

Building Codes—Doors. Building codes related to doors, exits, and passageways leading to doors are specific to ensure the safety of the occupants exiting the building in an emergency. Exits and passageways must be designed according to all applicable building codes to provide safe egress from a building. Specific code requirements for doors, exits, and passageways are based on the type of occupancy, such as residential or commercial, and the anticipated occupancy of the building.

A wall with a revolving door must also have a hinged swinging door within 10′ of the revolving door.

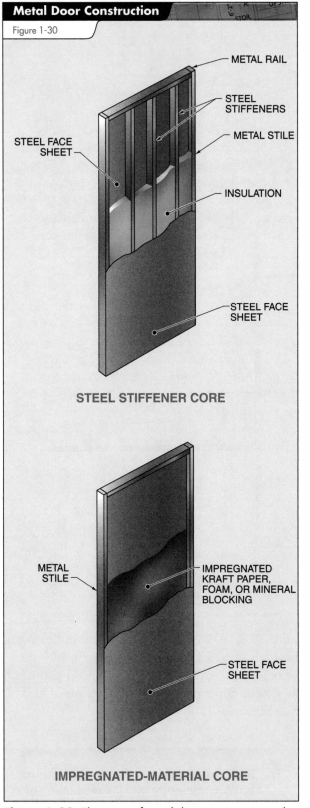

Metal Door Construction

Figure 1-30

METAL RAIL

STEEL STIFFENERS

METAL STILE

STEEL FACE SHEET

INSULATION

STEEL FACE SHEET

STEEL STIFFENER CORE

METAL STILE

IMPREGNATED KRAFT PAPER, FOAM, OR MINERAL BLOCKING

STEEL FACE SHEET

IMPREGNATED-MATERIAL CORE

Figure 1-30. The cores of metal doors are constructed of steel stiffeners or impregnated material.

Per the *International Residential Code,* each dwelling unit must have at least one exit door to provide direct egress from the habitable rooms of the building without going through a garage. Exit doors should be at least 3′-0″ × 6′-8″ × 1¾″, and must be readily openable from the side on which occupants are exiting. The minimum width of hallways and other exit passageways is 3′-0″. A floor or landing must be provided on each side of an exit door except for sliding doors. The floor or landing at the door should not be more than 1½″ below the top of the threshold and must be at least 36″ long measured in the direction of travel.

Per the *International Building Code,* which applies to commercial construction, the minimum width of doors should provide a clear width not less than 32″ and must be sufficient for the occupancy load of the building. The clear width of the door is measured between the door face and the stop with the door opened 90°. When double doors without a mullion are installed, one of the doors must provide a clear width not less than 32″. The maximum width of a swinging door is 48″. Additional building exits (other than elevators) are required where occupancy loads exceed a minimum number of people. Special doors, such as revolving doors, sliding doors, and overhead doors, may not be used as permitted exits. Exit passageways must be at least 44″ wide except when serving an occupancy load of less than 50. For occupancy loads less than 50, exit passageways should not be less than 36″ wide. See Figure 1-31. Landings must be provided at all doors and should not be less than the width of the door. Doors in the fully opened position should not reduce the required landing dimension by more than 7″. Landings must be at least 44″ long measured in the direction of travel.

In commercial buildings, location of exits and distance to exits are determined by the size and layout of the room or building. For example, a classroom with an occupancy load of over 50 people must have two doors placed a distance apart that is not less than one-half the maximum overall diagonal length of the classroom.

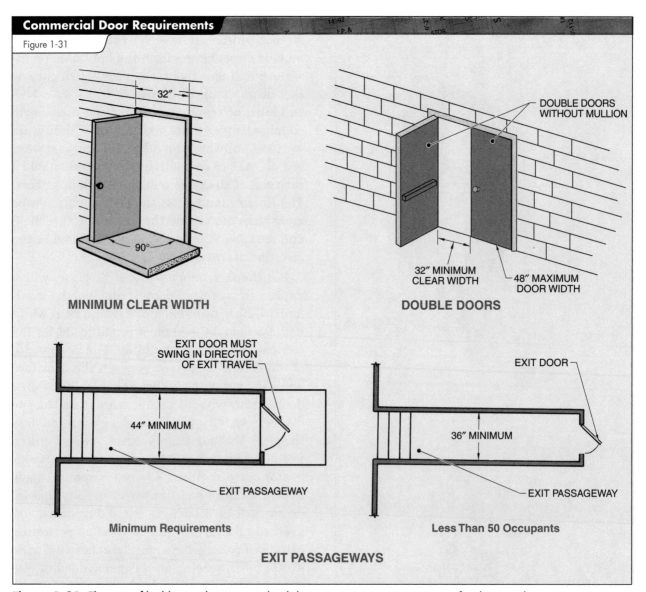

Figure 1-31. The type of building and occupancy load determine minimum requirements for doors and exit passageways.

Exit doors serving hazardous areas or with occupancy levels of 50 people or more must swing in the direction of exit travel. The force required to open these exit doors should not exceed 30 lb applied to the latch side. Exit doors must be openable from the inside without using a key or special effort, or applying any special knowledge.

Stairways

Stairways are typically represented on plan views using a series of parallel lines indicating the risers. Notations such as "14 R UP" (14 risers up)

and "13 R DOWN" (13 risers down) indicate the number of risers to the floor immediately above or below. An arrow with the notation points up or down, depending on the direction of travel. See Figure 1-32.

Stairways within a dwelling unit must have a minimum of 10 footcandles of illumination at every tread nosing. A footcandle (fc) is a measure of illuminance equal to 1 lumen/sq ft.

The *total rise* of a stairway is the vertical distance from the surface of the lower floor to the surface of the floor above. The *total run* of a stairway is the horizontal distance from the face of the bottom riser to the face of the top riser. The *unit rise* is vertical distance from the top of one tread to the top of an adjoining tread in a stairway. The *unit run* is the width of a stair tread not including the nosing.

Local building codes usually provide a means of calculating safe and proper stair ratios. A *stair ratio* is the relationship between riser height (R) and tread width (T) in a stairway. Two common stair ratio formulas are as follows:

$$T + R = 17'' \text{ to } 18''$$

$$T + R + R = 24'' \text{ to } 27''$$

Applying the first stair ratio formula, riser heights and tread widths commonly specified are as follows:

Riser		Tread		Total
6″	+	11″	=	17″
6½″	+	11½″	=	18″
6¾″	+	11¼″	=	18″

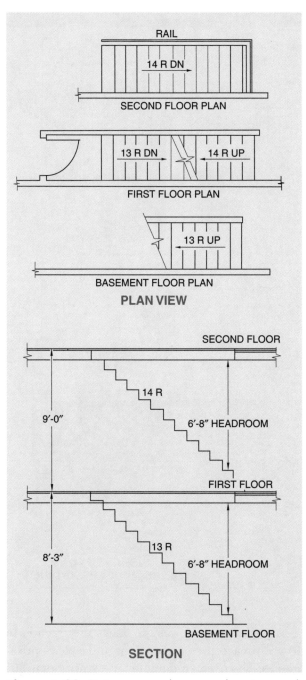

Figure 1-32. Stairways are shown on plan views and sections.

In multistory buildings, stairs may be straight-run, straight-run with a landing, L-shaped with a landing, U-shaped with a landing, L-shaped with winders, U-shaped with winders, circular, or spiral. See Figure 1-33. Other shapes may be developed through combinations of the basic shapes.

American Hardwood Export Council

Building codes specify minimum tread depths and maximum riser heights for stairways.

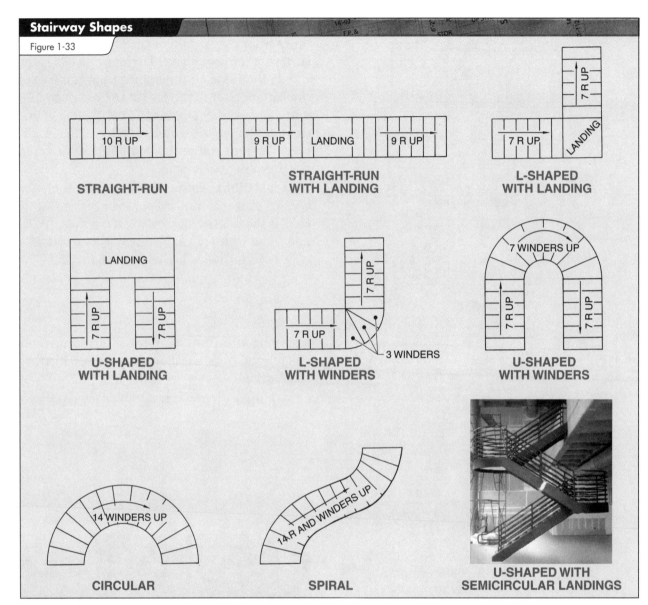

Figure 1-33. Stairway shapes are shown on plan views.

Riser form boards should be beveled at the bottom to allow the entire tread to be troweled.

Architects must design risers and treads to fit within accepted dimensions and code requirements. The preferred angle for a stairway is 30° to 35°. Less of an angle produces large total runs. Steeper angles do not facilitate easy climbing. See Figure 1-34.

Building Codes—Stairways. Stairways with two or more risers must comply with building code requirements. Commercial and residential stairways have different building code requirements. Commercial stairways have additional requirements based on the anticipated building occupancy and use of the stairway.

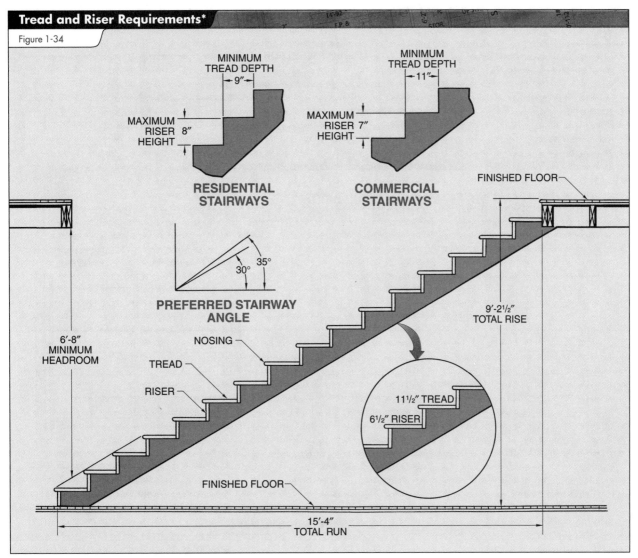

Tread and Riser Requirements*

Figure 1-34

MINIMUM
TREAD DEPTH
←9"→

MINIMUM
TREAD DEPTH
←11"→

MAXIMUM
RISER 8"
HEIGHT

MAXIMUM
RISER 7"
HEIGHT

**RESIDENTIAL
STAIRWAYS**

**COMMERCIAL
STAIRWAYS**

FINISHED FLOOR

35°
30°

**PREFERRED STAIRWAY
ANGLE**

NOSING

TREAD

RISER

9'-2½"
TOTAL RISE

6'-8"
MINIMUM
HEADROOM

11½" TREAD

6½" RISER

FINISHED FLOOR

15'-4"
TOTAL RUN

* *based on the* International Residential Code *and* International Building Code

Figure 1-34. Minimum headroom for stairways is 6'-8". The preferred stairway angle is 30° to 35°.

Per the *International Building Code,* maximum riser height is 7" and minimum riser height is 4" measured vertically between leading edges of adjacent treads. Minimum tread depth is 11" measured horizontally between the foremost projections of adjacent treads. See Figure 1-35. The difference in riser heights and tread depths in a stairway should not exceed ³⁄₁₆". The minimum headroom for all portions of a stairway is 80" measured vertically from an inclined plane formed by adjacent tread nosings. A landing or floor must be provided at the top and bottom of stairways. The landing width should not be less than the stairway width. Landings must have a minimum dimension measured in the direction of travel equal to the stairway width, and should not exceed 48" where the stairway has a straight run. A stairway should not have a vertical rise greater than 12'-0" between floors or landings.

Always refer to the building code in effect in the particular jurisdiction regarding information about permitted stairway dimensions.

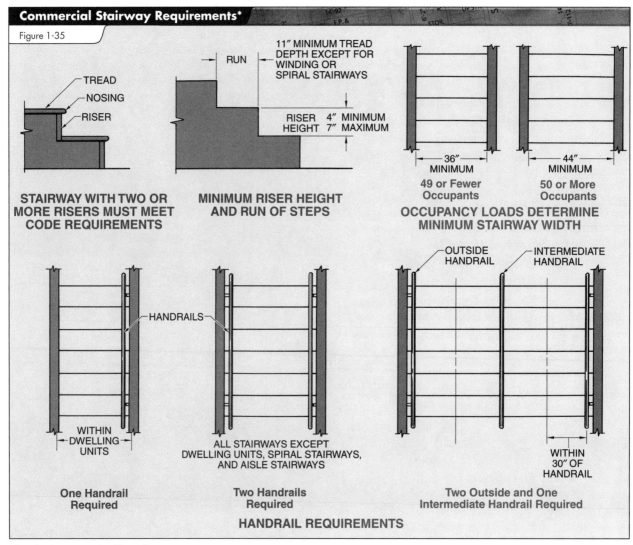

Figure 1-35. Commercial stairway requirements differ from residential stairway requirements. Stairways with two or more risers must comply with minimum requirements.

National Wood Flooring Association
Handrails must be provided for stairways with two or more risers.

Stairway width is based on the building occupancy. Stairways in buildings equipped with sprinkler systems are not required to be as wide as stairways in buildings without sprinkler systems. Stairways serving occupancy loads of 49 people or less must have a minimum width of 36″. Handrails must be provided for stairways with two or more risers. One handrail is required for stairways within dwelling units, spiral stairways, and aisle stairways. Handrails must be provided on both sides of all other stairways. Intermediate handrails are required on wide stairways so all portions of the stairway width are within 30″ of a handrail. The handrail height must be a minimum of 34″ and a maximum of 38″ above the tread nosings. A clear space not less than 1½″ must be provided between the adjacent wall and handrail.

Per the *International Residential Code,* which applies to one- and two-family dwellings, maximum riser height is 7¾″, which is measured vertically between leading edges of adjacent treads. Minimum tread depth is 10″, which is measured horizontally between the foremost projections of adjacent treads. The difference in riser heights and tread depths in a stairway should not exceed ⅜″. Minimum headroom for all portions of a stairway is 6′-8″ measured vertically from the inclined plane formed by adjacent tread nosings. A landing or floor must be provided at the top and bottom of stairways. The landing width should not be less than the stairway width and have a minimum dimension of 36″ measured in the line of travel.

Residential stairways should be a minimum of 36″ wide and handrails must not project more than 4½″ on either side of the stairway. Minimum clear stairway width should not be less than 31½″ when a handrail is installed on one side or 27″ when handrails are installed on both sides of the stairway. Handrails must be provided on at least one side of the stairway a minimum of 34″ and a maximum of 38″ above the tread nosings. A clear space not less than 1½″ must be

provided between the adjacent wall and handrail. Ends of handrails must return or be terminated at newel posts or safety terminals. The cross-sectional area of a handrail must be 1¼″ minimum or 2″ maximum. See Figure 1-36.

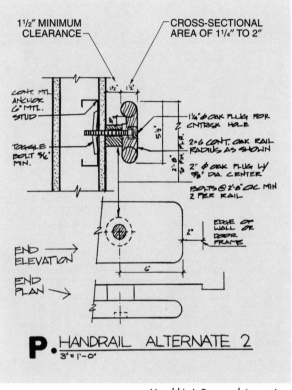

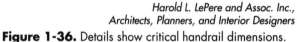

Harold L. LePere and Assoc. Inc.,
Architects, Planners, and Interior Designers

Figure 1-36. Details show critical handrail dimensions.

Printreading **Review Questions**

Name _____ Date _____

Multiple Choice

_____*C*_____ **1.** A ___° angle is formed between the axes in isometric drawings.
  A. 60
  B. 90
  C. 120
  D. 180

_____*B*_____ **2.** Cutting planes for sections are generally shown on ___.
  A. elevations
  B. floor plans
  C. details
  D. all of the above

_____*A*_____ **3.** Orthographic projections are also referred to as ___ drawings.
  A. multiview
  B. pictorial
  C. isometric
  D. oblique

_____*A*_____ **4.** For a hazardous area or when the occupancy load of a building exceeds 50 occupants, ___.
  A. exit doors must swing in the direction of travel
  B. force required to open exit doors shall not exceed 40 lb
  C. exit doors must swing inward
  D. none of the above

_____*A*_____ **5.** Dimensions on a print show ___.
  A. size
  B. location
  C. size relationship of parts
  D. all of the above

_____*B*_____ **6.** The most commonly used scale for working drawings is ___.
  A. ⅛″ = 1′-0″
  B. ¼″ = 1′-0″
  C. 1′-0″ = ⅛″
  D. 1′-0″ = ¼″

_____ **7.** Finished grade is shown on a plot plan with ___ contour lines.
   A. solid
   B. dashed
   C. dotted
   D. broken

_____ **8.** ___ is a method of viewing an object in a pictorial form.
   A. Layering
   B. Modeling
   C. Wire-framing
   D. none of the above

_____ **9.** The conventional representation for stairways on plan views is a series of ___.
   A. horizontal lines representing treads
   B. vertical lines representing risers
   C. parallel lines representing risers
   D. parallel lines representing runs and risers

True-False

T	F	**1.** Blueprints have white lines on a blue background.
T	F	**2.** Written information is often found in the title block.
T	F	**3.** Dimensions indicating the exact room size should be shown in each room on a floor plan.
T	F	**4.** As the space between contour lines increases, the lot becomes steeper.
T	F	**5.** The most common sections are taken through exterior walls.
T	F	**6.** All information about windows is shown on floor plans or section views.
T	F	**7.** Dimensions should not be repeated on prints unless marked REF.
T	F	**8.** Floor plans are generally the most used plans in a set of prints.
T	F	**9.** Exit passageways must be at least 44″ wide except when serving an occupancy load of less than 50.
T	F	**10.** Interior doors generally require only two hinges.
T	F	**11.** Hollow-core doors have a core of wood blocks.
T	F	**12.** Four elevations are generally sufficient to clearly show exterior walls of a building.
T	F	**13.** Door hand is the direction in which a door swings.

Completion

_____ **1.** All visible print lines are shown with ___ lines.

_____ **2.** Dimension lines are terminated by ___ lines.

_____ **3.** An architect's scale is ___ in shape.

_____ **4.** Interior frame partitions with a gypsum board finish on floor plans are usually indicated as ___" thick.

_____ **5.** A legal ___ is required to establish the corners of a building lot in relation to official points of measurement in the vicinity.

_____ **6.** Building ___ specify types of materials that must be used for particular aspects of construction.

_____ **7.** The location of all exterior walls and interior ___ are shown on floor plans.

_____ **8.** The ___ Elevation is the view of the south side of a building, not the direction a person faces to see that side of the building.

_____ **9.** A ___ block is the logical place to begin reading a set of prints.

_____ **10.** The three classifications of ___ are fixed-sash, sliding-sash, and swinging-sash.

_____ **11.** Complex building parts such as doors and windows are simplified and drawn as ___.

_____ **12.** When determining door hand, the viewer is considered to be standing on the ___ of the door.

_____ **13.** Flush doors may be either solid-core or ___-core.

_____ **14.** Interior doors for one-family and multifamily dwellings must be at least ___" thick.

_____ **15.** The vertical distance between residential stairway landings should not exceed ___'.

_____ **16.** Hidden lines are drawn with ___" dashes and ¹⁄₃₂" spaces.

_____ **17.** A right-hand door hinges on the right and opens ___.

_____ **18.** When using the architect's scale, the ___ should always be placed on the beginning of the line being scaled.

_____ **19.** Extension lines define size or ___.

_____ **20.** The abbreviation for foundation is ___.

Math

_____ **1.** A partition is framed with 2 × 4 studs and finished with ½" gypsum board on both sides. What is the actual thickness of the partition?

Refer to the plot plan for Highland Office Supply to answer questions 2 through 7.

Local ordinances require the following for commercial office buildings:

Setbacks—40'-0" from front street curb; 25'-0" on each side; 20'-0" on back

Parking—two 200 sq ft parking spaces per 1000 sq ft of office space

Green space—10% minimum of total lot size

Maximum building size—40% of total lot size

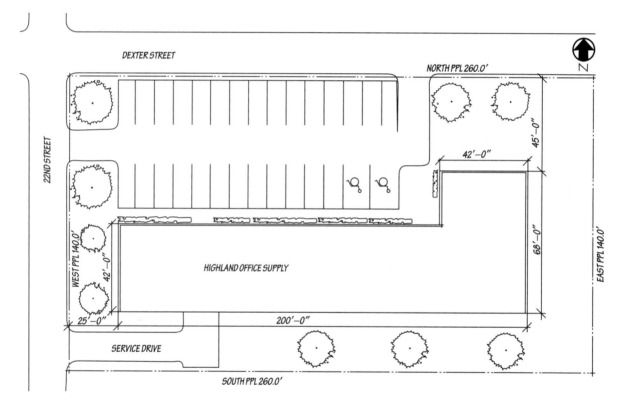

_____ **2.** Are front and back setbacks sufficient to meet local ordinance requirements?

_____ **3.** What is the east setback?

_____ **4.** How many square feet does the building contain?

_____ **5.** Is the number of parking spaces sufficient to meet local ordinance requirements?

_____ **6.** What is the south setback?

_____ **7.** What is the area (in square feet) of the lot?

Identification

_____ **1.** Straight-run stairway

_____ **2.** Total rise

_____ **3.** Circular stairway

_____ **4.** Straight-run stairway with landing

_____ **5.** Finished floor

_____ **6.** Riser

_____ **7.** Tread

_____ **8.** Total run

_____ **9.** Headroom

_____ **10.** Stair angle

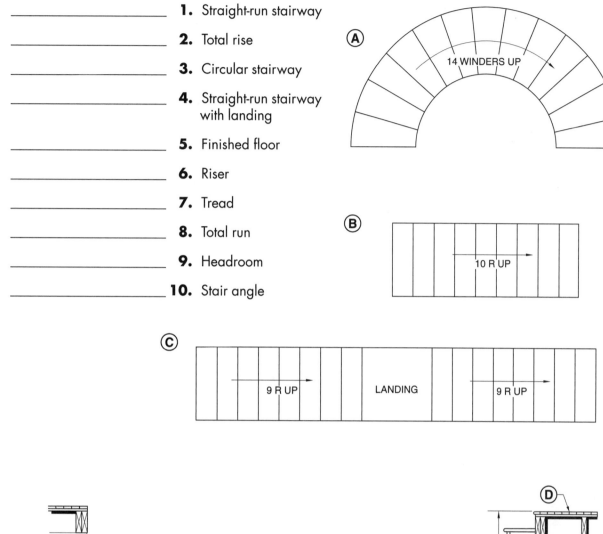

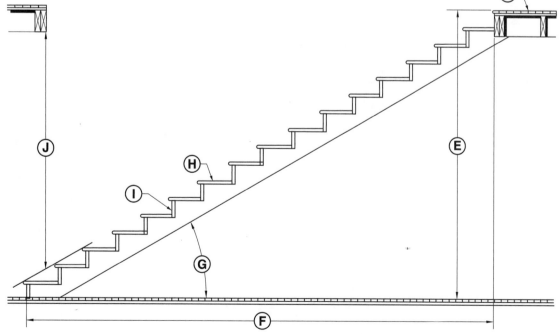

51

Identification

_____ **1.** Leader with open arrowhead

_____ **2.** Section line

_____ **3.** Long break line

_____ **4.** Hidden line

_____ **5.** Object line

_____ **6.** Short break line

_____ **7.** Cutting plane

_____ **8.** Leader with closed arrowhead

_____ **9.** Centerpoint

_____ **10.** Centerline

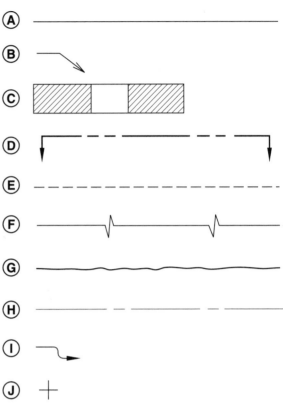

Identification

_____ **1.** Left-hand

_____ **2.** Left-hand reverse

_____ **3.** Right-hand

_____ **4.** Right-hand reverse

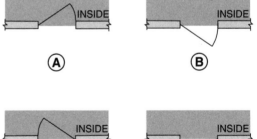

52

Construction Materials

2

A variety of materials are used to construct residential and light commercial buildings. These materials include wood, concrete, masonry, metal, insulation, plastics, glass, and gypsum products. Various materials are used for electrical and mechanical systems.

WOOD

Wood is a common construction material used for structural and finish applications. However, wood is flammable and subject to the flaws developed during growth and processing.

Wood is divided into two main classes—softwood and hardwood. Softwood lumber is manufactured from softwood trees called conifers. Conifers have thin needles and bear cones. Common softwood species are Douglas fir, pine, and redwood. Hardwood lumber is manufactured from broad-leaved deciduous trees, which lose their leaves in the autumn. Common hardwood species are maple, oak, and birch.

Each wood species has unique properties. Certain pine, hemlock, and fir species have excellent structural properties and are used for rough framing members. Maple and oak, commonly used for finish applications, are hard, wear-resistant, and fine-grained. Mahogany is commonly used as a veneer for flush doors. Birch and certain pine species are used for trim members. Trim members are commonly finger-jointed to create longer lengths from shorter pieces. Walnut and fruitwoods such as cherry are generally used for furniture because of their beauty, but are rarely used for trim members in buildings due to their cost.

Southern Forest Products Association
Wood is commonly used for structural applications including studs, headers, plates, and joists.

Rough lumber is available in 2' increments and is described by its nominal size, such as 2×4, 2×6, and 1×6. The *nominal size* is the dimensions of a piece of lumber before it is dried and surfaced. Nominal sizes are not actual sizes but are used for descriptive purposes. For example, a piece of lumber with a nominal size of 2×4 has an actual size of $1\frac{1}{2}'' \times 3\frac{1}{2}''$.

The symbol for wood-framed walls and interior partitions on plan views is two parallel lines (representing the two faces of the wall or partition) with a space between the two lines. See Figure 2-1. Walls are generally considered to be load-bearing while partitions are considered to be non-load-bearing. Alternate symbols may be used to represent wood on display drawings or remodeling drawings. Wavy lines may be used to fill wall and partition cavities on display drawings to allow the walls to be shown more prominently. In remodeling drawings, parallel lines may be used to fill wall and partition cavities to show parts that are new or require changes. See Figure 2-2.

Symbols are also used to represent wood members in sections and construction details. See Figure 2-3. End views of rough framing members are indicated with crossing diagonal lines within each piece. Face views of framing members are shown with two parallel lines. Finish wood members, such as moldings and trim, are shown with freehand lines to represent wood grain. Plywood drawn at a small scale is shown using the same symbol as wood trim members. When the scale is large, horizontal lines are added to indicate the plies but no attempt is made to show the exact number of plies.

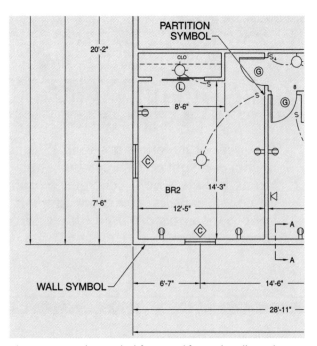

Figure 2-1. The symbol for wood-framed walls and partitions is two parallel lines with space between them.

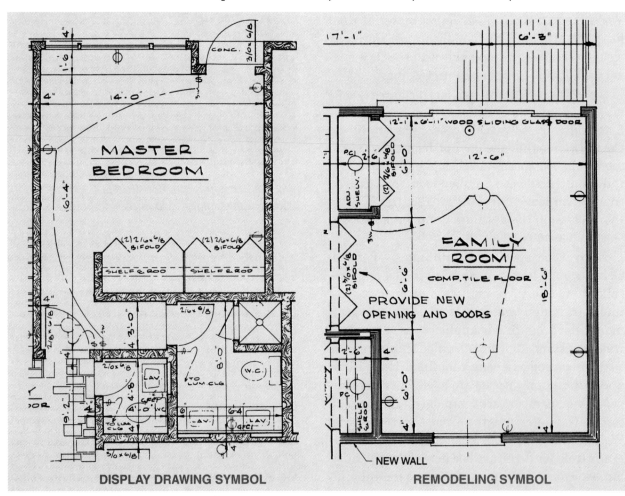

DISPLAY DRAWING SYMBOL　　　　**REMODELING SYMBOL**

Figure 2-2. Wall and partition symbols for display drawings and remodeling can be filled in with wavy or parallel lines.

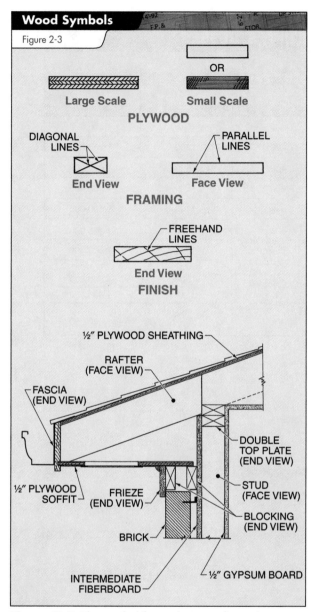

Figure 2-3. The symbol for end views of wood members in sections and details is diagonal lines drawn through the member.

Structural Properties of Wood

Proper specification and use of wood in construction is the responsibility of the architect and tradesworker. An architect must determine the available wood species that has the best structural properties for the job. One factor that must be considered when specifying wood species is the maximum allowable unit stresses of the wood. See Figure 2-4. The table identifies the maximum allowable unit stresses (in pounds per square inch [psi]) for common wood species, plywood, and glued laminated (glulam) timber used in construction.

When stresses such as loads are applied to wood members, the wood fibers react to the applied stress. *Extreme fiber stress* is the resistance to the shortening and lengthening of wood fibers when a wood member is placed in a position where it may bend under a load. *Horizontal shear* is the resistance of wood fibers sliding past one another lengthwise when a wood member is placed in a position where it may bend under a load. The fibers may also be compressed when loads are applied. Compression across the grain is the resistance to compression at right angles to the axis of the wood member. Compression parallel to the grain is the resistance to compression parallel to the axis of the wood member. Compression parallel to the grain is always significantly greater than compression across the grain due to the fiber structure and arrangement. The *modulus of elasticity* is the relationship of the unit stress to unit elongation. When a member is placed under stress, it will elongate at a uniform rate until it reaches its limits of elasticity, after which it will no longer return to its original length.

Architects calculate the size of floor joists required to span a certain distance and make similar decisions regarding the sizes of other structural members. Tradesworkers must read, interpret, and follow the prints and specifications regarding materials and their installation, and are responsible for properly framing and finishing the building.

Fastening information is often included in the specifications or a fastening schedule is included on the prints. Minimum fastening requirements are based on Subsection 2304.9 of the *International Building Code.* For example, two 16d common nails are used to fasten a top plate to a stud.

MAXIMUM ALLOWABLE UNIT STRESSES					
Species and Commercial Grade	Extreme Fiber Stress and Tension Parallel to Grain*	Horizontal Shear*	Compression across Grain*	Compression Parallel to Grain*	Modulus of Elasticity*
Cypress	1300	120	300	900	1,200,000
Douglas Fir	1300	100	325	1200	1,600,000
Plywood (fir)	1500	100	400	1500	1,600,000
Glulam timber	1100	75	400	1500	1,600,000
Hemlock	1000	90	350	1100	1,400,000
Oak	1300	120	600	1000	1,500,000
Redwood	1100	75	300	1000	1,200,000
Southern Pine Longleaf	1300	120	450	1000	1,600,000
Shortleaf	1100	120	400	900	1,600,000
Spruce, Sitka or Eastern	1100	75	300	800	1,200,000

* in psi

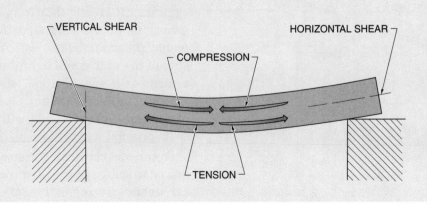

Figure 2-4. The maximum allowable unit stresses must be considered when specifying wood for construction.

American Hardwood Export Council

Trim members enhance the finished appearance of a room.

Trim Members

Many types and shapes of wood trim members are available for residential and commercial construction. See Figure 2-5. Finished wood trim members, such as moldings, are produced in standard sizes and shapes at a mill or manufacturing plant. Wood trim members are cut to width and length and molded from hardwood or softwood lumber. Trim members are available unfinished, primed, or prefinished. Softwood molding with a primed finish is typically used for applications where a painted finish is required. Hardwood molding is usually installed where the trim members are to remain a natural finish.

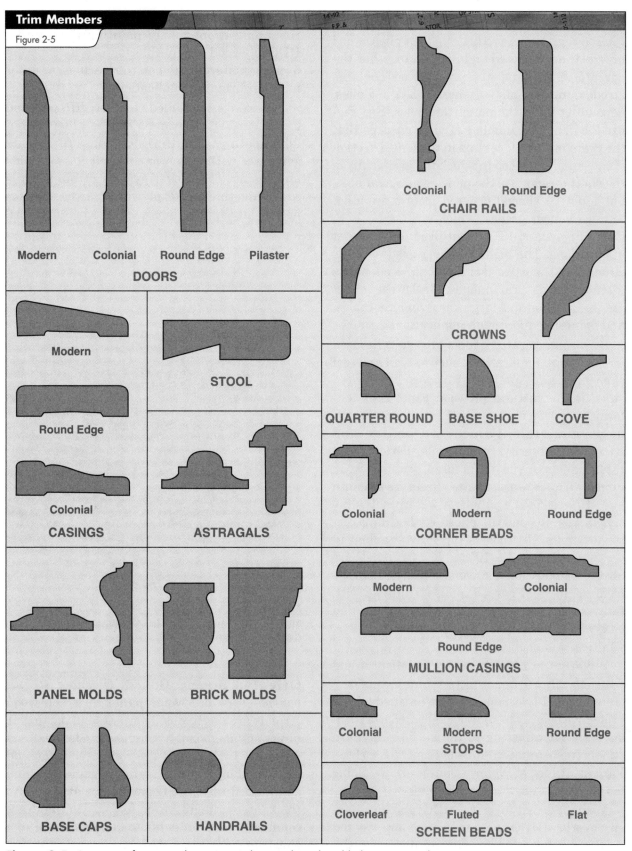

Figure 2-5. A variety of trim members are used in residential and light commercial construction.

Plywood and Wood Panel Products

Plywood is a panel product made of plies (wood layers) that are glued and pressed together under intense heat and pressure. Plywood contains an odd number of plies—generally 3, 5, or 7 plies, depending upon the panel thickness. See Figure 2-6. The odd number of plies ensures that the grain on each face runs in the long direction of the panel. Plywood in which the grain runs in the short direction of the panel is also available, but must be special ordered from a supplier. Various veneer grades, which include N, A, B, C, C Plugged, and D, are utilized for different applications. The highest veneer grade—N—is either 100% heartwood or 100% sapwood, and is intended for natural finishes. The lowest veneer grade—D—contains large knots and knotholes, and is intended for rough applications.

Performance rated panels are typically used for structural applications, such as wall and roof sheathing and subfloor. A *performance rated panel* is a structural plywood panel that conforms to performance-based standards for dimensional stability, bond durability, and structural integrity, for example. Performance rated panels are manufactured from softwood lumber. The softwood species affects the strength and stiffness of the panels. A waterproof adhesive is used to bond the plies together for structural panels. Plywood is typically supplied in 4′ × 8′ panels, but 4′ × 10′ and 5′ × 12′ panels are also available. Common panel thicknesses range from ¼″ to ⅞″. Plywood is also available with finish surface veneers such as birch, maple, and oak, which are used for wall paneling, cabinets, vanities, and shelving.

Plyform® is a performance rated plywood panel specifically manufactured for use as concrete forms. Plyform panels are finished with a protective overlay to allow for repeated use without concrete adhering to the surface. Plyform panels create a smooth-finished concrete surface. Various grades of Plyform panels are available for various strength requirements.

Medium density overlay (MDO) and high density overlay (HDO) plywood panels are treated on their surface veneer with an opaque resin. MDO plywood is used for siding and other exterior applications where painting is required. HDO plywood is suitable for use as concrete forming material, kitchen countertops, or other high-performance applications.

Fiberglass reinforced plastic (FRP) plywood has a surface treatment of fiberglass-woven fabric saturated with resins, glass fiber mats saturated with resins, or chopped glass strands and resins. These overlays vary from 25 mils to 60 mils thick. FRP plywood may be used for heavy-duty applications such as concrete forms.

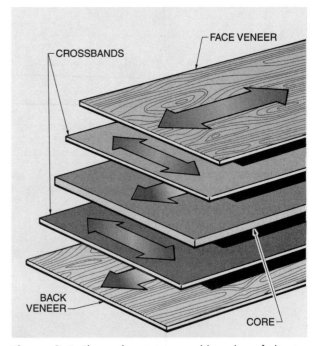

Figure 2-6. Plywood contains an odd number of plies to ensure that the grain on each face runs in the long direction of the panel.

Oriented Strand Board. *Oriented strand board (OSB)* is a wood panel in which wood strands are mechanically oriented in particular directions and bonded with resin under heat and pressure. OSB panels are composed of an odd number of layers running in the same direction as plywood plies. OSB panels are available in thicknesses ranging from 5⁄16″ to 1⅛″, and are commonly used for subfloors and wall and roof sheathing. See Figure 2-7.

Wood I-Joists and Rim Boards. A *wood I-joist* is a load-bearing structural member that consists of an OSB or plywood web between two pieces of dimensional lumber, forming an I. Wood I-joists are used for floor and ceiling joists and rafters in residential and light commercial construction. Rim boards are installed at the ends of wood I-joists in a manner similar to the manner in which header joists are installed at the ends of solid wood joists. Rim boards are manufactured from OSB in sizes that correspond to sizes of wood I-joists. Up to 24′ lengths can be spanned with rim boards.

Nonstructural Panels. Nonstructural panels, such as particleboard, fiberboard, and hardboard, are comprised of sawmill residue or various wood byproducts that are mixed with binders or other resins and formed into sheets under intense heat and pressure. Particleboard panels are used for underlayment, shelving, and cabinet components. Medium-density fiberboard (MDF) is a nonstructural panel product used for siding, moldings, shelving, and cabinet components. Hardboard is a nonstructural panel product used for wall paneling, cabinet components, underlayment, and siding.

Structural Insulated Panels. A *structural insulated panel (SIP)* is a structural member consisting of a thick layer of rigid foam insulation pressed between two OSB or plywood panels. Expanded polystyrene is commonly used as insulating foam. Structural insulated panels are available in sizes from 4′ × 6′ to 8′ × 24′. SIPs are structurally rated to provide lateral strength and uniform load capacity throughout the panel, and are used for roofs and walls of buildings. See Figure 2-8.

Parallel Strand Lumber. *Parallel strand lumber (PSL)* is an engineered wood product manufactured from wood strands or flakes and waterproof adhesives and cured under intense heat and pressure. Parallel strand lumber is manufactured to the same dimensions as solid lumber such as 2 × 10s. PSL is commonly used for load-bearing applications such as headers and beams.

ORIENTED STRAND BOARD (OSB)

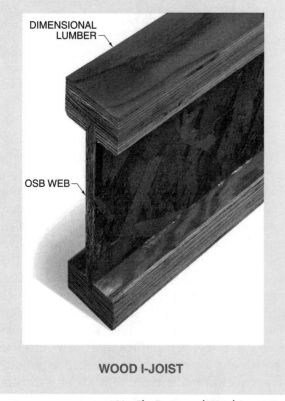

DIMENSIONAL LUMBER

OSB WEB

WOOD I-JOIST

APA—The Engineered Wood Association

Figure 2-7. Oriented strand board (OSB) and the web of wood I-joists are composed of wood strands that are mechanically oriented in particular directions.

Structural Insulated Panel Association

Figure 2-8. A structural insulated panel (SIP) is a structural member consisting of two outer skins, commonly OSB, with a core of insulating foam sandwiched between them.

Glulam Timber. *Glued laminated timber (glulam)* is an engineered wood product comprised of layers of wood members (lams) that are joined together with adhesive to form larger members. Glulam timbers are manufactured in many standard and custom sizes and shapes. Long spans are possible with glulam timbers. Glulam timber surfaces are often exposed in finished construction.

The use of glulam timber dates back to the early 1900s when the first patents for glulam were issued in Switzerland and Germany. One of the first glulam timber structures in the United States was built for the USDA Forest Products Laboratory in 1934. Since that time, glulam timber has become one of the most widely used engineered lumber products.

CONCRETE

Concrete is a mixture of cement, fine and coarse aggregate, and water. *Cement* is a mixture of shells, limestone, clay silica, marble, shale, sand, and other materials that are ground, blended, fused, and crushed to a powder. Cement is the binding agent in concrete. *Aggregate* is hard granular material, such as sand and gravel, that is mixed with cement and water to provide structure and strength in concrete. Aggregate includes uniformly sized crushed stone or gravel, cinders, slag, or other mineral products such as expanded mica (vermiculite). Lightweight concrete uses lightweight aggregate such as perlite, pumice, or vermiculite. Concrete is a strong, durable material when properly prepared and placed.

The proportions of a concrete mixture affect the properties of the final concrete structure or member. A concrete mixture is determined by the ratio of the concrete ingredients. A ratio of

1:2:4 indicates 1 part cement, 2 parts sand, and 4 parts gravel (or other aggregate). Concrete gains an initial set during the first 12 to 24 hours after placement, depending on the atmospheric temperature, size of the concrete mass, and other factors. Concrete forms are generally stripped (removed) after three or four days. The chemical process of hydration, during which concrete develops its load-bearing properties and design strength, primarily occurs within the first 28 days after concrete placement.

Chemical admixtures may also be added to concrete to obtain the desired effects. An *admixture* is a substance other than water, aggregate, or cement that is added to concrete to modify its properties. A variety of admixtures may be used in concrete mixtures. An *air-entraining admixture* is an admixture that provides greater resistance to freezing and high early strength properties. A *superplasticizer* is an admixture that significantly reduces the amount of water required in a concrete mixture and increases the workability of the concrete. A *retarder* is an admixture that delays the setting and hardening of concrete. An *accelerator* is an admixture that shortens the setting time and increases early strength of concrete.

Concrete footings bear the load of the foundation walls and the building, including its contents, and are designed according to the load and the type of soil on which they bear. Concrete can withstand great compressive stress, but is relatively poor in counteracting bending or tension forces. Reinforcement, such as rebar, welded wire reinforcement, or fibers, provides tensile strength properties to concrete to counteract bending or tension forces. Rebar (steel reinforcing bars) are placed in footings and foundation walls to provide tensile strength and to tie together adjacent parts of foundations, walkways, and concrete stairways. Welded wire reinforcement, also known as welded wire fabric, is a grid of heavy-gauge wire that is placed in concrete slabs for reinforcement. Fiber-reinforced concrete utilizes steel, glass, or plastic fibers that are introduced into the concrete mixture during initial mixing. Fibers can be used as the sole means of reinforcement or can be used in conjunction with rebar.

Portland Cement Association

Concrete is a construction material consisting of cement, fine and coarse aggregate, and water.

Tradesworkers must properly read and interpret the specifications and prints to ensure the formwork is constructed to the proper dimensions. Formwork must be constructed so that it will retain the plastic, almost liquid, concrete during placement and until it sets, yet must be easily disassembled when the concrete has set. Rebar must be properly positioned and supported as shown on the prints to provide the strength for which the structure is designed. The concrete and rebar symbols are shown on sections. See Figure 2-9.

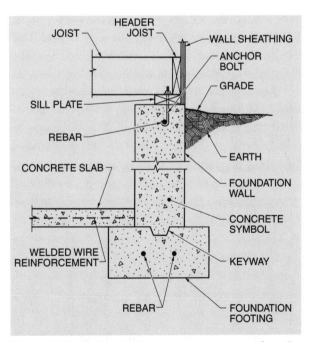

Figure 2-9. The symbol for concrete is a series of small dots and random triangles.

Hollow-core concrete masonry units (CMUs) are commonly used to construct interior and exterior walls in light commercial buildings.

Many light commercial buildings utilize precast concrete components. Precast concrete components include beams, columns, walls, pipes, or other structures that are formed, placed, and cured off-site, transported to the construction site, and set or lifted into their final position using a crane. Steel reinforcement, connectors, and openings are formed into precast components as the concrete is placed. Tilt-up concrete construction is a type of precast concrete construction in which walls are formed and concrete is placed at the job site and allowed to properly set. The walls are then tilted up into place. Lifting anchors are embedded in tilt-up walls to allow for a crane line and the proper rigging to be connected.

Cast-in-place or precast concrete may also be used for rough or finished floors in residential and light commercial construction. In slab-on-grade construction, concrete is placed over a bed of sand or gravel at or near grade level. A vapor barrier, typically polyethylene plastic sheets, is positioned directly below the concrete to prevent moisture from the ground from seeping through the slab. Slab thicknesses are specified on the plans. For some applications, finish flooring is laid on the concrete slab. A terrazzo floor finish

may also be applied. *Terrazzo* is a mixture of cement and water with colored stone, marble chips, or other decorative aggregate embedded in the surface. After the concrete sets, the surface is ground and polished to a smooth finish.

MASONRY

Various masonry materials are used in residential and light commercial construction for structural support and decorative purposes. Masonry materials include brick, concrete masonry units (CMUs), terra cotta, stone, and other materials laid as individual units and bound together with mortar. Many standard sizes and types of masonry material are available with a variety of face textures and appearances, providing unlimited opportunities for its use. Masonry material provides low maintenance cost, good weather resistance, and outstanding appearance.

Brick

A *brick* is an individual rectangular unit made from clay or a clay mixture that is hardened by drying in a kiln. The raw materials for brick are readily available in many parts of the country. Clay or shale is ground and mixed with water to the proper consistency and then placed in molds and formed into brick. Brick can also be made by the extrusion process in which clay is forced through a die and cut off to make individual bricks. Brick manufactured using either process are dried to the proper moisture content before being placed in the kiln. The brick are then fired at a high temperature for 40 to 150 hours.

A building brick, also referred to as common brick, is manufactured from local clay or shale and is available in many colors. Face brick is made of select clay to impart distinctive uniform colors and is treated to provide a special surface. Firebrick is manufactured of refractory ceramic material that resists high temperatures without disintegrating.

Individual brick are rarely shown on prints except when showing a large-scale plan view or section, or when showing a detail where brick is involved or when brick is to be laid in a specific decorative pattern. Brick is indicated on small-scale plan views, such as floor plans, by 45° crosshatching representing a specific type of brick. For example, common brick is shown on plan views with widely spaced 45° crosshatching. Face brick is shown with the crosshatching spaced closer together, and firebrick is shown as crosshatching with additional lines drawn in the opposite direction. See Figure 2-10. Horizontal lines represent brick on exterior elevations. A notation indicating the type of brick used, such as face brick, is included on the print.

Modular or nonmodular brick may be used in masonry construction. A *modular brick* is a brick in which the nominal dimensions are based on a 4″ unit. Nominal dimensions are equal to the actual dimensions of the brick plus the intended mortar joint. For example, the nominal dimensions of a closure modular brick are 4 × 4 × 8, but its actual dimensions are approximately 3⅝″ × 3⅝″ × 7⅝″. See Figure 2-11. Brick dimensions are expressed as the width by height by length. A *nonmodular brick* is a brick in which the actual dimensions are used to express the size. For example, the actual size of a closure standard nonmodular brick is 3½″ to 3⅝″ × 3½″ to 3⅝″ × 8″. Although nominal dimensions are

only indicated for modular brick, the heights of modular and nonmodular brick are the same.

Brick size and mortar joint thickness must be considered when laying brick to ensure the accuracy of the horizontal and vertical dimensions of a wall or other structure. For multistory buildings, accurate and uniform mortar joints are important since the floor-to-floor height is fixed and the brickwork must exactly fill the space. Bricklayers or stonemasons must refer to the prints to ensure all measurements work out accurately. Corners and openings must be perfectly vertical (plumb) and each course perfectly level. Mortar joints should coincide with the bottoms of windowsills, tops of windows, and floor levels. Brickwork should be laid out carefully for the openings and corners to use as many complete units as possible.

The Brick Industry Association (BIA) is the national trade association representing distributors and manufacturers of clay brick and suppliers of related products and services. The BIA is the recognized national authority on brick construction.

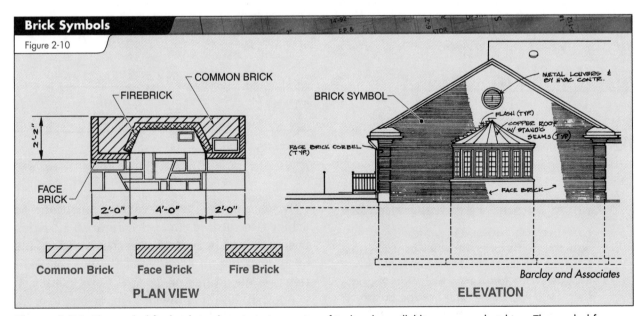

Figure 2-10. The symbol for brick in plan views is a series of inclined parallel lines or crosshatching. The symbol for brick in elevations is a series of horizontal lines.

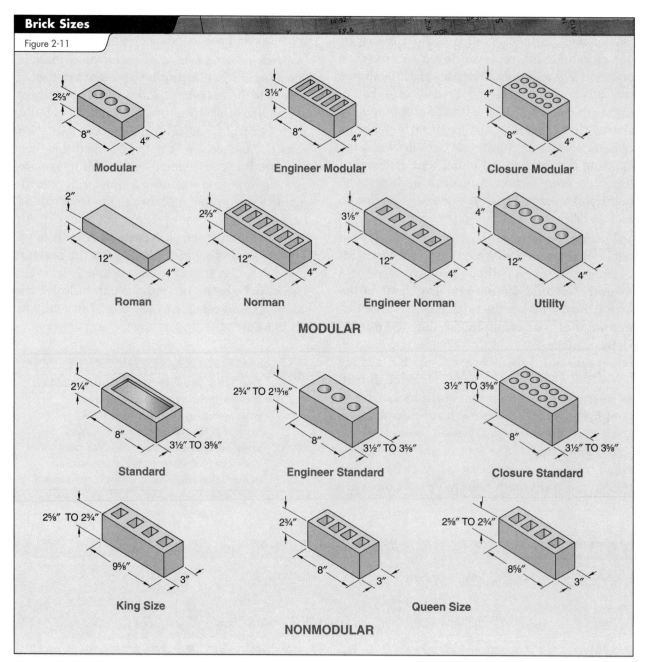

Brick Sizes

Figure 2-11

MODULAR

NONMODULAR

Figure 2-11. Modular and nonmodular brick are used in masonry construction.

Fasteners can be used to attach equipment, fixtures, or other components to masonry material. Masonry fasteners include screw (expansion) shields, toggle bolts, screws, sleeve and wedge anchors, lag shields, masonry nails, and powder-driven fasteners.

Brick can be laid in various positions to achieve the desired effect. See Figure 2-12. Brick positions may be indicated in the specifications or by showing an example of the desired positions on elevations or details. For example, a windowsill laid in a rowlock course or the brick over a window laid as a soldier course may be shown on elevations or details.

Brick Positions

Figure 2-12

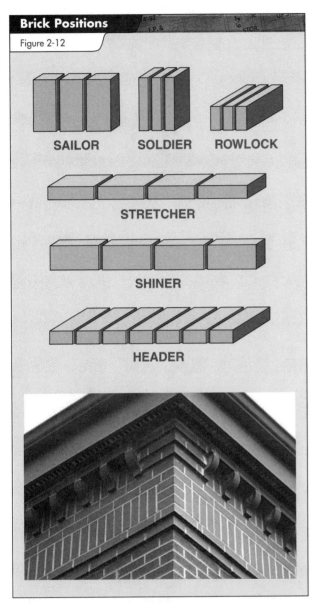

Figure 2-12. Brick can be laid in various positions.

In addition to brick being laid in different positions, brick can also be laid in various bonds. A *bond* is an arrangement of masonry in a pattern to provide a desired architectural effect and/or additional structure. A common bond is the most frequently used brick bond. A common bond has a header course every sixth course to tie the front and back wythes of brick together. See Figure 2-13. A *wythe* is a single, continuous, vertical masonry wall that is one unit thick. Flemish and English bonds are used in buildings or garden walls to provide a desired architectural effect. A Flemish bond is made with alternating headers and stretchers in each course with the headers tying the wythes together. An English bond is made with alternate header and stretcher courses. A stack bond is primarily used for decorative purposes.

Brick Bonds

Figure 2-13

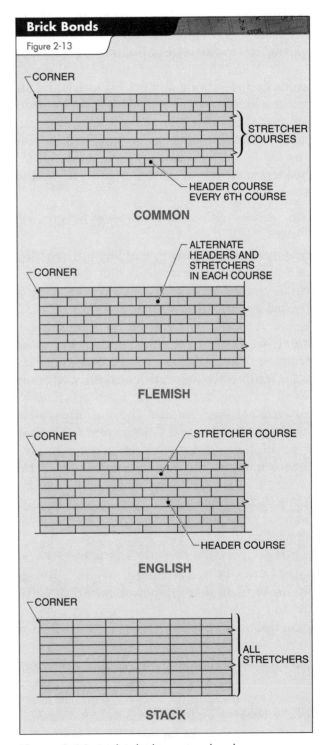

Figure 2-13. Brick is laid in various bonds.

Brick Veneer. Brick veneer may be used to finish frame or masonry walls. *Brick veneer* is a brick facing applied to the exterior wall surface of a frame structure or other type of structure. The backing wall and brick wall are separated by a 1″ air space for ventilation and moisture control. The backing wall and brick wall are secured together using fixed or adjustable galvanized metal ties. See Figure 2-14. In frame construction, the ties are fastened to the wall studs and sheathing and extend across the air space where they are embedded in the mortar joints of the brick-veneer wall. Brick veneer can also be tied to the face of a CMU wall with similar ties laid into horizontal mortar joints. CMU headers may also be used to tie a CMU wall to the brick.

Stone

Natural stone is used in building construction as veneer, as facing, or to provide a desired architectural effect. When used as veneer, stone is backed up with brick, structural clay tile, CMUs, or concrete. When used as facing, thin pieces of stone are fastened to other masonry or steel framing. Natural stone is used because of its color, compressive strength, and beauty, whether used as rough stones or with a smooth, cut-and-polished surface. Granite, limestone, sandstone, marble, and slate are commonly used types of stone. Cast stone, made of concrete, possesses many of the same qualities of natural stone. Stone is indicated on plan views by a sprinkling of dots. Lines indicate cast stone or rubble. Refer to the Appendix. Stone is shown on elevations with lines to resemble the stone.

Stone size varies greatly and is directly related to the desired architectural effect. Rough stone is fashioned by a tradesworker with greater regard for its aesthetic quality than its dimensions or shape. Cut stone is available in a variety of uniform sizes and shapes. When preparing details of a stone wall, an architect must consider the backing being used. When masonry is used as a backing, the horizontal mortar joints in the backing and stone must align so galvanized metal ties can be installed to fasten the stone to the backing.

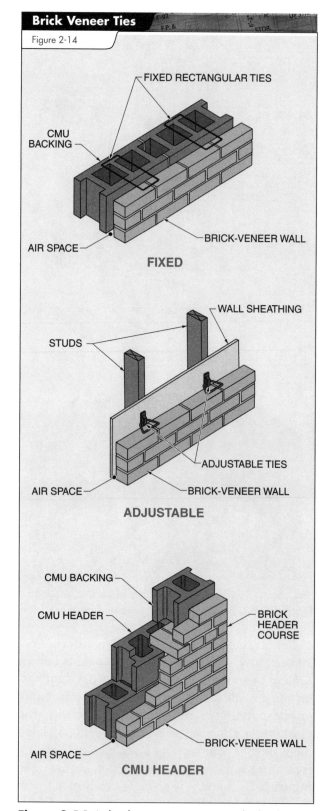

Figure 2-14. In brick-veneer construction, the backing and veneer are tied together using fixed or adjustable ties, or by using a CMU header into which a brick header course is placed.

Stone Classifications. Rubble, squared stone, and ashlar are the most common stone classifications used for construction. *Rubble* is rough, irregular stone that is used as fill or to provide a rustic appearance. Rubble is usually obtained locally as field stone or blasted in a quarry. *Squared stone* is rough stone made approximately square either at a quarry or at the job site. *Ashlar* is stone cut to precise dimensions according to the prints. When rubble or squared stone is to be installed on a building, an architect shows the general arrangement of the stone on elevations. Details are typically not required. A stonemason's skill and artistry are used to create the desired architectural effect. When ashlar is to be installed, an architect draws elevations and details showing each stone in place. Shop drawings are then created, which provide exact dimensions, finish, and anchors to be used. Each stone on the drawings is assigned a number. The shop drawings are submitted to the architect for approval before the stone is cut.

Stone is also classified by the bond created by the arrangement of stone. Basic stone bonds are random, coursed, and broken range. See Figure 2-15. A random bond is created with various sizes of stone placed in a random arrangement without maintaining courses or ranges. A *range* is a course of any thickness that extends across the face of a wall, but not all courses need to be the same thickness. A coursed bond is created with stone arranged in courses or ranges with vertical joints aligned on alternating rows. Each course of a coursed bond can consist of a different thickness of stone as long as the range remains unbroken. A broken range bond is created with stone so the range is broken with larger stone. Horizontal mortar joints break against larger stone. When working with ashlar, even in random bonds, a mason is required to follow the prints carefully to achieve precise mortar joints. Anchors specified on the prints or in the specifications are designed to provide proper support for the stone.

Concrete Masonry Units

A *concrete masonry unit (CMU)* is a precast hollow or solid masonry unit composed of portland cement and fine aggregate and formed into modular or nonmodular dimensions. CMUs are specified by width by height by length. The actual dimensions of standard modular CMUs are $7\frac{5}{8}'' \times 7\frac{5}{8}'' \times 15\frac{5}{8}''$. When combined with a $\frac{3}{8}''$ mortar joint all around, the nominal dimensions are $8'' \times 8'' \times 16''$. CMUs can be used as the finished surface, or stone, brick, or tile veneer can be applied to the face. Mortar joints in the veneer should align with joints in the CMU wall to allow galvanized metal ties to tie the materials together. CMUs are shown on elevations as courses using the concrete symbol with a series of lines to distinguish them from monolithic concrete. See Appendix.

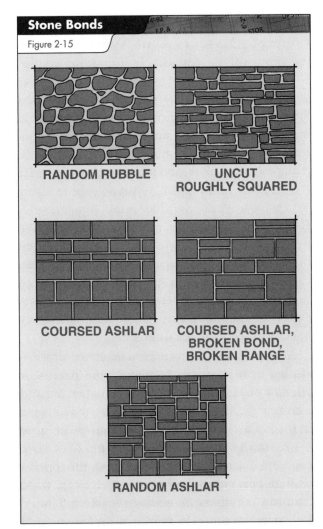

Stone Bonds

Figure 2-15

RANDOM RUBBLE

UNCUT ROUGHLY SQUARED

COURSED ASHLAR

COURSED ASHLAR, BROKEN BOND, BROKEN RANGE

RANDOM ASHLAR

Figure 2-15. Elevations of stone show whether it is rubble, roughly squared, or ashlar. The type of bond is also shown.

Hollow-core CMUs reduce weight to a minimum yet provide the desired strength and fire-resistance properties. The number of cores and their size and shape vary. Two-core CMUs are commonly used since they are lightweight and easily produced. Two-core CMUs are available in 4″, 6″, 8″, 10″, and 12″ widths, 4″ and 8″ heights, and 16″ and 18″ lengths. With many CMU widths available, wall thickness can be easily adjusted to the desired dimension. One wythe of modular 12″ CMUs laid in a stretcher position is used to form foundations or exterior walls. Narrower CMUs, such as 8″ CMUs, are used as backing for brick or stone. Two different thicknesses of CMUs can also be used to construct a wall to the required dimensions with galvanized metal ties securing the walls together.

Concrete Masonry Unit Types. Concrete masonry units are available in various shapes to serve different functions. See Figure 2-16. A *stretcher CMU* is a concrete masonry unit used for running walls. A *corner CMU* is a concrete masonry unit used at square corners. A *double corner CMU* is a concrete masonry unit used to make columns, piers, and pilasters. A *jamb CMU* is a concrete masonry unit with an extended ear to receive a window or door jamb. A *metal sash CMU* is a concrete masonry unit used to receive a metal window unit. A *header CMU* is a concrete masonry unit with a portion of its shell removed to receive header courses of brick or stone to secure the wall together. A *partition CMU* is a concrete masonry unit used as a masonry backing or to form partitions.

A *lintel CMU* is a concrete masonry unit installed over openings to make bond beams. A window buck or other bracing is constructed and a course of lintel CMUs is laid. Rebar is placed in the hollow of the blocks and concrete is placed to create the bond beam. A *solid top CMU* is a concrete masonry unit used to finish the top of a wall and provide a flat bearing surface for wood framing members or brick or stone masonry. Lightweight concrete masonry units, made of concrete with one of several lightweight aggregates, are also available.

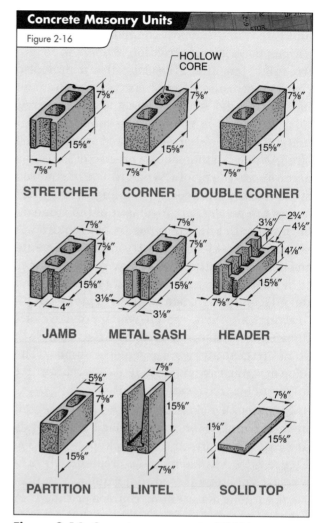

Figure 2-16. Concrete masonry units (CMUs) are available in various shapes to serve different functions.

Miscellaneous Masonry Products

A variety of other masonry products are commonly used in the construction of residential and light commercial buildings including decorative masonry units, clay facing tile, structural facing tile, terra cotta, fiber-cement boards and panels, and tile. Decorative masonry units are not intended for load-bearing structural purposes. Decorative CMUs form interesting designs when laid in a wall and also provide privacy for patios.

A *clay facing tile* is a masonry unit made of clay and fired in a kiln. Clay facing tile are used for interior facing material. Some types of clay facing tile, primarily used in applications where sanitation or moisture is a problem, have a high glaze, which is achieved by coating the faces of the tile with salt, chemicals, ceramic glazes, or enamel before firing. Food manufacturing plants, locker rooms, and swimming pools are commonly finished with clay facing tile.

A *structural facing tile* is a clay masonry unit with one face colored and glazed, and is used for load-bearing applications. Structural facing tile are produced in large dimensions. The color and glaze are achieved by coating the tile with salt, chemicals, ceramic glazes, or enamel before firing it in the kiln. Structural tile is nominally 6″ × 12″ and 2″, 6″, or 8″ deep. A variety of thinner shapes are available for fitting around window and door openings, and as base and corner trim.

Terra cotta is a masonry building material produced by firing molded units of clay in a kiln. The symbol used on plan views for terra cotta is similar to the symbol for cast stone. Terra cotta is colored and glazed and is primarily used for wall coping, although it also provides colorful exterior wall facings. Wall coping is produced in pieces up to 36″ long. See Figure 2-17. Terra cotta facing is fastened to the face of a building by applying mortar to the face of the backing and pressing the terra cotta into it. Terra cotta may also be anchored with galvanized wire or metal ties. Terra cotta facing material is available in several sizes.

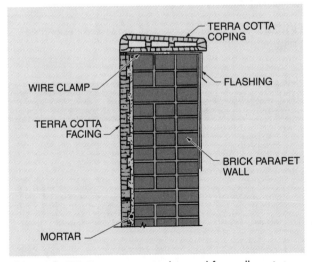

Figure 2-17. Terra cotta may be used for wall coping and facing.

Fiber-cement boards and panels may be used as exterior siding on buildings. Fiber-cement boards and panels are manufactured from cellulose fiber-reinforced material, and the exterior face is finished with a primer coat for application of paint. Fiber-cement siding is available in boards varying in widths from 5¼″ to 12″ and in 4′ × 8′, 4′ × 9′, and 4′ × 10′ panels. Fascia, moldings, and other accessories are also manufactured from fiber-cement materials.

Ceramic tile is manufactured from clay that has been fired and has a glazed surface. Ceramic tile is available in a variety of colors and degrees of glaze. Ceramic tile is shown on elevations as squares or rectangles. The tile may be drawn to scale, showing the exact arrangement of tiles, or a small portion of the wall may be drawn to indicate tile. When large-scale sections are shown, ceramic tile is indicated with wavy lines. Ceramic tile is applied to a surface using a thin coat of mastic. When the mastic has properly set, grout is spread over the surface and pressed into the joints, and the excess is wiped off. Ceramic tile is available in a variety of individual sizes and is also available in large assembled units with a flexible backing that can be applied more quickly.

Mosaic tile is a type of ceramic tile used to cover walls or floors, and is available in 1″ square, 2″ square, and 1″ × 2″ sizes. The tile is attached to a paper or mesh backing with even spaces between each tile. The tile are embedded in mortar or mastic and properly leveled. Grout is then spread over the surface and pressed into the joints. The excess is wiped off the surface.

Quarry tile is made from natural clay and shale, and is used for floors and base trim. Quarry tile is available in a variety of colors with smooth or textured finishes. Common quarry tile sizes are 6″ × 6″ and 4″ × 8″, with ½″ or ¾″ thicknesses.

METAL

Metal is used in many aspects of the construction industry. Metal is commonly used for the framework of commercial buildings and as framing members in residential and commercial construction. Metal is also used in windows, doors, and exterior trim, and as wall and roof coverings. Metal gutters and flashing are used to prevent moisture infiltration and to protect buildings from water damage. Metal is also used for applications ranging from reinforcing steel to conduit, pipe, and ductwork. Information regarding conduit, plumbing pipe, and ductwork is presented later in this chapter.

When shown on elevations, metal is not represented with a special symbol; information about metal is usually included in a notation or described in the specifications. In plan views or sections, metal components are drawn as solid lines. However, various metal symbols are shown in the details. Structural steel members such as beams are indicated with a dot-dash line on plan views.

Structural Steel

Structural steel is available in several standard shapes and serves as load-bearing units in construction. See Figure 2-18. Structural steel members are manufactured to close tolerances to ensure accuracy of the product. In addition, the chemical properties of the steel are constantly monitored during manufacture to ensure the finished product has the required strength.

A *wide-flange beam* is a structural steel member with parallel flanges that are joined with a perpendicular web. The intersection of the web and flanges is filleted. Wide-flange beams, indicated with the letter W, are specified by the nominal measurement outside of the flanges and the weight per running foot. For example, a W14 × 34 beam measures 14″ outside the flanges and

weighs 34 lb/ft. Web and flange dimensions vary with the weight and size of the beam. A W14 × 30 beam is another wide-flange beam with similar basic dimensions. The difference in weight and strength is accounted for by the flange and web thickness. Dimensions for other beams can be found in steel construction manuals.

A *steel angle* is a structural steel member with an L-shaped cross section with equal- or unequal-width legs. Steel angles are specified by the width of the legs measured along the back of the angle and the thickness of the legs. For example, a ∠6 × 6 × ⅞ steel angle measures 6″ along the back of each leg and is ⅞″ thick. See Figure 2-19.

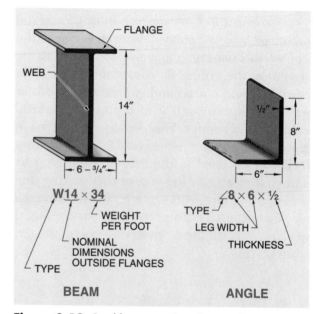

Figure 2-19. Steel beams and angles are designated using abbreviated descriptions.

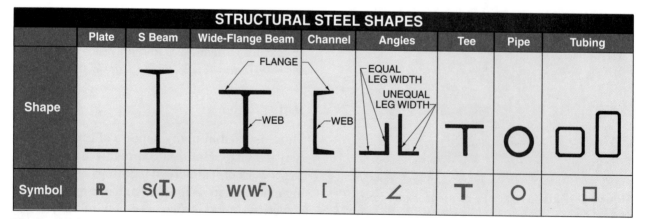

Figure 2-18. Symbols designate typical steel shapes used in residential and light commercial construction.

An *open web steel joist* is a structural steel member constructed with steel angles and bars that are used as chords with steel angles or bars extending between the chords at an angle. Open web joists are used extensively in light commercial construction to support floors and roofs. See Figure 2-20. Open web steel joists are discussed in greater detail in Chapter 3.

Steel Reinforcement

Steel reinforcement is steel wire, bars, or strands embedded in concrete to provide additional tensile strength to concrete structural members. Two primary types of steel reinforcement are used in residential and light commercial construction—rebar (reinforcing bar) and welded wire reinforcement. *Rebar* is steel reinforcing bar with deformations on the surface to allow the bar to interlock with concrete. Identifying marks on rebar indicate the manufacturer, type of steel, grade (or tensile yield point), and rebar size. Rebar size is indicated in eighths of an inch. No. 4 rebar is ⁴⁄₈″, or ½″ diameter. See Figure 2-21. Rebar is shown on plan views with solid lines and on sections with filled circles.

Rebar is bent in a fabricating shop to form rebar cages for round or square columns or beams. The bent rebar are tied to adjoining straight pieces of rebar to form a reinforcing structure that provides maximum tensile strength for the concrete. Straight pieces of rebar are installed for most common applications where tensile strength is required for an individual building unit, such as cast-in-place concrete footings.

Portland Cement Association

Straight and bent rebar are used to reinforce concrete used for roads and curbs.

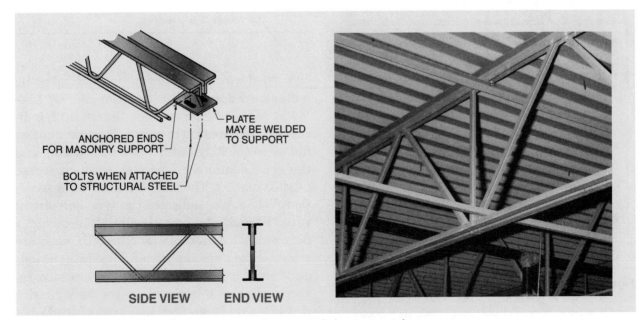

Figure 2-20. Open web steel joists support wide spans in light commercial construction.

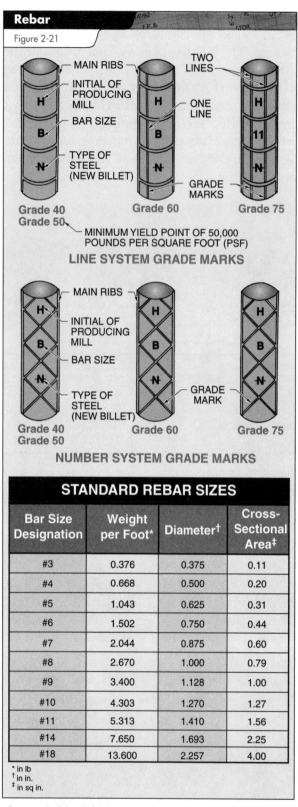

Rebar

Figure 2-21

LINE SYSTEM GRADE MARKS

- MAIN RIBS
- INITIAL OF PRODUCING MILL
- BAR SIZE
- TYPE OF STEEL (NEW BILLET)

Grade 40
Grade 50
MINIMUM YIELD POINT OF 50,000 POUNDS PER SQUARE FOOT (PSF)

TWO LINES
ONE LINE
Grade 60
GRADE MARKS
Grade 75

NUMBER SYSTEM GRADE MARKS

- MAIN RIBS
- INITIAL OF PRODUCING MILL
- BAR SIZE
- TYPE OF STEEL (NEW BILLET)

Grade 40
Grade 50
Grade 60
GRADE MARK
Grade 75

STANDARD REBAR SIZES			
Bar Size Designation	Weight per Foot*	Diameter†	Cross-Sectional Area‡
#3	0.376	0.375	0.11
#4	0.668	0.500	0.20
#5	1.043	0.625	0.31
#6	1.502	0.750	0.44
#7	2.044	0.875	0.60
#8	2.670	1.000	0.79
#9	3.400	1.128	1.00
#10	4.303	1.270	1.27
#11	5.313	1.410	1.56
#14	7.650	1.693	2.25
#18	13.600	2.257	4.00

* in lb
† in in.
‡ in sq in.

Figure 2-21. Rebar is identified using a line system or number system of grade marks. The manufacturer's identification, size, type of steel, and tensile yield point are indicated on rebar.

Concrete floors and slabs are reinforced with welded wire reinforcement. *Welded wire reinforcement (WWR)* is heavy-gauge wire joined in a grid and used to reinforce and increase the tensile strength of concrete. Welded wire reinforcement is placed in position and supported with chairs before concrete is placed. Welded wire reinforcement is available in sheets and rolls.

Two types of welded wire reinforcement are smooth and deformed. When using smooth wire, anchoring properties in concrete are achieved by the welded intersections. When using deformed wire, anchoring properties are achieved by deformations and the welded intersections. ASTM International specifies the use of the letter "W" to designate smooth wire and the letter "D" to designate deformed wire. Smooth wire has a lower tensile strength and yield strength and a higher shear strength than deformed wire.

Welded wire reinforcement (WWR) must be properly placed to perform effectively. WWR should be placed in the middle third of a 4″ to 6″ slab; 2″ below the surface is recommended in most cases. WWR is properly positioned using chairs, or by placing concrete in two courses with the WWR laid in place between the courses.

Welded wire reinforcement is specified using a standard designation, for example, 6 × 12—W12 × W5. The first two numbers, 6 × 12, indicate the wire spacing in inches. The first number indicates the longitudinal (length) spacing and the second number indicates the transverse (width) spacing. The last portion of the designation, W12 × W5, indicates the type and size of wire. "W" indicates smooth wire; "D" designates deformed wire. In this example, both wires are smooth. The numbers 12 and 5 indicate the longitudinal wire size and transverse wire size, respectively. Cross-sectional area of the W12 wire is 0.12 sq in. Cross-sectional area of the W5 is 0.05 sq in. See Figure 2-22.

Welded Wire Reinforcement

Figure 2-22

TRANSVERSE WIRES

LONGITUDINAL WIRES

ROLLS

SHEETS

LONGITUDINAL SPACING (IN IN.)

TRANSVERSE SPACING (IN IN.)

W = SMOOTH WIRE
D = DEFORMED WIRE

$$6 \times 6 \text{—} W2.9 \times W2.9$$

LONGITUDINAL WIRE SIZE (CROSS-SECTIONAL AREA)

TRANSVERSE WIRE SIZE (CROSS-SECTIONAL AREA)

WIRE SIZE COMPARISON

W & D Size Number		Area*	Nominal Diameter†	American Steel and Wire Gauge Number
Smooth	Deformed			
W8.5		.085	.329	
W8	D8	.080	.319	
W7.5		.075	.309	
		.074	.3065	1/0
W7	D7	.070	.298	
W6.5		.065	.288	
		.063	.283	1
W6	D6	.060	.276	
W5.5		.055	.264	
		.054	.2625	2

* in sq in.
† in in.

COMMON STOCK SIZES OF WELDED WIRE REINFORCEMENT

New Designation (W-Number)	Old Designation (Wire Gauge)	Diameter*	Weight†
6 × 6 — W1.4 × W1.4	6 × 6 — 10 × 10	⅛	21
6 × 6 — W2.0 × W2.0	6 × 6 — 8 × 8	5/32	29
6 × 6 — W2.9 × W2.9	6 × 6 — 6 × 6	3/16	42
6 × 6 — W4.0 × W4.0	6 × 6 — 4 × 4	¼	58
4 × 4 — W1.4 × W1.4	4 × 4 — 10 × 10	⅛	31
4 × 4 — W2.0 × W2.0	4 × 4 — 8 × 8	5/32	43
4 × 4 — W2.9 × W2.9	4 × 4 — 6 × 6	3/16	62
4 × 4 — W4.0 × W4.0	4 × 4 — 4 × 4	¼	85

* in in.
† in lb per 100 sq ft

Figure 2-22. Welded wire reinforcement (WWR) is designated by a numbering system related to the cross-sectional area of the wire.

Light-Gauge Metal Framing Members

Light-gauge metal framing members, such as C shapes, channels, and tracks, are commonly used in residential and light commercial construction. C shapes are the most common metal framing member and are used for load-bearing and non-load-bearing walls and partitions as studs and joists. See Figure 2-23.

The *Prescriptive Method for Residential Cold-Formed Steel Framing* is a standard that provides construction details and other information for the construction of one- and two-family dwellings using light-gauge steel framing members.

Figure 2-23. Light-gauge metal framing members are commonly used in residential and light commercial construction.

Light-gauge metal framing members are manufactured by cold forming, in which the steel is rolled, hammered, or stretched at low temperatures. Metal framing members are galvanized to prevent corrosion. Metal framing members are available in several thicknesses. C shapes used for studs and joists are typically 14 ga, 16 ga, or 18 ga steel. Channels are available in widths ranging from 2½″ to 6″ and in 1″ and 1⅜″ depths. C shapes used for studs are available in widths ranging from 2½″ to 8″ and in 1¼″, 1⅜″, 1½″, and 1⅝″ depths. U channels and furring channels are also manufactured from light-gauge cold-rolled steel. C shapes, tracks, U channels, and furring channels are typically joined using self-tapping screws or powder-actuated fasteners. Light-gauge metal framing members are discussed in greater detail in Chapter 3.

Heavy-gauge framing members used for load-bearing studs, floor joists, and window and door frames are also produced using the cold-rolling process. Heavy-gauge framing members range in thickness from 20 ga to 14 ga, and are galvanized to prevent corrosion.

Miscellaneous Metal Building Products

Metal products are commonly used in construction for weather protection, ductwork, facing, and ornamental work. Thin metal sheets can be cut and bent with ease and shaped into gutters and downspouts. Metal flashing protects wood and masonry from water damage. Metal siding is easy to apply, is maintenance-free, and also provides fire protection for a building. Ductwork used in an HVAC system can also be fabricated from thin metal.

INSULATION

Insulation is a material used as a barrier to inhibit thermal and sound transmission. Insulation is available as loose fill, flexible, rigid, and foamed-in-place. Loose fill and flexible insulation, such as blankets and batts, are commonly used in residential and light commercial construction. Loose fill insulation is granular mineral wool or pellets made from glass, slag, rock wool, or expanded mica poured or blown into place. Flexible insulation is blanket and batt insulation composed of mineral fiber, vegetable fiber, or glass wool attached to a waterproof paper and manufactured in widths to fit exactly between studs and joists. Batt insulation is 48″ long, and blankets are available in longer continuous rolls. Loose fill and flexible insulation is placed in frame wall cavities and over the ceiling in the attic space. See Figure 2-24.

CertainTeed Corporation

LOOSE FILL INSULATION

FLEXIBLE INSULATION

Figure 2-24. Loose fill or batt insulation is placed between framing members.

Rigid insulation board is produced from expanded plastic foam and is available in ½″ and ²⁵⁄₃₂″ thicknesses. Rigid insulation board may be used as foundation wall insulation or exterior wall sheathing, or installed under concrete slabs to minimize thermal infiltration. Rigid foam insulation is attached to vertical surfaces using mechanical fasteners, powder-actuated fasteners, and/or adhesives.

Foamed-in-place insulation is a chemical foam that is poured or sprayed into wall cavities. As the foam is poured or sprayed, it expands to fill the opening, making it useful in hard-to-reach or unusually shaped areas. Excess foam is trimmed away with a long blade. In addition to possessing excellent insulating properties, foamed-in-place insulation seals a surface well against air infiltration.

Insulation is rated by R value. The *R value* is a value that represents the ability of a material to resist heat flow. Higher R values represent a greater resistance to heat flow. Buildings in colder climates require insulation with higher R values. A comparison of required R values for two areas of the United States follows:

	North Central	Southeast
Walls	R-18	R-13
Floors	R-25	R-13
Ceilings with attic	R-49	R-49

PLASTICS

Plastics are used for many construction applications, including countertops, wall and floor coverings, piping, and housewraps. Plastics can be combined with other materials to increase durability of the product. For example, thin plastic overlays can be bonded to plywood panels to provide greater durability, chemical resistance, and abrasion resistance. A variety of products is available, each having different physical and chemical properties.

Plastics are usually manufactured as thin material and are shown on prints by a solid line or by two lines spaced close together to indicate the two faces. When the material has significant thickness, the architect may use a symbol of choice. A designation or note is included, with an arrow pointing to the material in place.

Plastic Laminates

Plastic laminates are available in a variety of designs, colors, and textures such as simulated stone. Plastic laminate is used for countertops and cabinet facings. The laminate is bonded to a subsurface such as plywood or hardboard using an adhesive. Plastic laminates are available in sheets in stock sizes up to 5′ × 12′.

Plastic laminates may also be bonded to hardboard panels and used as interior wall coverings. The wall coverings are available in a variety of colors, patterns, and textures, and provide excellent durability.

Finish Flooring

Resilient finish flooring and laminate flooring are installed in high-traffic areas such as kitchens, dining areas, hallways, and entries due to their durability and ease of cleaning. Resilient finish flooring is commonly manufactured from vinyl material. Resilient finish flooring is available in tile ranging from 9″ × 9″ to 36″ × 36″ and as sheets in 6′, 9′, and 12′ widths. Resilient finish flooring must be installed over an underlayment surface that is smooth and free from bumps and indentations.

Laminate flooring is a composite material that consists of a transparent top layer, decorative layer, carrier layer, and bottom layer. See Figure 2-25. The top layer and decorative layer, where the pattern is placed, are plastic materials that provide excellent durability. The carrier layer is fiberboard or particleboard, and the bottom layer is a stiff paper-based material.

Solid-surface countertops, manufactured from composite resin materials, are popular for kitchens and bathrooms.

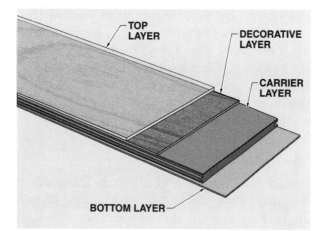

Figure 2-25. Laminate flooring is a plastic composite material.

Figure 2-26. Vinyl siding, gutters, and downspouts are commonly used as finish materials on residential and light commercial buildings.

Exterior Finish Products

Exterior vinyl siding, gutters, and downspouts are commonly used as finish materials on residential and light commercial buildings. Siding may be smooth or textured to provide a wood-grain pattern. Vinyl siding, gutters, and downspouts are durable and maintenance-free. See Figure 2-26. The color of vinyl products extends completely through the product. Vinyl products can be cut and assembled using simple hand tools and joined using an adhesive. Siding pieces lock together with grooves and notches that are part of the siding design. Vinyl siding is available in 8″, 10″, and 12″ widths and 12′-6″ lengths. Siding and window and door components are available with a vinyl covering bonded to the wood to provide permanent weather resistance and a colorfast surface.

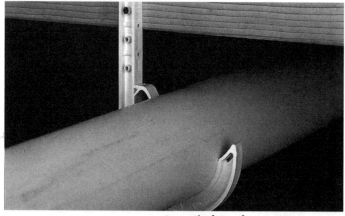

Sioux Chief Manufacturing Company, Inc.

Polyvinyl chloride (PVC) pipe is the most commonly used plastic plumbing pipe.

Plastic Pipe and Fittings

Plastic pipe and fittings are used for water supply and drainage, waste, and vent systems in residential and light commercial buildings. Four basic types of plastic pipe and fittings used for plumbing applications are acrylonitrile-butadiene-styrene (ABS), polyvinyl chloride (PVC), chlorinated polyvinyl chloride (CPVC), and cross-linked polyethylene (PEX). *Acrylonitrile-butadiene-styrene (ABS) pipe and fittings* are black plastic pipe and fittings used for sanitary drainage and vent piping, and aboveground and underground stormwater drainage. ABS pipe is available in diameters ranging from 1¼″ to 6″ and 10′ and 20′ lengths. *Polyvinyl chloride (PVC) pipe and fittings* are plastic pipe and fittings used for sanitary drainage and vent piping, aboveground and underground stormwater drainage, water mains, and water service lines. PVC pipe is the most common type of plastic plumbing pipe used in residential and light commercial buildings. PVC pipe is available in diameters ranging from 1¼″ to 6″ and 10′ and 20′ lengths. *Chlorinated polyvinyl chloride (CPVC) pipe and fittings* are cream-colored thermoplastic materials specially formulated to withstand higher temperatures than other plastics. CPVC is commonly used for water supply systems, and is available in diameters from ½″ to 12″ in 10′ lengths. *Cross-linked polyethylene (PEX) tubing* is flexible thermosetting plastic used for water service piping and water distribution piping. See Figure 2-27. PEX is available in diameters from ¼″ to 2″, and in straight lengths of 20′ and flexible coils ranging from 100′ to 1000′.

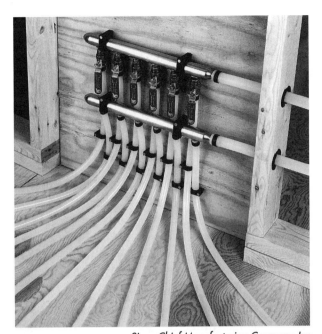

Sioux Chief Manufacturing Company, Inc.

Figure 2-27. Cross-linked polyethylene (PEX) tubing can be used for water service piping and water distribution piping.

Miscellaneous Plastic Building Products

A variety of other building products, including vapor barriers, housewraps, and light diffusers, are manufactured from plastic. A *vapor barrier* is a thin, moisture-resistant material placed over the ground or in walls to retard the passage of moisture into a building. Large plastic sheets of polyethylene film are positioned over sand or gravel fill before a concrete slab is placed to retard the passage of moisture from the ground. Vapor barriers may also be installed on exterior walls to reduce the passage of moisture into the building. A vapor barrier must be placed on the warm side (inside surface) of an exterior wall to prevent moisture accumulation in the insulation.

A *housewrap* is a translucent spun-plastic sheet material that is tightly wrapped around a building to prevent water and air penetration into the building while allowing moisture vapor and gases from a building interior to move outward. See Figure 2-28. Housewrap is available in 3' and 9' wide rolls and is fastened to the exterior wall sheathing using staples. Translucent plastic is also fabricated into a variety of shapes and sizes for use as ceiling light panels, light fixtures, and skylights.

Figure 2-28. Housewrap is tightly wrapped around a building to prevent water and air penetration into the building.

GLASS

Glass is a hard and brittle material made by melting silica to produce a flat glass by a controlled cooling process. Two basic types of glass are used for building construction—sheet glass and float glass. *Sheet glass* is glass manufactured by drawing it vertically or horizontally and slowly annealing (cooling) it to produce a high-gloss surface. Sheet glass is the most common type of glass used in residential and light commercial construction, and is available in three thicknesses: single strength (³⁄₃₂″ thick), double strength (⅛″ thick), and heavy sheet (from ³⁄₁₆″ to ⁷⁄₁₆″ thick). *Float glass* is glass manufactured by floating liquid glass on a surface of liquid tin and slowly annealing it to produce a transparent, flat glass. Float glass has excellent optical properties and is used in mirrors, architectural windows, and specialty applications.

Insulating glass is window glass made of two pieces of sheet glass that are separated by a sealed air space. The edges are sealed on all four sides by a glass, metal, or plastic closure. A typical piece of insulating glass measuring ⁷⁄₁₆″ thick is composed of two sheets of double strength glass (⅛″) with a ³⁄₁₆″ air space and a glass closure. See Figure 2-29. Insulating glass windows may be coated or the air space may be filled to provide additional insulating properties. A *low-emittance (low-E) coating* is a metal or metallic oxide coating that reduces the passage of heat and ultraviolet rays through windows. Argon or krypton gas may be used to fill the air space to reduce the passage of heat from one piece of glass to the other.

Pella Corporation

Windows provide light and ventilation for the interior of a building.

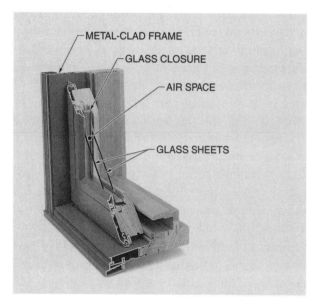

METAL-CLAD FRAME

GLASS CLOSURE

AIR SPACE

GLASS SHEETS

Marvin Windows and Doors

Figure 2-29. Insulating glass is made of two pieces of sheet glass that are separated by a sealed air space.

Other types of glass, such as tempered, patterned, and laminated glass, may be indicated on the prints or in the specifications. *Tempered glass* is glass produced by heating a sheet of glass during the manufacturing process to near its softening point and then quickly cooling the glass under carefully controlled conditions. Tempered glass is significantly stronger than sheet or float glass, has a high resistance to thermal stress, and has high impact resistance. Tempered glass is required for use in patio doors, entrance doors, sidelights, and other hazardous locations. Tempered glass cannot be cut, drilled, or modified after manufacture. Therefore, the required size must be specified when ordering tempered glass.

Patterned glass is glass that has one side finished with a fine grid or an unpolished surface so the glass is translucent. Patterned glass is used in office partitions and for doors and windows when privacy is desired. *Laminated glass* is specialty glass produced by placing a clear sheet of polyvinyl butyral (PVB) between two sheets of glass and subjecting the composite to intense heat and pressure. Laminated glass is used in schools and other public buildings where safety is a concern, and is similar to the glass used in automobiles. When laminated glass is broken, the particles generally adhere to the plastic sheet. *Wire glass* is glass embedded with wire mesh to provide additional security. When wire glass is broken, the wire mesh holds the glass pieces together. *Cathedral glass,* or stained glass, is a type of art glass available in a wide range of colors and with many surface treatments. Cathedral glass is cut into small pieces and then reassembled using lead channels. Windows made from cathedral glass are often used in churches and public buildings.

A *glass block* is a hollow opaque or transparent block made of glass and is used in non-load-bearing walls and partitions. Steel lintels are installed above masonry wall openings to be filled with glass block so the weight of the masonry above will not rest on the glass block. Glass block is available in 6″, 8″, and 12″ (nominal) squares and assorted thicknesses. The nominal sizes allow for a ¼″ mortar joint. Glass block is occasionally used to provide light in rooms when ventilation is not a factor and as interior partitions.

Glass in elevations is generally shown as blank rectangles. Since glass is thin, it is shown on plan views and sections as a thin line. When large-scale details are drawn, glass is shown with a series of closely drawn parallel lines.

GYPSUM PRODUCTS

Gypsum is a soft mineral used as the core for gypsum board and gypsum lath, and may also be used as an ingredient in plaster. Gypsum board is used for interior and exterior finish applications. No special symbol is required when showing gypsum board on plan views, sections, and details. When a masonry wall is to be plastered, a line is added to represent the thickness of the lath and plaster. A solid plaster wall is represented by a wavy line and a sprinkling of dots. See Figure 2-30. When lath and plaster or gypsum board is shown on large-scale details, the symbol used is an overall pattern of dots.

National Gypsum Company

Gypsum joint compound and reinforcing paper are applied to the joints between panels.

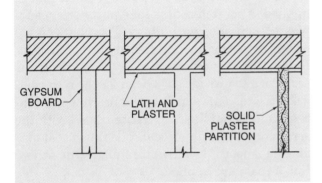

Figure 2-30. Special symbols are not used to represent gypsum board on plan views. A line indicates lath and plaster on a masonry wall. A solid plaster partition is represented with wavy lines and dots.

Gypsum Board

Interior gypsum board, or drywall, consists of a fire-resistant gypsum core encased with heavy paper on both sides. The core and heavy paper may be treated to provide water resistance and greater dimensional stability. Exterior gypsum board has a treated core to provide water resistance, and may have fibers embedded in the surface to create a better bond with the finish material. Gypsum board is available in a variety of thicknesses and lengths. Gypsum board thicknesses range from ¼″ to 1″, with ½″, ⅝″, and ¾″ thicknesses used for interior applications. Coreboards and liner boards for shafts, firewalls, and stairways are commonly ¾″ or 1″ thick. See Figure 2-31. Gypsum board is available in 4′ × 8′ sheets, but 12′ and 14′ lengths are more common because less installation time is required.

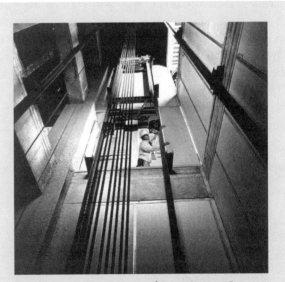

United States Gypsum Company

Figure 2-31. Gypsum board is used for interior and exterior applications.

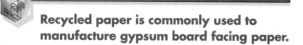

Recycled paper is commonly used to manufacture gypsum board facing paper.

Gypsum board is fastened to wood studs or joists using an adhesive and nails or self-tapping (drywall) screws. Screws are used to fasten gypsum board to metal studs and joists. The nails or screws are driven in so a slight indentation is created around the nail or screw head without breaking the paper covering. Gypsum joint compound and reinforcing paper is applied to the joints between panels and corners. See Figure 2-32. Compound is also applied over the nail or screw heads. After the compound has properly set, the surface is sanded and additional joint compound is applied and sanded after it has set until a smooth finish is achieved.

More than one layer of gypsum board may be applied to a wall or ceiling to provide additional security and resistance to sound transmission. The first layer is fastened to the supporting structural members using conventional means. The second layer is bonded to the first layer at a right angle using construction adhesive or gypsum joint compound.

Lath and Plaster

Gypsum lath is a gypsum product composed of an air-entrained gypsum core pressed between two sheets of absorbent paper. Gypsum lath is used as a base for plaster and is available in ⅜″ and ½″ thicknesses measuring 18″ × 48″. The 48″ lengths allow the lath to extend across three studs. The lath is clipped or nailed to the studs leaving approximately ½″ between the upper and lower edges of the lath. As plaster is applied to the surface, it is forced into the preformed holes of the lath and spaces between the lath to create a bond with the lath.

The traditional method of plastering is the three-coat method. After the lath is properly fastened to the studs and joists, a scratch coat is applied. A scratch coat is lime putty or gypsum plaster combined with fibers. The fibers create a bond between the scratch coat and brown coat. Before the scratch coat is dry, the surface is scratched to provide good bond for the next coat. The second coat, which is the brown coat, contains additional fibers to create a bond with the scratch coat and finish coat. The finish coat provides a smooth, level, white finish. One or two finish coats are applied.

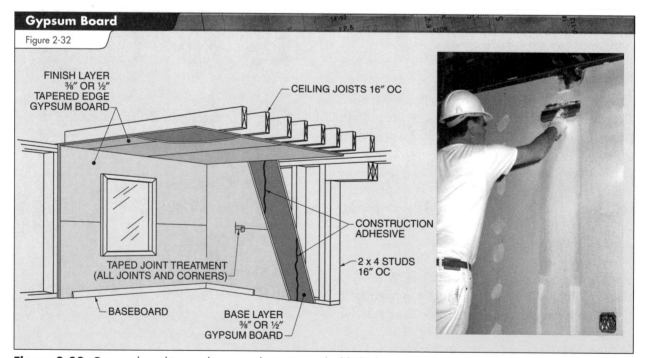

Gypsum Board

Figure 2-32

FINISH LAYER ⅜″ OR ½″ TAPERED EDGE GYPSUM BOARD

CEILING JOISTS 16″ OC

CONSTRUCTION ADHESIVE

2 × 4 STUDS 16″ OC

TAPED JOINT TREATMENT (ALL JOINTS AND CORNERS)

BASEBOARD

BASE LAYER ⅜″ OR ½″ GYPSUM BOARD

Figure 2-32. Gypsum board is taped to cover the joints. In double-thick applications, gypsum board is placed at a 90° angle to the base sheets.

Exterior Insulation and Finish Systems

An *exterior insulation and finish system (EIFS)* is an exterior finish system consisting of insulation board, reinforcing mesh, a base coat of acrylic copolymers and portland cement, and a finish of acrylic resins. See Figure 2-33. Insulation board is extruded or molded expanded polystyrene, which provides thermal insulation and flexibility in the structure to minimize cracking. Insulation board is attached to a wood, concrete, or masonry substrate using mechanical fasteners or construction adhesive. A ¼″ thick base coat is troweled onto the surface of the insulation board and reinforced with one or two layers of an open-weave glass fiber reinforcing mesh. After the base coat has properly set, the textured finish of acrylic resin is troweled or sprayed onto the structure to create the desired finish.

ROOFING

A variety of roofing materials is used on residential and light commercial buildings including asphalt and fiberglass shingles, wood shingles and shakes, roofing tile, and built-up and elastomeric roofing materials. Asphalt shingles are produced from asphalt-saturated felt that is covered with mineral granules. Fiberglass shingles are produced from fiberglass mats that are covered with mineral granules. Asphalt and fiberglass shingles are available in strips of three-tab shingles (12″ wide × 3′ long) in a variety of patterns and colors. See Figure 2-34.

Asphalt shingles were first used as a roofing material in the late 1800s.

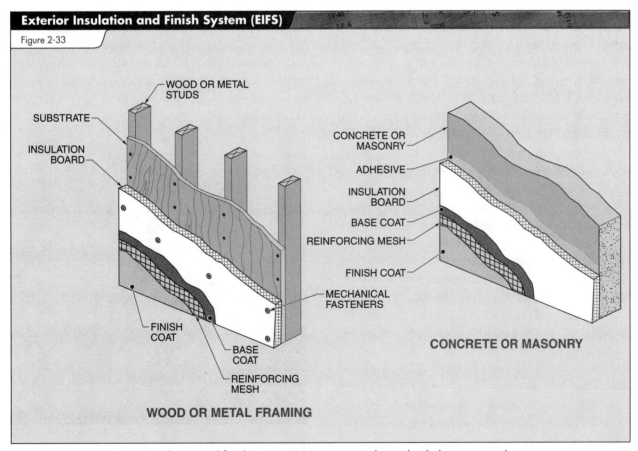

Figure 2-33. An exterior insulation and finish system (EIFS) is commonly used in light commercial construction.

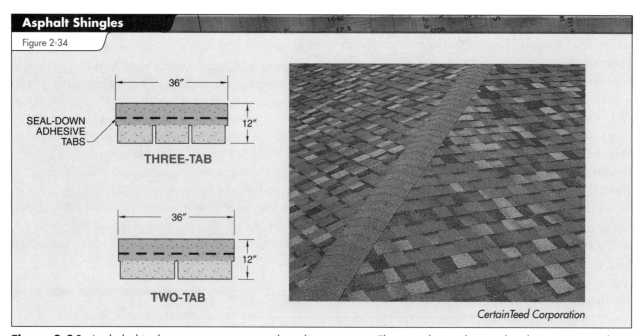

Asphalt Shingles

Figure 2-34

36″

SEAL-DOWN
ADHESIVE
TABS

12″

THREE-TAB

36″

12″

TWO-TAB

CertainTeed Corporation

Figure 2-34. Asphalt shingles are common on residential construction. Three- and two-tab strip shingles are commonly installed on new construction.

Wood shingles and shakes are one of the oldest types of roof coverings. Wood shingles have a smoother finish than shakes since shingles are sawn from cedar logs and shakes are split from the logs. Wood shingles are available in random widths ranging from 3″ to 14″ and in standard lengths of 16″, 18″, and 24″. Wood shakes are available in random widths starting at 4″ and in standard lengths of 18″, 24″, and 32″.

Clay and concrete roofing tile are available in a variety of colors and profiles. Roofing tile is durable and highly fire-resistant. Clay tile is lighter than concrete tile; however, concrete tile is more durable and is used more often than clay tile. Roofing tile may have a flat or roll profile. Accessory tiles, such as ridge and hip tile, rake tile, and apex tile, have different profiles to accommodate different applications.

Built-up roofs consist of three, four, or five individual layers of asphalt-saturated roofing felt bonded together with hot tar or asphalt. See Figure 2-35. The final layer of roofing felt is coated with gravel. Built-up roofs are used for flat roofs.

Elastomeric roofs are formed from rubber sheets that are chemically welded together at the edges with the proper cement/adhesive. Elastomeric roofs provide excellent weatherability and resistance to chemicals and ultraviolet radiation.

Ethylene propylene diene monomer (EPDM) roofing is a type of elastomeric roofing material that consists of a single membrane measuring 30 mil to 60 mil thick that is either reinforced with fabric or unreinforced. EPDM roofing may be laid loose on the roof deck, mechanically fastened, or adhered to the roof deck, depending on the application.

CertainTeed Corporation

Figure 2-35. Built-up roofs are commonly used on flat roofs. The asphalt-saturated felt layers are bonded together with hot tar or asphalt.

ELECTRICAL AND MECHANICAL SYSTEMS MATERIALS

Electrical and mechanical systems are comprised of three primary components—the generation or main energy sources, distribution systems, and receptacles, switches, and luminaires. The proper coordination of the components in electrical and mechanical systems provides for safe operation of the equipment and the system. Standard sizes are established for many electrical and mechanical system components, ensuring compatibility and interchangeability with components produced by other manufacturers.

Electrical Materials and Components

The basic categories of electrical materials and components include service panels; distribution materials such as conduit, junction boxes, wire, and various cable materials; and electrical devices such as switches, receptacles, and luminaires. Electrical materials are manufactured in compliance with provisions of the National Electrical Code® and Underwriters Laboratories to ensure safety and the ability to handle the imposed electrical loads.

Sources. Electrical power enters a building from a transformer through a main service drop or lateral. The primary component of the service is the main service panelboard. See Figure 2-36. A *panelboard* is a wall-mounted distribution cabinet containing overcurrent and short-circuit protection devices. Panelboards consist of an enclosure (tub) and an interior on which circuit breakers or fuses are mounted and connected to busbars. Panelboard interiors are commonly assembled at a manufacturing facility according to specific requirements. Panelboards are rated by their total load capacity (in amperes).

A panelboard contains overcurrent protection devices such as fuses and circuit breakers. A *fuse* is an overcurrent protection device with a fusible link that melts and opens a circuit when an overload condition or short circuit occurs. A *circuit breaker* is an overcurrent protection device with a mechanism that automatically opens a circuit when an overload condition or short

circuit occurs. Fuses and circuit breakers are rated by the current that can flow through the device without interrupting the circuit. The interrupting (trip) mechanism within a circuit breaker is operated thermally, magnetically, or by a combination of the two. Most circuit breakers use a combination thermal/magnetic trip mechanism.

Figure 2-36. Panelboards provide a connection for power distribution and circuit protection.

Distribution Systems. Electrical cables and raceways (conduit) extend from the main service panelboard to electrical luminaires. The prints and/or specifications specify the types of electrical cable and raceways to be installed.

A *conductor* is a wire that is used to control the flow of electrons in an electrical circuit. Article 100 of the NEC® provides three definitions for a conductor. Conductor size is designated by an American Wire Gauge (AWG) number that indicates the diameter. The higher the gauge number, the smaller the conductor diameter. See Figure 2-37. The NEC® recognizes three types of conductors for electrical installations—copper, aluminum, and copper-clad aluminum. Copper conductors offer the most ampacity. Bare copper conductors are available in gauges ranging from No. 14 to No. 4/0. Bare copper conductors are most commonly used for electrical system grounding wires. Three grades of copper wire are soft drawn, medium hard drawn, and hard drawn temper. Aluminum conductors are a lightweight wire, and are commonly used for service conductors and feeders for circuits from distribution switchboards to lighting and power panels. Aluminum wire is susceptible to oxidation when exposed to the atmosphere. Oxidation results in resistance to current flow that may lead to overheating at connections. Anti-oxidation materials may be applied prior to completion of the installation to protect against oxidation and overheating.

Conductors can be bare, covered, or insulated. Bare conductors do not have an outer covering that encases the actual conductor. Covered conductors are covered by a material that has not been evaluated or recognized as having a specific insulation rating and are rarely used in electrical systems. Insulated conductors are covered with a material that has been recognized by the NEC® as an insulation material. Insulation used with conductors includes the following:

- Moisture-resistant thermoplastic (TW). TW conductors are used in wet and dry applications. TW insulation does not have an outer covering and is used with No. 14 solid or stranded conductors. TW conductors have a maximum operating temperature of 140°F.
- Heat-resistant thermoplastic (THHN). THHN conductors have a nylon or equivalent coating and are used in dry locations. THHN insulation is used with No. 14 solid or stranded conductors and has a maximum operating temperature of 194°F.
- Moisture- and heat-resistant thermoplastic (THW). THW conductors are used in wet and dry locations. THW conductors do not have an outer covering and are used with No. 14 solid or stranded conductors. THW conductors have a maximum operating temperature of 194°F when used with lighting equipment of 1000 V or less.
- Moisture-resistant thermoset (XHHW). XHHW conductors have a fire-resistant synthetic polymer insulation and do not include an outer covering. XHHW conductors are used in wet and dry locations, are made with No. 14 solid or stranded conductors, and have a maximum operating temperature of 167°F in wet locations and 194°F in dry locations.
- Moisture-, heat-, and oil-resistant thermoplastic (MTW). MTW conductors have thick (Type A) or thin (Type B) insulation coatings. Type A insulation has no outer covering. Type B insulation has a nylon covering. MTW conductors are

COPPER CONDUCTOR RATINGS*		
AWG	Ampacity	Diameter*
• 18	—	40
• 17	—	45
• 16	—	51
• 15	—	57
• 14	20	64
• 12	25	81
• 10	30	102
• 8	40	128
• 6	55	162
• 4	70	204
• 3	85	229
• 2	95	258
• 1	110	289
• 0	125	325
• 00	145	365
• 000	165	410

*@ 60°C

Figure 2-37. Conductor size is designated by an American Wire Gauge (AWG) number that indicates diameter.

commonly used for machine tool wiring in wet locations and have a maximum operating temperature of 140°F. MTW conductors are made with No. 14 stranded conductors.

- Thermoplastic-covered fixture (TF). TF conductors have a thermoplastic insulation with no other covering. TF conductors are made with No. 16 or No. 18 solid or stranded conductors and have a maximum operating temperature of 140°F. TF conductors are commonly used for wiring electrical fixtures.

- Thermoplastic-covered fixture wire—flexible stranded (TFF). TFF conductors have similar characteristics to TF conductors but are made only with stranded conductors.

- Heat-resistant thermoplastic-covered fixture (TFFN). TFFN conductors are used for fixture wiring and have a maximum operating temperature of 194°F.

A *cable assembly,* or cable, is a flexible assembly of two or more conductors with a protective outer sheathing. The most common cable assemblies used in residential and light commercial construction are armored cable (AC), metal-clad cable (MC), nonmetallic-sheathed cable, and service-entrance cable. See Figure 2-38.

Armored cable (AC) is an assembly that contains one or more conductors wrapped in a flexible metallic covering. Armored cable is available with single or multiple conductors ranging from No. 4 to No. 14. AC may only be used in dry locations and must be supported every 4'-6" and within 12" of outlets and fittings. Armored cable is commonly referred to as Type AC or BX.

Metal-clad cable (MC) is an assembly of one or more conductors, with or without fiber-optic members, and enclosed in an armor of interlocking metal sheath, or smooth or corrugated metal sheath. Metal-clad cable is installed as services, feeders, and branch circuits for power, lighting, and control and signal circuits. MC cable cannot be used where exposed to destructive corrosive conditions such as direct burial in the earth or in concrete, or where exposed to cinder fill. MC cable must be supported every 6' and within 12" of boxes, cabinets, fittings, or other cable terminations.

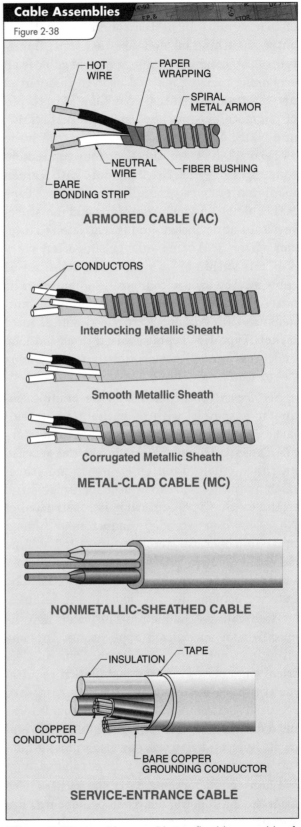

Cable Assemblies

Figure 2-38

HOT WIRE
PAPER WRAPPING
SPIRAL METAL ARMOR
NEUTRAL WIRE
FIBER BUSHING
BARE BONDING STRIP

ARMORED CABLE (AC)

CONDUCTORS

Interlocking Metallic Sheath

Smooth Metallic Sheath

Corrugated Metallic Sheath

METAL-CLAD CABLE (MC)

NONMETALLIC-SHEATHED CABLE

INSULATION
TAPE
COPPER CONDUCTOR
BARE COPPER GROUNDING CONDUCTOR

SERVICE-ENTRANCE CABLE

Figure 2-38. A cable assembly is a flexible assembly of two or more conductors with a protective outer sheathing.

Nonmetallic-sheathed cable is an assembly of two or more insulated conductors with an outer sheathing of moisture-resistant, flame-retardant, nonmetallic material. NM cable is an economical wiring method used in residential and light commercial construction. Three types of nonmetallic-sheathed cable are NM, NMC, and NMS. NM cable, also known in the trade as Romex®, has two, three, or four conductors ranging in size from No. 2 to No. 14 with a green insulated or bare grounding conductor. Type NM cable has a flame-retardant and moisture-resistant outer jacket, and is restricted to interior wiring. NM cable must be supported every 4'-6" and within 12" of outlets and fittings. NM cable may be used with metallic or nonmetallic boxes. Type NMC cable has a flame-retardant, moisture-, fungus, and corrosion-resistant outer jacket. Type NMS cable is used in closed-loop and programmed power distribution systems ("smart houses").

Service-entrance cable is a single- or multiconductor assembly, with or without an overall jacket. Two types of service-entrance conductors are Types USE and SE. Underground service-entrance cable (Type USE) has a moisture-resistant jacket and can be used for direct burial in the earth. Type USE cable is constructed of No. 12 solid or stranded conductors and has a maximum operating temperature of 167°F. Type SE cable is made with one or more conductors with gauges ranging from No. 12 to No. 4/0. The outer covering is fire- and moisture-resistant.

High-voltage conductors and cable may be specified for specialized applications. In some situations, detailed specifications from an electrical engineer concerning installation requirements, safe applications, and testing are required. Cable manufacturers can provide technical data and pricing for high-voltage wire and cable. Independent testing agencies provide quotations for specialized high-voltage cable testing.

Large conductors that carry electrical service from the main power source to panelboards are specified by the number of conductors, wire gauge, number and gauge of grounding conductor, and overall cable diameter. For example, a notation of 4#4, 1#10 GRD, 1¼ indicates four

No. 4 conductors, one No. 10 grounding conductor, and an overall cable diameter of 1¼". See Figure 2-39.

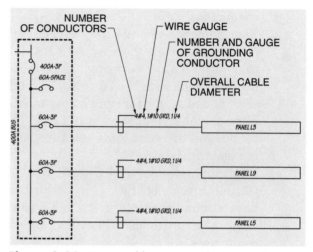

Figure 2-39. Heavy cables are specified according to the number of conductors, wire gauge, number and gauge number of grounding conductors, and overall cable diameter.

A *raceway* is an enclosed channel for conductors. Raceways include all enclosures used for conductors including switches, panels, controllers, and cabinets. Raceways provide protection for conductors and give the system flexibility in that existing conductors can be removed and new conductors pulled in. Conduit is a common type of raceway used in residential, commercial, and industrial installations. Metallic and nonmetallic conduit is available in rigid and flexible forms. See Figure 2-40. Conduit is secured in position using fasteners that fasten the conduit to structural members. Manufacturer specifications and the NEC® provide information about fastener spacing and fastening requirements.

RACEWAYS		
	Abbreviation	**Size**
Rigid metal conduit	RMC	½" to 6" in 10' lengths
Rigid nonmetallic conduit	RNMC	½" to 6" in 10' and 25' lengths
Electrical metallic tubing	EMT	½" to 4" in 10' lengths
Flexible metal conduit	FMC	⅜" to 4" in 25', 50', or 100' coils

Figure 2-40. Common raceways installed in residential and light commercial buildings include rigid metal conduit, rigid nonmetallic conduit, electrical metallic tubing, and flexible metal conduit.

Rigid metal conduit (RMC) is a heavy conduit made of metal. RMC is considered to be the universal raceway and is permitted for use in all atmospheric conditions and types of occupancies. RMC is available in 10′ lengths with a coupling threaded on one end and in ½″ to 6″ diameters.

Rigid nonmetallic conduit (RNC) is conduit made of materials other than metal. Rigid polyvinyl chloride (PVC) conduit is the most common rigid nonmetallic conduit. PVC conduit is a nonconductive conduit that is not permitted to be installed in hazardous locations or air plenums. Rigid PVC conduit is available in 10′ lengths and ½″ to 6″ diameters. PVC conduit is available in thin wall (Schedule 40) and thick wall (Schedule 80). Fittings, such as couplings, are fastened to PVC conduit with a special cement. PVC conduit is also available in power and communications (P&C) grade for use in power and communication applications. P&C grade PVC conduit is available in 25′ lengths and ½″ to 6″ diameters.

Electrical metallic tubing (EMT), commonly referred to as thin wall or steel tube conduit, is a lightweight tubular steel raceway without threads on the ends. EMT is available in 10′ lengths and ½″ to 4″ diameters. EMT is galvanized or electroplated to resist corrosion. EMT must be supported every 10′ and within 3′ of each outlet box, junction box, cabinet, or fitting. Different EMT fittings are available to facilitate connections, including compression and set screw couplings and compression and set screw connectors.

Flexible metal conduit (FMC), or Greenfield, is a raceway of metal strips that are formed into a circular cross-sectional raceway. The metal strips are helically wound, formed, and interlocked. FMC is manufactured in ⅜″ to 4″ diameters, and is available in coils of 25′, 50′, or 100′, depending on the diameter. Diameters range from ⅜″ to 4″. FMC must be supported every 4′-6″ and be securely fastened within 12″ of each box, cabinet, or conduit body. A variety of connection fittings are available.

Cable and conduit are connected at electrical boxes. A *box* is a metallic or nonmetallic electrical enclosure for electrical equipment, devices,

and pulling or terminating conductors. Boxes protect connections, provide access to wiring, and provide a method for mounting switches, receptacles, and luminaires. Nonmetallic boxes are permitted only when using nonmetallic-sheathed cable, nonmetallic raceways, open wiring on insulators, and concealed knob-and-tube wiring. Boxes are available in a variety of sizes and types for mounting switches, receptacles, and other devices. Knockouts are provided in boxes to allow conductors and conduit to be inserted. Common electrical boxes include utility (handy), square, switch, octagonal, and masonry boxes. See Figure 2-41.

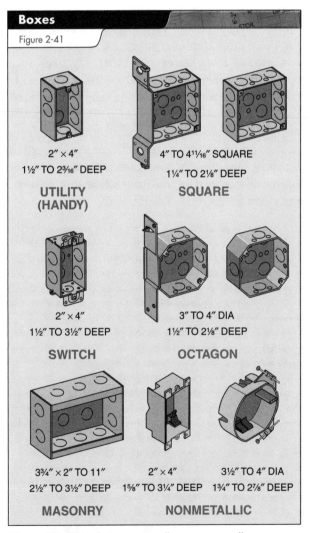

Figure 2-41. A box is a metallic or nonmetallic electrical enclosure used for equipment, devices, and pulling or terminating conductors.

The National Electrical Code® is revised and updated every three years.

Switches, Receptacles, and Luminaires. Switches, receptacles, and luminaires (lighting fixtures) are typically shown on floor plans using various symbols and abbreviations. See Figure 2-42. A *switch* is a device with a current and voltage rating, used to open or close an electrical circuit. Switches are classified according to the number of poles, number of closed positions, method of operation, and similar considerations. Common switches include single-pole, double-pole, three-way, four-way, key-operated, momentary-contact, maintain-contact, dimmer, photoelectric, and safety switches. A *receptacle* is a contact device installed at an outlet for the connection of equipment to an electrical system. A *luminaire (lighting fixture)* is a complete lighting unit including the components that distribute light, position and protect the lamps, and provide connection to the power supply. Types of luminaires include surface-mounted, ceiling-mounted, recessed, track lighting, bracket-mounted, pole-mounted, and exit lights. Electrical plans and schedules may be provided for fixture installation.

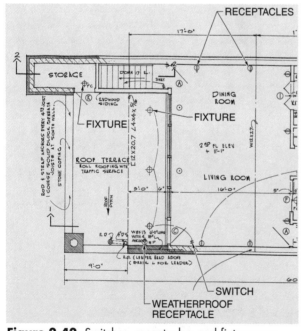

Figure 2-42. Switches, receptacles, and fixtures are typically shown on floor plans.

Mechanical Materials

Mechanical systems include the heating, ventilating, and air conditioning (HVAC) and plumbing systems. A variety of sources are used to heat, cool, and properly treat the air in an HVAC system. In a plumbing system, a centrally located water heater or on-demand water heater may be used to heat the water supply. Air and water are conveyed throughout a building using a variety of ductwork, pipes, connectors, and valves. The air and water are distributed into the living space using various fixtures including radiators and grilles for HVAC systems and lavatories and water closets for water supply.

Sources. Municipal water supplies or private wells are the primary sources for water in an HVAC or plumbing system. The location of the municipal water supply connection is shown on plot plans. In a plumbing system, a water service pipe extends from the municipal water supply connection to the water meter. A water meter measures the volume of water passing through the water service pipe. A tee is installed in the cold water main, diverting a portion of the available water to a water heater. Gas or electric water heaters, sized by their capacity (in gallons) and recovery rate, supply hot water to plumbing fixtures throughout the building. On-demand, or tankless, water heaters may be installed near fixtures to heat water as it is delivered to the fixtures.

Two common types of HVAC systems are hydronic and forced-air systems. A *hydronic heating system* is a heating system that uses water to convey heat from the source to the point of use. A circulating pump conveys water from the source (typically a boiler), through the piping system, terminal devices (radiators), and return piping of the system. A *boiler* is a pressurized vessel that safely and efficiently transfers heat to water. Boilers are available as low-pressure or high-pressure boilers. A *low-pressure boiler* is a boiler that has a maximum allowable working pressure (MAWP) of 15 pounds per square inch (psi). Low-pressure boilers are common in residential applications and light commercial applications such as warehouses and schools. A *high-pressure boiler* is a boiler that has an MAWP above 15 psi. High-pressure boilers are common in industrial operations and electricity generation.

In forced-air systems, a furnace or air conditioner provides heating and cooling, respectively, by changing the temperature of the air at the source and conveying the warmed or cooled air into the living space. A *furnace* is a self-contained heating unit that includes a blower, burner, and heat exchanger or electric heating elements, and controls. See Figure 2-43. A furnace transfers heat from the point of combustion or electric heating elements to the surrounding air. In combustion furnaces, fuel is burned in the firebox. In electric furnaces, electric current flows through a high-resistance wire to create heat, which is transferred to the surrounding air. Forced-air furnaces are categorized by the direction of air flow, fuel or energy used, dimensions, and heating capacity.

An *air conditioner* is a component in a forced-air air conditioning system that cools the air. See Figure 2-44. An air conditioner contains an evaporator, compressor, condenser, and expansion valve. An *evaporator* is a heat exchanger that absorbs heat from the surrounding air and adds the heat to low-pressure refrigerant liquid. Air is passed over the evaporator and distributed to areas to be cooled. A *compressor* is a

mechanical device that compresses refrigerant. The pressurized refrigerant vapor is discharged into the condenser. The *condenser* is a heat exchanger that removes heat from high-pressure refrigerant vapor. The refrigerant condenses and is circulated through an expansion valve. An *expansion valve* is a device that reduces the pressure on liquid refrigerant by allowing the refrigerant to expand.

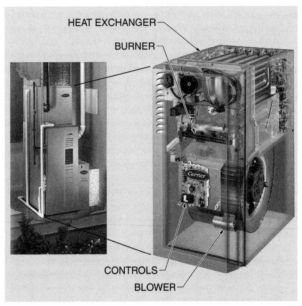

Carrier Corporation

Figure 2-43. A furnace includes a blower, burner, and heat exchanger or electric heating elements, and controls.

Carrier Corporation

Figure 2-44. Air conditioners are available in a variety of sizes to meet different cooling load requirements.

Distribution Systems. A variety of materials is used to distribute heated or cooled water or air, or other liquids or gasses, to the living area or point of use. Common pipe and tubing materials used to convey liquids or gases are plastic, copper, brass, steel, cast iron, and ductile iron. Pipe and tubing are available in various diameters and grades for different applications.

Piping for plumbing and HVAC systems is not generally shown on residential and light commercial building prints. However, an isometric plumbing diagram may be included that shows water supply and drainage systems. Single lines represent each pipe in the system with the nominal pipe diameters specified. See Figure 2-45.

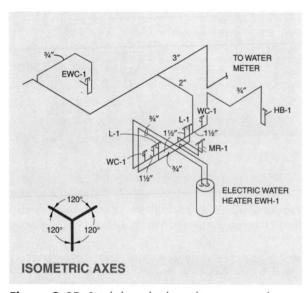

Figure 2-45. Single-line plumbing diagrams may be included in a set of prints to show water supply and drainage systems.

Plastic pipe and tubing are lightweight, inexpensive, and easily joined to plastic fittings. Plastic pipe and tubing are resistant to most chemicals including acids and other corrosive materials. In addition, plastic pipe and tubing have low thermal conductivity, allowing liquids being conveyed to maintain more uniform temperatures. Plastic pipe and tubing also do not conduct electricity and are not subject to galvanic or electrolytic corrosion. A variety of plastic pipe and tubing materials are used in construction including acrylonitrile-butadiene-styrene (ABS),

polyvinyl chloride (PVC), chlorinated polyvinyl chloride (CPVC), and cross-linked polyethylene (PEX). Plastic pipe and tubing are available in nominal diameters ranging from ¼" to 12", and are joined using heat fusion, flanged joints, or solvent cement. Thicker plastic pipe may be joined by threading.

Copper tube and fittings are used for water supply and distribution systems, drainage, waste and vent systems, fire suppression systems, and HVAC systems. Copper tube is available as either drawn or annealed. *Drawn copper tube,* also known as hard copper tube, is copper tube that is manufactured by pulling copper through a die or series of dies to achieve a desired diameter. *Annealed copper tube,* also known as soft copper tube, is drawn copper tube that is heated to a specific temperature and cooled at a predetermined rate to impart the desired hardness and strength properties. Copper tube is manufactured in many different wall thicknesses or types including Types K, L, M, DWV, G, ACR, and medical gas. Types K, L, M, and DWV are used for plumbing applications. Types K, L, and M are primarily used for potable water service, HVAC applications, and noncritical laboratory gases. *Potable water* is water that is free from impurities that could cause disease or harmful physiological effects. Type DWV copper tube is used for drainage, waste, and venting applications, and has the thinnest wall of any copper tube. Type G copper tube is used for natural gas and liquefied petroleum (LP) gas applications. Type ACR copper tube is used for air conditioning and refrigeration applications. Medical gas copper tube is used for medical gas applications. Nominal diameters of copper tube range from ¼" to 8", with a variety of wall thicknesses depending on type and diameter. Copper tube is joined by soldering, brazing, and flanged or flared joints.

Brass pipe is composed of an alloy of copper and zinc, and may be used for potable water supply and distribution systems. Brass pipe is available in standard and extra-strong weights. Nominal diameters for brass pipe range from ⅛" to 6" in a variety of wall thicknesses depending on grade and diameter. Brass pipe is joined by soldering, brazing, or flanged fittings.

Steel pipe may be seamless or welded pipe. Seamless steel pipe is available in nominal diameters ranging from ⅛″ to 48″. Welded steel pipe is available in nominal diameters ranging from ⅛″ to 24″ and is used for standard water, gas, air, or steam applications. Seamless and welded steel pipe are available in several weights (indicating wall thickness) including standard, extra-strong (XS), and double extra-strong (XXS). Stainless steel pipe is used in pharmaceutical, chemical, and food-processing industries where corrosion resistance and freedom from contamination are required. Stainless steel pipe is available in nominal diameters ranging from ⅛″ to 12″.

Cast iron pipe is primarily used for aboveground and underground sanitary drainage, vent, and stormwater drainage piping. Cast iron pipe is manufactured by pouring molten gray cast iron into a spinning pipe mold where centrifugal force propels the molten iron against the mold, causing it to solidify and form the pipe walls. Cast iron is leakproof, nonabsorbent, and corrosion-resistant, and is easily cut with the proper tools. Cast iron pipe is available in no-hub and bell-and-spigot designs. No-hub cast iron pipe is joined using a mechanical coupling consisting of a neoprene sleeve and stainless steel band equipped with screw clamps that secure the sleeve in position. No-hub cast iron pipe is available in nominal diameters ranging from 1½″ to 15″, and is used primarily for aboveground applications. Bell-and-spigot cast iron pipe is available in nominal diameters ranging from 2″ to 15″ and is used primarily for underground applications and for applications where long, straight pipe runs are required.

Ductwork is the distribution system for forced-air systems. See Figure 2-46. Ductwork is manufactured from galvanized sheet metal, ductboard, plastic, or fabric. Most residential and light commercial buildings use sheet metal or ductboard for rigid ductwork. Plastic or fabric ductwork is primarily used for commercial buildings where flexibility is required. Ductwork may be internally or externally insulated to absorb vibrations and pulsations that may otherwise cause noise and minimize heat loss.

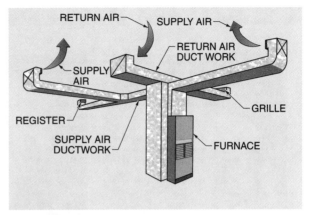

Figure 2-46. Ductwork is used to distribute warm or cool air throughout a building.

Fixtures. A *fixture* is a receptacle or device that is temporarily or permanently connected to the water distribution system, demands a supply of potable water, and discharges the waste directly or indirectly into the sanitary drainage system. Common plumbing fixtures include lavatories, water closets, and water coolers. See Figure 2-47. Plumbing fixtures are manufactured from durable, corrosion-resistant, and nonabsorbent materials such as vitreous china, enameled cast iron, enameled steel, stainless steel, fiberglass, and plastic resins. A fixture schedule may be included on commercial building prints. Notations on plan views are keyed to the fixture schedule. Information included on a fixture schedule may include the manufacturer name and product number, sizes, fittings, and general notes.

Ductsox

Ductwork conveys heated or cooled air to registers located at various points around the interior of a building.

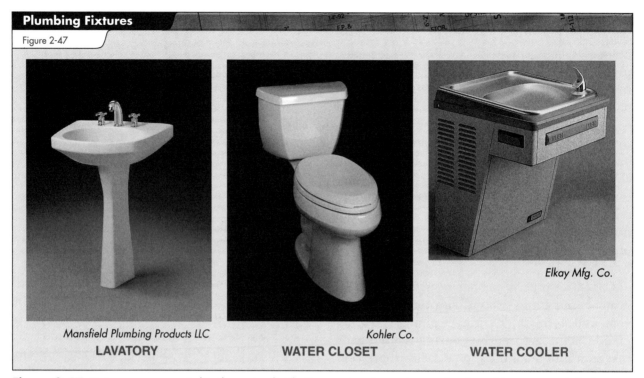

Plumbing Fixtures

Figure 2-47

Mansfield Plumbing Products LLC
LAVATORY

Kohler Co.
WATER CLOSET

Elkay Mfg. Co.
WATER COOLER

Figure 2-47. Fixtures are connected to the water distribution system, demand a supply of potable water, and discharge the waste directly or indirectly into the sanitary drainage system.

In a hydronic heating or air conditioning system, a *terminal device* is a device that transfers heat or coolness from the water in a piping system to the air in the living space. A circulating pump circulates water from the source, through the piping system and terminal device, and back to the source. A *radiator* is a type of terminal device used in a hydronic heating system. In a hydronic air conditioning system, the terminal device holds cold water from the chiller. Blowers move air through the terminal device to cool the air. Terminal devices for hydronic air conditioning systems include cabinet and unit air conditioners.

In forced-air systems, a *register* is a device that covers the opening of air supply ductwork. Registers commonly contain a damper for controlling air flow into the living space. A *damper* is a movable plate that controls and balances air flow in a forced-air system. A *grille* is a device that covers an opening of return ductwork. Grilles do not contain a damper.

Name _____ Date _____

Multiple Choice

_____ **1.** ___ is a type of raceway used in residential and light commercial buildings.
   A. Rigid metal conduit
   B. Flexible metal conduit
   C. Electrical metallic tubing
   D. all of the above

_____ **2.** ___ is the resistance to the shortening and lengthening of wood fibers when a wood member is placed in a position where it may bend under a load.
   A. Horizontal shear
   B. Extreme fiber stress
   C. Modulus of elasticity
   D. none of the above

_____ **3.** A(n) ___ is a structural member consisting of two outer skins with a core of insulating foam sandwiched between them.
   A. oriented strand board (OSB)
   B. wood I-joist
   C. nonstructural panel
   D. structural insulated panel (SIP)

_____ **4.** ___ is an engineered wood product comprised of layers of wood members that are joined together with adhesive to form larger members.
   A. Oriented strand board (OSB)
   B. Parallel strand lumber (PSL)
   C. Glued laminated timber (glulam)
   D. Plywood

_____ **5.** A(n) ___ can be added to concrete as an admixture.
   A. accelerator
   B. superplasticizer
   C. retarder
   D. all of the above

_____ **6.** ___ brick is made of select clay to impart distinctive uniform colors and is treated to provide a special surface.
   A. Common
   B. Fire
   C. Modular
   D. Face

93

_____ **7.** ___ is rough, irregular stone that is used as fill or to provide a rustic appearance.
   A. Ashlar
   B. Squared stone
   C. Rubble
   D. Cast stone

_____ **8.** ___ is steel wire, bars, or strands embedded in concrete to provide additional tensile strength to concrete structural members.
   A. Ductwork
   B. Structural subflooring
   C. Steel reinforcement
   D. Range

_____ **9.** A ___ is a clay masonry unit with one face colored and glazed, and is used for load-bearing applications.
   A. mosaic tile
   B. structural facing tile
   C. clay facing tile
   D. quarry tile

_____ **10.** A ___ CMU is a concrete masonry unit used to finish the top of a wall and provide a flat bearing surface for wood framing members or brick or stone masonry.
   A. metal sash
   B. solid top
   C. lintel
   D. header

_____ **11.** ASTM International specifies the use of the letter "___" to designate smooth wire and the letter "___" to designate deformed wire.
   A. W; D
   B. W; S
   C. S; D
   D. D; S

True-False

T   F   **1.** Pine species can be used for both rough framing and trim members.

T   F   **2.** Partitions are generally considered to be non-load-bearing.

T   F   **3.** Special symbols are used to represent gypsum board on plan views.

T   F   **4.** Switches, receptacles, and luminaires (lighting fixtures) are typically shown on floor plans using various symbols and abbreviations.

T   F   **5.** End views of framing members are shown with freehand lines to represent wood grain.

T   F   **6.** Plywood always contains an odd number of plies.

T   F   **7.** Plywood with a surface veneer such as oak is used for cabinets.

T	F	**8.** Medium density overlay (MDO) plywood is used for concrete forming material.
T	F	**9.** Many light commercial buildings utilize precast concrete components.
T	F	**10.** Sections show concrete and rebar symbols.
T	F	**11.** Steel, glass, or plastic fibers are added to concrete as reinforcement during initial mixing.
T	F	**12.** Brick are manufactured by firing them in a kiln for 24 hours.
T	F	**13.** Brick positions may be indicated in the specifications or by showing an example of the desired positions on elevations or details.
T	F	**14.** Insulation is a material used as a barrier to inhibit thermal and sound transmission.
T	F	**15.** When large-scale sections are shown, wavy lines are used to indicate ceramic tile.
T	F	**16.** Quarry tile is used for exterior wall facing.

Completion

_____ **1.** The ___ size is the dimensions of a piece of lumber before it is dried and surfaced.

_____ **2.** Moldings are a type of finished wood ___ member.

_____ **3.** The ___ is a value used to indicate the ability of a material to resist heat flow.

_____ **4.** ___ pipe is the most common type of plastic plumbing pipe used in residential and light commercial buildings.

_____ **5.** A(n) ___ is a thin, moisture-resistant material placed over the ground or in walls to retard the passage of moisture into a building.

_____ **6.** ___ consist of three, four, or five individual layers of asphalt-saturated roofing felt bonded together with hot tar or asphalt.

_____ **7.** A(n) ___ is a wall-mounted distribution cabinet containing overcurrent and short-circuit protection devices.

_____ **8.** A(n) ___ is an enclosed channel for conductors.

_____ **9.** A(n) ___ is a device with a current and voltage rating, used to open or close an electrical circuit.

_____ **10.** A(n) ___ contains an evaporator, compressor, condenser, and expansion valve.

_____ **11.** ___ is water that is free from impurities that could cause disease or harmful physiological effects.

_____ **12.** ___ is heavy-gauge wire joined in a grid and used to reinforce and increase the tensile strength of concrete.

_____ **13.** ___ is a single or multiconductor assembly, with or without an overall jacket.

_____ **14.** A(n) ___ is a self-contained heating unit that includes a blower, burner, and heat exchanger or electric heating elements, and controls.

_____ **15.** A(n) ___ is a heat exchanger that absorbs heat from the surrounding air and adds the heat to low-pressure refrigerant liquid.

_____ **16.** ___ is the distribution system for forced-air systems.

_____ **17.** A(n) ___ is a receptacle or device that is temporarily or permanently connected to the water distribution system, demands a supply of potable water, and discharges the waste directly or indirectly into the sanitary drainage system.

_____ **18.** A(n) ___ is a movable plate that controls and balances air flow in a forced-air system.

_____ **19.** ___ is hard granular material, such as sand and gravel, that is mixed with cement and water to provide structure and strength in concrete.

_____ **20.** A(n) ___ is a precast hollow or solid masonry unit composed of portland cement and fine aggregate, and formed into modular or nonmodular dimensions.

Matching—Conductors

_____ **1.** Moisture-resistant thermoplastic

_____ **2.** Heat-resistant thermoplastic

_____ **3.** Moisture- and heat-resistant thermoplastic

_____ **4.** Moisture-resistant thermoset

_____ **5.** Moisture-, heat-, and oil-resistant thermoplastic

_____ **6.** Thermoplastic-covered fixture

_____ **7.** Thermoplastic-covered fixture wire

_____ **8.** Heat-resistant thermoplastic-covered fixture

A. XHHW

B. THW

C. THHN

D. TFF

E. TF

F. MTW

G. TW

H. TFFN

Name _____ Date _____

True-False

T   F   **1.** Pine species can be used for both structural and trim members.

T   F   **2.** Maximum allowable unit stresses for most wood species (other than plywood) are the same.

T   F   **3.** Brick are manufactured by molding or extrusion.

T   F   **4.** In frame construction with brick veneer, galvanized metal ties are fastened to the wall studs and sheathing and extend across the air space where they are embedded in the mortar joints of the brick-veneer wall.

T   F   **5.** Buildings in colder climates require insulation with higher R values.

T   F   **6.** Open web steel joists are used extensively in light commercial construction to support floors and roofs.

T   F   **7.** U channels are the most common metal framing member and are used for load-bearing and non-load-bearing walls and partitions as studs and joists.

T   F   **8.** Higher R values represent greater heat flow.

T   F   **9.** An exterior insulation and finish system is an exterior finish system consisting of reinforcing mesh, a base coat of acrylic copolymers and portland cement, and a finish of acrylic resins.

T   F   **10.** Built-up roofs are used for flat roofs.

T   F   **11.** NM cable is an economical wiring method used in residential and light commercial construction less than four stories high.

T   F   **12.** Grilles contain a damper.

T   F   **13.** Compression parallel to the grain of wood is always significantly greater than compression across the grain.

T   F   **14.** OSB panels are composed of an odd number of layers running in the direction opposite to that of plywood plies.

T   F   **15.** FRP plywood may be used for heavy-duty applications such as concrete forms.

T   F   **16.** PSL is commonly used for load-bearing applications such as headers and beams.

T	F	**17.** Squared stone is stone cut to precise dimensions according to the prints.
T	F	**18.** CMUs can be used as a finished surface.
T	F	**19.** Hollow-core CMUs are no longer used because of deficiencies in strength and fire resistance.
T	F	**20.** When shown on elevations, metal is not represented with a special symbol.
T	F	**21.** Both light- and heavy-gauge metal framing members are manufactured by cold forming.
T	F	**22.** Resilient finish flooring must be installed over a smooth underlayment.
T	F	**23.** The color of vinyl extends completely through a vinyl product.
T	F	**24.** Gypsum board is used for interior and exterior finish applications.
T	F	**25.** No special symbol is required when showing gypsum board on plan views, sections, and details.
T	F	**26.** Float glass is manufactured by drawing it vertically or horizontally and slowly annealing it to produce a high-gloss surface.
T	F	**27.** Piping for plumbing systems is not generally shown on residential and light commercial prints.
T	F	**28.** In a plumbing diagram, single lines represent each pipe in the system.

Completion

_____ **1.** When symbols are used to represent wood members in sections and construction details, two ___ lines indicate face views of framing members.

_____ **2.** A(n) ___ is an arrangement of masonry in a pattern to provide a desired architectural effect and/or additional structure.

_____ **3.** Thin pieces of stone fastened to other masonry or steel framing are called ___.

_____ **4.** A(n) ___ bond is created with various sizes of stone placed in a random arrangement without maintaining courses or ranges.

_____ **5.** ___ or ___ gas may be used in insulating glass to fill the air space to reduce the passage of heat from one piece of glass to the other.

_____ **6.** A(n) ___ is a slender wire that is used to control the flow of electrons in an electrical circuit.

_____ **7.** Conduit is a common type of ___ used in residential, commercial, and industrial installations.

_____ **8.** In a(n) ___ system, a circulating pump conveys water from the source, through the piping system, terminal devices, and return piping of the system.

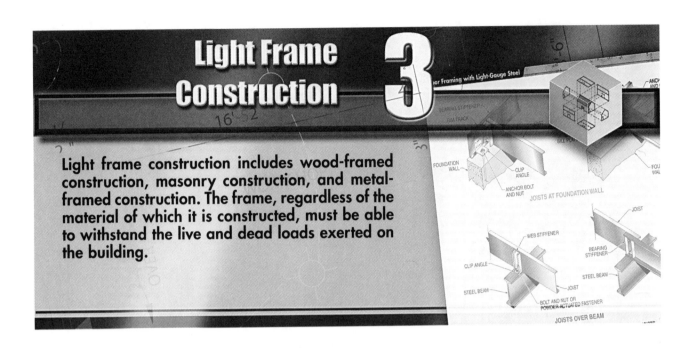

Light Frame Construction 3

Light frame construction includes wood-framed construction, masonry construction, and metal-framed construction. The frame, regardless of the material of which it is constructed, must be able to withstand the live and dead loads exerted on the building.

FRAME CONSTRUCTION

The framework of a building forms a skeleton on which the exterior and interior finish are applied. The framework is designed to withstand the live and dead loads exerted on the building. A *live load* is a moving or changing load that may be placed on different sections of a building. Live loads include the building inhabitants, furnishings, snow, and wind. A *dead load* is the weight of the permanent structure of a building and includes the materials that make up the wall, floor, ceiling, and roof units. Several construction methods have been developed for light frame structures, each with its own advantages. The construction methods are designed to use available materials and labor efficiently and economically.

Platform Framing

The most common type of light frame construction is platform framing. *Platform framing*, or western framing, is a framing method in which each story of a building is framed as a unit consisting of walls, joists, and a subfloor. See Figure 3-1. Platform framing is an efficient and inexpensive method for assembling and erecting residential and light commercial buildings.

Wood or light-gauge steel framing members form the framework in platform framing.

In typical platform framing, a sill plate is fastened to the top of the foundation wall using anchor bolts embedded in the wall. Anchor bolts are available in ⅜″ to ¾″ diameters and 6″ to 24″ lengths. Flat washers and nuts secure sill plates to foundation walls. See Figure 3-2. Anchor bolts are commonly placed 4′-0″ or 6′-0″ on center (OC).

Anchor bolts are placed in fresh concrete. After the concrete has properly set, sill plates are secured to the anchor bolts using flat washers and nuts.

Platform Framing

Figure 3-1

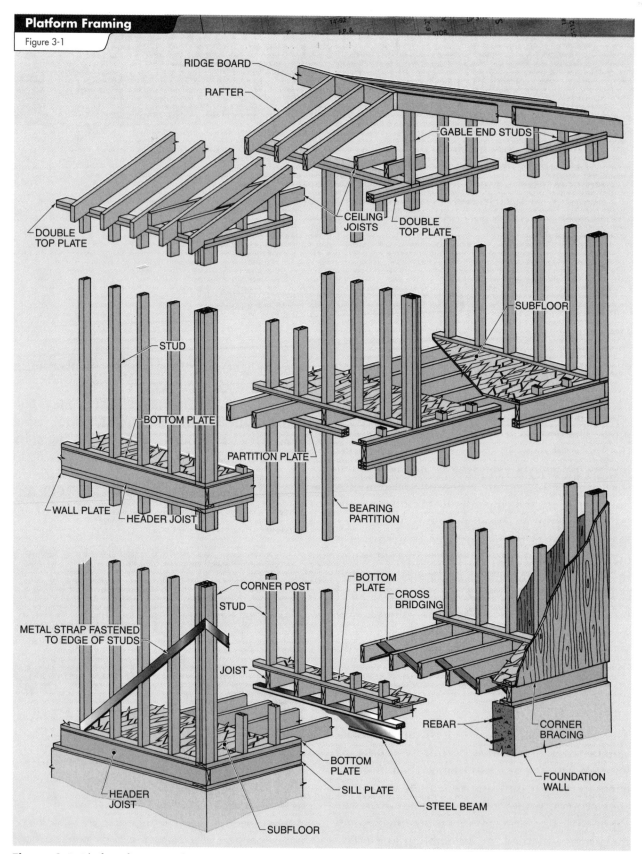

Figure 3-1. Platform framing is the most popular type of light frame construction.

floor. The subfloor extends to the outer edge of the joists and header joists on all sides to form a platform.

When the subfloor has been securely fastened to the joists, exterior walls and interior partitions are constructed. The framing members for walls and partitions, including studs and top and bottom plates, are a nominal 2″ thick. Exterior walls and interior partitions are assembled on the subfloor and raised into position. Walls and partitions are constructed with studs (usually spaced 16″ OC), a single bottom plate, and a double top plate that is constructed so the members overlap at corners and intersections to provide solid connections. For wide spans, a bearing partition may be placed near the center of the building. A *bearing partition* is an interior partition capable of supporting heavy loads. Small walls and partitions are often constructed in one piece and tilted up into position. Longer sections are made in lengths that can be conveniently handled. The wall sections are aligned with chalk lines snapped on the subfloor and are temporarily tacked and braced in position until other walls have been erected.

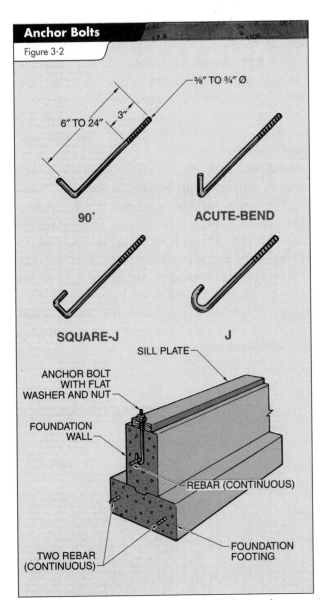

Anchor Bolts

Figure 3-2

⅜″ TO ¾″ Ø

6″ TO 24″   3″

90°   ACUTE-BEND

SQUARE-J   J

SILL PLATE

ANCHOR BOLT WITH FLAT WASHER AND NUT

FOUNDATION WALL

REBAR (CONTINUOUS)

TWO REBAR (CONTINUOUS)

FOUNDATION FOOTING

Figure 3-2. Anchor bolts secure the sill plate to the foundation wall.

Joists rest on the sill plates. The two outside joists align with the outer edges of the sill plates. The ends of all joists butt against a header joist. In wide spans, joists are supported by a steel or wood beam at the center of the building. An oriented strand board (OSB) or plywood subfloor is placed over and fastened to the joists using screws or nails. See Figure 3-3. OSB or plywood panels are arranged in a staggered pattern at a right angle to the joists. In addition, construction adhesive may be used to secure the subfloor in position to provide a very strong and quiet

Senco Products, Inc.

Figure 3-3. The subfloor is fastened to the joists using nails or screws.

When the exterior walls and interior partitions are erected, the bottom plates are securely fastened to the subfloor and into the joists below where possible. The bottom and top plate corners and intersections are then fastened together.

While this assembly is stable and plumb, it must be permanently braced to withstand strong winds and other external stresses. Plywood or OSB sheathing or metal straps may be used to brace exterior walls. See Figure 3-4. Plywood or OSB panels are fastened to the studs at each end of the wall to provide lateral strength. The remainder of the wall is sheathed with fiberboard, rigid foam insulation, or plywood or OSB panels. Diagonal metal straps are fastened to the exterior edge of the studs at a 45° angle in each corner. Sheathing is placed directly over the metal straps and fastened to the studs and plates.

The basic structure is modified to provide stairwell and chimney openings in floors, window and door openings in walls, and additional strength under bearing partitions. Floor openings for stairwells or chimneys must be located according to the prints, regardless of the joist arrangement. Appropriate joists are cut and reinforced by double trimmers (double joists) at the side and double headers at the ends. Door and window openings, regardless of size, are located as shown on the prints, even though the studs are spaced 16″ OC. Where door and window openings are required, the studs are removed and replaced by trimmer studs at the sides to support headers over the opening. Framing door and window openings can be accomplished in several ways, but the principle involved is to transfer the load imposed above the opening to the floor below and to provide the proper size rough opening. See Figure 3-5. Where bearing partitions are placed parallel to floor joists, double or triple joists are placed under the partition to carry the load transferred from the structure above.

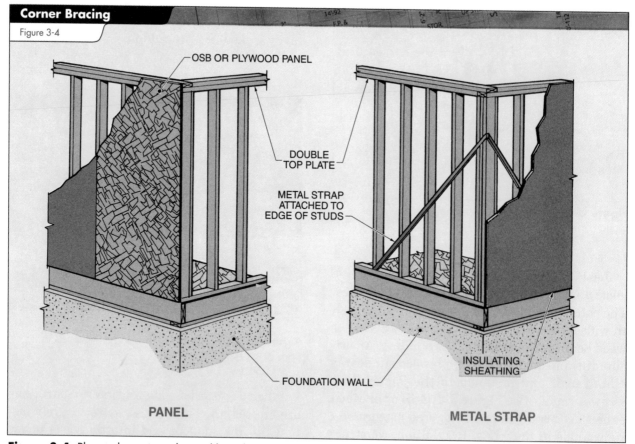

Figure 3-4. Plywood or oriented strand board (OSB) sheathing or metal straps are used to brace corners in a platform-framed building.

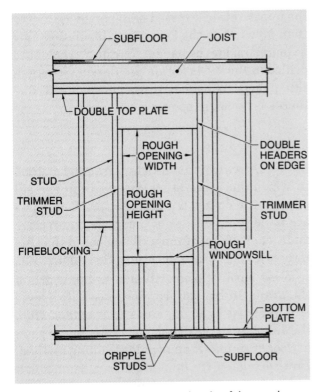

Figure 3-5. Trimmer studs at each side of the rough opening support the header and provide a nailing surface for the trim. Full studs maintain 16″ OC spacing.

Ceiling joists, which are nominal 2″ thick members placed on edge, are positioned 16″ OC with ends resting on the exterior walls and bearing partitions. Bearing partitions may not always be placed near the center of the building; the joist span on one side of the partition may be much longer than on the other side. However, the floor plan indicates the proper size joist to support imposed loads and be within the allowed deflection (bending) limits. Joist sizes are specified so they do not deflect more than a prescribed amount when subjected to live and dead loads. Excessive deflection results in cracks in the interior finish. When there is a second floor on the building, a subfloor is installed on the first floor walls to act as both a first floor ceiling structure and a second floor subfloor. Second floor exterior walls and interior partitions are then constructed and tilted up into place.

Prefabricated Components. Some components for platform-framed buildings may be prefabricated off-site and shipped to the job site.

The components are precisely constructed in a prefabrication facility. Prefabrication facilities are common in all parts of the country to supply builders with the required components.

Floor and roof trusses are prefabricated components commonly used in a platform-framed building. See Figure 3-6. Roof trusses are available for flat, gable, hip, and other roof types. Roof trusses are constructed at a prefabrication facility, transported to the job site on a truck, and lifted into place with a mobile crane.

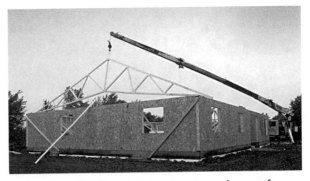

Figure 3-6. Prefabricated components, such as roof trusses, are built off-site and quickly erected on the job site.

Some prefabricated framing components, such as box beams or stressed-skin panels, consist of plywood panels applied over wood structural frames. A *box beam* is a hollow horizontal member used for floor and roof supports or to span wide distances over openings. See Figure 3-7.

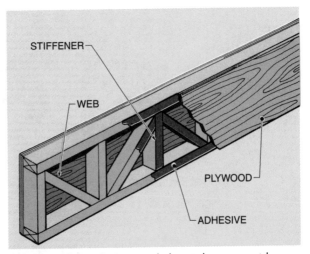

Figure 3-7. Box beams are lightweight, yet provide strong support.

Wood Truss Council of America

Prefabricated components, such as roof trusses, are commonly specified for residential and light commercial buildings.

A *stressed-skin panel* is a structural unit used in floor, wall, and ceiling systems that consists of plywood panels nailed and glued to a wood frame. Typically, stressed-skin panels are framed with 2 × 4s spaced 16″ OC and covered on each side with plywood. See Figure 3-8. Plywood on the upper side of stressed-skin panels is thicker than plywood on the lower side. Insulation may be placed inside the panels. Ventilation holes are drilled in the 2 × 4s for air circulation. Stressed-skin panels are primarily used to span wide distances between supports.

Balloon Framing

Balloon framing is a multistory framing method in which one-piece studs extend from the sill plate to the double top plate. Upper floor joists are nailed to the sides of the studs and receive additional support from a ribbon board that fits into notches cut into the studs. See Figure 3-9.

Wood shrinks primarily across the width of the grain. In balloon framing, wood shrinkage is minimized by using studs that extend from the sill plate to the double top plate. In the past, balloon framing was a popular framing method. However, due to the limited availability and high cost of long wood studs, balloon framing is not as common today. In split-level residences, balloon framing may be used in the central section of the house.

Balloon framing provides passageways for ductwork and raceway systems through the open stud spaces from floor to floor. However, the stud spaces can also act as flues, enabling fire to spread quickly, unless fireblocking is installed near the floor levels.

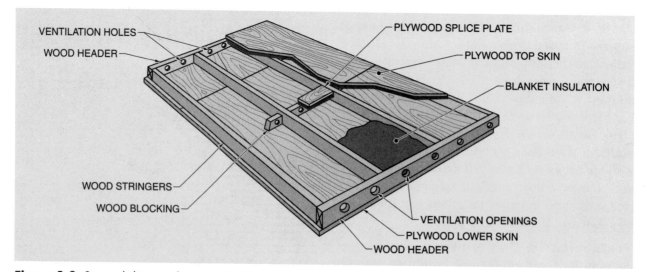

Figure 3-8. Stressed skin panels span wide distances, and are used in floor, wall, and roof systems.

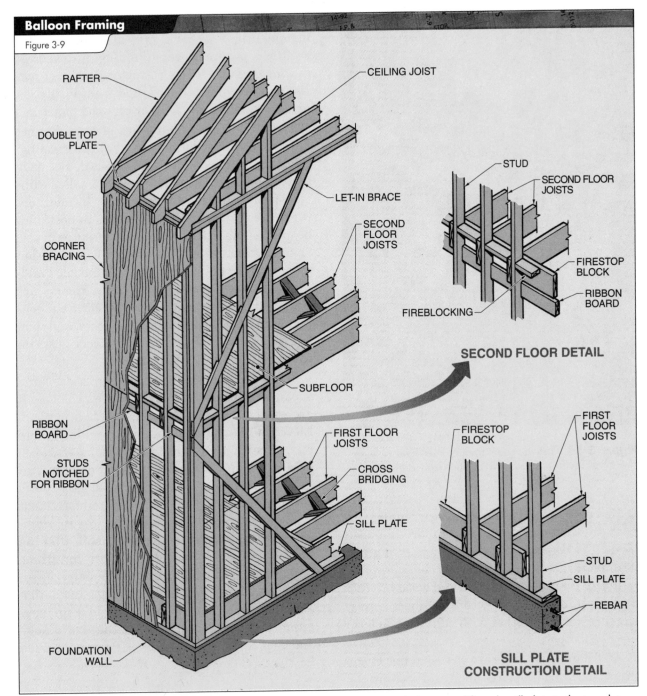

Balloon Framing

Figure 3-9

- RAFTER
- CEILING JOIST
- DOUBLE TOP PLATE
- LET-IN BRACE
- STUD
- SECOND FLOOR JOISTS
- SECOND FLOOR JOISTS
- CORNER BRACING
- FIRESTOP BLOCK
- RIBBON BOARD
- FIREBLOCKING
- **SECOND FLOOR DETAIL**
- SUBFLOOR
- RIBBON BOARD
- FIRST FLOOR JOISTS
- FIRESTOP BLOCK
- FIRST FLOOR JOISTS
- STUDS NOTCHED FOR RIBBON
- CROSS BRIDGING
- SILL PLATE
- STUD
- SILL PLATE
- REBAR
- FOUNDATION WALL
- **SILL PLATE CONSTRUCTION DETAIL**

Figure 3-9. Balloon framing minimizes shrinkage by the use of continuous studs that extend from the sill plate to the top plate.

Post-and-Beam Framing

Post-and-beam framing is a framing method in which the basic framework of the building consists of vertical posts and horizontal or sloping beams. Post-and-beam framing is characterized by wide expanses of glass, high ceilings that are actually the underside of the roof planks, and heavy support members. See Figure 3-10. The ceilings are finished to show the beauty of the wood itself. The unique structural features of post-and-beam framing are posts at the outside walls, beams below the floor and beams above supporting the roof planks, and posts supporting the roof ridge.

support 2″ thick planks for the roof. Structural insulated panels (SIPs) may also be used as a roof for a post-and-beam building. A *structural insulated panel (SIP)* is a structural member consisting of a thick layer of rigid foam insulation pressed between two OSB or plywood panels.

Post-and-beam framing has several distinct differences from platform and balloon framing. Since post-and-beam exterior walls do not have studs spaced 16″ OC, windows are installed without special framing for openings. In addition, there are few structural members in post-and-beam framing and only minor differences in size or shape among them. One critical consideration for an architect designing a post-and-beam building is properly locating the posts. Rooms are usually planned so partitions run down the center of the building to enclose the posts, and then out to exterior walls where they meet posts located between window units.

While post-and-beam framing provides large expanses of open area and glass, a few challenges are associated with this construction method. Electrical wiring and ductwork are difficult to conceal since there are few interior partitions. Wiring and ducts above floor level must be run in the central partition or concealed along posts between windows. Additional floor reinforcement under heavy equipment and fixtures in kitchens and bathrooms is difficult to install after the floor is installed. In addition, post-and-frame buildings are more difficult to adequately insulate than platform-framed buildings. Insulating glass is used on exterior walls. Rigid foam insulation may be placed between the roof planks and roof finish material, or SIPs may be used for the roof.

Southern Forest Products Association

Figure 3-10. Post-and-beam framing uses heavy structural members to achieve an open appearance.

Heavy floor and roof beams are required in post-and-beam framing to support imposed loads. The beams may be solid timbers or glued laminated (glulam) timbers. A *glued laminated (glulam) timber* is an engineered wood product comprised of layers of wood members (lams) that are joined together with adhesives to form larger members.

All framing members are spaced at fixed wide intervals, providing large open areas within the building. The construction at the sill plate resembles platform framing. Floor beams are used in place of floor joists. Floor beams are spaced from 6′-0″ to 8′-0″ apart and support the floor planks. Floor planks, typically 2″ thick with a tongue-and-groove joint, provide structural strength. Thicker planks with floor beams spaced farther apart are used for heavy construction. Posts used to support top plates and roof beams are spaced the same as floor beams. Roof beams

Post-and-beam construction was introduced to North America around 1620 when English settlers began arriving. Early post-and-beam structures consisted of a framework of posts and beams, with the spaces between filled with an intertwined mixture of reeds and branches, known as wattle, which was covered with mud.

A-Frames

An A-frame is a type of construction typically used for vacation homes. See Figure 3-11. Heavy framing members spaced 4'-0" to 6'-0" apart are the main structural members. The framing members resemble the roof beams of post-and-beam framing except that they are placed at a steep slope and extend from the foundation, where they are firmly fastened, to the ridge. Roof planks are strong enough to carry the roof load over the span between the structural members. The exterior sides of an A-frame are actually roof surfaces and the two gable ends. The gable ends include windows and doors for light, ventilation, and access.

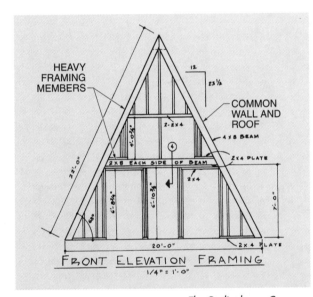

The Garlinghouse Company

Figure 3-11. In A-frame construction, heavy framing members form a common wall and roof.

The living area of an A-frame is commonly left open to the roof above, creating a cathedral ceiling effect that is upward sloping. Extensive use of glass in the gable end walls opens up the living space to the outdoors. A loft, typically containing bedrooms and an additional bathroom, is often placed in the house. The open space of the living area allows good sight lines and an open feeling between the loft deck and the space below. Circular or steeply pitched straight-run stairs commonly lead to the loft.

MASONRY CONSTRUCTION

Masonry construction is divided into two broad classifications—monolithic concrete construction and unit masonry construction. In monolithic concrete construction, concrete is formed as a single, continuous member. Monolithic concrete construction is used for residential and light commercial construction, but is most prevalent in heavy construction. Brick, stone, concrete masonry units (concrete block), and structural and facing tile are used in unit masonry construction. Unit masonry construction is most prevalent in residential and light commercial construction. Monolithic concrete and unit masonry construction are often combined for construction projects.

Monolithic Concrete Construction

Monolithic concrete construction is typically used for load-bearing footings and foundation walls. Concrete, when properly mixed and placed in the forms, provides structurally sound continuous footings and walls that last for many years. Concrete may also be used for above- and below-grade walls of buildings.

Forms for monolithic concrete construction must be properly located as specified on the prints and constructed to the desired shape before concrete is placed in the forms. Concrete is mixed according to the specifications at a batch plant and delivered to the job site in transit-mix trucks. All voids in the concrete must be removed during concrete placement, typically using a mechanical vibrator. When the concrete has properly set and hardened, the forms are carefully removed so as not to damage the concrete. Bricklaying or framing can then begin. However, since concrete does not develop its full strength until approximately 28 days after placement, care must be taken when laying brick or framing the building.

Footings. Prior to concrete being placed for the footings, the forms must be properly laid out. A tradesworker lays out the building lines from a point of beginning on the lot. A *point of beginning (POB)* is a fixed location on a building site used as a reference point for horizontal dimensions and vertical dimensions. The locations of building lines are marked on batterboards set back from the foundation location so they will not be disturbed during excavation. See Figure 3-12. Earth-moving equipment, such as a bulldozer, is used to excavate the lot to the specified depth. Sufficient room is provided along the sides of the excavation for tradesworkers when erecting the forms. Where required, the sides of the excavation must be shored up or excavated to the proper angle of repose to prevent cave-ins. The foundation footings must be placed on undisturbed earth or earth that has been compacted to the proper specifications.

Building lines representing the faces of the foundation wall are strung horizontally between the batterboards. Plumb lines are extended down from the intersections of the building lines to locate points from which the foundation footing forms can be located. Metal or wood form boards spaced to the proper footing width and adjusted for the specified height are erected and braced. Rebar are placed in the footing according to the foundation wall section of the prints. Wire chairs and/or other devices may hold the rebar in position when concrete is placed.

Foundation Walls. Foundation walls are constructed of concrete masonry units or concrete. When concrete foundation walls are specified, several formwork methods may be used, depending on builder preference and the foundation wall thickness and height.

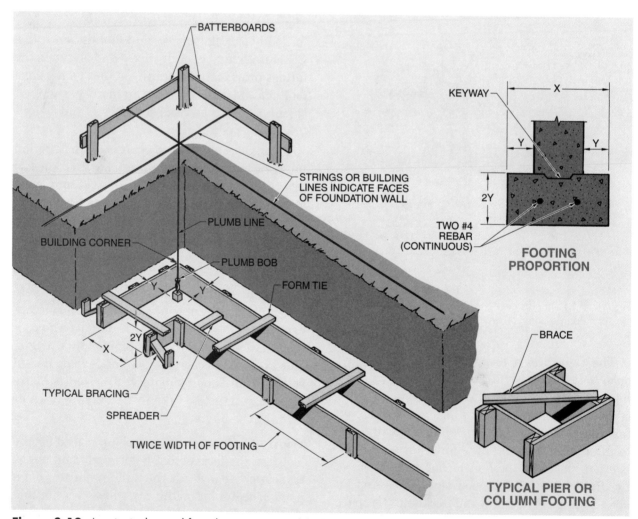

Figure 3-12. A point is dropped from the intersection of the building lines and placed on a stake. The footings and the face of the foundation wall are located from this point.

Basements with habitable space must have at least one openable escape window or exterior door opening.

Most foundation forms are panelized forms that can be reused many times. See Figure 3-13. Job-built or patented panel forms are used to form foundation walls. Job-built forms are constructed of plywood panels that are framed with 2 × 4s. Patented panel forms are available from several manufacturers and are easily assembled. Patented panel forms are constructed with Plyform® or high density overlay (HDO) plywood panels and interlocking metal tabs or with metal frames faced with Plyform panels. Regardless of the type of patented panel form, manufacturer recommendations for panel placement and bracing must be carefully followed.

Foundation wall forms are placed on the footing and tied together with snap ties. A *snap tie* is a patented tie system with spreader cones to maintain form wall spacing and tie the walls together when concrete is placed. See Figure 3-14. Snap ties are broken off (snapped) at the breakback after the forms are stripped.

Foundation walls often have windows and doors to provide ventilation and access to the outside of the building. In most cases, finish metal window frames and doorjambs are installed in the form walls and secured in place with temporary fasteners. The metal frames and jambs remain in the concrete wall after the forms are removed. Another method to provide door and window openings is to construct a buck, which is framing around an opening, installed in the form walls and secured in place with duplex nails. The bucks are removed when the forms are stripped.

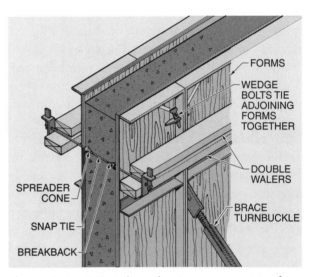

Figure 3-14. Patented panel systems use a variety of holding devices, such as snap ties, to maintain wall spacing when concrete is placed.

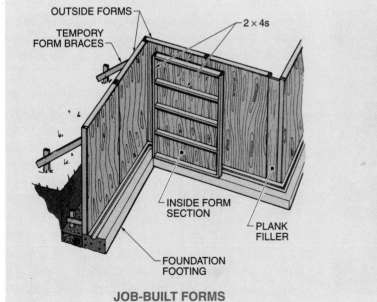

JOB-BUILT FORMS

PATENTED PANEL FORMS

Figure 3-13. Job-built or patented panel forms can be reused many times.

Insulating concrete forms (ICFs) may be used to form concrete foundation walls in residential and light commercial construction. An *insulating concrete form (ICF)* is a specialized forming system that consists of a layer of concrete sandwiched between layers of insulating foam material on each side. See Figure 3-15. Advantages of ICF construction include minimal air infiltration, reduced heating and cooling loads, and better fire resistance. ICF components are designed with interlocking edges that fit together or utilize adhesive to hold them in place during concrete placement. Plastic or steel ties maintain the ICF spacing as concrete is placed. The form walls remain after the concrete is placed, eliminating form removal time.

Waterproofing Foundations. Solid concrete walls are highly resistant to water penetration, but can still absorb moisture if not properly waterproofed. CMU foundation walls have less resistance to water penetration since they are constructed with individual units. Regardless of the material, foundation walls should be treated with waterproofing materials from the bottom of the wall to the finish grade.

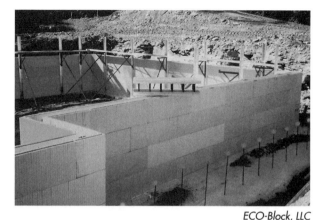

ECO-Block, LLC

Figure 3-15. Insulating concrete forms (ICFs) are used to form foundation walls and also provide wall insulation.

Foundation walls and footings are waterproofed in various ways, depending on the soil condition, footing depth below grade, and the general climatic conditions of the area. Methods for waterproofing foundation walls include liquid membranes, asphalt sheet membranes, and rigid foundation waterproofing panels. See Figure 3-16. Liquid membranes are applied by spraying or mopping the foundation wall and footing with tar or asphalt. In some situations, wide sheets of polyethylene film are placed over the liquid membrane to form an overlapping waterproofing cover. Asphalt sheet membranes are self-adhesive 60 mil sheets of rubberized asphalt laminated to polyethylene film. Asphalt sheet membranes provide good waterproofing capabilities when properly applied. Rigid foundation waterproofing panels are placed over a liquid membrane which holds the panels in position until the foundation is backfilled.

Drain tile is perforated pipe installed along the outer edge of foundation footings to collect storm water and surface water and move it away from the foundation. Various types of drain tile are available. The most common types of drain tile are flexible high-density polyethylene (HDPE) drain tile and rigid polyvinyl chloride (PVC) drain tile. Both types have slots or holes around the circumference. Surface water enters slots or holes along the upper portion of the tile and is directed away from the foundation. In some cases, the tile may terminate at a sump pump that expels the surface water from a sump well to an area where it can drain properly.

Vertical and horizontal rebar is placed in insulating concrete forms (ICFs) prior to concrete being placed.

Waterproofing Foundations

Figure 3-16

WATCHDOG WATERPROOFING®

LIQUID MEMBRANES

ASPHALT SHEET MEMBRANES

TUFF-N-DRI®

RIGID FOUNDATION WATERPROOFING PANELS

Figure 3-16. Foundation walls and footings are waterproofed in various ways including the use of liquid membranes, asphalt sheet membranes, and rigid foundation waterproofing panels placed over a liquid membrane.

Concrete Stairways. Concrete stairways are formed in several ways, depending on their design. One method of constructing concrete stairway forms is to erect Plyform or HDO plywood panels along the sides and place riser form boards between the panels. The riser form boards are beveled along the bottom edge to allow a tradesworker to properly finish the concrete tread. The panels and riser form boards are properly braced to resist the pressure of the concrete as it is placed. See Figure 3-17.

Unit Masonry Construction

Unit masonry construction provides durable and easily maintained walls. When properly constructed of sound material, unit masonry provides a structure with unlimited service. The units must be laid properly to form a strong wall and care must be taken to ensure a waterproof wall.

Unit masonry materials include brick, concrete masonry units (CMUs), stone, and tile. Brick and CMUs are commonly used for bearing-wall construction. Brick walls are constructed as solid brick walls with no backup, brick walls with backup, cavity walls, or brick veneer over a wood frame.

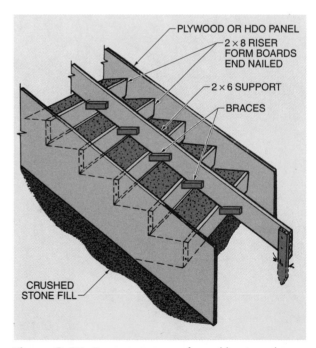

PLYWOOD OR HDO PANEL

2 × 8 RISER FORM BOARDS END NAILED

2 × 6 SUPPORT

BRACES

CRUSHED STONE FILL

Figure 3-17. Concrete stairs are formed by risers that are held in place with braces.

Solid Brick Walls with No Backup. Solid brick walls can be constructed to carry the load of the floor and roof joists. See Figure 3-18. The walls are laid with two wythes of brick bonded together every sixth course by a header course. A *wythe* is a single continuous vertical masonry wall that is one unit thick. Some building codes require a 12″ wall of three wythes for buildings more than one story tall. Joist ends are fire cut (cut on an angle) to rest in the brick wall. In the event of a severe fire, the burned-out joist would drop without disturbing the wall. A square-cut joist end would exert a prying action, forcing the wall to fall outward. The joists are tied to a masonry wall using twisted steel plate joist anchors placed at every fourth joist. The anchors pull out of the wall in case of fire. The remainder of the structure is constructed in the same manner as platform framing.

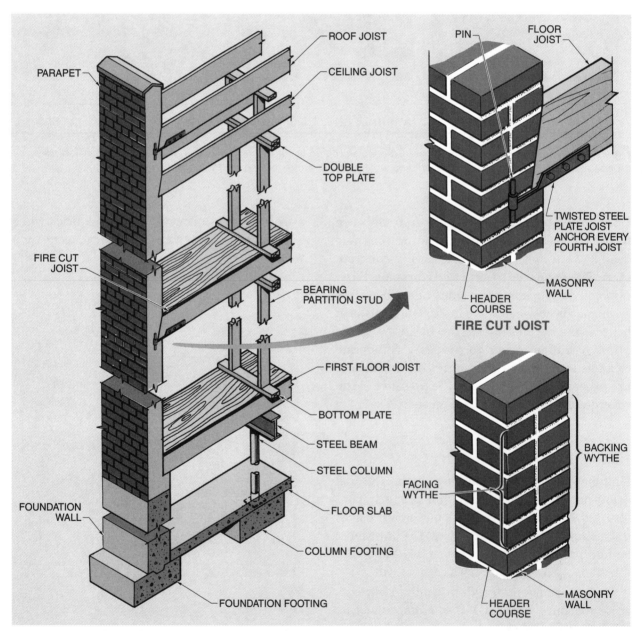

Figure 3-18. Solid brick walls carry the load of the floor and roof joists. Joist ends are fire cut to rest in the brick wall.

A load-bearing wall with only a single wythe of brick may be constructed using SCR brick. An *SCR brick* is a solid masonry unit with nominal dimensions of 6″ × 2⅔″ × 12″. SCR brick is primarily used for one-story structures, although the brick may be used for high, load-bearing walls. SCR brick saves time when constructing a masonry wall since the brick is larger than building brick and is laid without backup material. In order to provide sufficient bearing for the joists, the wall is corbeled. A *corbel* is a short projection from the face of a wall formed with successive courses of masonry to provide bearing space for the joists.

Furring strips or metal channels are usually installed on the inside of masonry walls to provide a flat and true surface for finish materials such as gypsum board. See Figure 3-19. Furring strips (2″ × 2″) or metal channels are fastened to the brick using powder-actuated fasteners. The space between the gypsum board and brick wall provides ventilation for the wall. Moisture within the wall caused by condensation runs down to the flashing and is directed out of the building through weep holes in the mortar joints directly above the flashing.

Brick is generally selected for its color, texture, and size. Face brick requirements are detailed in ASTM C216—*Standard Specification for Facing Brick*.

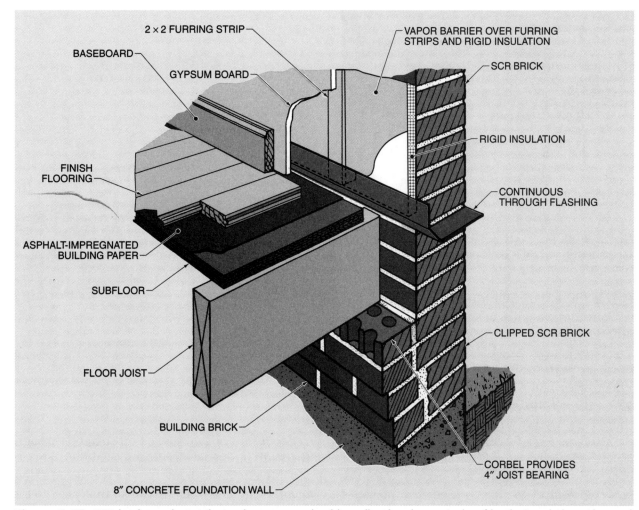

Figure 3-19. SCR brick may be used to make a strong, durable wall with only one wythe of brick. A corbel may be used to provide a bearing surface for the joists.

Adjustable brick ties can be used to tie together an exterior stud wall and brick facing.

Another typical framing method for building with masonry walls is to use steel columns and beams to support floor joists or open web steel joists in place of a bearing partition. In this type of construction, the structural steel members support the roof loads, and the masonry walls between the steel columns provide a low-maintenance and highly secure divider. See Figure 3-20. Masonry construction combined with steel columns and beams is used for light commercial buildings such as strip malls.

Figure 3-20. Masonry construction combined with structural steel support is commonly used for light commercial buildings.

Brick Walls with Backup. Brick is often used in conjunction with a backup material of a different size such as CMUs. See Figure 3-21. The brick courses and backup material must be arranged so the wall is tied together at intervals. When brick and CMUs are laid to make up a 12″ wall, a full-cut header and brick header course are used to tie the wall together. A *full-cut header* is a special concrete masonry unit that is notched to receive the brick header course. The backing wythe is parged with mortar. *Parging* is a thin coat of mortar on a vertical masonry surface that is used to provide additional waterproofing. See Figure 3-22.

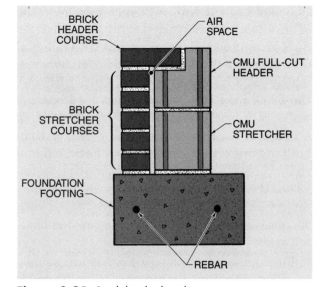

Figure 3-21. Brick backed up by concrete masonry units (CMUs) is tied together with a full-cut header and header course.

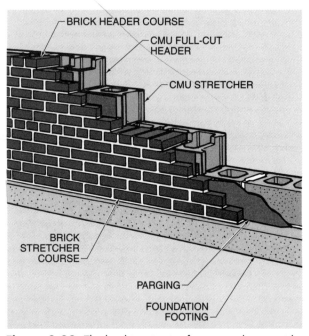

Figure 3-22. The backing tier is often parged to provide additional waterproofing.

Stone may be laid so the units extend through the wall, but generally they are laid with brick or CMUs to back them up. The wythes are tied together in a manner similar to that used to tie together masonry walls using brick and other materials for backup.

Cavity Walls. Cavity walls are constructed using two wythes of brick. A *cavity wall* is a masonry wall with at least a 2″ air space between adjacent faces. The air space increases resistance to thermal and sound transmission. Ladder, individual, or truss ties are used to tie the wythes together. See Figure 3-23. Individual ties are usually embedded in the mortar joints of every sixth course at 24″ OC. Continuous flashing is provided in the same manner as for SCR brick. The core of the cavity wall may be filled with insulation to further increase the resistance to thermal and sound transmission. Furring strips are applied to the interior walls to provide a flat and true surface for finish materials. Cavity wall construction is commonly used in buildings where the inside face of exterior walls is finished with exposed brick.

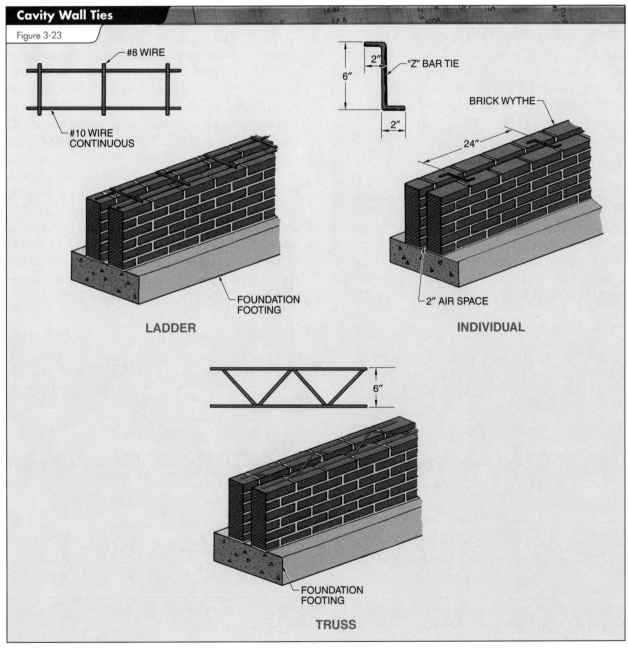

Figure 3-23. A cavity wall contains two wythes of brick separated by a 2″ air space and is tied together every sixth course using ladder, individual, or truss ties.

Brick-Veneer Walls. In brick-veneer construction, one wythe of brick is used as a skin over wood- or metal-framed walls. Stone may also be used to cover the framed walls. The foundation must be wide enough to support the sill plate for the joists and the brick or stone. See Figure 3-24. The building framework is erected first and provides the supporting structure for floor joists, ceiling joists, and rafters. The brick is then laid and tied to the frame wall with clips. One clip is required for each 2 sq ft of area. A 1″ air space is provided between the wall sheathing and the back of the brick because a slight movement between the brick and the frame wall will result due to shrinkage of the wood members. The air space also provides ventilation for the wall. Flashing is used to divert any moisture toward the weep holes placed in brick joints.

METAL FRAMING

Metal framing is a method of constructing the framework of a building using light-gauge steel framing members. Light-gauge steel framing members are lightweight, straight, and strong. The framing members are not affected by insects such as termites, and are more fire-resistant than comparable wood framing members.

Light-gauge steel framing members are available in various shapes, thicknesses, and strengths. Common light-gauge steel framing member shapes include C-shapes, tracks, U-channels, and furring channels. See Figure 3-25. C-shapes are the most common shape produced for light-gauge steel framing, and are used for studs and joists. Tracks are fastened to the ends of studs and joists in a manner similar to wall plates and header joists, respectively, used in wood-framed construction.

Non-load-bearing walls constructed with C-shapes and tracks are commonly used for interior partitions in residential and light commercial construction. Wall sections are either laid out on the subfloor and tilted up into position or constructed in place by fastening the top and bottom tracks in position and installing the C-shapes between them. Tracks are fastened to the floor and ceiling with nails, screws, or powder-actuated fasteners, depending on the surface material. The studs are snapped into place at the specified on-center spacing (commonly 24″ OC) and fastened with screws or crimped to stay in position. Gypsum board is attached to the C-shapes and tracks using self-tapping screws. Door frames are installed in the framework wherever specified on the prints. See Figure 3-26.

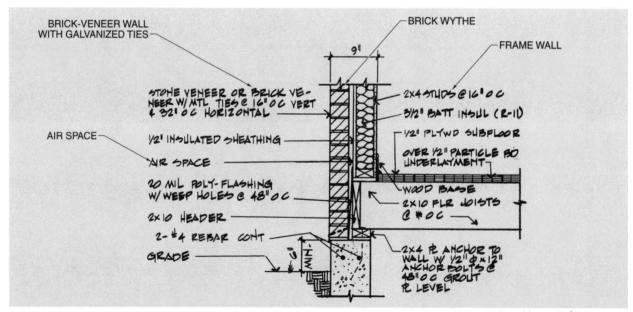

JonesMayer Architecture, Inc.

Figure 3-24. A brick veneer wall contains one wythe of brick secured to the frame wall with galvanized ties. An air space separates the brick from the frame wall.

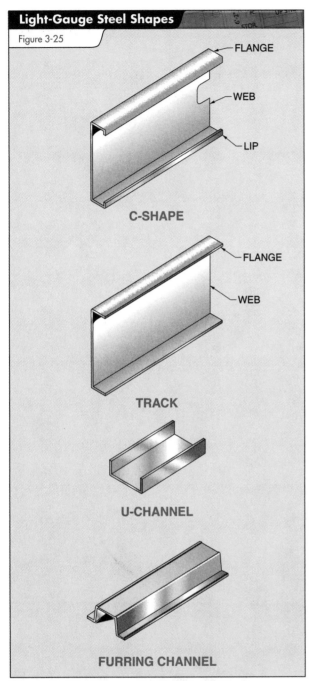

Light-Gauge Steel Shapes

Figure 3-25

FLANGE
WEB
LIP

C-SHAPE

FLANGE
WEB

TRACK

U-CHANNEL

FURRING CHANNEL

Figure 3-25. Common light-gauge steel framing member shapes include C-shapes, tracks, U-channels, and furring channels.

Floor Systems

Floor systems for metal-framed buildings are constructed in a manner similar to wood-framed buildings. C-shapes are used for joists, and are available in several depths (6″ to 12″) and several metal thicknesses. Metal joists can rest directly on the foun-

dation wall or on a sill plate attached to the wall. See Figure 3-27. When joists rest directly on the foundation wall, clip angles are used to attach the rim track to the wall. When joists rest on a wood sill plate, a metal plate is used to fasten the rim track to the sill plate. Bearing stiffeners are installed at the joist ends to prevent the ends from being crushed when loads are applied.

A conventional steel beam, built-up wood beam, or engineered wood beam is used to support long spans of steel joists. The joists may be continuous over the beam or overlap over the beam. Web or bearing stiffeners provide additional support for the floor above. For spans of 12′ or more, solid blocking or cross bridging is required at the centers of the spans to prevent the joists from twisting.

Floor openings using steel joists are framed in a manner similar to wood-framed floor openings. Trimmer joists, which support the ends of headers, are constructed of C-shape and track members. Common joists are attached to the headers using clip angles.

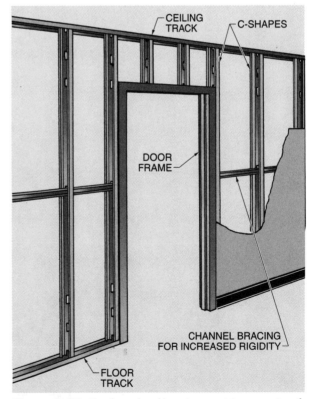

CEILING TRACK
C-SHAPES
DOOR FRAME
CHANNEL BRACING FOR INCREASED RIGIDITY
FLOOR TRACK

Figure 3-26. Steel non-load-bearing partitions consist of floor and ceiling tracks and C-shape studs.

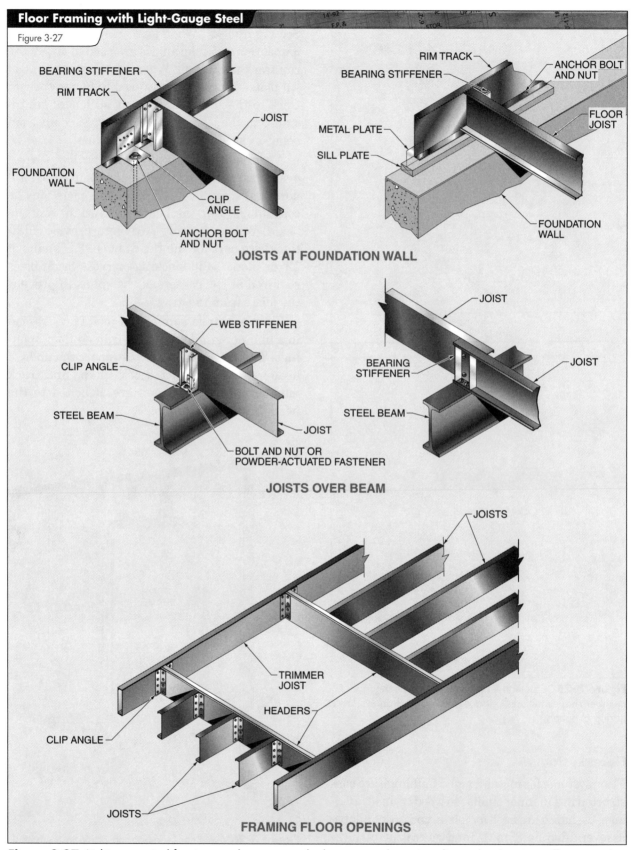

Floor Framing with Light-Gauge Steel

Figure 3-27

BEARING STIFFENER

RIM TRACK

JOIST

FOUNDATION WALL

CLIP ANGLE

ANCHOR BOLT AND NUT

RIM TRACK

BEARING STIFFENER

ANCHOR BOLT AND NUT

FLOOR JOIST

METAL PLATE

SILL PLATE

FOUNDATION WALL

JOISTS AT FOUNDATION WALL

WEB STIFFENER

CLIP ANGLE

STEEL BEAM

JOIST

BOLT AND NUT OR POWDER-ACTUATED FASTENER

JOIST

BEARING STIFFENER

JOIST

STEEL BEAM

JOISTS OVER BEAM

JOISTS

TRIMMER JOIST

HEADERS

CLIP ANGLE

JOISTS

FRAMING FLOOR OPENINGS

Figure 3-27. Light-gauge steel framing members are attached to one another using clip angles, bearing stiffeners, and web stiffeners. The stiffeners also prevent framing members from being crushed.

An OSB or plywood subfloor is applied over the joists. Subfloor material and thickness are specified based on the local building code. Ends of the subfloor panels are staggered in a manner similar to a wood-framed building. Self-drilling screws are used to secure the subfloor in place as they will penetrate the panels without lifting them.

Wall and Roof Systems

Exterior walls are placed on the floor joists and subfloor. Exterior walls consist of load-bearing studs, often referred to as heavy-gauge framing members, with top and bottom tracks. Solid C-shapes or C-shapes with knockouts punched in the webs are used as studs. Studs with knockouts allow the passage of plumbing pipes or electrical conduit. Studs are spaced at the on-center spacing specified on the prints. In-line framing is commonly utilized when constructing load-bearing walls. *In-line framing* is a framing system in which all joists, studs, and roof rafters are in a direct vertical line with one another, allowing loads to be directly transferred to the foundation. See Figure 3-28. Racking loads (distortions diagonally across the wall) are counteracted by using structural wall sheathing at the corners or by using diagonal tension straps.

> **Steel framing member thickness is usually expressed as gauge. The higher the gauge number, the thinner the steel.**

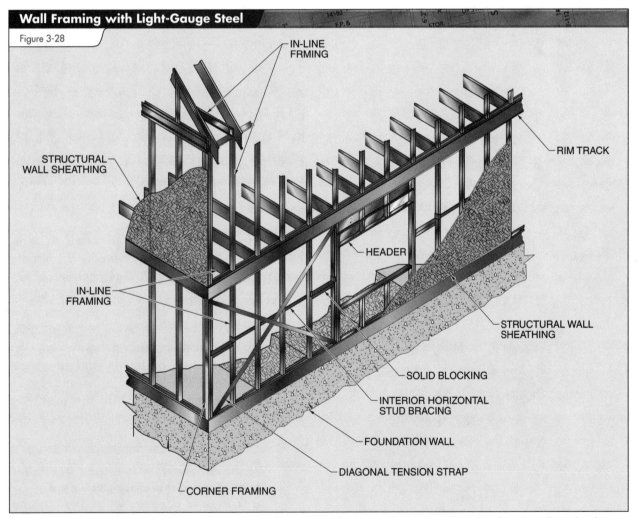

Wall Framing with Light-Gauge Steel

Figure 3-28

IN-LINE FRMING

STRUCTURAL WALL SHEATHING

RIM TRACK

HEADER

IN-LINE FRAMING

STRUCTURAL WALL SHEATHING

SOLID BLOCKING

INTERIOR HORIZONTAL STUD BRACING

FOUNDATION WALL

DIAGONAL TENSION STRAP

CORNER FRAMING

Figure 3-28. Metal-framed wall construction is similar to wood-framed wall construction. In-line framing allows loads to be directly transferred to the foundation.

Reinforced headers are required in load-bearing walls. Headers are constructed with two equal-size C-shapes forming box beam or back-to-back headers, or with one or two angle pieces that fit over the top track forming L-headers. See Figure 3-29. Box beam headers should be properly insulated before installation.

Non-load-bearing interior partitions are generally constructed of lighter gauge metal studs. See Figure 3-30. When load-bearing interior partitions are required, heavier gauge studs are used. Gypsum board is then applied using self-tapping screws.

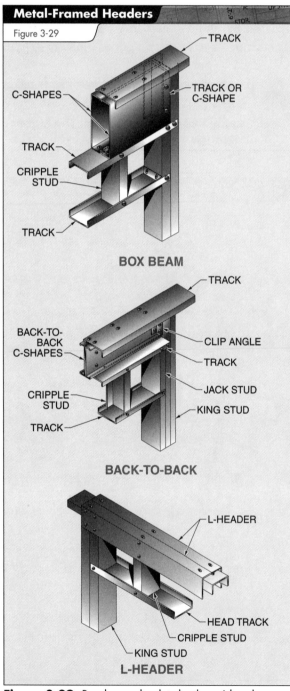

Metal-Framed Headers

Figure 3-29

TRACK

C-SHAPES

TRACK OR C-SHAPE

TRACK

CRIPPLE STUD

TRACK

BOX BEAM

TRACK

BACK-TO-BACK C-SHAPES

CLIP ANGLE

TRACK

JACK STUD

CRIPPLE STUD

KING STUD

TRACK

BACK-TO-BACK

L-HEADER

HEAD TRACK

CRIPPLE STUD

KING STUD

L-HEADER

Figure 3-29. Box beam, back-to-back, or L-headers are installed above door and window openings.

Figure 3-30. Interior partitions are framed with lighter gauge metal studs.

Open web steel joists are often used in conjunction with metal framing systems and masonry construction. An *open web steel joist* is a structural steel member constructed with steel angles and bars that are used as chords with steel angles or bars extending between the chords at an angle. Open web steel joists provide structural support for floors and roofs of buildings, and allow passage and concealment of pipes, ducts, and electrical conduit within the depth of the joist. See Figure 3-31.

Longspan and deep longspan steel joists are lightweight prefabricated steel trusses used between walls, beams, and main structural members for direct support of floor or roof slabs or decks.

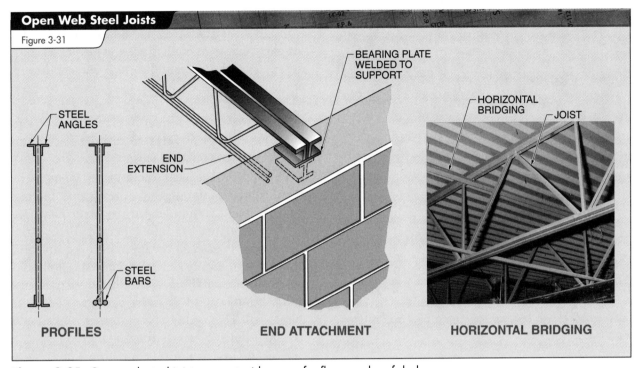

Figure 3-31. Open web steel joists support wide spans for floors and roof decks.

Standards developed by the Steel Joist Institute establish the depths, spans, and load-carrying capacities of open web steel joists. K series open web steel joists range in depth from 8″ to 24″, in 2″ increments, and are available in spans up to 60′-0″. The span of K series steel joists must not exceed 24 times their depth. K series open web steel joists are most commonly used in light commercial construction. Long-span steel joists (LH series) and deep long-span steel joists (DLH series) can span up to 96′-0″ and 144′-0″, respectively, without center support. The span of LH and DLH series steel joists must not exceed 24 times their depth for roofs and 20 times their depth for floors.

Open web steel joists are spaced so the load on each joist does not exceed the allowable load for that particular joist. In general, joists are spaced 24″ OC for floors and up to 30″ OC for roofs. Joist spacing is specified on the prints. Open web steel joists must be properly braced using horizontal or diagonal bridging before construction loads are placed on the joists. Bridging prevents lateral movement of the top chord during construction and secures the joists in

position. Horizontal bridging consists of two continuous horizontal steel members, with one member attached to the top chord and the other attached to the bottom chord. The horizontal bridging is bolted or welded to the joists. For joists longer than 40′-0″, a row of horizontal bridging must be bolted in place before crane hoisting lines are released.

When a finished ceiling is specified under open web joists, end extensions may be installed to allow ceiling materials to be applied. End extensions are bolted or welded to the bottom chord and, in some situations, the exterior wall of the building. Ceiling supports can be suspended from or mounted directly to the bottom chords of joists. Suspended ceilings are commonly used with open web steel joists due to variations in actual joist depths.

Floors supported by open web steel joists are usually 2½″ to 3″ of concrete placed on steel decking. Concrete thickness can be increased to accommodate electrical conduit and raceways for communications systems. Precast concrete, gypsum planks, or plywood can also be used for floor systems over open web steel joists.

CertainTeed Corporation

Roofing felt is applied to a built-up roof using heat and asphalt roofing compound.

Roofs over open web steel joists are commonly constructed with steel decking and left exposed or topped with lightweight concrete or rigid insulation board. For exposed metal deck roofs, fiberglass insulation is installed on top of the open web steel joists prior to installing the roof deck. A covered roof is finished with built-up roofing felt covered with gravel or a single-ply roofing membrane covered with gravel. On flat roofs or roofs with a slight pitch, roof drainage must be carefully evaluated. The rigid insulation board can be sloped, or joists can be sloped to direct water flow on the roof.

REGIONAL VARIATIONS

A variety of footing and foundation designs may be used for a building, depending on the climatic, moisture, and soil conditions. In cold climates, the depth of the frost line affects the foundation design. Moisture from rain and snow penetrates the ground and freezes during the winter season. Freezing and thawing cycles of the soil cause the soil to expand and contract. Footings must be placed below the frost line to prevent foundation movement during the freezing and thawing cycles. Moisture also affects foundation design.

Excessive moisture may enter the building through the foundation if the foundation is not properly waterproofed. Since the load of a building rests on the surrounding soil, soil conditions must be considered when designing a foundation. Certain soil types, such as sand and gravel, compact less when a load is placed upon them and allow surface water to drain better than other soil types such as clay.

Foundation designs include full basement, crawl space, slab-on-grade, and grade beams. Full-basement foundations are constructed where soil and moisture conditions permit. Basements are commonly used for the mechanical equipment, laundry, and family or recreation room. Foundation walls are solid concrete or concrete masonry units. Foundation walls also serve as the basement wall. The top of the foundation wall should extend at least 8″ above the finish grade.

A crawl-space foundation does not have a basement area. Crawl space refers to the distance between the bottoms of the floor joists and the ground, and is typically 18″ or more. Foundation walls for crawl-space foundations are solid concrete or concrete masonry units. Footings and foundations for crawl-space foundations extend below the frost line in cold climates to prevent foundation movement. Crawl-space foundations provide better insulation for the first-story floors than slab-on-grade floors, but do not need the deep excavations required for full-basement foundations.

Slab-on-grade foundations are used extensively in warmer climates and areas with high water tables, but may also be used in colder climates. In colder climates, a footing and short rim wall that extends below the frost line supports the floor slab. In warmer climates, a thickened perimeter footing is used since there is no foundation movement caused by the freezing and thawing cycles of the soil. See Figure 3-32.

Welded wire reinforcement is heavy steel wire welded together in a grid pattern. Welded wire reinforcement is used to reinforce concrete slabs.

Slab-on-Grade Foundations

Figure 3-32

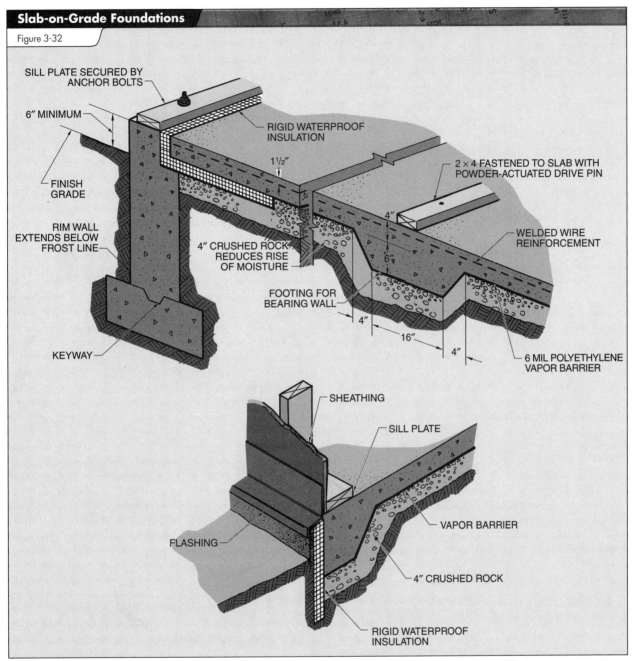

SILL PLATE SECURED BY
ANCHOR BOLTS

6" MINIMUM

RIGID WATERPROOF
INSULATION

1½"

2 × 4 FASTENED TO SLAB WITH
POWDER-ACTUATED DRIVE PIN

FINISH
GRADE

4"

RIM WALL
EXTENDS BELOW
FROST LINE

WELDED WIRE
REINFORCEMENT

4" CRUSHED ROCK
REDUCES RISE
OF MOISTURE

6"

FOOTING FOR
BEARING WALL

KEYWAY

4"

16"

4"

6 MIL POLYETHYLENE
VAPOR BARRIER

SHEATHING

SILL PLATE

VAPOR BARRIER

FLASHING

4" CRUSHED ROCK

RIGID WATERPROOF
INSULATION

Figure 3-32. A slab-on-grade floor requires a short rim wall and edge insulation when used in cold climates. A simple perimeter support suffices in warmer climates.

Grade beam foundations are used where unstable soil conditions exist. Grade beam foundations receive their support from piers spaced at regular intervals that extend deep into the ground. See Figure 3-33. Grade beam foundations can be used on level or steeply sloped lots.

The bottoms of all grade beam piers must extend below the frost line and rest on firm soil. Steel dowels or rebar for tying into the grade beam are positioned when concrete is placed.

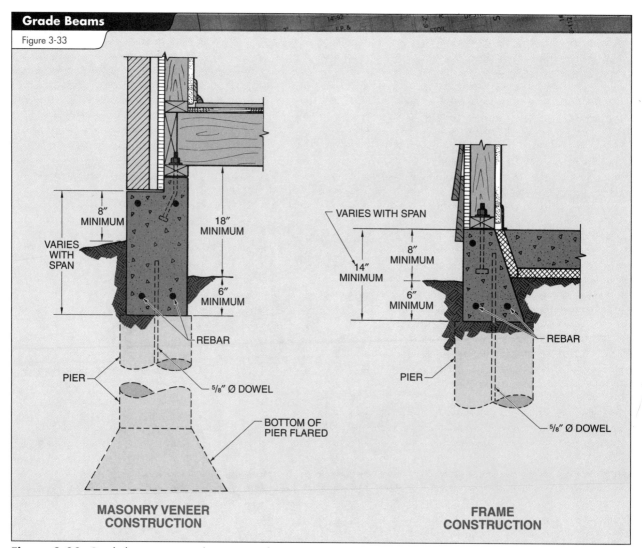

Figure 3-33. Grade beams receive their support from piers.

In many regions of the country, wood-boring insects such as termites can cause structural damage to wood-framed buildings. Precautions must be taken to prevent insects from damaging the building. While most insect infestation occurs after construction is completed, precautions taken during excavation and foundation construction can minimize insect damage. Pressure-treated lumber should be used for wood members close to or in contact with the ground. Termite shields can be installed between the sill plate and top of the foundation wall. A termite shield should be made of 24 ga galvanized metal and extend down 2″ on each side of the wall at a 45° angle. Soil treatment can also be used to prevent

insect infestation. Soil poisons are applied to the ground during construction and form a chemical barrier against the insects.

Due to engineering requirements, the basic building structure, whether wood, metal, or masonry, does not vary greatly between different regions of the country. However, precautions must be taken in regions subjected to excessively high winds or where there is danger of earthquakes (seismic risk zones) to ensure that buildings can withstand great stresses. Rebar is required in all concrete or masonry foundation walls constructed in these regions. In addition, special ties or other structural reinforcement may be required to fasten the foundation to the building framework and to fasten the various framing members together. See Figure 3-34. Wall rigidity is increased by using strong diagonal braces and thicker sheathing.

In seismic risk zones, buildings are designed to counteract horizontal shear forces in the framework. Shear walls with a variety of specialized tiedown and anchoring systems provide structural protection against forces exerted during an earthquake. The tiedown and anchoring systems provide a frame that is not rigid at the connecting points. See Figure 3-35.

Holddowns tie together floors of a building in seismic risk zones. The threaded rod extends through to the upper floor where it is secured to another holddown.

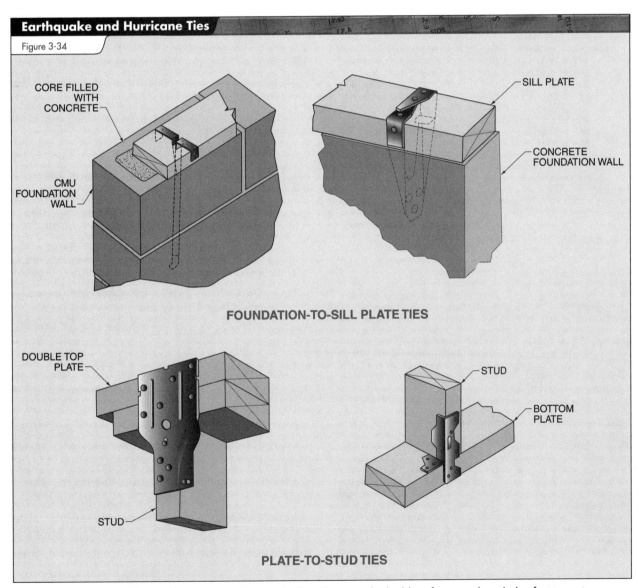

Figure 3-34. Earthquake and hurricane ties fasten the foundation to the building framework and also fasten various framing members together.

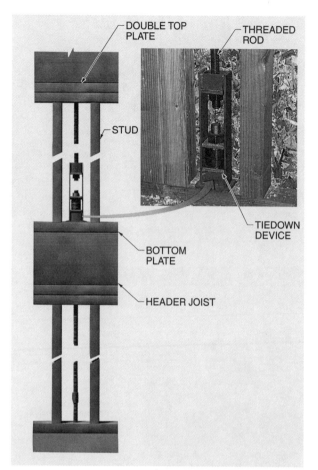

Simpson Strong-Tie Company, Inc.

Figure 3-35. Shear wall construction uses a variety of specialized tiedown and anchoring systems.

CertainTeed Corporation

Blown-in-blanket insulation consists of a spun polypropylene fabric that is attached to studs and joists into which loose fill insulation is placed.

A gable roof, constructed using rafters or trusses for support, is the most common roof type used in residential construction. Roof trusses are typically prefabricated in a shop and delivered to the job site ready to lift and secure in place. Asphalt shingles are widely used as finish roof covering over pitched roofs. Flat roofs are common for light commercial construction. Flat roofs are commonly finished using roofing felt and hot tar or asphalt. Other roof types can also be installed, depending on the desired architectural effect. Snow and ice on roofs pose special problems which can be solved by increasing the protection at the eaves and insulating the attic space to prevent heat loss through the roof. Snow and ice protection may include snow guards installed on the roof over door openings to prevent snow and ice masses from sliding off the roof or the installation of low-voltage electrical heating elements installed over the finish roofing material to melt snow and ice on the roof.

Fire-resistant roof finish materials, such as tile roofing or metal roof coverings, may be required in areas prone to fire. Tile roofing is manufactured from clay or concrete in a variety of styles and colors. Clay tile is lighter than concrete tile, but concrete tile is more durable. Metal roof coverings include aluminum and steel shingles and standing-seam metal panels.

The primary cause for regional variations in building materials and construction methods is climate. Construction materials are rated by R value. See Figure 3-36. The *R value* is a value that represents the ability of a material to resist heat flow. Most insulation products have an R value listed on the packaging. The higher the R value, the greater the resistance to heat flow. The total R value of a wall includes the R value of the framing and sheathing material plus the insulation placed in the wall. An air space, such as the one between the wythes in a masonry cavity wall, adds to the total R value of the wall.

R VALUES OF COMMON BUILDING MATERIALS		
Material	Thickness*	R Value
Masonry Units		
Lightweight concrete masonry units	12	2.27
Face brick	4	0.44
Common brick	4	0.80
Building Materials—General		
Wood sheathing or subfloor	¾	0.94
Fiberboard sheathing, regular density	½	1.32
Fiberboard sheathing, intermediate density	½	1.14
Fiberboard sheathing, nailbase	½	1.14
Plywood	⅜	0.47
Plywood	½	0.62
Plywood	¾	0.93
Vertical tongue-and-groove (cedar or redwood)	¾	1.00
Gypsum board	⅜	0.32
Gypsum board	½	0.45
Interior plywood paneling	¼	0.31
Building paper, permeable felt	—	0.06
Unfaced foam insulation board	1	5.40
Foil-faced foam insulation board	1	7.20
Tyvek® (on 2 × 4 framed wall)	—	11.00
Insulating Materials		
Fiberglass batts	2 to 2¾	7.00
Fiberglass batts	3 to 3½	11.00
Fiberglass batts	5 to 5¼	19.00
Wood		
Fir, pine, and similar softwoods	¾	0.94
Fir, pine, and similar softwoods	1½	1.89
Fir, pine, and similar softwoods	2½	3.12
Fir, pine, and similar softwoods	3½	4.35
Maple, oak, and similar hardwoods	1	0.91

* in in.

Figure 3-36. The R value is the ability of a material to resist heat flow.

Name _____ Date _____

Identification

_____ **1.** Header joist

_____ **2.** Bottom plate

_____ **3.** Metal strap

_____ **4.** Gable end studs

_____ **5.** Rafter

_____ **6.** Sill plate

_____ **7.** Ridge board

_____ **8.** Cross bridging

_____ **9.** Ceiling joists

_____ **10.** Foundation wall

_____ **11.** Steel beam

_____ **12.** Bearing partition

_____ **13.** Double top plate

_____ **14.** Partition plate

_____ **15.** Corner post

_____ **16.** Joist

_____ **17.** Subfloor

_____ **18.** Rebar

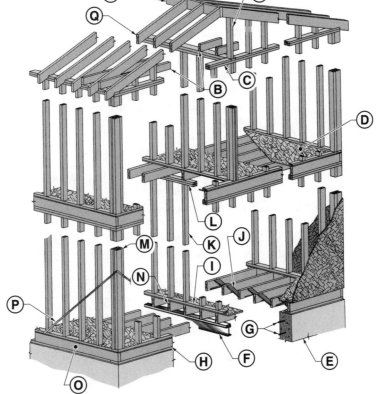

Completion

_____ plate _____ **1.** A double top ___ is the top member of an interior partition.

_____ **2.** A(n) ___ stud is placed at each side of the rough window opening to support the header.

_____ **3.** Shrinkage is minimized in ___ framing through the use of continuous studs from the sill plate to the double top plate.

_____ **4.** Stairs in A-frame houses generally have a(n) ___ pitch.

_____ **5.** ___ ties are used to maintain spacing in foundation walls during concrete placement.

_____ **6.** A(n) ___ is a brick ledge designed to support a load.

_____ **7.** Brick veneer is ___ wythe(s) thick.

_____ **8.** The ___ load is the weight of the permanent structure of a building.

_____ **9.** The double top plates of walls and partitions in platform framing are ___ at the corners and intersections for nailing.

_____ **10.** ___ framing provides an open architectural effect.

_____ **11.** A(n) ___ insulated panel consists of a layer of insulating foam between two OSB or plywood panels.

_____ **12.** ___ are used as top and bottom plates in metal wall framing.

True-False

T   F   **1.** SCR brick is used for cavity walls.

T   F   **2.** Brick walls backed by concrete masonry units are tied together with header courses of brick.

T   F   **3.** Cavity walls are brick walls made of two wythes with an air space between the wythes.

T   F   **4.** Brick veneer is combined with wood or metal framing.

T   F   **5.** The brick in a brick-veneer wall supports the rafters or roof trusses.

T   F   **6.** Windows and doors are difficult to design into metal-framed buildings.

T   F   **7.** Walls of metal-framed buildings are strengthened by diagonal straps or the use of plywood or OSB sheathing at the corners.

T   F   **8.** An advantage of open web steel joists is the ease of installing raceway systems.

T   F   **9.** Crawl-space foundations are limited to the southern part of the country.

T   F   **10.** A ranch dwelling is built with the same type of foundation in all parts of the country.

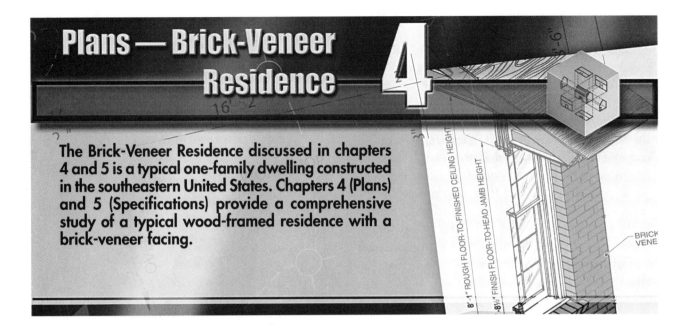

Plans — Brick-Veneer Residence 4

The Brick-Veneer Residence discussed in chapters 4 and 5 is a typical one-family dwelling constructed in the southeastern United States. Chapters 4 (Plans) and 5 (Specifications) provide a comprehensive study of a typical wood-framed residence with a brick-veneer facing.

DESIGN FACTORS IN PRINTS

A residence should provide for the needs and lifestyles of the inhabitants and provide space for all inhabitants and their activities. The design must be flexible enough so the residence continues to be useful over a long period of time. Formal areas, work areas, recreational areas, and rest areas, each with their own special features, must be provided. See Figure 4-1.

Another design factor to consider is the outward appearance of a residence. All parts of the residence should fit together into a harmonious whole. A residence is attractive when attention is paid to all details and their effect on the overall appearance. A residence has added appeal if it is designed to fit its surroundings and is properly located on a building site.

The cost of a residence must also be considered during design. Cost is determined by the choice of the building lot, overall size of the residence, size of individual rooms, and the equipment and materials used in construction. The mechanical and electrical systems selected for the residence also affect the cost of the residence. Plumbing and electrical components should be within the budget for total cost of the structure. Heating and cooling systems must be properly sized to carry the loads imposed by climatic conditions.

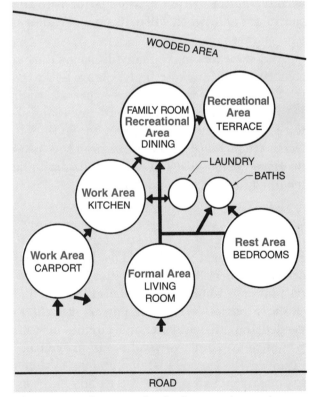

Figure 4-1. The areas of a dwelling are designed to provide for the needs of the inhabitants.

READING PRINTS

Tradesworkers strive to be skillful and efficient in their work. Being efficient means that tradesworkers avoid wasting effort or time. Building materials should always be applied as intended, with a minimum of waste. Many building trades skills are evident in the finished building. Well-laid brick and stone work, interior finish, custom-designed and constructed cabinetwork, and properly laid floor coverings all contribute to a quality finished product. Other building trades work that is hidden in walls, floors, or ceilings is equally important because it can provide an owner with many years of trouble-free service.

Tradesworkers must understand all parts of working drawings and specifications that directly concern them and also have an overall knowledge of the structure. Tradesworkers are responsible for following the plans exactly as drawn. If tradesworkers find errors or discrepancies, or have other suggestions about the construction, they should consult the contractor. The architect, after discussing the matter with the contractor and owner, will determine any necessary changes.

Tradesworkers make many decisions during construction. Many specific details are left to the tradesworkers because they are experts in their field and perform the work every day. Plans often call for measurements to be made on the job. Notes are included on the prints or in the specifications stating that building details are to be modified to meet job conditions.

Construction procedures and techniques are the responsibility of the tradesworkers. In very few instances is the rough structure detailed to show carpenters the wall and floor framing, joist arrangement, or roof truss or rafter layout. Electricians run conduit or nonmetallic-sheathed cable to outlets wherever power or light is needed and efficiently arrange circuits for convenience so that overloading is prevented. Plumbers design and install plumbing systems to properly provide potable water, and safely convey wastewater and waterborne waste from the residence. See Figure 4-2. Heating and cooling systems must be carefully planned and installed since walls, floors, and structural members must be carefully cut to accommodate ductwork. Frequent adjustments are made on the job while the building is in progress. Accurately reading plans and extensive trade knowledge are keys to doing a good job.

Figure 4-2. Electricians install conduit to outlets wherever power or light is required. Plumbers install water supply, waste, and vent piping.

Orientation

Orientation is the process of visualizing and getting acquainted with the prints. When the prints for the dwelling to be studied in this chapter are spread out and examined individually, it is immediately evident that there is a great deal of information to be studied. Prints are designed to be read by tradesworkers who are familiar with construction procedures and techniques and are able to quickly locate the necessary information.

The plans for study are for a Brick-Veneer Residence. This set of plans contains five sheets. Each sheet is identified in the title block in the lower-right corner. The sheets and their contents are as follows:

Sheet 1: Basement Plan
Floor Plan
Typical Basement Column detail

Sheet 2: Exterior Elevations
Right Side Gable Overhang detail
Carport Gable Wall detail

Sheet 3: Sections
Exterior Sections
Interior Elevations
Details

Sheet 4: Plot Plan
Interior Elevations
Piping Diagram
Light Fixture and Door Schedules

Sheet 5: Floor Framing Plan
Roof Framing Plan

BRICK-VENEER RESIDENCE

The construction project titled Brick-Veneer Residence is a one-family dwelling. See Figure 4-3. A *dwelling* is one or more rooms for the use of one or more persons as a housekeeping unit with space for eating, living, and sleeping, and permanent provisions for cooking and sanitation. The dwelling is on a cul-de-sac; therefore, the front lot line is curved. A *cul-de-sac* is a street with only one outlet and a large circular area for turning around.

The Plot Plan, Sheet 4, shows the location of the house on the lot. The house faces northeast and is located on an irregularly shaped lot that extends 213′ deep along the Carport end on the house and 164′ along the bedroom wing. The lot is 227′ wide at the rear. The driveway is not part of the contract.

Figure 4-3. The Brick-Veneer Residence is a three-bedroom dwelling with a Carport and exterior finishes of siding and brick veneer.

The exterior walls of the Brick-Veneer Residence are brick over wood framing members.

Elevation points are not shown on this plot plan. A septic tank with tile field is located between the bedroom wing and the northwest property line.

The Floor Plan of the first floor, Sheet 1, shows the shape, size, and relationship of rooms. The exterior entrance to the Living Room is from a sheltered Porch. The Living Room has a fireplace at the Carport end of the dwelling. This fireplace is also shown on the Basement Plan, Sheet 1, Exterior Elevations, Sheet 2, and Section B-B, Sheet 3.

Sufficient natural lighting throughout the dwelling is available from the large windows. The Kitchen, which is the work center of the house, is designed for efficiency. The large windows above the Kitchen sink provide natural light. A breakfast area is included in the Kitchen. Direct entrance to the Kitchen from the Carport allows groceries to be carried in easily and trash to be removed from the Kitchen without passing through other rooms of the dwelling.

Convenient access is provided from the Kitchen to the Family Room, which includes a Dining Area. The Dining Area and Kitchen are adjacent and are designed with a wide counter opening between the two areas. The washing machine and dryer are located behind bifold doors along the Passage.

The Family Room contains a large expanse of glass, allowing the inhabitants to stay in close touch with the outdoors throughout the year. The adjacent open Terrace, which is a 4″ thick concrete slab, provides an outdoor living space.

The bedroom wing provides quiet, privacy, adequate light, cross ventilation, and ample closets. Three bedrooms are entered from a common Hall. Bath #2 is accessible from the Hall while Bath #1 is only accessible from Bedroom #1, which is the master bedroom. Each bathroom has a lavatory, water closet, and bathtub. The plumbing fixtures in the bathrooms are backed up to a common wall.

The Basement extends under part of the Kitchen and Living Room and is reached by a stairway from the Carport. The Basement contains the furnace, water heater, sump pump, and room for storage. The balance of space below the living area of the dwelling is crawl space.

The Exterior Elevations, Sheet 2, and Figure 4-4, complete the orientation to the house. Front, Rear, Right Side, and Left Side Elevations are shown on Sheet 2. The exterior walls of the dwelling are constructed of brick veneer. Wood trim at cornices, wood siding on the exterior wall outside the Living Room, and the Carport are stained. The change in material along the front of the dwelling, the gable roof with raised ridge over the central portion, and the double-hung windows toward the road divided by muntins give the dwelling a traditional character.

The rear of the dwelling cannot be seen from the road and faces the woods. Wide expanses of insulating glass provide unobstructed views of the natural setting toward the southwest. The Terrace at the rear of the house promotes use of the rear yard.

Exterior elevations provide information about roof and wall finish and the elevation of each floor, but contain few horizontal dimensions.

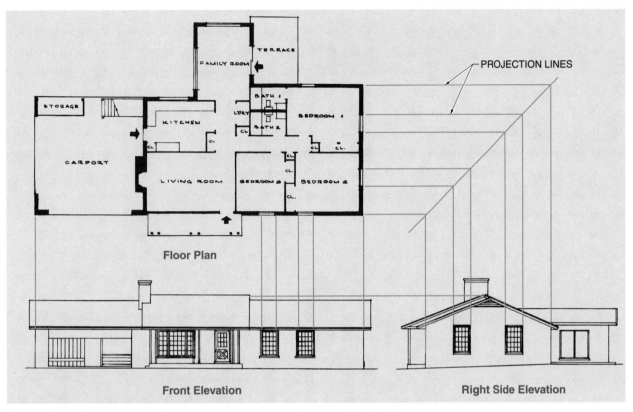

Figure 4-4. Floor plans and elevations provide an overall view of the dwelling.

Living Room

The plan view of the Living Room, Figure 4-5, is taken directly from Sheet 1. The dimensions of the Living Room are 12'-10" × 20'-2" to the rough framing members (studs). The 4" dimension on partitions and the exterior wall of the Living Room represents the nominal measurement. A 2 × 4 actually measures 1½" × 3½". Lumber shrinks after being seasoned (air-dried or kiln-dried), and surfacing at the planing mill further reduces its measurements to its nominal size. When determining the actual wall thickness, the framing member width is added to the wall finish material thicknesses. In the exterior wall, the framing member width (3½"), interior wall finish material thickness (½" gypsum board), and exterior sheathing and siding thicknesses (½" and ¾") are added to determine the final wall thickness (3½" + ½" + ½" + ¾" = 5¼"). See Figure 4-6. In some situations, the wall thickness is rounded to the nearest whole inch for ease in calculations.

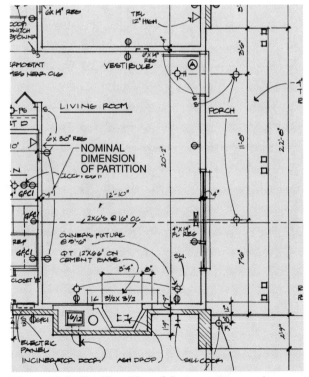

Figure 4-5. The Floor Plan of the Living Room indicates building materials, structural items, and finishes.

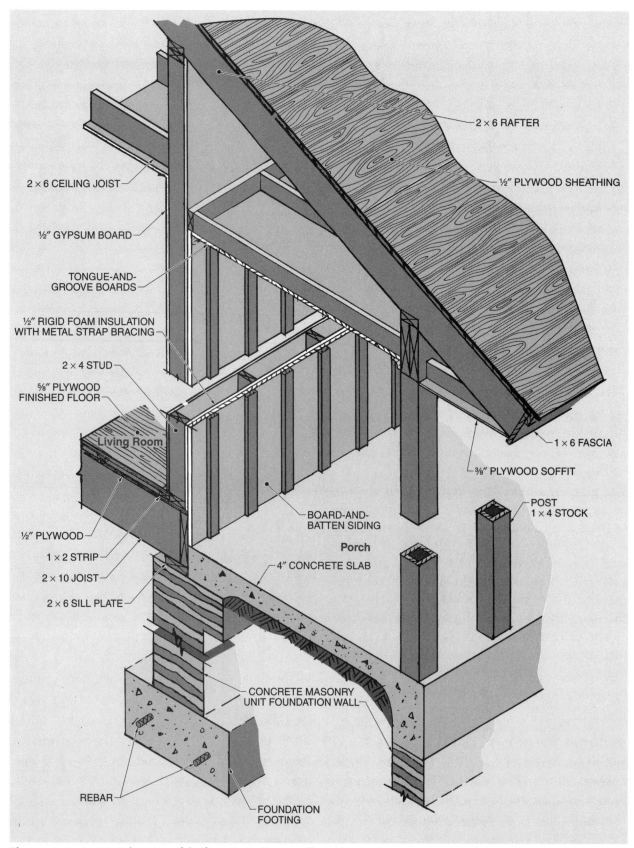

Figure 4-6. A pictorial section of the front Living Room wall and Porch shows construction details.

The Living Room floor has ½″ plywood laid as the subfloor over 2 × 10 floor joists. Strips (1 × 2s) are nailed to the subfloor to provide an air space between the subfloor and the underlayment for the finished floor for thermal insulation. The underlayment is ⅝″ plywood.

In some situations, it is necessary to refer to several sheets to gather all of the required information. Dimensions on the Floor Plan, Sheet 1, horizontally locate the windows to the right of the front entrance. The symbol on the Floor Plan indicates the type of window to be installed. The Front Elevation, Sheet 2, shows how the windows are arranged with a larger lower sash and muntins (dividing bars). The dimensions shown on the upper sashes 36/24 are light sizes (glass sizes) measured as though there were no muntins. The first number (36) is the width and the second number (24) is the height of the windows.

The remaining dimension for proper placement of the windows is the height above the floor. The Typical Wall Section, Sheet 3, and Figure 4-7 provide the height-above-floor information for all double-hung windows in the dwelling. The Typical Wall Section is a section cut through the brick-veneer exterior wall. A dimension of 6′-8½″ from the finished floor to the underside of the head jamb of the double-hung window is shown in the section. Information about the double-hung windows in the Living Room is shown on the Floor Plan, Sheet 1, the Front Elevation, Sheet 2, and Section A-A, Sheet 3.

The only door in the Living Room is the front entrance door. The door symbol indicates the side of the door with butts (hinges). The "A" designation refers to the Door Schedule, Sheet 4, which describes the size, type, and door material as well as information about the frame and casing. The Front Elevation, Sheet 2, shows that the door is a crossbuck door with nine lights surrounded with trim. Details 3 and 4, Sheet 3, provide information about the door frame including the jambs, trim, and rough framing.

The fireplace and chimney are shown in the Living Room on the Floor Plan, Sheet 1. For additional information, refer to Sections A-A and

B-B, Sheet 3, and the Basement Plan, Sheet 1. The section through the Living Room, Section A-A, shows the face of the wall and wall below extending to the Basement floor where the cleanout is located. The bricklayer will provide and install the cleanout door. The section through the Carport, Section B-B, is viewed looking toward the chimney. The section shows the flues with hidden lines.

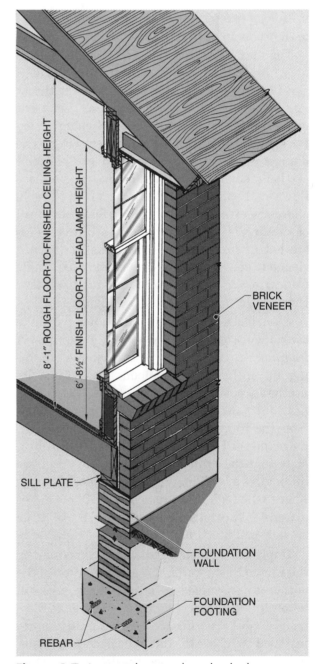

Figure 4-7. A pictorial section through a bedroom window shows brick-veneer construction.

The section through the Living Room, Section A-A, shows the appearance of the fireplace. The fireplace will have a brick face with $1\frac{1}{8}'' \times 2\frac{3}{4}''$ oak finish molding on the sides and top. See Section A-A and Fireplace Trim detail, Sheet 3. The Floor Plan, Sheet 1, shows the chimney masonry, which extends almost to the corner of the room. The masonry is concealed by wall finish as indicated by the line that passes in front of it. The Floor Plan shows all dimensions required by a bricklayer except the height of the opening, which is shown on Section A-A, Sheet 3.

The round flue, constructed of 8″ tile, is used as a furnace flue. See Basement Plan, Sheet 1. The flue for the fireplace begins above the throat and does not show on the Floor Plan. The *throat* is the opening at the top of the fire chamber extending into the smoke chamber where the damper is located. If there were an attic plan or a section taken through the chimney, the fireplace flue would appear in place. Section B-B, Sheet 3, shows the arrangement of the two flues, back wall of the fireplace, and throat. An ash drop is installed in the hearth of the fireplace with a cleanout opening in the Basement. Steel angle iron with $3\frac{1}{2}''$ legs supports the masonry above the fireplace opening. See Floor Plan, Sheet 1.

Electrical features in the Living Room include convenience outlets and switched luminaires. A *luminaire (lighting fixture)* is a complete lighting unit including the components that distribute light, position and protect the lamps, and provide connection to the power supply. Switches near the front entrance door control the luminaires on the Porch and above the entrance door. Note that the symbol shown indicates that the luminaires are ceiling lights. Letter designations refer to the Light Fixture Schedule, Sheet 4. For example, the letter H indicates a No. 1716 surface-mounted luminaire with one 60 W bulb.

Duplex convenience outlets are shown along the Living Room walls. The exact location of the outlets is determined by the electrician, who will follow applicable sections of the National Electrical Code®. See Figure 4-8. Wall outlets are installed 16″ above the finished floor. The grounding plug of the receptacle usually is located on the lower side of the receptacle.

Two air supply registers and one return air grille for the Living Room are shown on the Floor Plan, Sheet 1. One $4'' \times 14''$ register is installed in the floor in front of the windows. The other supply register, measuring $6'' \times 14''$, is installed in the wall near the front entrance door. A $6'' \times 30''$ return air grille is installed in the wall adjacent to Closet D. The actual location of registers and grilles is determined by the heating, ventilating, and air conditioning (HVAC) subcontractor based on placement of wall studs, floor joists, and ceiling joists. In addition, the HVAC subcontractor locates the registers and grilles to provide proper air flow.

The designation 2×6s @ 16″ OC in the Living Room refers to the size and spacing of the joists in the ceiling above. The arrows below the designation show the direction of run for the ceiling joists. The Roof Framing Plan and Floor Framing Plan are shown on Sheet 5. The Roof Framing Plan indicates $2 \times 6 \times 14'$ rafters spaced 16″ OC above the Living Room. The Floor Framing Plan indicates $2 \times 10 \times 14'$ floor joists spaced 16″ OC below the Living Room.

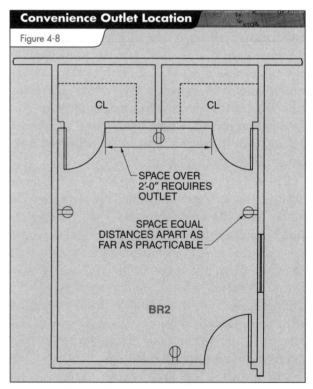

Convenience Outlet Location

Figure 4-8

CL

CL

SPACE OVER 2'-0″ REQUIRES OUTLET

SPACE EQUAL DISTANCES APART AS FAR AS PRACTICABLE

BR2

Figure 4-8. Installation of wall outlets must comply with applicable sections of the National Electrical Code®.

Bedroom Area

The bedroom wing is enclosed in brick-veneer walls. See Figure 4-9 and the Typical Wall Section, Sheet 3. A brick-veneer building is essentially a frame building covered with brick. The framework of the Brick-Veneer Residence is 2×4 studs with wood floor joists, ceiling joists, and rafters supported using conventional means. The dwelling is sheathed with ½″ rigid foam insulation panels. A 1″ air space is provided between the frame wall and the brick wall for ventilation to prevent moisture accumulation. The 4″ brick wall rests on the foundation wall and is tied to the frame wall with anchors that bridge the air space. One anchor is provided for each 2 sq ft of wall area. The brick are laid around window and door openings to give the appearance that the wall is solid brick masonry. The wall is built up right to the cornice, but does not support the structure above. On the gable end, the brick-veneer wall is built past the soffit. See Right Side Gable Overhang detail, Sheet 2. The window is shown in place on the Typical Wall Section detail, Sheet 3, which shows the rough framing and trim. The 9″ wall thickness, shown on the Floor Plan, Sheet 1 and Figure 4-9, is comprised of a 3½″ stud, ½″ rigid foam insulation panel sheathing, 1″ air space, and 4″ brick. The ½″ gypsum board interior wall finish is not included in the 9″ wall thickness.

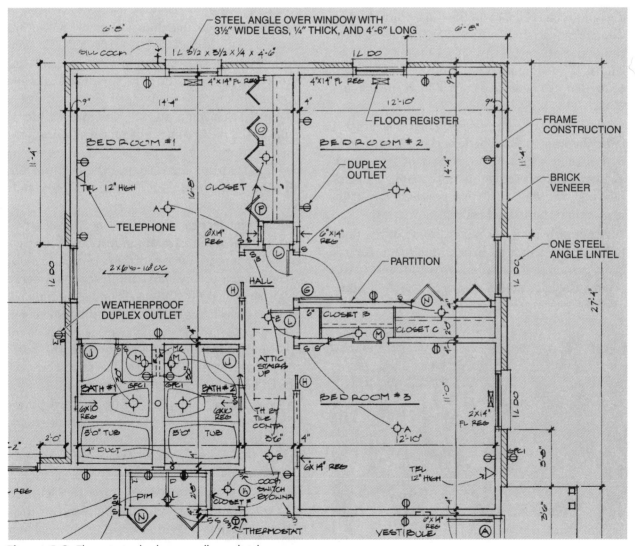

Figure 4-9. The exterior bedroom walls are brick veneer.

All bedroom windows are identical and are shown on the Front, Right Side, and Rear Elevations, Sheet 2. Two sash sizes are used in each window—36/24 and 36/36. Each sash is equipped with insulating glass.

Doors are identified on the Floor Plan using circled letters. The letters refer to the Door Schedule, Sheet 4, where additional information is provided. Pocket doors are installed at the entrances to Bedrooms #1 and #3. Closets A and C are equipped with bifold doors, shelves, and hanger rods. The doors for Closet A in Bedroom #1 are O and P doors. Both doors are 8'-0" high, have one solid panel and open louvers, are made of pine, and have oak trim and jambs. The O doors are 4'-0" wide and the P doors are 5'-0" wide. The doors for Closet C in Bedroom #2 are designated as N doors on the Floor Plan. N door dimensions are 5'-0" × 6'-8" × 1⅜". N doors have the same style and finish as O and P doors. Closet B has bypass doors that are designated as M doors. M doors are paired doors measuring 2'-0" × 6'-8" × 1⅜" each.

Wall switches control ceiling and closet lights in the bedrooms. Telephone outlets are provided in Bedrooms #1 and #3. A pair of three-way switches control the lights in the Hall. A disappearing stairway, providing access to the attic, is installed in the Hall ceiling.

Air supply registers are installed in the floor beneath the windows in each bedroom. Air return grilles are installed in walls across the rooms. Register size is shown on the floor plan.

Duct frames are attached to the studs in preparation for the ductwork.

Ceiling joists above the bedrooms are 2 × 6s spaced 16" OC. Arrows on the Floor Plan, Sheet 1, and lines on the Roof Framing Plan, Sheet 5, indicate the joist size and direction.

Bathrooms

The layout of fixtures in Baths #1 and #2 are similar, but reversed. See Floor Plan, Sheet 1, and the detailed, large-scale elevations on Sheet 4. A 6" thick plumbing wall accommodates the supply, waste, and vent piping for the bathrooms. The air supply is provided through registers on the long walls across from the fixtures. Exhaust fans, which are controlled from the wall switches, are provided in the ceiling and have ducts extending into the attic space.

The notation "4" DUCT" over the bathtub in Bath #1 refers to an exhaust duct for the clothes dryer. The notation "TH BY TILE CONTR" indicates that the tile contractor is responsible for supplying and installing the threshold between the bathroom and Hall needed because of a change in flooring material. The interior elevations of the bathroom walls on Sheet 4 indicate where ceramic tile is to be installed. Tile extends 6'-4" up from the floor around the bathtub. On all other bathroom walls, ceramic tile extends 4'-2" up from the floor.

Base and door casing and the location of accessories are also shown on the elevations. A tile cove base is applied at the base of the ceramic tile walls. Wood casings are used to trim the doors. Refer to the Door Schedule, Sheet 4, for information on J doors. A towel bar, tumbler and toothbrush holder, and soap dish are shown above the water closet and vanity. The medicine cabinets in the bathrooms are not fully recessed because they are placed back-to-back on the common wall.

Floor joists below the bathrooms are shown on the Floor Framing Plan, Sheet 5. Since loads imposed on the floor in this area may be greater due to the weight of the fixtures and water in the bathtubs, the spacing of the floor joists has been decreased to 12" OC from the 16" OC spacing specified for remainder of the dwelling. Closer spacing provides greater support per square foot.

Kitchen

Many factors are involved in the planning of an efficient kitchen. Proper location of the sink, refrigerator, range, oven, and counter space allows the inhabitants to save steps and provides convenience. The three major areas in a kitchen are for storage, preparation, and cooking. Storage areas include base and wall cabinets, pantries, refrigerators, and freezers. Preparation areas include sink and adequate counter space. Cooking areas include stoves, grills, countertop units, and ovens. Microwave ovens, whether freestanding or built-in, must also be considered when planning kitchens. In addition to the three major areas of a kitchen, adequate cleanup facilities must be provided. Sinks and portable or built-in dishwashers are utilized in cleanup. A built-in dishwasher is installed under the counter adjacent to the sink for user convenience and short plumbing runs.

An efficient kitchen is designed so work is minimized and steps are saved. The lengths of three sides of a triangle drawn on the floor plan of an efficiently designed kitchen should total 12′-0″ to 21′-0″. See Figure 4-10. Distances less than 12′-0″ result in crowding of the kitchen appliances. Distances over 21′-0″ require too much walking between areas.

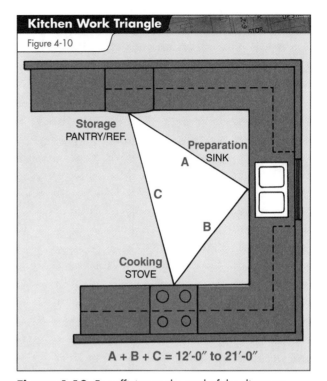

Figure 4-10. For efficiency, the total of the distances between storage, preparation, and cooking areas should equal 12′-0″ to 21′-0″.

Cabinet space should be adequate for the needs of the family. Base cabinets are 24″ deep and 36″ high. The countertop overhangs the base cabinet by 1″. A minimum of 5 running feet of drawers is required for a kitchen. As the number of base cabinets increases, the number of drawers should also increase. All-drawer base cabinets provide additional drawer space. Special base cabinets, such as corner units, may also be utilized. Base cabinets are shown on floor plans with solid lines.

Wall cabinets with an open space above them are 12″ deep and 30″ high. Three shelves provide storage space. Wall cabinets extending to an 8′-1″ finished ceiling are 42″ high and generally have a smaller door at the top. Other wall cabinets vary in height according to their particular use. For example, wall cabinets above a stove are generally 18″ shorter than other wall cabinets in the kitchen. Wall cabinets are shown on floor plans with hidden lines. The recommended vertical clearance between base and wall cabinets is 18″. See Figure 4-11.

Merillat Industries

The lengths of the sides of a kitchen work triangle should total 12′-0″ to 21′-0″.

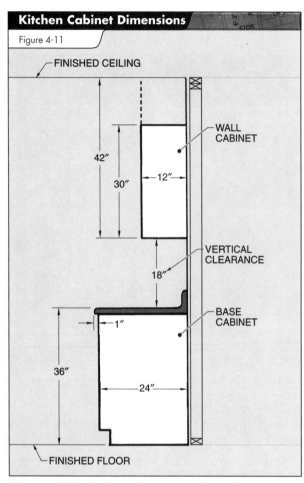

Figure 4-11. Kitchen cabinets typically conform to standard dimensions.

Kitchen windows provide light and ventilation for the dwelling. Windows are commonly placed above a kitchen sink. A valance (decorative molding strip) is often placed between wall cabinets and above the kitchen sink for continuity and to provide mounting space for light fixtures above the sink.

Special provisions are made for larger electrical appliances, such as ranges and dishwashers, and small appliances and ventilation fans. Counter-mounted receptacles in residential kitchens shall be protected with a GFCI (ground-fault circuit interrupter) per the NEC®. Space for a table and chairs is often provided in the kitchen. Access to a formal dining area should be convenient. Kitchens are frequently planned with access to a carport or garage so groceries and other household supplies can be brought in with maximum convenience.

Additional information about the Kitchen is included in the prints. See Figure 4-12 and the Kitchen Cabinets Elevations, Sheet 3. Section A-A, Sheet 3, is drawn through the Kitchen and provides additional information. The Rear Elevation, Sheet 2, provides details of the windows.

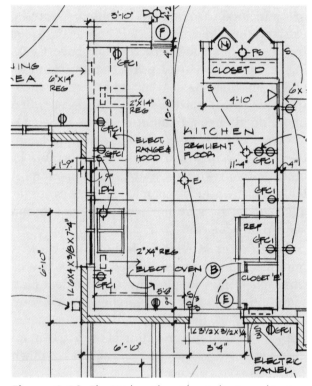

Figure 4-12. The Kitchen Floor Plan indicates cabinet and appliance layout.

The Kitchen windows are shown on the Floor Plan and Rear Elevation view as triple casement sash with the center window fixed. The rough opening for the windows is 1'-10½" × 3'-2¼". Optional sizes are available from different manufacturers. The glass in the windows is insulating glass. The height of the windows above the floor or countertop is not given directly, but the interior elevation of the Kitchen cabinets shows the top of the window trim touching the soffit at a height of 7'-1". The exterior door leading to the Carport is shown on Section B-B, Sheet 3. The Door Schedule, Sheet 4, indicates the exterior door is a steel-clad door with a urethane core.

The Floor Plan, Sheet 1, shows an L-shaped arrangement along one side of the Kitchen consisting of the oven, corner cabinet, sink, and dishwasher. The utility closet (Closet E), space for refrigerator, refrigerator cabinet, base and wall cabinet, and space for a kitchen table are shown on the other side. The Kitchen Cabinet elevations, Sheet 3, provide detailed views of three sides of the Kitchen. A base cabinet is shown at the far left side of Elevation A. This base cabinet has a maple countertop and a plastic laminate backsplash. A wall cabinet with one fixed and two adjustable shelves is shown above the base cabinet. Note that only the two adjustable shelves are called out in the notation, as one fixed shelf (the bottom shelf) is required in the construction of a wall cabinet.

The soffit begins above the wall cabinet and continues around the Kitchen to the corner nearest the Family Room. A refrigerator space is provided next to the base and wall cabinets. Note the cabinets above the refrigerator space. The minimum recommended width of a refrigerator space is 32″. The cabinet supplier should verify the refrigerator size before constructing or ordering the Kitchen cabinets. Closet E is located between the refrigerator space and the Carport. The Door Schedule, Sheet 4, indicates that the E door is a 1′-8″ × 6′-8″ × 1⅜″, hollow-core flush oak door.

Elevation B shows Door B (refer to Door Schedule, Sheet 4) and the oven space, with a cabinet above and below the oven space. A wall cabinet with two adjustable shelves and a lazy Susan (revolving) base cabinet finished with plastic laminate top and backsplash is shown. Elevation B meets the cabinet on the adjacent wall at the corner.

Elevation C shows the wall with the window, sink location, dishwasher, range top with hood above, and cabinets with shelves and drawers or doors. A special drop-in cutting board is located over the dishwasher. A portion of the wall at the far right is open, providing a pass-through to the Family Room. The wall cabinet with doors on either side is accessible from the Kitchen and the Family Room.

Appliance dimensions must be verified prior to ordering cabinets.

Building codes may require the use of firestopping materials, such as firestopping caulk, around floor and wall openings.

Basic dimensions are provided on the Floor Plan, Sheet 1, and on the Kitchen Cabinet elevations, Sheet 3. The window, pass-through opening, utility closet, soffit, and wall finish are built or installed before accurate measurements for cabinets can be taken.

Power outlets for the range, oven, and clock outlet are shown on the Floor Plan, Sheet 1. The clock outlet is installed 6′ above the finished floor. A three-way switch controls the ceiling light from two locations. The electrical panel is installed in the utility closet.

The air supply enters the Kitchen through registers in the toekick under the base cabinets as shown on the Floor Plan, Sheet 1 and the Kitchen Cabinet elevations, Sheet 3. An exhaust fan is part of the range hood. A vent extends from the hood through the wall cabinet and exits through the roof.

Family Room

The appearance of the Family Room, Sheet 1, is enhanced by large windows and the sliding glass doors leading to the Terrace. See Figure 4-13. The windows and doors are shown on the Rear, Right Side, and Left Side Elevations, Sheet 2.

Item C in the Door Schedule, Sheet 4, describes the sliding glass doors, one of which is fixed (stationary). Tempered insulating glass is used in the doors. The door height is 6'-8" with a threshold of ½", placing the head jamb 6'-8½" above the floor. The window head jambs are set at the same height as the door head jamb.

Air supply registers, measuring 4" × 14", are installed in the floor under the rear window and in front of the fixed door. The return air grille, measuring 6" × 14", is located on the wall under the pass-through.

Luminaires (lighting fixtures) in the Family Room are recessed. The recessed luminaire in the Dining Area is installed 2'-4" from the wall. Another recessed luminaire (lighting fixture) is installed 3'-6" from the rear window and 2'-4" from the finished wall adjacent to the Terrace. The main recessed luminaire (lighting fixture) is located in the center of the Family Room. Light fixtures are controlled from switches near the Passage.

Three closets are located next to the Passage. Closet F, Sheet 1, faces the Hall and is equipped with a luminaire (lighting fixture) that is controlled by a door switch. Closet D, Sheet 1, is a guest closet in the Passage near the Living Room. The closet is equipped with a luminaire (lighting fixture) that is controlled by a pull switch. The closet in the Passage has a receptacle for the dryer and a 4" duct to vent dryer exhaust to the outside. The luminaire (lighting fixture) above the washing machine and clothes dryer is controlled by a wall switch to the right of the doors.

Carport

A *carport* is a covered shelter with one or more open sides. The Carport, Sheet 1, has a 4" thick concrete slab with solid brick masonry at three corners. The slab slopes ¼" per foot for proper water drainage. A W12 × 27 beam supports the roof structure over the wide opening. The roof is

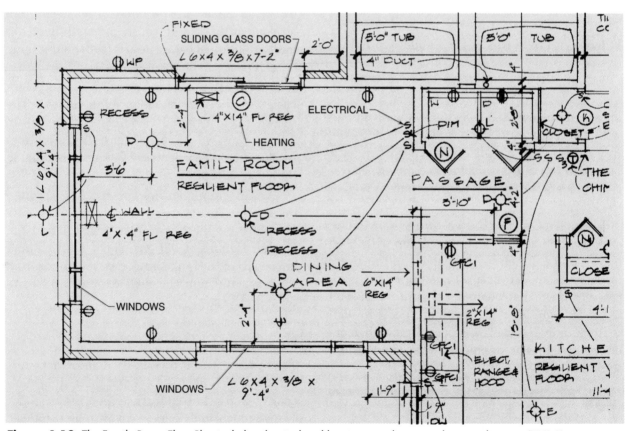

Figure 4-13. The Family Room Floor Plan includes electrical and heating, ventilating, and air conditioning (HVAC) information.

supported at the rear by 6 × 6 posts. See Rear Elevation, Sheet 2. Siding on a wood framework with screen wire mesh panels encloses the left side of the carport. The Storage wall is covered with siding. See Detail 2, Sheet 2. A wire mesh screen is installed near the Basement stairs. A single wall switch along the Kitchen door controls the lights in front of the Carport. A three-way switch inside the Kitchen door and another three-way switch on the brick wall outside the door control the ceiling light and the light at the head of the stairs in the Carport.

Elevations

Elevations show the building materials used on the exterior of the dwelling. The roof is covered with asphalt shingles. The pitch symbol indicates a 4½″ on 12 slope for the roof. All roofs of the dwelling have the same pitch. Metal diverters are indicated on the Rear, Right Side, and Left Side Elevations to divert water into the valleys of the intersecting gable roofs. There are no gutters or downspouts on the dwelling. Wood louvers are installed in both gable ends of the main roof to ventilate the attic space. The louvers are shown on the Right Side and Left Side Elevations.

Steel angle lintels support the brick above the heads of windows such as on the right side gable end, at the sliding glass doors in the Family Room, the end windows in the Family Room, and the Kitchen windows. The lintels are shown on the Floor Plan, Sheet 1. For example, the lintel over the end windows in the Family Room is 6″ × 4″ × ⅜″ × 9′-4″ long.

Information concerning the chimney is shown on the Front and Left Side Elevations, Sheet 2. The chimney extends 3′-0″ above the main roof ridge and measures 2′-5″ × 5′-6″. Metal flashing is shown at the intersection of the chimney and roofs.

Wood board-and-batten siding is used as exterior finish for the wall between the front entrance door and the Living Room windows. See Front Elevation, Sheet 2. Three pairs of wood posts are shown across the front porch.

The elevations of the Carport on Sheet 2 provide additional information about the materials used for exterior finish. The redwood siding,

posts, and railing shown on the Front Elevation, Sheet 2, are for the Storage area and the stairway at the rear of the Carport. The wire mesh screen and wood siding, shown on the Rear Elevation, Sheet 2, form the back wall with an open space between them. The Left Side Elevation, Sheet 2, shows wood siding with wire mesh screen panels above.

Rough Structure

The elements that comprise the rough structure of the dwelling are the footings and foundation; wood framework of floor joists, walls, partitions, ceiling joists, and roof; and brick and brick veneer. Several sheets of the plan must be studied to review the rough structure.

The footings are shown with hidden lines on the Basement Plan, Sheet 1, the four elevations on Sheet 2, and Sections A-A and B-B and the Typical Wall Section, Sheet 3. The foundation wall is shown on the Basement Plan, Sheet 1, with two thicknesses—8″ and 1′-0″. The footing width varies accordingly. Footing dimensions increase when there is an added load, such as at garage corners. The footing under the chimney is a large rectangular pad. Square footings are provided under each column in the crawl space. The wall footings are 12″ thick and reinforced with two continuous #4 rebar. Additional reinforcement is placed across the chimney footing. The bottoms of the footings are set at four different elevations as shown in the Left and Right Side Elevations, Sheet 2.

Concrete foundation footings and walls are common for residential and light commercial construction. Sill plates are attached using anchor bolts projecting from the top of the foundation wall.

One portion of the deep footing is around the Basement, which extends under the Living Room and Porch. See Figure 4-14. Other footing elevations provide for the change in grade of the lot. The ground slopes toward the front of the building. Provision for the grade change is achieved with a stepped footing on each side.

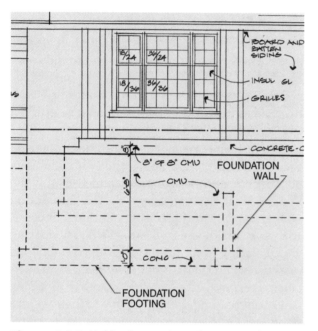

Figure 4-14. Hidden lines indicate footings and basement foundation walls.

The foundation walls consist of concrete masonry units (CMUs) laid on the footings according to the Basement Plan, Sheet 1, and the elevations on Sheet 2. The bricklayer must study the elevations because the foundation wall is not built to the same elevation (height) all around. The Right Side Elevation, Sheet 2, shows that the top of the foundation wall is stepped so the brickwork follows the grade closely. The Basement Plan, Sheet 1, shows that the wall toward the crawl space is 4'-0" high. The foundation wall around the Carport is modified to compensate for the grade change, to give direct support to the corner piers that are built before the floor is placed, and to provide for a concrete grade beam at the front opening. Steel reinforcement is required between alternate CMU courses. See the notation next to the Basement Plan, Sheet 1, and Figure 4-15.

Figure 4-15. Steel reinforcement provides additional lateral strength for a concrete masonry unit foundation wall.

Steel members supporting the floor joists are W8 × 17 beams resting on pipe columns and masonry walls. See the Typical Basement Column detail, Sheet 1. The top CMUs are filled with concrete, and anchor bolts are placed at 6'-0" intervals. Sill plates are shimmed to level around the building. The sill plates are secured in place by tightening nuts on the anchor bolts and grouted in place to maintain level. *Grout* is a fluid mortar mixture consisting of cement and water with or without aggregate. Care must be taken to ensure building dimensions, as shown on the Floor Plan, Sheet 1, are followed accurately and that corners are square. After the beams and sill plates are installed, the joists are then placed and fastened. The Floor Framing Plan, Sheet 5, provides information about the joist size and spacing. Note that the joists under the bathrooms are placed 12" OC. Cross bridging is required at the center of each span. See Figure 4-16.

Bridging between joists maintains joist alignment and helps to distribute the load carried by the floor unit. Bridging is typically required when joist spans are greater than 8'-0". Wood cross bridging, solid wood bridging, or metal cross bridging may be used with wood-framed buildings. When installing cross bridging, the upper ends are fastened into place before the subfloor is placed. The lower ends are fastened into place after the subfloor is placed and loads are imposed on the floor.

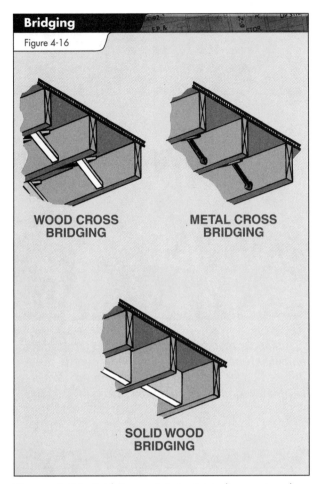

Bridging

Figure 4-16

WOOD CROSS BRIDGING

METAL CROSS BRIDGING

SOLID WOOD BRIDGING

Figure 4-16. Bridging maintains joist alignment and strengthens floors by distributing loads across several floor joists.

Based on the Typical Wall Section, Sheet 3, the next operation is subfloor installation. The subfloor is ½″ plywood that extends to the outside of the header joist, which is located at the ends of the joists. The subfloor is screwed or nailed and glued to the joists. When the subfloor is in position, wall framing begins. Lines are snapped on the subfloor indicating wall positions and dimensions. Wall sections are then constructed on the floor with the bottom plate and double top plates nailed to the studs. The double top plate allows the wall sections to be tied together at intersections and corners. See Figure 4-17.

The Typical Wall Section, Sheet 3, shows two 2 × 10s on edge to form a header over the window. The Typical Wall Section depicts headers for the double-hung windows in the bedrooms. Ceiling joists rest on the wall plates and the load-bearing partition that extends the length of the house near the center. One row of solid bridging is required in each span to provide rigidity and to prevent the joists from twisting.

The roof rafters, shown on the Typical Wall Section, Sheet 3, are notched to fit over the wall plate and extend down to form support for the overhang. The Roof Framing Plan, Sheet 5, indicates the layout and spacing of the rafters. See Figure 4-18. Although Figure 4-18 is not a schematic of the Brick-Veneer Residence, it is

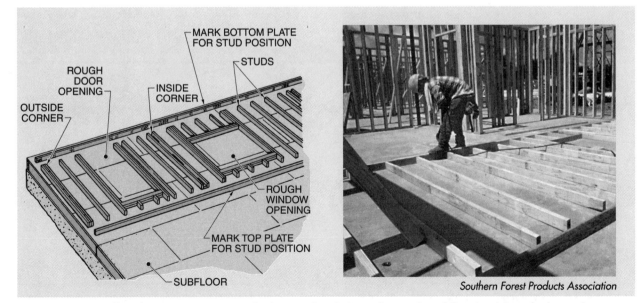

Southern Forest Products Association

Figure 4-17. Wall and partition sections are laid out and nailed together on the subfloor, and then tilted into place.

included for clarity and shows the major roof components. The elevations on Sheet 2 show the roof appearance. Note the varying ridge heights and the valleys over the Family Room. The elevations indicate the eaves are at varying heights around the dwelling, making it necessary to extend some of the rafters. Part of the roof over the Family Room is supported by partitions below.

Bricklaying can start as soon as the frame walls are finished, rough window openings are installed, and sheathing is applied. The brick corners of the Carport and the chimney are built at the same time. Placing concrete for the Carport, Terrace, and Porch slabs is among the last outdoor tasks to be performed. The Basement Plan, Sheet 1, and Section B-B, Sheet 3, show a grade beam for the front of the Carport slab reinforced with two rebar. The other two sides of the Carport and Porch slabs are made with edges thicker than the slabs themselves to provide additional support. The Section Views, Sheet 3, provide information on the slabs.

ATAS International, Inc.
Standing seam metal roofs can be used for residential and light commercial buildings. Snow guards are installed on the roof over door openings to prevent large snow and ice masses from sliding off the roof.

Roof Framing

Figure 4-18

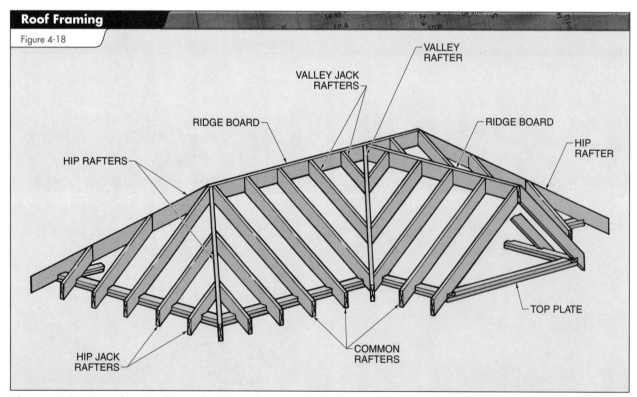

Figure 4-18. A combination hip and gable roof, commonly known as an intersecting roof, is composed of several types of rafters.

Print Details

The Typical Basement Column detail, Sheet 1, shows the steel columns installation, the first floor construction, and the bearing partition framing. The Right Side Gable Overhang detail, Sheet 2, shows the continuation of the brick-veneer wall above the soffit. The detail also shows lookouts used to support the last rafter, soffit, and trim at the right end wall over the bedrooms. The Carport Gable Wall detail, Sheet 2, is for the gable at the opposite side of the building. For framing above the openings in the screen, 2 × 6s are used. The construction of the Carport screen is also shown on the Cornice at Carport Entrance detail, Sheet 3. The detail also provides information on the rafters and cornice supporting the steel beams and the wall finish. The Porch detail, Sheet 3, shows important trim features for the dwelling.

Plumbing and Electrical

An examination of the Floor Plan, Sheet 1, and the Water Piping Diagram, Sheet 4, reveals that the plumbing has been carefully arranged for efficiency and economy. The Floor Plan shows that the Kitchen fixtures have been placed in line with one another. The sink, dishwasher, washing machine, and fixtures for Baths #1 and #2 are laid out on the same plumbing partition. The sillcock outside Bedroom #1 is also approximately in line with the main plumbing run. In addition to these fixtures and appliances, the Water Piping Diagram includes the water heater and the supply line for the sillcock in the Carport. The soil pipe—4″ PVC—is shown on the Basement Plan, Sheet 1, running to the septic tank. The septic tank and tile field are indicated on the Plot Plan, Sheet 4. Water along the perimeter of the basement is removed by drain tile along the footings. See Basement Plan, Sheet 1, and Section A-A, Sheet 3. The tile extends back to the Family Room and to the floor drain at the foot of the stairway. The water is diverted into a tile settling basin to reduce the silt and then expelled by a sump pump to drain tile under the lawn.

The electrical system has been shown as each outlet appeared for the first time in relation to its use in the building. The Light Fixture Schedule, Sheet 4, refers to catalog descriptions of the luminaires (lighting fixtures) selected for each location.

True-False

T	F	**1.** Wall cabinets may have adjustable shelves.
T	F	**2.** The rough structure of a building is generally very detailed so that carpenters can locate each measurement.
T	F	**3.** A set of plans always contains an even number of sheets.
T	F	**4.** Exterior elevations show complete kitchen details.
T	F	**5.** The primary areas of a residence include formal areas, work areas, and recreational and rest areas.
T	F	**6.** The abbreviation OC indicates off-center.
T	F	**7.** Air supply registers may be located in floors or walls.
T	F	**8.** Kitchen wall cabinets are generally 30" or 42" high.
T	F	**9.** The recommended vertical clearance between base and wall cabinets is 18".
T	F	**10.** Elevations may be either interior or exterior.
T	F	**11.** Window head jambs in a building are normally set at the same height.
T	F	**12.** Solid wood bridging should not be installed to prevent joists from twisting.
T	F	**13.** Floor registers are often placed below windows.
T	F	**14.** The three primary areas of a kitchen are the storage, preparation, and cooking areas.
T	F	**15.** Details and floor plans are drawn to the same scale for uniformity.

Completion

_____ **1.** A(n) ___ plan shows the location of the house on a lot.

_____ **2.** The light size of a window refers to the size of ___.

_____ **3.** A section is made by passing a cutting ___ through an object.

_____ **4.** A brick-___ building is essentially a frame building covered with brick.

_____ **5.** The standard depth for wall cabinets is ___″.

_____ **6.** The furred-down area above kitchen cabinets is the ___.

_____ **7.** A(n) ___ switch controls lights from two locations.

_____ **8.** The standard door height is ___.

_____ **9.** The ___ is the highest point of a gable roof.

_____ **10.** Roof ___ are notched to fit over the top plate.

_____ **11.** The standard depth for base cabinets is ___″.

_____ **12.** The actual size of a 2 × 4 stud is ___.

_____ **13.** The first number in a window notation indicates the ___ of the glass.

_____ **14.** Wall cabinets are shown on floor plans with ___ lines.

_____ **15.** Electrical wall outlets must be spaced no more than ___ apart, measured along the wall.

Identification

Refer to Appendix.

_____ **1.** Sillcock

_____ **2.** Centerline

_____ **3.** Concrete (section)

_____ **4.** Pull switch

_____ **5.** Hidden line

_____ **6.** Earth (section)

_____ **7.** Telephone

_____ **8.** Steel (section)

_____ **9.** Lighting panel

_____ **10.** Duplex convenience outlet

Ⓐ – – – – – Ⓑ

Ⓒ Ⓓ

Ⓔ —— · —— Ⓕ Ⓢ

Ⓖ Ⓗ

Ⓘ Ⓙ

T	F	**26.**	Sill plates in exterior walls are 2 × 8s.
T	F	**27.**	The basement floor is a 6" slab.
T	F	**28.**	All siding on the dwelling is applied vertically.
T	F	**29.**	A double top plate is shown on rear walls.
T	F	**30.**	Closet B is larger than Closet A.

Completion

_____ **1.** The telephone jack in Bedroom #3 is ___" high.

_____ **2.** The Terrace has ___ electrical convenience outlets.

_____ **3.** Exhaust fans in the Baths are controlled by ___ switches.

_____ **4.** The concrete slab for the Terrace slopes ___" per foot.

_____ **5.** The foundation wall at the bedroom end of the dwelling is ___ in length.

_____ **6.** Basement columns are ___" diameter standard pipe.

_____ **7.** Registers in toekicks of Kitchen base cabinets are 2" × ___".

_____ **8.** ___ flashing is placed around the chimney.

_____ **9.** Brick veneer is anchored to the house frame every ___ sq ft.

_____ **10.** ___" exterior grade plywood is used for the soffit at the porch.

_____ **11.** The scale for Section A-A is ___" = 1'-0".

_____ **12.** The fireplace opening is ___ high.

_____ **13.** Plumbing supply lines inside the residence are ___.

_____ **14.** Door ___ is a sliding door with tempered, insulating glass.

_____ **15.** Ceramic tile is placed to a height of ___ around bathtubs.

_____ **16.** Brick-veneer walls are flashed with ___" aluminum flashing.

_____ **17.** A(n) ___ step is shown at Door B leading to the Carport.

_____ **18.** Kitchen cabinet elevations are drawn at a scale of ___" = 1'-0".

_____ **19.** The concrete slab is thickened to ___" at the front entrance of the Carport.

_____ **20.** Section B-B is drawn to a scale of ___" = 1'-0".

_____ **21.** The septic tank is located ___' from the bedroom end of the dwelling.

_____ **22.** Hot and cold water pipes to the washer are ___" in diameter.

_____ **23.** Ridge boards in roof framing are 2 × ___s.

_____ **24.** Floor joists over the Basement are spaced ___″ OC.

_____ **25.** Foundation footings under the main structure are ___ wide.

_____ **26.** The front Porch is supported by ___ 6 × 6 posts.

_____ **27.** A(n) ___″ hood is placed above the drop-in cooktop.

_____ **28.** The Family Room has a(n) ___ floor.

_____ **29.** Bedroom ___ measures 14′-4″ × 16′-8″.

_____ **30.** The crawl space is excavated to the top of the ___.

_____ **31.** The concrete stairway leading to the basement has ___ risers.

_____ **32.** Access to the attic is located in the ceiling of the ___.

_____ **33.** The electrical panel is located in Closet ___.

_____ **34.** Soil beneath the Terrace is ___.

_____ **35.** The front entrance door is Door ___.

_____ **36.** Bedroom #3 is 11′-0″ × ___.

Identification

_____ **1.** Soffit

_____ **2.** Foundation wall

_____ **3.** Bottom plate

_____ **4.** Sill plate

_____ **5.** Ceiling joist

_____ **6.** Pitch symbol

_____ **7.** Floor joist

_____ **8.** Foundation footing

_____ **9.** Window apron

_____ **10.** Brick veneer

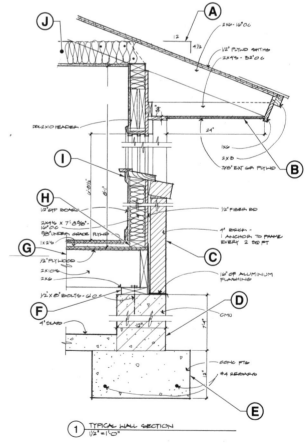

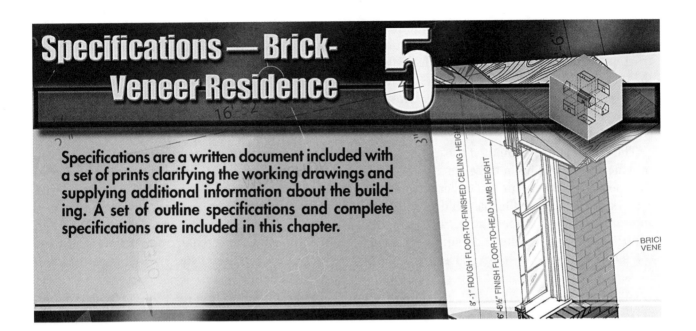

Specifications — Brick-Veneer Residence 5

Specifications are a written document included with a set of prints clarifying the working drawings and supplying additional information about the building. A set of outline specifications and complete specifications are included in this chapter.

SPECIFICATIONS

Specifications provide written descriptions of many building components and procedures in conjunction with the prints. Specifications include information in written form that describes the building to be constructed, the materials to be used, and the responsibilities of those involved.

Even the simplest construction job has specifications. These specifications consist of short statements about the work to be done and the materials to be used. Specifications are included with a sketch or a working drawing and a written contract, and these all become the basis for agreement between the owner and the contractor. Complete specifications are written to give detailed information about the job.

Specifications provide the general conditions of the contract and outline the responsibilities of the owner, architect, contractor, and subcontractors. Guarantees of performance are included. Specifications also supplement the prints with detailed technical information about the work to be done, and specify the materials, equipment, and fixtures to be used. In addition, specifications serve, with the contract agreement and the working drawings, as the legal basis for the transaction of erecting the building from start to finish.

Specifications supplement the set of prints with data that describes the construction job in a general sense. The set of prints and the specifications are intended to be in agreement. In the event of any discrepancy or conflict between the prints and specifications, the specifications take precedence.

The architect, who is responsible for the specifications, carefully accounts for all the details in writing. Specifications spell out the architect's role in the project and the personal responsibility that must be assumed for inspection.

The owner uses the specifications to verify that materials specifically desired in the building are provided and to obtain a specific and detailed overview of the finished building. The owner reviews the various guarantees of performance for future reference in the event that the structure or its equipment does not prove satisfactory.

The specifications provide the contractor and subcontractors with detailed information for estimating the costs of labor and materials when bidding competitively. Suppliers of building materials, such as roofing, lumber, and insulation, are able to determine the quality and types of materials to be used. Equipment and fixture suppliers obtain detailed descriptions, with catalog numbers or names, for plumbing fixtures, furnace and air conditioning equipment, and similar items from the specifications. Subcontractors bid their work based upon codes referred to in the specifications. For example, electricians comply with the requirements of the National Electrical Code® when estimating costs for specific materials.

The building department of the city or county in which the building is to be constructed uses the specifications and prints to determine their compliance with all applicable building codes and zoning ordinances to meet structural, fire, and health standards. Banks and loan agencies use the same information to appraise the building to determine its value. When governmental agencies such as the Veterans Administration (VA) or the Federal Housing Administration (FHA) provide part of the financing, they require a copy of the specifications for their approval. Certain sections of the specifications must be written on forms supplied by the individual agency when either VA or FHA financing is used.

Specifications have a very important role in the complete set of construction documents. Specifications are part of the legal contract and may be used in court in the event of a lawsuit. If the working drawings are correct, and the specifications written with care, the likelihood of problems arising during the construction project is diminished.

Writing Specifications

The architect is responsible for writing the specifications so they are consistent with the prints. New developments in construction materials and methods must be studied so an architect can recommend specific products to be used and building techniques to be followed. When preparing the specifications, an architect includes the exact materials to be used and lists the equipment by catalog numbers or suggests an alternative. This process requires experience acquired from specifying and observing the performance of materials and equipment and watching for new developments.

The architect has an extensive library of catalogs supplied by manufacturers as well as literature from other sources. One of the most

useful tools for acquiring material and equipment information is the *Sweet's Architectural Catalog File,* which is a series of volumes consisting of manufacturer catalogs organized as a ready reference. *Sweet's Architectural Catalog File* (commonly referred to as *Sweet's Catalogs*) is organized according to the Construction Specification Institute's MasterFormat™, with product manufacturers' specific catalog material providing technical information such as size, color, and application. Sweet's information is readily accessible on compact disc (CD) and on the Internet. These electronic formats provide for quick searches of the most current information available.

Another example of reference material that an architect consults is the *Building Materials Directory* published by Underwriters Laboratories Inc. Product classifications are identified alphabetically, followed by manufacturers of those particular products. Underwriters Laboratories Inc. also publishes a number of other directories, including the *Electrical Construction Equipment Directory* and *Electrical Appliance and Utilization Directory,* which are updated annually.

The American Institute of Architects (AIA) provides standard forms and overall directions for specification writing. These materials are particularly useful in stating the general conditions. The general conditions are stated at the beginning of the set of specifications, but they govern all of the separate areas of construction. The general conditions also provide uniform legal language, which protects all of the participants in a construction project including the owner, architect, general contractor, subcontractors, and suppliers.

CSI MASTERFORMAT™

The Construction Specifications Institute (CSI) is an organization of individuals and organizations such as architects, engineers, constructors, specifiers, and suppliers of construction products. One of the primary documents developed by CSI is the MasterFormat™. The *MasterFormat*™ is a uniform system of numbers and titles for organizing information about construction requirements, products, and activities into a standard sequence. See Figure 5-1. MasterFormat™ is used for organizing information in project manuals, for organizing cost data, for filing product information and other technical data, for identifying drawing objects, and for presenting construction market data. The MasterFormat™ was produced jointly by the CSI and Construction Specifications Canada (CSC) with extensive public review and coordination with industry and trade organizations.

Groupings

The numbers and titles in MasterFormat™ are grouped under the following general headings:

- Introductory Information (00001 to 00099)
- Bidding Requirements (00100 to 00499)
- Contracting Requirements (00500 to 00999)
- Facilities and Spaces (no numbering)
- Systems and Assemblies (no numbering)
- Construction Products and Activities (Division 1 to 16)

Divisions

The MasterFormat™ organizes related construction products and activities into 16 level one titles, called divisions. The numbers and titles of the divisions are the following:

- Division 1—General Requirements
- Division 2—Site Construction
- Division 3—Concrete
- Division 4—Masonry
- Division 5—Metals
- Division 6—Wood and Plastics
- Division 7—Thermal and Moisture Protection
- Division 8—Doors and Windows
- Division 9—Finishes
- Division 10—Specialties
- Division 11—Equipment
- Division 12—Furnishings
- Division 13—Special Construction
- Division 14—Conveying Systems
- Division 15—Mechanical
- Division 16—Electrical

CSI MasterFormat™ Numbering

Figure 5-1

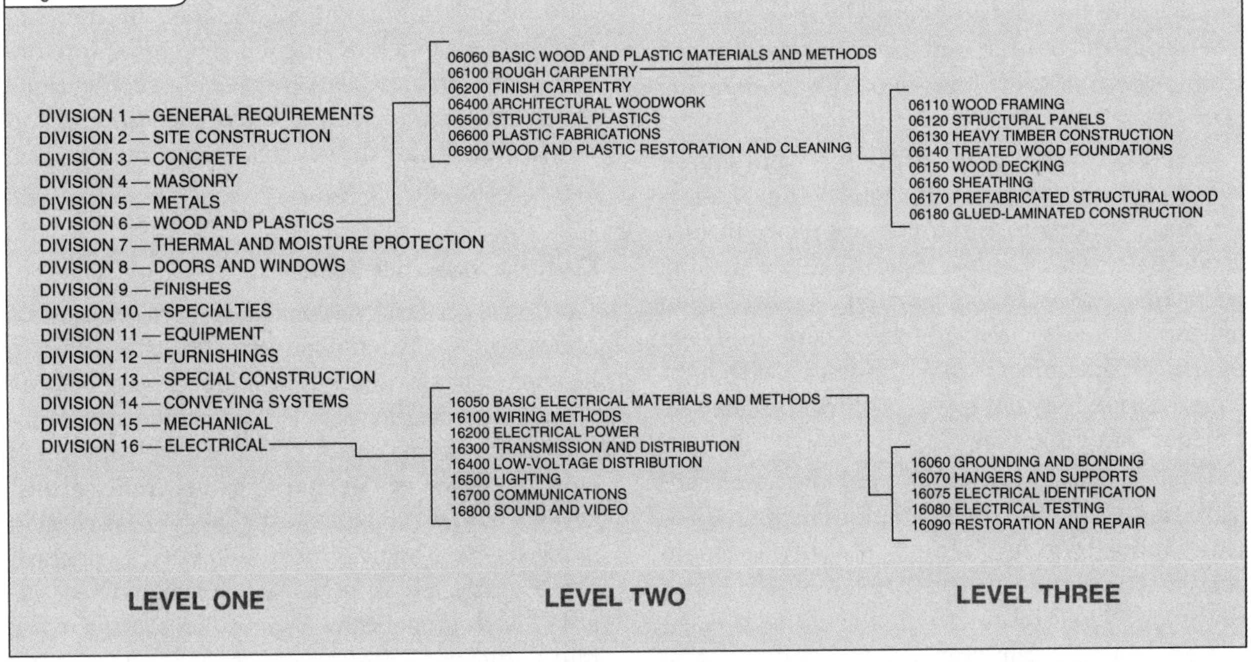

Figure 5-1. The CSI MasterFormat™ is divided into 16 divisions, with each division providing specific information about various materials.

Electrical systems are included in Division 16 of the CSI MasterFormat™.

Level two titles of the MasterFormat™ identify clusters of products and activities that have an identifying characteristic in common. For example, the level two notation 06100—Rough Carpentry includes products such as sill plates, floor joists, and studs, as well as activities such as methods of framing and blocking. Level two titles are the highest level used in titling and arranging units of construction information.

In the MasterFormat™, level three notations include both numbers and titles. Level three numbers are presented as the last three digits of the five-digit designation in boldface type.

The MasterFormat™ suggests level four titles, but does not indicate numbers. Users should create numbers by interpolating between assigned numbers when using level four titles or creating new titles.

Sweet's Architectural Catalog File and manufacturer catalogs generally follow the MasterFormat™ organization so reference to products is made with relative ease. Specifications written according to the MasterFormat™ organization are similar in the arrangement of content. However, specifications for small buildings with light construction may not always follow the MasterFormat™ organization.

Certain divisions may not apply for some construction projects. For example, Division 14—Conveying Systems may not apply to some construction projects and, consequently, is not included. The architect can write the specifications using a condensed form and arrange the divisions to fit the particular building being planned.

TYPES OF SPECIFICATIONS

The specifications for a construction project begin with conditional statements, such as the responsibility for examining the site, the liability due to delay in the work, periodic cleaning of the construction area, and similar items. The remainder of the specifications is devoted to technical information about the divisions of work to be done. Each technical division covering an area of work should contain four parts as follows:

- Scope—information that is included in this section of the work
- Materials—specific materials to be used in each instance
- Applications—special instructions concerning material applications and usage
- Guarantee—a statement binding the contractor to a certain quality of work over a specified time. The guarantee can be general, applying to all the trade groups, and inserted in the general conditions.

Specifications are prepared in several ways to serve different purposes. Minimum specifications (for a minor repair job or remodeling) might consist of a sketch showing the work to be done and a simple statement about the materials to be used. Some specifications are prepared to give general information about the construction and the features of a building without going into detail about procedure. A full set of specifications covers every conceivable area of the building and the building site that is not shown in detail on the working drawings.

Outline Specifications

Outline specifications consist of short statements about the work to be done and the materials to be used in construction. See Figure 5-2. One type of outline specification is that which accompanies stock plans. Stock plans are well-designed working drawings prepared by an architectural service to meet the needs of a large cross section of prospective owners located in various parts of the country. Stock plans are sold for a reasonable fee to prospective owners. In order for the plans and specifications to meet local building code requirements, they should be reviewed and revised as required by a local architect.

OUTLINE SPECIFICATIONS

Brick-Veneer Residence

This specification is a brief outline of building features. Cost estimates and construction are to be based on the detailed specifications and the working drawings.

1. Foundation:	Cast-in-place footings formed to size and shape as shown on the working drawings. Basement walls of concrete masonry units with horizontal metal reinforcing. Outside of basement walls to be waterproofed with pitch and membrane. Chemical termite protection shall be applied as directed. Slabs to be a minimum of 4″ concrete with a reinforced grade beam at the carport entrance.
2. Walls:	Building. Face brick veneer as shown on elevations. Wall at living room to have board-and-batten siding. Carport. Solid brick piers at corners. Storage room with board-and-batten siding. Stair windbreak screen of metal. Chimney. Concrete masonry units with brick veneer and solid brick masonry as shown on the plans.
3. Rough Framing:	Steel beams on steel posts support 2 × 10 floor joists. Studs 2 × 4. Ceiling joists and roof rafters 2 × 6. Spacing 16″ OC for all framing members except under baths 12″ OC.
4. Roof:	Asphalt shingles over plywood sheathing.
5. Floors:	Plywood subfloors. 1 × 2 inch furring strips. Finish floor underlayment-grade plywood. Ceramic (mosaic) tile in baths.
6. Resilient Floors:	Vinyl sheet goods and cove base in passage, kitchen, and family room.
7. Interior Finish:	Gypsum board walls and ceilings. Ceramic tile bathroom walls as shown on the working drawings.
8. Windows:	Wood windows with insulating glass.
9. Doors:	Front and rear entrance doors of insulated steel. Exterior basement door is wood panel with lights. Interior doors to be flush hollow core except one louvered closet door.
10. Kitchen:	Wood custom-built kitchen cabinets. Equipment includes oven and range top. Vented hood above range. Dishwasher by owner.
11. Bathrooms:	Built-in vanities with laminated plastic countertops. Vent fans in ceilings.
12. Heating:	Gas-fired, forced warm air system, with 55 gal. capacity electric water heater.
13. Electricity:	200 A service
14. Painting:	Two coats oil-base paint on exterior except where stain is specified. Interior painting not included in contract.

Figure 5-2. Outline specifications include short statements about the work to be done and the materials to be used.

Sioux Chief Manufacturing Company, Inc.

Copper tubing is specified in the complete specifications for water supply piping in the Brick-Veneer Residence.

A residential builder for prospective buyers prepares another form of outline specifications. These specifications feature the details for the houses available in the subdivision or development.

Description of Material Specification Forms. Governmental agencies such as the Federal Housing Administration (FHA) and the Veterans Administration (VA) require the use of a standard form, entitled *Description of Materials,* as part of the procedure for obtaining a mortgage. See Figure 5-3. The *Description of Materials* form requires the architect to make decisions in the choice of materials and gives the governmental agency a uniform and quick check on the contents. The *Description of Materials* form cannot be considered a complete set of specifications because it does not contain the general conditions nor outline the work to be done.

> Standard forms published by governmental agencies are updated and revised on a regular basis.

Complete Specifications

Complete specifications are provided for the building studied in Chapter 4. See Figure 5-4. Complete specifications follow the Master-Format™ division sequence. The specifications, however, can be arranged in some other sequence, depending on the architect's preference. The two primary objectives are to make the specifications complete and concise. Complete specifications are generally broken down into divisions of trade areas and written in detail so a contractor is assured that everything has been covered in estimating labor and material costs.

References are generally made to specific products. Specifying material may take several forms and often includes optional choices. In some cases, a product that has a recognized level of quality may be indicated. For example, "Formica® or equal" indicates that Formica® brand plastic laminate or its equal must be used. In other cases, several choices may be given in this manner: "Windows by Andersen, Pella, or ROW." In other cases, a product may be specified by name and catalog number because it will function best in the particular situation.

The complete specifications for the Brick-Veneer Residence are arranged with the divisions used in the MasterFormat™ to parallel the numbering system in *Sweet's Architectural Catalog File* and literature from manufacturers. Four divisions—10, 12, 13, and 14—are omitted because they do not apply to the Brick-Veneer Residence. When a set of specifications is lengthy and covers a large number of items, the MasterFormat™ level two sections are carefully followed.

Senco Products, Inc.

Pneumatic tools, such as a finish and brad nailer, are commonly used for finishing operations.

Description of Materials

U.S. Department of Housing and Urban Development
Department of Veterans Affairs
Farmers Home Administration

HUD's OMB Approval No. 2502-0192 and 2502-0313

Public reporting burden for this collection of information is estimated to average 30 minutes per response, including the time for reviewing instructions, searching existing data sources, gathering and maintaining the data needed, and completing and reviewing the collection of information. This agency may not collect this information, and you are not required to complete this form, unless it displays a currently valid OMB control number.

The National Housing Act (12 USC 1703) authorizes insuring financial institutions against default losses on single family mortgages. HUD must evaluate the acceptability and value of properties to be insured. The information collected here will be used to determine if proposed construction meets regulatory requirements and if the property is suitable for mortgage insurance. Response to this information collection is mandatory. No assurance of confidentiality is provided.

☐ Proposed Construction ☐ Under Construction No. _____ (To be inserted by HUD, VA or FmHA)

Property address (Include City and State)

Name and address of Mortgagor or Sponsor

Name and address of Contractor or Builder

Instructions

1. For additional information on how this form is to be submitted, number of copies, etc., see the instructions applicable to the HUD Application for Mortgage Insurance, VA Request for Determination of Reasonable Value, or FmHA Property Information and Appraisal Report, as the case may be.
2. Describe all materials and equipment to be used, whether or not shown on the drawings, by marking an X in each appropriate check-box and entering the information called for each space. If space is inadequate, enter "See misc." and describe under item 27 or on an attached sheet. **The use of paint containing more than the percentage of lead by weight permitted by law is prohibited.**

3. Work not specifically described or shown will not be considered unless required, then the minimum acceptable will be assumed. Work exceeding minimum requirements cannot be considered unless specifically described.
4. Include no alternates, "or equal" phrases, or contradictory items. (Consideration of a request for acceptance of substitute materials or equipment is not thereby precluded.)
5. Include signatures required at the end of this form.
6. The construction shall be completed in compliance with the related drawings and specifications, as amended during processing. The specifications include this Description of Materials and the applicable Minimum Property Standards.

1. **Excavation**
   Bearing soil, type _Clay, some sand, bearing capacity 2500 lb/sq ft_

2. **Foundations**
   Footings concrete mix _5 bag mix_ strength psi _2500_ Reinforcing _2-#4 rebar_
   Foundation wall material _Concrete masonry units_ Reinforcing _Horiz steel, alt courses_
   Interior foundation wall material _N/A_ Party foundation wall _N/A_
   Columns material and sizes _3½" STD pipe col_ Piers material and reinforcing _N/A_
   Girders material and sizes _W8 x 17_ Sills material _2 x 6_
   Basement entrance areaway _CMU walls, conc fl_ Window areaways _N/A_
   Waterproofing _1 coat pitch, polyethylene sheet_ Footing drains _Drain tile, sump pump for basement_
   Termite protection _Chlordane termite treatment_
   Basementless space ground cover _N/A_ insulation _N/A_ foundation vents _N/A_
   Special foundations _Stepped footings at R & L sides. Fireplace footing conc 2-#5 rebar 12'-0" lg_
   Additional information _Grade beam at garage entrance 2-#4 rebar_

3. **Chimneys**
   Material _Face brick & CMU_ Prefabricated (make and size) _N/A_
   Flue lining material _Tile & VIT Tile_ Heater flue size _8" VIT Tile_ Fireplace flue size _12 x 12_
   Vents (material and size) gas or oil heater _N/A_ water heater _N/A_
   Additional information

4. **Fireplaces**
   Type ☒ solid fuel ☐ gas-burning ☐ circulator (make and size) _N/A_ Ash dump and clean-out _10"_
   Fireplace facing _Face brick_ lining _Face brick_ hearth _Q Tile_ mantel _N/A_
   Additional information

Retain this record for three years Page 1 of 6 ref. HUD Handbook 4145.1 & 4950.1 form HUD-92005
VA Form 26-1852 and form FmHA 424-2

Figure 5-3. Standard forms, such as the *Description of Materials,* are commonly used by governmental agencies.

5. Exterior Walls

Wood frame wood grade, and species _#2 Pine_ ☒ Corner bracing   Building paper or felt _Housewrap_

    Sheathing _Rigid foam_ thickness _½_ width _4 x 8_ ☐ solid ☐ spaced _N/A_ o.c. ☐ diagonal _N/A_

    Siding _Board & batten_ grade _D select_ type _N/A_ size _1 x 8, 1 x 2_ exposure _____ fastening _Gal. case. nails_

    Shingles _N/A_ grade _N/A_ type _N/A_ size _N/A_ exposure _N/A_ fastening _N/A_

    Stucco _N/A_ thickness _N/A_ Lath _N/A_ weight _____ lb.

    Masonry veneer _Face brick_ Sills _Face brick_ Lintels _St. Angles_ Base flashing _Al. Sisalkraft_

Masonry ☒ solid ☐ faced ☐ stuccoed total wall thickness _8 & 12_ facing thickness _N/A_ facing material _N/A_

Backup material _N/A_ thickness _N/A_ bonding _N/A_

Door sills _N/A_ Window sills _N/A_ Lintels _N/A_ Base flashing _N/A_

Interior surfaces dampproofing, _N/A_ coats of _N/A_ furring _N/A_

Additional information

Exterior painting material _Pigmented stain except doors, windows, and frame oil paint_ number of coats _2_

Gable wall construction ☒ same as main walls ☐ other construction _____

6. Floor Framing

Joists wood, grade, and species _2 x 10 16" OC, #2 pine_ other _____ bridging _Steel cross_ anchors _Metal_

Concrete slab ☒ basement floor ☐ first floor ☒ ground supported ☐ self-supporting mix _6 bag mix_ thickness _4"_

    reinforcing _N/A_ insulation _N/A_ membrane _N/A_

Fill under slab material _Crushed stone_ thickness _4"_

Additional information

7. Subflooring (Describe underflooring for special floors under item 21)

Material grade and species _Construction grade_ size _½"_ type _Plywood_

Laid ☒ first floor ☐ second floor ☐ attic _N/A_ sq. ft. ☐ diagonal ☒ right angles

Additional information _Stagger joints and lay long way across joists. 1 x 2 furring 16" OC_

8. Finish Flooring (Wood only. Describe other finish flooring under item 21)

Location	Rooms	Grade	Species	Thickness	Width	Bldg. Paper	Finish
First floor	All	Underlay	N/A	⅝	N/A	N/A	
Second floor							
Attic floor	sq. ft.						

Additional information _For carpeting or vinyl sheet goods_

9. Partition Framing

Studs wood, grade, and species _#2 Pine_ size and spacing _2 x 4 16" OC_ Other _N/A_

Additional information

10. Ceiling Framing

Joists wood, grade, and species _#2 Pine 2 x 6_ Other _____ Bridging _Solid_

Additional information

11. Roof Framing

Rafters wood, grade, and species _#2 Pine 2 x 6_ Roof trusses (see detail) grade and species _____

Additional information

12. Roofing

Sheathing wood, grade, and species _Construction ½" Fir Plywood_ ☒ solid ☐ spaced _N/A_ o.c.

Roofing _Asph Shingles_ grade _240 #_ size _3 tab_ type _Class C_

Underlay _Roofing felt_ weight or thickness _15 #_ size _____ fastening _Zinc ct nail_

Built-up roofing _N/A_ number of plies _N/A_ surfacing material _N/A_

Flashing material _Gal St_ gage or weight _26 gage_ ☐ gravel stops ☐ snow guards

Additional information

13. Gutters and Downspouts

Gutters material ___N/A___ gage or weight ___N/A___ size ___N/A___ shape ___N/A___

Downspouts material ___N/A___ gage or weight ___N/A___ size ___N/A___ shape ___N/A___ number _____

Downspouts connected to ☐ Storm sewer ☐ sanitary sewer ☐ dry-well ☐ Splash blocks material and size _____

Additional information ___Metal diverters at rear valley___

14. Lath and Plaster

Lath ☐ walls ☐ ceilings material ___N/A___ weight or thickness ___N/A___ Plaster coats ___N/A___ finish ___N/A___

Dry-wall ☒ walls ☒ ceilings material ___Gyp Bd___ thickness ___¹/₂___ finish ___Smooth___

Joint treatment ___Tape and spackle; sand smooth___

15. Decorating (Paint, wallpaper, etc.)

Rooms	Wall Finish Material and Application	Ceiling Finish Material and Application
Kitchen	Paint 3 coats	Paint 3 coats
Bath	Ceramic tile, Paint 3 coats above	Paint 3 coats
Other	Paint 3 coats	Paint 3 coats

Additional information

16. Interior Doors and Trim

Doors type ___HC Flush & louvered___ material ___Flush oak, louvered pine___ thickness ___1³/₈-1³/₄___

Door trim type ___Solid___ material ___Oak___ Base type ___Stock___ material ___Oak___ size ___N/A___

Finish doors ___Stain & varnish___ trim ___Stain & varnish___

Other trim (item, type and location) ___Mantel trim oak stain & varnish___

Additional information

17. Windows

Windows type ___DH & casement___ make ___Andersen___ material ___Pine___ sash thickness ___1³/₈___

Glass grade ___Insulating___ ☐ sash weights ☒ balances, type ___Spring___ head flashing ___N/A___

Trim type ___Wood casing___ material ___Oak___ Paint ___Stain & varnish___ number coats ___2___

Weatherstripping type ___Friction___ material ___ST/ST___ Storm sash, number ___N/A___

Screens ☒ full ☐ half type ___Aluminum___ number ___N/A___ screen cloth material ___N/A___

Basement windows type ___N/A___ material ___N/A___ screens, number ___N/A___ Storm sash, number ___N/A___

Special windows _____

Additional information

18. Entrances and Exterior Detail

Main entrance door material ___Pease steel clad___ width ___3'-0"___ thickness ___1³/₄"___ Frame material ___Pine___ thickness ___1³/₈"___

Other entrance doors material ___Pease steel clad___ width ___3'-0"___ thickness ___1³/₄"___ Frame material ___Pine___ thickness ___1³/₈"___

Head flashing ___N/A___ Weatherstripping type ___Friction___ saddles ___N/A___

Screen doors thickness ___N/A___ number ___N/A___ screen cloth material ___N/A___ Storm doors thickness ___N/A___ number ___N/A___

Combination storm and screen doors thickness ___1¹/₈___ number ___2___ screen cloth material ___Al.___

Shutters ☐ hinged ☐ fixed Railings ___Wood___ Attic louvers ___2 #2 Pine___

Exterior millwork grade and species ___D select (West Coast)___ Paint ___Pigmented stain___ number coats ___2___

Additional information ___Oil paint windows, doors, and trim___

19. Cabinets and Interior Detail

Kitchen cabinets, wall units material ___Oak___ lineal feet of shelves ___28'___ shelf width ___12"___

Base units material ___Oak___ counter top ___Laminated plastic___ edging ___Laminated plastic___

Back and end splash ___Broderick 3309___ Finish of cabinets _____ number coats _____

Medicine cabinets make _____ model _____

Other cabinets and built-in furniture ___2 Bathroom vanities; laminated plastic top; oak stain and varnish___

Additional information

ref. HUD Handbook 4145.1 & 4950.1 form HUD-92005
VA Form 26-1852 and form FmHA 424-2

20. Stairs

Stair	Treads Material	Thickness	Risers Material	Thickness	Strings Material	Size	Handrail Material	Size	Balusters Material	Size
Basement	CONC		CONC		CONC		Pipe	2"	N/A	
Main										
Attic										

Disappearing make and model number ___Super Simplex folding stair (wood)___

Additional information ___

21. Special Floors and Wainscot (Describe Carpet as listed in Certified Products Directory)

Floors

Location	Material, Color, Border, Sizes, Gage, Etc.	Threshold Material	Wall Base Material	Underfloor Material
Kitchen	3/16" Vinyl sheet goods	Al.	Vinyl	1/2" Plywood
Bath	3/16" Vinyl sheet goods	Al.	Vinyl	1/2" Plywood

Wainscot

Location	Material, Color, Border, Cap. Sizes, Gage, Etc.	Height	Height Over Tub	Height in Showers (From Floor)
Bath	Ceramic tile; see Elevations	4'-2"	6'-4"	N/A

Additional information ___2 Soap dishes, 2 tumbler holders, 4 towel bars, 2 toilet paper holders___

22. Plumbing

Fixture	Number	Location	Make	MFR's Fixture Identification No.	Size	Color
Sink	1	Kitchen	Crane	ST. ST 2 comp 2 DRBD	5'-6"	SS
Lavatory	2	Bath	Crane	with vanity		as selected
Water closet	2	Bath	Crane	Siphon jet w/ tank		as selected
Bathtub	2	Bath	Crane		5'-0"	as selected
Shower over tub△	2	Bath	Crane			
Stall shower△	N/A					
Laundry trays	N/A					
Dishwasher		Kitchen	By Owner			
Food waste disposer		Kitchen	Insinkerator	77	1/2 hp	
Washer/Dryer		Closet	By Owner			

Bathroom accessories ☐ Recessed material _____ number _____ ☐ Attached material _____ number _____

Additional information ___

△ ☒ Curtain rod ☐ Door ☐ Shower pan material _____ * (Show and describe individual system in complete detail in separate drawings and specifications according to requirements.)

Water supply ☒ public ☐ community system ☐ individual (private) system*

Sewage disposal ☐ public ☐ community system ☒ individual (private) system*

House drain (inside) ☐ cast iron ☐ tile ☒ other ___PVC___ House sewer (outside) ☐ cast iron ☒ tile ☐ other _____

Water piping ☐ galvanized steel ☒ copper tubing ☐ other _____ Sill cocks, number _____

Domestic water heater type ___Electric___ make and model ___Rheem___ heating capacity _____ gph. 100° rise.

Storage tank material ___Glass___ capacity ___55___ gallons

Gas service ☐ utility company ☐ liq. pet. gas ☐ other _____ Gas piping ☐ cooking ☐ house heating

Footing drains connected to ☐ storm sewer ☐ sanitary sewer ☐ dry well ☐ Sump pump make and model _____

capacity _____ discharges into _____

Additional information ___

23. Heating

☐ Hot water ☐ Steam ☐ Vapor ☐ One-pipe system ☐ Two-pipe system

☐ Radiators ☐ Convectors ☐ Baseboard radiation Make and model _____

☐ Radiant panel ☐ floor ☐ wall ☐ ceiling Panel coil material _____

☐ Circulator ☐ Return pump Make and model _____ capacity _____ gpm.

Boiler make and model _____ Output _____ Btuh. net rating _____ Btuh.

Additional information

Warm air ☐ Gravity ☒ Forced Type of system _Ducts in basement_ _____

Duct material supply _Sheet metal_ return _Sheet metal_ Insulation _N/A_ thickness _N/A_ ☐ Outside air intake

Furnace: make and model _Lennox G4IUF-36C-090_ Input _____ Btuh. output _80,000_ Btuh.

Additional information

☐ Space heater ☐ floor furnace ☐ wall heater Input _____ Btuh. output _____ Btuh. number units _____

Make, model _____

Additional information

Controls make and types _Johnson electric for above furnace_ _____

Additional information

Fuel: ☐ Coal ☐ oil ☐ gas ☒ liq. pet. gas ☐ electric ☐ other _____ storage capacity _500 gal._

Additional information

Firing equipment furnished separately ☒ Gas burner, conversion type ☐ Stoker hopper feed ☐ bin feed

Oil burner ☐ pressure atomizing ☐ vaporizing _____

Make and model _____

Control _____

Additional information

Electric heating system type _____ Input _____ watts @ _____ volts output _____ Btuh.

Additional information

Ventilating equipment ☐ attic fan, make and model _____ capacity _____ cfm.

☐ kitchen exhaust fan, make and model _Thermador_ _____

Other heating, ventilating, or cooling equipment _2 Bath fans, Tradewind model 1201_ _____

Additional information

24. Electric Wiring

Service ☒ overhead ☐ underground Panel ☐ fuse box ☒ circuit-breaker make _Bryant_ AMP's _200_ No. circuits ___

Wiring ☒ conduit ☐ armored cable ☐ nonmetallic cable ☐ knob and tube ☐ other _____

Special outlets ☒ range ☒ water heater ☒ other _oven, clothes dryer_ _____

☐ Doorbell ☒ Chimes ☐ Push-button locations _Front & back doors_ _____

Additional information

25. Lighting Fixtures

Total number of fixtures _12_ Total allowance for fixtures, typical installation, $ _____

Nontypical installation _____

Additional information

ref. HUD Handbook 4145.1 & 4950.1 form HUD-92005
VA Form 26-1852 and form FmHA 424-2

26. Insulation

Location	Thickness	Material, Type, and Method of Installation	Vapor Barrier
Roof	N/A		
Ceiling	6"	Foil-faced fiberglass	
Wall	2"	Foil-faced fiberglass	
Floor	N/A		

27. Miscellaneous: (Describe any main dwelling materials, equipment, or construction items not shown elsewhere; or use to provide additional information where the space provided was inadequate. Always reference by item number to correspond to numbering used on this form.)

Hardware (make, material, and finish.)

Schlage, bronze

Special Equipment (State material or make, model and quantity. Include only equipment and appliances which are acceptable by local law, custom and applicable FHA standards. Do not include items which, by established custom, are supplied by occupant and removed when he vacates premises or chattles prohibited by law from becoming realty.)

Countertop range, food waste disposer, built-in oven

Porches

4" concrete slab and covered porch at front door

Terraces

4" concrete slab with trowel finish

Garages

Walks and Driveways

Driveway width __N/A__ base material _____ thickness _____ surfacing material _____ thickness _____

Front walk width __N/A__ material _____ thickness _____ Service walk width _____ material _____ thickness _____

Steps material __N/A__ treads _____ risers _____ Cheek walls _____

Other Onsite Improvements

(Specify all exterior onsite improvements not described elsewhere, including items such as unusual grading, drainage structures, retaining walls, fence, railings, and accessory structures.)

Entire site to be fine-graded.

Landscaping, Planting, and Finish Grading

Topsoil __4"__ thick ☒ front yard ☒ side yards ☒ rear yard to __15__ feet behind main building

Lawns (seeded, sodded, or sprigged) ☐ front yard __N/A__ ☐ side yards _____ ☐ rear yard _____

Planting ☐ as specified and shown on drawings ☐ as follows:

__N/A__ Shade trees deciduous _____ caliper   __N/A__ Evergreen trees _____ to _____ B & B

__N/A__ Low flowering trees deciduous _____ to _____   __N/A__ Evergreen shrubs _____ to _____ B & B

__N/A__ High-growing shrubs deciduous _____ to _____   _____ Vines, 2-year _____

__N/A__ Medium-growing shrubs deciduous _____ to _____   Other

__N/A__ Low-growing shrubs deciduous _____ to _____

Identification—This exhibit shall be identified by the signature of the builder, or sponsor, and/or the proposed mortgagor if the latter is known at the time of application.

Date (mm/dd/yyyy)_____ Signature _____

Signature _____

Retain this record for three years — Page 6 of 6 — ref. HUD Handbook 4145.1 & 4950.1 form HUD-92005 VA Form 26-1852 and form FmHA 424-2

COMPLETE SPECIFICATIONS FOR
A BRICK-VENEER RESIDENCE

INDEX

DIVISIONS 10, 12, 13, and 14 do not apply.

GENERAL CONDITIONS

The latest edition of the standard form of "General Conditions of the Contract" published by the American Institute of Architects shall be understood to be a part of this specification and shall be adhered to by the Contractor (the General Contractor).

1

Figure 5-4. Complete specifications follow the CSI MasterFormat™ division sequence.

SPECIAL CONDITIONS

Sec. 1.   EXAMINATION OF SITE. It is understood that the Contractor has examined the site and is familiar with all conditions which might affect the execution of this contract and has made provisions therefor in his bid.

Sec. 2.   TIME FOR COMPLETION. The work shall be completed within 150 calendar days after written Notice to Proceed is issued to the Contractor.

Sec. 3.   EXISTING TREES. Existing trees within 15 feet of the foundation line for the new structure shall be carefully protected by the Contractor from injury which might result from any operation connected with the execution of this contract.

Sec. 4.   GUARANTEE. The acceptance of this contract carries with it a guarantee on the part of the Contractor to make good any defects in the work of the building arising or discovered within one year after completion and acceptance of same by the Architect, whether from shrinkage, settlement, or faults of labor or materials.

Sec. 5.   RESPONSIBILITIES OF CONTRACTOR. Except as otherwise specifically stated in the Contract, the Contractor shall provide and pay for all materials, labor, tools, equipment, water, light, heat, power, transportation, temporary construction of every nature, taxes legally collected because of the work, and all other services and facilities of every nature whatsoever necessary to execute the work to be done under this contract and to bring the building to completion in every respect within the specified time, all in accordance with the drawings and specifications. The Contractor shall carry public liability, workmen's compensation, and vehicular insurance. The Contractor shall coordinate all trades.

DIVISION 1—GENERAL REQUIREMENTS

1.01   SUMMARY OF THE WORK

1.01.1   Work under the Contract shall include all work shown on the drawings and indicated in these specifications. All work shall conform to local rules and ordinances. The General Contractor shall complete all work within the allotted time as indicated in the Method of Bidding.

1.01.2   The carpenter shall do cutting of wood necessary for other trades and shall erect ladders inside of building. Scaffolding shall be erected, maintained, and removed by Contractor for whose work it is necessary. Ditches for mechanical trades shall be dug and refilled by Contractor for whose work they are necessary.

1.01.3   Items provided by Owner are shown on the drawings and will be installed by Owner unless noted to be installed by the General Contractor.

1.01.4   Owner occupancy shall occur at the completion of the work. The General Contractor must complete the work within 30 days after the substantial completion. (Substantial completion date is the date when owner, architect, and contractor go over a checklist of things in the contract.)

1.1   PROGRESS AND PAYMENT (Project meetings)

1.1.1   Progress of the work for payment purposes shall be determined by the Architect. The Contractor shall submit his claim for payment to the Architect for approval. The Architect shall determine that the work in place meets the quality specified and the claim for payment is for the work in place and material stored at the building site.

1.1.2   Payment to the Contractor shall be made by the Owner within ten (10) days of the Architect's approval of the claim for payment.

1.2   SUBMITTALS

1.2.1   Shop Drawings and Samples of finish materials shall be submitted to the Architect for his approval before shop fabrication.

1.2.2   Cost Breakdown for purposes of payment shall be submitted within 30 days of the signing of the contract.

1.3   TEMPORARY FACILITIES AND CONTROLS

1.3.1   Utilities for temporary use shall be provided by the Contractor.

1.4   PROJECT CLOSEOUT

1.4.1   Cleaning up shall be the responsibility of the General Contractor. All rubbish shall be removed from the building and hauled to the city landfill site each week. Floors, walls, windows, and all other surfaces shall be cleaned ready for occupancy. Turn over building broom clean. The owner will wash windows and the plumbing fixtures.

1.4.2   Final Inspection shall be held with the Owner, Contractor, and Architect, or a representative of each, present. Within one week (7 days) the Contractor shall correct all items found to be defective.

DIVISION 2—SITE CONSTRUCTION

2.1   SUBSURFACE EXPLORATION

2.1.1   Subsurface Soil Data from previous projects in the area indicate an allowable bearing load of 2500 lb/sq ft. The Contractor shall notify the Architect, who shall inspect the excavation prior to placing of footings.

2.2   CLEARING

2.2.1   Topsoil Stripping and Storage. Strip all topsoil up to a depth of 6 inches and stockpile within the site. Keep topsoil free from all trash. See plot plan.

2.3   EARTHWORK

2.3.1   Site Grading. Do all cutting, filling, backfilling, and grading required to bring the entire project area outside of buildings to subgrade. Subgrade for lawn and planting areas is 4 inches below finished grade.

2.3.2   Trench for footings and carport foundations allowing sufficient room for formwork. Place footings and foundations upon undisturbed and firm bottoms.

2.3.3   Excavate for basement and crawl space to 18 inches outside of foundation line.

2.3.4   Backfill and compaction against foundation wall shall be trash-free material in 8 inch lifts. Rough grade around building to be 4 inches below top of foundation. Care must be taken not to damage the foundation walls or the dampproofing and waterproofing.

2.3.5   Waste Material Disposal. Remove from the site, and dispose of, all debris and all excavated materials not suitable or needed for fill.

2.3.6   Finish grading shall be to elevations shown on the drawings. Use topsoil from stockpile on the site. Slope all work away from the building with no abrupt changes.

2.4   SOIL POISONING

2.4.1   Chemical—Chlordane applied in oil solution or water emulsion, 1.0% concentration.

2.4.2   Apply at rate of 1 gallon per $2\frac{1}{2}$ linear feet of depth along both sides of basement and crawl space foundation walls.

2.4.3   Under floors of basement, carport, basement stairs, and porches and around column footings in crawl space, apply overall treatment at rate of 1 gallon per 10 square feet.

2.4.4   In voids of unit masonry foundation walls, apply at rate of 1 gallon per 5 linear feet.

2.4.5   Treatment shall not be made when the soil or fill is excessively wet or immediately after heavy rains. Unless treated areas are to be immediately covered, take precautions to prevent disturbance of treatment.

2.5   PAVEMENTS AND WALKS

not in contract

2.6   LANDSCAPING

not in contract

4

DIVISION 3—CONCRETE

3.1   CONCRETE FORMWORK

3.1.1   Forms for footings and edges of slabs shall conform to the shapes, lines, and dimensions called for on plans and be substantial and tight to prevent leakage of concrete. Prior to placing concrete, concrete forms shall be thoroughly oiled.

3.1.2   Remove forms without damage to concrete.

3.2   CONCRETE REINFORCEMENT

3.2.1   Provide and install reinforcing bars as indicated on drawings.

3.3   CAST-IN-PLACE CONCRETE

3.3.1   Portland cement shall conform to ASTM C150, *Standard Specification for Portland Cement.*

3.3.2   Aggregates for concrete shall conform to ASTM C33, *Standard Specification for Concrete Aggregates.* Grade course aggregate from 1 inch to $1\frac{1}{2}$ inches.

3.3.3   Water shall be clean and free from injurious amounts of deleterious substances.

3.3.4   Place concrete only on undisturbed earth. Concrete shall be ready mixed and shall comply with ASTM C94, *Standard Specification for Ready-mixed Concrete.*

3.3.5   All debris and ice shall be removed from the space to be occupied by the concrete. Reinforcement shall be free of ice and other coatings and shall be thoroughly cleaned.

3.3.6   Compacted fill under basement and carport slabs shall be approved by the Architect. A 95% compaction is required.

3.3.7   The 4 inch porous fill under the slab shall be composed of gravel or crushed stone of uniform size particles, $\frac{3}{4}$ inch in size, compact and level. Cover this fill with a vapor barrier polyethylene sheet 6 mil nominal thickness.

3.3.8   Concrete for slabs and steps shall not be less than 4 inches thick. Concrete floor finish shall be true and level as called for by the drawings with maximum tolerance of $\frac{1}{8}$ inch in 6 feet. Pitch basement floor to drain. Pitch porch floors away from building. Trowel finish slabs.

3.3.9   Concrete shall be maintained in a moist condition for at least 7 days by water curing or membrane curing.

DIVISION 4—MASONRY

4.1   MORTAR

4.1.1   Mortar: Proportioning. By volume, one part portland cement, one part lime putty, six parts sand.

4.1.2   Mortar consistency shall be as wet as can be conveniently handled. Do not use stiffened mortar.

4.2   ANCHORS AND TIES

4.2.1   Brick veneer shall be secured to backing with corrosion-resistant ties. Install one metal tie for each 2 square feet of area.

4.3   CONCRETE MASONRY UNITS

4.3.1   Build foundations of concrete masonry units accurately as shown on drawings. Key mesh or Durowall reinforcing in alternate CMU courses. Bond walls together at intersections.

4.3.2   Fill voids in top units with concrete. Install anchor bolts 6 feet-0 inches OC.

4.4   BRICK VENEER AND BRICK WALLS

4.4.1   Build brick veneer walls and solid brick walls as shown on drawings.
Figure $_____ per thousand for brick delivered to the job as selected by the Owner.

4.4.2   Build walls straight and plumb, courses level. Fill all joints with mortar as units are laid. Full head joints. Tool exposed brick joints with concave tool. Lay solid brick walls with common bond.

4.4.3   Install lintels furnished by other contractor under Division 5.

4.5   CHIMNEY AND FIREPLACE

4.5.1   Build chimney as shown on drawings.

4.5.2   Install vitrified tile flue for furnace, and tile flue for fireplace.

4.5.3   Build fireplace as shown on drawings. Line with firebrick, face with same brick as on exterior. Install ratchet-type cast iron damper, ash drop. Mason contractor is responsible to make fireplace operate properly.

4.5.4   Furnish and install two iron cleanout doors. Install lintels furnished by others.

4.6　　　　　CLEANING MASONRY

4.6.1　　　　Clean brick from top down with a solution of nonstaining soap and clean water or solution of one part muriatic acid to ten parts water. Scrub surface with stiff bristle brushes and rinse well with clean water.

DIVISION 5—METALS

5.1　　　STRUCTURAL STEEL

5.1.1　　　Basement beams, steel pipe columns, carport entrance beam, and lintels as shown on drawings.

5.1.2　　　All steel shall be painted one shop coat of rust-inhibiting paint.

DIVISION 6—WOOD AND PLASTICS

6.1　　　CARPENTRY

6.1.1　　　Workmanship shall conform to FHA standards. Interior finish shall be installed by trim carpenters. Trim shall be set level and plumb, well joined. Set nails.

6.2　　　ROUGH CARPENTRY

6.2.1　　　Material: Sill plates, floor joists, ceiling joists, studs, and rafters shall be construction grade Douglas fir or No. 2 or better yellow pine. Subfloor shall be utility-grade west coast wood or yellow pine sheathing or $1/2$ inch CD plywood. Roof boards same. Wall sheathing $1/2$ inch rigid foam insulation panels. At both sides of four corners of house, install $1/2$ inch plywood sheathing.

6.2.2　　　Methods of Framing

6.2.2.1　　　Lay out carpenter work as called for by the drawings. Cut and fit for conditions encountered. All work shall be plumbed, leveled, and braced with nails, spikes, bolts, etc., to ensure rigidity. Steel cross bridging for floor joists. Solid bridging for ceiling joists.

6.2.2.2　　　Clearance around chimneys and flues shall conform to National Bureau of Fire Underwriters (NBFU) Building Code and local code.

6.2.2.3　　　Bottom plate framing members shall be single, 2 inch nominal thickness members for all walls and partitions.

6.2.2.4　　　Studs shall be 2 × 4 inch wood at 16 inch OC, doubled at openings and tripled at corners, placed to provide end nailing for sheathing and wallboard. Toenail to bottom plate with two 8d nails on each side face of each stud. One stud per 4 feet of exterior wall shall be fastened by means of 19 gauge zinc-coated metal anchor, as per manufacturer's instructions.

6.2.2.5　　　Top plates shall be double, 2 inch nominal thickness members for all partitions.

6.2.2.6   Plates shall be same width as studs and form continuous horizontal ties. Ends of bottom plates shall be provided with splice plates, nailed to studs and corner posts. Top plates shall be nailed together with 16d nails at 24 inches OC. Two 16d nails shall be used at ends of upper members. No joint in upper member shall occur over a joint in a lower member. Lintels shall occur over openings in walls and bearing partitions. Plate splices shall not occur where plate forms part of a lintel.

6.2.2.7   All wood members shall be anchored and fastened together to ensure sound, sturdy construction.

6.2.3   <u>Wood Blocking</u>

6.2.3.1.   Wood blocking, nailers, and grounds shall be provided for woodwork, cabinets, and other finished items.

6.3   FINISH CARPENTRY

6.3.1   Material: Fascia boards and siding shall be D select west coast lumber. Plywood soffit AB exterior-grade plywood. 6 × 6 posts shall be standard grade fir or No. 2 yellow pine. Top flooring shall be underlayment-grade $5/8$ inch plywood on 1 × 2 inch strips 16 inches OC. Face nail with 8d ring or coated nails 12 inches OC and 6 inches OC at edges. Stock oak jambs and stops. Stock $2^1/4$ inch ranch-type oak casings.

6.3.2   Vanities by Owner to be installed by this Contractor. Oak mantel trim. Install window trim, base, closet plywood partitions, shelves, hanging rods as shown on drawings.

6.3.3   Custom-built oak kitchen cabinets to be built and installed by kitchen cabinet sub-contractor.

6.4   <u>Methods of Framing</u>

6.4.1   Exterior millwork and trim shall be installed with tight joints, securely nailed with galvanized case nails. Interior trim and finish lumber shall be fastened in place with finishing nails, the heads set for putty, and finish sanded.

6.4.2   Millwork shall be in long lengths with jointing where solid fastenings can be made. Corners shall be mitered or coped as is standard practice.

6.5   WOOD TREATMENT

6.5.1   All sill plates in contact with concrete shall be treated with preservative meeting Federal Specifications TTW571.

DIVISION 7—THERMAL AND MOISTURE PROTECTION

7.1   FOUNDATION WATERPROOFING

7.1.1   Outside of foundation walls around basement and crawl space and basement stair. Crawl space side of wall between crawl space and basement.

7.1.2   Apply one heavy coat of pitch. Over this apply 6 mil polyethylene sheets in as wide widths as practical, well lapped.

7.2   DAMPPROOFING

7.2.1   Vapor barrier applied over plywood sheathing shall be housewrap.

7.2.2   One-ply felt on walls.

7.3   INSULATION

7.3.1   Between studs in outside walls install 2 inch foil-faced fiberglass batts. Between ceiling joists install 6 inch foil-faced fiberglass batts or blow in fiberglass to joist depth. If blown-in insulation is used, install foil-backed gypsum board on ceilings.

7.4   ROOFING

7.4.1   Cover roofs with 15 lb roofing felt. Over this install 12 × 36 inch 240 lb asphalt shingles, class C label, standard color as selected by Owner. Five inch exposure, six nails per shingle, zinc-coated nails.

7.5   FLASHING AND SHEET METAL

7.5.1   Install flashing around chimney and where carport roof meets gable wall. Diverters where shown on drawings. 26 gauge galvanized iron. Install 20 × .019 inch aluminum valley flashing in valleys.

7.6   CAULKING AND SEALANTS

7.6.1   Caulking shall conform to Federal Standard TT-C-598 Grade 1, color to be selected by Architect.

7.6.2   Sealant to be polysulfide.

7.6.3   Set all thresholds in sealant. Caulk and seal all windows, doors, and joints.

7.6.4   Apply materials with pressure gun.

DIVISION 8—DOORS AND WINDOWS

8.1   METAL DOORS

8.1.1   Outside entrance doors. Insulated steel doors. (Pease Co.) Keyed alike. Owner to choose style.

8.2   WOOD DOORS

8.2.1   Basement door wood panel door per schedule. Key alike with entrance doors.

8.2.2   Interior doors, premium-grade hollow-core flush oak doors or stock pine louver doors with panels, as scheduled.

8.2.3   Interior and exterior door frames pine, stock design.

8.2.4   Install all doors to fit snugly without binding. All faces, edges, tops, and bottoms to be finished. $1/16$ inch clearance at top and sides and $1/2$ inch at the bottom.

8.3   SPECIAL DOORS

8.3.1   Wood sliding glass doors, 6 feet wide minimum sash opening, stock type by Andersen, Pella, or ROW, with $5/8$ inch tempered insulating glass and manufacturer's screen.

8.3.2   Provide and install attic access door, stock type.

8.4   WOOD WINDOWS

8.4.1   Double-hung by same manufacturers of similar stock types, with insulating glass, grilles, and manufacturer's full screens. Casement window same, no grilles, roto-operators.

8.4.2   Provide screen louvers for right and left gable ends, stock type.

8.5   HARDWARE

                All material and work in this section by carpentry contractor.

8.5.1   Rough hardware, nails, screws, hangers, anchor bolts, and fastening as required.

8.5.2   Tracks and associated hardware for bifold and bypass sliding doors. Pocket door frames. Hinges, lock and latch sets, cabinet hardware, medicine cabinets. Bedroom and bathroom doors shall have pushbutton knob locks. Allow $_____ Contractor's cost for same as selected by Owner. Install same.

8.5.3   Aluminum thresholds with vinyl inserts at two outside doors. Weatherstrip jambs. Caulk around all outside masonry openings with best grade caulking paste.

DIVISION 9—FINISHES

9.1   GYPSUM BOARD

9.1.1   Gypsum board. Basement ceiling, ¹/₂ inch fire-rated board. Bathroom walls, ¹/₂ inch water-resistant type. On ceilings and other walls and partitions, ¹/₂ inch gypsum board for taping. Install metal beads at outside corners. Apply per manufacturer's instructions. Tape joints, putty nail heads, and corner beads to smooth finish job. No taping in basement.

9.2   CERAMIC TILE

9.2.1   Conform to specifications of Tile Council of America. Standard colors and patterns as selected by Owner. Same in both baths.

9.2.2   On bathroom floors install mosaic tile floors by thin set method over plywood installed by others. On bathroom walls install 4¹/₄ × 4¹/₄ inch tile on water-resistant gypsum board installed by others. See drawings. Allow $_____ for accessories as selected by Owner.

9.2.3   Tile hearth. Quarry tile, 12″ × 6″ on 1¹/₄ inch cement base by this Contractor.

9.3   RESILIENT FLOORS

9.3.1   Apply materials as per manufacturer's directions. Lay out for minimum number of seams, which shall be tight. Fit tight to base, door jambs, and casings, etc. Check condition of floors before starting work. If not satisfactory, report to general contractor for correction.

9.3.2   In kitchen, passage, and family room, install Armstrong Chateau Villa II sheet goods in 12 foot widths. All same pattern, as selected by Owner.

9.4   PAINTING

9.4.1   General

9.4.1.1   Furnish labor and materials to complete painting of all surfaces: gypsum board, wood, and metal as hereinafter specified and shown on the drawings. Prime window and door frames.

9.4.1.2   Materials: Paint shall be best grade oil-base house and interior paint as made by Moore, O'Brien, Pittsburgh, Sherwin-Williams, or as approved by Owner. Cabot's oil stain and Galvinoleum as specified in Painting Schedule.

9.4.1.3   Architect shall furnish a color schedule showing where various colors are used. Owner will give final approval of colors.

9.4.1.4   Each coat of paint shall be slightly darker than preceding coat unless otherwise directed. Undercoats shall be tinted similar to finish coats.

9.4.1.5   Commencing of work indicates acceptance of surfaces by painter.

9.4.1.6   Cover materials and surfaces, including floors, adjoining or below work in progress, with clean drop cloths or canvas. Remove hardware, accessories, plates, lighting fixtures, and similar items or provide protection by masking. Upon completion, replace above items or remove protection and clean.

9.4.1.7   Before applying paint or finish, surfaces, including floors, shall be clean, dry, smooth, and free of loose dirt and dust.

9.4.2   <u>Workmanship</u>

9.4.2.1   Brush, spray, or roll on materials smoothly in solid, even colors without drips, runs, lumps, defective brushing, discoloration, or any other faulty workmanship.

9.4.2.2   Coats shall be thoroughly dry before applying succeeding coats. Allow 48 hours drying time between coats for exterior work and 24 hours for interior work.

9.4.3   <u>Painting Schedule</u>

9.4.3.1   <u>Exterior Finish</u>

9.4.3.1.1   Window sash and frames, paint two coats. Two wood doors and frames, same.

9.4.3.1.2   Two outside entrance doors, wood frames, paint two coats. These doors are metal. Paint one coat red Rustoleum, one coat house paint.

9.4.3.1.3   Fascias, soffits, siding, porch woodwork, two coats Cabot's oil stain. Chimney flashing, one coat Galvinoleum, one coat house paint.

9.4.3.1.4   Check colors with Owner or Architect before applying paint or stain.

9.4.3.2   <u>Interior Finish</u>

9.4.3.2.1   Kitchen and bath walls: one coat primer, one coat semi-gloss.

9.4.3.2.2   Other walls and ceilings: one coat primer, one coat alkyd flat.

9.4.3.2.3   Interior wood: one coat stain; two coats dull varnish.

9.4.3.2.4   Check colors with Owner or Architect before applying paint or stain.

DIVISION 11—EQUIPMENT (RESIDENTIAL)

11.1   KITCHEN EQUIPMENT

11.1.1   Electric cooktop surface unit shall be Kenmore 42484 or equal.

11.1.2   Built-in oven shall be Kenmore double oven 41389 or equal.

11.1.3   Dishwasher shall be furnished by the Owner.

11.1.4   Refrigerator shall be furnished by the Owner.

11.1.5   Food waste disposer shall be stainless steel.

11.1.6   Kitchen cabinets, backsplashes, and countertops shall be by Brammer or equal. Oak wood finish and hardware by manufacturer.

11.2   LAUNDRY EQUIPMENT

11.2.1   Laundry equipment shall be one washer and one dryer by GE or equal. Washer shall be 12-cycle washer No. WBSE3120BWW. Dryer shall be gas dryer No. DVL223GBWW.

DIVISION 15—MECHANICAL

15.1   GENERAL PROVISIONS

15.1.1   <u>Scope of Work</u>

15.1.1.1   All plumbing, heating, and air conditioning for a complete job as specified and on the drawings.

15.1.1.2   It is not the intention of the specification to mention specifically each and every item shown on the plans and, therefore, this does not excuse the Contractor from the responsibility of furnishing or having the proper subcontractor furnish and install such items without extra cost to the Owner.

15.1.2   <u>Codes and Standards</u>

15.1.2.1   All codes of the local and state jurisdiction shall be applied and shall take precedence over any item mentioned in this specification. Conform to International Plumbing Code.

15.1.2.2   Standards of the trades and materials shall be the highest quality.

15.1.2.3   The General Conditions and General Requirements shall apply to this Division.

15.2   PLUMBING

15.2.1   Provide complete systems as called for and/or shown or specified including but not limited to the following items.

15.2.2   Electrical work by others. Waterproof patch where plumbing pipes are cut through foundation walls.

15.2.3   Sewerage. Four inch PVC pipe inside of building and to 4 feet outside, then closed 4 inch tile to 1000 gallon concrete septic tank. Tile field as required by seepage tests. Install 200 feet of agricultural tile in gravel, or more if required.

15.2.4   Drain tile. Install 4 inch perforated plastic pipe or agricultural tile set in crushed stone at footings as indicated on plan. Connect to 21 inch tile settling basin and sump. Iron covers and concrete bottoms for same.

15.2.5   Sump pump, Weil SS 605 automatic submersible, $\frac{1}{3}$ hp with automatic reset over load protection, waterproof power cord with heavy-duty plug and grounded lead. $1\frac{1}{4}$ inch galvanized steel pipe to 20 feet from building, discharge into 20 feet of 4 inch perforated plastic pipe. Set in gravel or crushed stone, about 2 feet deep.

15.2.6   Wastes and vents shall be ABS-DWV with corresponding fittings or galvanized steel with cast iron soil stack.

15.2.7   Two inch water main is at front of lot. Tap into same with $\frac{3}{4}$ inch tap. Water pipe in earth or concrete shall be copper, elsewhere copper with copper fittings or galvanized steel schedule 40 with galvanized malleable fittings. Shutoff valve where service pipe enters building. See piping diagram.

15.2.8   Hot water to sink, dishwasher, clothes washer, lavatories, bathtubs. Cold water to same except dishwasher, and to water closets, water heater, and to sillcocks, with shutoff valves. Valve dishwasher riser. (Dishwasher by Owner) Provide recessed metal panel at clothes washer with hot and cold water faucets, drain, and electric receptacles for washer and dryer. Insulate pipes in danger of freezing.

15.2.9   Water heater, as made by Rheem, Ruud, or A. O. Smith, 55 gallon electric, glass liner, with temperature and pressure relief valve. Send manufacturer's guarantee to Owner before final payment for this contract.

15.2.10   Fixtures. Stops at all fixtures. Crane, Eljer, American Standard, or Kohler, with manufacturer's chrome or stainless steel trim. Check selection with Owner before ordering.

15.2.11   Bathtubs. Color as selected by Owner. Five foot, 14 inches high, built-in, cast iron; built-in shower with diverter spout, pop-up waste, curtain rod.

15.2.12   Lavatories. Color as selected by Owner. About 17×14 inches oval, vitreous china, for building into countertop. Include stainless steel sink rim. Combination faucet, pop up waste.

15.2.13   Water closets. Color as selected by Owner. Close coupled, round front, floor mounted, siphon jet with tank, plastic seat and cover to match.

15.2.14   Five foot, 6 inch sink. Stainless steel two compartment, drainboard, with mixing faucet like Moen, hose spray. Disposer, Insinkerator model 77, $\frac{1}{2}$ hp.

15.2.15   Connect Owner's dishwasher

15.2.16   Floor drain at basement stair shall be cast iron, Blake, Wade, Crane, or equal, black body and cover.

15.2.17   Install all appliances as called for in Division 11.

15.2.18   Testing and cleaning of all plumbing, soil, waste, drain, vent piping, and sewers shall be as required by the City Plumbing Inspector.

15.2.19   Verify locations of the city and utility company services. Secure and pay for all permits, fees, inspections, etc., required by the city or utility company.

15.2.20   Materials shall be new and of the grade and quality specified. Work shall be performed by trained, experienced workers, skilled in their various crafts.

15.2.21   All openings in roof shall be flashed with galvanized sheet metal in one piece, extending under and over the shingle roof at least 12 inches, measured with the vertical.

15.2.22   All excavation and backfilling required shall be done for the proper installation of the work.

15.2.23   All work shall be in accordance with the plumbing ordinances of the city.

15.2.24   The entire installation shall be guaranteed against defects in workmanship and material for the period of one year from the date of final acceptance. The installation shall be guaranteed against water hammer, rattling of pipes, gurgling of traps, and to be a complete and noise-free installation.

15.3   HEATING

15.3.1   Provide complete blower system warm air heating system for the residence including, but not limited to, the following:

15.3.2   LP gas furnace.

15.3.3   All piping and electrical connections and disconnect switch.

15.3.4   Thermostat.

15.3.5   Supply and return duct system.

15.3.6   Grilles and registers.

15.3.7   Guarantee to heat all rooms to 70 degrees in 0 degree weather. Design and installation shall conform to standards of the Heating, Refrigeration, and Air Conditioning Institute. Design system for addition of future air cooling. A complete layout showing sizes of pipe, thermostat location, register location, ducts, distribution system, size, and type of furnace shall be submitted before award of contract. The owner shall accept or reject the heating bids on the basis of quality as well as price.

15.3.8   Include electrical work for heating. Fused disconnect near furnace furnished by others. Include one plain room thermostat.

15.3.9   LP forced air furnace, 84,000 Btu/hr output. Include filters, fan controls, limit control, and safety controls.

15.3.10   Place tank near rear lot line, with necessary piping projecting above slab near house wall.

15.3.11   Ducts all full lined aluminum and/or galvanized iron, adequate size, tightly joined. Dampers as required to balance system. Floor and wall registers, where indicated on plan, with dampers and adjustable vanes. Include register in ductwork to provide warm air to basement.

15.3.12   Thermostat shall be Johnson Controls or equal electric system.

15.3.13   Workmanship shall be such as to require a minimum of cutting and patching.

15.3.14   Secure and pay all required heating permits and inspections required by the city and the utility company and all other fees, etc.

15.3.15   Put system into operation, lubricated and adjusted, balance room temperatures.

15.3.16   The Contractor shall guarantee the system in writing to be and remain in good working condition for one year from the date of the first heating season, beginning October 1. The guarantee shall state that all rooms shall be heated to 70 degrees in 0 degree weather.

15.3.17   Include ducts between three fans and roof jacks installed by others. Include 4 inch round duct and roof jack for dryer vent.

DIVISION 16— ELECTRICAL

16.1   GENERAL PROVISIONS

16.1.1   Scope of Work

16.1.1.1   Items provided by the Owner or other trades shall be checked carefully so as to avoid duplicating material or labor provided by others. Electrical installation shall include, but not be limited to, the following:

16.1.1.2   New 120/240 volt, 1 phase, 3-wire overhead service and main switch.

16.1.2   Codes and Standards

16.1.2.1   Equipment, devices, apparatus, and installation shall be in full compliance with applicable standards, requirements, rules, regulations, codes, statutes, ordinances, etc., of the city, county, state, and the utility company.

16.1.2.2   Electrical equipment, wiring, etc., shall comply with National Bureau of Fire Underwriters requirements and National Electrical Code® requirements for the particular type of installation, and labeled UL approved.

16.1.3   Guarantee and Testing

16.1.3.1   The entire installation shall be guaranteed for workmanship and material for a period of one year from acceptance.

16.1.3.2   The entire conduit system and the solid neutral wires shall be tested for shorts and grounding in the presence of the Architect.

16.1.3.3   The Contractor must guarantee that all joints are soldered or tightly screwed and that all wire joints are thoroughly insulated as specified.

16.2   BASIC MATERIALS AND METHODS

16.2.1   All materials shall be new and of the grade and quality specified. Work must be performed by trained, experienced workers, skilled in their various crafts.

16.2.2   The location of all outlets, switches, convenience outlets, and devices shall be as shown on the plans and as directed by the Architect.

16.2.3   Do all excavation and backfilling required to install the work properly.

16.2.4   Wiring shall be electrical metallic tubing (EMT). Wiring in concrete slabs or in fill shall be galvanized rigid conduit and moisture-proof. Wiring shall be concealed in construction except in attic, basement, and carport. Cut in straps or receptacle boxes to make a flush surface for drywall.

16.2.5   Install branch circuits for lighting, complete with wire, receptacles, wiring devices, silent switches. Dimmer switch as noted on plan, like Moe 6502, 600 watt. Install circuits for convenience outlets, complete with wire, wiring devices, receptacles, cover plates. All plugs three point for grounding. Cover plates at switches and convenience outlets, chrome in kitchen and baths, prime coat elsewhere. Outlet boxes shall be stamped steel octagonal or square, of suitable and ample sizes, mounted with hangers, of same finish as conduit. Junction and pull boxes shall be of adequate size and of correct gauge steel to meet requirements of the National Electrical Code® (NEC®). Wiring devices, switches, convenience outlets, etc., shall be of Hubble, Hageman, or approved equal, 125V.

16.2.6   Furnish and install bathroom ceiling fans. Provide roof jacks. Ducts by others. Kitchen range hood and fan, same.

16.2.7   Provide and install chimes with transformer and pushbuttons.

16.2.8   Set lamppost in concrete near front of lot. Install waterproof cable underground to same. Install photoelectric control to operate lamppost lamp.

16.2.9   Kitchen exhaust range hood shall be special "Thermador," as shown on the drawings, complete with duct through ceiling and roof. Bathrooms shall be exhausted with "Trade Wind," Model 1201, complete with electrical connection to light switch and 4 inch round duct to attic space.

16.2.10   Install fused disconnect for furnace. Heating wiring by others. Make electric connections to water heater and disposer, furnished by others, and range top and oven.

16.3   SERVICE AND DISTRIBUTION

16.3.1   Three-wire 200 ampere single-phase. Install galvanized iron pipe conduit for same.

16.3.2   Install circuit breaker panel with 200 ampere main breaker and 20 breakers as follows: One 30 amp each to range top, water heater, clothes dryer; 50 amp to oven. One 20 amp each to dishwasher, food waste disposer, refrigerator, furnace, and two circuits for kitchen convenience outlets. Four 20 amp for convenience outlets, and four for lighting outlets, two spares. Label circuits on circuit breaker panel.

16.4   LIGHTING

16.4.1   Provide and install light fixtures with lamps as scheduled.

16.5   DOORBELL SYSTEMS

16.5.1   Provide transformers and low-voltage lines for door chimes. Provide lighted pushbuttons at front and rear doors. Owner will provide chimes to be installed by Contractor. Divide system to indicate different signal from each door.

16.6   COMMUNICATIONS

16.6.1   Telephone outlets as indicated on plan, with 1/2 inch thin wall conduit from outlet to below floor.

18

Name _____ Date _____

Matching

_____ **1.** Division 1   **A.** Concrete

_____ **2.** Division 2   **B.** Electrical

_____ **3.** Division 3   **C.** General Requirements

_____ **4.** Division 4   **D.** Wood and Plastics

_____ **5.** Division 5   **E.** Doors and Windows

_____ **6.** Division 6   **F.** Metals

_____ **7.** Division 7   **G.** Thermal and Moisture Protection

_____ **8.** Division 8   **H.** Site Work

_____ **9.** Division 15   **I.** Mechanical

_____ **10.** Division 16   **J.** Masonry

True-False

T   F   **1.** When there is a conflict between the information shown on the prints and the specifications, the specifications are to be followed.

T   F   **2.** The working drawings, specifications, and contract are considered the legal documents.

T   F   **3.** The owner decides on all of the materials to be used in the building and informs the architect, who then writes the specifications.

T   F   **4.** All MasterFormat™ divisions must be included in the specifications for a building.

T   F   **5.** Small remodeling jobs should have specifications.

T   F   **6.** Outline specifications do not tell how material is to be applied.

T   F   **7.** The *Description of Materials* form is used mainly to provide information on which to base a mortgage loan.

T   F   **8.** Complete specifications cover the ordering of specific materials, suitable options, and equivalent products.

T   F   **9.** Information in *Sweet's Architectural Catalog File* is organized alphabetically by product.

True-False

Refer to Outline Specifications for the Brick-Veneer Residence, Figure 5-2.

T   F   **1.** No information is given about the concrete mix or about formwork.

T   F   **2.** Exterior finish above the first floor level shall be brick veneer or wood siding.

T   F   **3.** Vanities may be either plastic laminate countertop or marble, depending on cost.

T   F   **4.** Floors in the bathrooms and family room are to be mosaic tile.

T   F   **5.** Doors are made of wood or steel.

T   F   **6.** The roof is finished with asphalt shingles.

T   F   **7.** The electrical service for this house is 200 A.

T   F   **8.** The kitchen cabinets are factory built.

T   F   **9.** The electric water heater has a 65 gal. capacity.

T   F   **10.** Interior painting is not included in this contract.

True-False

Refer to Description of Materials for the Brick-Veneer Residence, Figure 5-3.

T   F   **1.** The concrete mixes are a 5-bag mix for the footings and a 6-bag mix for the basement slab.

T   F   **2.** The chimney is built with face brick and firebrick.

T   F   **3.** The exterior is finished with D select siding using 1 × 8 boards with 1 × 2 battens.

T   F   **4.** Floor joists are placed on 12″ or 16″ centers.

T   F   **5.** Underlayment-grade plywood is used for the finished wood floor.

T   F   **6.** Cross bridging is used between floor and ceiling joists.

T   F   **7.** Stock roof trusses are used to support the roof.

T   F   **8.** The roofing is 240 lb asphalt shingles over 15 lb roofing felt.

T   F   **9.** Interior and exterior finish coating consists of three coats of paint.

T   F   **10.** Exterior doors are 1¾″ thick.

T   F   **11.** Folding stairs are provided to reach the attic space.

T   F   **12.** The heating section includes information on the make and model of hood and vent fans.

T   F   **13.** Gutters and downspouts are vinyl-clad metal.

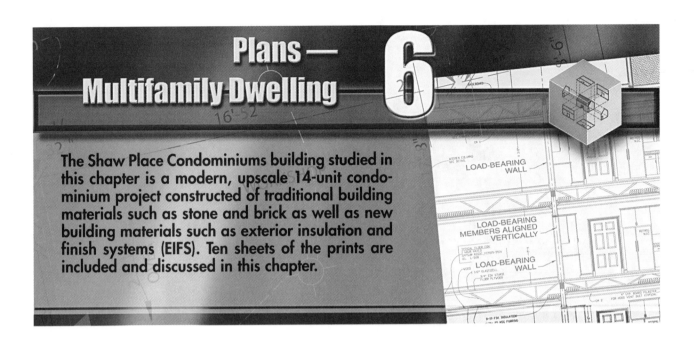

Plans — Multifamily Dwelling 6

The Shaw Place Condominiums building studied in this chapter is a modern, upscale 14-unit condominium project constructed of traditional building materials such as stone and brick as well as new building materials such as exterior insulation and finish systems (EIFS). Ten sheets of the prints are included and discussed in this chapter.

INTRODUCTION AND GENERAL DESCRIPTION

Multifamily dwellings have changed in size and appeal to residents. Traditional multifamily dwellings were primarily apartment buildings designed for individuals who could not afford a home purchase or needed temporary living arrangements. With the advent of condominium living, more features are being incorporated into multifamily settings to make high-quality residential features available to those who choose not to own a single-family residence.

Chapter 6 is based on a partial set of prints for a luxury condominium development. The prints for the Shaw Place Condominiums describe a 3½ story, 14-unit condominium project. See Figure 6-1. Because of the potential for 100 people or more to occupy the condominiums at any one time, sound isolation and fire protection features are incorporated throughout the building.

The complete set of drawings for the Shaw Place Condominiums includes 73 sheets. Ten of the more representative sheets—a Site Plan, Foundation Plan, Penthouse Floor Plan, Roof Plan, interior and exterior elevations, sections, and details—are discussed in this chapter.

SITE PLAN, SHEET A1.1

Sheet A1.1 includes a title block, list of abbreviations used on the prints, information concerning the building, information related to the building code as it relates to the prints, and Site Plan for the project including overall building dimensions, utility locations, and site finish information.

John Deere Construction & Forestry Company

A site plan contains information regarding the proper site elevations and position of the building on the lot.

Figure 6-1. Condominiums have become a popular choice, providing many of the benefits of home ownership while offering advantages associated with rental properties. The Shaw Place Condominiums are constructed of traditional building materials such as stone and brick as well as new building materials such as exterior insulation and finish systems (EIFS).

Title Block

The title blocks, which are similar for each sheet of the prints, provide general information about the Shaw Place Condominiums, including the address of the condominiums, architect information, and sheet number. The condominiums are located at #15 Topton Way in Clayton, Missouri. The architect is Barry R. Nelson and Associates, located in St. Louis, Missouri. The sheet number, A1.1, indicates the sheet is the first sheet in the set of architectural prints (indicated with an "A"). The complete set of prints contains architectural prints (A), civil engineering prints (C), electrical prints (E), mechanical prints (M), plumbing prints (P), and structural prints (S).

Abbreviations

The list of abbreviations included on Sheet A1.1 is organized to some extent according to the type of work to be performed. The list of abbreviations is generally organized by terms used on the Site Plan, terms used on the Foundation Plan, terms used on the Floor Plan and Elevations, terms used to represent finish materials, terms related to the Structural Plan, and terms related to electrical and mechanical systems. The groups of terms are not mutually exclusive, and a tradesworker reading the prints may need to check throughout the list to identify the appropriate abbreviation.

Code Information

Building code information is shown in the upper-right corner of Sheet A1.1. The Shaw Place Condominiums prints are based on the 1996 edition of the Building Officials and Code Administrators (BOCA) building code. The building code title and edition are important to note on a set of prints or specifications, as that code and edition are applicable to all work on the project. Often, municipalities take several years after the publication of a new edition of a building code to complete their review and adoption of the most recent code. The building occupancy is listed as R-2, which is a residential building containing more than two dwelling units where the occupants are primarily permanent. An R-2 classification includes condominiums, apartments, dormitories, and nontransient boarding houses. The total floor area per floor is 11,728 sq ft. The building is equipped with automatic sprinklers, which are supplied with water by the municipal water supply. The building includes 14 dwelling units and 28 parking spaces for the occupants.

Site Plan

The Site Plan provides information about the placement of the building on the property. The scale of the Site Plan is 1″ = 10′-0″. Two North arrows are shown on the Site Plan—True North and Plan North. True North is based on the exact compass bearing, while Plan North is a more general bearing, which allows the drawing to properly fit on the sheet. Also, the use of Plan North when referring to various elevations or directions associated with the prints avoids confusion when referring to a particular face of the building.

Compass bearings of the building lot are shown on the northwest, northeast, and southeast corners of the lot. Building layout begins at the northwest corner with the benchmark located at 0.22° East 0.59° South. The west property line along Topton Way is 229.75′ long at a radius of 870.00′. The south property line is composed of three sections. The longest section is 82.61′ long at a bearing of N42°52′22″E. See Figure 6-2. An iron pipe is located at the east end of the south property line, from which the property line continues 31.68′ at a bearing of S29°00′52″E. The south property line continues 27.00′ at a bearing of S42°48′07″W, ending at an iron pipe. The east property line is 172.65′ long at a radius of 750′. A final iron pipe is located at the northeast corner of the property at 0.30° East 0.81° South.

Basic information shown on site plans or plot plans is derived from a survey plat drawn by a licensed surveyor. A survey plat shows a division of land divided into streets and lots.

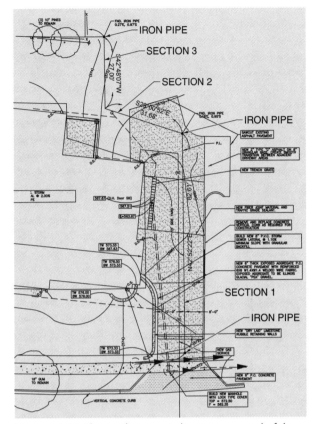

Figure 6-2. The south property line is composed of three sections with a bearing and linear measurement provided for each section.

Overall Building Dimensions and Orientation. The Site Plan indicates that the overall building dimensions are 188.83′ × 68.00′. The Shaw Place Condominiums are to be built on Topton Way, a street that is 60′ wide. The building is set back 25′ from the west property line, measured at a point between the main entrances. The northwest corner of the building is 26.52′ from the west property line and 17.12′ from the north property line. The first floor elevation is 577.33′ and the basement floor elevation used as the parking garage is 567.67′. See Figure 6-3.

Utility Information

Existing gas and water service utility lines are shown under Topton Way. Electrical service to a street lamp is shown in the parkway in front of the building. The main electrical transformer is shown near the northwest corner of the building. The electrical service for the building enters through the north wall of the building. See Figure 6-4.

David White Instruments

Figure 6-3. Surveying instruments, such as laser levels and builder's levels, are used to accurately position a building on a job site.

The gas service extends from the gas main under Topton Way, runs along the south side of the building under the driveway, and enters the building at the southeast corner. A 6″ water service for domestic use and fire protection extends from the water main under Topton Way, and is routed through an underground vault along the west side of the building. The water service then extends to the west side of the building between the main entries. Storm water is collected from the downspouts around the building perimeter, routed through a 6″ PVC storm sewer lateral at 2.00% minimum slope, and piped to an 8″ PVC storm sewer lateral on the south side of the building under the driveway. Two new manholes are to be constructed on the southwest corner of the lot. One of the manholes provides access to the storm sewer connection as indicated by the hidden lines representing the 8″ PVC storm sewer lateral pipe. Although not indicated on this drawing, the other manhole may be used to access the sanitary sewer connection.

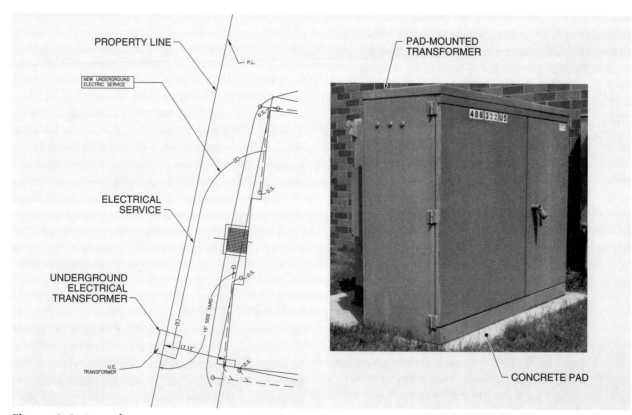

Figure 6-4. A transformer converts power at one voltage and current rating to a voltage and current rating that is usable by building inhabitants. The electrical service enters the building through the north wall.

Site Finish Information

Landscaping and other hard surface finishes are indicated on the Site Plan. Eleven trees are shown that are to remain on the property—four oak trees, three pine trees, three gum trees, and one maple tree. Care must be taken during construction to avoid damaging the trees or the soil surrounding the trees.

Contour lines show the finished grade of the lot around the building perimeter. The elevation along the west side of the building is 576'. Contour lines along the south side of the building indicate the finished elevation of the driveway to ensure proper drainage.

New "dry laid" limestone rubble retaining walls are to be constructed along the north side of the driveway. See Figure 6-5. Various notations designate the elevations at the top and bottom of each wall. A general notation indicates that the layout of the front entry sidewalks and limestone retaining walls must be field-coordinated with the architect prior to construction.

Hard surface paving for the Shaw Place Condominiums includes four exposed-aggregate patios on the east side of the building, an exposed-aggregate driveway on the south side of the

building, two entry sidewalks, and a 4' wide by 4" thick sidewalk along Topton Way. An apron and curb will also be installed at the intersection of the driveway and the street. A small section of asphalt pavement is to be placed at the southeast corner of the property as a transition between adjoining driveway areas. The 2" thick asphalt pavement is to be placed on 6" of granular fill. The two entry sidewalks are 4' wide and made of 4" thick exposed-aggregate concrete using Illinois glacial "pea" gravel.

FOUNDATION PLAN, SHEET A1.3

Sheet A1.3 contains the Foundation Plan for the south half of the Shaw Place Condominiums and Typical Downspout @ Grade Detail. Due to the overall size of the building and the scale required to properly show details, only half of the building is shown on Sheet A1.3. A match line is indicated along the left side of the plan. A *match line* is an aligning mark on a print that is used when a drawing is too large to be contained on one sheet. Drawings on two individual sheets are laid next to one another and aligned to show the entire building.

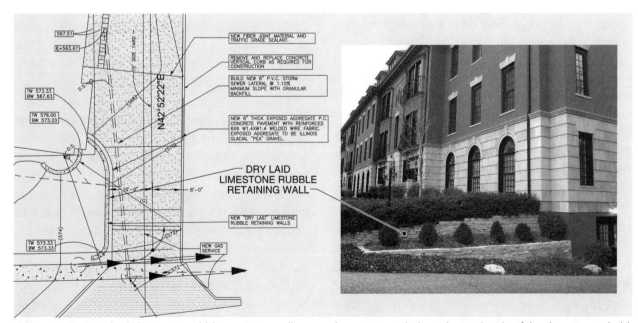

Figure 6-5. "Dry laid" limestone rubble retaining walls are to be constructed along the north side of the driveway to hold back earth.

Columns shown on the Foundation Plan are laid out on a 20′ horizontal grid. Grid lines that extend vertically across the drawing are identified by numerical designations (7 through 13). Grid lines that extend horizontally across the drawing are identified as A, B, and C.

A key to the symbols used on Sheet A1.3 appears in the lower-right corner of the sheet for reference when reading the prints. Since architectural firms use a variety of symbols on drawings, each sheet should be scanned for a symbol legend when initially reviewing the prints.

Foundation Supports

The building is supported by a 12″ thick cast-in-place concrete foundation wall on the east and west sides of the building. The south foundation wall is 12″ thick and is comprised of 4″ brick veneer over an 8″ concrete wall. Footing information is not shown on this sheet, but appears on sections such as Section 1, Sheet 3.2. Intermediate support for the building is provided by concrete columns that are erected over concrete piers on the grid lines. Columns on grid lines 8 and 9 are slightly offset.

Each column is supported by a 3′-0″ diameter cast-in-place concrete pier. Isolation joints, also known as expansion joints, are formed around the concrete columns to allow for movement of the concrete floor and column caused by expansion and contraction of the concrete as well as by loads imposed on the slab and columns. Isolation joints pass completely through the thickness of the concrete slab. A piece of asphalt-impregnated fiber material is used in the isolation joint to provide space for the concrete movement. Concrete beams 3′-0″ wide are placed in a north/south direction. Additional information about the concrete piers, columns, and beams and isolation joints is obtained from the structural drawings (not included with this set of prints).

Interior Finish

The finished floor elevation of the Garage concrete slab varies from 90′-0″ at the floor drains to 90′-4″ at the perimeter of the slab. The lower elevation at the floor drains provides proper drainage of the Garage area. Hidden lines indicate slope lines to the floor drains. The 5″ tinted concrete slab is to receive a swirled magnesium float finish. A clear sealer is applied to the slab to protect it from salt damage. Contraction joints (CJ) are indicated at various locations around the slab to create a weakened plane and control the location of cracking due to imposed loads. Contraction joints are tooled into fresh concrete or sawn into the slab after it has hardened.

Storage lockers are provided for building occupants along the east and west side of the Garage. A 4″ thick elevated area, which extends 6′ from the east and west foundation walls, provides an area for storage lockers and adjacent work area. The elevated area also forms a curb and permits easy access to storage lockers since vehicles cannot be parked tight against the locker doors. The elevated areas slope 1″ toward the curb to provide proper drainage. Bold numbers painted on the floor indicate parking space and storage locker numbers.

Other floor finishes include a 4″ thick plain concrete slab in the elevator entry area and Equipment Room and a compacted earth-filled area in the southeast corner. The compacted earth-filled area is a base for the first floor terraces. Concrete-filled steel bollards are located inside and outside of the overhead door to protect the edges of the opening. Bollards are also to be installed at various locations around the foundation.

Walls in the garage area include Type 1 walls that are designated by the architect to provide for resident storage lockers around the perimeter of the garage. For many light commercial buildings and multifamily dwellings in which several types of walls of similar construction are constructed, an architect may specify walls as "Types" and provide a key or legend that describes or illustrates the wall construction. For example, Type 1 walls may be framed with 2 × 4s and sheathed on the outside surface with plywood. This convention of representing wall construction reduces the number of notations required on a drawing.

A Trash Room in the southwest corner of the Garage is partitioned off using two walls constructed of 6″ concrete block and painted. Four 8″ cast-in-place concrete walls create an elevator shaft. Other interior walls in the Garage include Type 4, 2-hour fire-rated walls between the Lobby and Garage, Equipment Room walls, and Lobby walls. Doors installed in fire-rated walls, such as G02, H02, and G04, must also be fire-rated. The fire rating on doors and walls indicates the amount of time these building components can withstand fire without structural failure. Dimensions for wall and partition placement are included throughout the drawing. For example, the 3′-0″ dimension in storage locker 20 indicates the face of the storage locker walls is 3′-0″ from the interior face of the concrete foundation wall. Centerlines extending vertically from the concrete columns pass through the center of every other storage locker wall. Therefore, the storage locker walls are 10′-0″ OC, which is typical for the other storage lockers.

Door identifier codes are shown at each door opening. See Figure 6-6. Details regarding each door are included in a door schedule (not included with this set of prints). A pair of 6′-0″ × 6′-8″ bypass sliding doors is installed at the entrance to each locker. Single swinging doors are shown at the entrances to the Trash Room and Lobby. The door in the Trash Room measures 3′-0″ × 6′-8″, with the rough opening located 4′-0⅜″ from the inside of the concrete wall. The door at the entrance to the Lobby measures 3′-0″ × 7′-0″. A set of 6′-0″ × 7′-0″ double doors is to be installed at the Trash Room and Equipment Room entrances. The doors along the south side of the building are centered on the offset wall. The doors leading into the Equipment Room are 1′-6″ from the interior wall of the lobby. A 16′-0″ × 7′-0″ motorized overhead door is to be centered in the south wall opening to provide access for vehicles into and out of the Garage.

Three plywood shelves are installed in each closet of the Trash Room. No window openings are shown on Sheet A1.3.

A fire door is a fire-resistant door and assembly, including the frame and hardware, and is commonly equipped with an automatic door closer.

DOOR SCHEDULE			
Door	Size	Type	Remarks
G02	3′-0″ × 7′-0″	Fire-rated door	
G04	6′-0″ × 7′-0″	Interior double swinging doors	
G05	3′-0″ × 6′-8″	Swinging door	Steel
G06	6′-0″ × 7′-0″	Exterior double swinging doors	
G14–G19	6′-0″ × 6′-8″	Double sliding doors	Painted with rust preventer paint
G29–G36	6′-0″ × 6′-8″	Double sliding doors	Painted with rust preventer paint
H02	3′-0″ × 7′-0″	Exterior swinging security door	

Figure 6-6. Door information, such as door size and type, is provided in a door schedule.

The interior finish of the Lobby is determined from the Interior Finish Schedule. A flight of stairs extends from the Garage floor to the stairway landing. The flight of stairs includes seven treads, each measuring 11″ deep, for a total stairway run of 6′-5″. A 3′-0″ × 7′-0″ swinging door at the top of the stairway provides access to the east side of the building through a rear entry door. The concrete landing outside the rear entry door and exterior stairway has a 4″ floor drain to prevent moisture from accumulating at the bottom of the stairway.

Mechanical Systems

The mechanical equipment shown on the plan is located in the Lobby and Equipment Room along the east side of the Garage. Per the Americans with Disabilities Act (ADA), a minimum of one elevator is required in new construction for buildings that are more than three stories tall or have more than 3000 sq ft per story. A cast-in-place concrete elevator shaft with 6′-6½″ × 8′-4″ inside dimensions is constructed 15′-10″ from the inside of the foundation wall. Due to requirements of the building code and the weight of the elevator and its inhabitants, elevator shaft walls are constructed differently than other building partitions. The elevator shaft walls are 8″ thick concrete to withstand fire and properly support elevator support members such as the rails, guides, and elevator car support system.

An elevator sump pump is installed in an 18″ square by 18″ deep sump pit in the Equipment Room floor. The sump pit is connected to the elevator pit using two pieces of 6″ diameter PVC conduit, which are positioned below the floor slab. Overflow from the elevator pit drains into the sump pit, where it is ejected from the building. Elevator hydraulic equipment is commonly placed in a recessed pit below the elevator car. Hydraulic lift equipment varies with each elevator manufacturer. Hydraulic lift equipment ensures safe operation of an elevator within specified loading conditions. A sump pump is provided to ensure that the elevator hydraulic drive system and electrical controls remain dry and operational. A disconnect box for the elevator is located on the west wall of the Equipment Room.

Another sump pit is located next to storage locker 13 to collect storm water from drain tile surrounding the building foundation. A sump pump ejects the storm water outside and away from the building.

Wall Sections

Four wall sections are referenced on the east and south foundation walls. The upper number in the section reference indicates the section number and the lower number indicates the sheet number on which the section is located. The triangle points in the direction of sight for the section. The sections show construction details for the garage and other floors of the building.

Typical Downspout Detail @ Grade, Sheet A1.3

Four downspouts, designated with a small circle and the abbreviation "D.S.," are indicated along the west and south walls of the building. The Typical Downspout Detail @ Grade shows the transition of a 3″ × 4″ downspout to 4″ diameter PVC pipe that extends underground to direct storm water from the roof away from the building. A 3″ × 4″ corrugated downspout is connected to a 4″ PVC drain pipe with a 3″ × 4″ downspout shoe, which is set 8″ below the first floor elevation and tight against the building. The shoe is connected to a 45° wye fitting equipped with a 3″ cleanout plug. Four-inch diameter PVC pipe is connected to the outlet of the wye and a strap anchor is used to secure the assembly to the building.

PENTHOUSE FLOOR PLAN, SHEET A1.11

Sheet A1.11 contains the floor plan for the penthouse on the south side of the fourth floor (4S). Each fourth floor penthouse consists of over 3800 sq ft of living space. A key to the symbols is included in the lower-right corner of the sheet for reference. Boxed numbers shown on the print refer to the Architectural Notes in the lower-right corner of the sheet. This method of notation provides the necessary information, but does not clutter the drawing and obstruct construction details.

A match line is shown along the left side of the drawing for alignment with the north penthouse floor plan. The match line is aligned with the common wall between the adjoining fourth floor penthouses.

Room Layout

The primary entrance to the fourth floor penthouse is from the elevator through the Lobby and into the Foyer located in the middle of the condominium unit. The elevator has doors on opposing sides, allowing inhabitants to enter the fourth floor penthouse through the Foyer or through the stairway landing and into the Kitchen. The elevator shaft has a Type 5 wall with a 2-hour fire rating and the Lobby has a Type 3 wall with a 2-hour fire rating. The Lobby measures 5'-2½" wide by 5'-1¼" deep and has mechanical chases for HVAC ductwork on the north and south sides. A *chase* is an enclosure in a structure that allows for the placement of piping and wiring for plumbing, mechanical, and electrical systems. Crown molding (CM3) is applied as the ceiling finish material in the lobby.

Foyer. The Foyer is entered from the Lobby through a 3'-6" × 7'-0" door (S01). The overall measurements of the Foyer are 10' × 13'. The corners of the Foyer are angled at 45° approximately 2'-6" from each corner. The perimeter of the ceiling is 10'-0" high and the 6'-0" × 6'-0" area of the ceiling surrounding the 4'-0" square skylight tapers up from 10'-0" height to the skylight height. The raised ceiling area also receives angled corners to coincide with the room design. The corners are angled 9⅞" in from each corner. The Foyer ceiling is finished with crown molding (CM2).

A 4' × 8' opening to the north of the Foyer, designated S27, leads to a set of 4'-0" × 7'-0" double doors that provide access to the private living areas of the condominium unit including the Den/Study and the bedrooms. Another 4' × 8' opening to the south of the Foyer (S32) leads into the main living space through the south hallway.

Guest Lavatory. A Guest Lavatory is located adjacent to the west wall of the Foyer and is entered through the 3'-0" × 7'-0" opening (S26).

A 2'-8" × 7'-0" pocket door (S16) is installed in the south wall of the Lavatory. The Lavatory has 9' ceilings and is finished with crown molding (CM3). A water closet is to be installed along the east wall of the Lavatory and a vanity with a sink is to be installed along the west wall. Per Architectural Note 3, the soffit above the vanity is framed to 8'-0". A ¼" thick by 48" high plate glass mirror is to be installed on the wall behind the vanity (Architectural Note 7). Notes 12 and 13 refer to a towel bar and paper holder that are to be installed in the Lavatory.

A 2'-0" deep linen closet, located in the short hallway leading to the Lavatory, is accessed through a 3'-0" × 7'-0" door (S06). Per Architectural Note 9, 16" wide plastic laminate shelves and a chrome hanger pole are to be installed in the linen closet.

South Hallway. The south hallway is 5' wide by 13'-2½" long, and has a 10'-0" ceiling. The hallway provides access to the Kitchen, Great Room, Dining Room, and Foyer. The 04 notation refers to the room number of the hallway in the interior finish schedule. A 3'-0" × 7'-0" double-acting door (S05) leads from the south hallway to the Kitchen. A *double-acting door* is a door that swings in two directions. Openings designated S31 and S29 lead from the south hallway to the Great Room and Dining Room, respectively.

Crown molding, which is installed along the intersection of walls and ceilings, is specified for use throughout the Shaw Place Condominiums.

Kitchen. The Kitchen measures 17′-4″ wide by 21′-7″ long, and has a 10′-0″ ceiling. Access to the Kitchen is attained through the fire-rated door (S03) between the stairway landing and Kitchen, through the swinging door leading to Terrace 2, or through the swinging door leading to the Utility Room (S04).

Kitchen appliances are located primarily along the north and west walls, with the ovens to be installed in the southwest Kitchen corner. An island cabinet is installed 3′-11″ from the cooktop and 3′-4″ from the ovens. Interior Elevation 2, Sheet A5.3 (not included with this set of prints) provides additional information about cabinet and appliance layout.

Terrace 2. Terrace 2 is 17′-4″ wide by 9′-4″ long. One Type M window and one Type L window are installed in the wall between Terrace 2 and the Kitchen. An additional Type L window is installed in the door also located in the wall between Terrace 2 and the Kitchen. Additional information about the window wall is shown on Details 1 and 2, Sheet A4.6 (not included with this set of prints) and on the Right Side Elevation. Fixed glass windows are installed in the east wall along with a swinging door leading into the Kitchen. The interior face of the Terrace walls is finished with exterior insulation and finish system (EIFS), which is finished with a copper cap and a painted metal railing.

Utility Room. The Utility Room measures 9′-4″ wide by 31′-7¼″ long and has an offset that increases the room width to 11′-0¾″. An Elastizell™ floor is installed in the Utility Room. Elastizell is a lightweight concrete mixture composed of water, cement, and preformed foam. The concrete mixture is pumped into place and finished prior to setting. The ceiling of the Utility Room is sloped to match the roof above and finished with gypsum board. Mechanical equipment located in the Utility Room includes a horizontal furnace and a water heater (WH). A mechanical chase used to route supply and return air ductwork and electrical wiring is shown in the northeast corner of the Utility Room.

Great Room. The Great Room measures 25′-10½″ wide by 21′-0¾″ long and has an 11′-0″ tray ceiling. A *tray ceiling* is a horizontal ceiling with angled sides around the perimeter so as to resemble an inverted tray. The angled sides follow the roofline from the wall to the horizontal portion of the ceiling. The Great Room is designated Room 17 on the interior finish schedule. Two Type M doors installed in the south wall provide access to Terrace 3 from either side of the fireplace. Fixed glass windows are installed along the Type M doors on the side opposite the fireplace. The fireplace, which measures 7′-2¾″ wide, is constructed with a Type 3 1-hour fire-rated exterior wall. Note 1 indicates that the fireplace is a Majestic No. BR42 gas log fireplace. The flue is located on the west side of the firebox.

Terrace 3. Terrace 3 measures 22′-5″ wide by 12′-2½″ long, and is finished with materials similar to those used to finish Terrace 2. Additional information about the Terrace wall construction is on Detail 6, Sheet A 4.5 (not included with this set of prints). Information regarding terrace construction shown on Section 1, Sheet A 3.2 also applies to Terrace 3.

Dining Room. The Dining Room, designated Room 19, has a 10′-0″ tray ceiling and walls that are angled in 1′-9¹⁵⁄₁₆″ at each corner. Access to the Game Room from the Dining Room is gained through a 6′-0″ × 7′-0″ opening (S30) between the rooms. The Dining Room is the only room providing access to the Game Room.

Game Room. The Game Room, designated Room 18, measures 9′-0″ wide by 12′-10″ long, and has a 9′-0″ high ceiling. The Penthouse Floor Plan shows one Type O window in the west wall of the Game Room. The window is installed in the dormer, which projects through the roof. The window is also shown on the Front Right Elevation, Sheet A2.1 as a three-panel window with a fixed glass window in the center and a casement window on each side. Dormers are utilized for upper floor rooms to provide additional living space and minimize the amount of building space allotted to attics. Dormers require a roof with a steep slope and a high ridge.

Private Living Areas. The private living areas of the condominium, including the Den/Study and bedrooms, are north of the Foyer. Access to the private living areas is gained through the hallway leading from the Foyer or through the door leading from Stair 2B and into the Den/Study. A short hallway (04) is located immediately off the Foyer. A set of swinging double doors (S07) leads to the Den/Study. Another set of double doors (S08) leads to the bedroom hallway.

The Den/Study is comprised of two adjoining areas that are connected through a 6'-0" × 7'-0" opening (S28). The main area of the Den/Study measures 14'-7¾" wide by 17'-6" long, and has a 10'-0" tray ceiling. An offset and chase in the southwest wall accommodates chimney flues from living spaces below. A 3'-0" × 7'-0" 90-minute fire-rated door (S02) provides access to Stair 2B from the main area of the Den/Study. Type 4 2-hour fire-rated gypsum board is used as finish material in the stairwell. A pocket door (S17) is installed in the opening in the north wall of the Den/Study to provide access to a bathroom.

The west area of the Den/Study measures 9'-0" wide by 9'-4" long, and has a 9'-0" ceiling. One Type O window is installed in the west wall. A Typical Dormer Section is referenced along the west wall as 1/A4.3. See Figure 6-7.

The north hallway, designated 06, provides access to both bedrooms, the Laundry, and Utility Room through three 3'-0" × 7'-0" swinging doors. The hallway has a 10' flat ceiling and is finished with crown molding (CM3).

The Master Bedroom, designated Room 14, is entered from the north hallway through a 3'-0" × 7'-0" swinging door (S09). The Master Bedroom measures 17'-4¾" wide by 21'-5" long, and has an 11'-0" tray ceiling. The east wall of the Master Bedroom has a Type M window and two Type L openings. Further information about the Type L openings in the Master Bedroom should be obtained from the Door Schedule and Rear Elevations (not included with this set of prints). A swinging door in the east wall provides access to Terrace 1. The wall finish on Terrace 1 is similar to that on the other two terraces, with the primary finish material being EIFS. The fireplace in the Master Bedroom, measuring 3'-5" × 7'-0", is a gas log fireplace. Pocket doors on both sides of the fireplace (S21 and S23) provide access to the Master Baths and Dressing Rooms.

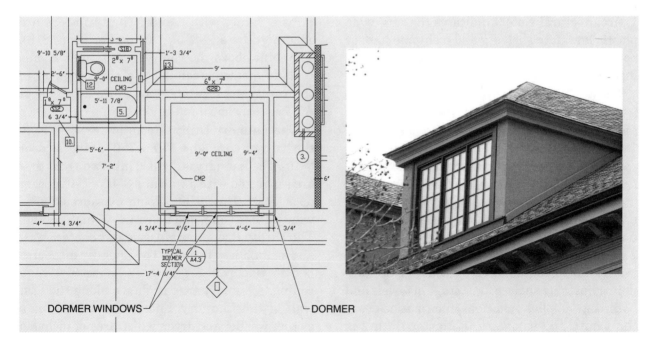

Figure 6-7. Dormers project from sloping roof surfaces to provide additional living area and allow light into the living area.

Master Bath 1 and Dressing Room 1 have 9'-0" ceilings throughout. Crown molding is installed in Master Bath 1 and the soffit in Dressing Room 1 is framed to 8'-0". Master Bath 1 includes a bathtub on the east wall and a vanity with lavatory (sink) on the west wall. A backsplash composed of 12" × 12" ceramic tile is installed around the bathtub and a 24" towel bar is installed at the foot of the bathtub 54" above the floor. A recessed medicine cabinet is installed along the side of the vanity with the bottom set 48" above the finished floor. A ¼" × 48" high plate glass mirror is installed along the full width of the vanity. A 2'-8" × 7'-0" swinging door (S15) leads to the toilet area. A paper holder is to be installed in the toilet area 18" above the finished floor.

A reference for Detail 9, Sheet A5.4 is indicated in Master Bath 1. Detail 9 provides information about the bathroom cabinets and vanity.

A custom common shower with doors opening into each bathroom is directly north of the fireplace. The shower head is along the north wall, allowing the piping to be installed in a common wall with the water closet piping.

Dressing Room 1, which measures 14'-11⅞" wide by 6'-3¾" long, is accessed from Master Bath 1 through a 3'-0" × 7'-0" pocket door (S24). A 1-hour Type 3 fire-rated wall surrounds a the chase in the southwest corner of Dressing Room 1. Architectural Note 9 indicates that 16" wide plastic laminate shelving and a chrome hanger pole placed 66" above the finished floor are to be installed in Dressing Room 1.

Master Bath 2 and Dressing Room 2 also have 9'-0" ceilings throughout. Master Bath 2 is entered from the Master Bedroom through a 3'-0" × 7'-0" pocket door (S21). Four doors in the bathroom provide access to the common shower, toilet area (S14), Dressing Room 2 (S22), and closet (S13). The mirror, towel bars, paper holder, and medicine cabinet are installed in similar locations to those in Master Bath 1. Dressing Room 2 has shelves on three walls. The closet, which is 1'-7¼" deep, contains five 16" wide plastic laminate adjustable shelves for storage of towels and bathroom supplies. Additional information about the vanity and cabinetry in Master Bath 2 is shown on Detail 9, Sheet A5.4.

The three basic plumbing systems installed in a building are the potable water supply system, the sanitary drainage and vent piping system, and the stormwater drainage system.

Bedroom 2 (designated 07) and the adjoining room have 9'-0" high ceilings. The ceiling of the area connecting Bedroom 2 and the adjoining room is 8'-0" high. The north wall of Bedroom 2 is the common wall with the next condominium unit, and is a Type 6 wall that is 10½" thick and has a 1-hour fire rating. Two closets are shown along the west wall of Bedroom 2. One closet, measuring 2'-2" × 6'-2", is enclosed with a pair of sliding bypass doors (S25) and the other closet, measuring 2'-2" × 2'-4", is enclosed with a swinging door (S12). Architectural Notes 9 and 10 specify the shelving arrangements in the closets. A pocket door (S19) on the south wall provides access into the Bath.

The Bath between Bedroom 2 and the Den/Study is divided into two areas. The west area, which contains the water closet and bathtub, has a 9'-0" ceiling. A wainscot of 12" × 12" ceramic tile is laid 96" high around the bathtub. A paper holder and towel bar are also to be installed in the west area. The east area of the Bath contains a vanity with a sink. The two areas are separated by a 2'-8" × 7'-0" pocket door (S18). The soffit above the vanity is 8'-0" high. A mirror and medicine cabinet are also installed in the vanity area. A reference to Detail 9, Sheet A5.4 is also shown in the Bath.

The Laundry/Utility Room is accessed from the hallway through a 3'-0" × 7'-0" swinging door (S10). The Laundry is divided into two areas that are separated with a wall and 3'-0" × 7'-0" pocket door (S20). The Utility Room measures 8'-5⅜" wide by 5'-0" long, and has an 8'-0" high ceiling. The Utility Room contains a water heater (WH) and an auxiliary furnace. The Laundry measures 8'-5⅜" wide by 9'-6¾" long, and has a 9'-0" high ceiling. A laundry tray is shown along the east wall of the Laundry. Space is provided for a clothes washer and dryer, which are not included in the contract (NIC).

ROOF PLAN AND DETAILS, SHEET A1.12

Sheet A1.12 contains a Roof Plan for the entire condominium building and a variety of roof details. The Roof Plan is drawn at a scale of ⅛″ = 1′-0″ and shows six dormers on the west side of the building, six penthouse terraces on the south, west, and north sides, and a mechanical area in the center of the roof. See Figure 6-8. The terraces are numbered 1, 2, and 3 for each condominium unit.

Roof Plan, Sheet A1.12

The majority of the roof is finished with asphalt shingles. Mineral rolled roofing is to be installed in the mechanical area, while standing-seam copper roofing is to be installed as accents on the north, west, and south sides of the building. Fireplace flues are terminated with copper chimney caps. Two additional fireplace flues are shown on the Roof Plan. A single-flue chimney serving the Master Bedroom in the Penthouse is shown along the Terrace 1 opening at the north end of the roof. A double-flue chimney is shown along the Terrace 3 opening at the south end of the roof.

Other caps, flashing, and crickets are shown at several roof locations. Copper chimney caps

provide aesthetic appeal. Painted metal flue caps prevent rain from entering the chimney and animals and debris from blocking the flues. Two galvanized metal caps are shown at the common flues in the central portion of the roof. Aluminum flashing is installed as required on the roof including the tops of parapets and ridge boards on the dormers, valley flashing along the dormer and roof valleys, and along the chimneys. Crickets are installed along the upper sides of chimneys at the intersection with the roof to prevent the accumulation of rainwater, ice, or snow behind the chimney that would create the potential for leaks. A match line is shown near the middle of the Roof Plan. The match line aligns with an expansion joint in the Garage concrete slab.

A variety of mechanical equipment is shown in the mechanical area in the center of the roof. Rooftop units 1 and 2 (RTU-1 and RTU-2) are positioned directly above the elevator shafts. Sixteen air conditioning condensers are shown in the mechanical area. The two 4′-0″ square skylights in the Foyers of the penthouses are represented on the print as a square with an X. Roof access to the mechanical equipment is provided by a 4′-0″ × 5′-0″ roof hatch door.

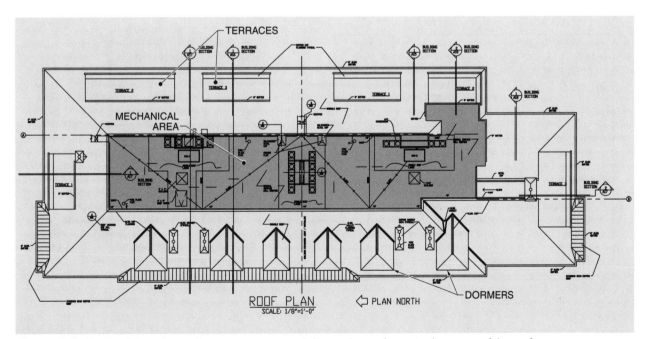

Figure 6-8. The Roof Plan shows dormers, terraces, and the mechanical area in the center of the roof.

Approximately 40% of the heat loss from a building can occur through the roof. For flat roofs, rigid foam insulation is usually applied to the upper surface of the rafters.

The flat roof on which the mechanical equipment is mounted is sloped 6″ to provide proper drainage of the roof area. Slope is indicated using solid lines with arrows along their length. Five-inch gutters are indicated along the south and southeast edges of the flat roof. Two scuppers—one at the northeast corner of the mechanical area and the other along the east side of the mechanical area—provide drainage for the majority of the mechanical area. A notation near the west parapet indicates that the roof slopes down 6″ from the roof ridge in this area. The mechanical area of the roof is finished mineral surface roll roofing, with a double layer placed beneath the air conditioning and rooftop units.

Six-inch aluminum gutters are to be installed around the perimeter of the roof. Five-inch gutters are to be installed along the edge of the sloping roof above the terraces to prevent water from draining onto the terraces.

Details 1 through 6 are included on Sheet A1.12. Four of the six details are referenced on the Roof Plan. Several sections are also referenced on the Roof Plan and are included on other sheets in the set of prints.

Detail 1, Sheet A1.12

Detail 1 shows the method for mounting the air conditioning condenser units in the center of the mechanical area on the rooftop. See Figure 6-9. Mounting pylons for the units are constructed of 2×12s spaced 24″ OC with three 2×12 posts on each end. Type X gypsum board is installed on the mounting pylon wall to provide fireproofing and prevent air infiltration into the supporting structure. Detail 1 provides additional information concerning the sloping sleeper and roof trusses on either side of the mounting pylon. Sleepers are 2× material fastened to each side of horizontal roof trusses to form the mechanical area of the roof. The sleepers are installed to provide the 6″ roof slope specified on the prints.

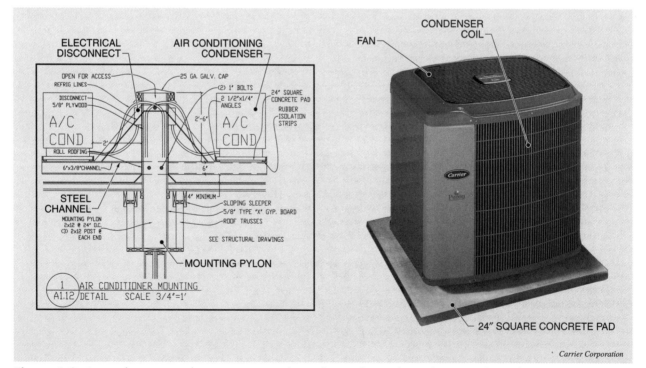

Figure 6-9. Air conditioning condensers are mounted on pylons in the mechanical area on the rooftop.

Two 6″ × ⅜″ steel channels are attached to the mounting pylon a minimum of 4″ above the roof surface with two 1″ bolts. Rubber isolation strips are installed between the steel channels and 24″ square concrete pad to minimize transfer of air conditioner vibration and noise to the living areas. Eight air conditioning condensers are placed on top of the concrete pads. The concrete pad and isolation strips are supported by ½″ × ¼″ × 24″ angle brackets on each side. Refrigerant lines pass down through the mounting pylons. The pylons are finished with ⅝″ plywood, roll roofing, and a 25 ga galvanized metal cap. A disconnect switch is installed on each side of the support for each air conditioning condensing unit as required by the National Electrical Code®.

Detail 2, Sheet A1.12

Detail 2 shows the proper construction of a typical flue shaft as it penetrates the roof. Detail 2 is referenced on the Roof Plan just north of the match line. One-hour fire-rated walls are used to line the flue shaft for the auxiliary furnace. One-inch Type X gypsum board is used as a fire separator between the furnace flue and air intake. Two 12″ × 18″ grilles are installed in each flue shaft penetration to provide fresh air to the building. The flue cap is painted to match the chimneys.

The top surfaces of the flue shafts are finished with 25 ga metal, which is soldered to prevent leakage. Flashing is installed at the top of the parapet where the roof ridge intersects the short vertical wall and on the horizontal portion of the gas furnace flue enclosure.

A cant strip is installed where the roof sheathing meets the vertical wall. A *cant strip* is a triangular member, commonly wood, installed under the finish roofing material at the intersection of a parapet and roof. Cant strips minimize the angle over which roofing material is applied to prevent cracking or breakage of roll roofing material and also channel water away from a sharp corner and leak area. Roll roofing extends across the cant strip and up the face of the flue shaft wall to a point where it can be enclosed at the top by galvanized flashing material.

Detail 3, Sheet A1.12

Two roof scuppers are shown on the Roof Plan. The scuppers direct storm water that collects on the flat center portion of the roof toward two downspouts to convey the water away from the building. The scupper shown along the match line is 3′-0″ wide, and will direct the majority of the storm water from the flat roof. The scupper is framed with 2 × 8s spaced 24″ OC and covered with 2½″ of ISO95 insulation, ¾″ fiberboard, and roll roofing. The front of the scupper is 7″ high, creating minimal visual interruption in the appearance of the roof. The upper interior portion of the scupper is finished with ½″ MDO plywood. A 4″ aluminum drip flashing is installed along the upper edge of the scupper under the shingles to prevent storm water from flowing up under the shingles.

Detail 4, Sheet A1.12

Detail 4, which depicts the roof ridge vent, is drawn to a scale of 3″ = 1′-0″ to provide additional clarity for the construction details. This construction technique is utilized at all points where the roof ridge intersects the parapet surrounding the mechanical area of the roof. The detail indicates how the framing and finish members are installed to provide air circulation in the attic of the building. Plywood is attached to the exterior face of the framing members and roll roofing is extended from the flat roof to the top of the plywood. The top of the plywood panel is secured in position with a roof clamp bar. A 1½″ opening is provided for airflow and is covered with continuous insect screen. A ¾″ wood spacer is installed at the peak of the ridge and a prefinished 7½″ × 10″ aluminum ridge cap is fastened in place using gasketed screws spaced 12″ OC. The base of the ridge cap is tied into the continuous hook strip fastened to the roof sheathing. The 10″ drop of the ridge cap prevents storm water from entering the vent opening.

Detail 5, Sheet A1.12

Detail 5, drawn to the scale of 1½″ = 1′-0″, shows the proper means of mounting the air conditioning condensers next to the elevators (RTU-1 and

RTU-2). An extra layer of roll roofing is applied to the roof surface below cedar 4 × 4s. The 4 × 4s are set in mastic and 2½″ × 2½″ × ⅜″ angles are fastened to the 4 × 4s as mounting rails. Neoprene rubber strips are placed on the angles and the condenser is set into position.

Detail 6, Sheet A1.12

Detail 6, drawn at a scale of 1½″ = 1′-0″, shows the roof hip venting detail referenced at the northwest corner of the Roof Plan. A 1″ × 12″ vent slot is cut into the top of each 2 × 10 rafter, 8″ from the hip rafter. The slots allow air to flow through the enclosed portion of the roof up to the roof ridge vents. The roof is sheathed with ¾″ plywood and insulated with R-19 FSK insulation. *Foil, scrim, and kraft (FSK) insulation* is a type of batt insulation that receives three facings to incorporate fireproofing characteristics, a reinforcing fabric, and a kraft paper face.

> Condensation can occur beneath the roof if water vapor is unable to escape through the roofing material.

EXTERIOR ELEVATIONS, SHEET A2.1

Sheet A2.1 contains three elevations showing the west and south sides of the condominium. The west side of the building is shown in two parts: Front Left Elevation and Front Right Elevation. See Figure 6-10. A match line indicates the adjoining edges of the elevations. The south side of the building is shown in the Right Side Elevation. All three elevations are drawn to the scale of ³⁄₁₆″ = 1′-0″.

Front Left Elevation, Sheet A2.1

The Front Left Elevation shows the north half of the west side of the condominium. Finished floor heights of 11′-8″ appear along the left side of the drawing. For ease of design and construction, the floor plans for the first, second, and third floors are similar. Windows on each level align vertically since the floor plans are similar. Double-hung, casement, and fixed windows are shown on the elevations. The hinged sides of casement windows are indicated by the apex of the hidden lines.

Figure 6-10. Sheet A2.1 includes the Front Left, Front Right, and Right Side Elevations.

The shingled and copper-covered roof areas indicated on the Roof Plan are shown on the Front Left Elevation. Several details and sections are referenced on the Front Left Elevation and are included on other sheets of the set of prints. Section 1, Sheet 3.2 is included with the set of prints provided with this book.

The exterior finish material for the second and third floors is painted brick, while stone veneer is used as the finish material for the first floor. Stone keystones and window sills are installed above and below the windows, respectively. A stone belt course is included as a decorative element between the first and second floors and to provide a transition between the stone veneer and brick veneer. Exterior chimney surfaces are finished with EIFS.

Front Right Elevation, Sheet A2.1

The Front Right Elevation provides additional information about the materials used for building. Shingle roofing is indicated and the aluminum ridge cap described in Detail 4, Sheet A1.12 is shown. EIFS is indicated as finish material on chimney flues, fourth floor dormer walls, and portions of the walls along the sides of the dormer windows. The second and third floor exterior wall finish is painted brick with stone trim above the single casement windows. Stone keystones and sills are to be installed above and below all double-hung windows, respectively. A stone belt is installed around the perimeter of the building slightly below the second floor elevation. Stone veneer is applied as the finish material to the wood-framed first floor walls.

Decorative molded brackets are installed 2'-0" OC around the soffit of the building. A canvas awning is installed over the main entry doors to provide protection while entering the building during inclement weather. First floor terrace railings and balustrades are manufactured from Fypon™. See Figure 6-11. Fypon is a high-density polymer material that is cast around steel pipes in balusters or posts to provide the desired finish and design. The second and third floor balconies above the first floor terraces are not intended for occupation. Wrought iron railings are

installed around the windows to provide the desired aesthetic appearance. Various notes provide additional references for wall and window sections on other detail drawings from additional drawing sheets.

Downspouts are to be installed at three locations as shown in the Front Right Elevation. Dimensions indicated for downspout locations correspond to the downspout locations shown on Sheet A1.3. The stone belt used as wall finish is to be notched to avoid offsets along the length of the downspout.

Figure 6-11. Balusters and posts are made of a high-density polymer that is cast around steel pipes.

Right Side Elevation, Sheet A2.1

The Right Side Elevation shows the south side of the building, and features the garage entrance, terraces, and the penthouse roof line. Overall wall finish for the south side of the building is painted brick. Casement and fixed windows and doors that lead to the terraces are shown on the Right Side Elevation. Stone sills and soldier header courses of brick are specified for window trim. Stone veneer and a stone belt course, which tie into the stone veneer and stone belt course on the Front Right Elevation, are used as the first floor exterior finish material along the front of the building. Stone sills and stone keystones are indicated as window trim on the west portion of the elevation. EIFS is indicated as finish material on chimney flues, fourth floor dormer walls, and penthouse walls.

A 16′ × 7′ overhead garage door and entry doors to the Trash Room appear on the lower level. Rowlock courses of brick are indicated above the overhead door. Detail 4, Sheet A3.3 and Detail 5, A4.5 (not included with this set of prints) are referenced on the overhead and entry doors, respectively.

The Right Side Elevation shows the inhabitable terraces for the first, second, and third floors. Wrought iron terrace railings and painted wood columns are used to finish the terraces.

Shingle roofing is specified as the roof finish material. The flue caps are painted metal. Copper flashing is installed on top of the chimneys around the flues. Additional copper flashing is installed on the offset roof sections above the Trash Room doors to provide the appearance of a standing-seam copper roof.

A notation in the lower-left corner of the elevation references civil drawings for information regarding the retaining wall. A dry laid limestone retaining wall is to be built along the north side of the driveway to the garage. The individual limestone pieces in a dry laid wall are not bonded together using mortar or adhesives.

SECTION THRU DECKS, SHEET A3.2

Sheet A3.2 contains the Section Thru Decks, which is referenced as Section 1, Sheet A3.2 on Sheets A1.3, A1.11, and A2.1. Refer to the sheets again to visualize the location and direction of sight indicated by the section reference.

Foundation

The building foundation consists of concrete piers, columns, and beams, which provide the central structural supports, as well as 12″ cast-in-place concrete foundation walls that provide structural support around the perimeter of the building. A ¾″ minus crushed limestone base is provided below the 5″ tinted concrete slab. Note the raised areas of the concrete slabs, which provide curbs along the storage lockers. Profiles of the storage locker walls are shown on the section. Four-inch perforated PVC drain tile is laid in 1½″ river gravel along the foundation walls.

Filter fabric is placed over the drain tile to prevent sand or soil from entering the tile.

A 4″ perforated PVC drain tile is installed below the limestone base toward the middle of the slab. Filter fabric is installed over the drain tile. The drain tile conveys storm water to the storm sewer system.

The terraces on the east side of the building are supported by 18″ concrete piers. The first floor terrace, which is at finished grade level, is supported by compacted fill and a minimum of 3′ of 1½″ crushed limestone backfill. A waterproofing material is sprayed on the foundation walls and 4″ perforated PVC tile is installed in the backfill to prevent storm water from entering the building. A downspout drain is also placed in the limestone backfill to convey storm water from garage floor drains to the storm sewer. A 45° layback is indicated for foundation excavation to provide safe working conditions while setting concrete wall forms with existing soil conditions.

Floors 1 through 3

The first floor consists of a cast-in-place concrete floor, which is strengthened with cast-in-place concrete beams over the concrete columns. Voids are cast in the beams to provide room for electrical wiring. Wood trusses spaced 24″ OC support the upper floors of the building. Additional truss information concerning loading capacities, web depth, and spans is shown in details, schedules, and structural drawings (not included in this set of prints). The second, third, and fourth floors are 1-hour fire-rated construction, and have a ¾″ CDX plywood subfloor covered by 1½″ of Elastizell (lightweight concrete).

References for Details 1 through 5, Sheet A4.3 (not included with this set of prints) are shown along the left side of the drawing. Detail 1 describes construction at the intersection of the roof and fourth floor walls. Detail 2 shows construction at the fourth floor roof offset. Detail 3 illustrates construction at the third floor exterior wall. Detail 4 provides a detail of the attachment of the wrought iron railing and the second floor offset. Detail 5 provides information on the first floor balustrade. Rough opening heights along the west wall range from 5'-0⅛" at the fourth floor to 8'-10⅝" at the first floor. The 5'-0⅛" rough opening height accommodates the casement and fixed window combination units in the fourth floor penthouses. The rough openings for the first floor are higher to accommodate the circletop windows. A Majestic Model No. BR42 fireplace is to be installed in the Master Bedroom of each condominium unit on the first, second, and third floors. Each fireplace includes a custom-size mantel and marble trim and plinth block.

In-line framing is utilized from the Garage through the third floor; load-bearing walls for the first, second, and third floors are directly aligned with the concrete beams, columns, and piers in the Garage. See Figure 6-12. Walls on the fourth floor are offset to accommodate the roof line and to maximize the floor space available in the penthouse. A six-panel door is shown on each side of framed openings on the first, second, and third floors. Openings leading from room to room are framed with wooden columns and lowered soffits.

A framed opening appears on the fourth floor elevation. Ceiling heights are indicated and details concerning the crown molding (CM3 and CM4) are provided. Ceilings are framed of 2 × 6 ceiling joists 24" OC supported by 2 × 4 hangers from the roof trusses. The 2 × 4 hangers are spaced a maximum of 6' OC. R-19 FSK insulation is installed in addition to FSK paper applied continuously across the face of the exposed trusses.

Kitchen details are shown to the right of the east load-bearing wall. Base cabinets measure 34½" high and are finished with 1½" granite countertops. Wall cabinets are 3'-6" high, with the tops of the cabinets 8'-0" above the finished floor. A six-panel door is installed between the Kitchen and stairway landing and elevator entrance. The cabinet layout includes wall cabinets with doors, base cabinets with drawers and doors, and a built-in microwave oven. Granite backsplashes measuring 1½" thick by 4" wide extend across the back of the countertop. The refrigerator is not provided in the contract.

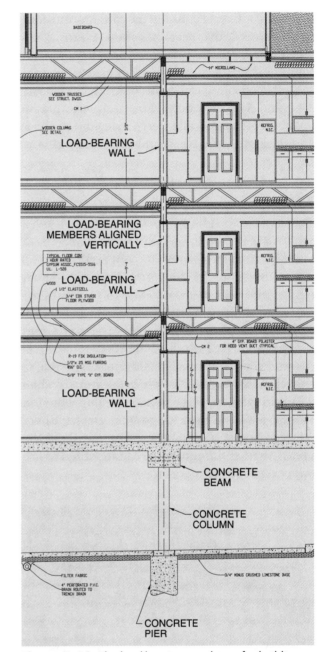

Figure 6-12. The load-bearing members of a building are aligned in in-line framing.

A pilaster finished with gypsum board is built out from the face of the Kitchen soffit above the microwave oven to provide room for the hood vent. This installation is typical throughout the building. A notation also indicates that CM2 crown molding is to be installed in the Kitchen.

The outer corners of the terraces are supported with Permacast™ columns. Permacast columns are manufactured from a fiber-reinforced polymer composite, making the columns durable, weatherproof, and insect-resistant. Plain 12″ diameter Permacast columns are used for first floor columns and 10″ diameter columns are used for second floor columns. Details 6 through 9, Sheets A4.3 and A4.5 provide construction information about the roof and wall intersection, and the floor and deck construction on the first, second, and third floors.

Roof

The Section Thru Decks, Sheet A3.2 provides roof construction details including the proper location of vent slots, insulation, and roof truss and ceiling framing. As shown on Section 6, Sheet A1.12, roof rafters are notched to maintain air passage for proper ventilation of the attic. R-19 FSK insulation is installed between the roof rafters, and the bottom of the roof structure is covered with continuous FSK paper. The roof is sheathed with ¾″ CDX plywood and finished with shingles over 30 lb asphalt-impregnated roofing felt. The Roof Ridge Vent Detail, Sheet A1.12 provides additional information about the prefinished aluminum ridge cap installed at the upper ends of the roof rafters.

Metal ties are used to secure a brick-veneer wall to a backing wall.

Underslung roof trusses are installed to support the flat area of the roof that houses the mechanical equipment. An *underslung truss* is a roof or floor truss that is supported by the top chord. Sleepers are attached to the tops of the trusses to provide the proper roof slope for storm water drainage. The upper surface of the west side of the flat roof is to be 6″ above the east side of the roof so storm water flows toward scuppers along the east side of the roof. A layer of 2½″ ISO 95 rigid foam insulation is placed over the sleepers followed by ¾″ wood fiber insulation. Mineral-surfaced asphalt rolled roofing is applied to the wood fiber insulation on the roof and up the side walls.

DETAIL SECTIONS AND ELEVATIONS, SHEET A4.1

Sheet A4.1 includes three vertical sections through the front wall, a horizontal section through the main entry, and a detail elevation of the main entry. Detail and section references are shown on the Front Left Elevation, Sheet A2.1. Note that features on Sections 1, 2, and 3 align horizontally with features on the elevation. Features on Section 5 align vertically with features on the elevation. Alignment of the sections and elevations assists in reading and interpreting the drawings.

Section 1, Sheet A4.1

Section 1 is a section of the front cornice of the building. The standing-seam copper roof at the cornice projects out from the shingled portion of the roof. A 6″ aluminum gutter is supported by a ¾″ × 11¼″ (1 × 12) wood gutter board, also known as a finish fascia board. Fiber-reinforced polymer trim members comprise the remainder of the cornice trim. Polymer trim members are available in a variety of sizes and designs, and are attached to a building with mastic and mechanical fasteners, such as screws or nails, as specified by the manufacturer. See Figure 6-13. The stone belt, brick, and concrete masonry units above the window opening are supported by a 4″ × 5″ × 5/16″ steel angle lintel. The rough opening height for Type F windows is 4'-7¹⁄₁₆". A stone arch, which projects ½" from the face of the wall, is installed along the upper portion of the window.

Section 2, Sheet A4.1

Section 2 shows construction details of the window sill and wall finish at the third floor. A 3" stone sill is installed as exterior window trim at the bottoms of the windows. The stone sill is sloped ³⁄₈" away from the window to allow proper water drainage. The 4" concrete masonry unit backing and painted brick veneer are supported by two galvanized 4" × 5" × ⁵⁄₁₆" steel angles. The overall wall thickness including the brick veneer, CMU backing, studs, and interior finish material is 1'-4".

A two-piece decorative stone jack arch projects ½" from the face of the wall. The stone keystone, which fits between the stone jack arches, projects 1" from the face of the wall.

Natural stone is used as a veneer or facing on a building. The physical, structural, and aesthetic qualities must be considered when selecting stone.

Type E windows are custom fixed-sash windows. A 3'-4" wide by 9'-9³⁄₁₆" high masonry opening is required for Type E windows. Wood casing around the second floor windows is 5½" wide.

Section 3, Sheet A4.1

Section 3 is a detail section through the main entry of the building. The section is referenced on the Front Left Elevation, Sheet A2.1. The header above the entry door includes a concrete masonry unit (CMU) lintel reinforced with two #5 rebar and filled with concrete. Two courses of 12" CMUs are laid on top of the lintel. A stone belt is laid on top of the CMU courses and the face of the wall above is finished with painted brick. The face of the CMU lintel and 12" CMU wall is finished with the stone keystone, which is projected ¾", and stone trim.

The wall shown in Section 3, Sheet A4.1 is framed with 2 × 6s and insulated with batt insulation as shown in Section 5, Sheet A4.1. Window and door headers are parallel strand lumber (PSL) or laminated veneer lumber (LVL), which provide greater dimensional stability than dimension lumber. More information regarding the headers is included on the structural drawings.

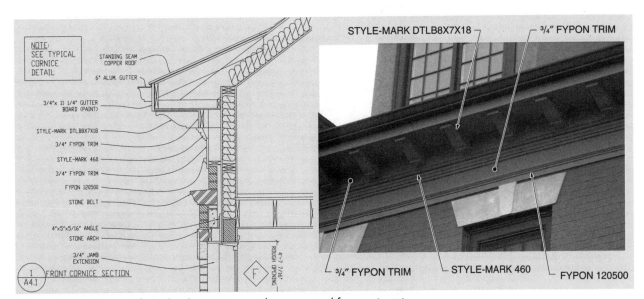

Figure 6-13. Fiber-reinforced polymer trim members are used for cornice trim.

The main entry canopy is attached to the stone trim per the manufacturer specifications. The canopy is constructed of a framework of 1″ welded steel tubing that divides the 180° canopy into nine segments. The framework is covered with Sunbrella™ fabric. A 2¼″ × 3′-4″ × 6′-8″ Honduras mahogany entry door is installed in a wood door frame. The door is a 15-light beveled tempered glass door with brass muntins, a 12″ high polished brass kickplate, and a mortised sweep at the bottom. The door is composed of a bottom rail that is 1′-4″ high, a 4′-8″ section comprised of five rows of beveled tempered glass lights with brass muntins, and an 8″ high top rail. Door stiles are 5½″ wide. A circletop piece of art glass with brass beading is installed above the entry door. The door and circletop art glass are enclosed with mahogany casing. Detail 5, Sheet A4.1 provides additional information about the main entry construction.

The base of the main entry is placed directly over the area of the west foundation wall, which is widened to 1′-8″ to support the entry. The concrete slab for the first floor rests on 8″ of the foundation wall. A 6″ thick by 1′-4″ wide stone sill with ½″ slope is grouted in place as a base for the entry. An 8″ wide ADA-compliant bronze saddle is used as a threshold between the stone sill and the concrete first floor slab. Concrete hangers support and tie the concrete walk to the foundation and support the stone sill to prevent settling. The concrete hangers are tied to the foundation wall using rebar and project from the face of the wall. Additional information concerning the specific design of the concrete hangers is shown on the structural plans.

Detail 4, Sheet A4.1

Detail 4 is an elevation of the front entry from the finished grade to the lower edge of the roof. The detail provides a significant amount of information regarding the materials to be used for the main entry. See Figure 6-14. Three decorative fixed windows are to be installed on the third floor. The Type F windows are 1′-1″ wide, with the middle window centered directly over the main entry door. The two outer windows are installed 11⅝″ from the middle window. The windows are trimmed with stone arches that project ½″ and stone sills. See Figure 6-15.

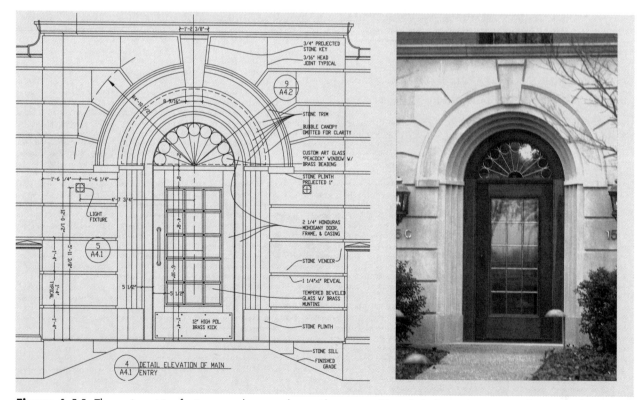

Figure 6-14. The main entries feature a mahogany door with tempered beveled glass, a custom circletop art glass window with brass beading, and stone trim with a stone keystone projected ¾″ from the surface.

Figure 6-15. Three decorative fixed windows, complete with stone arches and sills, are centered directly over the main entry doors.

One Type E custom fixed-sash window is to be installed on the second floor. The Type E window is installed in a 3'-4" × 9'-9⁹⁄₁₆" masonry opening. A 5½" molded casing is to be installed around the window. The top of the window is to be finished with two stone jack arches that project ½" and a stone keystone that projects 1" from the wall face. Section 2, Sheet A4.1 provides additional information about the fixed-sash window opening.

A 6" wide stone belt is installed along the front and sides of the building to provide a transition from the painted brick veneer to the stone veneer. The stone veneer and stone keystone at the top of the main entry door extend to the bottom edge of the stone belt.

The bubble canopy, which is attached to the stone trim, is omitted from Detail 4 to fully show the entry door detail. The exterior face of the first floor is finished with 1'-3" wide stone veneer with a 1¼" × 1" reveal. Layout of the stone and stone trim around the main entry door is based on a point at the center of the top casing of the door and 6'-10" above the first floor sill. Edges of stone veneer courses are angled toward the top of the circular stone trim, forming an arch with a radius of 4'-10½" to the outer edge. Full courses of stone veneer continue to the edges of the stone trim arch. A tapered stone keystone measuring 8⁹⁄₁₆" at the base and 1'-2⅜" at the top is centered above the door and window and projects ¾" from the wall face. A ³⁄₁₆" head joint is placed on both sides of the keystone.

A 2¼" × 3'-4" × 6'-8" swinging door with tempered beveled glass and brass muntins is installed in the entry. A custom art glass window with brass beading is installed above the main entry door. Additional information about the main entry arch is shown in Section 9, Sheet A4.2.

Light fixtures are to be installed on both sides of the main entry door. The lights are located 4'-7¾" from the door opening centerline and 5'-11⅜" above the first floor sill.

Section 5, Sheet A4.1

Section 5 provides additional information about the stone trim at the main entry. The setbacks and offsets of the stone trim members along the sides and top of the door are noted. Setbacks range from 3⁵⁄₁₆" to 4¹³⁄₁₆"; offsets range from 2½" to 4". A 5½" wide mahogany wood trim member extends along each side of the entry door (H03) and above the art glass window. Section 5 shows the CMU and stone veneer exterior wall, air space, wood-framed wall with exterior sheathing, insulation, and interior gypsum board. The overall thickness of the front wall at the main entry door is 1'-10½".

WALL AND WINDOW DETAILS, SHEET A4.2

Sheet 4.2 contains a variety of sections, details, and elevations that are referenced on other sheets in the set of prints including the exterior elevations, Sheet A2.1, and Detail 4, Sheet A4.1. Details 1, 2, 3, and 4 are aligned vertically to allow the prints to be more easily visualized in relation to each other, and are referenced from Details 5 and 10, Sheet A4.2.

Detail 1, Sheet A4.2

Detail 1 is a horizontal section looking down through the stone veneer corner and the window jamb. The wood-framed wall is constructed of 2 × 6 framing members, which are covered on the exterior side with plywood sheathing. Tyvek™ housewrap is used to cover the plywood sheathing to minimize air infiltration through the walls. A 4" concrete block and stone veneer wall is laid up and reinforced with 1" × ¼" galvanized anchors spaced 16″ OC both ways. The anchors are anchored to the plywood sheathing, extend through the 4″ concrete block, and are embedded in the mortar joints of the stone veneer wall. An air space is provided between the housewrap and concrete block to provide additional insulation and to prevent thermal transfer.

The 2″ stone veneer has shiplap joints along the upper and lower edges to secure together the edges of the veneer. The corner pieces of stone veneer receive a quirk mitre at the outside corners. A *quirk mitre* is a type of joint used at the outside corners of adjoining members in which the acute miter corners are trimmed flat at the ends to provide relief for the joint and prevent the ends from splitting.

Window trim member details are also given. A 1 × 8 and 2 × 4 are fastened to the wall sheathing and concrete block wall, respectively, to be used as a base for the wood trim members. Two high-density polymer trim members (Fypon 126200 and Style-Mark 226) are fastened in the position shown on the detail. Joints along the trim members are to be caulked to waterproof them.

Fypon does not absorb moisture, warp, or crack. However, it will expand and contract with temperature changes.

Detail 2, Sheet A4.2

Detail 2 is a vertical section through the stone belt course that provides specific dimensions for the stone members that form the belt course around the building. The stone belt course provides transition between the stone veneer and brick veneer exterior finishes. Four-inch concrete block are laid up from the foundation wall, and stone veneer is installed along the lower portion of the wall. A detailed cut stone belt with a sloping upper surface is installed at the top of the 4″ concrete block wall, with the lower edge of the stone sill overlapping the upper edge of the stone veneer. An undercut and a drip on the underside of the sill prevent water from flowing back against the wall surface. Painted brick veneer is installed above the stone belt.

A notation along the interior side of the wall indicates that the gypsum board ceiling is suspended from 25 ga × ½″ resilient furring channels. Resilient furring channels reduce sound transmission between adjoining floors. See Figure 6-16.

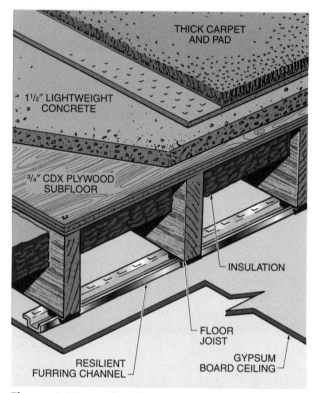

Figure 6-16. Resilient furring channels are fastened to the bottoms of floor joists to reduce sound transmission between adjoining floors.

Detail 3, Sheet A4.2

Detail 3 provides a view through the stone veneer and 4″ concrete block wall. Details 2 and 3 show the continuation of the stonework and wall framing. Galvanized steel anchors used to tie together the wood-framed and stone-veneer walls are also shown.

R-19 blanket insulation is installed in the wood-framed walls, and the walls are finished with ⅝″ gypsum board. Aquaseal™ flashing is provided near the bottom of the first floor wall to divert moisture away from the wood-framed wall and toward weep holes in the stone veneer. Aquaseal flashing is a self-adhesive flashing tape that provides a durable weatherproof bond.

Detail 4, Sheet A4.2

A 4½″ thick by 1′-3½″ wide stone base is grouted solid into place at the bottom of the stone veneer wall. A 4″ shoulder must be formed in the foundation wall to accept the stone base. The base stone supports the 4″ concrete block and 2½″ stone veneer.

Detail 5, Sheet A4.2

The detail elevation shown on Detail 5 includes a partial view of the third floor window, and complete views of the first and second floor windows. Second and third floor windows are identical windows, with manufacturer number 2836-1. The first floor window is manufacturer number 3632-1. The first floor double-hung window and circletop window are identified on the window schedule as U and Z, respectively.

Wood and stone trim surround the double-hung and circletop windows. A 5½″ mahogany casing is installed along the sides of the window and continues up and around the circletop window. A 2″ thick stone haunch is installed at the top of the sixth course of stone veneer and a 6¹¹⁄₁₆″ wide stone arch is installed around the wood casing. A *haunch* is a trim member installed at the termination of an arch. Edges of stone veneer courses are angled toward the top of the stone arch, expanding the arch with a radius of 3′-3¼″ to the outer edge. A stone keystone, which is 6″ wide at the bottom and 10″ wide at the top and projects 1″, is centered above the wood casing arch. Detail 1, Sheet A4.2, described earlier, provides additional information about the windows and trim.

Detail 6, Sheet A4.2

Detail 6 is referenced on Detail 5, Sheet A4.2. Detail 6 is a detail section through the first floor window arch molding, and includes dimensions for the stone arch molding. The molding is 1⅜″ thick along the window opening and increases in thickness to 2½″ at the outer edges. Additional dimensions are provided for the stone fabrication. Polymer and wood trim members are used

to finish the window. Note where caulking must be applied to ensure that storm water does not enter the building.

Detail 8, Sheet A4.2

Detail 8 is a section taken through the center of the window shown in Detail 5, and is aligned horizontally with Detail 5 to assist in reading the section. The window header, which is parallel strand lumber (PSL) or laminated veneer lumber (LVL), is installed 8′-8½″ above the finished floor. The top of the double-hung window is 6′-11⁵⁄₁₆″ above the finished floor and the top of the circletop window is 1′-8¹¹⁄₁₆″ above the double-hung window, providing a ½″ gap for fitting and shimming.

The 2″ thick stone base is grouted solid into a recess formed in the foundation wall and a set-back in the concrete floor. A 4″ concrete block is set in position on top of the stone base and a shiplapped piece of stone veneer is applied to the face of the block. A 2¾″ thick by 8½″ wide window sill is supported by the block and stone structure. Aquaseal flashing is installed along the upper edge of the stone base. Additional information concerning the stone veneer, wall framing, and insulation is provided on the structural drawings.

Detail 9, Sheet A4.2

Detail 9 is a detail section through the main entry arch, and includes detailed information for proper fabrication of the stone trim members above the main entry door. Detail 9 is referenced on Detail 4, Sheet A4.1. When the trim members are properly fabricated, Detail 9 is then used for proper installation by providing specific offsets and setbacks. Specific dimensions for the stone sill/belt are shown on Detail 1, Sheet A00 (not included in this set of prints).

A wood-framed structural wall with a header, studs, plates, and insulation is shown along the right side of Detail 9. Information regarding construction of the wood-framed wall is included on the structural drawings. A concrete block lintel with two rebar and filled with concrete is installed above the stone arch as a header for the two 12″ concrete blocks above. The concrete block structure provides a base for the stone sill/belt and stone veneer.

Detail 10, Sheet A4.2

Detail 10 is a section through the first floor exterior stone veneer wall. Each stone veneer course is 1'-4" high with shiplapped top and bottom edges to minimize air and water infiltration. The 1'-4" dimensions also are referenced when installing wall ties. Details 2, 3, and 4, Sheet A4.2 are referenced on Detail 10. Detail 10 can serve as a typical wall section for the first floor showing the interior room finish, wall framing, fireblocking, insulation, exterior sheathing, CMU, and stone veneer. The wood-framed wall is composed of 2 × 6 studs with a single bottom plate that is grouted into place, a double top plate, and fireblocks at the bottom of the floor trusses and at the midpoint of the wall. A *fireblock* is a wood member nailed between studs, joists, or trusses to restrict air movement and reduce the spread of fire within walls. The crown molding is referred to in the interior finish schedule.

The aluminum downspouts are fastened tight against the stone veneer. The downspouts terminate at a 3" × 4" PVC downspout shoe, which provides a transition from a rectangular downspout to the 4" diameter PVC drainage pipe. The 4" diameter PVC pipe is anchored to the foundation wall with expansion anchors set into the face of the wall.

STAIRWAY DETAILS, SHEET A5.1

Sheet A5.1 includes a variety of details regarding the stairways throughout the condominium. Plan views, elevations, and sections are used to describe the stairway construction. The stairway designs comply with building codes for multifamily dwellings in effect in the jurisdiction.

Detail 1, Sheet A5.1

A steeply sloped ship's ladder is constructed of 1 × 10 yellow pine treads mortised into 2 × 10 yellow pine stringers. The ship's ladder is installed in the fourth floor attic and provides access to the roof hatch shown on the Roof Plan, Sheet A1.12. The mortise depth for each tread is ¾". Unit rise is 10" and unit run is 6". The surface of each tread receives a 4" wide strip of nonskid material. The lower surface of the stringers is finished with ½" A-C grade birch plywood and ⅝" gypsum board. The handrail is made of oak and supported by steel brackets 4' OC attached to the adjoining wall. All wood members have a varnish finish.

Detail 2, Sheet A5.1

Detail 2 is a section through the rear stairway. The rear stairway is constructed of four 2 × 12 stringers (carriages) and 1" yellow pine treads. The stairway has an 11" unit run and a 7" unit rise, with a ½" nosing. A 1 × 12 finish stringer is installed on each side of the stair treads along the walls. Handrail brackets are supported by 1 × 6 blocking installed between the studs in the wood-framed walls. A 1¾" diameter oak handrail, similar to that used on the ship's ladder, is used for the rear stairs.

Detail 3, Sheet A5.1

Detail 3 is a plan view of the front stairway at the second floor landing. Detail 3 is referenced on Detail 6, Sheet A5.1. The unit run for the stairway is 11". Hidden lines indicate the stair risers. An Arcway A6700 railing is specified for the enclosed side of the stairway. The width of the rough framing for the stairs is 3'-8" and the stair return is 1'-6¼". An Arcway A-4315P newel post and A-6700 railing are specified for the open side of the stairway and stair return. Detail 5, Sheet A5.1 provides additional information about this portion of the stairway.

Detail 4, Sheet A5.1

Detail 4 is a continuation of the front stairway shown in Detail 3 and shows the stairway at the first floor level. Details 3 and 4 are aligned to assist in visualizing the details. The bottom tread of the stairway is a red oak bullnose tread that extends below the bottom newel post and custom volute. The center of the newel post and volute, which is used in the layout of the balusters, is 3½" from the centerline of the stairway and 6" from the front edge of the tread. Volute baluster spacing and angles are noted on the detail. Detail 7, Sheet A5.1 provides additional information about this portion of the stairway.

Detail 5, Sheet A5.1

Detail 5 is a section taken through the front stairway at the second floor and provides additional construction information for this portion of the stairway. Detail 5 is referenced in Details 3 and 6, Sheet A5.1. A 2 × 12 stringer is installed at the open side of the stairway to support the balusters and handrail. A double 2 × 12 is framed on the open side of the 3'-8" wide landing area, with a cutout stringer set between the 2 × 12s.

The newel post on the open side of the stairway is anchored with ½" × 4" lag bolts spaced 22" OC and staggered up and down. The handrail height at floor level is 3'-6". Recessed light fixtures are centered and installed between the middle stairway stringers.

Additional stair trim members including handrail members, balusters, and stringer finishes are identified with manufacturer names and code numbers. The stair trim members are prefabricated at a shop specializing in stair construction, primed for a paint finish coat, and delivered to the job site as sections and individual pieces to allow for ease of installation.

Gypsum board is installed along the bottoms of the 2 × 12 stair stringers. CM2 crown molding is installed along the intersection with the wall on both sides of the stairway. A chair rail is to be installed on both stairway walls. A ¾" thick by 3½" square plinth block is used to terminate the chair rail where it abuts the handrail brackets. Handrail brackets are placed 4'-0" OC.

Detail 6, Sheet A5.1

Detail 6 is a section taken through the front stairway at the second floor level. Details 3 and 5, Sheet A5.1 are indicated on Detail 6 and should be referred to when reviewing Detail 6. Information similar to that indicated on Detail 5 is also included on Detail 6. Additional features of Detail 6 include the metal hangers used to attach the stairway stringers to the landing, crown molding installed under the stairway soffit, and ¾" CDX tongue-and-groove plywood used as a base for the Elastizell lightweight concrete flooring. The typical height from the finished floor to the top edge of the chair rail is 2'-9½". Railings around stairway landings are 3'-6" high.

Detail 7, Sheet A5.1

The primary feature of Detail 7 is the attachment of the stairway stringers to the concrete floor. A short piece of 2 × 4 is anchored to the concrete floor along the outside stringers using ½" expansion bolts. The stringers are then nailed or screwed to the 2 × 4s. See Figure 6-17. The starting tread and riser are red oak and receive a varnish finish; the remainder of the treads and risers are vertical grained yellow pine. The typical vertical distance from the nosing of each tread to the top of the handrail is 3'-0". Detail 4, Sheet A5.1 is referenced on Detail 7.

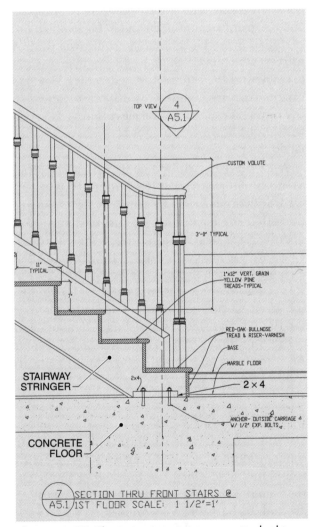

Figure 6-17. The stairway stringers are attached to a 2 × 4 anchored to the floor using ½" expansion bolts.

BATHROOM AND POWDER ROOM ELEVATIONS, SHEET A5.4

Sheet A5.4 includes a variety of interior elevations of the bathrooms and powder rooms throughout the building. Many of the condominium units have different bathroom layouts and fixtures; therefore, multiple elevations are required. Architectural Notes in the lower-right corner provide additional finish information for the bathrooms and powder rooms.

Elevation 1, Sheet A5.4

The North Wall and South Wall elevations of the Master Bathroom in Unit "A" are shown in Elevation 1. Two 36" wide by 21" deep cabinets are installed along the south wall with a drawer unit between them. The area below the cabinets is open. A granite countertop and 4" backsplash are installed over the cabinets and drawer unit. A mirror, which is ¼" thick by 48" high, spans the area behind the countertop and vanity. Beveled mirror trim in 2" and 3" widths is fastened to the mirror as shown on the elevation. A 21" wide soffit built down to a height of 8' above the finished floor is shown.

A 72" long by 36" wide bathtub is installed along the north wall of the Master Bathroom. Cabinets measuring 15" wide by 21" deep are installed on both ends of the bathtub, and granite tops are installed over the cabinets. Ceramic tile measuring 12" × 12" are installed as a backsplash around the bathtub. A 2'-8" × 7'-1" custom shower is installed in the adjoining area of the bathroom. The wall opening for the shower door is 8'-0" high. The overall ceiling height is 9'-4". Details 4 and 5, Sheet A5.5 provide additional information regarding shower construction.

Detail 2, Sheet A5.4

Detail 2 is an elevation of Bath 2 in the unit "A" condominium unit. A 66" long by 36" wide bathtub is installed along the far wall of the bathroom and 12" × 12" ceramic tile are installed around the bathtub. A 45" wide by 21" deep vanity with a cultured marble countertop and 4" backsplash are installed next to the bathtub. A

water closet is installed next to the vanity. A paper holder is installed 18" above the finished floor. A medicine cabinet is installed along the adjacent wall with the bottom set 48" above the finished floor. The crown molding is designated CM3.

Detail 3, Sheet A5.4

Condominium units "B" and "C" have the same configurations for the Master Bath and Bath 2. The North Wall Elevation of unit "C" is similar to the right side of the South Wall Elevation in Detail 1, Sheet A5.4. The elevation of the Master Bath for unit "B" is a mirror image of the elevation for unit "C."

The South Wall Elevation shows a six-panel swinging door, a 60" × 42" bathtub, and a custom shower. A backsplash around the bathtub is created using one course of 12" × 12" ceramic tile that is finished with a wood cap. Details 4 and 5, Sheet A5.5 provide additional information regarding shower construction.

Detail 4, Sheet A5.4

Detail 4 is an elevation of Bath 2 in condominium units "B" and "C." A 36" wide by 21" deep vanity with a cultured marble countertop and backsplash is installed next to the water closet. A 66" × 36" bathtub is installed against the north wall and is finished with 12" × 12" ceramic tile to a height of 96".

Detail 5, Sheet A5.4

Detail 5 is an elevation of a typical powder room, which could be installed in several of the individual condominium units depending on the particular floor plan. The floor-mounted vanity has short legs and feet to give the vanity more of a furniture appearance. Baseboard is installed on the wall prior to installing the vanity. A 48" high plate glass mirror is installed above the vanity. An 18" wide towel bar is installed on the adjacent wall at the toilet area 54" above the finished floor. The paper holder is installed 18" above the finished floor. A 21" wide soffit is built to a height of 8'-0" above the finished floor. The full ceiling height is 9'-4". CM3 crown molding is also to be installed in the Powder Room.

Detail 6, Sheet A5.4

Detail 6 is an elevation of the Master Bath for condominium unit "D," and includes elevations for the north wall and the south wall. The vanity and countertop area of the Master Bath in unit "D" is similar to the vanity and countertop area in the Master Bath of unit "A." The water closet in unit "D" is installed against an angled wall in the Master Bath. The South Wall Elevation shows a shower on the left, a 72″ × 36″ tub in the middle, and a three-panel door leading to a linen closet on the right.

Details 7 and 8, Sheet A5.4

The elevations shown in Details 7 and 8 are similar in layout except for the bathtub shown in the Bath 2 Elevation and the shower shown in the Powder Room Elevation. A 36″ × 21″ vanity is installed in Bath 2 and the Powder Room. A cultured marble countertop and backsplash are installed in Bath 2 and a granite countertop and backsplash are installed in the Powder Room. Symbols representing the plumbing fixtures, such as the shower nozzle and hand mixing valve, are shown.

Detail 9, Sheet A5.4

Detail 9 includes the west wall elevations of Master Bath 1 and Master Bath 2 in the north and south penthouses. Both baths have larger cabinets than the other condominium units, including granite countertops and backsplashes. A 42″ × 21″ vanity is installed in Master Bath 1, with an area on the left side open to the wall. Information about the custom shower is provided in Details 4 and 5, Sheet 5.5.

A 45″ × 21″ vanity with granite countertop and backsplash is installed in Master Bath 2. A six-panel door is shown to the right of the vanity.

Detail 10, Sheet A5.4

The vanity in Bath 3 of the penthouses is the widest bathroom cabinet in the building, measuring 60″ wide. The overall ceiling height is 9′. A 21″ wide soffit is constructed along the east wall, with the bottom of the soffit 8′ above the finished floor. CM3 crown molding is to be installed along the ceiling.

Name _____   Date _____

True-False

T F **1.** Isolation joints pass completely through the thickness of a concrete slab.

T F **2.** FSK insulation is a type of spray-on foam insulation.

T F **3.** The individual stones in a dry laid limestone wall are bonded together with mortar.

T F **4.** Polymer trim members are attached to a building using mastic and mechanical fasteners.

T F **5.** Cant strips minimize the angle over which roofing material is applied to prevent cracking or breakage of roll roofing material.

T F **6.** The central portion of a tray ceiling is constructed at the same pitch as the roof rafters.

T F **7.** The title block provides general information about the set of prints including the name of the architect.

T F **8.** The letter "E" in a title block on a set of prints denotes engineering drawings.

T F **9.** A fireblock is installed between studs, joists, or trusses to restrict air movement and reduce the spread of fire within the walls.

T F **10.** Plan North is based on the exact compass bearing of the job site.

Multiple Choice

_____ **1.** A(n) ___ truss is a roof or floor truss that is supported by the top chord.
   A. top loaded
   B. upper type
   C. underslung
   D. horizontal

_____ **2.** A ___ is a trim member installed at the termination of an arch.
   A. corbel
   B. soldier
   C. quoin
   D. haunch

235

_____ **3.** The abbreviation "NIC" means ___.
  A. National Insulation Code
  B. not included in the contract
  C. notching in concrete
  D. near inside center

_____ **4.** A(n) ___ line is an aligning mark on a print that is used when a drawing is too large to be contained on one sheet.
  A. dimension
  B. match
  C. section
  D. extension

_____ **5.** A cant strip is ___ in cross section.
  A. square
  B. rectangular
  C. triangular
  D. oval

Completion

_____ **1.** A(n) ___ mitre is a type of joint used at the outside corners of adjoining members in which the corners are trimmed flat at the ends to prevent the ends from splitting.

_____ **2.** A(n) ___ is an enclosure in a structure that allows for the placement of wiring and piping for plumbing, mechanical, and electrical systems.

_____ **3.** The ___ on doors and walls indicates the amount of time these building components can withstand fire without structural failure.

_____ **4.** The abbreviation "PSL" represents parallel ___ lumber.

_____ **5.** Isolation joints are also known as ___ joints.

_____ **6.** An undercut and a(n) ___ on the underside of a sill prevent water from flowing back against the wall surface.

_____ **7.** When installed along the bottom edges of floor joists, resilient furring ___ reduce sound transmission between adjoining floors.

_____ **8.** A(n) ___ door is a door that swings in two directions.

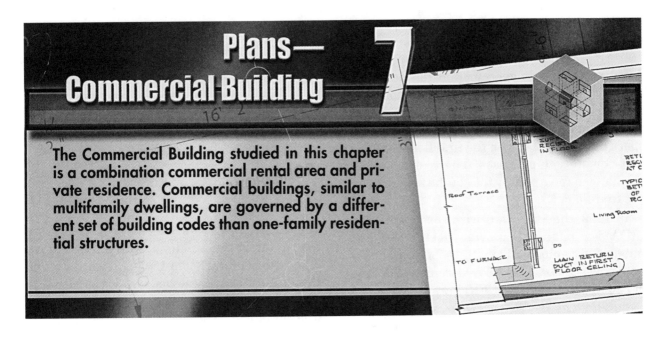

Plans— Commercial Building 7

The Commercial Building studied in this chapter is a combination commercial rental area and private residence. Commercial buildings, similar to multifamily dwellings, are governed by a different set of building codes than one-family residential structures.

DESIGN

For the combination commercial and residential building discussed in this chapter, the architect was commissioned to design a commercial building on a narrow lot with the following general requirements:

- The first floor is to be designed for commercial rental. It must be adaptable to suit the needs of different types of businesses, and must comply with the American with Disabilities Act (ADA) guidelines.
- The foundation will be a slab-on-grade with the outside edges of the slab placed on short rim walls.
- The second floor is to be an apartment with private front and rear entrances. The second floor should be the equivalent of a five-room apartment with the option of combining the living and dining areas. The living room shall be at the rear of the structure, opening onto a roof terrace.
- Heating is to be forced warm air.

The prints, Sheets A-1, A-2, and A-3, represent the final solution that was developed by the architect and accepted by the client.

The commercial rental area and apartment are well planned within the limitations that the lot is narrow and the two side walls have no openings except for the kitchen window. The longitudinal section, designated Section 1-1, shows many construction features including the stairway arrangement. The prints include many details showing a variety of construction and building features.

The Front Elevation, Sheet A-2, is laid out as a symmetrical arrangement of doors and windows, with redwood siding between the openings. As shown in the First Floor Plan, Sheet A-1, the brick walls and roof soffit extend beyond the face of the front wall to allow the storefront to be set back from the sidewalk.

A set screw connector joins a box and conduit in an electrical system.

The First Floor Plan, Sheet A-1, shows the large rectangular space for commercial use. The rear wall has an exterior door and an overhead door that provides a wide opening for merchandise or equipment. Although not open to the commercial area, the stairways for the apartment are shown and dimensions are provided. The space under the stairs on the first floor is available for storage purposes. The restroom and mechanical room occupy the southeast corner of the first floor.

In 1992, the Americans with Disabilities Act (ADA) was enacted to provide greater access to public and commercial buildings for individuals with physical disabilities. The document, 28 Code of Federal Regulations (CFR) Part 36—*Nondiscrimination on the Basis of Disability by Public Accommodations and in Commercial Facilities,* establishes guidelines for accessibility to places of public accommodation and commercial facilities by individuals with disabilities. The guidelines are to be applied during the design, construction, and alteration of public buildings and commercial facilities. The International Code Council (ICC) in conjunction with the American National Standards Institute (ANSI) has developed illustrations and explanatory text based on the guidelines, published in ICC/ANSI A117.1—*Accessible and Usable Buildings and Facilities.* The restroom shown on the First Floor Plan, Sheet A-1, is accessible for individuals with physical disabilities.

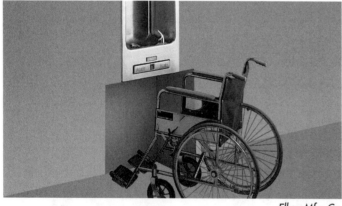

Elkay Mfg. Co.

Greater access to public and commercial buildings is mandated in 28 CFR Part 36—Nondiscrimination on the Basis of Disability by Public Accommodations and in Commercial Facilities.

While restroom and fixture design standards were included in the first edition of the ICC/ANSI A117.1 standard, wheelchair bathroom standards for residences were not included until the 1981 edition.

The Second Floor Plan, Sheet A-1, shows two bedrooms facing the street and the Dining Room-Living Room area at the rear of the second floor. The Kitchen, Bath, and closets are placed across the center of the building. Both stairways ascend to the Dining Room-Living Room area. The Dining Room-Living Room area is connected to the bedrooms by the hallway, which is flanked by a closet wall. The compact Kitchen is located adjacent to the Dining Room. Light and ventilation are provided for the Dining Room-Living Room area by a window wall to the south. A roof terrace provides for outdoor access and is partially protected by the projecting roof.

The Rear Elevation, Sheet A-2, provides information about window and door openings for both levels and shows the exterior of the stair tower and chimney. Section 1-1, Sheet A-2, is a longitudinal section. The First Floor Plan, Sheet A-1, shows that the cutting plane is parallel to and near the east wall, passing through the front stair hallway, the commercial area, the restroom, and the mechanical room. The Second Floor Plan, Sheet A-1, shows the cutting plane passing through Bedroom 2, the linen closet over the stairs, the Living Room, and the Roof Terrace. The door shown on the Roof Terrace provides access to a Storage area.

Rear Stair Section 2-2, Sheet A-2, is taken through the rear stairwell near the west wall. Rear Stair Section 2-2 combined with Section 1-1 shows foundation and footing construction and provides information regarding the steel, wood, and brick structure. The stairway arrangement is shown in both sections. The stairway arrangement required a careful study of adequate headroom and resulted in sloped soffits over the stairways. The manner in which the roof projects over the Roof Terrace is shown in Section 1-1, Sheet A-2.

Sheet A-3 contains the Plot Plan that provides lot and building dimensions and construction details for the Commercial Building. Detail 1 (Typ Foot'g Det—East & West Walls), Sheet A-3, provides information about the special footings under the east and west foundation walls. Rebar in the footings and foundation wall and welded wire reinforcement in the floor are shown.

Detail 2 (Wall Section Thru Front Door and Wall), Sheet A-3, is a section through the front wall from the first floor to the roof taken at a point passing through one of the front doors. Detail 2 shows steel members, rough wood members, wall and floor finish, trim members, and roof details.

Detail 3 (Front Window Det), Sheet A-3, is a section taken through the front windows of the commercial rental area and provides information needed to prepare the window opening, set the frame, and install the glass.

Detail 4 (Typ Roof Bm Framing), Sheet A-3, shows the rough construction used to support the roof members. Roof beam framing occurs at the two beam locations shown in Section 1-1, Sheet A-2.

Detail 5 (Typ Fascia Front & Rear), Sheet A-3, shows information about supporting the ends of roof joists over the front of the building with a steel channel. Detail 5 also provides information about the fascia and soffit.

Detail 6 (Typ Bearing Det at Ends of Fascia & Outer Walls), Sheet A-3, shows the steel channel anchoring in the brick walls.

Detail 7 (Detail at Door to Roof Deck), Sheet A-3, indicates how the wall is supported and shows the construction details to compensate for the difference in floor heights at the door to the roof deck.

Detail 8 (Rear Window Details), Sheet A-3, describes the windows in the rear wall at the Dining Room-Living Room area. Detail 9 (Soffit Detail), Sheet A-3, identifies the ducts that run in the ceiling of the commercial rental space to supply heat to the second floor and provide for the return of cold air. The First Floor Plan, Sheet A-1, shows the supply air duct along the west wall and the return air duct along the east wall.

Three small-scale interior elevations are shown on Sheet A-2. The Kitchen Elevations show the cabinet arrangement, soffit, and wall finish in the Kitchen. The East Bath Elevation indicates the placement of the Bathroom fixtures and wall finish in the Bathroom.

Sioux Chief Manufacturing Company, Inc.
Elevations indicate the location of bathroom fixtures for which water supply and waste piping is provided.

CONCRETE WORK

Plan views of the foundation wall and footings were not included in the set of prints because the building is rectangular and has a simple slab-on-grade foundation. The only unique challenge is that the building is built on the east and west property lines, which prevents centering the foundation wall on the footing. See Detail 1, Sheet A-3, and Front Elevation, Sheet A-2. The foundation wall and footing dimensions are shown on Section 1-1, Sheet A-2. The foundation wall extends approximately 3″ above grade. The hidden lines for the foundation in Section 1-1, Sheet A-2, and also on the Front and Rear Elevations indicate the footing and foundation wall. A concrete post and footing is placed under the Lally column at the front stairway hallway and is shown on Section 1-1, Sheet A-2, and on the First Floor Plan, Sheet A-1.

Rebar increases the tensile strength of concrete. The rebar arrangement ties together the foundation footings, walls, and slab. See Figure 7-1. Rebar for the foundation wall and footing are #4 and #5. To determine the actual rebar diameter, multiply the number by ⅛″. For example, #4 rebar are actually ½″ diameter, while #5 rebar are actually ⅝″ diameter (4 × ⅛″ = ⁴⁄₈″ or ½″; 5 × ⅛″ = ⅝″). The designation #4 @ 15″ indicates a ½″ rebar spaced at 15″. The designation 2 #5 CONT indicates two ⅝″ rebar running continuously through the foundation wall. The reinforcing steel in the floor is made of wire welded in a square or rectangular pattern. The notation 6 × 6—W2.9 × W2.9 WWR indicates welded wire reinforcement with 6″ wire spacing using wire with a .029 sq in. cross-sectional area.

ROUGH STRUCTURE

The rough supporting structure includes brick and concrete masonry unit walls on the east, west, and south sides and a frame wall on the north side. Steel members, including wide-flange beams and channels, are placed at right angles to the east and west walls. Wood joists run at right angles to the steel members.

Exterior Walls

Information about the masonry is indicated at several places on the prints. The First and Second Floor Plans, Sheet A-1, show that brick is used and backed up by concrete masonry units. The brick is returned into openings at the doors at the rear to provide a finished appearance. Solid face brick is used at the front part of the side walls since the brick project under and beyond the storefront. As shown in Section 1-1, Sheet A-2, building (common) brick is used for the parapet. A *parapet* is a low protective wall at the edge of a balcony or roof. The parapet of the Commercial Building extends 2′-10″ above the second floor steel beams. The chimney is constructed with concrete masonry units and brick to the second floor ceiling. Only brick is used from this elevation to the cap.

The elevations shown on Sheet A-2 provide information for a bricklayer including the required vertical dimensions. The plan views provide horizontal dimensions and information about the steel lintels. A *lintel* is a horizontal structural member installed above a door or window and used to distribute the weight from the structure above to either side of the opening. Further information about the brickwork and

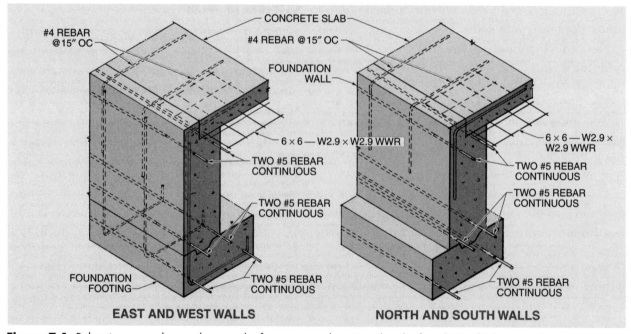

Figure 7-1. Rebar increases the tensile strength of concrete and ties together the foundation footings, walls, and slab.

steel members is provided in Details 3, 6, and 9, Sheet A-3. Detail 3, Sheet A-3, shows the face brick laid in a single wythe under the storefront windows. The masonry walls support and provide anchorage for some of the steel and wood structural members. See Details 6 and 9, Sheet A-3. Note 1 on Sheet A-1 describes the firm base for beam ends.

The front wall of the Commercial Building is a wood-framed wall. The storefront wall is supported by 2 × 6s. See the Detail 3 (Typ Vert Mull section), Sheet A-3. The front wall of the second floor part is a typical wood-framed wall using 2 × 4s. The wall is supported by a steel plate welded to the wide-flange beam, which is located above the storefront. See Detail 2, Sheet A-3. The storefront wall carries little structural load because of the large wide-flange beam over the storefront. The roof load at the front of the building is supported by a wide-flange beam (W12 × 27) that is 17'-0" in from the front of the building and a steel channel (⊏ 12 × 20.7) in the fascia. See Details 4 and 5, Sheet A-3.

Steel Structure

The structural steel members used to support the second floor and the roof are shown on the First Floor Plan and Second Floor Plan, Sheet A-1. Details 2, 4, 5, 6, and 7, Sheet A-3, provide detailed information. See Figure 7-2.

Wide-flange beams are indicated with the letter W on the prints.

The description and location of second floor beams and roof beams are shown on the First Floor Plan and Second Floor Plan, Sheet A-1, respectively. Wide-flange beams, indicated with the letter W, are described by the nominal measurement outside of the flanges and the weight per running foot. A W14 × 34 beam is 14" high and weighs 34 lb per running foot. For both beams used in the Commercial Building, the height is the actual dimension as well as the nominal dimension. Channels are designated by the actual dimension outside of the flanges and

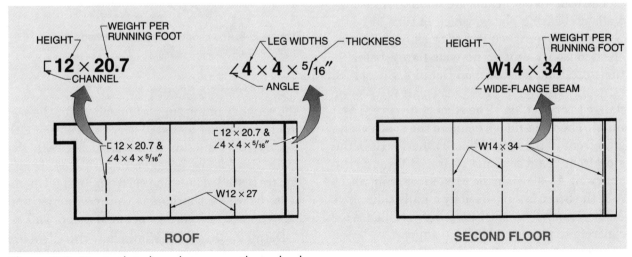

Figure 7-2. Structural steel members support heavy loads.

the weight per running foot. See Figure 7-3. The *Manual of Steel Construction,* published by the American Institute of Steel Construction, can be consulted to determine structural steel dimensions.

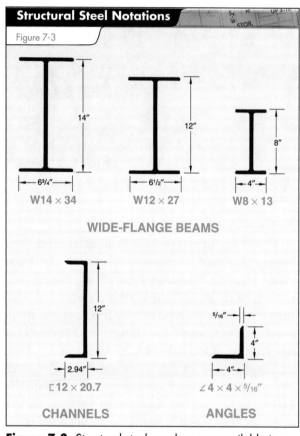

Figure 7-3. Structural steel members are available in a variety of shapes and sizes.

The wide-flange beams are set in the masonry walls on bearing plates, which in turn are supported by several courses of brick or solid concrete masonry units. The wide-flange beam at the storefront, as shown on Detail 2, Sheet A-3, is modified by welding a ⅜″ steel plate to its lower flange to project 3½″. The steel plate serves as a lintel. The wide-flange beam to the south of the storefront in the second floor is shorter than the storefront beam so as not to project through the stairwell. As shown in the First Floor Plan, Sheet A-1, the beam is supported by a Lally column. A *Lally column* is a steel post that is filled with concrete to provide additional support.

Details 5 and 6, Sheet A-3, call attention to the special construction used at the fascia at the

north and south ends of the roof. At each location two steel members are required—a channel and an equal-leg angle—that are tack welded together. As shown in Detail 6, Sheet A-3, the channel supports the ends of the roof joists and must be anchored solidly in the masonry of the side walls. See Figure 7-4. Wide-flange beams, which are 4′ long and 8″ wide, are embedded in the masonry wall and fastened to the fascia channels with bolts through clip angles.

Other structural steel members specified for the Commercial Building are the lintels constructed of three angles, which are located over the door and window openings in the rear wall and the second floor west wall. One angle supports the brick wythe and two angles support the concrete masonry units.

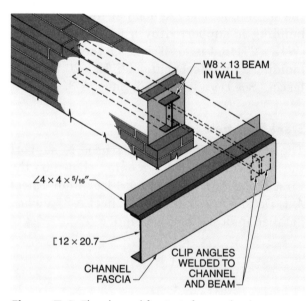

Figure 7-4. The channel fascia is fastened to beams embedded in the brick wall.

Wood Framing Members

The rough framing support members for the second floor consist of 2 × 10 joists spaced 16″ OC. Metal cross bridging is installed between the joists. See Figure 7-5. Two rows of cross bridging are installed between each pair of steel members, between the beams and channels, and between the wide-flange beam and end wall.

Detail 7, Sheet A-3, shows how the joists are cut to permit them to rest on the lower flange of the wide-flange beam to allow the gypsum board

Metal Cross Bridging

Figure 7-5

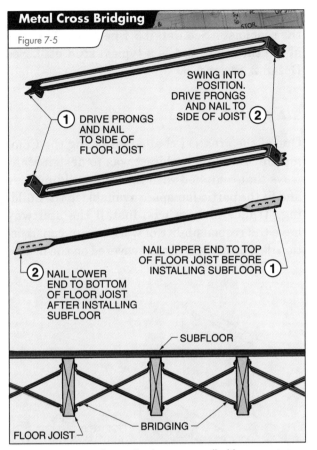

① DRIVE PRONGS AND NAIL TO SIDE OF FLOOR JOIST

② SWING INTO POSITION. DRIVE PRONGS AND NAIL TO SIDE OF JOIST

① NAIL UPPER END TO TOP OF FLOOR JOIST BEFORE INSTALLING SUBFLOOR

② NAIL LOWER END TO BOTTOM OF FLOOR JOIST AFTER INSTALLING SUBFLOOR

SUBFLOOR

FLOOR JOIST

BRIDGING

Figure 7-5. Metal cross bridging is installed between joists to maintain their alignment and prevent them from twisting.

for the ceiling to pass directly below the steel beam. See Figure 7-6. The three joists nearest to the east and west walls are tied together at 6′-0″ intervals with metal strips embedded in the masonry wall. See Detail 9, Sheet A-3.

Solid blocking is placed between the ends of each pair of joists to maintain their alignment. The 2 × 4s are spaced 16″ OC at right angles to the joists to support the plywood subfloor and to provide a 3½″ space in which to run ducts for the second floor. See Detail 9, Sheet A-3.

Detail 7, Sheet A-3, indicates the Roof Terrace floor construction to provide for the change in elevation from the finished second floor and to provide slope for proper drainage for the floor. The 2 × 2 blocking is ripped into increasingly narrow pieces until the plywood finished floor and roof sheathing are in contact with each other.

Metal cross bridging has a galvanized finish to prevent corrosion and is available in 16-, 18-, 20-, and 22-ga thicknesses. Bridging must be installed tightly to reduce or eliminate floor movement.

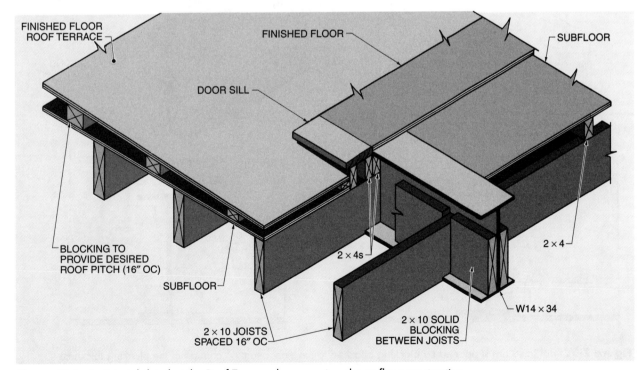

FINISHED FLOOR ROOF TERRACE

FINISHED FLOOR

SUBFLOOR

DOOR SILL

BLOCKING TO PROVIDE DESIRED ROOF PITCH (16″ OC)

SUBFLOOR

2 × 4s

2 × 4

2 × 10 JOISTS SPACED 16″ OC

2 × 10 SOLID BLOCKING BETWEEN JOISTS

W14 × 34

Figure 7-6. A pictorial detail at the Roof Terrace door opening shows floor construction.

In the construction of the roof supporting structure, the upper surfaces of the steel beams are to be kept at the same elevation (+19'-10⅜"). Detail 4, Sheet A-3, shows how the joists are cut to provide maximum bearing on the blocking, which is bolted to the beams. See Figure 7-7. Blocking is placed between beams to maintain joist alignment and prevent the joists from twisting. The blocking under the joists is modified at each beam so that the roof slopes 3" from front to rear. See Section 1-1, Sheet A-2.

Joists over the front of the building are hung from the steel channel. See Details 2 and 5, Sheet A-3. The gypsum board ceiling is supported by 2 × 4 ceiling joists, which are suspended from the roof joists. See Detail 5, Sheet A-3. The wall above the storefront is a typical stud wall. See Detail 2, Sheet A-3.

STAIRWAYS

One of the greatest challenges facing the Commercial Building architect was to design stairways that complied with the local building code and fit the particular space available in the building. Tradesworkers who install the stairway have the responsibility of working out construction details not specifically covered on the prints,

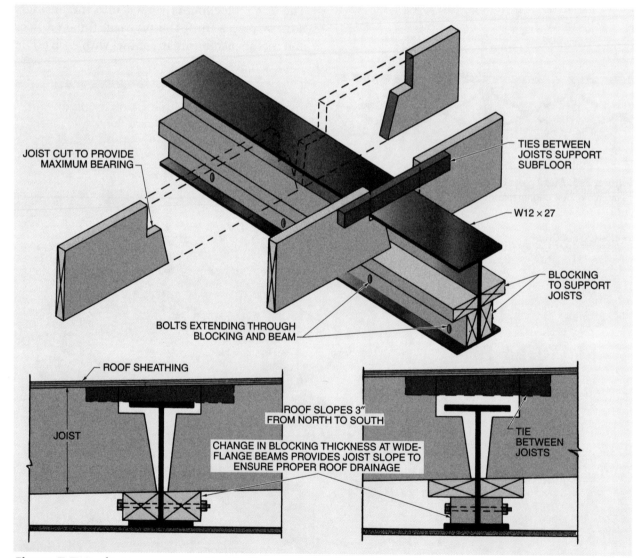

Figure 7-7. Roof joists are supported by blocking attached to the steel beam. A change in the blocking thickness provides the proper roof pitch.

including adequate support for the stairway and framework for the soffit above. Custom-built stairways are often prefabricated in a shop that specializes in stair work. Custom-built stairways require accurate machining to rout out the stringers to receive the treads and risers. See Figure 7-8.

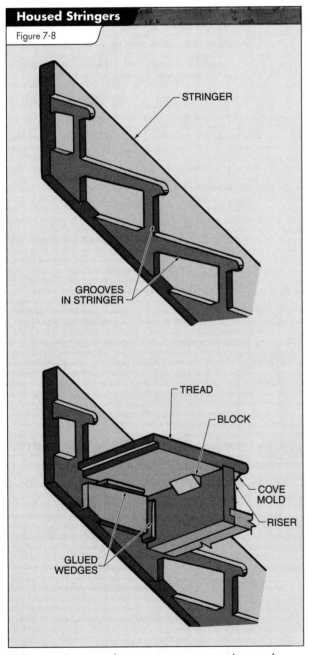

Figure 7-8. Housed stair stringers receive the treads, risers, and wedges. Glued wedges and blocks reinforce the treads.

Stairway Codes

Local building codes for stairways vary. However, the codes provide information regarding the permitted riser height, tread depth, headroom, and stairway landing restrictions. Different requirements are specified for residential and commercial building stairways. The following stairway requirements are based on the *International Residential Code for One- and Two-Family Dwellings*™ and *International Building Code*® published by the International Code Council (ICC). The ICC is a nonprofit organization dedicated to developing a single set of comprehensive and coordinated national model construction codes. The founders of the ICC are Building Officials and Code Administrators International, Inc. (BOCA), International Conference of Building Officials (ICBO), and Southern Building Code Congress International, Inc. (SBCCI). At one time, BOCA, ICBO, and SBCCI published separate regional model codes that were used throughout the United States. The three organizations developed and published the *International Residential Code* and *International Building Code,* which have been adopted by the majority of states.

> Stringers must be laid out so that a set of stairs has a safe and comfortable angle of ascent and descent. The preferred angle for a stairway is 30° to 35°. The minimum safe angle is 20° and the maximum safe angle is 50°.

International Residential Code for One- and Two-Family Dwellings. The *International Residential Code for One- and Two-Family Dwellings* addresses the design and construction of one- and two-family dwellings and townhouses. This code is compatible with the BOCA *National Codes,* ICBO *Uniform Codes,* and SBCCI *Standard Codes.* The following requirements apply to stairways for one- and two-family dwellings:

- Risers. Maximum riser height is 7¾", which is measured vertically between leading edges of adjacent treads. The difference in riser heights in a stairway should not exceed ⅜".

- Treads. Minimum tread depth is 10″, which is measured horizontally between the foremost projections of adjacent treads. The difference in tread depths in a stairway should not exceed ⅜″.
- Headroom. The minimum headroom for all portions of a stairway is 6′-8″ measured vertically from the inclined plane formed by adjacent tread nosings.
- Stairway width. Stairways should be a minimum of 36″ wide.
- Landings. A landing or floor must be provided at the top and bottom of stairways. The landing width should not be less than the stairway width and have a minimum dimension of 36″ measured in the line of travel.
- Handrails. Handrails must be provided for stairways with two or more risers. Handrails must be provided on at least one side of the stairway a minimum of 34″ and a maximum of 38″ above the tread nosings. A clear space not less than 1½″ must be provided between the adjacent wall and handrail.

International Building Code. The *International Building Code* establishes minimum regulations for building systems. The *Code* is based on broad-based principles, making possible the use of new materials and building designs. The following requirements apply to multifamily and nonresidential stairways:

- Risers. Maximum riser height is 7″ and minimum riser height is 4″ measured vertically between leading edges of adjacent treads. The difference in riser heights in a stairway should not exceed ⅜″.
- Treads. Minimum tread depth is 11″, which is measured horizontally between the foremost projections of adjacent treads. The difference in tread depths in a stairway should not exceed ⅜″.
- Headroom. The minimum headroom for all portions of a stairway is 80″ measured vertically from the inclined plane formed by adjacent tread nosings.
- Stairway width. Stairway width is based on the occupancy of the building. Stairways in buildings equipped with sprinkler systems are not required to be as wide as stairways in buildings without sprinkler systems. Stairways serving occupancy loads of 50 people or fewer must have a minimum width of 36″.
- Landings. A landing or floor must be provided at the top and bottom of stairways. The landing width should not be less than the stairway width. Landings must have a minimum dimension measured in the direction of travel equal to the stairway width, and should not exceed 48″ where the stairway has a straight run. A stairway should not have a vertical rise greater than 12′-0″ between floors or landings.
- Handrails. Handrails must be provided for stairways with two or more risers. Handrails must be provided on both sides of the stairway a minimum of 34″ and a maximum of 38″ above the tread nosings. Intermediate handrails are required on wide stairways so all portions of the stairway width are within 30″ of a handrail. A clear space not less than 1½″ must be provided between the adjacent wall and handrail.

The International Codes specify maximum riser height and minimum tread depth. Local building codes usually provide a means of calculating safe and proper stair ratios. A *stair ratio* is the relationship between riser height and tread depth in a stairway. Two common stair ratios, expressed as formulas, are as follows:

$$T + R = 17″ \text{ to } 18″$$

$$T + R + R = 24″ \text{ to } 27″$$

A riser height of 7½″ and a tread depth of 9½″ satisfies both of these stair ratios. In general, a stairway with the lowest riser height and widest tread depth that complies with building code requirements is preferred. A low riser height provides comfortable ascent. Rear Stair Section 2-2, Sheet A-2, indicates that the floor-to-floor height for the Commercial Building is 10′-9⅝″, or 129.62″. The following riser heights could be used for the stairs:

$$129.62″ \div 18 = 7.20″ \text{ or } 7\frac{3}{16}″ \text{ riser height}$$

$$129.62″ \div 17 = 7.62″ \text{ or } 7\frac{5}{8}″ \text{ riser height}$$

$$129.62″ \div 16 = 8.10″ \text{ or } 8\frac{1}{8}″ \text{ riser height}$$

In multifamily and nonresidential stairways, maximum riser height is 7″ and minimum riser height is 4″.

The riser height selected for the Commercial Building was 7⅝″, each with a tread depth of 9″. The riser height and tread depth produce a 16⅝″ stair ratio. The tread depth indicated on the prints is less than the minimum tread depth for the ICC model codes. However, a variance was granted to the local building code by the local building authorities, permitting the specified stairway to be constructed. Variances may be granted in cases where there are historic considerations, a constrained building lot size, zoning requirements, or other unusual circumstances. The owner and architect usually initiate a request for a building code variance and appear before a public hearing of the local building commission in order to obtain approval.

A landing is shown at the top of the fifth riser on the front stairs because it provides a break in the stairway and there is ample room. See Section 1-1, Sheet A-2, and First Floor Plan, Sheet A-1. The landing is 3′-9″ × 3′-0″. Less room is available for the rear stairway. A landing is provided at the top of the rear stairway for safety.

Headroom is measured vertically from a line through the upper edge of the nosings to the ceiling above. Tradesworkers usually construct the soffit framework before a stairway is installed. The stairwell is framed with headers, which the stair stringer rests against, as well as strong side members. The headroom dimensions shown on Section 1-1 and 2-2 comply with code requirements and provide a sufficient allowance so there is no need to cut into the ceiling or vertical wall above when the sloped soffit is formed.

WINDOWS AND DOORS

Windows and doors are often described in schedules that provide sizes and special characteristics. When there are a limited number of doors and windows, the information is included on the prints and in the specifications. Information provided on the First Floor Plan, Sheet A-1, and Detail 3, Sheet A-3, is used to prepare the openings for the tempered glass to be installed after the frame is ready. The front and rear windows on the second floor and the steel sash window in the Mechanical Room are stock windows ordered from a manufacturer catalog.

Dimensions are provided on the prints for the size and location of the overhead door. The name of the manufacturer and descriptive information are stated in the specifications. Other doors throughout the building are described on the door schedule or by a note on Sheet A-1. Width and height dimensions are shown either on the door schedule or at their location on the First and Second Floor Plans.

A stairway should not have a vertical rise greater than 12′-0″ between floors or landings.

HEATING

The building is heated with a forced warm air system designed using a long supply duct along the west wall at the ceiling of the commercial rental space and a return duct along the east wall. See First Floor Plan, Sheet A-1, and Detail 9, Sheet A-3. The greatest heat loss is at the windows and doors on the north and south walls. The heat loss is counteracted by supply registers in the floor in the Dining Room-Living Room area and in the bedrooms. Heat is supplied to the kitchen by a register in the soffit above the cabinets. See Figure 7-9.

Return air flows through grilles in the bedroom partition and at two locations in the Dining Room-Living Room area. The ducts are installed under the floor in the space between the joists in a north-south direction, then turn toward the return trunk at the east wall. The ducts are installed in the space between the joists and the floor in an east-west direction. No return is required from the Kitchen or the Bathroom; the Kitchen air is exhausted through the range hood and the Bathroom has an exhaust fan in the ceiling. Both have ducts that pass through the roof.

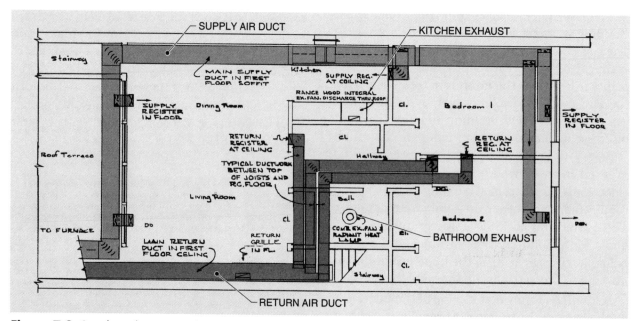

Figure 7-9. Supply and return air ducts are installed in the space under the floor or between the joists. Kitchen air is exhausted through the range hood and Bathroom air is expelled through an exhaust fan in the ceiling.

Name _____ Date _____

Completion

_____PLOT_____ **1.** A(n) ___ plan contains lot and building dimensions.

_____5/8"_____ **2.** A #5 rebar is ___" in diameter.

_____ **3.** A(n) ___ section runs from the front to the back of a building.

_____ **4.** The designation 6 × 6—W2.9 × W2.9 WWR indicates ___ wire reinforcement with a 6" wire spacing.

_____ **5.** Building brick is also known as ___ brick.

_____ **6.** ___ provide vertical dimensions needed by a bricklayer.

_____ **7.** A W14 × 34 steel beam weighs ___ pounds per running foot.

_____ **8.** Steel channels are designated by the actual dimension ___ the flanges and the weight per running foot.

_____ **9.** A concrete-filled steel post is commonly referred to as a(n) ___ column.

_____ **10.** A(n) ___ is a horizontal structural member installed above a door or window and used to distribute the weight from the structure above to either side of the opening.

_____ **11.** ___ are the vertical parts of a stairway.

_____ **12.** ___ are the horizontal parts of a stairway.

_____ **13.** The minimum width for interior stairways in one-family and two-family dwellings is ___".

_____ **14.** A stairway should not have a vertical rise greater than ___ between floors or landings.

_____ **15.** ___ for stairways is measured vertically from the inclined plane formed by adjacent tread nosings to the ceiling directly above.

_____ **16.** The symbol for a supply air register is a rectangle with ___ diagonal lines.

_____1/2"_____ **17.** The notation #4 @ 15" indicates ___" rebar spaced 15" apart.

_____ **18.** A tradesworker obtains ___ dimensions from plan views.

_____ **19.** The Americans with ___ Act was enacted in 1992 to provide greater access to public and commercial buildings for individuals with physical disabilities.

_____ **20.** The *International Building Code,* which is a commercial building code, is published by the International Code ___.

True-False

T   F   **1.** Metal cross bridging cannot be used with wood joists.

T   F   **2.** Steel angles are described by the size of each leg and the steel thickness.

T   F   **3.** Rebar should not be completely concealed in foundations.

T   F   **4.** A landing or floor must be provided at the top and bottom of a stairway.

T   F   **5.** A tread and riser stair ratio of 17″ to 18″ produces a stairway that is within safe limits.

T   F   **6.** Window and door sizes are always specified in schedules on the prints.

T   F   **7.** A return air grille is drawn as a rectangle with one diagonal line.

T   F   **8.** The tradesworker who installs stairways should work out any details of construction not specifically covered in the prints.

T   F   **9.** Heating and air conditioning ducts may be concealed in soffits.

T   F   **10.** Handrails must be provided for all stairways.

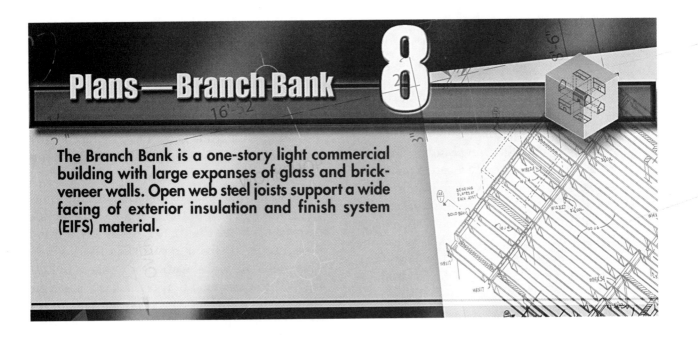

Plans—Branch Bank 8

The Branch Bank is a one-story light commercial building with large expanses of glass and brick-veneer walls. Open web steel joists support a wide facing of exterior insulation and finish system (EIFS) material.

GENERAL DESCRIPTION

The Branch Bank is located at a corner of a major highway and a street near the center of a small community. The bank is positioned on the highest portion of the lot, away from the highway and street, to create an open feeling and to provide ample customer parking. The exterior of the Branch Bank has wide expanses of tall glass windows and brick walls. Cantilevered open web steel joists support a wide facing of exterior insulation and finish system (EIFS) material that projects beyond the building on three sides.

The Branch Bank is constructed of open web steel joists supported by structural steel, a slab-on-grade foundation, metal-framed windows and window walls, and masonry combining brick and concrete masonry units. A heat pump is used for heating and cooling the building. A *heat pump* is a refrigeration system designed to carry heat to a transfer medium to provide cooling in the summer and to absorb heat for heating in the winter through a one-duct system.

Five sheets are included in the set of prints for the Branch Bank, providing all of the essential information required to complete the structural portion of the building. The heating, cooling, plumbing, and electrical drawings are not included. The specifications are also not included with this set of prints.

When studying a particular sheet of the prints, reference may be made to other sheets for further information. The prints for the Branch Bank will be studied in the following order:

1. Site Plan, Sheet A-1. A study of the site, location of the building, elevations, grades, driveways, and walkways.
2. Floor Plan, Sheet A-2. A study of the room layout, walls and partitions, windows, roof soffit, concrete work, and equipment.

HVAC equipment and ductwork are suspended from steel beams.

3. Elevations, Sheet A-5. A study of the elevations as they relate to the Floor Plan, windows, doors, roof projections, footings, foundation, and concrete curbs.
4. Foundation Plan, Sheet A-1. A study of the footings and foundation, the auto teller pit, and under-slab plumbing.
5. Steel Structure, Roof, and Lintels, Sheet A-3. A study of the structural steel members supporting the roof, roof slab, and lintels.
6. Sections, Sheet A-4. Orientation of sections in relation to other working drawings in the set of prints.
7. Details, Sheets A-1 to A-4. A review of the construction details related to the building.
8. Schedules, Sheet A-3. A study of the Interior Finish Schedule and the Door Schedule.

Site Plan, Sheet A-1

The Site Plan identifies the property lines and the corners, locates the building in relation to the property lines, establishes elevations (in particular the elevation of the finished floor), and indicates the finish grade elevations at various points on the lot. Existing and new walkways, curbs and driveways, and the locations of utility poles, gas lines, sewers, and large trees are often included on site plans. If the building lot is steeply sloped, the building site contour may also be shown. The Site Plan, Sheet A-1, for the Branch Bank shows new walkways, driveways, and a complete layout of the parking lot.

> Soil type must be considered when designing the foundation of a building. The four major soil groups are clay, silt, sand, and gravel, with particle sizes ranging from .0002″ to 3″ in diameter.

A licensed surveyor who is legally responsible for the accuracy of the survey provides the basic information about the lot in its preconstruction state. A survey drawing establishes the property lines and corners and also provides a means of determining elevations from a benchmark. A *benchmark,* or datum point, is a stable reference point marked with the elevation above mean sea level from which differences in elevation are measured. Benchmarks are established at intervals across the United States by the U.S. Geological Survey. A survey drawing provides information about present walkways, curbs, and streets and usually indicates the lot slope using contour lines of grade elevations. Using the survey drawing as a base, an architect draws the site plan for the building.

Location. A survey drawing includes information that is critical to the location of the building on the lot. See Figure 8-1. Generally, a point of beginning (POB) is designated from which measurements and elevations are taken. In Figure 8-1, it is assumed that point A is a mark on the pavement for horizontal measurements. A mark on the curb across the street is used for elevations (Curb Top 94.4′). The surveyor sets a surveying instrument over point A in a true north-south bearing, then moves it through an angle of 9°-07′-28″ in a northwesterly direction to sight point B, which is 194.28′ away. The angle is measured in degrees (9°), minutes (07′), and seconds (28″). A *degree* is an angular measurement equal to $\frac{1}{360}$ of a circle. A *minute* is an angular measurement equal to $\frac{1}{60}$ of a degree. A *second* is an angular measurement equal to $\frac{1}{60}$ of a minute.

Distances on plot plans are typically expressed in feet and hundredths of a foot. The tape measure used to measure these distances is divided into tenths and hundredths of a foot to facilitate accurate measurement. A stake or marker is then placed at point B. The surveyor sets up the surveying instrument over point B, takes a bearing of 89°-26′-57″ from a north-south line, and locates point C, which is 151.78′ away. The remaining stakes (points D, E, and F) are then located in sequence until the final bearing returns to point A. None of the corners of the lot for the Branch Bank are right angles, nor are any two sides parallel.

When an architect draws a site plan, the building location must comply with local ordinances regarding setback from the street, and side and rear property lines. The building is located for overall efficiency while providing convenient driveways and parking within the legal limitations. The Branch Bank is located on a line drawn parallel to and 55'-0" away from the west lot line. The line is extended to cross the north lot line. From the point of intersection, a measurement of 40'-0" locates the northwest corner of the Branch Bank. Other corners of the building are established using a surveying instrument and a long tape measure.

Elevations and Grades. The proper elevations and grades must be established on the lot. The Branch Bank benchmark designated by the building authorities is a mark on a curb across the

street at an elevation of 94.4' above the local datum. The surveyor has provided grade elevations at a number of points, which are recorded on the Site Plan. The rough contour of the lot slopes down from the north to the south.

The architect establishes elevations for the building, driveway, and other pavements, taking advantage of the natural slope of the lot. This reduces the amount of earth cut and fill and provides proper drainage around the building and the parking areas. A sudden change in grade to the north and east would concern neighbors who would be affected by the runoff of the surface water.

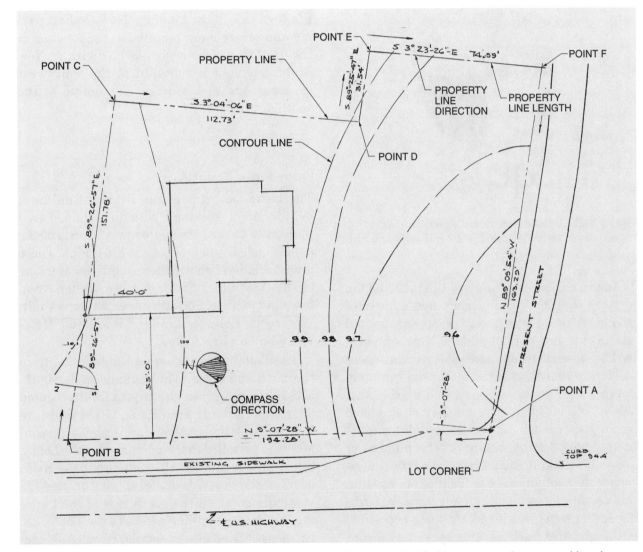

Figure 8-1. Lot corners are established by a surveyor. Property lines are identified by compass direction and length. Contour lines show the approximate slope of the lot.

Elevation symbols for the pavement on the Site Plan resemble a target. See Figure 8-2. The south parking area is to be level at 98.0'. The west parking lot is to rise from 98.0' to 99.6' to properly intersect the driveway that passes the north side of the building. The driveway is required to be at an elevation of 100.5' at the location of the auto teller island. Elevation symbols on the driveway show that the driveway and parking areas are sloped to allow surface water to run off to the south.

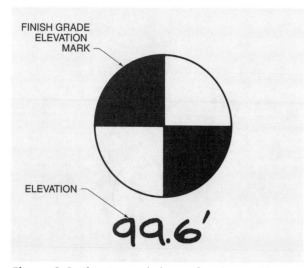

Figure 8-2. Elevation symbols are often shown with targets. Elevations are indicated in feet and tenths of a foot.

Additional information shown on the Site Plan includes location, arrangement, and number of parking spaces. Seven parking spaces are located on the east side of the building. Nine standard parking spaces and one accessible parking space are located on the south side of the building. Seven parking spaces are located on the west side of the building. The number of standard parking spaces for commercial buildings must comply with local ordinances. The number of accessible parking spaces is based on the Americans with Disabilities Act guidelines, which state that parking lots with 25 or fewer standard parking spaces must provide at least one accessible parking space. Each parking space has a concrete bumper to prevent vehicles from driving too far into the space.

Triangles indicate the direction of vehicular traffic flow. Two-way traffic is permitted in the main parking area to the south of the Branch Bank. One-way traffic is indicated from the south parking area to the auto teller and continues to the northwest exit to the highway. One-way traffic is also indicated in the west parking area. Vehicles may enter or exit from the southeast and southwest driveways. The northwest driveway is for exiting only.

Sidewalks leading to the front and side entrances of the Branch Bank are 6'-0" wide. Sidewalks along the south and west parking areas are 5'-0" wide. An accessible ramp is provided adjacent to the accessible parking space. An existing sidewalk is shown along the highway on the west side of the building. New asphalt paving and concrete are required at the junction of the northwest driveway and the highway. New asphalt paving is required at the southwest driveway and new concrete is required at the southeast driveway.

Floor Plan, Sheet A-2

The basic footprint of the Branch Bank is a 40'-0" × 56'-0" rectangle with an L-shaped area projecting toward the highway. All areas of the bank are clearly defined on the Floor Plan. These areas include a Lobby, Automated Teller Machine (ATM) Vestibule, Closing Office, Teller Area, Manager's Office, Secretary Area, Storage Vault, Workroom, Lounge, Janitor Closet, and Men's and Women's Restrooms.

The Lobby extends across the building from the north wall to the ATM Vestibule on the south. The Lobby comprises the largest uninterrupted floor area in the Branch Bank. Glass walls are located along the south and west and large windows are installed in the north wall of the Lobby. The Lobby is entered through either the main doors on the west side of the building or the ATM Vestibule doors on the south side of the building. All doors providing access to the Lobby are "A" doors. The Door Schedule, Sheet A-3, provides detailed information about the doors in the Branch Bank.

The ATM Vestibule provides access to the ATM when the Branch Bank is closed. The interior set of "A" doors is secured when the Bank is closed and the exterior set of doors remains unlocked.

The Closing Office provides privacy for business transactions. This large office area can be entered through two "C" doors located directly across the Lobby from the Teller Area. The Door Schedule, Sheet A-3, provides detailed information about the "C" doors. The wall separating the Closing Office from the Lobby is gypsum board over 2 × 6 wood studs spaced 16″ OC. Additional information concerning finish for the Closing Office is provided on the Interior Finish Schedule, Sheet A-3.

Most of the business of the Branch Bank is conducted at the counter in the Teller Area. The counter is conveniently located on the east side of the Lobby and is in view when entering from either set of entrance doors. Detail 8 and Interior Elevation 10, Sheet A-4, contain dimensions and other information required to complete the counter.

Banking activities in the customer areas can be observed through the glass partitions in the Manager's Office. The Interior Finish Schedule, Sheet A-3, notes that the partitions are ¼″ plate glass in bronzed, anodized aluminum frames. The "B" door of the Manager's Office is detailed in the Door Schedule, Sheet A-3.

The Secretary Area is open to the Lobby and immediately adjacent to the Manager's Office and the Teller Area. The location of the Secretary Area provides the secretary with an excellent view of the banking activities. A railing, shown on Detail 9, Sheet A-4, separates the Secretary Area from the Teller Area. The 3′-4″ high railing is framed with 2 × 4s and capped with ¾″ thick oak. A 2′-0″ gate in the railing provides entrance into the Teller Area. The wall separating the Secretary Area from the Lounge is constructed with gypsum board over 2 × 6 wood studs spaced 16″ OC. The "E" door located in this frame wall is detailed in the Door Schedule, Sheet A-3.

The Storage Vault is immediately behind the Teller Area, and is consequently isolated from inadvertent entry by unauthorized personnel. Note the wall material and thickness of the Storage Vault. Section 1, Sheet A-4, provides additional information concerning the vault floor, walls, and ceiling. The "J" door of the Storage Vault is stainless steel and can swing 180°.

The Workroom is located directly behind the Teller Area and between the Storage Vault and Lounge. The Floor Plan indicates 1 × 2 furring strips on the 1′-0″ core-filled concrete masonry unit wall separating the Storage Vault and Workroom. Gypsum board is applied to the furring strips. A 2′-0″ deep closet is located behind a "G" door. The closet contains a shelf and rod. The Workroom is entered through a "D" door.

The Lounge, designed for employee use, can be entered through an "E" door from the Secretary Area or through an "F" door from the rear of the Teller Area near the Workroom. A 39″ kitchen area unit is located in one corner of the Lounge and the Janitor Closet is behind the east wall. A gypsum board soffit is installed over the kitchen area unit.

The Janitor Closet contains a mop sink, 30-gallon electric water heater, and electrical panels for the Branch Bank. A "G" door provides entry into the Janitor Closet.

The Men's and Women's Restrooms are located off a short hallway from the Lounge. Each Restroom contains a water closet and vanity-mounted lavatory. A floor drain, indicated by the abbreviation "FD," is located in each Restroom. The Restrooms are entered through "H" doors. Both Restrooms are designed to provide access to employees with disabilities.

In a built-up roof, wide-flange beams support open web steel joists for the roof decking.

The Floor Plan must be studied in conjunction with other sheets in the set of prints to gain detailed knowledge of the Branch Bank construction. For example, while the Floor Plan, Sheet A-2, shows all doors, their location, and their direction of swing, the Door Schedule, Sheet A-3, must be studied to determine size, type, material, frame, casings, and hardware for each door.

Exterior Walls. The exterior walls are face brick with concrete masonry unit (CMU) backing. With the exception of the Storage Vault walls, all exterior walls are 1'-0" thick. The exterior walls of the Storage Vault are 1'-4" thick and are made of 1'-0" CMUs in which the cores are filled solid with concrete. The CMU wall is then faced with 4" brick. Wood furring is installed on the interior surface of the exterior walls except for the Storage Vault. Gypsum board is applied to the furring strips as a finish. Walls and partitions for the Storage Vault are specially constructed and reinforced for security. Cutting planes are indicated through the masonry exterior walls in two locations. Additional information regarding these sections is shown in Sections 1 and 2, Sheet 4.

Glass Walls, Windows, and Exterior Doors. Fixed glass walls and windows are shown on the west and south sides of the Branch Bank. Fixed glass walls and windows do not open. Dimensions to locate glass walls and windows are provided on the Floor Plan, Sheet A-2. Cutting planes denoting Sections 3 and 4, Sheet A-4, are shown on the Floor Plan. These sections provide additional information about the glass walls, doors, and windows.

Exterior doors and ATM Vestibule doors are "A" doors, and are referenced to the Door Schedule, Sheet A-3. Door size, type, material, frame, and hardware are noted. "A" doors are the only paired doors for the Branch Bank.

Federally insured banks and savings institutions are regulated under the Bank Protection Act, which specifies minimum construction requirements for vault floors, walls, and ceilings.

Partitions. Most full-height partitions are constructed with 2 × 6 wood studs and covered with gypsum board. The Finish Schedule, Sheet A-3, indicates the finish that is to be applied to the walls and partitions in all rooms. The partition between the Men's and Women's Restrooms and the Manager's Office is constructed differently than other wood-framed partitions in the Branch Bank. See Detail 1, Sheet A-2. This partition is constructed with 2 × 6 plates with 2 × 4 studs spaced 16" OC in an offset arrangement to form a thicker partition, allowing insulation to be placed around the offset studs. Vinyl-covered fiberglass blanket insulation is placed in the partition to provide better sound-deadening properties.

Two partitions for the Manager's Office are glass. The Finish Schedule, Sheet A-3, indicates the partitions are ¼" plate glass in bronzed, anodized aluminum frames. The glazing is flush. These glass partitions provide an open look to the main customer area of the Bank while providing the manager a certain amount of privacy.

Roof. The 3½" pipe columns along the west wall and in the partition behind the Secretary's Area are shown on the Floor Plan, Sheet A-2. The footing for a 3½" column is shown in Detail 2, Sheet A-1. The Roof Plan, Sheet A-3, shows column location and notes the size and location of connecting structural steel.

The roof extends beyond the face of the building. A wide soffit begins at the exterior wall outside of the Janitor Closet, surrounds three sides of the building, and ends at the northwest corner. The soffit is shown with a hidden line on the Floor Plan since the soffit is more than 5'-0" above the finish floor elevation. The underside of the soffit is finished with waterproof gypsum board to withstand exposure to the weather. Detail 7, Sheet A-4, shows the soffit details. The roof overhang is also shown on Detail 6 and Sections 1 to 4, Sheet A-4.

Concrete Work. The location of a future island and auto teller installation is shown on the Floor Plan, Sheet A-2. The window and counter for the auto teller are to be installed during initial construction. The note "FUTURE" indicates that the auto teller will be installed at a later date. The canopy over the island will also be installed later. The Foundation Plan, Sheet A-1, provides additional information about the auto teller.

Concrete walkways are shown on the Floor Plan, Sheet A-2. Additional information regarding the walkways is obtained from the Site Plan, Sheet A-1. Both walkways leading to the building are 6'-0" wide. An accessible ramp with a nonslip finish is provided along the accessible parking space.

A concrete curb is shown along the north wall of the Branch Bank per the Site Plan, Sheet A-1, Floor Plan, Sheet A-2, and Section 3, Sheet A-4. The curb is 10" wide at the northeast corner and extends to 2'-0" wide at the northwest corner. The curb ensures adequate clearance between the north wall of the building and vehicular traffic on the driveway. The night depository, located in the north exterior wall, is also protected by the concrete curb.

 Hardware such as grab bars is required for restrooms in commercial and public buildings and must be installed according to ADA guidelines.

Equipment. Built-in counters for the Teller Area are shown on the Floor Plan, Sheet A-2. Notations shown by the counter on the Floor Plan refer to Detail 8 and Interior Elevation 10, Sheet A-4. The details provide dimensions for building the counter.

The water heater, mop sink, and electrical panels are located in the Janitor Closet. The kitchen unit shown in the Lounge is a compact unit containing a stove, refrigerator, and sink. Compact units are often used for commercial applications where space is limited or larger equipment is not required for the number of employees in the building.

Detail 2, Sheet A-2, shows an elevation of the Women's Restroom wall. The maximum heights specified conform to the ADA guidelines. The Men's Restroom, in which the fixtures are laid out on the opposite hand, is also finished as shown in this elevation. Tile on the Restroom

wall extends 4'-0" above the finished floor. Information about the surface-mounted mirror and wall-hung lavatory is provided.

Elevations, Sheet A-5

The Elevations, Sheet A-5, are based on the Floor Plan, Sheet A-2, and are drawn at the same scale for easy reference. Foundation walls and footings are indicated with hidden lines on the four elevations on this sheet. While information concerning footings is provided, Sections 1 to 4, Sheet A-4, should be referred to for additional information. Details regarding the overhang structure finishes and other exterior wall finishes are provided on all elevations.

The West Elevation shows the front of the Branch Bank, which faces the highway. The doors and window wall shown in the West Elevation are part of the Lobby. Sign letters are to be applied to this wall. The upper row of letters is 8" high and the lower row of letters is 6" high. The North Elevation shows a window in the Closing Office, the north Lobby windows, and the auto teller window. The night depository is also located on the north wall. The South Elevation shows the ATM Vestibule exterior entrance doors, part of the Lobby window wall, and a window in the Closing Office. The East Elevation is a solid wall with no openings.

The concrete curb is shown on the Site Plan, Sheet A-1.

Insulation board of an exterior insulation and finish system is placed on walls in a running bond pattern so joints are staggered and do not occur over sheathing joints. Edges of insulation board are interlocked at the corners.

Windows and Doors. Fixed-sash windows in the Closing Office and in the north wall of the Lobby are ¼″ polished plate glass with a horizontal bar located 2′-6″ above the finished floor. The window for the auto teller counter is made of bullet-resistant glass and is to be supplied by the auto teller manufacturer.

Fixed-sash glass window walls are placed along the south and west sides of the Lobby.

Glass doors are integral parts of the metal frames for the window walls. Square metal members, which conceal the pipe columns supporting the roof, measure 5″ × 5″.

Roof Projection. The roof projection is referenced to Details 6 and 7, Sheet A-4. The details show the open web steel joists and the rough wood framework required to support the facing and the soffit. Exterior insulation and finish system (EIFS) is specified for the wide facing along the roof projection. An *exterior insulation and finish system (EIFS)* is an exterior finish system consisting of exterior sheathing, insulation board, reinforcing mesh, a base coat of acrylic copolymers, and a finish of acrylic resins. See Figure 8-3. The bottom of the soffit is supported from 2 × 6 lookouts and is finished with waterproof gypsum board.

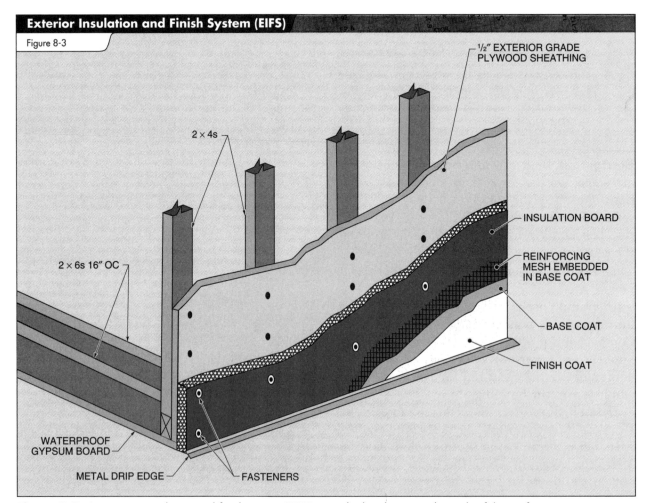

Exterior Insulation and Finish System (EIFS)

Figure 8-3

½″ EXTERIOR GRADE PLYWOOD SHEATHING

2 × 4s

2 × 6s 16″ OC

INSULATION BOARD

REINFORCING MESH EMBEDDED IN BASE COAT

BASE COAT

FINISH COAT

WATERPROOF GYPSUM BOARD

METAL DRIP EDGE

FASTENERS

Figure 8-3. An exterior insulation and finish system (EIFS) is applied to the vertical panels of the roof projection.

Footings and Foundations. The finished floor, finish grade, and footing elevations are shown on the Elevations, Sheet A-5. The finished floor elevation is 6″ above the finished pavement on the north side of the building. See the West Elevation, Sheet A-5. The finish grade is at the same elevation on all Elevations except the North Elevation where the concrete curb is shown, and between the North and South Elevations where the driveway is shown. The driveway on the north side of the Branch Bank, which is 6″ below the finished floor elevation, follows the curb and the wall under the Closing Office window.

Hidden lines below each Elevation indicate the footings and foundation walls. Vertical hidden lines occur at foundation corners and are identified by referring to the Foundation Plan, Sheet A-1. The deep foundation shown on the North Elevation is for the auto teller equipment. The top of the foundation wall is 8″ below the finished floor elevation and 4″ below finish grade. Two rowlock courses of brick, with one course showing above grade, are placed under the Lobby windows and the windows in the Closing Office. Refer to Detail 2, Sheet A-1.

Foundation footings are shown on the Foundation Plan, Sheet A-1. Three #4 rebar run continuously in the footings. Four #4 rebar are placed in column footings. Masonry reinforcement is placed in alternate horizontal course joints in the CMU foundation walls as indicated on the Foundation Plan, Sheet A-1.

Steel Members. The locations of the ends of steel wide-flange beams that support open web steel joists are shown on the North and South Elevations, Sheet A-5. Beam sizes specified vary from 8″ to 14″.

Foundation Plan, Sheet A-1

The Foundation Plan, Sheet A-1, is drawn to the scale ¼″ = 1'-0″. Additional information about the foundation footings and walls, piers, and concrete slab is shown on the West Elevation, Sheet A-5, Details 1 and 2, Sheet A-1, and Section 2, Sheet A-4.

Foundation Footings. Foundation footings transfer the load of a building and foundation walls to the earth. Footing size increases as the load increases or as the load is concentrated in one area. A concrete footing 1'-0″ thick and 2'-4″ wide under 1'-0″ thick CMU foundation walls forms most of the foundation. Three #4 rebar run continuously throughout the footing. The footing varies in width under the Storage Vault foundation, under the non-load-bearing walls of the Lobby, and around the auto teller pit.

Steel columns supporting the roof structure are located in the window wall. These columns and other columns toward the rear of the building are supported on 16″ square piers.

Foundation Walls. The CMU foundation walls are 2'-8″ high. See South and West Elevations, Sheet A-5. CMU walls are 8″, 12″, or 16″ thick. Pilasters with an 8″ concrete cap are constructed where columns will be located in the Lobby walls. See Detail 2, Sheet A-1. Concrete columns, reinforced with four #4 rebar that extend into the footing, support the steel columns at the rear of the building. See Section 2, Sheet A-4. A liquid waterproofing membrane is applied to the outside of the foundation walls as detailed in the specifications. As shown in Detail 6, Sheet A-4, Styrofoam™ insulation, in 1″ thick by 24″ wide pieces, is fastened to the inside of the foundation walls.

Floor Slab. The concrete floor slab, which is 4″ thick, is placed over a 4 mil polyethylene (PE) vapor barrier and at least 4″ of crushed stone. The slab is reinforced with 6 × 6—W1.4 × W1.4 welded wire reinforcement. All under-slab piping, conduit, ducts, and other materials must be in place and verified before concrete for the slab is placed.

The slab termination at the walls is shown in Details 1 and 2, Sheet A-1, and in Detail 6 and all of the sections on Sheet A-4. Note that the slab is thickened at the column-bearing west wall.

As noted in the Foundation Plan, Sheet A-1, the slab is depressed below the restrooms, providing space to lay the thinset mortar bed and a ceramic tile floor, which will be flush with the top of the slab. A 4″ ABS drain line, which must be roughed-in prior to placing concrete for the depressed slab, extends to the sanitary sewer system.

Auto Teller. Electronic and electrical controls and pneumatic tubes are used to efficiently transport cash, checks, and other currency and papers between customer and teller. The auto teller for the Branch Bank is to be completed later. However, as many provisions as possible are included at the time of initial construction to reduce costs when the island and canopy are constructed. See the Site Plan, Sheet A-1.

Section 1, Sheet A-1, is related to the Foundation Plan, Sheet A-1. Note the cutting plane and the direction in which the section is taken in the Foundation Plan. Section 1 shows two walls of the auto teller pit and the masonry wall supported by a reinforced concrete beam. A PVC tube extends beyond the future island to provide space for the auto teller equipment. The notation on the Foundation Plan indicates an opening is to be provided in the floor of the Bank for the passage of the pneumatic tubes and wiring. The sump pump and the access hole indicated in the Foundation Plan do not show in the section because they are behind the cutting plane.

Underslung joists are supported by their top chords.

Under-Slab Piping. The notation on the Foundation Plan, Sheet A-1, "VERIFY THAT ALL UNDER-SLAB PIPING, CONDUIT, DUCTS, ETC., ARE IN BEFORE PLACING SLAB" alerts tradesworkers to the importance of this aspect of construction. Certain plumbing features are shown on the Foundation Plan. Downspouts convey rainwater from the roof through pipes in the masonry walls. A 3″ downspout is indicated in the north masonry foundation wall as shown on the Foundation Plan. The 3″ downspout connects to a 4″ polyvinyl chloride (PVC) pipe running south where the pipe connects with the discharge from the sump pump. Depending on the local building codes and ordinances, sump pumps may not be permitted to connect to the sanitary sewer. In areas where this connection is not permitted, the sump pump would be piped onto the ground surface or driveway away from pedestrian traffic. The 4″ PVC pipe passes under the floor slab, continuing out through a 6″ pipe to a storm sewer in the street at the south end of the lot. The soil pipe to the sanitary sewer system is shown in its approximate location. Other water supply lines to and drainage lines from the Restrooms, Janitor Closet, and kitchen unit are not shown.

Steel Structure, Roof, and Lintels, Sheet A-3

The main feature of the steel structure for the Branch Bank is the use of open web steel joists. Open web steel joists are a combination of angles that serve as top and bottom chords with diagonal bars for reinforcement, creating a truss effect. Open web steel joists are particularly useful in light construction because they can span great distances, are lightweight, and the open webs provide passage for conduit, pipes, and ducts.

The Roof Plan, Sheet A-3, and a variety of sections and details on Sheet A-4 provide information about the steel structure. The open web steel joists are supported by masonry walls and structural steel members. See Figure 8-4. A variety of sizes of open web steel joists are used and are selected based on their spans and the loads to be supported.

The most common type of open web steel joist is underslung. An *underslung joist* is a joist that is supported by its top chord. Refer to the joists over the Storage Vault at the northeast corner in Figure 8-4. The top chords of the joists rest on bearing (weld) plates that are securely anchored in the masonry.

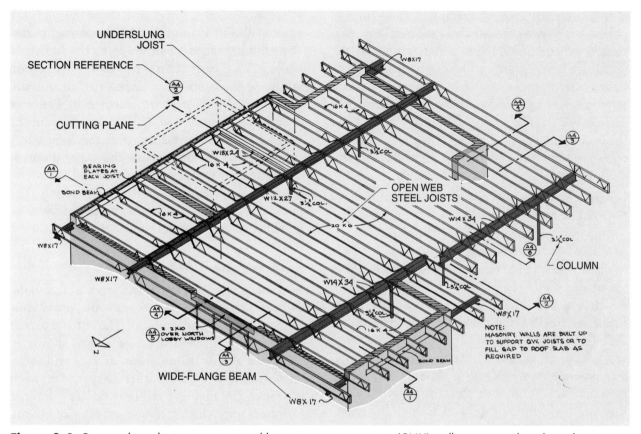

Figure 8-4. Open web steel joists are supported by concrete masonry unit (CMU) walls or structural steel members.

The top of the masonry wall is constructed using a reinforced concrete bond beam. The bond beam is formed using CMU lintels, which are filled with concrete and reinforced with rebar. See the exterior wall of the Storage Vault in Section 1, Sheet A-4. The bond beam ties the walls together into a single unit. After the joists are lifted into position, they are tack welded to maintain their alignment. Other underslung joists rest on the exterior wall and on wide-flange beams to which they are securely welded.

Wherever the joists cantilever (project beyond the wall) on the east or west side of the Branch Bank, they are modified with square ends to support the facing panels and soffit. See Detail 6 and Sections, Sheet A-4. Section 1 shows the joists where they pass through a masonry wall, and Detail 6 shows the support by a wide-flange beam over the glass window wall of the Lobby. The end joists at the north and south sides of the building are supported by short wide-flange beams embedded in the masonry and fastened with anchor bolts, and by the ends of a large W14 beam and W8 beams.

An 8″ masonry parapet is constructed surrounding the heat pump location as shown on the Roof Plan, Sheet A-3, and Section 2, Sheet A-4. A parapet is a low protective wall. The parapet rests on a W8 × 24 beam and a W12 × 27 beam. On the other sides, the parapet rests on a continuation of the masonry of the Storage Vault wall and the exterior wall. Two 12″ × 8″ openings at roof level are provided for roof drainage.

Special steel members include a W12 × 27 beam under the parapet where the heat pump is located. A ¼″ × 7″ steel plate is welded to the wide-flange beam to provide a wider base for the masonry above. Steel angles are used to frame the curbs for the Restroom fans and heat pump at the roof. See Details 1 and 2, Sheet A-3.

A corrugated steel deck is welded to the open web steel joists. See Details 6 and 7, Sheet A-4. Welded wire reinforcement (6 × 6—W1.4 × W1.4 WWR) is then laid into position and 2½″

of lightweight concrete, using perlite as an aggregate, is placed. *Perlite* is a volcanic siliceous rock, crushed and heated at a high temperature, which expands it into lightweight glassy particles. A five-ply built-up roof of tarred felt and pitch is then applied. The surface is finished with fine gravel. Details 6 and 7, Sheet A-4, show how the roof edge is formed with 4 × 4s that act as an edge form for the concrete and provide an installation surface for the metal fascia.

Lintels. The windows in the window wall on the West Elevation do not need lintels because the wall is non-load-bearing. Details 6 and 7, Sheet A-4, show the blocking required to close the gap to open web steel joists above and to provide a means for fastening ceiling and soffit material. A reference is made on the North Elevation, Sheet A-5 to Detail 5, Sheet A-4, for the lintel over the north Lobby windows. Detail 5 shows two 2 × 10s serving as a lintel over the windows. The masonry wall shown in Detail 5 is beyond the opening. Lintels over the auto teller window and the two windows in the Closing Office are made of CMU lintels, which are filled with concrete and reinforced with rebar. See Figure 8-5.

Details 1 and 2, Sheet A-3, show the roof slab against the heat pump and fan opening curbs. The slab is placed at an angle at the fan curb, while a 1 × 6 cant strip provides the transition at the heat pump curb. Three roof drains are shown on the Roof Plan, Sheet A-3. The roof drains are connected to 3″ diameter pipes in the space between the ceiling and roof and carry rainwater to downspouts in the walls. Four 4″ diameter overflow pipes, which extend 1½″ above the roof, pass through the roof projection. The manner in which the overflow pipes are installed and flashed is shown in Detail 7, Sheet A-4.

Sections, Sheet A-4

Sections show interior elevations and finish details and structural features of walls, partitions, foundation, and roof support. The cutting planes for sections in the Branch Bank are shown on the Floor Plan with direction arrows and reference numbers. As with other elements on a set of prints, the means used to note the reference numbers may vary from one set of prints to another. One convention used to express reference numbers specifies the sheet number first, followed by the detail or section number on the sheet. See Figure 8-6. Sheet A-4 contains four sections taken through the building and additional sections through the counter.

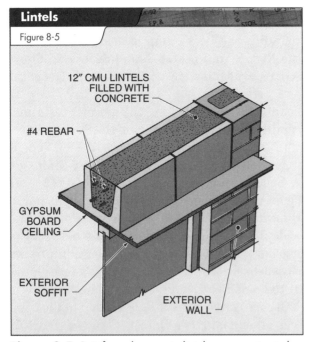

Figure 8-5. Reinforced concrete lintels are constructed for the Branch Bank.

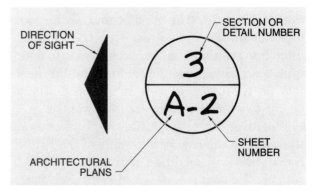

Figure 8-6. References key cutting planes to details and sections.

Section 1, Sheet A-4. Section 1 is a view taken parallel to the north wall looking toward the wall. The cutting plane passes through the Closing Office, Lobby, Teller Area, and Storage Vault.

See Floor Plan, Sheet A-2. Brick and the reinforced concrete bond beam are two structural features included in Section 1. The frame partition is shown extending above the ceiling and lower chord of the open web steel joists and is anchored by bolts. The ceiling over the auto teller area is dropped to a clear height of 8'-0" using suspended eggcrate luminous ceiling tile. A complete description of the reinforced concrete slab ceiling for the Storage Vault is provided. The edges of the ceiling project into the masonry walls.

Section 2, Sheet A-4. Section 2 is taken through the Workroom, Teller Area, and Lobby looking south. The cutting plane passes through the roof where the heat pump is located. The closet door is to the left. The next door to the right leads to the Lounge. The doors and window wall to the right are in the south wall of the Lobby. Details of the wood railing between the Teller Area and the Secretary Area are shown. This railing, which is shown on the Floor Plan, Sheet A-2, could be mistaken for a partition if Section 2 was not provided. Detail 9, Sheet A-4, provides additional information about the railing.

The glass partition and door for the Manager's Office appear beyond the railing. The suspended acoustical ceiling is shown with a reference to Detail 7, Sheet A-4, for more information. The ceiling height in the Workroom and Restrooms is 8'-0". The ceiling in the Janitor Closet extends to the joists. Parapet support and wall construction on the roof is indicated. The parapet is 8" solid brick and is capped with a 2 × 8 and finished with aluminum coping.

Section 3, Sheet A-4. Section 3 is taken through the Lobby looking west and shows the wide expanse of the window wall, including the double entrance doors in the ATM Vestibule and Lobby. The two doors to the right lead to the Closing Office. The concrete curb outside the north wall is shown with dimensions and reinforcement requirements.

Section 4, Sheet A-4. Section 4 is taken through the Lobby looking east to show the arrangement of the teller counter and details of the glass partition in the Manager's Office. The right side of the Teller Area shows the finished appearance of the counter. The suspended ceiling over the Teller Area is shown with gypsum board above. The doors from left to right are the Storage Vault door, Workroom door, and Lounge door. The railing to the right of the counter separates the Teller Area from the Secretary Area.

Detail 8, Sheet A-4. Detail 8 is taken through the counter in the Teller Area. The counter has two working surfaces. The surface used by the tellers is 40" high. The surface used by bank customers is 54" high. Plastic laminate is applied to these surfaces. Metal cabinets beneath the counter are not in the contract.

Interior Elevation 10, Sheet A-4. Interior Elevation 10 is taken as if looking at the teller side of the counter. The wood shelf unit is supplied by the general contractor. Letter and numerical designations refer to metal cabinets that are not part of the Branch Bank contract.

Details, Sheets A-1 to A-4

Details are generally sections that are enlarged to present detailed information that could not be clearly shown at a smaller scale. Details may also be plans, sections, or elevations.

Section 1, Sheet A-1. Section 1 shows a section taken through the auto teller pit. The detail is drawn to the scale of $\frac{3}{8}$" = 1'-0". Foundation footings are 1'-8" wide and 1'-0" high and are reinforced with three #4 rebar.

Drain tile is shown along the bottom of the foundation footing. Details of the 12" polyvinyl chloride (PVC) pipe for installation of future auto teller island equipment are also provided. Compacted fill is placed over the PVC pipe and covered with asphalt. Future work is indicated even though the auto teller is not part of this contract.

Detail 2, Sheet A-1. Detail 2 shows how the pipe columns in the Lobby window wall rest on a concrete base which forms the top of the foundation wall. The detail also shows the relationship between the brick masonry and the floor slab. The slab is increased in thickness from 4" to 8" and rests on the 8" concrete base. The Styrofoam™ insulation extends to the top of the foundation wall and is also installed behind the courses of brick. No scale is indicated for this detail.

Section 3, Sheet A-2. Section 3 is a section taken through the soffit over the teller counter. The detail is drawn to the scale of $\frac{1}{4}'' = 1''$, which is one-quarter size. The detail provides information about rough framing and methods used to suspend the soffit panels.

Gypsum board is also indicated on Detail 3. The eggcrate ceiling is suspended with exposed tees. One of the tees is shown at the corner. See Figure 8-7.

Other Details. Details 1 and 2, Sheet A-3, show the wood framing members, flashing, and opening dimensions. These details were previously described.

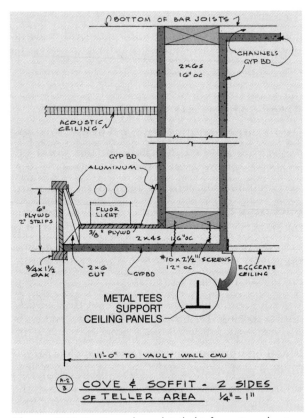

Figure 8-7. Sections show detailed information about construction of the soffit over the teller counter.

A number of references have been made to Details 5, 6, and 7, Sheet A-4. Sections 8 and 9, Sheet A-4, show sections through the teller counter and railing, and provide all of the information required to construct them. The rough framework, plywood, blocking, and finish are carefully detailed.

Detail 10, Sheet A-4, displays the arrangement of metal cabinets in the Teller Area shown from the teller's side. The manufacturer number is noted for each unit. Detail 10 and Section 4, Sheet A-4 should be compared to gain a better understanding of the counter construction.

Schedules, Sheet A-3

Schedules are an important component of a set of prints since they consolidate and readily display information about similar items. The schedules included in a set of prints vary with the complexity of the project. The Branch Bank plans contain an Interior Finish Schedule and a Door Schedule. A window schedule is not required since only fixed-glass windows are specified for the Branch Bank.

Interior Finish Schedule. The Interior Finish Schedule provides information about the finishes for floors, walls, and ceilings. The type and size of baseboards for walls are also indicated. Note that the carpet is not a part of this contract. Four different types of paint and stain finishes are detailed, and are noted as Finish 1, 2, 3, and 4.

Door Schedule. The Door Schedule describes each type and size of door completely, including the finish and frame. Reference numbers on the Floor Plan, Sheet A-3, identify the location of each door. Three pairs of entrance doors of aluminum are to be furnished with medium stiles. A stile is a vertical member of a door. "B" doors are solid wood doors with particleboard cores and ventilating louvers. A "G" door is specified for the Janitor Closet, and "H" doors are solid wood doors specified for the Restrooms.

The doors leading to the Manager's Office, Closing Office, and Restrooms have locksets. A *lockset* is a complete assembly of a bolt, knobs, escutcheon plates, and mechanical components for securing a door. Locksets are typically keyed and have rectangular or beveled bolts, or both. Doors "E," "F," and "G" have latchsets. A *latchset* is a mechanical device used to hold a door shut when it is closed. Latchsets usually have beveled bolts and are not keyed for security.

Name _____ Date _____

Completion

_____ **1.** A(n) ___ is a unit that provides heating or cooling for a building.

_____ **2.** The survey drawing provides a means of determining elevations from datum points or ___.

_____ **3.** The point of ___ is a point from which measurements and elevations are taken.

_____ **4.** ___ are drawn to a larger scale to show the object more clearly.

_____ **5.** A(n) ___ provides complete information on the type and size of doors specified.

_____ **6.** Studs in walls and partitions may be ___ to allow insulation to be placed around the studs.

_____ **7.** A(n) ___ has arrows on each end to indicate the direction of sight.

_____ **8.** ___ windows cannot be opened.

_____ **9.** Concrete foundation footings are usually reinforced with ___.

_____ **10.** A surveyor's tape measure is divided into tenths and hundredths of a(n) ___.

True-False

T   F   **1.** A section is commonly shown with closely spaced parallel lines drawn horizontally through the object.

T   F   **2.** A site plan locates and identifies the property lines and corners.

T   F   **3.** Floor plans showing room size and layout are drawn with the line of sight parallel to the floor.

T   F   **4.** Elevation symbols on prints often resemble a target.

T   F   **5.** The size of a foundation footing is increased as loads are concentrated in one area.

T	F	**6.** Concrete floor slabs must be poured at the same elevation throughout a building.
T	F	**7.** Downspouts should always be run on the outside of exterior walls.
T	F	**8.** A floor drain always requires the pumping action of a sump pump.
T	F	**9.** A W12 × 27 beam weighs more per foot than a W14 × 34 beam.
T	F	**10.** Hidden lines on floor plans indicate features over 5'-0" above the floor.
T	F	**11.** Wide-flange cannot be adequately supported by masonry walls.
T	F	**12.** Parapet may be wood-framed or masonry construction.
T	F	**13.** Acoustical ceilings must be suspended to prevent sound transmission.
T	F	**14.** Latchsets do not have keyed locks.
T	F	**15.** Door schedules describe each type and size of door, including the finish and frame.
T	F	**16.** Stiles are horizontal members of a door.
T	F	**17.** Locksets may have rectangular, beveled, or rectangular and beveled bolts.
T	F	**18.** Prints drawn to the scale of ¼" = 1'-0" are one-quarter actual size.
T	F	**19.** Site plans may be used to determine if property setbacks comply with local ordinances.
T	F	**20.** Open web steel joists may be utilized in constructing cantilevered roofs.

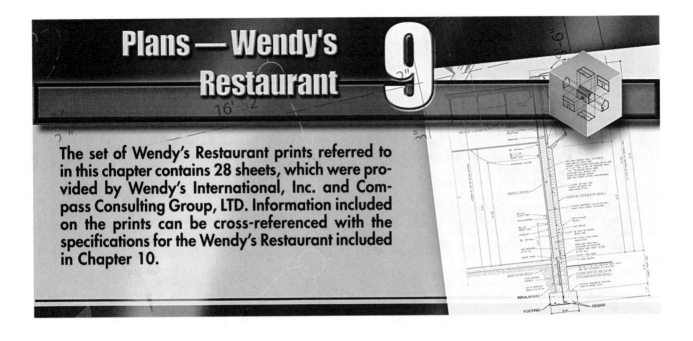

Plans — Wendy's Restaurant 9

The set of Wendy's Restaurant prints referred to in this chapter contains 28 sheets, which were provided by Wendy's International, Inc. and Compass Consulting Group, LTD. Information included on the prints can be cross-referenced with the specifications for the Wendy's Restaurant included in Chapter 10.

WENDY'S RESTAURANTS

Fast-food restaurants have become firmly established throughout the United States and across the world. Easily identified by their distinctive signs, fast-food restaurants attract local patrons as well as the traveling public. Offering quality food products quickly and at moderate prices, fast-food restaurants are located in cities, in suburbs, and along major highways. See Figure 9-1.

Fast-food restaurants are a vital part of a community's economy because they provide jobs for local citizens. From the work generated in the construction of a new restaurant to the serving of food, fast-food restaurants employ millions of people. Building tradesworkers, material and equipment suppliers, food and beverage purveyors, utility companies, employees, and numerous other groups of people benefit from the economic opportunities. In addition, government bodies at all levels receive taxes generated by the establishment and operation of these facilities.

Wendy's Restaurants, with corporate headquarters in Ohio, has established itself as one of the more popular fast-food restaurants. Their buildings are easily recognizable by their distinctive design and architecture. The prints in this chapter are actual prints that have been used to build many Wendy's Restaurants throughout

the United States. Clean, well-planned buildings designed for efficiency have helped to maintain customer loyalty.

PLANS

The scope of work detailed in the set of plans is for a new restaurant. Many types of drawings and specifications are utilized for construction of this project, including written specifications, civil engineering plans, foundation and floor plans, exterior and interior elevations, structural plans, electrical plans, HVAC plans, equipment plans, and a variety of schedules.

Wendy's Restaurants offer quality food products at moderate prices and provide a clean, family-oriented atmosphere.

Figure 9-1. Wendy's Restaurants are among the most popular fast-food restaurants and are easily recognizable by the distinctive design and architecture of their buildings.

The set of Wendy's Restaurant prints referenced in this chapter contains 28 sheets plus specifications. See Figure 9-2. (Specifications are included in Chapter 10.) Sheets 1 through F-1 were provided by Wendy's International, Inc. Sheets C-2, C-3, C-4, and C-6 were provided by Compass Consulting Group, LTD, a civil engineering firm in the Chicago area. The Photometric Plan was developed by LSI Industries and provided by Compass Consulting Group, LTD. When reading the prints, carefully check all portions of the prints, including schedules and elevations that are cross-referenced from one sheet to another, to ensure complete and accurate information exists.

GEOMETRIC PLAN AND PROJECT DETAILS, SHEETS C-2 and C-6

The Geometric Plan, Sheet C-2, provides information concerning the building lot and location and layout of the building on the lot. Details for various pavement markings and signage are shown on Sheets C-2 and C-6.

Building Lot Information

The building lot for the Wendy's Restaurant is Lot 5 in Parcel 1 of a growing commercial development property. The north and south property lines of the lot are parallel, but each is a different length. The north property line is 205.97′

while the south property line is 226.26'. The west property line, which is 174.54' long, is perpendicular (at a 90° angle) to the north and south property lines, and is directly aligned with the north/south meridian line as indicated by the compass reading of N00°00'00"E. The east property line is 175.72' long. A 12' wide public utility easement extends along the south, east, and west property lines. The Site Data indicates the building lot includes 0.866 acre, of which 0.722 acre is impervious area and 0.144 acre is pervious area. The total building area is 3362 sq ft. Impervious area is area that does not permit the direct passage of water, and includes the building and parking lot. The scale of the Geometric Plan is 1" = 20'.

Paving. Setbacks from the property lines are shown on the Geometric Plan. Pavement must be set back 3.5' from the north property line, 4' from the south property line, and 25' from the east property line. Pavement extends all the way to the west property line.

Notations regarding the pavement shown throughout the Geometric Plan relate to the Pavement Legend, Sheet C-2. For example, the proper composition of the 8" concrete pavement along the north side of the building is shown in the Pavement Legend. See Figure 9-3. The approximate quantity of each type of pavement is shown toward the bottom of Sheet C-2. For example, 1525 LF (linear feet) of type B-6.12 curb and gutter and 115 SY (square yards) of 5" thick concrete pavement are required. All concrete quantities should be verified by the contractor prior to ordering. Sheet C-6 indicates the dimensions, subsurface treatment, materials, expansion joint placement, and reinforcing for type B-6.12 curb and gutter. See Figure 9-4. Two #6 smooth rebar that are 18" long are placed in the premolded joints at 6" OC. The required concrete mix is a six-bag mix and has a strength of 3500 lb/sq in. The earth below the slab is compacted clay, which is covered with 2" compacted granular bedding material.

The overall curb height/depth is 15" and the overall width is 19". The radius at the top edge of the curb is 2" and provides a finished appearance. The radius at the drainage portion of the curb is 3" and the curb is sloped downward ¾" to direct storm water into the curb. Expansion joints are installed every 50' and contraction joints are spaced 25' on center. The minimum curb slope is 3%, or 3' vertical drop for each 100' linear feet.

INDEX OF DRAWINGS	
No.	**Description**
2	Site Details
3	Foundation Plan
4	Floor Plan
5	Exterior Elevations
6A	Interior Elevations / Dining Room
6B	Interior Elevations / Dining Room / Floor Tile / Carpet Plan
6C	Interior Elevations / Restrooms
6D	Interior Elevations / Backroom
6E	Interior Elevations / Backroom
7A	Wall Sections
7B	Wall Sections
8	Structural Plan
8A	Structural Details and Notes
9	Equipment Plan—Standard Grill

INDEX OF DRAWINGS	
No.	**Description**
10A	Register System and Outdoor Order Station
10B	Security Plan
11	HVAC Plan
12	Electrical Plan—Gas / Electric Cooking
13	Lighting and Reflected Ceiling Plan—Standard Grill
14	Electrical Distribution—Gas Heat–Gas / Electric Cooking
15	Plumbing Plan—Gas Heat–Gas Water Heater
15A	Plumbing Rough-In Plan and Ansul Fire Suppression System
F-1	Finish Schedules —Terra
C-2	Geometric Plan
C-3	Grading Plan
C-4	Utility Plan
C-6	Project Details
1 of 1	Photometric Plan

Figure 9-2. Twenty-eight sheets are included in the set of plans studied in this chapter. The specifications for the Wendy's Restaurant are included in Chapter 10.

PAVEMENT LEGEND

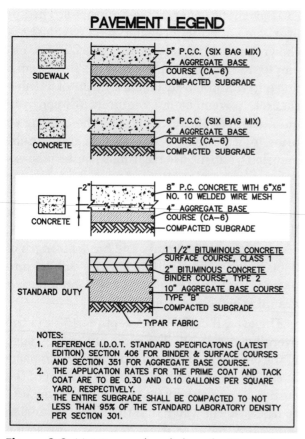

SIDEWALK
- 5" P.C.C. (SIX BAG MIX)
- 4" AGGREGATE BASE COURSE (CA-6)
- COMPACTED SUBGRADE

CONCRETE
- 6" P.C.C. (SIX BAG MIX)
- 4" AGGREGATE BASE COURSE (CA-6)
- COMPACTED SUBGRADE

CONCRETE
- 8" P.C. CONCRETE WITH 6"X6" NO. 10 WELDED WIRE MESH
- 4" AGGREGATE BASE COURSE (CA-6)
- COMPACTED SUBGRADE

STANDARD DUTY
- 1 1/2" BITUMINOUS CONCRETE SURFACE COURSE, CLASS 1
- 2" BITUMINOUS CONCRETE BINDER COURSE, TYPE 2
- 10" AGGREGATE BASE COURSE TYPE "B"
- COMPACTED SUBGRADE
- TYPAR FABRIC

NOTES:
1. REFERENCE I.D.O.T. STANDARD SPECIFICATONS (LATEST EDITION) SECTION 406 FOR BINDER & SURFACE COURSES AND SECTION 351 FOR AGGREGATE BASE COURSE.
2. THE APPLICATION RATES FOR THE PRIME COAT AND TACK COAT ARE TO BE 0.30 AND 0.10 GALLONS PER SQUARE YARD, RESPECTIVELY.
3. THE ENTIRE SUBGRADE SHALL BE COMPACTED TO NOT LESS THAN 95% OF THE STANDARD LABORATORY DENSITY PER SECTION 301.

Figure 9-3. Notations and symbols on the Geometric Plan, Sheet C-2, refer to the Pavement Legend. The 8" concrete pavement indicated along the North side of the building is highlighted here.

Additional paving information shown on the Geometric Plan includes dimensions, various radius cutouts, and striping. Entry into the parking lot is from the southwest corner of the building lot. The entry driveway is 25′ wide at its narrowest point. The entry driveway joins the 30′ wide public access road at the west property line, and a 20′ radius is formed along each side to assist drivers turning into the parking lot from the north or south. A 5′ radius on the south and 15′ radius adjoining a 3′ radius on the north complete the entry driveway. Vehicular traffic travels east through the parking lot and can park in the 9′-0″ wide parking spaces along the south or north side of the building, or continue around the building to enter the drive-through lane along the north and west side of the building. Many linear and radius dimensions are shown for the parking lot. The concrete pavement for the drive-through lane and pick-up area is 10.5′ wide to provide adequate room for larger vehicles. Concrete is to be used in this area to provide additional durability.

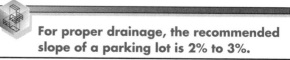

For proper drainage, the recommended slope of a parking lot is 2% to 3%.

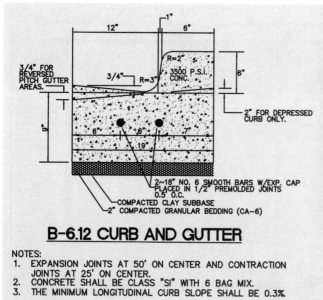

- 12"
- 6"
- 1"
- 3/4" FOR REVERSED PITCH GUTTER AREAS.
- 3/4"
- R=3"
- R=2"
- 3500 P.S.I. CONC.
- 6"
- 2" FOR DEPRESSED CURB ONLY.
- 6"
- 6"
- 6"
- 7"
- 19"
- 2~18" NO. 6 SMOOTH BARS W/EXP. CAP PLACED IN 1/2" PREMOLDED JOINTS 0.5 O.C.
- COMPACTED CLAY SUBBASE
- 2" COMPACTED GRANULAR BEDDING (CA-6)

B-6.12 CURB AND GUTTER

NOTES:
1. EXPANSION JOINTS AT 50′ ON CENTER AND CONTRACTION JOINTS AT 25′ ON CENTER.
2. CONCRETE SHALL BE CLASS "SI" WITH 6 BAG MIX.
3. THE MINIMUM LONGITUDINAL CURB SLOPE SHALL BE 0.3%.

Figure 9-4. Concrete curbs and gutters are placed according to specific dimensions.

Signage. Signage information includes pavement marker details, handicapped parking details, directional signs, and information about proper sign location on the building lot. As noted on the Geometric Plan, typical parking spaces are 9'-0" wide. A stripe extending 19.5' from the curb is painted between parking spaces. Various directional arrows and other markings are painted on the standard-duty pavement areas. A total of 43 parking spaces are provided for this Wendy's Restaurant—41 standard parking spaces and two handicapped-accessible parking spaces. The On Site Parking Data information indicates that the owner is required to provide 20 parking spaces for each 1000 sq ft of floor area. Floor area is equal to the building area multiplied by 85% (3362 sq ft × .85 = 2858 sq ft). For this Wendy's Restaurant, 57 parking spaces were required. However, the lot size and parking design only allowed for 43 parking spaces. The owner received a variance from Wendy's to allow the building to be built on the specified site with 43 parking spaces.

The Handicap Parking Detail indicates that handicapped-accessible parking spaces are 16.6' wide, which includes an 8' wide area for safely exiting and entering a vehicle. The handicapped-accessible parking space has a painted handicapped symbol and yellow striping spaced 3' OC. The Handicapped Painted Symbol Detail, Sheet C-6, shows the dimensions for the handicapped painted symbol. See Figure 9-5. A sign that indicates the handicapped-accessible space is 5' maximum from the curb of the parking space. Details indicating the sign height, post size and type, placement, and the content of the two signs are shown on the Handicapped Parking Sign Detail, Sheet C-6.

As shown on Sheet C-2, directional signs are 31" by 5" deep, and are typically mounted 16" above grade. The pick-up window sign is to be installed along the north edge of the entry driveway. The exit sign is to be installed along the north edge of the exit driveway. The enter sign is not specified for this building lot. The Wendy's monument sign is 4'-2" high by 6' wide, and is installed 1'-10" above finish grade on an 8' long brick base. The top of the monument sign is 6' above finished grade. The monument sign is shown on Sheet C-2 on the east side of the building. Additional signage includes the proposed menu board and preview board on the west side of the building.

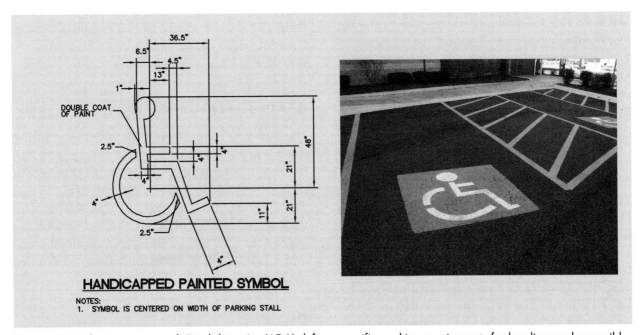

Figure 9-5. The Americans with Disabilities Act (ADA) defines specific marking requirements for handicapped-accessible parking spaces.

An outdoor order system allows drive-through customers to place their orders from a vehicle. Information concerning the outdoor order system is included on Sheet 10A. Per the Outdoor Order Station Notes, either an LCD pedestal or scoreboard order system is to be selected by the owner and coordinated with the contractor. In an LCD pedestal system, the drive-through customer places an order through a microphone in the pedestal and a list of ordered items is displayed on the LCD screen. In a scoreboard order system, a customer places the order through the microphone in the speaker column and an employee verifies the order by voice.

An AccuVIEW or Delphi LCD pedestal is required when an LCD pedestal order system is specified. Two slab details on Sheet 10A show the slabs required for the LCD pedestals. The AccuVIEW pedestal requires an 18½″ × 15″ × 32″ slab, while the Delphi pedestal requires a 26″ × 18″ × 36″ slab.

As shown on the LCD Pedestal Layout, Sheet 10A, a concrete base for the menu board is 18″ square by 36″ deep. However, the actual depth is based on the local building code and frost line. The concrete base for each sign cabinet is set 3′-4″ from the edge of the concrete slab. The sign cabinet is 8′-10¾″ long and set at a 45° angle to the curb line so it can be easily viewed. See Figure 9-6. The locations of the speaker column, electrical wiring, and 1″ conduit to connect the LCD pedestal and scoreboard to the restaurant for electrical and data transmission are shown. All conductors are routed in 1″ conduit below grade, with differing conduit configurations depending on the installation of either the LCD pedestal ordering system or scoreboard menu ordering system.

As shown on the LCD Pedestal Layout and Scoreboard Menu Layout, the concrete slab for each installation is 10′ wide by 20′ long. A vehicle is represented with phantom lines on the prints. The centerline of the LCD pedestal is to be 8′-9″ from the front corner of the concrete menu board base and 17″ from the curb line as shown on the LCD Pedestal Layout. The centerline of the scoreboard pedestal is to be 5′-1″ from the front corner of the concrete menu board base and 12″ from the curb line as shown on the Scoreboard Menu Layout. The speaker pedestal is 8″ wide and 3′-10″ high, and is mounted to a 12″ × 12″ × 36″ concrete base as shown on the Speaker Pedestal—Front and Side Elevations.

Figure 9-6. The menu board, installed along the drive-through lane, lists the restaurant's products and prices and includes a speaker and microphone.

Building Location

The overall dimensions of the Wendy's Restaurant are 47.0′ × 95.7′. The east edge of the building is set back 50.8′ (25.0′ + 17.0′ + 8.8′ = 50.8′) from the east property line. The south side of the building is set 52.0′ from the south property line (4.0′ + 19.5′ + 28.5′ = 52.0′).

GRADING PLAN, SHEET C-3

The Grading Plan, Sheet C-3, provides building site elevations and paving and utility information required in the construction of the restaurant. The drawing scale for Sheet C-3 is 1″ = 20′. The Grading Plan is used by excavating and paving contractors to determine cut and fill requirements for the building and parking areas and to determine pavement slope to ensure proper drainage.

Elevations

The site benchmark, which is a U.S. Geographical Survey (USGS) datum, is a cross cut in the top of a curb southwest of the building site. The benchmark, indicated as Benchmark #1, is 773.47'. The finished floor elevation of the building is 775.50', meaning the finished floor elevation will be 2.03' above the benchmark (775.50' − 773.47' = 2.03'). Elevations for the sidewalks, curbs, and paved areas are also shown. For example, the elevation at the top of the concrete walk leading to the west entrance door is 775.45'.

Existing elevations of the building lot are indicated with a lowercase "X" followed by the elevation reading. See Figure 9-7. For example, the existing elevation of the lot near the center of the building is shown as 774.43'. A contour line indicating the existing grade as 775' appears at the south edge of the parking lot.

The "FL" abbreviation indicates the flow line for the paved areas of the building site. The flow line is the lower horizontal portion of the curbs in which storm water flows. Unless otherwise specified, the top of the curb (TC) is 6" (.5') above the flow line. The flow line elevations are used as guides for paving around the perimeter of the parking lot. Proper flow line elevations ensure proper drainage of the paved areas.

Additional paving elevations are indicated with the letter "P." For example, the concrete drive at the pick-up area is noted with several elevations, the highest being P774.90'.

Two additional notations on the Grading Plan indicate the removal of 105 LF (linear feet) of existing curb and gutter for the entrance and 54 LF of existing curb and gutter for the exit drive. An Asphalt Driveway Apron Detail for entrance and exit driveways is provided on Sheet C-6. The existing curb and gutter is tied into the new one using two #4 rebar placed 6" OC.

Hidden lines and arrows around the parking lot indicate the highest elevations and the direction of slope toward parking lot drains. For example, the P774.80 elevation in the south parking lot indicates the pavement elevation at that point, and arrows indicate that the parking lot slopes away from this point toward the east and west.

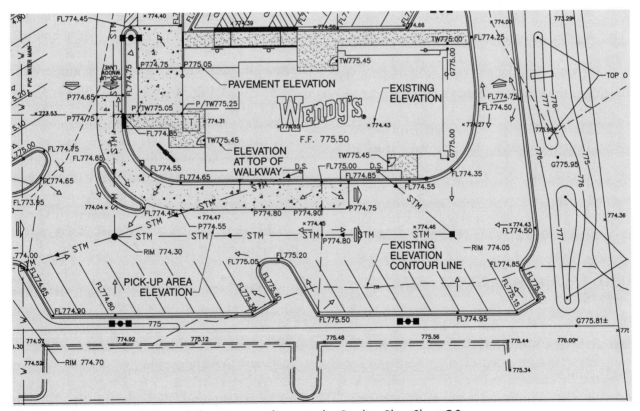

Figure 9-7. Existing and planned elevations are shown on the Grading Plan, Sheet C-3.

For this commercial development property, berms are required along the east side to separate vehicular traffic on the highway from restaurant patrons. A *berm* is a raised earth embankment. Three berms are formed in the utility easement area to fulfill the requirement. The minimum elevation at the top of the berms is 777.50′, placing the tops of the berms at least 2′ above the finished floor level. Vegetation planted on the berms will provide additional separation and protection.

Utilities

Elevations to the rim of each storm water catch basin are shown on the Grading Plan. For example, the elevation of the rim of the storm water catch basin in the northeast corner of the parking lot is 773.85′. Heavy lines with arrows labeled with "STM" represent the storm water drainage system in which rainwater and other natural precipitation flow. Water entering the downspouts (D.S.) on the building is directed to the storm water piping, which conveys the storm water to the storm sewer to the west of the property line. The rim of the curb inlet for the existing storm sewer connection is 772.60′, with the inflow at 776.31′. The only storm water from the parking lot that does not flow into the storm water drainage system on the property is water flowing into the street from the parking lot entrance and exit.

The water service (indicated with a "W"), which is installed under the surface of the parking lot, is shown on the west side of the lot. The water main is 12″ diameter PVC pipe and fittings. The sanitary sewer (indicated with "SAN"), runs along the west property line, with an access manhole indicated in the entrance drive.

UTILITY PLAN AND PROJECT DETAILS, SHEETS C-4 and C-6

Sheets C-4 and C-6 contain details regarding the installation of utilities for the Wendy's Restaurant. Sheet C-4 includes a Utility Plan and Profiles for Proposed Sanitary Sewer. Sheet C-6 provides details relating to the utilities to be installed on the property.

Utility Plan, Sheet C-4

The Utility Plan provides additional information relating to the Grading Plan, Sheet C-3, concerning sanitary sewer connections, and also indicates the storm water drainage system elevations. Storm water piping, sanitary sewer piping, electrical service, telephone service, and natural gas service are shown on the Utility Plan. Sheet C-6 also includes details for plumbing connections and trenches in which the utilities are to be installed.

Storm Water. Storm water piping is shown in the same configuration as on the Grading Plan, with additional information showing the sizes, materials, and slopes of the storm water piping and the sizes and types of catch basins and inlets. For example, the storm water pipe connecting the downspout to the inlet on the southeast corner of the building is approximately 35′ of 6″ diameter PVC pipe at a minimum 1% slope (1′ in 100′).

Details on Sheet C-6 show catch basin and inlet details. See Figure 9-8. Catch basins (CB) are constructed of precast reinforced concrete ring sections that are installed over a 6″ precast or cast-in-place concrete slab. The slabs are placed on 4″ of granular bedding material. Catch basins have inlet and outlet piping and are installed at intermediate points throughout the storm water drainage system. Inlets are constructed of precast reinforced concrete ring sections that are installed over a 4″ precast concrete slab. Four inches of granular bedding material is placed below the slabs. Inlets are installed at the two ends of the storm water drainage system on the property. A molded concrete invert is placed inside the inlets to divert storm water toward the outlet piping.

Sanitary. Sanitary sewer piping is indicated on the south side of the building using heavy lines with arrows labeled with "SAN." Two sections of 6″ diameter by 16′ long pipe project from the south side of the building, one leading to grease trap #2 and the other leading to manhole #1. The drop in pipe (D.I.P.) is 1% for the pipe leading to the grease trap and 2.56% for the pipe leading to the manhole. Information for each sanitary sewer connection indicates the rim elevation and the inflow and outflow elevations and directions. For example, the rim elevation of grease trap #2 is 774.85', the inflow from the building enters at an elevation of 770.29' on the north side of the trap, and the outflow exits the trap at an elevation of 770.12' on the west side.

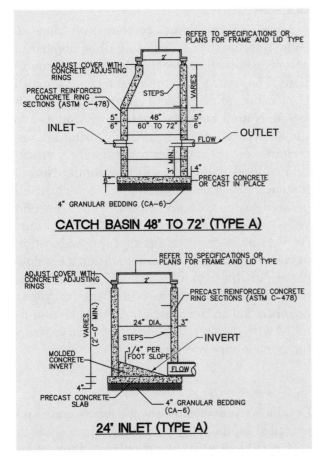

CATCH BASIN 48" TO 72" (TYPE A)

24" INLET (TYPE A)

Figure 9-8. Utility locations are carefully planned and installed prior to other construction operations. Catch basins and inlets are installed as part of the stormwater drainage system.

Sheet C-6 provides detail section drawings of the grease trap and manhole construction materials and installation. Grease traps are constructed of precast reinforced concrete ring sections that are installed over a 6" precast concrete base and 4" granular fill. In addition to inlet and outlet piping, a removable creosote-treated wood baffle, measuring 5'-6" high, is installed toward the bottom of the grease trap to allow the grease to settle out. Cleanouts are provided

at the inlet and outlet to provide access when removing obstructions from the pipe. Manholes are constructed of precast reinforced concrete sections that are installed on a 6" precast concrete base supported by 4" of granular bedding. The outsides of manholes should be moistureproofed with two coats of bituminous material.

As indicated on the Utility Plan, Sheet C-4, connection to the sanitary sewer is made at the manhole located in the entrance driveway. Contractors must adjust the existing rim height of the manhole from 768.13' to 773.85' The inlet and outlet connections of the manhole will be made with 8" PVC pipe with the inlet elevation at 768.06' and the outlet elevation at 768.03'.

Notations C01 and C02 are shown at the northwest and southwest corners of the building and are keyed to the Utility Crossings notations along the right side of Sheet C-4. C01 indicates that the 12" storm water piping is installed at an elevation of 769.91' and the sanitary sewer piping is installed at an elevation of 768.82', a difference of over 12". Notations C03 and C04 identify possible areas of conflict between the elevations of the water main and sanitary or storm sewers. The plumbing contractor must dip the water main below the sanitary and storm sewer piping if a minimum of 18" of vertical separation is required.

Profiles for Proposed Sanitary Sewer, Sheet C-4. The profiles are drawn using two different scales to show a maximum amount of information in a minimal area. The profiles are sections taken looking along the full length of the sanitary sewer installation in an east to west direction. In a manner similar to a typical wall section, the profiles show a vertical location of the pipe installation by taking a section below grade. The scale for each profile is 1" = 20' in a horizontal direction and 1" = 2' in a vertical direction. Elevations are listed along the right side of each profile in 2' increments. The 0+00 dimension on the profiles represents the location of the existing sanitary sewer manhole.

The profile on the left shows the finished floor of the building at 775.50', the proposed curb, gutter, and pavement, and the locations of the proposed electrical, telephone, and gas lines. The sanitary sewer lines exit the building at an elevation of 770.45′ and connect to Grease Trap #2 and Manhole #1. A 16′ length of 6″ pipe extends from the building to Grease Trap #2 and an 8′ length of 6″ pipe connects Grease Trap #2 to Manhole #1. The rim, inflow, and outflow elevations and directions are provided for the grease trap and manhole. After exiting manhole #1 and continuing toward the sanitary sewer manhole connection, the locations and elevations of the proposed 6″ PVC roof drain and 12″ RCP (round concrete pipe) storm sewer, and the existing 12″ water main must be considered. The existing 12″ water main is located at an elevation of 769.20, and is approximately 15′ from the existing sanitary manhole. The water main may be moved to a deeper location at an elevation of approximately 766′ to avoid conflict with the sanitary sewer system. For the existing sanitary manhole connection, the rim elevation and inflow elevation on each side of the manhole are given along with their direction. A typical water service connection is shown on the Typical Tap Service Piping Detail, Sheet C-6.

The detail on the right showing the Manhole #1 profile is similar to the detail on the left, with the only difference being the horizontal location of Manhole #1. Since Grease Trap #2 and Manhole #1 are located in the same horizontal alignment, the proper location could not be clearly shown on the profile on the left. The profile on the right shows the same elevations with the manhole placed in the proper horizontal location.

SITE DETAILS, SHEET 2

The Site Details provide information for construction of items located outside the building, such as the extruded curb, pavers, exterior pole lights, and trash enclosure. Curb construction and pavement marker details are also shown. The Standard Trash Enclosure Plan with sections, details, and an elevation indicate all dimensions and materials required for construction of the trash enclosure located at the rear of the building. Exterior signage footer and exterior pole light details are provided on Sheet 2. Note that four 1″ × 36″ anchor bolts are used to mount the exterior pole light on the footer. Double nuts and washers must be used when installing the pole light to allow air to circulate on the inside of the pole to prevent moisture accumulation. Details for the sidewalk ramp, sidewalk, and pavers complete the drawings on this sheet. Note that the scale used for the drawings on this sheet varies.

Four General Notes are shown on Sheet 2. Note 1 states that all signs shall be erected in accordance with all local codes and soil conditions. The signage erector must be familiar with the local building codes to ensure proper installation. Note 2 indicates that designs related to the structural integrity and anchoring are determined by the supplier and calls for verification of local wind and soil conditions. Note 3 instructs the general contractor to furnish all painted pavement markers, which are to be solid yellow. Note 4 indicates that a 24″ convex mirror is to be installed at an appropriate location to view customers at the order station if employees are unable to view vehicles directly from the pick-up window. The location of this mirror is not specified on the prints, but would be coordinated with the architect, owner, general contractor, and signage erector.

Curb Details

Details are provided on Sheet 2 for concrete and extruded asphalt curbs. Determination of which curb is to be used for a particular restaurant location is made in accordance with local requirements. In standard sets of prints utilized on a number of similar projects, architects may show a variety of curbs and other features that may be used on a project. The type of curb or other features installed on a particular job may not be shown on the prints but called out in the specifications or contracts with contractors and subcontractors on a job-specific basis. The curb selected will then be noted on the Site Details, Sheet 2.

Concrete Curb Detail, Sheet 2. The Concrete Curb Detail is drawn to the scale of 1″ = 1′-0″. The concrete curb is 6″ wide by 18″ high with

12" of the curb below grade. A continuous #4 rebar is run horizontally through the curb and is approximately centered in the 6" portion of the curb above grade. The corners of exposed curb receive a ¼" radius for a finished appearance. All concrete curbs must have expansion joints or saw cuts not more than 20'-0" apart. The Concrete Curb Detail is the standard curb drawing provided by Wendy's Restaurant. Civil drawings provided by a local engineering firm may vary from the standard drawings. Contractors should request clarification from the architect and project owner in cases of confusion or differences existing. Additional local concrete curb information is provided on Sheet C-6.

Extruded Curb Detail, Sheet 2. The Extruded Curb Detail is drawn to the scale of 1" = 1'-0". The curb is 8" wide by 6½" high, and is placed on 3" asphalt topping (compacted thickness) over 6" of crushed stone (compacted thickness). The symbol used to represent the extruded curb is the same as the asphalt paving, denoting that the curb is also asphalt. No. 3 rebar (⅜" diameter) are driven through the asphalt topping and crushed stone at 4'-0" OC to anchor the extruded curb to the topping pavement. An asphaltic bonding agent is also applied to the area between the curb and topping pavement to provide a good bond and to prevent water penetration that could deteriorate the curb structure.

Pavement Marker Details, Sheet 2

Pavement markers provide directional information to restaurant patrons. Two pavement marker details are shown, with each drawn to a scale of ½" = 1'-0". The PICK-UP WINDOW pavement marker is triangular in shape with a 6'-0" base and 30° sides, and is preceded by an 8" × 4'-8" rectangular bar placed 8" in front of the triangle. Eight-inch letters are located in front of the rectangular bar. The EXIT ONLY pavement marker is similar to the PICK-UP WINDOW marker and uses the same basic dimensions for the marker and lettering.

> The minimum turning radius for an average size private vehicle is 24'-0".

Standard Trash Enclosure Plan, Sheet 2

The plan view, elevation, sections, and details for the trash enclosure occupy a large portion of Sheet 2. Two sections (A/2 and B/2) and one elevation (Typical Front Elevation) are referred to on the Standard Trash Enclosure Plan. Details C and D, which provide information for the gate latch, are referred to in the Typical Front Elevation for the trash enclosure.

The Standard Trash Enclosure Plan is drawn to a scale of ⅜" = 1'-0". The trash enclosure is constructed over a 12'-0" × 38'-0" concrete slab. The slab is 6" thick and is reinforced with W2.9 × W2.9 wire mesh (welded wire reinforcement). The slab is sealed against grease absorption and slopes ¼" per foot from back to front to provide proper drainage for the slab. Expansion joints are provided at each of the seven post footings. An *expansion joint* is a joint that separates adjoining sections of concrete to allow for movement caused by expansion and contraction of the concrete. The joints are filled with asphalt-impregnated material. Corner posts are 6" × 6" treated cedar and are set in 6" from rear and sides of the slab. Wood gates are attached to two 3" square metal tubing posts installed next to the two front cedar posts. See Figure 9-9. The Hinge Tab detail indicates that ½" × 2" flat hinge tabs are welded to the metal tubing posts. Two 6" concrete-filled posts (bollards) are installed in front of the trash enclosure to protect the posts from vehicle damage. The trash dumpster area is separated from the grease barrel storage area by two additional 6" concrete-filled posts that are painted yellow. The grease barrel area is accessible through a single 4'-6" wide gate that is hinged on a square steel post similar to the front gates.

Cutting planes for Sections A/2 and B/2 are indicated on the Standard Trash Enclosure Plan. The Typical Front Elevation is aligned vertically with the Standard Trash Enclosure Plan for ease of interpretation.

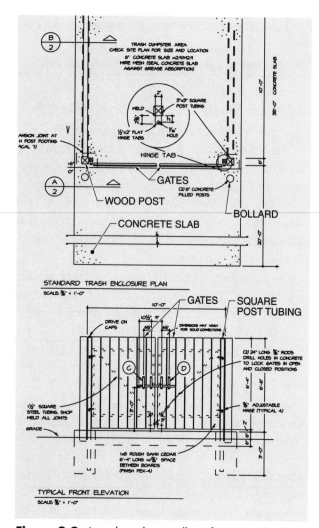

STANDARD TRASH ENCLOSURE PLAN
SCALE: ⅜" = 1'-0"

TYPICAL FRONT ELEVATION
SCALE: ⅜" = 1'-0"

Figure 9-9. A trash enclosure allows for access by trash removal services and conceals the dumpster from public view and access. The Standard Trash Enclosure Plan and Typical Front Elevation are aligned with one another for ease of visualization.

Section A, Sheet 2. Section A/2 is referred to in the Standard Trash Enclosure Plan and shows the gated end of the trash enclosure. See Figure 9-10. Section A/2 is drawn to the scale of ¾" = 1'-0". Concrete footings for the front posts are 12" × 18" × 36" and support the wood and steel posts. The tops of the footings are flush with the top of the 6" concrete slab, both of which are 6" above grade.

The 6" × 6" treated cedar posts are attached to the footings with Simpson CB66 post bases that are set 8" into the concrete footings. The posts are attached to the bases using two ⅝" diameter bolts at each base.

As shown in Section A/2, the 3" steel posts are placed 3" up from the bottom of the footing and 3½" in from the edge of the footing, and extend 6'-6" above the finished slab. Post tops are finished with drive-on caps that prevent moisture accumulation inside the pipe. The gate frame is fabricated from 1½" square steel tubing that is welded together. The gates are finished with 1 × 8 × 6'-4" rough sawn cedar spaced ⅜" apart and finished with a PEX-4 finish.

The PEX-4 finish specified for the trash enclosure is a solid-color latex acrylic stain that is Charleston brown.

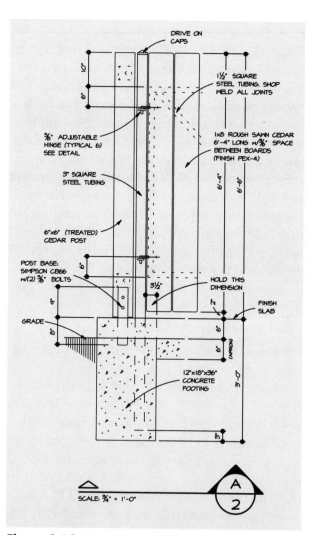

Figure 9-10. Sections provide detailed construction information about a variety of building components.

Section B, Sheet 2. Section B/2 is referred to in the Standard Trash Enclosure Plan and shows details of the thickened perimeter slab and the fence. The slab thickness is increased from 6″ to 12″ at its perimeter, with the thickened portion extending 8″ horizontally. The top surface of the slab is 6″ above grade. Welded wire reinforcement in the slab is indicated by horizontal hidden lines. The 12″ diameter footing, used to support the cedar fence posts, is shown with hidden lines.

The fence is constructed of 1 × 8 rough-sawn cedar boards which are stained. The boards are staggered and attached to each side of 4″ × 4″ top and bottom cedar rails. The staggered boards are overlapped 1″ to prevent direct sight through the fence while providing air flow. The bottoms of the boards are 2″ above the concrete slab to avoid direct contact with the slab. The top rail is 4″ below the top of the fence and the bottom rail is 9″ above the concrete slab.

Typical Front Elevation, Sheet 2. The Typical Front Elevation, drawn at a scale of ⅜″ = 1′-0″, provides basic information for construction of the front gates. The gates are constructed with 1 × 8 × 6′-4″ rough-sawn cedar boards that are attached to a 1½″ square steel tubing frame. A ⅜″ space is specified between boards on the gate. The 3″ square steel tubing posts are placed 10′-0″ apart. Height dimensions shown on the Typical Front Elevation include the footings, overall post heights, and latch information.

Dimensions for placement of the gate latch are noted on the Typical Front Elevation. The centers of the brackets are spaced 6½″ apart and the bottoms of the brackets are 3′-0″ above the top of the slab. A 3″ space is provided between the gates to allow them to easily open and close. A notation along the right side of the elevation specifies that two holes are to be drilled in the concrete to allow for ⅜″ diameter by 24″ long rods to hold the gates in open and closed positions.

Details C and D provide information about the gate latch used on the front gate. Detail C shows the ⅜″ × 1½″ × 30″ steel gate arm, which is secured by two gate latch arm supports on each gate. Each gate latch arm support is fabricated from ¼″ × 1½″ × 10″ steel plate with a 12″ brace welded to the latch. Spacers, measuring ⅜″ × 1½″, allow the steel gate arm to pivot in a vertical arc on the left gate and drop down into the two gate latch arm supports on the left gate. The latch supports are fastened to each gate using ⅜″ diameter bolts. Dimensions for locating the bolt holes are provided.

Detail D provides dimensions for the two open-top catches to receive the gate arm on the right side gate. The catches are fabricated from ¼″ × 1½″ steel plate. A ⅜″ × 1½″ spacer maintains spacing for the front catch lip. The front catch lip is formed of ¼″ × 1½″ × 3½″ steel plate. The top of the lip is slightly bent to allow for easier placement of the steel gate arm.

Signage Footer and Exterior Pole Lights Details

The Exterior Signage Footer and Exterior Pole Lights details provide information for the signage erector and electrical contractor. The number of signs required is not specified on Sheet 2. Rather, the number of signs and their specific locations are shown on the Geometric Plan, Sheet C-2.

Exterior Signage Footer Detail, Sheet 2. Dimensions for the concrete signage footer are determined by the signage erector and general contractor based on the signage requirements and the local building codes. Steel pipe used for mounting the signage is embedded in the concrete footer to within 3″ of the bottom. The top of the footer is ½″ above grade. The signage is furnished and installed by the sign erector. The Exterior Signage Footer is drawn to a scale of 1″ = 1′-0″.

Exterior Pole Lights Detail, Sheet 2. Exterior pole lights are used to illuminate the exterior of the Wendy's Restaurant. See Figure 9-11. The number and location of exterior pole lights is indicated on the Geometric Plan, Sheet C-2, and Photometric Plan, Sheet 1 of 1. The detail states that the 7′-0″ tall concrete pier is sized according to local codes and soil conditions. The pier extends 2′-0″ above grade. An air gap is provided between the pole light base and the top of the pier to allow moisture to escape.

Figure 9-11. Exterior pole lights illuminate the exterior of a building. Pole light location is indicated on the Geometric Plan, Sheet C-2.

The electrical contractor is responsible for furnishing and installing the exterior pole lights, including the concrete pier, anchor bolts, and bottom plate. The anchor bolt cover is to be provided by the lighting supplier. Lighting notes at the top of the drawing provide specific information about the type of lighting, including wattage, foot-candle lighting requirements, and ballast types. The light poles are a maximum of 30'-0" high. The Exterior Pole Lights Detail is drawn to the scale of ½" = 1'-0".

Sidewalk Details

Three additional details on Sheet 2 include the Sidewalk Ramp Detail, Sidewalk Finish Detail, and Paver Detail. None of these details are drawn to scale.

Sidewalk Ramp Detail, Sheet 2. Per the Americans with Disabilities Act (ADA), public places must provide unobstructed access for disabled individuals. Sidewalk ramps are provided for this purpose and also to provide easy access for delivery of goods. The run of the sidewalk ramp is a minimum of 36" wide. A 1 in 10 minimum slope is specified on each side of the ramp with a 1 in 12 slope specified for the central section. The surface of the ramp area is finished with a rough crosshatch concrete finish to improve traction. A notation also states additional slope requirements for narrower ramps. The Sidewalk Ramp Detail, Sheet 2, is a standard Wendy's ramp detail. The Handicap Ramp Detail, Sheet C-6, provides information about the ramp and surface finishes required for the handicapped-accessible sidewalk ramp for this particular restaurant. The handicapped-accessible sidewalk ramp shown along the north side of the building is detailed by a local engineering firm.

Sidewalk Finish Detail, Sheet 2. A ¾" contraction joint is required every 4'-0" in concrete sidewalks regardless of the sidewalk width. A *contraction joint* is a groove made in the concrete surface to create a weakened plane and control the location of cracking. The edges of each sidewalk section are trowel-finished and the field surface of each section receives a broom finish. The broom finish provides a nonslip finish for restaurant patrons. An elevation of the sidewalk is shown directly below the plan view. The sidewalk finish is also shown on the Project Details, Sheet C-6.

Paver Detail, Sheet 2. The Paver Detail indicates that 2" to 12" of coarse granular material is used as a base for the pavers. Actual thickness of the base varies with the site. A 4" concrete slab is placed over the base followed by a ½" sand bedding course. Brick pavers measuring 3⅛" thick are placed on the bedding course and the joints between the pavers are filled with sand. The Paver Detail is a standard Wendy's detail provided for consideration by all Wendy's Restaurant locations. There are no pavers specified for this particular restaurant.

PHOTOMETRIC PLAN, SHEET 1 OF 1

The Photometric Plan provides information on the proper placement of light poles and the required illumination levels. Four light poles are indicated on the plan, and their general lines of illumination are also shown. The Luminaire Schedule at the bottom of the sheet includes the symbols, quantities, labels, lighting arrangements, required lumens for each, and total watts. All poles are 30′ high and are mounted according to the requirements indicated on Sheet 2. Per the lighting notes on Sheet 2, all site lighting is to be 750 W pulse-start metal halide vertical burn fixtures.

A grid of points across the entire building lot indicates the minimum illumination levels required in the final luminaire (lighting fixture) installation. The corners and outlying portions of the lot are required to have minimal illumination. For example, the southwest corner of the lot is required to have at least 3.8 lumens and the southeast corner is required to have at least 2.2 lumens. A *lumen* is a measure of illumination. The customer entrances and delivery areas receive greater illumination. For example, the delivery area at the back of the building receives 10.3 lumens of illumination. The contractor is responsible for rotating the reflectors in each light to obtain the levels of illumination indicated on the Photometric Plan.

Two 320 W pulse-start metal halide floodlights are to be installed atop designated light poles. See Figure 9-12. The floodlights should be directed toward the building to provide increased illumination levels.

Figure 9-12. Each light is carefully adjusted to provide the required amount of illumination as specified on the Photometric Plan.

> **A minimum lighting level of 5 foot-candles is recommended for entrances.**

FOUNDATION PLAN, SHEET 3

The Foundation Plan provides dimensions and information about the foundation of the building. The Foundation Plan is drawn to the scale of ¼″ = 1′-0″. Overall building dimensions are 45′-0″ × 87′-8″. Unless otherwise noted, all footings are 20″ × 8″ with two #4 rebar running continuously. Footing depths must be verified to comply with local building code requirements. All concrete block (concrete masonry units) coursing begins at the top of the footing. Electrical and mechanical drawings included in the set of prints provide additional information for conduit and piping runs. Three #4 rebar that are 2′-0″ long are placed 12″ OC at all door openings. Concrete for the slab is then placed through the openings. A control joint is centered on the wall at all door openings.

Footings are designed for 3000 pounds per square foot (PSF) soil-bearing pressure. Local soil-bearing capacity must be verified before footings are placed. A notation assigns responsibility for the investigation of existing soil conditions to the contractor and owner. Anchor bolts measuring ½″ × 18″ with 3″ hooked ends are placed 32″ on center in stud walls. The CMUs should be grouted solid.

The floor slab area is unexcavated. The top of the finished concrete floor slab acts as 100.00′ for other elevations. The 4″ floor slab is placed over 4″ of granular fill, which is covered with a 6 mil vapor barrier. The slab is reinforced with 6 × 6—W1.4 × W1.4 welded wire reinforcement. Rebar is also placed in the slab along inside corners to prevent the slab from cracking. A notation indicates that ⅛″ control joints and/or construction joints are to be sawn into the slab within 24 hours of concrete placement.

Foundation walls are either 8″ or 12″ concrete block as shown in the various sections referred to on the Foundation Plan. Four cutting planes refer to Sections A, B, C, and D shown on Sheet 7A. Four additional cutting planes refer to Sections E, F, G, and H shown on Sheet 7B.

Section A, Sheet 7A is a section taken along the east wall of the building and includes information about the finish materials, including the Series II fascia system.

Section A, Sheet 7A

Section A is taken from a cutting plane through the east wall of the Public Area, Room 101. The room number is designated on the Floor Plan, Sheet 4, and the number and room name are indicated on the Room Finish Schedule, Sheet 4. Cutting plane A/7A is shown on the Foundation Plan, Sheet 3, and the Floor Plan, Sheet 4. Section A is drawn to the scale of ¾″ = 1′-0″.

Section A shows a 24″ × 12″ foundation footing with three #4 rebar running continuously through it and a 12″ concrete block foundation wall. See Figure 9-13. A course of 8″ concrete block is laid on top of the three courses of 12″ concrete block and is faced with brick. Two #5 hooked dowels are embedded in the concrete footing and extend up into the 8″ concrete block. Two anchor bolts, measuring 1¼″ diameter by 24″ long, are embedded in the concrete-filled cores of the concrete block and project through the 8″ concrete block. The anchor bolts are installed at each end of the sheer wall, and are secured with two Simpson HD20A holdowns to the foundation. A double nut and washer are placed at the bottom of the anchor bolt to secure it into the concrete masonry unit structure. After concrete for the footings is placed and the concrete block for the foundation wall are laid, 24″ wide pieces of Styrofoam insulation (R-5) are placed along the inside of the foundation walls. The insulation extends from the bottom of the second course of 12″ concrete block to the top of the 8″ block. The trench is backfilled with granular fill and the fill is spread across the unexcavated area to serve as a base for the concrete floor slab. A notation indicates the installation of through-wall flashing near the foundation between the wood-framed

wall and masonry wall. The flashing has a mortar screen and weep holes 24″ OC to allow for the escape of trapped moisture. Masonry ties start at the third course of masonry at the lowest point of the wood-framed wall.

The overall wall height above the finished floor, including the top of the parapet, is 15′-4″. The framed wall height is 14′-9½″ above the finished floor, and the brick-veneer wall extends 9′-0″ above the finished floor. The wall is framed with 2 × 6 studs spaced 16″ OC and is filled with R-19 insulation. A firestop is installed approximately 10′ above the finished floor to inhibit the spread of fire above the suspended ceiling. Exterior finish includes ½″ CDX plywood sheathing, one layer of 15 lb felt or building paper, and brick veneer with a split-faced block course. The fascia above the brick-veneer wall is provided by the owner and installed by the general contractor. The fascia extends from the top of the brick-veneer wall to the top of the parapet, and is fastened to 2 × 4 nailers running continuously around the building. Interior wall finish includes a vapor barrier, ⅝″ thick drywall (gypsum board), and various paneling, wall covering, and trim members. The suspended ceiling in this area is 9′-6″ above the finished floor.

A continuous doubled 2 × 8 is fastened to the inside of the framed wall to support the roof edge. The ends of wood I-joists (TJI roof joists) are shown on Section A. The height to the bottom of the roof system varies depending on the roof slope at various points around the building.

Shear walls provide additional support for structures to ensure structural integrity against unusual loading such as earthquakes or wind storms. Special features or components of this shear wall include additional anchoring to the foundation using two 1¼″ × 24″ anchor bolts with double nuts and a washer. The anchor bolts are used to secure the HD20A holdowns to the foundation. The holddowns are bolted to three 2 × 6 studs at the end of each wall. In addition, ½″ plywood sheathing is fastened to each side of the wall with solid blocking at all horizontal joints, and nailed 4″ OC using 10d nails, as shown on the Shear Wall Detail, Sheet 3. The shear wall sections extend 48″ from each end. Additional information regarding shear wall construction is included later in this chapter.

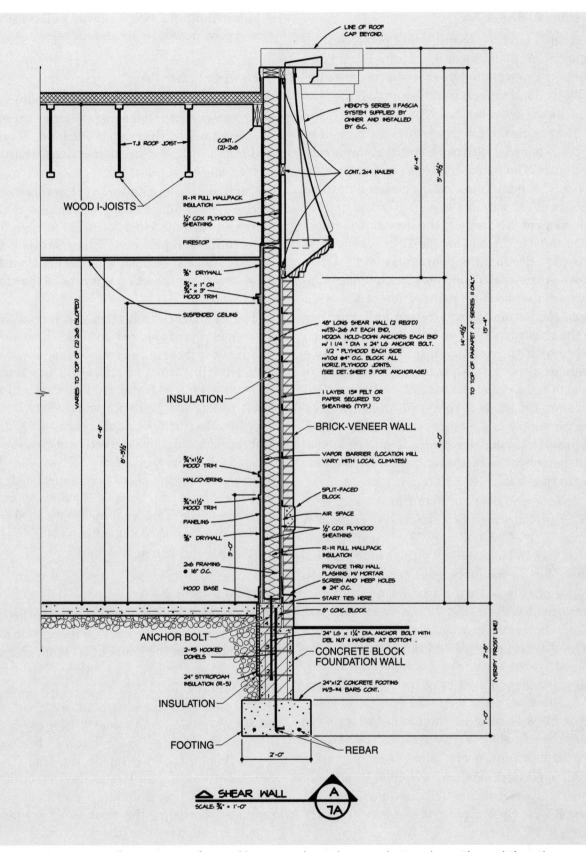

LINE OF ROOF CAP BEYOND.

WENDY'S SERIES II FASCIA SYSTEM SUPPLIED BY OWNER AND INSTALLED BY G.C.

CONT. (2)-2x8

CONT. 2x4 NAILER

TJI ROOF JOIST

WOOD I-JOISTS

R-19 FULL WALLPACK INSULATION

½" CDX PLYWOOD SHEATHING

FIRESTOP

⅝" DRYWALL

¾" x 1" ON ¾" x 3" WOOD TRIM

SUSPENDED CEILING

48" LONG SHEAR WALL (2 REQ'D) w/(3)-2x6 AT EACH END, HD20A HOLD-DOWN ANCHORS EACH END w/ 1 1/4" DIA x 24" LG ANCHOR BOLT. 1/2" PLYWOOD EACH SIDE w/10d @4" O.C. BLOCK ALL HORIZ. PLYWOOD JOINTS. (SEE DET. SHEET 3 FOR ANCHORAGE)

INSULATION

1 LAYER 15# FELT OR PAPER SECURED TO SHEATHING (TYP.)

BRICK-VENEER WALL

VAPOR BARRIER (LOCATION WILL VARY WITH LOCAL CLIMATES)

¾"x1½" WOOD TRIM

WALCOVERING

SPLIT-FACED BLOCK

AIR SPACE

¾"x1½" WOOD TRIM

PANELING

½" CDX PLYWOOD SHEATHING

⅝" DRYWALL

R-19 FULL WALLPACK INSULATION

2x6 FRAMING @ 16" O.C.

PROVIDE THRU WALL FLASHING W/ MORTAR SCREEN AND WEEP HOLES @ 24" O.C.

WOOD BASE

START TIES HERE

8" CONC. BLOCK

ANCHOR BOLT

24" LG x 1¼" DIA. ANCHOR BOLT WITH DBL NUT & WASHER AT BOTTOM.

2-#5 HOOKED DOWELS

CONCRETE BLOCK FOUNDATION WALL

24" STYROFOAM INSULATION (R-5)

24"x12" CONCRETE FOOTING W/3-#4 BARS CONT.

INSULATION

FOOTING

REBAR

VARIES TO TOP OF (2) 2x6 (SLOPED)

4'-8"

8'-5½"

3'-0"

6'-4"

5'-9½"

14'-9½"

15'-4"

TO TOP OF PARAPET AT SERIES II ONLY

4'-0"

2'-8" (VERIFY FROST LINE)

1'-0"

2'-0"

△ SHEAR WALL
SCALE: ¾" = 1'-0"

A / 7A

Figure 9-13. Exterior wall sections are referenced by cutting planes shown on the Foundation Plan and Floor Plan.

Section B, Sheet 7A

Section B is taken from cutting planes on the Foundation Plan, Sheet 3, and the Floor Plan, Sheet 4. The section shows the wall between the walk-in Cooler/Freezer and Room 108. Section B is drawn to the scale of ¾″ = 1′-0″.

The footing for this area is 20″ wide by 8″ deep and is reinforced with two #4 rebar running continuously. The foundation construction is similar to the foundation construction shown in Section A/7A, with the same anchoring and reinforcement. The edge of the floor slab is thickened to bear directly on the 12″ CMUs and to provide additional support for the 4″ CMUs above. A course of 8″ concrete block provides support for the wood-framed portion of the wall. Construction of the wood-framed wall is similar to the construction of the wall shown in Section A/7A, with the additional information that a pressured-treated (Wolmanized™) sill plate is used to resist decay. Blocking (2 × 6s) is installed between the studs of the wood-framed wall at the joint between the gypsum board and plywood to provide support for the ends of the panels. The height to the bottom of the suspended ceiling in this area is 10′-6″.

As shown on the Floor Plan, Sheet 4, a 12′-0″ × 15′-0″ prefabricated Cooler/Freezer is installed at the rear of the building. The Cooler/Freezer module is to be supplied by the owner and installed by the manufacturer. Four-inch concrete block veneer is tied to the wood-framed wall with corrugated wall ties set 16″ OC vertically and 32″ OC horizontally. An air space is provided between the framed wall and concrete block. The wall above the Cooler/Freezer module is flashed, has two courses of split-faced concrete block, and is finished with brick. Another course of split-faced block is set near the top of the wall followed by a final top course of brick. The parapet cap detail is provided on Sheet 8A.

An additional notation on Section B concerns shear wall construction. This note also applies to Detail A-7A. Special construction provisions are made to incorporate holddown anchors at each end of the wall for seismic and wind resistance.

Additional information on shear wall construction is provided later in this chapter.

Section C, Sheet 7A

Section C is taken from a cutting plane through the south exterior wall along the drive-through area as shown on the Foundation Plan, Sheet 3, and the Floor Plan, Sheet 4. Section C is drawn to the scale of ¾″ = 1′-0″.

The footing, foundation, roof, and exterior brick-veneer wall information is similar to that shown on Sections A and B, Sheet 7A. Since food preparation equipment, which generates a significant amount of heat, is placed against the exterior wall, construction of the wall differs from other walls.

The wall shown in Section C is framed with 18 ga metal studs spaced 16″ OC. The exterior and interior faces of the metal-framed wall are covered with Durock® wallboard. Durock wallboard is a cement board product that will not swell, soften, or delaminate, and is also noncombustible. Moisture-resistant plywood or ⅝″ thick Durock is required for the bottom 12″ of the interior face of the wall. Hidden lines show the fryer assembly, stainless steel exhaust hood, and a stainless steel panel supplied by the equipment contractor. The distance from the finished floor to the bottom of the exhaust hood is 5′-5″. The suspended ceiling height is 8′-10″.

Section D, Sheet 7A

The cutting plane for Section D is taken through the exterior wall of the Cooler/Freezer slab area and is shown on the Foundation Plan, Sheet 3, and the Floor Plan, Sheet 4. Section C is drawn to the scale of ¾″ = 1′-0″.

The footing in this area is 16″ × 8″, with two #4 rebar running continuously. The top of the footing is 2′-8″ below grade, but may be deeper depending on the frost line in the area. Three courses of 8″ concrete block are laid on top of the footing. The 4″ floor slab is thickened in this area and is supported by the block. A ½″ expansion joint is installed between the thickened floor slab and the exterior sidewalk.

Scupper Detail, Sheet 7A

While not referred to in any particular wall section on this sheet, the scupper detail is shown at ½" = 1'-0" scale. A *scupper* is an opening in a wall that allows rainwater to drain into the downspout and storm water drainage system. See Figure 9-14. The Scupper Detail indicates that the single-ply roofing system is returned around the top of the scupper opening. A sealant is used at the top and bottom of the wrapped area on the exterior of the wall. The termination bar and fastener for the scupper are supplied by the roofing manufacturer.

> **The number and size of scuppers must be carefully determined to prevent water from collecting on the roof. Rectangular scuppers convey more water than round scuppers.**

Section E, Sheet 7B

The cutting plane for Section E is shown on the Foundation Plan, Sheet 3, and the Floor Plan, Sheet 4. The section represents the north wall of the building in the general dining area of the restaurant and shows the framing and construction of the window openings. Section E is drawn to the scale of ¾" = 1'-0".

The foundation in this area is similar to other building areas including a 20" × 8" footing and the four courses of concrete block with anchor bolts embedded in the concrete-filled cores. The windowsill is 3'-0" above the finished floor. The wall below the window is constructed with 2 × 6 wood studs spaced 16" OC that are sheathed with ½" CDX plywood and finished on the exterior with a brick veneer. A course of split-faced concrete block is placed directly below the brick rowlock windowsill. The aluminum store window frame projects 1" out from the face of the ½" plywood wall sheathing. Flashing is installed above and below the window frame. The general contractor is to provide end dam flashing for the window frame. The window header is 9'-0" above the finished floor, and is constructed of three 2× wood members. The fascia system is supplied by the owner and installed by the general contractor.

The interior side of the wall is covered with a vapor barrier and ⅝" drywall (gypsum board). Paneling is installed below the window with wood trim, and wallpaper is applied to the drywall from the wood trim up to the suspended ceiling line. A ¼" × ¾" prefinished oak batten strip is installed along the edges of the storefront frame where the wallpaper meets the aluminum frame. R-19 insulation is installed in the wall cavity. The suspended ceiling is 9'-6" above the finished floor.

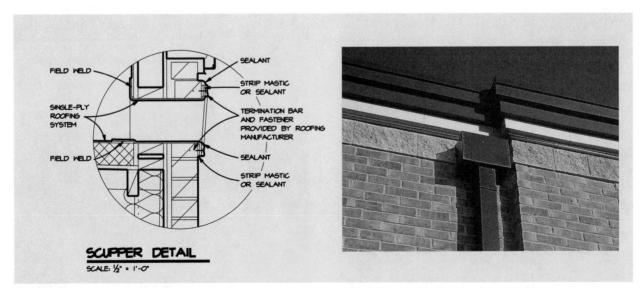

Figure 9-14. Scuppers collect rainwater from the roof and channel it into downspouts.

Section F, Sheet 7B

The cutting plane for Section F is shown on the Foundation Plan, Sheet 3, and the Floor Plan, Sheet 4. The section is taken through the exterior wall in Room 101A leading from the dining area to the restroom area. Section F is drawn to the scale of ¾" = 1'-0".

The foundation and exterior wood-framed brick-veneer wall are shown in Section F. Interior wall finish is shown in the section. Paneling is applied to the wall to a height of 2'-10½", with WC-C wall covering above the paneling. Moisture-resistant ⅝" plywood or Durock is applied to the lower 12" of the wall. Three horizontal trim members are applied to the wall. One trim member is 2'-10½" above the finished floor, another trim member is 9⅛" above the first member, and the top trim member is installed 4'-7⅞" above the second member. See Figure 9-15. The suspended ceiling height is 8'-10" above the finished floor in this area. Tile base is set with a J mold at the top.

Additional information supplied on Section F relates to the roof system. The roof is sheathed with ⅝" CDX plywood, which is covered with R-20 rigid insulation and finished with a single-ply roofing system. The roof system shown in Section F is typical of the majority of the building.

Section G, Sheet 7B

The cutting plane for Section G is shown on the Foundation Plan, Sheet 3, and the Floor Plan, Sheet 4. Section G is drawn to the scale of ¾" = 1'-0". The section shows the pick-up window treatment at the wall and the method for projecting this portion of the building out from the face of the rest of the building.

The foundation and wall framing below the pick-up window are similar to other parts of the building. The pick-up window is set 3'-0" above the finished floor and is 4'-4" high. The overall height of the pick-up window wall is 12'-0" (3'-0" + 4'-4" + 4'-8" = 12'-0"). The section above the window is framed using a triple 2 × 10 header with ½" plywood fillers, which are glued and nailed to form a single structural unit. The remainder of the upper portion of the wall is framed with 2 × 6s with a double top plate.

Figure 9-15. A variety of wall finishes and trim members are installed at specified heights as indicated on sections.

Figure 9-16. Pick-up windows project from the face of a restaurant to provide easier patron access.

Exterior wall finish above the pick-up window consists of $8'' \times 8''$ wall tile applied to $\frac{1}{2}''$ plywood sheathing. A $5'' \times 3\frac{1}{2}'' \times \frac{5}{16}''$ steel angle is attached to the face of the wall above the tile for use as a lintel for two courses of split-faced block and one course of brick. See Figure 9-16. The top of the wall is capped with a waterproofing system recommended by the roofing manufacturer.

The roof over the pick-up window area is constructed with 2×10 joists spaced $16''$ OC. The tops of the joists are cut to form a slight roof slope for water drainage. Four 2×12s, which are glued and nailed together, form a header to support the roof trusses and the parapet above the roof. A $6'' \times 3\frac{1}{2}'' \times \frac{5}{16}''$ steel angle is fastened to the ends of the wood I-joists to provide a base for the brick-veneer parapet. The parapet is finished with brick veneer, split-faced block, and a prefinished aluminum fascia. The overall wall height is 15'-4" to the top of the parapet.

Section H, Sheet 7B

As shown on the Foundation Plan, Sheet 3, and the Floor Plan, Sheet 4, Section H is taken through the side of the pick-up window area and shows a fixed window, which allows employees at the pick-up window to view oncoming patrons. Section H is drawn to the scale of $\frac{3}{4}'' = 1'\text{-}0''$.

The foundation in this area is similar to other portions of the building. A wood-framed brick-veneer wall is constructed below the window, with additional interior moisture protection at the bottom of the wall comprised of $\frac{5}{8}''$ moisture-resistant plywood or Durock. The fixed window is 4'-4" high, and is set 1" out from the face of the $\frac{1}{2}''$ plywood wall sheathing. A triple 2×10 forms the header above the window. A 2×4 is bolted to the wall studs for use as a ledger for the 2×10 joists shown on Detail G.

Detail A—Recessed Mop Basin, Sheet 3

Detail A refers to a mop basin area shown in the northwest corner of the floor slab. As shown on the Foundation Plan, Sheet 3, the mop basin area is 1'-6" × 2'-4", and is 3'-2" from the north wall and 4'-2" from the west wall. The floor slab in the mop basin area is thickened to 7", and 2"

high kitchen tile are placed around the perimeter of the recessed floor area. The mop basin recess slopes 1" toward the center where it connects to a 3" diameter drain line. Tile base extends up the adjoining wall.

Detail B—Shear Wall Detail, Sheet 3

A notation in the lower-right corner of the Foundation Plan refers to Detail B, Sheet 3, for information about the anchoring system for the shear wall. The Shear Wall Detail shows an enlarged 24" wide by 12" deep footing extending 8'-0" from the outside of the footing. See Figure 9-17. Three #4 rebar are placed 3" from the bottom of the footing. Two #5 hooked dowels are embedded in the footing and project up through the four courses of concrete block. The dowels are grouted solid in the concrete block. A $1\frac{1}{4}''$ diameter by 24" long anchor bolt is embedded in the concrete block between the two #5 hooked dowels. A Simpson HD20A holddown anchor is installed over the anchor bolt at each end of the shear wall. The holddown anchors are then bolted to three 2×6 studs with four 1" diameter bolts. A notation on Sheet 8 provides additional information about shear wall construction.

Holddown anchors, installed at the ends of shear walls, tie the foundation to wall framing members to prevent uplift from strong winds.

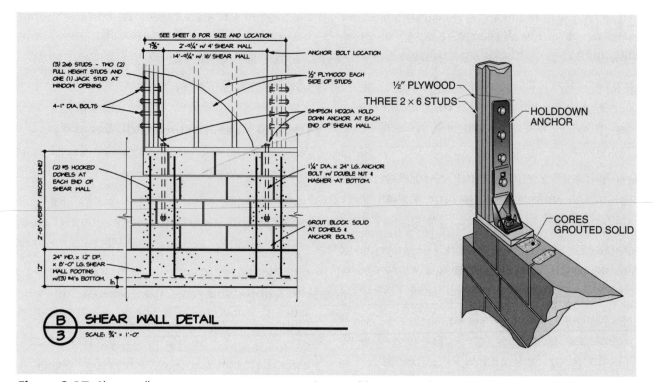

Figure 9-17. Shear wall construction requires proper anchoring of framing members to the foundation with approved holddowns or other devices.

STRUCTURAL PLAN, SHEET 8

The Structural Plan indicates placement of various structural members including walls and beams to support the roof and to provide for wide expanses of open space in the building. The design load is based on a 25 PSF live load and an 18 PSF dead load.

Walls

Several notations around the perimeter of the building indicate the wall heights required for truss bearing. Along the north side of the building, truss bearing heights are 11'-10" at the west end, 11'-8½" at the center recessed area, and 11'-10" high at the east end. Truss bearing heights are 11'-0" across the main portion of the south wall. Truss bearing height changes at the window wall in the Public Area to 11'-1½". Truss bearing heights change from the north wall to the south wall to provide proper roof drainage toward the scuppers and downspouts on the

south side of the building. The exterior walls must be constructed to the proper height before trusses are installed. Additional framing instructions are provided around the perimeter of the exterior walls to ensure proper structural support. For example, a notation along the east side of the building indicates that two full height southern yellow pine (SYP) 2 × 6 studs and two jack studs are required along the storefront walls.

Trusses and Headers

Trusses specified for the Wendy's Restaurant are wood I-joists, consisting of a solid or laminated upper and lower flange with an OSB web extending between the flanges. Truss spacing is indicated along the top of the Structural Plan. With a few exceptions, trusses are spaced 2'-8" OC. A Material List and Engineering Specs for the trusses appear in the upper-right corner of Sheet 8. The first column (QTY) indicates the number of each type of truss required for the building. The second column (TYPE) includes the truss identifier code, which is keyed to the Structural Plan. For example, five type T4A trusses are indicated on the Structural Plan at the west end of the building with three type T2 trusses placed to their right. The third column on the Material List and Engineering Specs shows the truss depth; all trusses in the building are 24″ deep. The fourth column (SERIES) indicates the manufacturer product numbers. Truss lengths are indicated in the fifth and sixth columns. The sixth column (P. LENGTH) indicates the lengths of the trusses as delivered to the job site. The fifth column indicates the final length of the trusses after being cut.

The List of Accessories describes various bracing and web stiffeners and the quantities required for the building. The products described as LTS12 are twist straps that provide a tension connection between two wood members and resist uplift at the ends of the trusses. The TB36 and TB48 tension bracing refers to metal tension bridging to prevent the trusses from twisting. Tension bracing must be installed in pairs. Web stiffeners, which are installed at the factory, are used to reinforce the webs of wood I-joists. See Figure 9-18.

> One advantage of wood I-joists over dimension lumber is their high strength-to-weight ratio. Wood I-joists are lighter and easier to handle than solid lumber joists required for the same span.

Two notations in the center of the Structural Plan indicate the required bridging for the trusses. Two continuous rows of 2 × 4s are fastened to the bottoms of the roof trusses using two 10d nails in each truss flange. See Detail F, Sheet 8A. Metal tension bracing is installed between alternating trusses as indicated on the Structural Plan, Sheet 8, and Detail F, Sheet 8A.

A variety of steel angles are shown at the building offsets on the Structural Plan to ensure proper roof support. Headers for roof openings are also shown throughout the drawing. Detail C, Sheet 8A, provides additional header detail information at the rooftop units. Detail C shows that roof trusses below the rooftop units are doubled and joined together with filler blocks as required at each joist hanger. Double 2 × 6 headers are installed at each rooftop unit opening and supported by joist hangers.

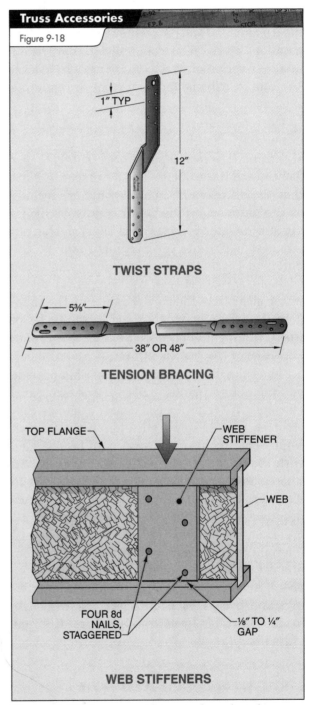

Truss Accessories
Figure 9-18

1″ TYP

12″

TWIST STRAPS

5⅜″

38″ OR 48″

TENSION BRACING

TOP FLANGE

WEB STIFFENER

WEB

FOUR 8d NAILS, STAGGERED

⅛″ TO ¼″ GAP

WEB STIFFENERS

Figure 9-18. Trusses must be properly anchored or braced using specified devices or methods.

Roof Plan, Sheet 8

The Roof Plan is drawn to a scale of ⅛″ = 1′-0″. The plan shows general locations for the exhaust fans (EF-1, EF-2, and EF-3), rooftop HVAC units (RT-1 and RT-2), and central makeup air unit (MUA-1). Exact locations and weights for each piece of equipment appear on the Structural Plan. Four-inch diameter roof openings are required for the ice machine and cookcenter condensers. Two notations on the Roof Plan indicate that the air intake on each rooftop HVAC unit must be at least 10′ from an exhaust fan to prevent recirculating exhausted air into the building.

The roof is covered with a single-ply roof membrane that is mechanically fastened to the roof sheathing. The roof slopes approximately ¼″ per foot toward the scuppers and downspouts. Note that the scuppers and downspouts are located on the south side of the building to avoid diverting storm water toward the primary patron entrances, which are on the north side of the building. Crickets are shown along the south edge of the roof between the scuppers to divert water away from the parapet and into the scuppers. The crickets are constructed as needed of wood framing and plywood decking and are installed over the roof sheathing.

General notes on the Structural Plan provide additional information about various structural elements. All tripled wood beams are to be constructed with ½″ plywood fillers between each solid wood member. Plywood is to be fastened with 10d nails 6″ OC on walls and roof areas. All wood is to be southern yellow pine (SYP) Grade #2 unless otherwise noted on the drawings. Additional structural notes are provided on Sheet 8A. The truss information provided is standard information that may vary in actual construction, and is provided only as a guide for takeoff purposes. A local engineer must finalize the drawings and truss layout and sizes. Varying snow loads and other loads could require different truss installations.

STRUCTURAL DETAILS AND NOTES, SHEET 8A

Eleven structural details, which are referred to on the Structural Plan, Sheet 8, are shown on Sheet 8A, along with six additional General Structural Notes. The notes include information about the minimum properties for various wood members, plywood installation, and wall studs.

Detail A—Curb Detail for Exhaust Fans, Sheet 8A

Detail A is drawn to the scale of ¾″ = 1′-0″ and shows the framing for each exhaust fan curb. The curb is a minimum of 26″ high, with minimum outside dimensions of 33″ in each direction. The curb is fabricated from one piece of 18 ga steel that is welded and insulated. The fan is mounted to a 23½″ square 18 ga curb adapter, and must have a minimum clearance of 40″ above the roof surface for proper ventilation. Type X ⅝″ gypsum board is extended up 6″ into the curb. The exhaust duct sleeve is an ETS Schaefer Flameshield™ blanket, which is installed per manufacturer specifications.

Detail B—Parapet Wall Detail (Brick), Sheet 8A

A parapet surrounds the flat roof of the building to conceal the mechanical equipment and exhaust fans mounted on the roof. A parapet wall cover is installed along the top of the parapet to prevent moisture from entering the building and to provide a finished appearance. See Figure 9-19. The majority of the components, including the sheet metal truss, top cap, stringer, and prefinished aluminum finish, are supplied by the owner and installed by the general contractor. Other components are supplied by the roofing manufacturer.

Figure 9-19. A parapet capped with a metal wall cover conceals mechanical equipment on the roof.

Detail C—Header Detail, Sheet 8A

Detail C, which relates to openings at rooftop units, is drawn to the scale of 1½″ = 1'-0″ to provide greater clarity. The 2 × 6 doubled headers are supplied by the general contractor and are supported by joist hangers at doubled roof trusses. Filler blocks are installed at each joist hanger and between roof trusses to permit the vertical load to be shared among the trusses and to force each joist to absorb an equal amount of the load and bend the same amount under the applied load. The roof trusses must be tied together by nailing through the webs and filler blocks with 16d nails and clinching them.

Detail D—Load Detail, Sheet 8A

Detail D is drawn to the scale of 1½″ = 1'-0″. When additional support members are required at the bottom of trusses, filler blocks are nailed to the truss webs and joist hangers are fastened to the filler blocks. A maximum of 500 lb can be added to the roof trusses as designed.

Detail E—Header Detail, Sheet 8A

Detail E shows the wood framing for headers above windows. The bottoms of the headers are 9'-0″ above the finished floor. A typical header is constructed with three 2 × 10 members with ½″ plywood fillers between each that are fastened with glue and nails. The headers are supported on each side with multiple 2 × 6 studs. The actual number of studs used to support the headers is noted on Sheet 8.

Detail F—Blocking and Bracing Details, Sheet 8A

Detail F is drawn to the scale of 1½″ = 1'-0″ and shows the various materials designed to distribute building loads across the roof truss system. Continuous 2 × 4s are nailed to the bottom of each roof truss with the flat (face) against the bottom of the truss flanges. Metal tension bracing is installed between alternate sets of trusses as indicated on the Structural Plan, Sheet 8. A hurricane anchor is installed at each stud to tie together the roof and wall systems. Doubled 2 × 8s support the outer edges of the ⅝″ CDX roof sheathing. The first 2 × 8 is nailed to the 2 × 6 studs with three 16d nails and the second 2 × 8 is fastened to the first 2 × 8 with two rows of 16d nails spaced 8″ OC.

Detail G—Truss Bearing Elevation, Sheet 8A

Detail G, drawn at a scale of ¾″ = 1'-0″, shows the method for fastening wall trusses to the tops of exterior bearing walls. Bearing walls are constructed with triple 2 × 6 plates at the required bearing elevations. The north walls have an 11'-10″ bearing elevation and south walls have an 11'-0″ bearing elevation as noted on other drawings in the plans. Parapets above the bearing walls are then constructed of 2 × 4 studs with a double top plate. The heights for the parapets are indicated on Sheets 7A and 7B.

Trusses are fastened to the wall plates using Simpson LTS12 metal fasteners and braced with Simpson TB36 tension bracing. The trusses are fastened to the triple top plate with a minimum of two 16d nails and with three 12d nails to a parapet stud provided at each truss. The trusses are sheathed with ⅝″ CDX plywood.

Detail H—Truss Bearing Section (Wood Studs), Sheet 8A

Detail H, drawn to the scale of ¾″ = 1'-0″, provides a side view of the same area of the building. The 2 × 6 bearing wall with triple top plate and 2 × 4 parapet with a double top plate are shown. Note that ½″ plywood is used as exterior sheathing and must overlap a minimum of 2'-0″ on either side of the joint between the bearing wall and parapet for structural support. Horizontal 2 × 4 blocking is to be installed between the tops of the joists in both a flat position on top of the trusses between the parapet studs and in an on-edge position between the trusses.

Detail J—Truss Bearing Section (Metal Studs), Sheet 8A

Detail J is drawn to a scale of ¾″ = 1'-0″. Metal studs are installed in an exterior wall and interior partition in the food preparation area adjacent to the pick-up window area. Different fastening methods are used where wood roof trusses bear on metal-framed walls. A 2 × 6 ledger is fastened to the top track of the metal-framed wall using ½" bolts spaced 32" OC. A continuous 5" × 3" × ¼" metal angle is screwed to the inside of the metal-framed wall to provide additional reinforcement. The top plate is 18 ga steel. A 1½" metal channel is installed as horizontal bridging between the metal studs throughout the entire height of the metal-framed wall at 3'-4" OC minimum. The bearing height of the metal-framed wall is noted at 11'-0" for the low end (south) bearing.

The parapet is framed in a manner similar to the other details, with 2 × 4 studs and a double 2 × 4 top plate. In addition, 2 × 4 blocking is installed both on-edge and flat at the tops of the trusses where they intersect the parapet. The trusses are braced with bearing stiffeners as required, and nailed in the same manner as shown in Detail H. A minimum of ½" clearance is required between the end of the roof trusses and the interior surface of the ½" plywood exterior sheathing.

Detail K—Non-Load-Bearing Partitions, Sheet 8A

Detail K is drawn to the scale of ¾" = 1'-0". The tops of non-load-bearing partitions are attached to the bottoms of roof trusses using methods shown in Detail K. A ½" gap is provided between the tops of the partitions and the bottoms of the trusses. When partitions are perpendicular to the roof trusses, a truss clip is installed to secure the top of the partition in place. When partitions are parallel with roof trusses, wood blocking is fastened between the trusses and roof truss clips are fastened to the blocking.

Detail L—Water Heater Platform Framing and Detail LL—Front Edge Detail, Sheet 8A

The water heater is placed near the recessed mop basin. Details L and LL show the framing necessary to support the water heater. As shown in Detail LL, the top of the water heater platform is 4'-0" A.S.F. (above the surface of the floor). Two layers of ¾" plywood form the deck of the platform, with fiberglass-reinforced polyester paneling on the top, front, and bottom of the platform. As shown in Detail L, the water heater platform is 2'-7½" deep by 5'-2½" wide. The platform is framed with 2 × 6 joists that are supported by jack studs installed adjacent to full-height wood studs.

FLOOR PLAN, SHEET 4

Sheet 4 contains the Floor Plan, Room Finish Schedule, Door and Hardware Schedule, Door Elevations, Door Detail A, Front Corner Detail, and General Notes. Several sections and details are referred to on the Floor Plan and shown on other sheets.

The Floor Plan contains overall dimensions of the building (44'-4" × 87'-0"), location dimensions, and size dimensions. A *location dimension* is a dimension that locates a particular feature in relation to another feature. For example, the partition separating Room 102 and Room 108 is 5'-2" from the inside of the west wall. A *size dimension* is a dimension that indicates the size of a particular feature or area. For example, the partition between Rooms 100 and 101 is 5'-4" long.

Cutting plane references, such as A/7A, are enclosed in circles and include an arrow to indicate the direction of sight. Sections referred to on the Floor Plan are shown on Sheets 7A and 7B. Detail references, such as K/7B, are enclosed in circles but do not contain direction of sight arrows. Details referred to on the Floor Plan are shown on Sheet 7B. Elevations are referred to on the Floor Plan using small diamonds that enclose circles. Interior elevations referred to on the Floor Plan are shown on Sheets 6A, 6B, 6C, 6D, and 6E. Room numbers, such as 100, are enclosed in rectangular boxes. Doors, such as A, are identified by a letter enclosed in a circle. See Figure 9-20.

Floor plans contain information related to various trades. Floor plans are considered to be among the most used working drawings in a set of prints.

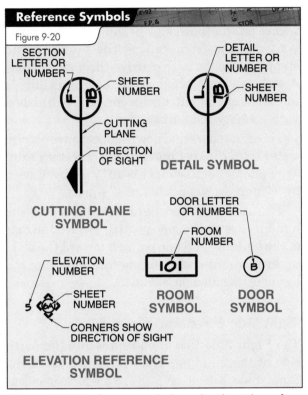

Figure 9-20. Reference symbols on the Floor Plan refer to specific views and schedules.

The General Notes on Sheet 4 apply to the entire Floor Plan. The General Notes provide information concerning partition framing, blocking, insulation, dimensioning, architectural symbols, and fire protection behind all cooking equipment. Specific notes such as "USE SELF CLOSING HINGE ON ALL ACCESSIBLE STALL DOORS" provide information pertaining to a specific feature or group of features.

All objects above 5′-0″ are shown on floor plans with hidden lines. For example, the furred-down soffit above the front counter in Room 105 is shown with hidden lines since the bottom of the soffit is 7′-1″ above the floor. Thick dashed lines indicate that ⅝″ plywood sheathing is to be installed to support wall shelving. Crosshatching along the south wall indicates the area where metal studs are required.

A room finish schedule indicates the finish materials to be used for each room of the building. The Room Finish Schedule, Sheet 4, designates a specific number for each space shown on the plans. Floor, base, wall, ceiling, trim, and door finishes are indicated on the Room Finish Schedule. Six specific notes are referred to in the Room Finish Schedule and specific instructions are provided. Sheet F-1 provides additional finish material information.

A Door and Hardware Schedule provides information regarding doors in the building and is keyed to the door symbols shown on floor plans. Door location and swing are indicated on the plans. The Door and Hardware Schedule, Sheet 4, designates a specific letter for each door shown on the Floor Plan, and the schedule provides additional information regarding door size, type, frame, hinges, latch-catches, and accessories. Ten specific notes are also referred to in the Door and Hardware Schedule.

Door Elevations, Sheet 4, contains letters identifying door types and notations and dimensions to clarify details. The letters used to identify door elevations are similar to those on the Door and Hardware Schedule. To avoid confusion, the letters in the fourth column of the Door and Hardware Schedule relate only to the Door Elevations shown to the right of the schedule. For example, an E door is similar to the door shown as Elevation C.

When studying the Floor Plan, first relate the four exterior elevations on Sheet 5 to the Floor Plan. The exterior elevations will help in visualizing the overall appearance of the building. Then, review each room on the Floor Plan in the order designated in the Room Finish Schedule along with the interior elevations, equipment, HVAC, electrical, lighting, and plumbing schedules as they apply to the particular room. A structured review of the Floor Plan and related information ensures that the building is properly laid out and constructed based on the set of prints. Additional study of specific plans is required for the actual construction.

Left Side Elevation, Sheet 5

The Left Side Elevation represents the south side of the building. The overall length of the Left Side Elevation is 87′-8″, which is calculated as the dimension shown plus two wythes of 4″ brick (87′-0″ + 4″ + 4″ = 87′-8″), as shown on the Floor Plan, Sheet 4. The Left Side Elevation is drawn to a scale of ¼″ = 1′-0″. Major features of this elevation are the pick-up windows and the entrance on the south side of the building.

The pick-up windows indicated on the Left Side Elevation are 4′-4″ high by 4′-0″ wide as shown on the Wall Sections and Floor Plan. Each pick-up window has a brick rowlock sill, 8″ × 8″ wall tile on both sides and above the windows, and metal flashing along the top. Each window also has a "Timelock" safe decal on the fixed window. The direction of movement for the operable pick-up window is shown with an arrow on the movable window. The three bollards shown are 6″ in diameter, project a minimum of 60″ above the surface of the sidewalk, and are painted yellow. See Figure 9-21.

Figure 9-21. A bollard protects a building from vehicular damage.

A railing is installed along the patron entrance on the south side of the building to prevent patrons from exiting the building and stepping into the path of drive-through patrons. A 48″ long by 36″ high wrought iron railing is installed at the entrance door, and is finished with a safety red paint.

Three scuppers and downspouts convey storm water from the roof into the storm water drainage system. Each scupper is 16″ wide by 6″ deep by 9″ high. Downspouts are 4″ square.

Two roof-mounted lights at the top of the building are shown, one pointed toward the rear of the building and one pointed toward the pick-up area. Additional information regarding the lights is included on Sheet 13.

Right Side Elevation, Sheet 5

The Right Side Elevation represents the north side of the building. The overall length of the Right Side Elevation is 87′-8″, which is calculated as the dimension shown plus two wythes of 4″ brick (87′-0″ + 4″ + 4″ = 87′-8″), as shown on the Floor Plan, Sheet 4. The Right Side Elevation is drawn to a scale of ¼″ = 1′-0″.

Features shown on the Right Side Elevation include the windows in the dining area (toward the left of the drawing), outline of the Cooler/Freezer module, and foundation footings and walls. Varying footing widths are shown where applicable. Notations indicate various masonry positions, materials, and fascia systems and their locations.

Rear Elevation, Sheet 5

The Rear Elevation represents the west side of the building. The overall length of the Rear Elevation is 45′-0″, which is calculated as the dimension shown plus two wythes of 4″ brick (44′-4″ + 4″ + 4″ = 45′-0″), as shown on the Floor Plan, Sheet 4. The Rear Elevation is drawn to a scale of ¼″ = 1′-0″. The Trash Enclosure Area is not shown on the Rear Elevation since it is not part of the building itself.

One feature of the Rear Elevation is the Cooler/Freezer area storage module with the notation, "STORAGE MODULE TO BE PRO-VIDED BY OWNER AND INSTALLED BY THE GENERAL CONTRACTOR." Flashing is provided by the general contractor to prevent water seepage between the module and back wall of the building. Additional features of the Rear Elevation are two roof-mounted light fixtures, two "Timelock" safe decals (one affixed to the rear entry door and the other to the sidelight along the door on the north side of the building), a security window in one door, and the fixed glass window at the drive-through area.

Front Elevation, Sheet 5

The Front Elevation represents the east side of the building, which faces the main thoroughfare (Illinois Route 31). The overall length of the Front Elevation is 38'-0", which is calculated as the dimension shown plus two wythes of 4" brick (37'-4" + 4" + 4" = 38'-0"), as shown on the Floor Plan, Sheet 4. The Front Elevation is drawn to a scale of ¼" = 1'-0".

The Wendy's sign and glass windows, which are the main features of the Front Elevation, are framed by brick-veneer walls and prefinished

aluminum trim and fascia. See Figure 9-22. The sign, with a copy length of 22'-6½", is supplied by the owner and installed by a sign installer. Dimensions at the top of the Front Elevation indicate placement of various sign components.

Face brick is used as the primary exterior finish material for the building. Courses of split-faced concrete block are laid below and above the window level and at the roofline. Dimensions along the left side of the Front Elevation indicate overall height of the building and the heights at which the split-faced concrete block are installed. Information about the light fixtures installed at the corners is provided on Sheet 13.

Mortar bonds masonry units into an integral structure and creates a tight seal between the units to prevent air and moisture infiltration. In addition, mortar bonds with steel reinforcement, ties, and anchor bolts to form a single integral unit with the masonry units.

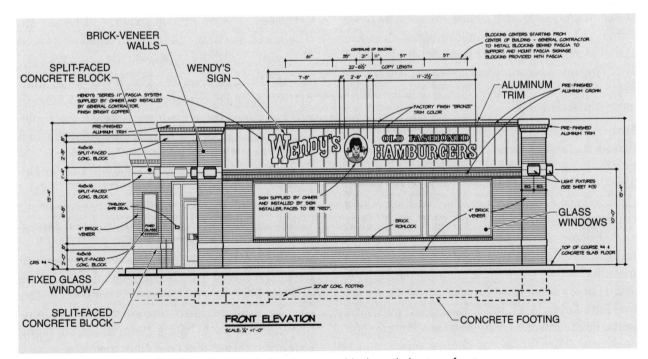

Figure 9-22. Exterior finish includes brick, split-faced concrete block, and aluminum fascia.

Vestibules, Room 100, Sheet 4

The vestibules shown at the north and south entrances on the Floor Plan provide entryways for patrons. Two entry doors are installed in each vestibule to minimize the amount of conditioned air escaping the building and to reduce drafts. Typical finishes for the vestibules are shown on Interior Elevations 8 and 9, Sheet 6B. The interior dimensions of the vestibules are slightly different. The Vestibule along the north side of the building is 4'-10" wide by 7'-6½" wide, while the Vestibule along the south side is 4'-10" wide by 7'-1½" wide.

A notation indicates that the framed wall between the Vestibule and the dining area is 36" high. Tempered glass is installed above the short wall to provide a line of sight from the Serving Area into the Vestibule. Tempered glass is a nonshattering glass that is significantly stronger than other types of glass and has high impact resistance.

Room Finish Schedules, Room 100, Sheet 4. The Room Finish Schedule indicates that the Vestibule floors are to be finished with decorative tile. Wall finish is paneling with vinyl fabric wallcovering. Baseboard is to be decorative tile. Ceiling height for the vestibules is 9'-6" and the ceiling is suspended acoustical tile. The wood trim is to be stained. Information about the stain is included in the Interior Finish Schedule, Sheet F-1. The finish is comprised of two coats of cherry stain finished with two coats of polyurethane satin-finish varnish.

Door and Hardware Schedule, Room 100, Sheet 4. Two doors are to be installed in each vestibule as shown on the Floor Plan, Sheet 4. The Vestibule along the north side of the building has type A and B doors; the Vestibule along the south side has type C and D doors. Type A and D doors, which are 3'-0" × 7'-0", have aluminum frames and tempered glass. A panel is installed across the middle of each door. Type A and D doors have pivot hinges, are self-closing, and have keyed locks. In addition, push-pull bars, panic hardware, and door stops are installed on each door. Thresholds and door sweeps are provided with the doors.

Tempered glass is produced by heating sheet glass to near its softening point and then quickly cooling the glass under controlled conditions. Tempered glass is required for entrance doors.

Type B and C doors are also 3'-0" × 7'-0" aluminum-framed, tempered glass doors. Type B and C doors are similar to type A and D doors except that they are not keyed and do not have panic hardware, door sweeps, thresholds, or panels across the middle.

Security Plan, Sheet 10B. The Security Plan indicates that a "Timelock" safe decal is to be applied to the sidelight next to the exterior Vestibule doors 48" above the finished floor (A.F.F.). An alarm system decal and closed circuit television (CCTV) decal are to be placed above and below each "Timelock" safe decal. The Security Plan also confirms information provided in the Door and Hardware Schedule, Sheet 4, such as that the exterior Vestibule doors have keyed locks and are self-closing. Door contacts (DC) are to be installed in the head frame on the latch side of the exterior Vestibule doors. If the door contacts are tripped when the alarm system is activated, a siren and/or strobe will be set off. The north Vestibule is in Security Zone #1 and the south Vestibule is in Security Zone #3.

HVAC Plan, Sheet 11. The HVAC Plan indicates that one 8" diameter duct from HVAC unit RT-2 supplies the air diffuser in each vestibule. An *air diffuser* is an air distribution outlet in a supply duct that is used to deflect and mix air. The "B" inside the hexagon refers to the Air Device Schedule, Sheet 11. The "150" inside the hexagon indicates the airflow (in cubic feet per minute or cfm) of the type B diffuser. A type B diffuser supplies 150 to 190 cfm of air. See Figure 9-23. A type B diffuser is a supply air diffuser that is laid into the suspended ceiling. The diffuser is white and has an 8" round neck. The supply air diffusers are also shown on the Lighting and Reflected Ceiling Plan, Sheet 13, using two intersecting diagonal lines inside a square and the letters "SA."

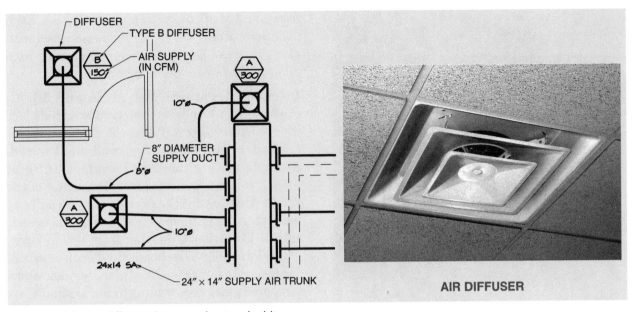

Figure 9-23. Air diffusers direct supply air to building spaces.

Lighting and Reflected Ceiling Plan, Sheet 13. The Lighting and Reflected Ceiling Plan indicates that fixture B-1 is to be installed in each vestibule. As indicated with the crosshatching, the B-1 Vestibule lights are on the night light circuit. The 2 × 4 lay-in fluorescent light fixtures provide 35 W per lamp and include three fluorescent lamps in each fixture. Supply conductors are two #12s with a #12 ground, which are run in ¾″ conduit.

Public Area, Room 101, Sheet 4

The Public Area used for dining is the largest area in the building. As indicated on the Equipment Plan, Sheet 9, the Public Area provides seating for 94 customers. The basic dimensions for the Public Area are 39′ × 33′ including the vestibules, condiment bar, and serving areas.

Coordinated wall, floor, and ceiling finishes are complemented by functional and attractive furniture placed for maximum use. The Room Finish Schedule and the Door and Hardware Schedule, Sheet 4, and Finish schedules, Sheet F-1, detail the finishes. Elevations 1, 2, 3, 4, 5, and 7 of Sheet 6A and Elevation 10 on Sheet 6B show finish details of the Public Area. The interior elevations on Sheets 6A and 6B are drawn to a scale of ½″ = 1′-0″ as shown in the title block

on each sheet. The Equipment Plan, Sheet 9; Security Plan, Sheet 10B; HVAC Plan, Sheet 11; Electrical Plan, Sheet 12; Lighting and Reflected Ceiling Plan, Sheet 13; and Plumbing Plan, Sheet 15, provide specific information for the various trades constructing the building.

Room Finish Schedule, Sheet 4. The dining portion of the Public Area is finished with carpet. The Room Finish Schedule refers to Sheet 6B for additional information regarding carpet installation. The Floor Tile/Carpet Plan, Sheet 6B, shows the carpet-seaming layout and provides installation notes. The first piece of carpet is installed adjacent to the tile with the seam running the width of the building. The pattern of the second piece of carpet is matched to the first piece. A third piece of carpet is cut into two strips and installed across the front of the building. A heavy line shows the transition strip between the carpet and decorative tile that covers the remainder of the floor in Room 101. See Figure 9-24. Decorative tile is installed in a pattern with the edges parallel to the front of the building. The Room Finish Schedule also refers to the Tile Base Detail, Sheet 6B, in which a decorative tile bullnose cove base and 1 × 2 wood base cap are shown for wall baseboards in Room 101.

Figure 9-24. Tile is commonly installed in areas with a high level of foot traffic, whereas carpet is utilized for dining areas. A transition strip is installed at the junction of the tile and carpet to provide a finished appearance.

Vinyl fabric, wood trim, and wood paneling are used to finish walls in the Public Area. Elevation 8, Sheet 6B, indicates that wood paneling is installed to a height of 2'-10½" above the floor. A 6" high tile base is capped with the 1 × 2 base cap, making the paneling exposure 2'-3". A 1 × 2 bottom chair rail is installed at this height and 6⅛" is provided for a strip of wallcovering WC-C. A 1 × 2 top chair rail is installed with the top of the rail 9⅛" above the bottom of the bottom chair rail. Additional wallcovering is installed to a height of 8'-3½", where a 1 × 2 on 1 × 4 crown molding is installed. Another piece of wallcovering is applied to finish the wall to the ceiling. See Figure 9-25.

As shown on the Room Finish Schedule, Sheet 4, and Section A, Sheet 7A, the suspended ceiling height in the Public Area is 9'-6". The acoustic ceiling is composed of lay-in panels. Trim in the Public Area is stained and doors are aluminum frames with glass.

Door and Hardware Schedule, Sheet 4. Doors B and C are exit doors from the Public Area into the vestibules. Both doors have an aluminum frame and are fitted with tempered glass. Each door measures 3'-0" × 7'-0" and is equipped with pivot hinges. The doors are self-closing with push-pull hardware and door stops.

Interior Elevations, Sheets 6A and 6B. Elevations 1, 2, 3, and 4 are referred to on the Floor Plan, Sheet 4. Sheet 6B provides additional information concerning the condiment stand. Booth details are shown in Elevation 10, Sheet 6B. Elevation 1 is viewed from the center of the Public Area toward the north wall. The hallway leading to the restrooms is shown on the far left side of Elevation 1. Moving from left to right, Elevation 1 shows the header and change in ceiling height, a tempered fixed glass window and a tempered glass door leading to the Vestibule, six fixed glass windows (with pairs of windows separated by piers), four decorative light fixtures (E-1), and a section of wall indicating the typical dining room finishes and dimensions. The point where the base transition occurs—where floor covering changes from tile to carpet and base changes from tile to 1 × 6 wood trim—is also indicated. Dimensions for trim placement are provided on Sheet 6B. A series of hanging planters is also shown on Elevation 1.

Elevation 2 is viewed from the center of the Public Area toward the east wall. Wall decor pieces 1 and 2, usually framed posters or photographs, are shown at each end of the wall. The fixed glass windows are the primary feature of Elevation 2. Note that a pair of windows are placed to each side of the triple fixed glass windows in the center. Light fixtures and hanging plants are suspended from the ceiling. Information about the lights and plants is provided on Sheet 13 and Sheet 9, respectively.

Fiberglass-reinforced polyester (FRP) paneling is a common finish material used in commercial kitchens, food preparation areas, and restrooms. FRP paneling is scratch-, impact-, and stain-resistant. In addition, FRP paneling will not corrode or support mildew, mold, or fungus growth.

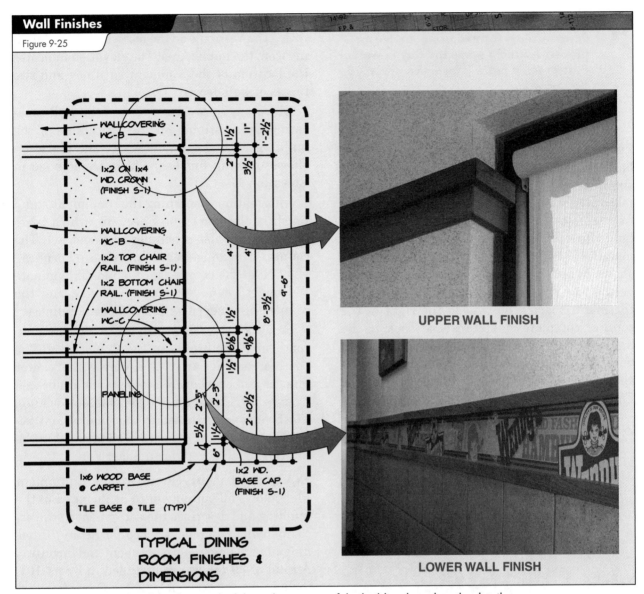

Figure 9-25. Typical wall finish is applied throughout areas of the building based on the detail.

Elevation 3 is viewed from the center of the Public Area toward the south wall of the building. Fixed glass windows are shown at the left side of Elevation 3. The base transition is shown to the left of the Vestibule door, along with the tempered glass Vestibule window. A base transition in elevation is shown below the waste receptacle. The patron traffic area and a portion of the Serving Area are shown to the right of the Vestibule door. A 21″ × 50″ rough opening which is centered vertically in the angled wall is provided for a recessed merchandiser. A merchandiser is an enclosed case, usually containing two or three shelves, that is used to market branded merchandise such as T-shirts or toys. Wood trim is to be installed around the merchandiser. Ceramic tile, which are installed in the Serving Area, are shown. Notations show a recessed merchandiser, and information concerning ceramic tile is provided. Two types of 4¼″ × 4¼″ wall tile—field tile and accent tile—are installed. Field tile are the tile that cover the majority of the wall. Accent tile are a different color than field tile and are arranged in a specified pattern at various locations. Detail J, Sheet 7B, provides information about the soffit over the counter.

Ceramic tile is formed using the plastic process (forming while the clay is wet) or dust-pressed process (using compressed clay powder).

Elevation 4 is viewed from the center of the Public Area west toward the Serving Area. The base cabinet and recessed merchandiser are shown on the left side of Elevation 4. The prefabricated service counter with the dropped soffit is prominently shown. The trim, Corian™, and laminate are provided by the kitchen equipment installer (KES). A portion of the menu board is shown behind the soffit, with ceramic wall tile on the face and bottom of the soffit supporting the menu board. The wall to the right of the counter completes the transition back to the hallway leading to the restrooms. The Americans with Disabilities Act (ADA) restroom sign is shown alongside the door to the Men's Room. See Figure 9-26.

Figure 9-26. Signage is placed according to dimensions provided on elevations or details.

Elevation 5 provides a view of the wall separating the Vestibule on the north side of the building from the Public Area. The elevation indicates the location of the comment card box and two pieces of wall decor.

Elevation 7 provides a view of the wall separating the Vestibule on the south side of the building from the Public Area. The elevation shows the wall finishes, which are detailed in Elevation 1.

Information concerning the condiment stand finish is also shown on Sheet 6B, which is related to the finish schedules on Sheet F-1. The counter trim and accent laminate are Formica™ #942 Nile, the counter face is plastic laminate Wilsonart™ #4663-60 Tawny Legacy, and the countertop is edged with a 3″ Corian bullnose.

Elevation 10, Sheet 6B, shows information concerning the booths in the Public Area. The booth assemblies are 9′-2″ square with a center planter and cantilevered tables that are braced from below. Each unit has four tabletops (R08). The booths are installed by the general contractor. Finishes for each booth are indicated in the interior finish schedule on Sheet F-1.

Equipment Plan, Sheet 9. The Equipment Plan shows all equipment to be included in the building and describes the equipment in the accompanying Equipment Schedule. Room 101 has a significant amount of equipment and furniture. A total of 39 tables are installed in Room 101, including eight accessible tables. Seventy-seven chairs (R05) are provided with this installation. Thirty-one 21″ × 24″ tabletops (R06) and table bases (R07) are to be installed in Room 101. See Figure 9-27.

Item B01 refers to the 120 sq yd of carpet required for the Public Area. Item B02 refers to the carpet-tile transition strip that separates the carpet from the decorative tile.

The bench seat (R10) is furnished and installed by the equipment suppliers. Item R15, the 36″ high serpentine rail that separates the dining area from the food ordering area, is furnished by the owner and installed by the general contractor. The handrail location and length are indicated on the Equipment Plan and a

Handrail Elevation is shown on Sheet 6B. The handrail is 3′-0″ high, made of various sizes of square metal tubing, and capped with a 2 × 4 oak handrail installed by the general contractor. Posts extend 4″ into the floor and a post protector is installed at the base. The ½″ × 1″ metal channel along the top of the rail is predrilled to allow the oak handrail to be properly attached. The arrangement of the zig-zag bars does not allow a 4″ diameter or larger sphere to pass between the bars. This design, primarily intended for child safety, ensures that adequate space is provided for passage and prevents entrapment.

The condiment stand (R03) is located between the Public Area and Serving Area. The condiment stand holds two napkin dispensers (C04), a scuffle cup dispenser (C05), and two condiment pumps (C15). Two countertops (B06) are installed at the ends of the condiment stand. Two booster chairs for children (R17) are stored under the condiment stand. A 102″ long bench seat (R10) is installed along the back of the condiment stand. Four table bases (R07) and tabletops (R06) with four chairs (R05) are placed along the bench seat.

Security Plan, Sheet 10B. The dining area is equipped with one emergency siren/strobe light, which is mounted near the middle of the room. The siren is positioned just above the suspended ceiling and the strobe is surface-mounted on the underside of the ceiling. The siren and strobe light are activated as an alarm in the event of a lapse in security.

HVAC Plan, Sheet 11. The Public Area is heated and cooled by a 10-ton roof-mounted HVAC unit. As shown on the HVAC Equipment Schedule, the unit, designated RT-2, is a 208 V, 3ϕ, 60 Hz unit with a 3 HP blower motor. Several manufacturer options are shown in the schedule, but specifications for the unit are consistent across manufacturers.

The HVAC system is designed to meet outside temperatures of 93°F in the summer and 0°F in the winter. All ductwork is installed above the suspended ceiling. Supply ducts and diffusers must be insulated. The HVAC Plan, Sheet 11, identifies the rooftop HVAC unit RT-2 and two 24″ × 14″ main supply air ducts. Round ducts branching off the main duct supply lay-in ceiling-mounted diffusers and surface-mounted registers. Twelve diffusers are supplied by 10″ diameter ducts. Diffusers designated A/300 have a 10″ diameter and provide 300, 350, or 400 cfm of air, depending on their location and setup.

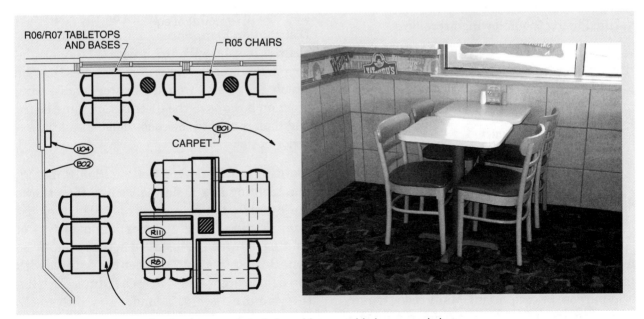

Figure 9-27. Equipment for the dining area includes tabletops, table bases, and chairs.

The General Notes on the HVAC Plan, Sheet 11, provide additional information about the HVAC system for the building. The HVAC system is designed to keep the restaurant comfortable in a range from 93°F to 0°F. The maximum allowable length of flexible duct is 7'-0", with the remainder of ductwork made of hard surface piping with 1" thick insulation. All ductwork must be concealed above the suspended ceiling system. The dimensions of all ductwork are the outside diameters, and all ductwork is insulated with 1½" thick duct wrap. Return air drops, such as those above the ceiling in Room 101, are lined with 1" insulation and all ducts are fitted with isolation duct connectors to minimize vibration and reduce sound transmission. Locations of the supply and return air diffusers are also indicated on the Lighting and Reflected Ceiling Plan, Sheet 13.

Electrical and Electrical Distribution Plans, Sheets 12 and 14. As shown on the Electrical Plan, three 120V, 1ϕ duplex receptacles are placed 14" above the finished floor in the Public Area. An additional receptacle is installed just outside the Closet door near Rooms 101 and 101A. Hidden lines connecting the receptacles indicate circuit wiring. The NEC® permits no more than 13 general-purpose outlets to be connected to a 20A circuit and no more than 10 general-purpose outlets to be connected to a 15A circuit. The permissible number of outlets is verified using the following procedure:

$$I = \frac{VA}{V}$$

$$I = \frac{180 \text{ VA}}{120 \text{ V}}$$

$$I = 1.5 \text{ A per outlet}$$

$$I = \frac{20 \text{ A CB}}{1.5 \text{ A}} = \textbf{13 outlets per circuit}$$

$$I = \frac{15 \text{ A CB}}{1.5 \text{ A}} = \textbf{10 outlets per circuit}$$

The National Electrical Code® must be referred to in order to determine the maximum number of lighting fixtures permitted on a general-purpose branch circuit. Many codes require a lighting outlet for a fixture to be computed at 1.5 A per outlet. For example, a maximum of 13 outlets are permitted to be connected on a 20 A circuit (20 A CB ÷ 1.5 A = 13.3).

A weatherproof duplex receptacle connected to circuit 31C is shown at rooftop HVAC unit #2 (RT-2). The letters "WP" placed near the receptacle symbol indicate that the receptacle is to be weatherproof. These receptacles are required by the National Electrical Code® to provide power for personnel servicing the HVAC equipment. Circuit 31 on panelboard C powers the two rooftop receptacles. Circuit 31 is a .8 kW circuit with a 20 A, single-pole circuit breaker. A notation indicates the power disconnect requirements for the HVAC suppliers and electrician. The HVAC Motors and Equipment Connections Schedule provides additional information for connection of the RT-2 unit and various circuit connections. The left column of the schedule shows the circuit number as 7C. The circuit identified as 7C on Sheet 14 is a 17.1 kW individual branch circuit. The disconnecting means for unit RT-2 is a 208/240 V, 3ϕ disconnect switch. A disconnect switch is required by the NEC® to protect personnel from electrical shock while servicing the unit.

An additional weatherproof receptacle is shown on the outside east wall. The receptacle is to be installed 14" above the finished floor level and connected to circuit 3A. Additional information about circuit 3A appears on the Electrical Distribution Plan, Sheet 14. Circuit 3 on panelboard A is a 1.0 kW circuit with a 20 A, single-pole circuit breaker. A notation indicates that the circuit is routed through a power-conditioning junction box above the distribution panelboard and then routed to the cash register and the exterior outlet.

Lighting and Reflected Ceiling Plan, Sheet 13. The Lighting and Reflected Ceiling Plan shows the layout for the ceiling grid and all lighting fixtures. Fixture B-2 is the most common type of lighting fixture to be installed in the Public Area. Type B-2 fixtures are 2 × 4 deep cell fixtures with three fluorescent lamps in each fixture. Each fixture requires two #12 conductors with a #12 ground wire and routed in ¾" conduit.

Two clusters of type C-1 lighting fixtures are indicated in the Public Area. The clusters consist of five 4' long fluorescent lights that are surface mounted. See Figure 9-28. Information about installation of the dropped lighting clusters is shown on Sheet 7B. Wiring requirements are the same as for type B-2 lights.

Figure 9-29. Emergency floodlights provide light in the event of an emergency.

Figure 9-28. Dropped lighting clusters consist of five 4' long fluorescent lights that are surface mounted.

Type E-1 lighting fixtures are shown around the perimeter of the Public Area. Type E-1 lighting fixtures are special fixtures with incandescent lamps, and are suspended from the acoustical ceiling grid at 6'-6" above the finished floor. All type E-1 fixtures are on circuit 23A. Elevations of the type E-1 lighting fixtures are shown on Sheet 6A.

Two emergency floodlights provide light for the Public Area in the event of a power outage. See Figure 9-29. The emergency floodlights, designated EM-1, are shown on the Lighting and Reflected Ceiling Plan. Lamps for the emergency floodlights are furnished with the fixtures. Where general lighting circuits and emergency lighting circuits enter fixture enclosures or other enclosures, separation must be provided between the circuits per the NEC®.

Emergency lighting equipment must include a rechargeable battery, a means to charge the battery, one or more lamps on the unit (or terminals for remote lamps), and a relay that automatically energizes emergency lighting when general lighting fails.

Exit lights are positioned near exit doors to clearly mark all exits. See Figure 9-30. Two exit lights, designated EX-1, are shown in the Public Area. The exit lights are ceiling-mounted fixtures that are furnished with lamps. Battery packs are permitted to be connected to the single-pole switch that controls a general lighting circuit in the same room as the battery pack. Per the NEC®, emergency and exit lighting circuits cannot be routed in the same conduit system that supplies illumination for required lighting.

Figure 9-30. Exit lights are installed at all exits of the building to clearly mark the doors.

Plumbing Plan, Sheet 15. Plumbing required for the Public Area is minimal. A floor drain (FD-1) is installed below the condiment area and 3″ sanitary waste piping extends from the drain to the 4″ sanitary waste piping that exits the building. Another floor drain is to be installed near the north Vestibule. Each FD-1 floor drain measures 5″ × 9″ and has an adjustable strainer, cast iron body, and 3″ bottom outlet.

A freezeproof wall-mounted hose bibb is to be installed on the exterior wall near the pick-up window. See Figure 9-31. The washerless hose bibb is mounted 18″ above the finished grade and is supplied by a ¾″ cold water line.

Figure 9-31. Freezeproof hose bibbs provide water for the exterior and ensure that water in the hose bibb will not freeze and rupture the pipe.

Restrooms, Rooms 102 and 103, Sheet 4

The Men's Room (Room 102) consists of an L-shaped area measuring 8′-11½″ × 8′-1″ and a separate area for a water closet measuring 5′-2″ × 5′-2″. The Women's Room (Room 103) is 12′-5″ long by 7′-9″ wide in the water closet area with an offset wall making the room 8′-3″ wide in the entry and lavatory area. Standard symbols indicate the locations of the urinal, water closets, and lavatories. The dashed circles in each restroom indicate the minimum 4′ diameter open space required for ADA compliance. The open space ensures adequate room for wheelchair access. In addition, 34″ wide stall doors are specified to provide adequate access to the stalls.

Room Finish Schedule, Sheet 4. Finish and equipment are similar in both restrooms with the exception of the urinal in the Men's Room. Restroom floors are finished with decorative tile and a decorative tile base. Restroom walls are finished with ceramic tile. Restroom ceilings are finished with drywall (gypsum board), which is hung 8′-0″ above the finished floor.

Door and Hardware Schedule, Sheet 4. Type E and F doors are installed in the Men's Room and Women's Room, respectively. The doors are identical except for their hand (swing direction). The restroom doors are shown as C doors in the Door Elevations, Sheet 4. Type E and F doors are aluminum-framed flush doors covered with plastic laminate and measuring 3′-0″ × 6′-8″. Per Note 1 in the Door and Hardware Schedule, the rough opening for plastic laminate-covered doors must be 2″ wider and 1″ taller than the door leaf. A MEN or WOMEN room sign is applied to the outside of each door. Self-closing mechanisms, push-pull hardware, and door stops complete the door hardware required for proper installation of the restroom doors.

Interior Elevations, Sheet 6C. Elevations 11, 12, 13, and 14 detail the walls in the Women's Room (Room 103). Elevations 15, 16, 17, and 18 detail the walls in the Men's Room (Room 102). Equipment in the restrooms is identified with a notation. Ceramic tile with a cove base and wall accent tile near the ceiling are shown on all walls in both restrooms. Typical Toilet Room Dimensions, Sheet 6C, provide specific information about tile and equipment placement in the restrooms.

Elevation 11 shows the north wall of the Women's Room and includes the toilet (water closet), toilet tissue dispenser, toilet partition, and Door F. Elevation 12 shows the east wall including the recessed electric hand dryer and side view of the lavatory vanity. Elevation 13 shows the front view of the lavatory vanity with a mirror above, and the toilet partition. Elevation 14 shows the two toilets, a toilet partition between the toilets (without the doors), and grab bars in the handicapped-accessible toilet area.

Elevation 15 shows the north wall of the Men's Room and includes the toilet partition and the urinal partition (partition immediately to the right of the urinal). Elevation 16 shows the east wall and includes the urinal, urinal partition, and Door E. Elevation 17 shows the face of the lavatory vanity in the Men's Room with a mirror above. A recessed electric hand dryer is to the left of the vanity. Grab bars are to be installed behind and to the right of the toilet. Elevation 18 shows the front view of the toilet partition and a side view of the lavatory vanity.

A Vanity Plan and Vanity Section are provided on Sheet 6C. The Vanity Plan indicates that a bone-colored Corian solid-surface material is used as the vanity surface, which has an integral sink bowl. The surface is to be supported by a 2 × 4 frame anchored to the surrounding wood-framed walls with lag screws. The Vanity Section indicates that the wood frame supports are set 2'-9¼" above the finished floor. The face of the 2 × 4 framing is covered with ⅝" plywood and finished with ceramic tile. The backsplashes and sidesplashes are also bone-colored Corian.

Equipment Plan, Sheet 9. Various pieces of equipment are specified for the restrooms. Each piece of equipment is referred to on the Equipment Plan with an item number. Item C02 indicates a soap dispenser in each restroom. Item C07 indicates toilet tissue dispensers in each restroom. The Women's Room contains two toilet tissue dispensers and the Men's Room contains one toilet tissue dispenser. Item M23 indicates electric hand dryers, which are furnished and installed by the electrical contractor. Specific information concerning the types of plumbing fixtures including the water closets, urinals, and lavatories is included in Division 15 of the written specifications.

HVAC Plan, Sheet 11. An 8" white air diffuser (type F) with a round neck is connected to an 8" duct above the ceiling in each restroom. The supply air is provided by RT-2. An 8" white register and 8" ducts run from the restrooms to Exhaust Fan 3 (EF-3).

Two E return registers are installed in the restrooms. The registers are fitted with 8" diameter ducts connected to Exhaust Fan 3 (EF-3), which is equipped with a 1½ HP, 115 V, 1φ, 60 Hz motor.

Electrical and Electrical Distribution Plans, Sheets 12 and 14. As shown on the Electrical Plan, electric hand dryers are to be installed in both restrooms. The hand dryers are also shown on Interior Elevations 12 and 14, Sheet 6C. A 120 V, 1φ junction box is to be installed 40" above the finished floor near the lavatory in each restroom to power the hand dryers. The hand dryer in the Women's Room is connected to circuit 11 of panelboard A and the hand dryer in the Men's Room is connected to circuit 9 of panelboard A. Each of these circuits are 2.3 kW with 20 A, single-pole circuit breakers. Each restroom has a 20 A, 120 V duplex receptacle fed by circuit 31 A. Circuit 31 of panelboard A is a 1.5 kW circuit with a 20 A, single-pole circuit breaker that also provides power to the dining room receptacles.

Lighting and Reflected Ceiling Plan, Sheet 13. Two B-3 luminaires (lighting fixtures) in each restroom provide illumination. As indicated in the Women's Room at the termination of the wiring run, the lighting fixtures are connected to circuit 15 of panelboard A. Type B-3 lighting fixtures each have three fluorescent lamps. The B-3 fixtures are mounted in the drywall ceilings and have the same wiring requirements as type B-1 and B-2 fixtures. Switch symbol 6 notes that these lights are controlled by switch number 6, which is installed near the inside of the rear entry door of the restaurant.

Plumbing and Plumbing Rough-in Plans, Sheets 15 and 15A. Plumbing fixtures are designated by letter and number on the plan and isometric views. See Figure 9-32. All restroom plumbing fixtures are provided by the plumbing contractor. The water closets (A-1 and A-2) are supplied by 1½" cold water pipes. Waste is directly discharged from the water closets through 4" waste outlets. The water closets are vented through a 2" vent pipe to a 4" vent through the roof. Water closet A-2 is handicapped-accessible.

Rough-in dimensions for plumbing fixtures, including water closets, urinals, and floor drains, are indicated on Sheet 15A. The rough-in dimensions are critical, especially when pipes are to be placed below a concrete slab and stubbed up in walls and partitions. The plumbing contractor will review the floor plans to determine wall placements and consult manufacturer specification sheets for rough-in dimensions for individual fixtures.

Restroom lavatories are designated as B-1. Lavatories are supplied by ½" hot and cold water lines. Note 8 indicates that the mixing valve type installed at the water heater outlet supplies regulated hot water of 110°F to all sinks. The lavatories have 1½" traps, direct waste outlets, and vent pipes. The mounting heights for supply and drain are as directed by the plumbing contractor.

The urinal (C-1) is supplied by a ¾" cold water line and is connected to a 3" waste pipe. The

urinal vent is a 1½" pipe. Sheet 15A shows the installation of a type ABC fire extinguisher near the entry to the Women's Room.

A floor drain (FD-1) is indicated in each restroom. The floor drains are 5" × 9" cast iron floor drains with adjustable strainers. The drains have 3" diameter bottom outlets, and a short piece of 3" pipe is installed between the drain and 4" sanitary lines.

Closet, Room 104, Sheet 4

Room 104 is a Closet measuring 4'-4" wide by 2'-9" deep, located adjacent to the Women's Room. A notation indicates that information about the wire shelving for the Closet is shown on Sheet 6A. The Closet is entered through a type H door, which is a 3'-0" × 6'-8" plastic laminate-covered flush door with a keyed lock and a door stop. Door hinges are attached to the jamb using 3½" screws.

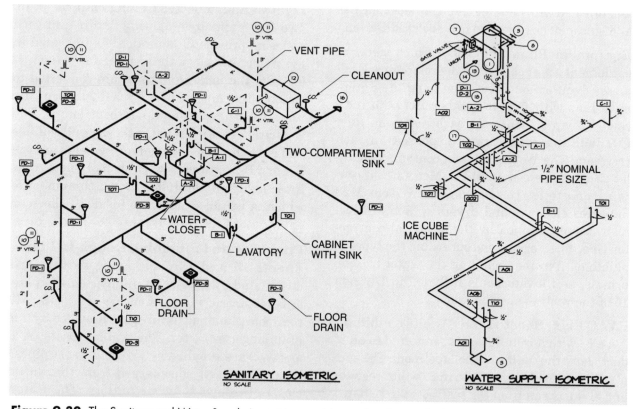

Figure 9-32. The Sanitary and Water Supply Isometrics provide an abundance of information for proper construction of the sanitary drainage, waste, and vent system and the water supply system, respectively. Vent pipes are indicated on the Sanitary Isometric using hidden lines. The cold water supply line is indicated with a "CW" while the hot water supply line is indicated with "110."

Interior Elevation 6, Sheet 6A. Interior Elevation 6 shows the door entering into the Closet. The door has an "EMPLOYEE" sign indicating this area is for employee use only. Three wire shelves are installed in the Closet. The lower shelf is 4'-0" above the finished floor, the middle shelf is 1'-0" above the lower shelf, and upper shelf 1'-0" above the middle shelf. The elevation also shows the door entering into the Women's Room and the proper locations of the fire extinguisher and ADA sign.

Equipment Plan, Sheet 9. The Equipment Plan indicates that three high chairs (R16) are stored outside the door leading into the Closet. The high chairs are used by infants in the dining area.

Serving Area, Rooms 105 and 106, Sheet 4

The Serving Area is the area where patrons place their food orders and employees prepare the orders. See Figure 9-33. The dimensions of Room 105 are 6'-2½" × 13'-10½". The dimensions of Room 106 are 12'-0" × 8'-10". A header installed in the ceiling 8'-3" above the slab (described on Detail J, Sheet 7B) separates Room 105 from Room 101 (Public Area). A soffit that is 7'-1" above the floor separates Room 105 from Room 107. Interior Elevations 19 and 20, Sheet 6D are referred to on Sheet 4.

Interior Elevations 19 and 20, Sheet 6D. The far left side of Interior Elevation 19 shows the fixed glass window at the pick-up windows. Equipment shown in this area includes the full-size warmer (V01), drive-through assembly counter (E12), undercounter refrigerator (Q06), point-of-sale monitor (D01), and portion pack dispenser (C13). A 1½" electrical conduit with junction boxes installed at 14" and 72" for connection to the cash register system is indicated. Ceiling height in the area near the pick-up window is 8'-10".

The cookcenter (E15) with an iced tea dispenser (A05), coffee warmer (A07), and portion pack dispenser (C13) is shown at the center of Interior Elevation 19. Stainless steel corner trim (L11-3) is indicated along the left side of the ceramic wall tile to protect the wall finish. See Figure 9-34. The 7'-1" high soffit is covered with ceramic wall tile on the sides and bottom, and contains the order boards for patron use.

Figure 9-33. Interior elevations and the Equipment Schedule provide detailed information about the equipment required in the food preparation and serving areas.

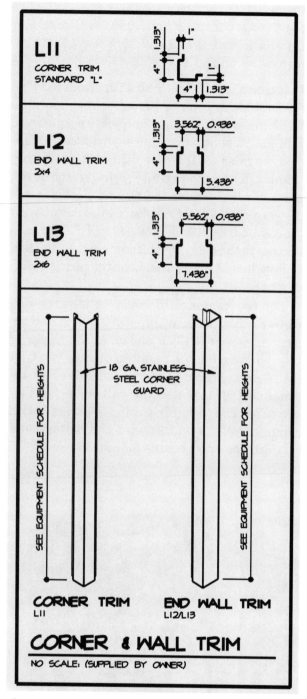

Figure 9-34. Stainless steel trim is specified for many corners and ends of walls to protect the wall finish.

The left side of Elevation 20 shows the wash sink unit (T01) over which a spray bottle rack for the dining room (S72-11) and the operations manual holder is mounted. The wash sink unit, rack, and holder are in a small unnumbered area

to the left of the Serving Area. Dimensions for the area are shown on the Floor Plan, Sheet 4. Stainless steel corner trim (L12-3) is indicated along the tiled wall. The center of Interior Elevation 20 shows the employee side of the serving counter with a drink tower (A01), two point-of-sale terminals (D02), two cup dispensers (C01), and two cash dump boxes (N02). The soffit separating this area from the dining room is finished with fiberglass-reinforced polyester paneling.

The fixed glass pick-up window is shown to the far right side of Interior Elevation 20. The ceiling height in this area is 8'-10". The wall is finished with fiberglass-reinforced polyester paneling and the bottom of the wall is finished with tile cove base. Equipment in the pick-up window area includes an iced tea dispenser (A05), coffee brewer (A06), undercounter refrigerator (Q06), Frosty machine (Q08), drink tower (A01), cup dispenser (C01), cash dump box (N02), and point-of-sale terminal (D02).

Detail J, Sheet 7B. Detail J shows the header construction over the serving counter. The header is framed with 2 × 4 wood members installed 16" OC and tied to the roof joists. The header is covered with ⅝" drywall. The suspended ceiling butts against both sides of the header. Sheet 6B provides details for the wood trim.

Equipment Plan, Sheet 9. Equipment for Room 105, identified on the Interior Elevations, Sheet 6D, is also identified on the Equipment Plan. In addition, equipment that cannot be shown in elevation is shown on the Equipment Plan, including the coffee warmer (A07), iced tea dispenser (A05), and cookcenter (E15). The Equipment Schedule lists each piece of equipment in numerical order and indicates the quantity and a brief description of the equipment. General Notes 1 through 4 relate to the Equipment Schedule.

Security Plan, Sheet 10B. The Security Plan and two details on Sheet 10B provide information about the security in Rooms 105 and 106. The Security Plan shows three cash dump boxes (CS), two cameras (C), two microphones (M), a monitor (TV), and window contacts (WC) at the pick-up window. Detail 1, drawn at a scale of ½" = 1'-0", shows the location of the security camera and monitor in Room 105. The camera is mounted 8″ below the ceiling and aimed toward the dining area and across the serving counter. A second camera is installed near the pick-up window and is aimed toward one of the fixed glass windows and the cash register in the pick-up window area. Detail 2, which is an interior elevation of the pick-up window, shows the location of security stickers on the window. Microphones are mounted in the ceiling over the serving and the pick-up window areas. The pick-up window areas are covered by Zone #7 of the security system.

HVAC Plan, Sheet 11. Two 10″ 350 cfm and one 400 cfm type A air diffusers provide the air supply for Room 105, with one near the Closet under MUA-1. A 10″ diameter duct connects both 350 cfm diffusers to rooftop unit 1 (RT-1) and a 10″ diameter duct connects the 400 cfm diffuser to rooftop unit 2 (RT-2). An additional 350 cfm type A diffuser provides the air supply in Room 106 near the pick-up window.

Electrical and Electrical Distribution Plans, Sheets 12 and 14. Circuits and home runs are shown for all equipment in Room 105. Circuits are indicated with dashed lines. Home runs, indicated with solid lines and terminated with arrowheads, are electrical conductors that extend from the power source to the point of use. Various types of electrical outlets are installed in this area to serve the variety of electrical equipment. For example, a notation near the pick-up window area indicates that a junction box for connection to cash registers is placed 24″ above the finished floor. The cable is protected by 2″ conduit. By following the dashed line indicating the circuit run, note that the circuit provides power to two additional outlets in the pick-up window area. At the termination of the dashed line, a notation indicates the circuit is fed from circuit 3 via a power conditioner box above the distribution panelboard. Sheet 14 indicates that circuit 3A is fed from electric panelboard A, which contains 225 A main lugs, 120/208 V, 3φ, four-wire service. Additional electrical information is provided in notations. For example, a notation on Sheet 12 indicates that the front counter is prewired for register outlets.

Register System and Outdoor Order Station Plan, Sheet 10A. Additional information related to the register system and outdoor order station is provided on Sheet 10A. The plan view shows various receptacles and conduit that are part of the outdoor order station. For example, ¾″ conduit is installed near the pick-up window for the outdoor menu speaker system. The general notes state that all conduit shown on this sheet is related to the cash register system. This plan must be cross-referenced with Sheet 12 to ensure the proper power systems and conduit are installed to provide the required electrical power to the point-of-sale ordering and sale systems. For example, the duplex receptacle shown near register 3 is installed 46″ above the finished floor to the center of the box as stated in the general notes. Additional information concerning this receptacle is included on Sheet 12, indicating the receptacle is powered by circuit 3 on panelboard A.

Lighting and Reflected Ceiling Plan, Sheet 13. A variety of lighting fixtures are utilized in Rooms 105 and 106. Three B-1 fixtures, each containing three fluorescent lamps, are recessed into the soffit above the serving counter. Three more B-1 fixtures are indicated in Room 106. The EM-1 light fixture is an emergency flood light that provides illumination in case of a power outage. Three type F-1 recessed can fixtures designed for use with incandescent lamps and utilizing compact fluorescent lamps are installed in Room 105. Two F-1 fixtures are installed in the bottom of the soffit and supplied by circuit 17A. One F-1 fixture is installed in the small Closet to the left of the serving counter and supplied by circuit 19A.

Switches 1, 2, 3, and 4 are installed in the Closet near the Serving Area. Switch 1 controls the lights above the Serving Area and the area near the condiment stand. Switches 2 and 3 control the two sets of lights in the Public Area. The hanging fixtures above the tables around the perimeter of the Public Area are controlled with switch 4. The switch 1 circuit is circuit 19 on panelboard A. The switch 2 circuit is circuit 21 on panelboard A. The switch 3 circuit is circuit 25 on panelboard A. The switch 4 circuit is circuit 23 on panelboard A.

Plumbing and Plumbing Rough-in Plans, Sheets 15 and 15A. Two floor drains (FD-1 and FD-3) are to be installed in the Serving Area and one floor drain (FD-3) is to be installed in the pick-up window area. The floor drains have 3″ bottom outlets and are connected to the sanitary waste system. Two drink towers (A01) are supplied with ¾″ cold water lines. The coffee machine and warmer (A06) is supplied with a ½″ cold water line. Heavy dashed lines extending from the drink towers to the back wall of the building indicate that 6″ schedule 40 PVC pipe is used as a conduit for beverage syrup lines. The Plumbing Fixture Schedule indicates that each drink tower is to have an indirect connection to the floor drain. The Indirect Drain Detail, Sheet 15, shows the indirect drain with the required air gap above the finished floor. See Figure 9-35. An *indirect drain* is a waste pipe that does not connect directly to the drainage system but conveys liquid waste by discharging it into a plumbing fixture, such as a floor drain or floor sink, that is directly connected to the drainage system. A backflow preventer is installed in the water supply line for each drink tower. A *backflow preventer,* or backflow prevention device, is a device used to protect the water supply from contaminated and undesirable substances entering the water supply system. The Plumbing Plan also shows a cleanout near the pick-up window to provide ready access to the sanitary waste system.

The hand sink near the pick-up window (T10) and the small sink in the Closet near the serving counter (T01) have ½″ hot and cold water lines. The Sanitary Isometric shows a 2″ sanitary line for sink T10 and a 3″ sanitary connection line for sink T01. Each of the sinks has a 1½″ sanitary vent as indicated by dashed lines on the Sanitary Isometric.

Serving Area, Room 107, Sheet 4

Room 107 is an activity-filled area between the food preparation area and the serving counter. Sandwiches and other food products are prepared and moved from the food preparation area (Room 108) to the serving areas at the pick-up window (Room 106) and serving counter (Room 105). Overall dimensions of Room 107 are 19′-10″ × 16′-9″.

Interior Elevations 22, 23, and 25 on Sheet 6D and Interior Elevations 27, 28, and 29 on Sheet 6E provide additional details about the layout of Room 107. The Room Finish Schedule, Sheet 4, indicates that the floor is quarry tile and the ceiling height is 8′-10″. A 3′-7″ long metal-framed partition disrupts the line of sight into the office (Room 109).

Long dashed lines in Room 107 on the Floor Plan indicate the location for Hood 1. Hood 1 measures 7′-0″ × 4′-0″ and is located 6′-0″ from the pick-up window offset and 7′-9″ from the inside of the exterior wall. A heavy dashed line on specific walls represents ⅝″ plywood sheathing that is to be installed to support wall shelving.

The Room Finish Schedule indicates that the floor and base in the Serving Area are finished with quarry tile. The walls are finished with FRP and the ceiling is finished with a washable suspended ceiling at a height of 8′-10″.

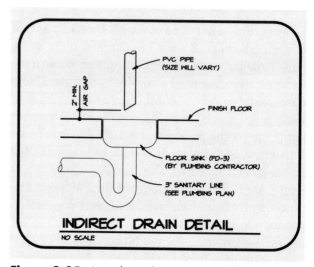

Figure 9-35. An indirect drain is required for certain equipment such as the drink towers. An indirect drain conveys liquid waste by discharging it into a plumbing fixture, such as a floor drain, that is directly connected to the drainage system.

Interior Elevations 22, 23, and 25, Sheet 6D. Elevation 22 is a view taken looking north from the center of Room 107. Rolling storage units (S90-1, S90-5, and S96-2) and the bun oven (K05) in the Dry Storage Area (Room 110) are shown on the left side of the elevation. A partition trimmed with stainless steel wall end trim (L12-6) separates Room 107 from Room 108. Equipment to the right of the partition includes a one-drawer MPHC (multipurpose heat cabinet) (V11), grill hood 1 (L03), 6' long grill with a double trough (K03), 6' long bun warmer (V09), point-of-sale monitor (D01), three-drawer MPHC (V13), cup dispenser (C01), coffee counter (E08), and hand sink (T10). The hood is to be installed 6'-6" from the finished floor.

Both sliding pick-up windows and the direction of travel for the windows are shown in Elevation 23. The front serving counter is shown along the left of the elevation. Equipment shown in Elevation 23 includes the headset backup, pick-up window (PUW) timers and chart holders, drink staging shelf (G15), assembly counter bin (G16), portion pack dispenser (C13), fry carton dispenser (C11), frydump cabinet (E06), fryer hood #2 (L05), four-vat open fryer (J06), pressure fryer (J04), stainless steel wall panel kit (L02), range/oven combination unit (K04), and the freezer (Q04). See Figure 9-36.

Figure 9-36. The serving area contains equipment used to prepare food, such as fryers, range/oven, and freezer.

Elevation 25 shows the rear of Room 107. The fixed glass window for the pick-up window area (Room 111), point-of-sale terminal (D02), change window shelf (E11), and cash dump box (N02) are shown at the left. The height of the junction box for the electrical connection to the cash register is indicated as 3'-10" above the finished floor. The window for the Office (Room 109) is shown, along with the location dimensions for a fire extinguisher. Walls are finished with fiberglass-reinforced polyester paneling. Stainless steel trim members (L11-6 and L12-6) are shown along with the bun racks (S80), lettuce cart (E22), knife holder (M20), two-compartment preparation sink (T09), bag and box rack (A03), storage unit (S90-4), and floor tool hooks (S74-5) in the Serving Area. The 84" dimension above the floor tool hooks indicates the installation height. The 82" dimension in the center of the elevation indicates the installation height of the sink module (S93-1).

Interior Elevations 27, 28, and 29, Sheet 6E. The north side of Rooms 110, 108, and 107 is shown on Elevation 27. (Information on Rooms 110 and 108 is provided later in this chapter.) The small Closet near the serving counter is shown on the right side of Elevation 27. Stainless steel trim (L06 and L09) is indicated on each side of the Closet opening. Although L06 and L09 are not included in the Equipment Plan, it is assumed that these items are also stainless steel trim like the other items in the L series of the Equipment Schedule. Ceramic wall tile surround the Closet opening. A Frosty machine (Q06), ice maker (Q02), safety equipment rack (X18), and night cover holder (G41) are shown to the right of the partition separating Rooms 107 and 108. The wall behind the ice maker is finished with fiberglass-reinforced polyester paneling and a J-mold where the panel butts against the tile cove base. A notation on Sheet 4 indicates that ⅝" plywood sheathing is to be installed for wall shelving support wherever walls are designated with heavy dashed lines.

Elevation 28 shows the pick-up window counter equipment at the left, the short divider wall, and the Office door at the right. Equipment pertaining to Room 107 includes a point-of-sale monitor (D01), 6' bun warmer (V09), a three-drawer MPHC (V13), grill hood #1 (L03), 6' grill (K03), and one-drawer MPHC (V11). This equipment is installed on the north side of the food preparation island. The 6'-6" dimension indicates the height of grill hood #1.

Elevation 29 shows the food preparation area (Room 108) at the left and the Serving Area (Room 107) at the right. Grill hood #1 (L03) is shown above the food preparation island. The only additional equipment shown on Elevation 29 is the freezer (Q04). The window at the right is one of the fixed glass pick-up windows.

Equipment Plan, Sheet 9. All equipment for Room 107 indicated on the interior elevations on Sheets 6D and 6E is also identified on the Equipment Plan. The Equipment Schedule lists each piece of equipment in numerical order and provides the quantity and a brief description of the equipment. General Notes 1 through 4 relate to the Equipment Schedule.

Security Plan, 10B. A motion detector is installed in Room 107. The motion detector provides 360° of coverage. A microphone, window contacts, counter safe, and security camera are installed near the pick-up window, along with decal installation information.

HVAC Plan, Sheet 11. Two exhaust fans, EF-1, and EF-2, are located in Room 107. EF-1 provides 2500 cfm of air movement and EF-2 provides 1350 cfm of air movement. Each exhaust fan is equipped with an exhaust hood that must be fabricated per NFPA 96 and local building codes. Per Note 3 on the Exhaust Hood Schedule, the hoods are to be fabricated from 16 ga black steel with continuous welded seams. A 16″ × 15″ duct leads from Hood 1 to EF-1 on the roof. A 10″ × 11″ duct leads from Hood 2 near the pick-up windows to EF-2 on the roof unit. Larger ducts are required in this area to remove smoke and odors.

Rooftop HVAC unit #1 (RT-1) provides supply air to Room 107 through five 22″ × 22″ diffusers and one 10″ diameter diffuser. Two 22″ × 22″ diffusers have 350 cfm capacity and three diffusers have 300 cfm capacity. The 10″ diameter diffuser, located near the pick-up window, has 350 cfm capacity. All ductwork for the diffusers is 10″ in diameter.

Electrical and Electrical Distribution Plans, Sheets 12 and 14. Circuits and home runs are shown for all equipment in Room 107. For example, the note 2B near the ice machine indicates that circuit 2 of electric panelboard B supplies power to the ice machine. Electric panelboard B contains a 225 A main on a 120/208 V, 3φ, four-wire service. The 208/240 V, 3φ disconnect switch near the ice machine is located 57″ above the finished floor.

Wiring for the two exhaust fans in Room 107 is shown on Sheet 12. Each exhaust fan has a 280/240 V, 3φ waterproof disconnect switch that is mounted on the roof near the fan. The disconnect switch allows the power to be turned off locally when servicing or maintaining the fans. As noted on the Electrical Distribution Plan, Sheet 14, Exhaust Fan 1 is powered by circuits 4, 5, and 6 on the Fan and Lighting Control. Exhaust Fan 2 is powered by circuits 10, 11, and 12 on the Fan and Lighting Control.

A series of five receptacles are installed on the exterior wall and east partition between the two pick-up windows. These are powered by control panelboard terminal 14. As shown on Sheet 14, these are the fry line receptacles. The four receptacles on the exterior wall are placed 14″ above the floor, while the receptacle on the east partition is installed 60″ above the floor.

A notation on Sheet 12 states that the cookcenter in the middle of Room 107 is prewired for register outlets and connected to a junction box above the ceiling. Sheet 14 shows the cookcenter panelboard at the right of the power riser detail. The cookcenter panelboard is 120/208 V, 3φ, four-wire, has a maximum load of 225 A, and is provided with the cookcenter equipment.

Lighting and Reflected Ceiling Plan, Sheet 13. A variety of lighting fixtures are to be installed in Room 107. Six B-1 fixtures are installed in this area. One B-1 fixture is shown with closely spaced diagonal lines, denoting that it is connected to the night light circuit. Type B-1 fixtures are 2′ × 4′ lay-in ceiling fixtures containing three fluorescent lamps. One emergency lighting fixture (EM-1) provides emergency lighting in this area. A junction box is to be installed above the ceiling for the hood lights.

Plumbing and Plumbing Rough-in Plans, Sheets 15 and 15A. Five floor drains serve Room 107—four type FD-1 and one type FD-3, which is to be installed near the ice machine. The rough-in dimensions for locating the centers of the floor drains are shown on Sheet 15A. For example, the floor drain nearest the Serving Area is 8′-8″ from the outside of the framed wall and 5′-3″ from the outside of the framed wall with the fixed window at the pick-up window area. Each floor drain location is identified in a similar manner on Sheet 15A. Placement of the drains and other utilities is critical to the equipment being positioned as designed.

The floor drains are connected to the sanitary sewer using 3″ pipe. Two cleanouts for the sanitary drainage system are installed in Room 107. A notation specifies that three of the floor drains shall be connected to the grease interceptor because of the high concentration of grease-producing cooking equipment in this area. Dimensions are provided on the plan for locating sanitary and water supply stubs. The isometrics specify pipe sizes and indicate vents with hidden lines. Vent dimensions and layout are also shown on the Plumbing Plan. A 2″ vent is installed under the floor, starting at a point past the cleanout in the floor. The vent pipe is sloped under the floor up to the wall and then continued as a 2″ vertical riser inside the framed wall.

A 2″ gas line is indicated on Sheet 15 under the floor between the food preparation island and the Office wall. The Gas Distribution to Range/Oven and Fryers Detail, Sheet 15A, indicates the gas distribution service required for the gas-fired equipment. Four separate gas connections are made from the main gas distribution line. Two gas lines provide fuel for the French fryers, one fuels the pressure fryer, and one fuels the range/oven. A gas cock is provided at each piece of equipment. Sheet 15 shows that this manifold configuration is placed on the exterior wall near the rear pick-up window (Room 111). The manifold and gas lines are supplied and connected by the plumbing contractor. The fire suppression general notes also indicate that electric gas valves are to be installed at Hood #1 and

Hood #2. The valves are to be provided by the hood system supplier and installed by the plumbing contractor. The hood system installer then activates the final connection.

The Pyrochemical/Ansul Fire Suppression System Detail, Sheet 15A, shows the method for installing the fire suppression system at Hood #1 and Hood #2. Dimensions show the locations of all equipment required for the fire suppression system. The fire cabinet is placed near Hood #2. Three tanks supplying the fire suppression chemicals are installed near Hood #2. Four type 6 nozzles are installed near the fire cabinet, each 17″ from the adjoining nozzle. Other nozzles in the installation are shown on the Equipment Schedule with numbered designations. A series of five nozzles are installed at Hood #1, with a type 4 nozzle in the center, two type 3 nozzles 36″ apart, and two type 5 nozzles near the ends of Hood #1. Notations indicate that all piping for the fire suppression system is ⅜″ black iron pipe except where exposed. Exposed pipe is chrome sleeved and has stainless steel fittings.

A fire suppression system is installed under Hood #1 and Hood #2.

Preparation Areas, Rooms 108 and 108A, Sheet 4

The overall dimensions for Rooms 108 and 108A are 14'-5" × 10'-5½" and 5'-2" × 5'-2", respectively. The dimensions for Room 108 are calculated by adding cumulative dimensions (11'-3½" + 4½" + 2'-9" = 14'-5" and 6'-9" + 4½" + 3'-4" = 10'-5½"). The interior partitions in these rooms are sheathed with ⅝" plywood to provide additional wall shelving support. A pair of hidden lines between Rooms 108 and 108A indicate a 5½" wide header to be installed 8'-3" above the finished floor. Interior Elevations 27 and 29, Sheet 6E, provide additional information about Rooms 108 and 108A. The room finishes for these rooms are the same, with the exception of the ceiling heights. Each area has a quarry tile floor and base, fiberglass-reinforced polyester panel walls, and a washable suspended ceiling. The ceiling height in Room 108 is 8'-10" and the ceiling height in Room 108A is 10'-6", separated by a 5½" wide header at 8'-3" above the floor.

Interior Elevations 27 and 29, Sheet 6E. Interior Elevation 27 shows the north walls of the food preparation areas. A door to the Cooler/Freezer is shown at the left of the elevation. Stainless steel trim is specified along the edges of the door. Bun racks (S80) are shown to the right of the Cooler/Freezer door. The header above the entrance to Room 108A is shown above the hot water tank (T11). The water meter location is indicated on the exterior wall of Room 108A adjacent to the hot water tank. The depressed mop sink (T06) is indicated with hidden lines with two faucets above. The walls in Room 108A and adjacent walls are finished with fiberglass-reinforced polyester paneling and tile cove base. A rolling storage unit (S90-4), plastic wrap box holder (G42), and chili workstation (S95-1) with the appropriate shelf heights are also shown on this elevation.

Interior Elevation 29 shows the east walls of the food preparation areas. Beginning at the left of the elevation, the elevated hot water tank (T11) and depressed mop sink (T06) are shown. A chemical storage shelf (G40) and hydrofoamer

rack are immediately above the tile cove base. Two sets of faucets (T03) are installed above the mop sink and their heights are indicated as 36" and 54". A spray bottle rack for the kitchen is installed above the faucets. A chemical blend station (T12) is connected to the upper set of faucets to deliver chemicals to the faucets for cleaning and sanitizing the food preparation area. The interior partition along the right side of Room 108A is trimmed with stainless steel edge trim (L11-3). A side view of the chili workstation (S95) is shown to the right of the partition with a knife holder (M20) fastened to the wall along the right side. A three-compartment power soak sink (T02) equipped with a chemical blend station (T12) is shown to the right of the chili work station. A sink module (S93-04) is to be installed above the power soak sink. A chemical storage shelf (G40) is located below the power soak sink for use with the chemical blend station. A Sparkle Station hand sink (T07) is to be installed next to the power soak sink along with three glove box holders (G32). Locating glove boxes near the hand sink promotes the use of gloves. Walls in this area are finished with fiberglass-reinforced polyester paneling and tile cove base.

Equipment Plan, Sheet 9. In addition to the equipment shown on Interior Elevations 27 and 29, other equipment to be installed in this area includes a 30" × 72" worktable (S94) with a slicer (W21) and a plastic wrap box holder (G42) adjacent to the chili workstation.

HVAC Plan, Sheet 11. Heated or cooled air is supplied to Rooms 108 and 108A with one 10" diameter supply duct, which feeds a 350 cfm air diffuser. Two 16" diameter return air ducts are shown with 20" × 20" louvered grilles. The ductwork is routed to rooftop unit 1 (RT-1).

Electrical and Electrical Distribution Plans, Sheets 12 and 14. Circuits and home runs are shown for all equipment in Rooms 108 and 108A. For example, the 33B notation near the hot water tank (T11) indicates that circuit 33 supplies the electrical power for the hot water tank from panelboard B. Panelboard B contains 225 A main lugs, 120/208 V, 3ϕ, four-wire service. As indicated on Sheet 12, the 208/240 V 3φ disconnect switch is located 72″ above the finished floor, and a duplex receptacle is to be installed for a gas water heater.

Lighting and Reflected Ceiling Plan, Sheet 13. Lighting for Rooms 108 and 108A is supplied by four 2 × 4 deep cell fluorescent fixtures (B-1), which are on the same circuit as the lights in the restrooms. A junction box for the Cooler/Freezer lights is to be installed on the west wall of Room 108. The junction box is on circuit 27 of panelboard B.

Plumbing Plan, Sheet 15. The water supply enters the building in Room 108A through a 1½″ diameter pipe. Specific information is provided for Rooms 108 and 108A in the form of Plan Notes. Notes 1, 3, 4, 7, 8, 13, 14, 17, and 18 on the Plumbing Plan refer to equipment in Rooms 108 and 108A. The capacity of the gas-fired water heater is 82 gal. and must have an expansion tank for safety. Freezeproof hose bibbs are required on exterior walls to prevent water from freezing inside the bibbs and cracking the fixture. Gas lines to the water heater must be located in conjunction with the mechanical contractor. The water meter must be fitted with a double backflow preventer valve to prevent contaminated water from harming the potable water supply system. The mixing valve installed where the hot water leaves the hot water tank is set to deliver water at 110°F, and is installed in a metal panel that is locked to prevent tampering. The water supply lines are 1½″ diameter from the building service to the water main. Plumbing pipe is to be covered with an escutcheon plate at each wall penetration.

Another item shown in Room 108A is the floor drain (FD-1) installed at the bottom of the depressed mop sink area. Also note that the condensate line from the Cooler/Freezer is extended through the wall to the floor drain (FD-3) in Room 108.

Office and Equipment Closet, Rooms 109 and 113, Sheet 4

The dimensions of the Office and Equipment Closet are 12'-1″ × 7'-9″ and 2'-8″ × 6'-9½″, respectively.

The Office provides space for planning, purchasing, recordkeeping, and other management activities. The Equipment Closet provides storage room for the bulk CO_2 tank and shortening management system. Interior Elevations 30, 31, 32, 33, and 34, Sheet 6E, are referred to on the Floor Plan. The office/training module acts as a room divider between the Office, which is utilized by the manager and supervisory staff, and the area near the Equipment Closet, which is used for employee training and storage.

Room Finish Schedule, Sheet 4. The Office floor is finished with quarry tile and quarry tile base. Walls are finished with fiberglass-reinforced polyester paneling. The ceiling is suspended 8'-10″ above the finished floor. Washable panels are installed in the suspended ceiling grid. Walls in the main area of the Office are sheathed with ⅝″ plywood behind the fiberglass-reinforced polyester paneling to better support shelving in this area. A 48″ wide by 36″ high fixed glass office window is installed in the east wall to allow for observation of the Serving Area. The top of the window is installed at 6'-8″ above the floor. The color of the frame is to match the exterior and is provided as part of the storefront package.

Reed Manufacturing Co.
A direct tapping machine is used to drill and tap water mains while the main is under pressure. A corporation cock is threaded into the tapped hole to provide a connection for the building water system.

Door and Hardware Schedule, Sheet 4. The Office has one door, which is shown as a G door on the Floor Plan, Sheet 4. The Office door is a plastic laminate-covered flush door measuring 3'-0" × 6'-8" and equipped with a keyed lock, door stop, and vision panel. The Equipment Closet has a double 3'-0" × 6'-8" plastic laminate-covered flush door. The Equipment Closet doors are equipped with a keyed lock, door stop, and surface-mounted bolt.

Interior Elevations 30, 31, 32, 33, and 34, Sheet 6E. Elevation 30, which is a view facing north, shows the fiberglass-reinforced polyester paneling around the door opening. The office/training module (N15) is shown to the right of the door. Office wall cabinets (N16), Office computer rack (N10), and Office desk top (N03) are also shown on the elevation. A security system can be installed above the door opening in the Office.

Elevation 31 is taken looking toward the east wall of the Office. The Office desk assembly including the Office desk top (N03), computer rack (N10), and money safe (N05) are shown. Two Office wall cabinets (N16) and a pigeonhole cabinet (N17) are installed on the sides of the Office window. The wall cabinet on the left includes a midheight shelf. An Office overhead shelf (N18) supports the music system controls. The installation heights of the cabinets are indicated along the right side of Interior Elevation 31.

Elevation 32 shows a profile view of the Office desk assembly with wall cabinets above at the left. The office/training module (N15) is used to separate the Office area from the Equipment Closet. The wall is finished with fiberglass-reinforced polyester paneling. Horizontal and vertical display folders are fastened to the wall. Two wall-mounted coat racks (N09) are to be installed, with the lower rack 3'-0" above the finished floor and the upper rack 3'-0" above the lower one. The bulk CO_2 tank (A04) is shown in the Equipment Closet.

Elevation 33 shows the east side of the office/training module (N15) between the Office and the Equipment Closet. The elevation shows the arrangement of cabinet doors and management informational items. Cabinet doors are shown with dashed lines converging at the hinged side. Shelf heights are provided along the right side of the elevation.

Elevation 34 shows the west side of the office/training module between the Office and Equipment Closet. Two cabinets with hinged doors and shelves are provided for employee use. A TV-VCR combination unit (D12) is provided for training purposes.

Equipment Plan, Sheet 9. Other equipment shown on the Equipment Plan for the Office and Equipment Closet includes chairs (N06 and R05) and the shortening management system (X15). The Equipment Plan provides a good plan view of the separation between the Office and Equipment Closet by the office/training module.

Security Plan, Sheet 10B. The control panelboard for the security system (CP) is installed above the door entering the Office. A monitor (TV), wall-mounted motion detector (MW), and VCR mounted inside the upper cabinet (VC) are also shown on the Security Plan. The Office is designated as Zone #4 in the security system.

HVAC Plan, Sheet 11. A white air diffuser with an 8" diameter neck supplies heated and cooled air to the Office. An 8" diameter duct is used to connect the air diffuser to the rooftop HVAC unit RT-1.

Electrical and Electrical Distribution Plans, Sheets 12 and 14. The Office and Equipment Closet contains a variety of receptacles for the computer and other office equipment. Most of the receptacles are placed near the fixed window and are supplied by circuit 35 on panelboard A. Circuit 35 is a 1.5 kW circuit with a 20 A, single-pole circuit breaker. A telephone outlet is also shown along the window wall. Additional notations on the Electrical Plan refer to the cash register system installation. A 1½" conduit for the cash register system is installed at the inside Office partition. A notation indicates that additional information is provided on Sheet 10A and in various technical manuals provided by the system manufacturer. A remote test station of the makeup air unit is installed in the Office area 36″ above the finished floor. A receptacle 100″ above the finished floor above the door provides power for the security system.

Lighting and Reflected Ceiling Plan, Sheet 13. The Office is illuminated with two fluorescent fixtures (B-1) which are recessed into the ceiling. One of the fixtures provides light for the manager's area, while the second fixture provides light for the training area and Equipment Closet. Both lights are controlled by switch 7, which is installed on the wall between the Equipment Closet and Dry Storage Area. The lights are on circuit 13 of electric panelboard A.

Plumbing and Plumbing Rough-in Plans, Sheets 15 and 15A. While plumbing is not required in the Office or Equipment Closet, the gas lines enter the building in this area. The gas meter and gas lines are installed tight against the exterior wall. Note 5 indicates that the gas company requirements must be taken into consideration before gas line installation. The main gas service is a 2½″ diameter line. A Type K fire extinguisher is installed in the Office.

Dry Storage Area, Room 110, Sheet 4

The Dry Storage Area measures 17′-1½″ × 12′-4½″. The 4′-2″ wall along the east side of the Dry Storage Area is sheathed with ⅝″ plywood to provide additional shelf support. The interior surface of the west brick-veneer wall is furred out to accommodate the electric panels. The Framing Elevation @ Electric Panels Detail indicates the stud spacing and arrangement along the west wall. Four 2 × 6s are used to frame the left side of the panelboard wall, with two of the studs used for framing the door opening. Two 2 × 6 studs are framed in place, allowing a 20″ clearance for Panelboard C. Two more studs are framed in place, allowing a 24″ clearance for the main distribution panelboard (MDP). Two more sets of 2 × 6 studs are then framed in place, allowing 20″ clearances for panelboards A and B. Interior Elevations 24 and 26, Sheet 6D, and Elevation 27, Sheet 6E, describe the appearance of the room.

Room Finish Schedule, Sheet 4. Floors in the Dry Storage Area are finished with quarry tile with a quarry tile base. Walls are finished with fiberglass-reinforced polyester paneling. The suspended ceiling is installed 8′-10″ above the finished floor.

Door and Hardware Schedule, Sheet 4. An exterior door, designated as J, is a 3′-6″ × 7′-0″ door set in a steel frame. For security purposes, the door does not contain any exterior hardware. The door is installed with security hinges and 3 ½″ screws. The door is equipped with a door kick panel, heavy-duty closer, door stop, vision panel, and panic hardware. Door accessories include a threshold, door sweep, and chime.

> Steel doors are available in most standard sizes and in 1⅜″ and 1¾″ thicknesses. Other sizes and thicknesses can be ordered. Steel doors are classified into four levels: Level I—Standard Duty, Level II—Heavy Duty, Level III—Extra Heavy Duty, and Level IV—Maximum Duty.

Interior Elevations 24 and 26, Sheet 6D. Interior Elevation 24 shows the rear entry door in the center of the elevation. The L11-6 notations indicate the stainless steel corner trim to be installed on the corners of the walls on both sides of the rear entry door. The Equipment Closet with double doors and various display boards is shown to the left of the door. Four electric panels, noted as A, B, C, and MDP, are shown to the right of the door. The panels are described in greater detail later in this section of the chapter. A junction box for the register circuit is installed 8′-0″ above the floor to the center of the junction box.

Interior Elevation 26, which is a view taken looking south, shows the arrangement of movable storage units in the Dry Storage Area. Shelf heights are indicated.

Equipment Plan, Sheet 9. Four storage units (S90) are shown in the center of the Dry Storage

Area. Three additional bun racks (S80) are shown between the Dry Storage Area and the Cooler/Freezer. A bread/bun work station (S96) with a bun oven (K05) are adjacent to the storage units. The time clock (D07) and fire extinguisher cabinet (N01) are placed near the door entering the Office from the Dry Storage Area. A first aid kit (M15) is also to be installed in the area near the back door. The shortening management system (M15) is placed at the exterior wall near the rear entry door.

Security Plan, Sheet 10B. The keypad (KP) for operation of the security system is installed on the wall between the Dry Storage Area and Office. The Security Keypad Location Detail, Sheet 10B, shows a keypad is to be placed to the left of the door and 65″ above the finished floor. The Security Sign Location Detail shows the security features at the rear entry door including the information sticker, back door viewer, and location of the door contacts. The sticker, which consists of white letters on a red background, is to be mounted below the back door viewer. The back door viewer, which is usually 5′-0″ from the bottom of the door, is used to view people wishing to enter the building through the back door. The rear entry door is designated as Zone #5 on the security system.

Fluke Corporation

Meters are used to check the voltage, current, and other electrical properties.

HVAC Plan, Sheet 11. Heated or cooled air is provided to the Dry Storage Area with one type A 350 cfm air diffuser and one type B 150 cfm air diffuser. The type A diffuser is supplied by a 10″ diameter duct from rooftop HVAC unit 1 (RT-1). The type B diffuser is supplied by an 8″ duct from rooftop HVAC unit 1.

Electrical and Electrical Distribution Plans, Sheets 12 and 14. The Dry Storage Area contains a variety of receptacles, fixtures, and devices, as well as the distribution and electric panelboards. An electrical contractor is to install a pushbutton door buzzer near the rear entry door. The door buzzer is powered by a transformer connected to 24 V low-voltage wire. A waterproof receptacle is installed on the exterior wall and connected to circuit 42 on panelboard B. A junction box is also to be installed 96″ above the finished floor near the rear wall. Circuits 1 and 3 from panelboard A run through the junction box and allow access for future power conditioning for the cash register and office computer systems, which require additional safeguards to prevent damage to the computer equipment.

The short wall separating the Dry Storage Area from the Serving Area has two receptacles. One receptacle is a 20 A, 120 V, 1φ duplex receptacle located 20″ from the end of the wall. The other receptacle is a 208/240 V, 1φ duplex receptacle. Each receptacle is powered by a different circuit. The other side of this wall has three remote alarms for RTU-1, RTU-2, and MUA-1 smoke detectors.

The service equipment, which consists of a main distribution panelboard (MDP), electric panelboards A, B, C, and cookcenter panelboard are shown on the Power Riser Detail, Sheet 14. See Figure 9-37. Electric service is provided by a lateral from a transformer located on a pad outside the building. The service-entrance conductors are two sets of #350 kcmil THW copper conductors routed in two 3½″ conduits. The lateral is routed from the transformer to a waterproof current transformer (CT) enclosure mounted on the exterior wall of the building. An electric meter is mounted above and connected to the current transformer. Service-entrance conductors are routed from the current transformer enclosure and connected to the terminals of the 600 A main and distribution panelboard. Two separate 2/0 AWG copper grounding conductors are routed from the panelboard to two ⅝" copper grounding rods. The grounding rods are to be driven a minimum of 8' and 10' deep and no more than 4" from the building. The rods should be a minimum of 6' apart.

Panelboards A, B, and C and the cookcenter panelboard are to be installed adjacent to the distribution panelboard. Panelboards A, B, and C are 120/208 V, 3φ, 4-wire, with 225 A main lugs, and contain 42 circuit breaker spaces. Panelboard C and the cookcenter panelboard are connected to the distribution panelboard using four 3/0 THHN and #2 equipment grounding conductors routed in 2½" conduit. Panelboards A and B are connected to the distribution panelboard using four 1/0 THHN and #6 equipment grounding conductors routed in 2" conduit. The Framing Elevation @ Electric Panels Detail, Sheet 4, shows the framing details, spacing, and installation heights for

the panelboards. Panelboard A is set 10" above the floor line. Panelboards B and C and the main distribution panelboard (MDP) are installed with the tops of the panels 6'-0" from the floor. Panelboards A, B, and C are 20" wide. The main distribution panelboard is 24" wide.

Timeclock Settings and Photocell Controller Settings Details, Sheet 14, are also shown in relation to the Electrical Plans. The timeclock controls a few of the electrical functions of the building. When properly set, the timeclock will take the HVAC out of night setback and allow power to be applied to the photocell control that provides power for the parking lot lights. The timeclock also has a bypass switch that allows electrical functions to be activated manually. Photocell settings for the lights are set to the 20 to 2000 footcandle setting. Lighting controls at the bottom of the panelboard are set manually at the time when additional lighting is required, and set to the point where the red adjustment lights at the top of the panelboard become illuminated.

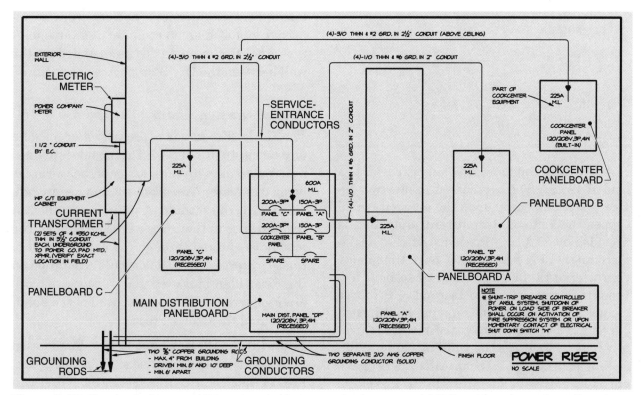

Figure 9-37. The electrical power supply is provided by a main distribution panel (MDP) and four electrical panelboards.

The arrangement of the 42 lugs on each panelboard is indicated and the equipment or lighting fixtures supplied by each, the kilowatt ratings, breakers, and circuit numbers are shown. Circuits are traced through the Electrical Plan, Equipment & Connections Schedule, and HVAC Motors & Equipment Connections Schedule, Sheet 12, and the electrical distribution information on Sheet 14, to determine conductor size, overcurrent protection device type, conduit size, and method of termination.

To determine that conductors specified are sized properly to carry the circuit load, multiply the kW by 125% and divide by the voltage (208 V $\times \sqrt{3}$) to obtain the amperage rating. When calculating three-phase problems, use the following values to eliminate one step from the mathematical computation:

- for 208 volts × 1.732, use 360
- for 230 volts × 1.732, use 398
- for 240 volts × 1.732, use 416
- for 440 volts × 1.732, use 762
- for 460 volts × 1.732, use 797
- for 480 volts × 1.732, use 831

For example:

$$I = \frac{VA}{V}$$

$$I = \frac{12,000 \text{ VA} \times 125\%}{360} = 41.66 \text{ A}$$

$$I = \textbf{42 A}$$

A #6 copper conductor will supply power to a load of 42 A. A 50 A overcurrent protection device is selected based upon the ampacity of #6 copper conductors. Overcurrent protection is provided by 50 A LPN fuses installed in a 60 A disconnect. LPN fuses do not have time-delay characteristics, but are designed to hold five times their rating for ¼ to 2 seconds. LPN fuses cannot be used with loads having high inrush current. The inrush current of motors is usually four to six times the running current. Resistant heating loads (as specified here) have only 10% of the full-load current ratings of the heating elements.

All circuits should be traced in the preceding manner to determine that they comply with the minimum requirements of the NEC® and local codes. Always consult the authority having jurisdiction if discrepancies arise.

Lighting and Reflected Ceiling Plan, Sheet 13. Four B-1 light fixtures provide illumination for Room 110. One of the B-1 lights is on the night light circuit. The exit light (EX-1) fed by circuit 39 on panelboard A is also shown above the rear entry door. A photoelectric sensor for control of the rooftop exterior lighting is to be installed on the roof to the parapet. The sensor is to be connected to the fan control wire. A wall-mounted waterproof light is to be installed above the rear entry door and connected to circuit 37 on panelboard A. Switches 5, 6, and 7 are placed for easy access inside the rear entry door to control various fixtures. Switch 5 controls lights in Rooms 107 and 110. Switch 6 controls the lights in the bathrooms and Room 108. Switch 7 controls lights in the Office and pick-up window areas.

Plumbing Plan, Sheet 15. One floor drain (FD-1) is shown in the Dry Storage Area near the Cooler/Freezer entrance. The floor drain is connected to a 4″ diameter sanitary sewer line. A type ABC fire extinguisher is installed on the wall between the Dry Storage Area and Office.

Cooler/Freezer, Room 112, Sheet 4

The Cooler/Freezer is a prefabricated module measuring 15′-0″ × 12′-0″. The module is divided into two areas, with the smaller of the two areas being the freezer. Two doors—K and L—are provided with the module. A ramp is installed at the entrance to the freezer area at door L. The module is entered through the exterior wall of the Dry Storage Area (Room 110). A notation on the Floor Plan indicates that 4″ concrete block are used to finish the exterior wall of the building behind the Cooler/Freezer.

Foundation Plan, Sheet 3. The Foundation Plan shows the unexcavated area for the Cooler/ Freezer slab. The 4″ concrete slab is reinforced with 6 × 6—W1.4 × W1.4 welded wire reinforcement over a 6 mil vapor barrier and 4″ granular fill. Details of the slab and footing are shown in Sections B and D, Sheet 7A. The Right Side and Rear elevations, Sheet 5, provide additional information.

Interior Elevations 35, 36, 37, 38, and 39, Sheet 6E. These interior elevations provide information about the various pieces of rolling equipment in the Cooler/Freezer. The heights of the shelves for each of the rolling racks are shown on the elevations. For example, on Elevation 35, the cooler storage unit (S91-2) has shelving heights of 10½″, 45½″, 55½″, 65½″, and 77½″. The other elevations provide similar information concerning shelf spacing on the various rolling storage racks.

Equipment Plan, Sheet 9. Five cooler storage units (S91) are shown in the cooler area. Four freezer storage units (S92) are shown in the freezer area.

Security Plan, Sheet 10B. Two walk-in panic buttons (WP) are installed in the Cooler/Freezer, one near the door in the cooler and one near the door in the freezer. The panic buttons are to be installed 12″ to 18″ above the finished floor. The Walk-in Panic Button Detail, Sheet 10B, indicates the location of the panic buttons. The panic buttons are activated in the event that an employee becomes trapped in the module. The panic buttons are in Zone #6 on the Security Plan.

Electrical and Electrical Distribution Plans, Sheets 12 and 14. The cooler and freezer areas are each equipped with electric motors and 208/240 V, 1φ weatherproof disconnect switches. The disconnect switch in the freezer area is routed to circuit 14 of panelboard B. The disconnect switch in the cooler area is routed to circuit 8 of panelboard B. The three-phase loads are protected by a 20 A, three-pole circuit breaker that provides simultaneous tripping should a short circuit or ground fault occur.

Name _____ Date _____

Identification—Architectural Symbols

Refer to Appendix.

_____ **1.** Concrete

_____ **2.** Wood trim member

_____ **3.** Concrete masonry unit

_____ **4.** Brick

_____ **5.** Rough wood member

_____ **6.** Earth

_____ **7.** Bronze or brass

_____ **8.** Steel

_____ **9.** Shingles

_____ **10.** Insulation

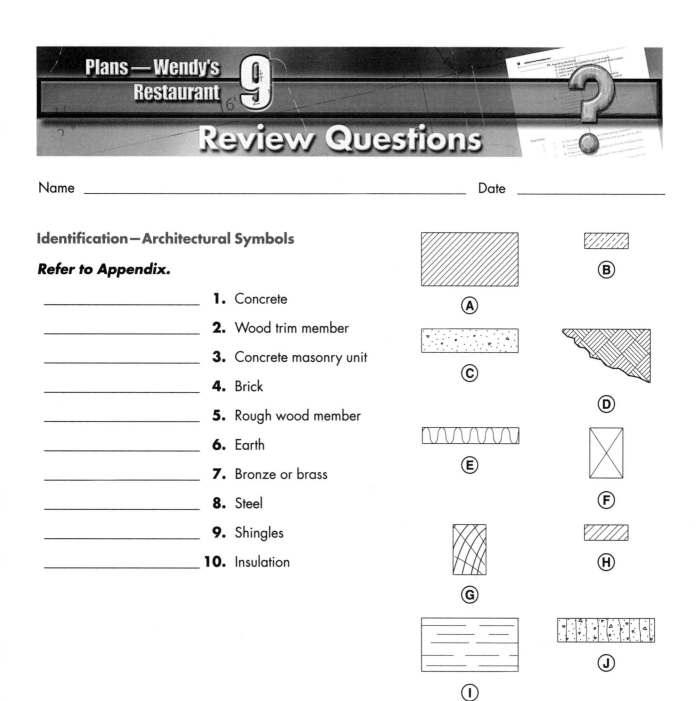

True-False

T   F **1.** A site benchmark is commonly a USGS datum.

T   F **2.** A construction joint is a groove made in a concrete slab to create a weakened plane and control the location of cracking.

T   F **3.** Pavers are installed over a sand or gravel base.

T   F **4.** Anchor bolts are used to secure gypsum board to wood or metal studs.

T	F	**5.** Wood members are pressured-treated to resist decay.
T	F	**6.** When a standard set of prints is utilized on several similar projects, architects show a variety of options and features that may or may not be used on a particular project.
T	F	**7.** An air diffuser is a return air duct for an exhaust system.
T	F	**8.** The arrow on a cutting plane reference indicates the direction of sight for the section.
T	F	**9.** An engineer is required to finalize standard drawings for local conditions and codes.
T	F	**10.** A 1% slope is equal to 1″ vertical drop for each 10′ of horizontal distance.

Identification—Plumbing Symbols

Refer to Appendix.

_____ **1.** Safety valve

_____ **2.** Water closet

_____ **3.** Grease separator

_____ **4.** Water heater

_____ **5.** Gas line

_____ **6.** Urinal

_____ **7.** Vent

_____ **8.** Hose bibb

_____ **9.** Above-grade soil and waste piping

_____ **10.** Handicapped lavatory

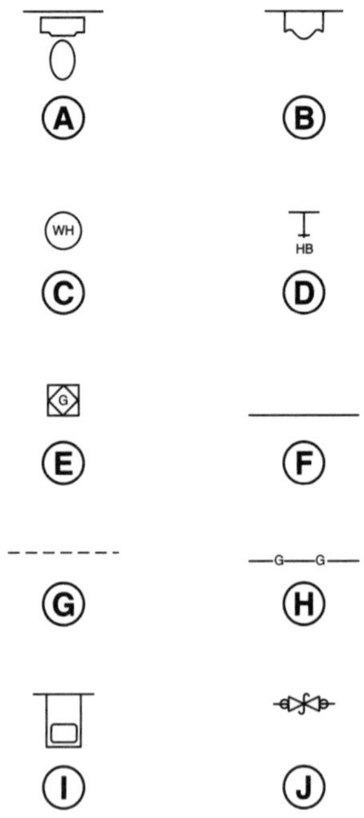

(A)   (B)

(C)   (D)

(E)   (F)

(G)   (H)

(I)   (J)

Completion

_____ **1.** ___ receptacles are identified using a standard receptacle symbol and the letters WP.

_____ **2.** A(n) ___ dimension locates a particular feature in relation to another feature.

_____ **3.** The NEC® permits no more than 13 general-purpose outlets to be connected to a(n) ___ A circuit.

_____ 4. A(n) ___ line is the lower horizontal portion of a curb in which stormwater flows.

_____ 5. A room finish ___ indicates the finish materials to be applied in each room of a building.

_____ 6. Stormwater and sanitary sewer piping, and electrical, telephone, and natural gas service are shown on a(n) ___ plan.

_____ 7. A(n) ___ is an opening in a wall that allows rainwater to drain into the downspout and stormwater drainage system.

_____ 8. A(n) ___ bonding agent is applied between an asphalt curb and topping pavement to prevent water penetration that could deteriorate the curb structure.

_____ 9. A(n) ___ joint separates structural supports, such as posts, from surrounding concrete slabs.

_____ 10. A(n) ___ is a concrete-filled post that protects buildings from vehicular damage.

_____ 11. ___ walls provide additional structural support to prevent building failures under unusual loading such as earthquakes or wind storms.

_____ 12. A(n) ___ is a short wall that surrounds a flat roof to conceal mechanical equipment mounted on the roof.

_____ 13. Installation of electrical equipment must conform to all local codes and the ___.

_____ 14. ___ glass is nonshattering glass that has high impact resistance.

_____ 15. Emergency lighting circuits cannot be routed in the same ___ supplying illumination for required lighting.

_____ 16. ___ runs are electrical conductors that extend from the power source to the point of use.

_____ 17. ___ duct connectors minimize vibration and reduce sound transmission between HVAC equipment and the structure.

_____ 18. A(n) ___ drain is a waste pipe that does not connect directly to the drainage system but discharges into a floor drain or floor sink directly connected to the drainage system.

_____ 19. A (n) ___ preventer in a water supply line protects the water supply from contamination by undesirable substances entering the water supply system.

_____ 20. A raised earth embankment is a(n) ___.

Identification—Electrical Symbols

Refer to Appendix.

_____ **1.** Three-way switch

_____ **2.** Computer data outlet

_____ **3.** Disconnect switch

_____ **4.** Outdoor pole-mounted fixture

_____ **5.** Split-wired triplex receptacle

_____ **6.** Emergency battery pack with charger

_____ **7.** Electric motor

_____ **8.** Pushbutton

_____ **9.** Weatherproof switch

_____ **10.** Duplex receptacle

(A) (B) (C) (D) (E) (F) (G) (H) (I) (J)

Math

Use I = VA/V to solve problems 1 to 3.

_____ **1.** I = 20 A; V = 120 V. Find VA.

_____ **2.** I = 15 A; VA = 1800 VA. Find V.

_____ **3.** VA = 7200 VA; V = 240 V. Find I.

The Specifications for the Wendy's Restaurant encompass 12 of the 16 divisions of the CSI MasterFormat, including Site Construction, Concrete, Wood and Plastics, Mechanical, and Electrical. The Specifications correspond to the plans for the Wendy's Restaurant discussed in Chapter 9.

alternates —

SPECIFICATIONS

Specifications are written instructions used to supplement the prints when constructing a building. Specifications may be included as part of the prints or bound in book form. General Requirements included at the beginning of a set of specifications define the relationships and assign the responsibilities of the owner, architect, contractor, subcontractors, and material suppliers. The General Requirements also describe some of the technical construction requirements for completing the job. The remainder of the specifications provides specific information regarding the types, sizes, and locations of materials and equipment used to construct the project. If a discrepancy should occur between the prints and the specifications, the specifications take precedence.

The Construction Specifications Institute (CSI) revises the MasterFormat every five to seven years to keep it current. A new edition of the MasterFormat, titled MasterFormat 04, reflects the rapidly growing volume and complexity of information generated for nonresidential building projects.

Specifications for the Wendy's Restaurant follow the standardized MasterFormat, developed by the Construction Specifications Institute (CSI). In the MasterFormat, 16 divisions, based on trade groups such as masonry, wood and plastics, and electrical, are the primary organizational headings. Depending on the size and complexity of the construction project, the number of divisions included in a set of specifications varies. For example, the specifications for Wendy's Restaurants contain 12 divisions.

Changes may need to be made during the course of construction. For example, an owner may decide to lengthen a room by an additional 6′. A change order is then issued to notify all affected trades and individuals involved in the project of the change. A *change order* is the formal, legal process authorizing any changes in location, layout, size, construction methods, or materials. Change orders are most commonly issued by an architect or owner, but a contractor, subcontractor, or supplier may also seek to make changes. Change orders are routed through the architect, who verifies compliance with all local, state, and national requirements, ensures owner approval of any additional project work and costs, and completes documents that ensure completion and payment of the change order.

INDEX TO SPECIFICATIONS

DIVISION 1—GENERAL REQUIREMENTS

Specifications of Construction Contract with Wendy's International, Inc.
Americans with Disabilities Act (ADA) New Construction Checklist

DIVISION 2—SITE CONSTRUCTION

Excavation, Backfilling, Grading
Asphalt Paving
Concrete Paving   *Soil balancing*
Striping and Parking Blocks
Curbs
Landscaping
Plant Guarantee and Replacement
Utilities

DIVISION 3—CONCRETE

Footings
Slabs and Footings
Sidewalks and Ramps
Sidewalk Pavers
Paving
Concrete Pads

DIVISION 4—MASONRY

General
Mortar for Face Brick
Brick and Block

DIVISION 5—METALS

Wrought Iron Railing (Outside—Required)
Wrought Iron Railing Serpentine Rail (Interior)

DIVISION 6—WOOD AND PLASTICS

Rough Carpentry
Structural Lumber
Nailing Schedule
Roof Joists
Finish Carpentry
Walk-in Cooler/Freezer/Dry Storage

DIVISION 7—THERMAL AND MOISTURE PROTECTION

Delivery
Handling
Storage
Overnight Cover
Roofing and Sheet Metal
Surface Preparation
Wood Decks
Membrane
Related Materials
Building Insulation
Insulation Attachment (Mechanical)
Flashing — *Keep moisture out*
Flash and Counter

Perimeter Laps
Caulking
Caulking Materials
Project/Site Clean-up
Inspections
Contractor Qualification Assurance
Warranty
Series II Fascia Panel System

DIVISION 8—DOORS AND WINDOWS

Aluminum Entrance Doors and Storefront
Prefinished Doors
Steel Service Doors and Frames
Pick-up Window

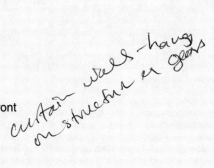

DIVISION 9—FINISHES

Stucco Brick
Floor and Wall Tile Installation
Exterior Decorative Wall Tile
Interior Floor Tile
Interior Wall Tile
Gypsum Drywall
Suspended Ceiling System
Carpet
Carpet Installation
Wall Covering
Fiberglass-Reinforced Polyester (FRP) Panels
Painting
Workmanship
Preparation of Surfaces
Inspection
Paint Schedule

DIVISION 10—SPECIALTIES

Exterior Trash Enclosure
General Signage
Building Signs
Menuboards
Kitchen Equipment
Hood Fire Suppression System and Portable Fire Extinguishers
Communication System
Public Restroom Doors/Partitions
Public Restroom Accessories
Room Identification Sign
ADA Restroom Identification Sign
Stainless Steel Corners
Wall Decor
Silk Plant Package
Floor Mats

DIVISION 15—MECHANICAL

Plumbing
Heating and Ventilation

DIVISION 16—ELECTRICAL

* Divisions 11, 12, 13, and 14 do not apply.

DIVISION 1—GENERAL REQUIREMENTS

Wendy's International, Inc. Construction Contract
This contract is made this day _____ of 200_ between Wendy's International, Inc.
(Wendy's) of 4288 W. Dublin-Granville Road, Dublin, Ohio 43017 and
_____ ("Contractor") of _____. In
consideration of the promises set forth below, the parties agree as follows:

ARTICLE I—CONTRACTOR'S WORK

1. Contractor shall construct (such construction referred to herein as the "work") on the
   premises, as defined in Article II below, a Wendy's restaurant and other improvements in
   accordance with the described plot plans, plans and specifications, described by sheet
   numbers and revision dates as provided by exhibit "A" and incorporated into this contract.
2. Contractor hereby acknowledges receipt of all of such construction documents, in duplicate, and has
   initialed one of such sets, which initialed set contractor shall deliver to Wendy's within five (5)
   business days hereof, all of which are hereby incorporated into this contract.

ARTICLE II—THE PREMISES

The restaurant shall be constructed on that real property (the "premises") commonly known as
_____ , in the city of _____ county of
_____ state of _____, as is more
particularly described on that certain survey of such parcel dated _____
made by _____, receipt of a copy of which survey contractor hereby
acknowledges.

ARTICLE III—CONTRACT SUM

1. Wendy's shall pay contractor the sum of _____ dollars
   $ _____ (the contract sum) in accordance with the terms of this contract. The contract
   sum includes and contractor shall be solely responsible for all federal, state and local taxes,
   including without limitation excise taxes, use taxes and retailers occupational taxes.
2. The contract sum does not include the purchase price and shipping cost of the items listed on
   exhibit "B" hereto, but does include installation of such items by contractor as noted thereon.
   Contractor shall be responsible for receiving, unloading, inventorying, warehousing, protecting,
   insuring, assembling and installing same in the same manner as purchased by contractor.

ARTICLE IV—START DATE

1. Contractor shall commence construction within five (5) calendar days after written notice from
   Wendy's.
2. Substantial completion of the work shall be no later than _____ calendar days after
   contractor is given notice to commence work, for purposes of the paragraph, substantial
   completion shall be the earlier of the date the restaurant opens for business or the date a certificate
   of occupancy is issued.

3. Written requests for extensions of time shall be given to Wendy's by contractor within five (5) days after the occurrence of the basis for the extension request. No such request shall be deemed granted unless expressly agreed to by Wendy's in writing.

ARTICLE V—PERFORMANCE AND CONTRACT BOND/LETTER OF CREDIT

1. When required by Wendy's, contractor shall provide Wendy's with a contract bond or letter of credit in the full amount of contract sum. The bond shall name Wendy's as obligee and if letter of credit, shall be made in Wendy's favor and shall be on a form and with a surety company or bank approved by owner. The bond and letter of credit shall ensure well and faithful performance of each and every condition of this contract; and, shall indemnify Wendy's against all damages suffered by failure to perform under this contract.
2. At Wendy's request, contractor shall furnish Wendy's, within five (5) business days of such requests, information deemed necessary by Wendy's to show that contractor is financially solvent and capable of fully performing under this contract. If, in Wendy's sole judgment, contractor is found not financially responsible or capable, then Wendy's, by written notice, may terminate this contract without further obligation to contractor other than to pay contractor for the value of the work in place at the time of termination.

ARTICLE VI—PERMITS

Contractor shall obtain all licenses, permits, approvals and certificates (collectively, the "permits") necessary to complete the work in compliance with all applicable rules and regulations, unless obtained by Wendy's.

ARTICLE VII—INSURANCE

1. Prior to commencement of work, contractor shall furnish Wendy's with certificates of insurance, naming Wendy's as an additional insured, as their interests may appear, evidencing that contractor has obtained the insurance coverage stated below from companies holding a general rating of "A" or better as set forth in the most current issue of best key rating insurance guide, such certificates will provide that Wendy's will receive at least thirty (30) days prior written notice of any material change in, or cancellation of, such insurance.

   A. Comprehensive general liability insurance including a broad form endorsement and a broad form property damage endorsement with limits not less than $1,000,000 combined single limit. If appropriate, contractor shall also maintain scaffolding and demolition insurance.
   B. Workers compensation insurance in accordance with applicable state requirements.
   C. Employers' liability insurance in an amount not less than $100,000.
   D. Comprehensive automobile liability insurance including owned, non-owned and hired coverage in an amount not less than $500,000 combined single limit.
   E. Contractor shall also satisfy any insurance requirements necessitated by any pertinent governmental authority.
   F. Contractor shall maintain builder's risk covering the premises, such insurance shall be written on an all risk basis, and will cover all work until Wendy's final acceptance of same.

2. At its election, Wendy's may waive the requirement that contractor maintain the insurance set forth in paragraph 7.1-f in such instances, Wendy's will bear the risk of loss to the building structure and any equipment or fixtures attached or installed to the building structure. Wendy's will not be responsible for any equipment or personal property of the contractor or its agents under these circumstances.

ARTICLE VIII—RISK OF LOSS

With the exception of the risk of loss assumed by Wendy's when the requirement to maintain the insurance set forth in paragraph 7.1-f is specifically waived by Wendy's, contractor assumes all risks, hazards, and conditions in connection with the Performance of this contract, and contractor shall be solely responsible for the work until final acceptance of the completed work by Wendy's.

ARTICLE IX—CONTRACT DOCUMENTS/CUSTODY OF PLANS

The agreement and each of the contract documents are complementary, and they shall be interpreted so that what is called for by one shall be as binding as if called for all. Should the contractor observe any conflicts within the contract documents, he shall bring them to Wendy's attention for decision and revision at once. The contractor shall secure written instruction from Wendy's before proceeding with any work affected by conflicts, omissions or discrepancies in the contract. Contractor shall retain sole custody of (except as required for the performance of the work), all drawings, plans, specifications and any copies thereof furnished to contractor by Wendy's. A consigned set of such drawings, plans, and specifications shall be kept on the premises at all times during the course of construction. All drawings, plans specifications and copies thereof furnished by Wendy's shall remain Wendy's and shall be returned to Wendy's at the completion of the work, together with a complete set of "as-built" plans.

ARTICLE X—METHOD OF PAYMENT

1. Upon satisfactory progress of the work and Wendy's receipt of completed and signed progress payment requests, Wendy's will make payments on the contract except when in Wendy's opinion it is necessary to protect Wendy's from loss due to defective work not remedied, claims or liens on the premises, failure of contractor to make payment promptly to subcontractors or material suppliers, or unsatisfactory progression of the work.
2. Throughout the course of this contract, contractor shall draw up not more than four (4) progress payment requests for submission to Wendy's when that portion of the work associated with each respective payment request has been completed. Each request shall be submitted on Wendy's application and certificate for payment form.
3. The first progress request shall include a complete list of all subcontractors and material suppliers, including names, addresses and telephone numbers, used for the work.
4. Progress payments shall be in portions of the contract sum as shall reflect the value of the work in place (less amounts already paid to contractor), less the 10% retainage and any amounts necessary to complete the work.
5. Fourth and final payment: 10% of contract sum shall be paid after the restaurant is open, all furnished construction items (including punch list) are completed, and all test reports, certifications, warranties, permits and final change orders have been delivered to Wendy's.
6. Prior to release of the final payment, the following documents, completed and validly executed must be delivered to Wendy's.

    A. Contractor's final waiver of lien (fully executed by all subcontractors and suppliers certifying that there are no liens on the project and that all subcontractors and material suppliers) and other potential liens have been paid in full.
    B. Certificate of occupancy.
    C. As required by Wendy's in the bid document, concrete or asphalt paving certification (certifying sub-base, base and surface preparation and application).
    D. Copy of complete "as-built" plans.
    E. Certification of any other item or material reasonably requested by Wendy's.
    F. Contractor's concurrence with punch list as described below in article XII.

7. All items required in connection with the final payment shall be completed and submitted by contractor within thirty (30) days of restaurant opening.
8. In the event contractor does not timely comply with any of the requirements set forth above for the final payment, Wendy's shall retain all of the remainder of the contract sum to protect Wendy's against any lien rights or claims, until all requirements for the final payment have been satisfied.
9. All correctly completed requests for payment received and approved by Wendy's will be paid within twenty-one (21) days of Wendy's approval, except final retainage draw which shall be paid within forty five (45) days.
10. Notwithstanding the above, Wendy's may reasonably change the method of payment, including without limitation, payment by joint check, in the event Wendy's determines that another method would be more prudent.

ARTICLE XI—PAYMENT BY CONTRACTOR

Contractor shall pay subcontractors and material suppliers in a timely manner to prevent mechanic's or material supplier's liens being filed against the premises. If Wendy's receives a notice of claim to be filed or if a claim is filed as a result of contractor's nonpayment, Wendy's shall have the right, after five (5) days notice to contractor, to immediately pay the full amount of any such claim directly or indirectly to the claimant and deduct same from the contract sum. Contractor waives any and all claims or causes of action contractor has or may have against Wendy's for payments which are to be or may be made under this paragraph, Wendy's shall also have the right and option to require contractor to provide Wendy's with a bond insuring over such liens in an amount at least one and one-half times the amount of any such liens filed or notices of lien, and sufficient to cover Wendy's fees, interest and increased costs and expenses to enforce this contract, contractor shall promptly defend to conclusion Wendy's interest against each such claim.

ARTICLE XII—PUNCH LIST

1. Contractor shall meet with Wendy's and Wendy's construction manager, seven (7) days before the opening of the restaurant in order to establish a formal list of construction deficiencies (the "punch list"). If the punch list items are not corrected within seven days thereafter, Wendy's may hire an independent contractor to perform same and may deduct reasonable costs from the monies retained from the contractor draw or letter or credit/performance bond; or may bill contractor for such costs. Contractor agrees to pay immediately all such costs billed by Wendy's. If an item cannot reasonably be corrected within such seven (7) days, the reasons therefore shall be explained in writing on the punch list to Wendy's satisfaction.
2. The preparation of a punch list by Wendy's shall in no way waive or affect any other rights of Wendy's under this contract pertaining to warranties, latent defects, etc.

ARTICLE XIII—CHANGE ORDERS

1. Wendy's may alter this contract by adding to or deducting from or otherwise modifying the work, without invalidating this contract. All such changes shall be performed under the conditions of the original contract, except that no extra work or modification shall be done or paid for by Wendy's without a written order from Wendy's signed by the construction manager. The contract sum shall be increased or decreased by an amount agreed to in writing by the parties prior to the commencement of any such change, which amount shall not include more than 10% mark-up to contractor. Contractor shall provide adequate proof of cost of each such items.
2. Any extension of time for the completion of the work as a result of change order shall be agreed to in the written authorization for such change order.
3. All requests for payment under change order must be submitted to Wendy's within one week of substantial completion.

ARTICLE XIV—DEFAULT BY CONTRACTOR

If contractor fails or neglects to perform the work in accordance with the contract, Wendy's may, after seven (7) days written notice to contractor, make good the deficiencies and deduct the cost thereof from payments due contractor and may also terminate this contract by written notice to contractor. Upon such failure or neglect by contractor, Wendy's may exercise its right provided in article V herein.

ARTICLE XV—INSPECTIONS

Wendy's construction manager shall have the right to inspect the work and reject any work which does not conform to the plans and specifications. Wendy's also has the authority to stop the work for the purpose of performing special inspections or testing of the work. In these instances, Wendy's will grant an appropriate extension of time to contractor. Should any work be found faulty as a result of special inspections or tests, contractor shall repair the work immediately and pay the fees for said inspections or tests. Should the work be satisfactory, Wendy's will bear such costs.

ARTICLE XVI—CONSTRUCTION MANAGER

Wendy's engineering department shall be Wendy's construction manager and shall supervise the construction provided for hereunder in accordance with this contract and accepted industry practices.

ARTICLE XVII—CONTRACTOR'S ATTENDANCE

Contractor or its designated and qualified representative, with full authority to act on behalf of contractor under this contract shall, at all times during the progress of the work, be in attendance at the premises and supervising the work, contractor shall carefully study and compare all plans, specifications and other instructions and shall at once report to Wendy's any error, inconsistency or omission contractor may discover. Contractor shall do no work without appropriate plans, specifications or interpretations.

ARTICLE XVIII—PROTECTION OF WORK AND PROPERTY

1. Contractor shall continuously maintain adequate protection for all work from damage and the elements and shall protect and take all reasonable precautions to protect Wendy's, Wendy's property, any third party and the property of any third party from injury or loss during the course of the work.
2. Contractor shall comply with all applicable rules and regulations of any public authority having jurisdiction for the safety of persons or property. Contractor shall erect and maintain as required by existing conditions and progress of the work all reasonable safeguards for safety and protection, including posting danger signs, promoting safety regulations and notifying owners and users of adjacent utilities and properties.
3. If the severity of the elements makes it impossible to continue operations in a safe manner in spite of all reasonable precautions, contractor shall cease work and immediately notify Wendy's. All work damaged due to contractor's negligence shall be removed and replaced with new work at contractor's expense.
4. Contractor shall provide and maintain a watertight storage space, secure from theft, for storage of all equipment called for on the plans and specifications.

ARTICLE XIX—INDEMNITY

Contractor shall indemnify and hold Wendy's harmless from any and all liability, loss damage, cost and expense, including court costs and attorney's fees (whether or not litigation has commenced), of whatever nature or type that Wendy's may suffer or incur by reason of:

    A. Any injury or damage sustained or purported to have been sustained by any persons who are at any time during the course of construction on the premises under the direction, supervision, or sufferance of contractor, including but not limited to subcontractors, laborers and material suppliers.

    B. Any breach or default of contractor under this contract.

ARTICLE XX—COMPLIANCE WITH LAWS

Contractor shall fully comply with all applicable federal, state and local laws, codes, regulations, etc. (collectively, the "law") in its performance under this contract. Prior to commencing the work, contractor shall review the drawings and specifications to determine their conformance to the law. If contractor then or thereafter finds the drawings and specifications are at variance with the law, then contractor shall immediately notify Wendy's construction manager in writing before proceeding with the work. The cost of any necessary changes to comply with the law shall be agreed to by Wendy's before proceeding with the work. If any of the work is done contrary to the law contractor shall bear all costs required to correct the work.

ARTICLE XXI—CONTRACTOR'S WARRANTIES

1. Contractor warrants that all of the work shall be done in a first-class workmanlike manner and in accordance with the drawings and specifications with new, quality materials and warrants all work and materials against defects in the material or the workmanship for a period of one year from the opening date of the restaurant, unless stated otherwise in specifications. If a defect in material or workmanship or a deviation from the drawings and specifications is latent, hidden or not readily observable, contractor's warranty shall be extended for one (1) year from the date of discovery of the defect or deviation, within a reasonable time after written notice of a defect or deviation contractor shall without expense to Wendy's, remedy and repair same and any damage to other work resulting therefrom.

2. Contractor agrees to meet with Wendy's and the construction manager, at least fifteen (15) but not more than thirty (30) days prior to the expiration of one (1) year from the date of the commencement of the one-year warranty period for a warranty inspection of the work. All warranty deficiencies shall be noted and the list of deficiencies shall be given to contractor. Contractor agrees to correct all such deficiencies within thirty (30) days after the date of the meeting, if the deficiencies are not timely corrected, Wendy's may hire an independent contractor to do the work and shall be reimbursed promptly by the contractor.

3. If any item cannot, with reasonable diligence, be corrected within thirty (30) days, contractor agrees to set forth in writing a reasonable schedule for completion of the work. If the schedule is not met, Wendy's may immediately upon notice to contractor, complete the work and be entitled to prompt reimbursement from contractor.

4. No act or omission of Wendy's shall relieve contractor of contractor's responsibility for deficient workmanship and materials.

5. Contractor shall cause each of the subcontractors responsible for the items listed below to execute and deliver to Wendy's upon completion of the work a written warranty (reasonably satisfactory to Wendy's) covering all work performed by such subcontractors. Such warranty shall be for a period of one (1) year unless a warranty for a longer period of time is required under the specifications of the contract. All warranties included in or as part of the restaurant and supplied to contractors shall be assigned to Wendy's. Those subcontractors required to supply warranties to Wendy's including, but may not be limited to electricians, plumbers, pavers, roofers, insulators and HVAC suppliers and materials.

6. Contractor agrees to use only those subcontractors and material suppliers approved by Wendy's and shown on plans unless a change is first approved by Wendy's. In the event of an emergency contractor may, in contractor's good faith discretion, substitute a subcontractor or material supplier and shall notify Wendy's, and the construction manager of such change in writing within three (3) days.

376 Printreading for Residential and Light Commercial Construction—Part 2

ARTICLE XXII—NOTICES

All notices to be delivered under this contract shall be in writing, signed by the parties serving same and delivered personally or by registered or certified U.S. mail postage prepaid, or by reputable private delivery service postage prepaid and providing a receipt to sender, each such notice shall be deemed delivered upon actual delivery or refusal or forty-eight (48) hours after mailing which ever is earlier to the pertinent address as set forth below.

Notices to Wendy's shall be addressed as follows:

Wendy's International, Inc.
PO Box 256
4288 W. Dublin-Granville Road
Dublin, OH 43017
Attn: Engineering Department

and to contractor _____

_____

Attention: _____

ARTICLE XXIII—SPECIAL CONDITIONS

The terms of this contract are subject to Wendy's obtaining all rights of possession as may be required to legally perform the work at the premises. In the event Wendy's is unable to timely obtain such possession, Wendy's shall promptly notify contractor of such inability and this contract shall be null and void and of no further force or effect.

ARTICLE XXIV—MISCELLANEOUS PROVISIONS

1. This contract is not assignable without the prior written consent of Wendy's, and contractor shall not factor or pledge this contract.
2. No right or remedy conferred upon or reserved to Wendy's in this contract is intended to be exclusive of any other right or remedy herein or by law provided, but each shall be cumulative and in addition to every other right or remedy given herein or hereafter existing at law or in equity.
3. In the event of any conflict between this contract and the drawings and specifications this contract shall govern.
4. In the event any provision of this contract is found to be invalid or unenforceable, the remainder of this contract shall continue in full force and effect.
5. This contract shall be construed in accordance with the laws of the state in which the premises is located.
6. Contractor hereby warrants and represents that contractor does not and will not, during the course of the work, discriminate against any employee or applicant for employment based on race, color, sex, national origin, religion, age, handicap or other unlawful basis.
7. Time is of the essence of this contract
8. This contract is binding upon the parties, their heirs, successors and approved assignees.

ARTICLE XXV—LIQUIDATED DAMAGES

In addition to the damages Wendy's may recover from contractor for contractor's unexcused delay in substantially completing the work on or before the time for substantial completion as provided in article 4 above (or as extended in writing by Wendy's), Wendy's shall be entitled to recover liquidated damages from contractor in the amount of $250.00 for each calendar day that substantial completion is delayed. The parties agree that it would be difficult to assess the actual amount of additional damages for such delay, but that the stated amount is a reasonable estimate of same.

ARTICLE XXVI—WENDY'S RIGHT TO AUDIT

Wendy's shall have the right to inspect, with contractor's assistance and cooperation, contractor's books and financial records pertaining directly or indirectly to Wendy's, the work or contractor's financial condition, contractor shall retain such records for a period of three (3) years after final payment under this contract.

In witness whereof, Wendy's and contractor through their duly authorized signatories have executed this contract as set forth below.

Contractor: _____   Wendy's International, Inc.

By: _____   By: _____

Title: _____   Title: _____

Date: _____   Date: _____

Law Dept. _____

Contractor's affidavit

Pursuant to the terms of the stipulated sum construction agreement dated this _____ day of _____ 200_ between Wendy's International, Inc. (Wendy's) of 4288 W. Dublin-Granville Road, Dublin, OH 43017 and _____ (contractor) for the construction or modification of a Wendy's Old Fashioned Hamburger facility located at_____, the undersigned hereby agrees to abide by the following restrictions and requirements.

A.   All line item quantities, unit costs and total costs are exactly as listed on the final bid breakdown form and contain no hidden costs, incentives, or rebates to Wendy's, its employees, or its suppliers.
B.   All invoices will reflect the actual cost of work in place by subcontractors and overhead, profit and extras are exactly as listed on the payment request for in place.
C.   No incentives, inducements, trips, kickback or monetary payments of any kind have been or will be made to Wendy's or its representatives or employees for the contract awarded. Any services performed separately for a Wendy's employee or representative must be disclosed to the engineering department in writing at the time of contract signing.
D.   The undersigned and his subcontractors have not provided any cash, merchandise, awards, trips or consideration of any kind to any representative or employee of Wendy's as an incentive or as a requirement for the awarding of any contract or purchase related to the above contract.

Contractor _____

By: _____

Title: _____

State of: _____

County of: _____

Ss: _____

Sworn to and subscribed before me this _____ day of _____, 200_

_____

AMERICANS WITH DISABILITIES ACT (ADA) NEW CONSTRUCTION CHECKLIST

It is the responsibility of the general contractor to assure that each of the following items is answered positively and in compliance with ADA regulations and Wendy's plans and specifications. Any "no" answer signals a violation and must be corrected at the contractor's expense prior to their receipt of final contract payment.

SITE PLAN COMPLIANCE

Disabled parking spaces

1. Are the required number of disabled parking spaces provided as per the below chart? _____

Total spaces	Accessible
1 to 25	1 space
26 to 50	2 spaces
51 to 75	3 spaces
76 to 100	4 spaces
101 to 150	5 spaces
151 to 200	6 spaces

2. Are disabled parking spaces a minimum of 96" wide? _____
3. Is there a minimum 96" wide access aisle centered between two of the disabled parking spaces? _____
4. Is there a minimum 60" wide access aisle on the passenger side of any additional disabled parking spaces? _____
5. Are the disabled parking spaces closest to the accessible entrance or in the most level area of the parking lot? _____
6. Is each disabled parking space marked with the international symbol of accessibility? _____
   Are signs mounted at exactly 60" to the centerline of the sign? _____
7. Are there signs reading "Van Accessible" at the disabled parking spaces with a 96" wide access aisle? _____

Ramps

1. Is the width of the traveling surface of the ramp 36" minimum? _____

   A. Is the traveling surface level with the parking lot? _____
   B. If not, is the slope of the flared sides a maximum 1:12? _____
      (Slope is given as a ratio of height to length. 1:12 means that for every inch of curb height the flared side must provide 12 inches.
      Ex.: A 6" curb must have 72" flared sides) _____

2. Is the slope of the flared sides a maximum 1:12? _____
3. Is the curb cut ramp located at the top of the access aisle of the disabled parking spaces? _____
4. If the disabled parking spaces are located across a vehicular way, is there a 36" minimum striped crosswalk leading from the access aisle to the curb cut ramp? _____

Path of Travel

1. Is the accessible path of travel at least 36" wide? _____
2. Can all objects protruding into a path be detected by a person with a visual disability using a cane? _____

   (In order to be detected using a cane, an object must be within 27" of the ground. Objects hanging or mounted overhead must be higher than 80" to provide clear head room. It is necessary to remove objects that protrude less than 4" from the wall.)
3. Does the path of travel maintain a cross slope of less than 2%? _____
4. Are all areas of sudden elevation along the accessible path less than 1/4"? _____

Accessible Entrance

1. Are at least 50% of all public entrances accessible? _____
   (Not including delivery entrances or employee entrances)
2. Do all inaccessible entrances have signs indicating the location of the nearest accessible entrance?
   _____
3. Is the threshold level (less than 1/4") or beveled, up to 1/2" high? _____
4. Is there a clear and level landing area of 5' × 5' at each accessible entrance? _____

Registered Surveyor/Engineer _____ Date _____ Stamp

General Contractor _____ Date _____ Notary

BUILDING COMPLIANCE CHECKLIST

Access to Goods and Services

1. Is the height of the cash register counter 36" or lower? _____
2. Is the distance from the cash register counter to the first rail of the serpentine at least 42"?
   _____
3. Are all public spaces on an accessible path of travel at least 36" wide? _____
4. In the restrooms, is there a 5' circle or a T-shaped space for a person using a wheelchair to reverse
   direction? _____
5. Are all thresholds and transition strips level (less than 1/4")? _____
6. Are all aisles and pathways to goods and services (including aisles between tables and chairs) at
   least 36" wide? _____
7. Is carpeting low-pile, tightly woven, and securely attached along edges? _____
8. In routes through public areas, are all obstacles cane-detectable (located within 27" of the floor or
   higher than 80", or protruding less than 4" from the wall)? _____
9. Are there accessible tables or booths available in all dining areas (smoking, non-smoking, solarium,
   etc.) which equal 5% of all tops provided? _____
   (Accessible tables shall have a minimum clear space without obstruction of 30" wide and extending
   19" under the table. There must be 27" of knee height clearance beneath the table as measured
   from the floor AND a height of 28" to 34" to the top of the table as measured from the floor.)
   Generally, quad booths meet these requirements.
10. If there are stairs provided to a raised or sunken dining area, do treads have a non-slip surface (if
    applicable)? _____
11. Do stairs have continuous rails on both sides, with 12" extensions beyond the top and bottom stairs
    which are returned to the wall or floor (if applicable)? _____
12. Is there a maximum 36" high service counter adjacent to the cash register counter which is the
    same appearance of the cash register counter with no disabled symbol? _____
13. Is the condiment stand a maximum of 34" high with a 24" maximum reach to the centerline of the
    furthest product? _____

Restrooms

1. Is the corridor at least 48" wide as measured from baseboard to baseboard? _____
2. Do both restroom entrance doors provide 32" clear width? _____
3. Is there at least 18" of strike side clearance on the pull side of the door? _____
4. Do all fixtures have 30" × 48" clear floor space allowing for a forward or parallel approach? _____
5. Do signs utilize raised letters, Braille, and symbol of accessibility? _____ Are they
   mounted on the strike side of door at 60" exactly as measured to the centerline of the sign?
   _____
6. Is the clear width of the accessible stall door at least 32"? _____
7. Is the accessible stall door outward swinging and self-closing with a 3 second minimum sweep time?
   _____

8. Is accessible stall door hardware sliding or if twisting, with a large twist lever? _____
9. Is the accessible stall 5' wide × 5' deep? _____
10. Is the side grab bar mounted on the nearest side wall in a horizontal position at 33"–36" above the floor? _____

    A. Is the side grab bar at least 42" long, mounted at a maximum of 12" from the rear wall, and extending 54" minimum from the rear wall? _____
    B. Is the rear grab bar mounted in a horizontal position at 33"–36" above the floor? _____
    C. Is the rear grab bar a minimum of 36" long and mounted at a maximum of 6" from the nearest side wall? _____
    D. Does the rear grab bar allow space for finger gripping below the bottom of the bar and the toilet tank? _____

11. Is the distance from the nearest side wall to the centerline of the toilet 18"? _____
12. Is the toilet paper dispenser mounted at a 44" maximum height or a 19" minimum and 36" from rear wall to leading edge? _____

    A. Is 6" clearance provided to the grab bar if mounted above the grab bar? _____

13. Are the rest room accessories (paper towel and soap dispensers) mounted at 48" maximum to highest operable part? _____

    A. Is the mirror mounted at 40" to bottom of reflecting surface? _____

14. Is the height of the intended accessible lavatory 34" maximum? _____

    A. Is 29" of knee clearance provided (as measured from the floor to the bottom of the sink)? _____
    B. Are the pipes wrapped? _____

15. Is the urinal 17" maximum to the rim? _____

    A. Is the height to the flush valve 44" maximum? _____
    B. Is the distance from the back wall to the front most of the urinal rim 14"? _____
    C. Is the clear width of the stall 30" minimum? _____

16. Is the height to the top of the water closet seat between 17"–19"? _____
17. Is the trash can open topped? _____
18. Is the hand dryer recessed (not to protrude more than 4" from wall surface)? _____

General Contractor _____ Date _____ Notary

DIVISION 2—SITE CONSTRUCTION

EXCAVATION, BACKFILLING, GRADING

1. Remove all vegetation, refuse or existing structures in confines of building construction and paving areas prior to commencement of work.
2. Excavate as required to provide sufficient working room for the laying of foundation walls, excavation for all footings to be down to undisturbed earth with a minimum depth as shown on drawings unless

3. In the event that rock is encountered in the foundation excavation, and if this rock must be removed by dynamite or compressor, the owner will reimburse the contractor for the predetermined cost of these operations.
4. Backfilling of walls in interior areas where concrete slab will bear on grade shall be grits or bank run gravel, well compacted, brought to a subgrade of 8" below finish floor line.
5. Backfilling of exterior foundation walls shall be clean gravel well-compacted, brought to a subgrade of 8" below finish sidewalk paving.
6. Backfilling over utilities running under paved areas shall be of grits.
7. Remainder of site shall be graded to assure drainage of surface water from building.
8. Remove and legally dispose of excess soils from the site.
9. Grades not otherwise indicated on the plans shall be uniform levels or slopes between points where elevations are given, abrupt changes in slopes shall be well rounded. The contractor is responsible for positive site drainage, sloped away from building.
10. Soils test shall be performed by the contractor to ensure soil meet 3,000 psf design strength. Contractor shall notify Wendy's immediately if excavation on any part of the site reveals fill or ground water.
11. Site fill should be non-organic soils compacted in 6" lifts to a minimum 98% standard proctor density.

ASPHALT PAVING

All paving shall be installed in areas as indicated on site plan. Pavement design shall meet soil conditions, Wendy's construction engineer requirements, and details on site plan.

Soil Class

Poor	CBR = 3.5	Type: Plastic when wet such as clay, fine silt, or sandy loam
Medium	CBR = 7.0	Type: Hard silty—sands or sand gravels containing clay or fine silt
Good	CBR = 12	Type: Clean sand and sand gravel free of clay, silt, or loam

Minimum Pavement

Poor Soil	Medium soil	Good Soil
6" coarse asphalt	4" coarse asphalt	3" coarse asphalt
Base binder (1 1/2" aggregate)	Base (1 1/2" aggregate)	Base (1 1/2" aggregate)
Plus 1 1/2" aggregate	Plus 1 1/2" aggregate	Plus 1 1/2" asphalt topping
(maximum 1/2" aggregate)	(maximum 1/2" aggregate)	(maximum 1/2" aggregate)

CONCRETE PAVING

Specifications for any concrete paving required for this site is to be verified by Wendy's construction engineer.

STRIPING AND PARKING BLOCKS

Striping to be "Tuf-trac", OSHA safety yellow, by Sonneborn (available through Sherwin Williams).

Parking lot marking requirements will vary depending upon local city codes. Yellow is the most common color for lot striping and especially important for northern climates where snow is prevalent, since it will provide contrast from snow and salt-laden surfaces. If codes allow, white paint is permitted for parking space striping only. All hazards should be identified in "safety" yellow paint. The following areas should be properly identified:

Vehicle parking area identified with the appropriate marking as required by local municipal codes. Color—yellow or white.

Direction traffic flow arrows painted on the lot should identify the route of travel into and out of the parking lot from all public or private access roads. Color—yellow.

Outline the outside of the pick-up window traffic lane with a four-inch solid stripe. Color—yellow.

All curbs that extend from the parking lot entrance to any public or private roadway should be painted. Color—yellow.

Speed bumps should be identified with striping. It is not necessary to paint the entire area. Color—yellow.

Parking stops or blocks located next to the building or in the middle of the parking lot should be yellow recycled plastic. (See parking block note below) Color—yellow.

Sidewalk curbing directly in the travel path of the building entrances or exits should be identified with a two-inch stripe on the top edge of the curve for a length of three feet. Color—yellow.

If site conditions warrant, any steps should be identified with a two-inch line painted on the top and front edge of each step. Color—yellow.

If the site conditions warrant, crosswalks across the drive-through lane for entrances/exits that are perpendicular to the drive-through traffic pattern should be identified with diagonal stripes. Color—white or yellow to match striping.

All posts, poles, and their supports or guide wires that may be exposed to vehicle traffic should be painted at least sixty inches in height from the base. Color—yellow.

Stencil "Pick-Up Window" lane behind directional arrow. Color—white or yellow to match striping.

Any curb that represents a possible hazard to vehicles should be identified by painting a two-inch line on the top and side of the curb. Color—yellow.

Handicap ramps and handicap parking should be identified with ADA striping and stenciling per local codes. Note: painting the entire ramp or parking space as well as paint blocking background on stencils is not recommended unless specified by code.

Handicap sidewalk ramps should have the outside curbing that is changing in elevation identified with a two-inch line painted on the top and side edge of curb for the first three feet of incline starting from the lower surface level. Color—yellow.

Parking Blocks

100% recycled plastic parking blocks, yellow in color. Parking blocks shall be minimum of 6'-0" in length and a maximum of 5" in height specify for use on concrete or asphalt for correct hardware. Blocks shall be placed as shown on Geometric Plan.

CURBS

Concrete curbs shall be full 6" x 18" formed curbs with expansion joints or saw cuts not more than 20'-0" apart. All freestanding or integral curbs shall be reinforced with at least one #4 reinforcing bar continuous.

LANDSCAPING

Landscape bidder shall submit a written proposal and landscape plan to the owner for approval. Proposal shall indicate size and number of plants and exact area to be sodded. Proposal to show unit prices for each tree and shrub. Provide all labor, materials and equipment necessary to complete the seeding, sodding, and landscape planting, earthwork, and edging as shown on proposal.

General contractor shall be responsible for installing topsoil to grade and for all rough grading. No payments in excess of contract shall be made unless approved by owner in writing. Total proposal shall include all work including taxes where applicable.

PLANT GUARANTEE AND REPLACEMENT

All plants and sod areas shall be guaranteed for one year from date of installation. Any plants not in satisfactory vigor shall be replaced at no additional expense to owner.

UTILITIES

1. The general contractor shall furnish all materials, labor, tools, transportation, incidentals, and appurtenances to complete in every detail and leave in working order all utilities called for herein and/or shown on the construction documents. This includes but is not limited to: storm sewer, sanitary sewer, water service, gas service, electric service, roof drainage, etc.
2. All utilities including electric service to signs will be considered site work and brought to within five feet of the building perimeter.
3. Required grease trap regardless of location shall be considered as part of the building cost and so reflected in all bidding.
4. The general contractor shall verify all taps and furnish any city drawings required prior to construction.

DIVISION 3—CONCRETE

Furnish all labor, materials, and equipment necessary to complete all concrete work including excavation, trenching, formwork, reinforcing, cement finish, and precast concrete.

FOOTINGS

1. Refer to drawings for sizes, depths, and reinforcement. Earth trench will be permitted for footings if conditions are favorable. Sides of trenches shall be clean, even, vertical and true, and bottoms shall be level, clean and without fill.
2. Reinforcing shall be unpainted and uncoated, free from rust or scale, and shall be cleaned and straightened before being shaped and placed in position. Accurately position reinforcement and secure against displacement. Where there is delay in pouring, reinspect reinforcement and clean off any dried cement, mortar, or rust.
3. All reinforcement shall be of size and spacing as called for on the drawings or as per local codes.

SLABS AND FOOTINGS

1. 3000 psi concrete slabs to be reinforced with 6 x 6—W1.4 x W1.4 welded wire fabric installed in a manner that places it in center of the slab. (lap edges 6"). Alternate: 9/32 fibermesh (9/32 or equal), a 100% homopolymer virgin polypropylene fibrillated fibers containing no reprocessed olefin materials and are specifically engineered and manufactured to an optimum graduation for use as fibrous reinforcement for concrete.
2. Provide continuous 6 mil 'Visqueen' vapor barrier on level 4" gravel base under all building slabs. Lap edges 6" and seal (turn up at walls).
3. All concrete floors shall be poured level, except where floor drains occur, in which case they shall have a 36" to 48" radius sloped to drain. Total slope is not to exceed 3/4" below floor level.
4. This contractor shall build into concrete work the following materials which are furnished by other trades, and shall bed and secure same as required.

   A. All plumbing and syrup lines, electric conduit, concrete inserts, hangers, anchors, floor clips, sleeves for all piping, etc. and when required for all other trades, anchor bolts, plates, etc., for all equipment.

SIDEWALKS AND RAMPS

4000 psi air-entrained concrete, 4" thick, broom finish score with 3/4" deep contraction joints into approximately 4'-0" squares as shown on detail on Foundation Plan (Sheet 3).

SIDEWALK PAVERS

Monroe Concrete Paver by New World Pavers to be 6 cm (2 3/8") or 8 cm (3 1/8") thick, red and charcoal colors "antique blend" available through Oberfields (see approved supplier list).

A 4" concrete slab over stone base is recommended. A 1/2" inch bedding course of sand shall be spread over the slab (see detail, sheet 2). A standard 6" concrete curb should be installed at the drive and steel edge restraints used for transitions with landscape beds and concrete walks. The paved walk shall slope away from the building at approximately 1/4" inch per foot.

PAVING

Specifications for any concrete paving required for this site is to be verified by Wendy's construction engineer.

CONCRETE PADS

Black concrete pads at pick-up window and order station (refer to site plan). Cement or mortar shall be integrally colored with "Wendy's Black Chemtint", a dry preparation of commercially pure, metallic pigments of high tinctorial strength, cure and seal with "Safe-Cure and EPX", all in strict accordance with the directions of the manufacturer Chemasters, Madison, Ohio 44057. A trial slab shall be made, using the same materials that are to be used on the job to assure owner acceptance.

DIVISION 4—MASONRY

Provide all labor, materials, and equipment necessary to complete all masonry work including structural steel, wall ties, masonry reinforcing, etc.

GENERAL

1. All work to be laid true to dimensions, plumb, square, and in bond or properly anchored. All courses shall be level with joints of uniform width, no joints shall exceed specified size, and if necessary, clipped courses shall be provided to level off.
2. Perform all masonry work in accordance with best trade practices. Brace "green" walls and protect mortar from "washing-out" at end of day's work using planks, weighted canvas, or similar means to cover wall. Cooperate with other trades in jointly executed work and built-in items. Patch openings as required for passage of mechanical and electrical trades. "Uncored" units must be used at all exposed and or semi-exposed conditions of brick rowlock caps, sills, etc. Size and location shown on construction documents.
3. All lintels shall be of size and shape as shown or noted on the drawings and shall be structurally sound for the spans and loads involved.
4. Build into masonry all materials furnished by other trades, such as angles, anchor bolts, flashing, steel lintels and framing, vents, sleeves, door frames, miscellaneous steel work with anchors, etc.
5. All brick to be laid in a running bond with all field brick to meet ASTM C-216, type FBS, grade SW. Accent brick to meet either ASTM C-216 or ASTM C-652, type HBS, grades SW.
6. All brick to be laid with full mortar in the bed and head joints.
7. Concave tooled joint using a tool of larger than 1/2" diameter.
8. Wall ties shall be corrugated masonry strapping. Ties should be hot-dipped galvanized in accordance with ASTM A-153, class B-2.
9. Weep holes should be at least every 24".
10. Flashing to be plastic-coated aluminum by Dur-o-Wall or thin coated copper by York flashing. The flashing should penetrate the brickwork and be trimmed at the completion of the masonry work.
11. Clean and point all brick and concrete block work at end of each working day. At the completion of work as an entirety, wet walls thoroughly and clean all exposed brick work with cleaner and stiff bristle brushes. No metal scrapers or metal brushes shall be used on any type of masonry. Cleaning agent should be as recommended by brick manufacturer.

MORTAR FOR FACE BRICK

Mortar shall be one part cement (Portland cement, ASTM C-1 50, type 1 or 3), one part lime (hydrated lime ASTM C-207, type N), and five parts sand (ASTM C-144 and potable water). Do not use admixtures. In cold weather, heat the sand and water. If temperature drops to 30 degrees Fahrenheit, stop masonry work.

Mortar for split-faced block to be tinted to match block.

BRICK AND BLOCK

Face brick (standard building finish)
4" brick veneer by Bowerston Shale Co, Bowerston, Ohio:
Standard: Rosemist   Modular 3 5/8" x 2 1/4" x 7 5/8"

Split-faced block (standard building finish)
Split-faced block by Oberfields Concrete, Delaware, Ohio:
Standard: Color: Buff   Modular 4" x 8" x 16" single score solid
Alternate: Color: Buff   Modular 4" x 8" x 16" solid (w/o single score)

DIVISION 5—METALS

Provide all labor, material, and equipment necessary to complete the miscellaneous structural and decorative metal work indicated on the drawings. All materials to meet ASTM A-36.

Provide all structural steel members as indicated on the drawings. All work shall be in accordance with the standard of the industry and all local governing codes. Fabrication shall be furnished to those trades prior to the execution of their work by this subcontractor for proper incorporation into their work.

1. Shop drawings: submit four (4) sets of shop drawings to the architect for approval and checking as required.
2. Provide proper anchor bolts as indicated.
3. All structural metal items to receive one coat of rust-inhibitive shop primer.

WROUGHT IRON RAILING (outside—required)

Provide wrought iron railings as indicated on the drawings, railings shall be complete with newel posts, corners, flanged hose shoe, and fittings. Rail design shall be 1/2" square tubing at 6" OC. Top rail and newel post to be 1" square tubing (finished rail to be powder-coated safety red).

WROUGHT IRON SERPENTINE RAIL (interior)

Provide prefabricated sections of powder-coated wrought iron railing, railings shall be complete with 1" square upright posts with flanged hose shoe and fittings. Rail design shall be 1/2" square tubing with top 1/2" x 1" channel predrilled to receive 2 x 4 shaped oak cap (stain S-1) standard rail finish. (Refer to sheet 6B and finish schedules for details.)

DIVISION 6—WOOD AND PLASTICS

ROUGH CARPENTRY

Furnish all labor, tools, equipment, and materials to complete all work under this heading as indicated on the drawings and described in the specifications.

Provide and maintain temporary enclosures, and barricades as required by governing local ordinances. Provide temporary door and window enclosures as required. All interior framing to be either 3 5/8" metal studs and 5 1/2" metal studs, or 2 x 4 studs 16" OC and 2 x 6 studs 16" OC double at openings and triple at corners as shown on plan. Headers to be 36" with two (2) 2 x 6s set on edge. All other openings to be detailed on drawings.

STRUCTURAL LUMBER

1. All structural lumber shall be grade stamped per standard grading rules. Unless otherwise noted, all structural lumber shall be southern yellow pine No. 2 KD 15%. Interior non-bearing stud walls shall be stud grade.
2. Plywood shall be DFPA grade stamped, type CDX 5 ply with exterior glue unless otherwise noted on plans.
3. Roof framing and sheathing shall be inspected prior to placing on roof.
4. Predrill all holes for 20d and larger nails and lag bolts.
5. Double top plates on all exterior and bearing partitions (not otherwise detailed). Plates shall lap 4'-0" minimum at splices and have 6—16d nails minimum through each side of splice.
6. Bolt holes for wood connections shall be 1/32" larger in diameter than normal bolt size.
7. Lag bolts shall have lead holes bored before driving. Hole diameters to be as follows:

    A.   Shank portion—same diameter and lengths as shank
    B.   Thread portion—0.6 to 0.75 diameter of thread and same length.

8. All bolt head and nuts bearing on wood shall have steel washers.

NAILING SCHEDULE

All nailing shall be common wire nails conforming to the latest edition of OBBC or UBC. Where automatic nailing is used, nails shall not penetrate plywood sheathing. Connections listed are minimum permissible. Details govern over schedule.

1. Joist to sill or girder, toenail 3—8d
2. Bridging to joist or rafter, toenail each end 2—8d
3. Sub flooring sheathing at all bearing

    A.   1 x 6 or less, face nail 2—8d
    B.   1 x 8 or wider, face nail 3—8d
    C.   2 x - bind and face nail 2—16d

4. Sole plate to joist or blocking, face nail 16d @ 16" OC
5. Top plate to stud, end nail 2—16d
6. Stud to sole plate, face nail 4—8d
7. Double studs, face nail 16d @ 24" OC
8. Double top plates, face nail 16d @ 16" OC
9. Top plates, laps and intersections face nail 2—16d
10. Continuous header, two pieces (along each edge) 16d @ 16" OC
11. Ceiling joists or rafters to all bearings, toe nail 3—8d
12. Continuous header to stud, toe nail 4—8d
13. Ceiling joist, laps over partitions, face nail 3—16d
14. Ceiling joist to parallel rafter, face nail 3—16d
15. 1" brace to each stud and plate, face nail 2—8d
16. Built-up corner studs 16d @ 16" OC
17. Joist or rafter to sides of studs

    A.   Up to and including 8" depth 3—16d
    B.   For each additional 4" depth or less 1—16d

18. Ceiling strips

    A.   1" x 4" to underside of joists each bearing—one slant and one straight 2—8d
    B.   2" x 3" to underside of joist each bearing—one slant and one straight 2—16d
    C.   Use strong hold annular grooved at gypsum board ceilings.

ROOF JOISTS

1. Joists to be used are supplied by Trus Joist Macmillan.
2. Series used are TJI in lengths and depths as indicated on drawings.
3. Shop drawings, nailing schedules, and connection details will be provided to contractor along with shipment of every order.

FINISH CARPENTRY

Furnish all labor and materials to complete all work under this section as indicated on drawings and described in these specifications. All hardware dimensions are to be net size and not nominal size. Material for interior finish shall be as follows:

    A.   Dining room trim—all stained trim select red oak square stock with eased edges.
    B.   Countertops to be furnished and installed by kitchen equipment supplier.

WALK-IN FREEZER/COOLER/DRY STORAGE

Placement of prefabricated, walk-in freezer/cooler/dry storage shall be part of this contract. Unit will be supplied by owners and will be shipped direct to store location with all uncrating and erection coordinated by general contractor and walk-in manufacturer. Unit will be shipped complete with hardware and instructions. Flooring in freezer is prefabricated. Flooring in cooler and dry storage is ceramic tile by general contractor. Installation of refrigeration to be coordinated by general contractor and walk-in manufacturer and electrical hook-up by electrical contractor. See Equipment Plan of the construction documents.

DIVISION 7—THERMAL AND MOISTURE PROTECTION

All components of the manufacturer's roofing system shall be products of that manufacturer. Substitutes of their related materials must have prior acceptance by the manufacturer.

Any deviation from manufacturer's specifications and installation instructions shall void any warranty issuance unless the deviation is approved by a duly authorized representative of the manufacturer in writing.

Shop drawings are required for ordering, manufacturing, and final inspection of the roofing system. All shop drawings shall include roof outline, size, all roof penetrations, insulation type and thickness, piece layout, and parapet location. Orders and shop drawings shall be approved by roofing manufacturer and assigned a manufacturer number.

DELIVERY

All roofing and related materials shall be delivered to job site in original packaging and all shipping labels intact. If any shortages or damages are discovered upon delivery, do not accept them until the freight agent makes a damaged or short notation on your freight bill. In case of concealed loss or damage, it is necessary to notify your freight agent at once.

HANDLING

There shall be adequate personnel and equipment to lift roofing material for placement on the roof to prevent damage to material. The material shall be deposited on the roof near the ends of joists or other roof load-bearing members of the building frame and conveniently located for final placement.

STORAGE

All roofing material shall be stored in original packaging to protect membrane from getting wet or being damaged and soiled. Adhesives and sealants shall be properly stored and protected as recommended by their manufacturers.

OVERNIGHT COVER

A temporary water seal shall be performed each night to avoid water penetrating underneath the installed membrane and causing damage to the building and the insulation being used.

    A.   Installation: with the membrane extended over exposed insulation (if used), set into a water-resistant, non-bituminous sealant, generously applied over a dust, grease, and moisture-free substrate. Fasten 12" on center using termination bar.

ROOFING AND SHEET METAL

Furnish and completely install the roofing system per Wendy's approved supplier specifications and diagrams as outlined and furnished by the supplier. The roofing system shall be installed exclusively by a Wendy's approved manufacturer installer. Final inspection prior to warranty issuance shall be performed by an authorized quality control field inspector as per current specifications, installation and inspection policies.

SURFACE PREPARATION

The roof shall have an adequately prepared surface to receive the insulation, roofing, and flashing. Prior to onset of work the applicator shall inspect the entire area to be roofed, and any defects and improper conditions affecting the roof installation shall be corrected before application of the insulation.

WOOD DECKS

Roof shall be clean, smooth, and suitable for acceptance of the roofing system. Remove and replace all deteriorated wood nailers, roof curbs, and soured or badly deteriorated roof insulation. Any joint or cracks greater than 1/4" shall be repaired.

MEMBRANE

The membrane material shall be in accordance with approved manufacturer specifications.

RELATED MATERIALS

1. Drip edges, gravel stops, copings, and counterflashings to be compatible and installed according to roof manufacturer's specification. If products used are sheet metal, it must be a 26 ga (min) galvanized. All metal counterflashing, coping, drip edges, and gravel stops shall have a 3" overlap for expansion and contracting.
2. Roof scupper linings: cut roof scupper lining to fit roof scuppers, allowing adequate material for field welding to roof cover and base flashing. Apply approved adhesive to scupper, install lining in scupper, and make field welds to roof cover and base flashing. Apply approved sealant to all exterior edges of lining on exterior of wall, under and on top of the termination bar surrounding the edges.
3. Wood members: All lumber shall be #2 southern yellow pine, Douglas fir or other approved species, and it shall be free from warping, excessive knots and grade marked. It shall be "Wolmanized" (CCA) pressure-treated and shall bear the trade mark "Wolmanized" or an approved equal treatment.

BUILDING INSULATION

Furnish all labor, materials, and equipment necessary to complete all work as indicated on the construction documents and described in the specifications.

A.	Vapor barrier under slabs on grade 6 mil "Visqueen" furnished and installed by concrete contractor. See Division 3.
B.	Exterior wall insulation—6" thick fiberglass batts (without backing) in the 2 x 6 stud walls of all cavity walls. Vapor barrier shall be Griffolyn F-65 by Reef Industries, Inc. or equal. The material shall have a 3-ply, high-density polyethylene and nylon yarn laminate. Material shall have a reinforced non-woven grid with a PPT tear strength of at least 15.0 lbs. Vapor barrier shall be applied in the widest practical widths. Side and end joints shall be lapped at least 6". Laps shall be sealed using fab tape. Any punctures or tears are to be repaired using Griffoln's Griff tape, fab tape or equal. Vapor barrier must provide a complete seal to prevent moisture transfer. Note: for southern coastal areas, the vapor barrier should be used on the exterior of the wall. Where there is uncertainty, follow local practice.
C.	Rigid roof insulation—furnished and installed by the roofing contractor. Insulation to be two layers; each layer, 2.4" C-5 Ultragard premier. Rigid roof insulation board R-20 insulation board by International Permalite, Inc. is an acceptable equal.
D.	Perimeter insulation—1" thick Styrofoam or equal on exterior foundation wall as shown on construction documents.

INSULATION ATTACHMENT (MECHANICAL)

The roof insulation boards shall be installed with factory-approved fasteners and stress distribution plates. Length will vary to meet the job conditions. A minimum of 5/8" of the fastener must protrude throughout the plywood deck.

FLASHING

All flashing on parapet walls shall be fastened 12" on center along bottom on main deck with a minimum 6" lap weldable to deck membrane, covering approved fasteners. All parapet walls shall be covered minimum of 12" high.

Roofing contractor to provide and install bronze cap flashing for parapet walls and column tops (painted as shown on exterior elevations).

FLASH AND COUNTER

Flash all items that pass through the roof. Provide "pitch pockets" as required to form a complete job.

Provide all necessary mounting clips, closures, fastenings, etc., required to complete the counter-flashing, gravel stops, caps, and copings, indicated on the drawings.

PERIMETER LAPS

Any time a roof edge does not have a parapet wall or roof tie-in, (i.e. drip edge, water/gravel stop, termination bar on edge, gutter, etc.) then the roof section must have a lap 27" in from the edge and reversed. This helps reduce wind up-lift around perimeters, and reversing the lap allows contractor applicator to place roof section away from the edge.

CAULKING

All surfaces to receive caulking are to be dry and thoroughly cleaned of all loose particles of dirt and dust, oil, grease, or other foreign matter.

Caulk at exterior door frames, window frames, and elsewhere to ensure a weatherproof job using gun application.

CAULKING MATERIALS

Polysulfide polymer base compound shall conform to American standard specification A-116, 1960 class A or B, and equal to that manufactured by Sonneborn or Pecora (exterior joints).

Butyl sealant shall be butyl rubber base compound equal to that manufactured by Sonneborn or Pecora (all other caulking).

PROJECT/SITE CLEAN-UP

Upon completion, the roofing contractor shall remove all rubbish, waste materials, etc., from the roof, leaving the roof in a clean condition and further removing all such roofing debris from the work site. A rigorous inspection for watertight field seams shall be made after completion of job.

INSPECTIONS

Upon completion of each roofing job, contractor shall fill out inspection card and return to manufacturer. Each room shall be inspected by an authorized quality control field inspector to make sure application meets manufacturer's specifications, before issuance of warranty. Contractor shall accompany inspector on inspections and obtain signed warranty from customer and return to manufacturer, with no final payment being made until a Wendy's representative has warranty.

CONTRACTOR QUALIFICATION ASSURANCE

The roofing contractor shall be duly certified by roofing manufacturer for complete application and installation of this roofing system. To maintain roof warranty, future repairs and alterations shall be made by personnel duly certified by roofing manufacturer.

WARRANTY

The owner shall be furnished and will sign for acceptance of a standard roofing manufacturer's 15-year limited warranty.

SERIES II FASCIA PANEL SYSTEM

Exterior fascia panel system with standing seam ribs. Fascia panels are bright copper color with bronze color moldings accented in red, as manufactured by Vacuform Corporation or National Sign. Non-illuminated if following site lighting specifications. System shall be furnished by owner and installed by general contractor.

DIVISION 8—DOORS AND WINDOWS

ALUMINUM ENTRANCE DOORS AND STOREFRONT

Kawneer Company Specifications: Storefront system shall be Tri-Fab 450 (1 3/4 " x 4 1/2") for 1/4" glass and/or Tri-Fab 451 (2" x 4 1/2") for 1" glass framing system as manufactured by Kawneer. Doors shall be "190 Narrow Stile" door manufactured by Kawneer or equal. All entrance doors shall be installed with the following hardware: one pair offset pivots, "Norton 1605 BC" or "LCN 4040" surface closures with 8 1/2 pound operating force on closer with a delayed action feature, Wendy's personalized logo panels with offset tubular 1" diameter bronze pull handle (as required by local code), and "Dor-o-Matic 1990" concealed rod panics on exterior doors only, interior vestibule doors to have "Norton J8300" surface closers and offset tubular 1" diameter bronze pull handles (as required by local code) omit lock, cylinders and preparation for same, (**lock cylinder may be by Falcon or as specified by regional engineer) aluminum threshold, 1/2" in height with any beveled edges having a slope no greater than 1:2 ratio.

All material shall be Kawneer #26 light bronze, anodized. Hardware & sealant shall be a color to match.

All exterior glass shall be 1" solar bronze, all door lights and interior glass shall be 1/4", clear safety glass. All glazing must meet safety codes as required. Glass must have 5-yr warranty against seal failure.

Wendy's has approved shop drawings established by Kawneer National Account. These drawings comply with the products and hardware requirements stated herein and are to be used as a guide by the local supervising architect, general contractor, and authorized Kawneer glazing contractor to ensure compliance with this specification. Copies of the approved shop drawings and metal quotation may be obtained by contacting Kawneer Company.

Tubelite Specifications: Aluminum storefront system shall be series 4500 (1 3/4" x 4 1/2") for 1/4" glass and/or series 1400 2" x 4 1/2") for 1" glass framing system as manufactured by Tubelite division of Indal Inc. Doors shall be narrow stile as manufactured by Tubelite or equal. All entrance doors shall be installed with the following hardware: one pair offset pivots, "Norton 1605 BC" or "LCN 1460" (P1460) or "LCN 4040" surface closures with 8 1/2 pound operating force on closer with a delayed action feature, Wendy's personalized logo panels with offset tubular 1" diameter bronze pull handle (as required by local code), and, Dor-o-Matic 1990" concealed rod panics on exterior doors only, interior vestibule doors to have Dorma series 651 closers and offset tubular 1" diameter bronze pull handles (as required by local code) omit lock, cylinders and preparation for same, (**lock cylinders may be by Falcon or as specified by regional engineer) aluminum threshold, 1/2" in height with any beveled edges having a slope no greater than 1:2 ratio.

All material shall be Tubelite 4k champagne, anodized. Hardware and sealant shall be a color to match.

All exterior glass shall be 1" solar bronze. All door lights and interior glass shall be 1/4" clear safety. All glazing must meet safety codes as required. Glass must have 5-yr warranty against seal failure.

Wendy's has approved shop drawings established by Tubelite national account. These drawings comply with the products and hardware requirement stated herein and are to be used as a guide by the local supervising architect, general contractor and authorized Tubelite glazing contractor to insure compliance with the specification. Copies of the approved shop drawings and metal quotation may be obtained by contacting Tubelite.

United States Aluminum Specifications: Aluminum storefront system shall be series 4500 (1 3/4" x 4 1/2") for 1/4" glass and/or series 1400 2" x 4 1/2") for 1" glass framing system as manufactured by United States Aluminum. Doors shall be "250 narrow stile" as manufactured by United States Aluminum Corp. or equal. All entrance doors shall be installed with the following hardware: one pair offset pivots, "Dorma series 651" or LCN 4040" surface closures with 8 1/2 pound operating force on closer with a delayed action feature, Wendy's personalized logo panels with offset tubular 1" diameter bronze pull handle (as required by local code), and "Dor-o-Matic" 1990" concealed rod panics on exterior doors only, interior vestibule doors to have Dorma series 650 closers and offset tubular diameter bronze pull handles (as required by local code) omit lock, cylinders and preparation for same, (**lock cylinders may be by Falcon or as specified by regional engineer) aluminum threshold, 1/2" in height with any beveled edges having a slope no greater than 1:2 ratio.

All materials shall be United States Aluminum Corporation #11 champagne medium, anodized. Hardware and sealant shall be a color to match.

All exterior glass shall be 1" solar bronze. All door lights and interior glass shall be 1/4" clear safety glass, all glazing must meet safety codes as required. Glass must have 5-yr warranty against seal failure.

Wendy's has approved shop drawings established by United States Aluminum National Account. These drawings comply with the products and hardware requirements stated herein and are to be used as a guide by the local supervising architect, general contractor, and authorized United States Aluminum Corporation glazing contractor to insure compliance with this specification. Copies of the approved shop drawings and metal quotation may be obtained by contacting United States Aluminum Corporation.

Vista Wall Architectural Products Specifications: Storefront system shall be series FG-2000 (1 3/4" x 4 1/2")for 1/4" glass and/or series 451 (2" x 4 1/2") for 1" glass framing system as manufactured by Vistawall. Doors shall be "250 narrow stile" as manufactured by Vista Wall or equal, all entrance doors shall be installed with the following hardware: one pair offset pivots, "Norton 1600 Series" closures w/ 8 1/2 lb. operating force on closer w/ a delayed action feature, Wendy's personalized logo panels with offset, tubular diameter bronze pull handles (as required by local code) and "Dor-o-Matic 1990" concealed rod panics on exterior doors only. Interior vestibule doors to have Dorma series 650 closers and offset tubular 1" diameter bronze pull handles (as required by local code) — omit lock, cylinders and preparation for same. (**lock cylinders may be by Falcon or as specified by regional engineer) aluminum threshold, 1/2" in height w/ beveled edges having a slope no greater than 1:2 ratio.

All materials shall be Vistawall #699 champagne, anodized. Hardware & sealant shall be a color to match.

All exterior glass shall be 1" solar bronze. All door lights and interior glass shall be 1/4" clear safety glass. All glazing must meet safety codes as required. Glass must have 5-yr warranty against seal failure.

Wendy's has approved shop drawings established by Vista Wall National Account. These drawings comply with the products and hardware requirements stated herein and are to be used as a guide by the local supervising architect, general contractor, and authorized Vista Wall glazing contractor to insure compliance with this specification. Copies of the approved shop drawings and metal quotation may be obtained by contacting Vista Wall.

Finish Hardware: Doors shall be prepared to receive heavy-duty hardware. Panic hardware to be as manufactured by American Device series 6301 or Von Duprin, stainless finish 630 US32D furnish and install 40" x 20" stainless steel kick plate as shown on drawings. Door closure to be LCN 4024 closure, top jam mount on push side of door, regular arm.

Door Viewer: National Guard Products, 6" x 2" VGLF-WD security vision window.

PREFINISHED DOORS

Laminated Doors—to be 1 3/4" solid core pre-hung doors as manufactured by Marlite Products. All doors of this type to be finished in high-pressure laminate furnished complete with adjustable aluminum frame and hardware.

Hardware to be Schlage - "D" series: (or as specified by regional engineer)

Door E push/pull hdw door   Door J A53PD keyed lock

Door F push/pull hdw door   Door G D53PD all purpose lock

Closer hardware to be Dorma or approved equal 1461 LCN aluminum closer

STEEL SERVICE DOORS AND FRAMES

Steel door frames: shall be 18 ga steel welded vertical edge, mechanical interlock not accepted, as called for in the door schedule on the drawings (sheet 4) and as manufactured by Amweld Corporation series 1500, or equal if approved by architect. Steel hollow metal door shall be 1 3/4" thick, flush type, minimum 18 ga steel face door with polystyrene core, insulation, etc, and manufactured as frames above. Refer to drawings.

PICK-UP WINDOW

Description: Fully automatic sliding aluminum window. Units are typically 4'-4" high and 4'-0" wide with a 24" x 34" active light. Color to match storefront.

Glazing: Glass stops are extruded aluminum snap-in type for interior glazing of glass of panels 5/8" thick (custom stops for thicknesses up to an 1" are available) and have a fixed gasket of high-quality elastomeric material perimeter wool pile and elastomeric weatherstrip is factory applied. Glass must have 5-yr warranty against seal failure.

DIVISION 9—FINISHES

STUCCO BRICK

A. General

1. Scope: Provide and install stucco finish as shown. Includes all accessories required for a complete installation.
2. Related work: Stone masonry (section 04430). Sheathing at all stucco areas (section 06100). Exterior insulation and finish system (section 07240). Flashing and sheet metal (section 07600). Caulking (section 07920).
3. Quality assurance: Comply with ANSI A42.2 "Specification for Lathing and Furring for Portland Cement and Portland Cement-Lime Plastering Exterior (Stucco) and Interior." Comply with ASTM 826-86 "Specification for Portland Cement and Portland Cement-Lime Plastering, Exterior (Stucco) and Interior." Comply with ASTM C1 063-86 "Installation of Lathing and Furring for Portland Cement-Based Plaster."
4. Delivery, storage and handling: Deliver manufactured plastering products to job site in original, unopened packages, containers, or bundles bearing manufacturer's name brand, type, and grade. Keep materials dry until used. Store under cover and off the ground. Protect metal from rusting and damage.

B. Products

1. Materials

   A. General: provide standard products recommended by the manufacturer for the application indicated.
   B. Water: potable and free from impurities that affect plaster.
   C. Sand: provide bagged white graded silica sand for finish coat.
   D. Portland cement: ASTM C150, type I; gray for base coat, mortar and white waterproof for finish coat.
   E. Lime: ASTM C206, types; special finishing hydrated lime.
   F. Corner aid: galvanized, Stockton or equal.
   G. Metal reinforcement: hexagon woven wire mesh, 1" self furring key mesh, galvanized or 3.4 self-furring expanded galvanized diamond lath in accordance with ASTM C1063-86.
   H. Trim: galvanized, Keens, Penn Metals or Alabama metal lath.
   I. Asphalt felts: "all-purpose asphalt sheathing paper", graded as manufactured by Fortifiber.
   J. Accessories and miscellaneous materials: provide the types of accessory items recommended by the furring and lath manufacturer for the application indicated and as required to produce a complete installation of metal furring and lathing, complying with industry standards.
   K. Parex 3.10 primer for application of acrylic finish over cement plaster.
   L. Parch acrylic finish.
   M. Stucco brick colors: brick to match Benjamin Moore #1228 split-face block to match Benjamin Moore #1128

2.   Mixes

    A.   Base coat: Not leaner than one part portland cement (94 lb bag); 50 lb bag air
    B.   Brown coat: Portland cement and lime requirements same as base coat plus
         6 to 7 cubic feet mason's sand.
    C.   Finish coat: Job-mixed finish coat materials
         1. 1 bag at 94 lb each waterproof portland cement
         2. 1 bag at 50 lb each air-entrained lime
         3. 3 parts at 100 lb each white silica sand
    D.   Finish texture: To be selected.
    E.   Parex acrylic finish per manufacturer's application standards.

C.   Execution

  1.   Preparation

    A.   Inspect and accept all surfaces to receive stucco prior to start of installation.
         Do not proceed until all discrepancies have been corrected.
    B.   Do not apply cement plaster to surfaces containing frost and do not plaster
         work when there is a danger of temperature dropping below freezing.
    C.   Exercise care in application, protect exposed finished surfaces maintain,
         protective covering until completion of plastering work.

  2.   Installation

    A.   Install asphalt felts horizontally over all framed surfaces to receive stucco finish.
         Lap joints a minimum of 2" in single fashion to direct water away from building
         interior. Secure to framing with fasteners at each stud horizontally and 24" OC
         vertically.
    B.   Install furring and lathing systems as required. Form angles and corners true
         and smooth. Provide casing beads where required. Miter corners and install
         with tight, accurate joints.
    C.   Machine mix plaster. Measure materials accurately and mix thoroughly to a
         uniform consistency. Do not use lumpy, caked, or frozen materials.
    D.   Apply 3 coat work over metal lath. Brown coat lath may be applied the same
         day as base coat and at least five (5) days prior to applying the finish coat.
         Brown coat is to be floated when sufficiently set.
    E.   Base (scratch) coat and brown coat each to be 3/8" thick. Stucco finish coat to
         be 1/8" thick over portland cement base coat for a nominal thickness of 7/8".
         Parex acrylic finish to be installed after in lieu of standard cement plaster finish.
    F.   Cut, patch repair and point-up plaster as required and as necessary to
         accommodate other work. Point-up finish plaster surfaces around items which
         are built into or penetrate plaster surfaces.
    G.   Remove temporary coverings. Promptly remove plaster from adjacent surfaces.
         Repair surfaces which have been stained, marred, or otherwise damaged
         during the plastering work.

FLOOR AND WALL TILE INSTALLATION

A.   General

  1.   Provide all tile work complete in place as indicated on drawings, specified
     herein.
  2.   Tile work shall be subject to performance standards as set by the American
     National Standards Institute (ANSI) specification A-137J-80 for ceramic tile or CTI-69-5 for
     special-purpose tile and the Tile Council of America (TCA) current handlook for ceramic tile
     installation.
  3.   Deliver material to the job site and store in original unopened cartons with all labels intact
     and legible.
  4.   Tile should be stored in a dry covered area.

B.   Product

1. Tile shall be standard grade in accordance with specifications published by ANSI A-137J80 for ceramic tile or CTI-69-5 for special-purpose tile.
2. Thresholds: Provide thresholds to adjust between tile and other floor finishes.

C. Installation

1. Acceptability of surfaces: surfaces to be tiled shall be smooth and level for mortar bed at the required finish elevation, and a steel trowel finish with a light broom textured finish without more than the following maximum variations:

   Portland cement mortar: walls and ceilings—1/4" in 8" floors; 1/8" in 10'

   Dry set, latex and cement mortar: walls and ceilings—1/8" in 8" floors; 1/8" in 10'

2. Preparation: Prior to the start of laying tile, sweep or vacuum and wash all surfaces to be covered. Surface should be free from coating, curing compounds, oil, grease, wax, and dust.
3. Job conditions: A minimum temperature of 50 degrees F (10 degrees C) should be maintained during tile work and for seven (7) days thereafter. Provide adequate lighting for good grouting and clean-up.
4. Layout of work: Determine locations of all movement (expansion) joints before starting tile work. Lay out all tile work so as to minimize cuts less than one half tile in size. Locate cuts in both walls and floors so as to be least conspicuous.
5. Setting methods: set to Tile Council of America specifications for walls W242-98 and floors F113-98.
6. Grouting: Follow manufacturer's recommendations as to grouting procedures and precautions. Remove all grout haze, observing grout manufacturer's recommendations as to the use of various cleaners.
7. Finishing: Thoroughly rinse all tile work. Use neutral cleaners for final cleaning; acid cleaners are not recommended.

EXTERIOR DECORATIVE WALL TILE

Exterior decorative wall tile pattern at pick-up-window locations shall be as shown on Exterior Elevation (Sheet 5).

A. Tile shall be "frost proof" 8" x 8" as supplied by JVA VOGUE or DSA. Bullnose trim pieces as required. See finish schedule for tile color.

Tile to be set with Mapei Kerabond with Keralastic Polymer-Modified Additive (or equal by Laticrete) grout to be Mapei /Dal-Quality sanded #09 gray with plastijoint acrylic latex additive, (or equal by Laticrete #542 platinum, Laticrete drybond thinset w/ Laticrete super flex additive 333).

Following installation, use mixture of 75% water 25% Mapei Karaclean to clean tile surface. Apply and buff (or equal Laticrete TC-50 tile cleaner 1:3 dilution ratio).

INTERIOR FLOOR TILE

Interior wall and floor finish layouts and patterns for kitchen, restrooms, and dining room shall be as shown on interior elevations and floor tile plan (Sheets 6A–6E).

A. All floor tile shall be 8" x 8" porcelain-bodied tile with slip resistant Crossville Crossgrip and 6" x 8" cove base (see finish schedule item FT-1, FT-3, and FT-4).

All floor tile to be set with Mapei Kerabond (or equal by Laticrete or PCI). Grout to be Mapei/Dal-Quality #09 gray (alternate: Laticrete #542 platinum) with plastijoint acrylic latex additive.

Note: Post construction clean-up with another application of a neutral cleaner with abrasive additive (Walter G. Legge's "Texspar" or equal), and best accomplished with a deck brush or scrubbing machine.

Use phosphoric acid or sulfamic acid only for removal of any grout residue. Do not use muriatic acid.

INTERIOR WALL TILE

A. Wall tile for kitchen and restrooms shall be 4 1/4" x 4 1/4" glazed wall tile (see finish schedules. C-1 & C-3)
B. Wall tile for restroom accent shall be 4 1/4" x 4 1/4" glazed wall tile (see finish schedule. C-4)
C. Wall tiles to be set with type 1 Mastic, and grouted as noted on finish schedule (C-1.)

GYPSUM DRYWALL

Furnish all material and labor necessary to provide finished drywall surfaces in all areas scheduled to receive this finish on the drawings. Tape, spackle, and sand surfaces as to receive paint. Repeat as required.

All drywall over furring and wood studs shall be 5/8" firecode gypsum. Materials shall be standard products manufactured by US Gypsum, National Gypsum, or Gold Bond Gypsum Company.

SUSPENDED CEILING SYSTEM

Furnish all materials and labor to provide a complete suspended ceiling including ceiling tile, hangers, grid tees, and all moldings.

- A. The acoustical ceiling materials in the dining room shall be mineral fiber composition, type III material. Panels to be textured 24" x 24" x 5/8" reveal edge, foil backed panels (see finish schedule CT-1). Exposed ceiling grid and framing shall be cold rolled steel. Exposed surfaces prefinished w/ manufacturer's standard enamel paint.
- B. The acoustical ceiling in the kitchen shall be a gypsum core, washable vinyl material, firecode "C", white square cut 24" x 48" x 1/2" lay-in panels (see finish schedule. CT-2). Ceiling grid and framing shall be cold rolled steel, exposed surfaces prefinished white.

CARPET

All carpet to be supplied with equipment package and installed by a qualified carpet installer working for the general contractor. Refer to Sheet 6B (FL tile & carpet plan) for recommended seaming and finish specifications for carpet.

- A. Standard carpet: Custom patterned "Axminster" carpet of 100% nylon woven through a synthetic backer (12' x 90' rolls). Use with pad and W136 tack transition strip.
- B. Pad: Firm commercial 3/8" contract cushion (for use with Axminster carpet only)

Carpet/tile transition strip: Tack strip to be a one-piece aluminum extrusion with solid vinyl saddle, as manufactured by National Shapes Inc and supplied by kitchen equipment supplier. (see finish specifications—carpet)

CARPET INSTALLATION

A. Standard "Axminster"

Environment: The installer should have the areas to be carpeted available for their use and free from other trades and activities. During winter, the carpet must be stored in a heated space and areas to be carpeted must be kept at the proper temperature before, during, and after the installation.

Proper cushion and adhesive: A firm commercial Hartex 3/8" contract cushion or equal. Do not install Axminster carpet over, "rebond", "waffle," or prime urethane.

Method of seaming: Hand-sewing and/or pin tape and latex are the preferred methods, although premium hot-melt tape (Orcon super 3S or equal) may be used successfully under certain circumstances (see instructions).

Trimming of selvedges: In most installations, it will be necessary to trim at least one selvage edge (not face yarn) and in some cases both selvage edges in order to obtain a proper seam. The trimmed edges must then be sealed ("buttered") with latex.

Pattern matching: US Axminster utilizes 100% synthetic backing yarns which will not shrink or stretch substantially when wet as is the case with old fashioned jute and cotton backing. All rolls are carefully produced to enable excellent pattern matching by following the attached instructions. The pattern is to be squared and aligned in length and width before beginning. Begin square and you can end square. Each roll from US Axminster is coded with a match length (ML) which will help determine the best sequence of rolls for installation. These codes are on tags attached to the rolls as well as on the bill of lading. The installer must study these codes before laying out the job and/or cutting any rolls.

Power stretching: All Axminster carpet stretched in over cushion must be power stretched according to the attached instruction. US Axminster's installation specialist is available to answer questions and solve problems related to installation.

WALL COVERING

All wall covering indicated on the drawings to be supplied by kitchen equipment supplier and installed by general contractor. Refer to finish specifications "WC" for material specifications (contractor to verify quantities prior to start of construction).

Preparation: all surfaces must be structurally sound, smooth, clean, and dry. Moisture content of walls should not exceed (5%) 5 percent. Drywall surfaces must be finished as to receive paint. Apply one coat of a water-based primer such as Evans 01014 vinyl primer to seal and size the surface.

Installation: Apply vinyl wall coverings using a premixed vinyl adhesive with mildew inhibitor (Evans 00233 or equal). Brush or roll adhesive uniformly giving special attention to edges. Use approximately one gallon per 10-12 linear yards. Paste and roll, allowing material to stand for at least five minutes. Hang on wall using butt procedure. Roll seams lightly and smooth out blisters as required.
 It is critical that all excess adhesive be removed from the wall covering surface. Apply clear silicone caulking bead where all wall covering meets wood trim.

Alternate wall covering background for humid zones—painted wall finish.

FIBERGLASS-REINFORCED POLYESTER (FRP) PANELS

Sanitary wall systems to be ivory FRP panel. Install 4' x 9' x 1/8" panel with harmonizing PVC moldings. Adhesive and sealants in strict accordance with manufacturer's written installation instructions, as manufactured by Marlite or Kemlite.

*Note: it is the contractor's responsibility to determine the use of "class A" or "class C" material.

PAINTING

The work to be done by the painting contractor shall include the furnishing of all materials, labor, tools, and equipment required to complete the painting of building as specified. The submission of a bid by this contractor confirms an understanding of all conditions pertaining to this work and proper application of materials specified.

WORKMANSHIP

1. All materials shall be applied free from runs, sags, wrinkles, streaks, shiners, and brush marks.
2. All materials shall be applied uniformly. If any reduction of the coating's viscosity is necessary, it shall be done in accordance with the manufacturer's label directions.
3. New plaster and other masonry surfaces shall not be primed until it has been determined these substrates have dried sufficiently to safely accept paint. A reliable electronic moisture meter should be used to make this determination. Unacceptable moisture content should be reported to the architect or his representative.
4. A minimum interior temperature of 65 degrees F shall be maintained during the actual application and drying of the paint, and until occupancy of the building occurs. Adequate ventilation shall be maintained at all times to control excessive humidity which will adversely affect the curing of coatings. The general contractor is solely responsible for maintaining suitable temperatures and ventilation.
5. Before painting begins, all other crafts shall have completed their work and shall have removed all dirt and debris resulting therefrom. The rooms or areas are to be left in broom clean condition.
6. Enamel and varnish undercoats are to be sanded prior to the recoating. Top and bottoms of doors are to be finished in the same manner as door facing, after the carpenters complete fitting of them.
7. No exterior painting shall be undertaken if air or surface temperature is below 50 degrees F, nor immediately following rain or until frost, dew, or condensation has evaporated. Surfaces should always be tested with moisture meter before proceeding.

PREPARATION OF SURFACES

1. The painting contractor shall be wholly responsible for the quality of his work, and is not to commence any part of it until surface is in proper condition.
2. If the painting contractor considers any surface unsuitable for proper finishing, he is to notify the general contractor of this fact in writing. He is not to apply any material until corrective measures have been taken, or general contractor has instructed to proceed.
3. All surfaces are to be clean. If for any reason the surface cannot be cleaned, this condition shall be promptly reported to the general contractor and Wendy's.
4. If the painting contractor has been instructed by the general contractor to begin painting under conditions and circumstances he believes could result in poor performance and early failure of the coatings, he shall request a decision in writing from Wendy's.
5. The prime coat should be applied soon after surface preparation has been completed to prevent contamination of the substrate.

INSPECTION

1. Any work not conforming to the specifications or does not meet with the approval of the owner, shall be removed or corrected and/or repainted as approved by the owner.

PAINT SCHEDULE

A. Exterior trim

Downspouts and scuppers (PEX-3) Wendy's bronzetone. Color deep bronzetone (163-62) Prime: One (1) coat Moorwood exterior primer (094) Finish: Two (2) coats Ironclad Retardo (163-62) Fences & enclosures (PEX-4) one coat "Benjamin Moore" Moorwood No. 089-66 Charleston Brown. (vinyl acrylic stain)

B. Oak trim

Oak to be stained with "Minwax" wood finish stain & finished w/ two coats of "Minwax" fast-drying polyurethane, satin finish. Apply per manufacturer's product instructions. See finish schedule S-1.

C. Painted Drywall

Drywall to be primed with Benjamin Moore latex quick-dry prime seal (#201) and finished with two coats of Benjamin Moore's Regal Aqua Velvet White (#31901). See finish spec. P-3.

D. Painted Wall Finish

"Le Fleck" heavy-density coverage base coat @ 300 sq ft / gallon, finish coat @ 150 sq ft / gallon. Apply with conventional spray equipment. See finish schedules, SP-1, for custom colors. Alternate background for humid zones.

DIVISION 10—SPECIALTIES

EXTERIOR TRASH ENCLOSURE

Exterior trash enclosure (PEX-4)
Trash enclosure shall be as per specifications and drawings (Geometric Plan and sheet 2)

GENERAL SIGNAGE

All building, freestanding and directional signs will incorporate the cameo identity. Total signage including menu and speaker signs shall be furnished by owner and installed by licensed sign erector. See approved sign suppliers list.

BUILDING SIGNS

1. Buildings with series 2 fascia (36" "Wendy's" old-fashioned hamburgers w/cameo, red closed-face channel letters). To be installed per exterior elevations (Sheet 5). See approved sign suppliers list.

MENUBOARDS (interior and exterior)

All Buildings Require: (one) interior burgundy 8-panel menuboard (soffit-mounted)
(one) exterior burgundy menuboard with order confirmation system in speaker pedestal

KITCHEN EQUIPMENT

General contractor to receive and unload all kitchen equipment and set in proper place. Kitchen equipment serviceman will set up equipment with general contractor making all final hook-ups. (This would also include any purchased Webco kitchen equipment items).

HOOD FIRE SUPPRESSION SYSTEM AND PORTABLE FIRE EXTINGUISHERS

Hood fire suppression system shall be as per specifications and drawings (sheet 15A) manufactured by Ansul or Pyrochem (no substitutes). System shall be furnished and installed by hood manufacturer unless otherwise instructed by owner (verify with owner before construction). Portable extinguishers shall be furnished by hood manufacturer and shall be installed as directed by local fire control authority.

COMMUNICATION SYSTEM

Total communication system as indicated on drawings (sheet 10A) system shall be as manufactured by H.M.E. System shall be furnished and installed by owner. Contractor to furnish conduit, electrical connection and coordinate installation with electrician.

PUBLIC RESTROOM DOORS/PARTITIONS

Restroom stall doors shall be high-pressure laminate (HPL) door as manufactured by Marlite. Doors shall be 7/8" thick with #920 almond color laminate thermally fused to the face of 45 lb industrial particleboard. All external edges shall be banded with color matching PVC edge banding applied under high pressure with hot melt adhesive. See drawings for size and locations of doors.

PUBLIC RESTROOM ACCESSORIES

1. Hand dryers: "World Dryer" model No. R-A5 recessed, mounted w/louvered nozzle No. 462 white as furnished by owner and installed by electrical contractor.
2. 28" w x 42" h wall mounted plate glass mirror w/stainless steel frame.
3. Liquid soap dispensers: lavatory mounted type 304, stainless steel with bright polish finish. Bobrick model no. B-822 installed by general contractor.
4. Toilet tissue dispensers: lavatory mounted jumbo roll tissue dispenser by Kimberly Clark Model No. 09612 JRT installed by general contractor.
5. Handicapped grab bars: Bobrick series No. B-610 stainless steel with exposed mounting. Finish shall be smooth and furnished complete with mounting kit. All items shown on drawings shall be furnished and installed by general contractor.

ROOM IDENTIFICATION SIGN

3/4" thick sandblasted and painted identification signs furnished by owner and installed by general contractor.

ADA RESTROOM IDENTIFICATION SIGN

Sign shall be 6" x 8" beige with contrasting brown icons in compliance with section 4-30-6 of the ADA manual. Sign shall be mounted on wall (latch side of door). See Sheet 6A.

STAINLESS STEEL CORNERS

18 ga stainless steel wrap style corner protectors in kitchen area. Install prior to floor and wall tile in accordance with locations noted on Equipment Plan (Sheet 9). Supplied by S&G Metal Works and installed by general contractor.

WALL DECOR

Framed artwork to be mounted to walls with concealed security hardware supplied with decor package from Creative Palette. Locations and mounting heights are indicated on Sheet 6A, interior elevations.

SILK PLANT PACKAGE

The standard silk plant package includes pre-assembled hanging plants, floor plants, and drop-in inserts as required. Refer to Sheet 9/Equipment Plan for location and key. Mounting heights for hanging planters are indicated on Sheet 6A/Interior Elevations and installed by general contractor.

DIVISION 15—MECHANICAL

PLUMBING

1. Provide all labor, equipment, and materials necessary to execute the plumbing work indicated on the drawings, and as required by local codes and ordinances.
2. Pay all fees and arrange for execution of all taps, meters with required enclosures (if any), etc. inherent to the installation of new plumbing service.
3. Shall include all piping; domestic hot and cold water, sanitary and supply and hook-up of all fixtures scheduled on the drawings; and insulation of designated piping runs shall also include all gas piping and equipment connections where required.
4. All items, such as fittings, etc. not mentioned but understood to necessary to complete the plumbing system shall be included.
5. Soil, waste, and vent piping to be of material approved by local codes.
6. Provide cleanouts for soil and waste lines as shown on drawings, and of type approved by local codes.
7. All water supply piping below ground shall be type K soft copper tubing, (avoid fittings below slab whenever possible). All water supply piping above ground shall be type L hard copper tubing.
8. Provide for draining water system, and cap all stubs until finish work is installed. Install drain valve at water meter with 3/4" hose thread and vacuum breaker.
9. Provide stops on water supplies to each fixture.
10. Gas piping for heating systems with gas-fired equipment shall be included in this contract. Gas piping shall be standard weight, black steel pipe, schedule 40. Piping exposed to atmosphere or run below grade shall have polyethylene plastic coating. All gas piping, fittings and installation shall be in accordance with requirements of utility company and all governing bodies.
11. Insulate all cold and hot water piping with Armstrong company Armaflex 11" pipe insulation. Seal joints with Armstrong 520 adhesive. Important—hold all cold and hot water piping to warm side of insulation to prohibit freezing. Insulation shall meet flame spread and smoke developed ratings required by local codes.
12. Plumbing fixtures shall be furnished and installed where shown on the drawings. All fixture fittings and exposed fixture piping shall be brass chromium-plated. All traps shall be cast brass. All fixtures shall be white. Fixtures shall be as manufactured by American Standard, Kohler, or Crane and equal in all respects to fixtures specified. Closet seats shall be Bemis.

Water closet (A-1)
No. 3043.102	American Standard: elongated water-saver "Madera" vitreous china toilet 17" high
No. 169	McGuire flexible supply stop
No. 1055C	Elongated "Bemis" open front white seat. Not self-sustaining hinge.
No. 111YB	Sloan "Royal" flush valve (1.6 gal/flush)

Water closet (A-2)
No. 3043.102	American Standard: elongated water-saver "Madera" vitreous china toilet 17" high
No. 169	McGuire flexible supply stop
No. 1055C	Elongated "Bemis" open front white seat. Not self-sustaining hinge.
No. 111YB	Sloan "Royal" flush valve (1.6 gal/flush)

Lavatory (B-1)
Corian single integral vanity top and bowl w/ 2 7/8" backsplash and sidesplashes included.
Overall size 31" x 19 1/2 " (bowl position "C").
Corian integral vanity top w/ double bowl (if code required) w/ 2 7/8" backsplash and sidesplashes included. Overall size 49" x 22" (bowl position 12 1/2" -LR-12 1/2").

No. 8872	McGuire adjustable cast brass "P" trap with tubing drain to wall 1 1/4" inlet and outlet, cleanout plug escutcheon.

No. 8434	Moen "Sani-stream", single handle faucet with grid strainer waste or
No. 5401.1724H.002	American Standard: "Heritage" faucet with pop-up drain or
1340M.000/.002	Metering faucet w/ mixing valve or
1480-115	Automatic American Standard
No. 167	McGuire flexible tube riser, wheel handle stop, escutcheon, provide with wall hangers
Urinal (C-1)	
No. 6501.010	American Standard: "Washbrook" vitreous china, washout, 3/4" (inch) top spud, wall hung.
No.186YB	Sloan "Royal" flush valve with integral stop
Mop sink (D-1)	
No. MSB-2424	Finished w/ quarry tile (FT-2)
No. 8344-111	"Heritage" faucet with vacuum breaker

Fixtures and equipment (K-1 thru K-111)
Fixtures and equipment by others. Rough-in final connections of required waste, vent, and water supply piping by plumbing contractor. All supply piping shall be valved.

13. Water meter is a positive displacement meter of the nutating disc type as required by local utility company.

14. Water Heater

A. The gas water heater shall be universal model G82-156, manufactured by Rheem/Ruud, having gas input of 156,000 Btu/hr. and a recovery rate of 151 GPH at a 100 degree temperature rise when tested and certified at 80% thermal efficiency. Water heater shall have a storage capacity of 82 gallons. Power vent kit #PV kit 4 is to be installed in conjunction w/ this tank. Water heaters shall have the System Sentinel diagnostic control system. Each LED will correspond to the sequence of operation as unit is in operation. Water heater shall have the AGA seal of certification and supplied with a factory AGA rated temperature and pressure relief valve. Tanks shall be furnished with a tube bundle having a double coating of high temperature porcelain enamel and furnished with magnesium anode rods rigidly supported. Water heaters shall meet or exceed the thermal efficiency and standby loss requirements of ASHRAE Standard 90LB-1992. Tanks shall have a working pressure 150 psi, and shall be completely factory assembled, including a pressure regulator properly adjusted or operation on LP gas with stainless steel burners. Controls will be arranged for safety shutoff in event of pilot failure. Water heater shall have top, front and rear side inlet/outlet water connections. Water heater shall have a 5 year warranty against tank leaks.

B. Electric hot water heater shall be model ES85-36, Rheem/Ruud, having electrical input of 36 kW and a recovery rate of 149 GPH at 100 degrees rise. Water heater shall have a storage capacity of 85 gallons. Water heaters shall have UL seal of certification and be factory equipped with an AGA/ASME rated temperature and pressure relief valve. Tank shall have a double coating of high temperature porcelain enamel and furnished with magnesium anode rods rigidly supported. Water heaters shall meet or exceed the standby loss requirements of ASHRAE standard 90.LB-1992. Tanks shall have a working pressure of 150 psi, and shall be completely assembled. Water heaters shall be approved-listed and constructed in accordance with NSF standard. Water heaters shall equipped with Lifeguard screw-in type elements featuring stainless steel outer sheath on Inco-loy 840 material. Tank shall be insulated with 3" of rigid polyurethane foam insulation. Water heaters shall be constructed with a System Sentinel element diagnostic panel utilizing light emitting diodes. Each LED will correspond to the number and location of the heating elements and monitor their on/off function. Water heaters shall be provided with internal power circuit fusing, control circuit fusing, magnetic contactors, 120 volt control circuit transformer and surface mounted thermostat or immersion thermostat with manual reset high limit control. 1 1/2" inlet and outlet water connections shall be provided. Water heater shall have a 5 year warranty against tank leaks.

C. High efficiency gas (option) water heater shall be Advantage plus model HE-80-160. Heater shall have a gas input of 160,000 Btu/hr, and a recovery rate of 184 GPH at a 100 degree temperature rise when tested and certified at 95% thermal efficiency. Water heater shall have a storage capacity of 80 gallons. The water heater shall be a sealed combustion system, taking only, outside air for combustion and exhausting the flue gas with plastic pipe. The intake air shall be piped with plastic PVC or ABS pipe, 3" in diameter and the exhaust gas shall be piped with CPVC or ABS solid non foam core for the first 7 feet only, with the remaining pipe being schedule 40 or 80 CPVC solid - solid PVC non-foam core - ABS solid non-foam core. All related intake air and exhaust gas shall be approved for zero clearance to any combustible surface. The heater shall be constructed of 316L stainless steel. The heat exchanger shall be constructed of 90/10 cupronickel. The insulation is a water blown foam and shall be 2" thick with a rating of R14.3 and 3" on top of the heater rated at R21.3. Insulation be enclosed in a plastic shell. All components of the self-diagnostic electronic control panel with digital readout shall be located in the front of the heater for easy access for serviceability. All related hardware shall be constructed of stainless steel studs and brass nuts for serviceability. Water heater shall have a 5 year warranty against tank leaks.

15. Wall hydrants shall be freezeless automatic draining type as manufactured by Woodford, model 65 or equal by Zurn or Wade.
16. Coordinate all working with electrical and heating contractor.
17. This contractor shall guarantee all work installed under the contract to be free from any defective workmanship or materials, usual wear expected, and should any such defects develop within a period of one year after acceptance of the building by the owner, this contractor shall repair and/or replace any defective items and all damage resulting from failure of these items, at no expense whatsoever to the owner.
18. Backflow preventor to be installed when required by local code and is to be provided by and installed by the plumbing contractor.
19. Supply and install premade gas cooking equipment manifold as shown on Sheet 15A, supplied by S&G Metal Works.

HEATING AND VENTILATION

1. Provide all labor, materials and equipment necessary to complete the heating and ventilating work indicated on the drawings and as required by local codes and ordinances.
2. Included in this section is all work to install kitchen exhaust hoods and room vents as shown on the drawings. All hoods and fans are to be Wendy's standard, as listed on Sheet S-5, approved suppliers. Roof mounted exhaust fans to be installed on prefabricated curb furnished and installed by heating contractor.
3. Heating and cooling units as indicated on the drawings to be furnished and installed by heating contractor. Heating and ventilating units indicated on the drawings and hereinafter specified are designed to meet ASHRAE 90-65 based on Columbus, Ohio design conditions of 90°F summer and 0° F winter. (see note 15)
4. Diffusers, registers, and louvers shall be as per model and size indicated on drawings. No substitutes shall be accepted unless approved by the owner or architect in writing. Diffusers and louvers not meeting specification as shown on drawings shall be replaced at the heating contractor's expense.
5. Before final acceptance by owner, an owner's representative shall check entire HVAC system and submit a written report to the owner. Final balance of HVAC system shall be performed by mechanical contractor. No final payment will be made until the above report has been received and HVAC systems are in balance.
6. Where required by governing ordinances, provide fire dampers conforming to NFPA 90A. Supply ducts to have 1" fiberglass insulation. Exhaust installation shall conform to NFPA 96.
7. Where required, provide class "B" gas vent flues complete with cap, collar, and flashing.
8. Install thermostat complete with all necessary wiring and controls; location as indicated on the drawings. Thermostat shall provide for automatic and manual fan operation.
9. Install and connect the complete system in strict accordance with all governing codes, ordinances and the latest codes and manuals of the National Warm Air Heating and Air Conditioning Association.
10. Adjust all controls and equipment for proper operation. Lubricate and clean all equipment prior to acceptance of building owner.

11. Coordinate all work with electrical and plumbing contractors.
12. Furnish the owner with all operating manuals and maintenance instructions for equipment installed.
13. This contractor shall guarantee all work installed under the contract to be free from the defective workmanship and materials, usual wear expected, and should any such defects develop within a period of one year after acceptance of the building by the owner, this contractor shall repair and/or replace any defective items and all damage resulting from failure of these items, at no expense whatsoever to the owner.
14. HVAC contractor is responsible to notify general contractor of required changes in roof openings for roof top units due to change in equipment size dictated by appropriate option above.
15. HVAC contractor is responsible to notify general contractor, electrical, and plumbing contractors of changes in electrical and gas requirements due to changes in equipment capacities as dictated by appropriate option above.

DIVISION 16 ELECTRICAL

1. Provide a complete electrical system as indicated on the drawings and described herein.
2. Electric work shall comply with the latest National Electric Code as well as state and local governing codes.
3. Pay for all permits and inspections and provide a certificate of inspection.
4. Provide required service and equipment grounding systems. The conduit system shall be electrically continuous and shall be safely grounded at the distribution panel. All devices shall be bonded to the conduit system. Provide a separate grounding conductor in each conduit, #12 minimum or as shown on drawings.
5. Materials shall be new with manufacturer's name printed thereon and Underwriters Laboratories listed. The selection of materials and equipment to be provided under this contract shall be in strict accordance with the specifications and drawings. This contractor shall submit to the architect for approval 8 copies of equipment as follows: main distribution panel, panelboards, disconnect switches, and lighting fixtures.
6. Identify disconnect switches, with laminated phenolic nameplates with 1/4" minimum height letters.
7. Provide power wiring and hook-up for each mechanical and kitchen equipment item. This contractor shall mount, provide wiring, and make final connections to equipment control panels (which include prewired starters, relays, etc.) Furnish and install all starters which are not furnished as a part of mechanical equipment.
8. Provide devices, wiring and hook-up for the emergency kitchen shutdown system as described and specified on drawings. Wiring shall be in conduit.
9. Disconnect switches shall be the heavy-duty type in NEMA I enclosure or equal by Square D or Arrow Hart. Switches shall be quick-make, quick-break, externally operated and interlocked.
10. Switches shall be 20 amp Hubbell 1221-1 single pole or 1223-1 three way. Duplex receptacles shall be 20 amp Hubbell 5362-1. Pass and Seymour, Arrow Hart and Bryant shall be considered as equal. Ground fault interrupting shall be G.E. TGTR115F. Cover plates shall be Sierra (Pass and Seymour). Switch plates to be series #S-in, duplex plates to be series #S-in. Duplex plates in dining room to be #P-8, etc. All cover plates to have satin finish #302 stainless steel (except dining room plates)
11. Test electrical system for short circuits and megger test feeders and branch circuit wiring. Ensure low impedance ground system.
12. The electrical service to the site shall be verified by this contractor prior to bidding job. This contractor shall provide conduit, cable, concrete, connections, and other equipment required for an underground electrical system from the power company equipment to the new distribution panel "DP." It shall be the responsibility of this contractor to coordinate electrical service entrance work with the power company, securing contracts with power company for the installation of primary entrance, including charges by power company in bid; and performing work required by power company in accordance with power company rules and regulations to insure a complete electrical service.
13. This contractor shall verify power company requirements and charges prior to bidding and include such in bid.
14. For service and panel feeder wiring, use type THHN cable. Use THWN cable for interior branch circuit wiring except as noted. Design is based on copper conductors and all wiring shall be copper. Minimum #12 AWG. Wiring shall be in conduit. Splice wires #6 AWG and larger with approved olderless connectors such as ILSCO properly taped and insulated. Splice smaller wires with mechanical connectors such as 3M "Scotchlock" type R.

15. Provide rigid galvanized steel heavy wall conduit or plastic conduit for service and panel feeder conduits. Fittings shall be steel threaded, set-screw type with insulated throats. Furnish EMT conduit for interior wiring where physical damage is not a consideration. Minimum conduit size is 3/4" except for flexible conduit to fixtures, motors, etc. which may be 1/2".
16. Conduit shall be concealed wherever possible and shall be run parallel or perpendicular to building walls and ceilings.
17. Conduit installed in or below slab shall be galvanized rigid conduit/or plastic conduit. No conduit larger than 1 1/2" diameter will be installed in slab.
18. Provide structural steel framework and hanging rods with braces and accessories where required to hold equipment in final position. Provide steel shapes and frames to support wall-mounted equipment where normal wall strength may be inadequate.
19. Electrical devices, motor starters, disconnect switches, etc. shall be supported independent of and isolated from equipment vibration.
20. Coordinate with kitchen equipment supplier all interior wiring connections needed during assembly of kitchen equipment.
21. Provide power to cash registers with the following grounding requirements.

    A. System power and ground must be made only at the main entrance panel. The equipment grounding conductor must be of insulated wire equal in size to the power conductor (conduit may not be used as the equipment grounding conductor).
    B. The ground conductor must not be used as a return or neutral conductor for any equipment and must not be used as a ground for any equipment other than cash register equipment.
    C. Receptacles for the registers must be 2 pole, 3 wire, 115 volts, 20 amperes. The ground must be insulated from the mounting hardware.
    D. For additional information, if required, contact Wendy's International, Inc., 4288 W. Dublin-Granville Road, Dublin, OH.
    E. The register conduits must not be used for any other equipment.

22. Provide fixtures as listed on lighting fixture schedule. Provide necessary mounting hardware for a complete installation. Provide lamps, ballasts, and special controls.
23. Furnish and install empty conduit, outlets, and backboard to accommodate telephone company wiring and equipment as shown on drawings. Work shall be installed in strict accordance with telephone company requirements.
24. This contractor shall guarantee work installed under the contract to be free from any defective workmanship and materials, usual wear expected, and should any such defects develop within a period of one year after acceptance of the building by the owner, this contractor shall repair and/or replace any defective items and damage resulting from failure of these items, at no expense whatsoever to the owner.

Name _____ Date _____

Refer to Specifications for Wendy's Restaurant.

DIVISION 1—GENERAL REQUIREMENTS

Completion

_____ **1.** Based on the *Americans with Disabilities Act (ADA) New Construction Checklist,* ___ accessible parking spaces are required if the parking lot contains 140 parking spaces.

_____ **2.** Per ADA requirements, the clear and level landing area at each accessible entrance is ___' square.

_____ **3.** The construction manager is Wendy's ___ department.

_____ **4.** A contractor must commence construction of the building within ___ calendar days after written notice from Wendy's.

_____ **5.** Per ADA requirements, the maximum highest operable part of restroom accessories is ___".

_____ **6.** The comprehensive liability insurance has minimum limits of $___ combined single limit.

_____ **7.** No more than ___ progress payment requests may be submitted by the contractor.

_____ **8.** A formal list of construction deficiencies is referred to as a(n) ___ list.

_____ **9.** Wendy's is entitled to recover liquidated damages from a contractor in the amount of $___ for each calendar day substantial completion is delayed.

_____ **10.** The contractor warrants all work and materials against defects for a period of ___ from the opening date of the restaurant.

True-False

T   F   **1.** The owner can stop construction work at any time for testing and special inspections.

T   F   **2.** The owner must secure and pay for all permits, licenses, approvals, and certificates related to the job.

T   F   **3.** The contractor is responsible in the event of loss or damage to adjacent property during construction.

T   F   **4.** No work may be performed under subcontract without prior written approval by Wendy's.

T   F   **5.** The contractor shall commence construction within five calendar days of notice from the owner.

T   F   **6.** The contractor's sole remedy for delay is an extension of the contract by Wendy's.

T   F   **7.** Wendy's requires that the contractor secure a contracts bond or letter of credit prior to construction.

T   F   **8.** The contractor can draw up to seven progress payments throughout the project.

T   F   **9.** The contractor shall indemnify and hold harmless the owner from all claims due to injuries received on the job.

T   F   **10.** The contractor shall provide certificates of insurance for Workers' Compensation and automobile liability coverage.

DIVISION 2—SITE CONSTRUCTION

Completion

_____ **1.** All ___, refuse, and existing structures are removed prior to commencement of work.

_____ **2.** ___ excavations must be on undisturbed earth.

_____ **3.** Soil tests are taken to ensure that site soil will meet ___ PSF design strength.

_____ **4.** ___ soil is defined as clean sand and sand gravel free of clay, silt, or loam.

_____ **5.** All parking blocks must be no more than ___" high.

_____ **6.** Concrete curbs have saw cuts a maximum of ___' apart.

_____ **7.** The ___ is responsible for positive site drainage.

_____ **8.** Plants and ___ are guaranteed for one year from installation.

_____ **9.** All ___ to within 5'-0" of the building perimeter are considered site work.

_____ **10.** The general contractor must verify all plumbing ___ and furnish any city drawings required.

True-False

T   F   **1.** Backfilling of foundation walls in interior areas is to be brought to a subgrade of 8" below the finish floor line.

T   F   **2.** Crushed stone and sand must be used as backfill over utilities.

T   F   **3.** All parking blocks are at least 6'-0" long.

T   F   **4.** Concrete curbs shall be reinforced with two #4 rebar running continuously.

T   F   **5.** Topsoil is furnished by the landscape contractor.

T   F   **6.** All bidders for landscape work shall submit a written proposal and landscape plan to the general contractor for approval.

T   F   **7.** All storm and sanitary sewer work is the responsibility of the general contractor.

T   F   **8.** Electric service to signs is considered to be part of the site work.

T   F   **9.** The owner is responsible for verifying all utility taps.

T   F   **10.** Grease trap installation is not part of the contract.

DIVISION 3—CONCRETE AND DIVISION 4—MASONRY

Completion

_____ **1.** All ___ for footings must be unpainted and uncoated.

_____ **2.** Concrete slabs are reinforced with 6 × 6—___ WWF.

_____ **3.** Welded wire fabric edges are lapped ___" before placing concrete.

_____ **4.** The total slope leading to floor drains shall not exceed ___" below floor level.

_____ **5.** All concrete walks are 4" thick and are to receive a(n) ___ finish.

_____ **6.** Black ___ paving is colored with Wendy's Black Chemtint.

_____ **7.** All concrete floors must be poured ___.

_____ **8.** All "green" brick walls must be ___ at the end of each day's work.

_____ **9.** Bottoms of earth trenches must be without ___.

_____ **10.** ___ concrete masonry units are used in exposed conditions such as sills.

407

_____ **11.** All masonry work must cease when the temperature drops below ___°F.

_____ **12.** Mortar for face brick shall be one part cement, one part lime, and ___ part(s) sand.

_____ **13.** Field brick must conform to ___ specifications.

_____ **14.** All brick is to be laid with joints of ___ width.

_____ **15.** Brick shall be cleaned with a(n) ___ brush.

DIVISION 5—METALS AND DIVISION 6—WOOD AND PLASTICS

True-False

T   F   **1.** Four sets of shop drawings showing all structural steel must be submitted to the architect for approval.

T   F   **2.** Wrought iron railings shall have ½" square bars.

T   F   **3.** Wrought iron railing samples must be submitted to the architect for approval.

T   F   **4.** Interior railings have a 2 × 4 oak handrail.

T   F   **5.** All interior framing may be either metal studs or wood studs as shown on the plans.

T   F   **6.** Wood 2 × 4 studs are spaced 16" OC.

T   F   **7.** Wood studs must be tripled at all openings and corners.

T   F   **8.** Unless otherwise noted on the plans, all structural lumber shall be No. 2 southern yellow pine.

T   F   **9.** CDX plywood with five plies and exterior glue is specified.

T   F   **10.** All holes for 16d and larger nails are to be predrilled.

Completion

_____ **1.** ___ top plates shall be utilized on all exterior and bearing partitions unless otherwise detailed.

_____ **2.** Bolt holes for wood connections shall be ___" larger in diameter than normal bolt size.

_____ **3.** Steel ___ shall be placed under all bolt heads and nuts bearing on wood.

_____ **4.** Nailing ___ govern over nailing schedules.

_____ **5.** Bridging to joists or rafters shall be toenailed at each end with two ___ nails.

_____ **6.** Double top plates shall be face nailed with 16d nails spaced ___ " OC.

_____ **7.** Continuous ___ shall be toenailed to studs with four 8d nails.

_____ **8.** Roof joists are supplied by ___.

_____ **9.** Common wire nails shall conform to the ___ or ___.

_____ **10.** Dining room trim is to be ___.

_____ **11.** Gypsum board ceilings are fastened with ___ nails.

_____ **12.** Countertops are to be installed by the ___.

_____ **13.** The Cooler/Freezer is supplied by the ___.

_____ **14.** The general contractor coordinates the uncrating and ___ of the Cooler/Freezer.

_____ **15.** The Cooler/Freezer is to be shipped complete with ___ and instructions.

DIVISION 7—THERMAL AND MOISTURE PROTECTION

True-False

T   F   **1.** Caulking is to be applied to all exterior door frames and window frames to provide weatherproofing.

T   F   **2.** Fascia panels are bright red in color.

T   F   **3.** Caulking materials must conform to American Standard specification A-116.

T   F   **4.** All parapet walls are covered with flashing a minimum of 12" high.

T   F   **5.** All metal counterflashing shall have a 3" overlap for expansion and contraction.

T   F   **6.** All roofing wood members shall be chromated copper arsenate (CCA).

T   F   **7.** The roofing system has a full 20 year warranty.

T   F   **8.** A 6 mil thick vapor barrier is placed under concrete slabs.

T   F   **9.** Fiberglass batts 4" thick are to be placed in all exterior walls.

T   F   **10.** Two layers of 2.4" thick R-20 are used as rigid roof insulation.

Completion

_____ **1.** ___ drawings are required for ordering, manufacturing, and final inspection of the roofing system.

_____ **2.** Any joints or cracks greater than ___″ must be repaired prior to installing the roof membrane.

_____ **3.** If metal drip edges, gravel stops, copings, and counterflashings are used, they must be a minimum of ___ ga.

_____ **4.** Perimeter insulation is ___″ thick Styrofoam.

_____ **5.** Fascia panels are a bright ___ color with bronze color moldings accented in red.

DIVISION 8 — DOORS AND WINDOWS

True-False

T   F   **1.** All exterior glass for the storefront has a 30 year warranty.

T   F   **2.** A polystyrene core is used in steel service doors.

T   F   **3.** The door viewer from National Guard Products has a 6″ × 6″ vision window.

T   F   **4.** The active light in the pick-up window unit is 20″ × 36″.

T   F   **5.** A Schlage A53PD keyed lock is installed in a J door.

Completion

_____ **1.** Kewaneer Company aluminum entrance doors are ___.

_____ **2.** Interior vestibule doors must have ___″ diameter pull handles.

_____ **3.** The operating force on United States Aluminum entrance door closers is ___ lb.

_____ **4.** The glass color for Vistawall storefront systems is ___.

_____ **5.** Steel door frames are ___ ga steel.

_____ **6.** All exterior glass is to be ___″ solar bronze.

_____ **7.** All laminated doors are to be ___″ thick.

_____ **8.** The lock for ___ doors is a Schlage D53PD all-purpose lock.

_____ **9.** The pick-up window unit is ___′ wide.

_____ **10.** All prefinished doors have ___ frames and hardware.

DIVISION 9—FINISHES

True-False

T	F	**1.**	White graded silica sand is used for a stucco finish coat.
T	F	**2.**	Thresholds are not required between tile and other floor finishes.
T	F	**3.**	The exterior decorative wall tile pattern at the pick-up window is shown on Sheet 5.
T	F	**4.**	Muriatic acid should be used to remove grout residue.
T	F	**5.**	The Axminster carpet is provided in 12′ × 90′ rolls.

Completion

_____ **1.** All ___ over furring and wood studs must be ⅝″ firecode gypsum.

_____ **2.** Washable ceiling tiles are ___ faced.

_____ **3.** The maximum surface variation for wall tile is ___″ in 8″ for portland cement mortar.

_____ **4.** Restroom ___ tile is manufactured by Crossville.

_____ **5.** The carpet pad is ___″ thick contract cushion.

_____ **6.** All walls to which wall covering is to be applied must have a(n) ___ content of less than 5%.

_____ **7.** ___ adhesive is to be used when applying wall covering.

_____ **8.** ___ coat(s) of primer and two coats of high gloss enamel paint are specified for scuppers.

_____ **9.** A minimum indoor temperature of ___ must be maintained during painting.

_____ **10.** All interior wood is ___ and varnished.

DIVISION 10—SPECIALITIES

True-False

T	F	**1.**	Toilet and urinal partitions are manufactured by American Standard.
T	F	**2.**	Locations for hanging planters are shown on Sheet 6A.
T	F	**3.**	Handicapped grab bars are high-impact plastic.
T	F	**4.**	All room identification signs are supplied by the sign erector.

T	F	**5.** The restroom signs are in compliance with ADA section 6-30-4.
T	F	**6.** The communication system is manufactured by H.M.E.
T	F	**7.** No substitutes are acceptable for the hood fire suppression system specified.
T	F	**8.** Portable fire extinguishers are sized by the local fire control authority.
T	F	**9.** The plumber is to receive and unload all kitchen equipment.
T	F	**10.** The general contractor will make all final connections for kitchen equipment.

Completion

1. Restroom stall doors are to be manufactured of high-pressure ___.

2. The corner trim pieces are manufactured of ___ ga stainless steel.

3. Framed artwork used for wall decor is to be mounted to walls with ___ security hardware.

4. The communication system is shown on Sheet ___.

5. Room identification signs are ___" thick.

DIVISION 15—MECHANICAL

Completion

1. Soil, waste, and vent piping material must meet all local ___.

2. Type K soft ___ tubing is used for water supply piping installed below ground.

3. All water supplies to fixtures must be equipped with ___.

4. Schedule ___ black steel gas piping is to be used for all heating systems.

5. All water supply piping must be placed to the ___ side of insulation.

6. Traps for all plumbing fixtures are to be cast ___.

7. The urinal is to be ___ hung.

8. The water heater has a(n) ___ year warranty.

9. ___ hydrants must be freezeproof and automatic draining types.

10. The backflow preventor, if required by local code, is to be provided and installed by the ___ contractor.

True-False

T   F   **1.** The installation of kitchen exhaust hoods is covered in Division 15.

T   F   **2.** Heating and cooling units are designed to handle normal temperatures in Columbus, Ohio.

T   F   **3.** The final balance of the HVAC system shall be performed by the mechanical contractor.

T   F   **4.** All supply ducts must be wrapped with a minimum of 2" insulation.

T   F   **5.** The thermostat is required to provide manual operation only.

T   F   **6.** Diffuser types can be substituted by the HVAC contractor based on local supply availability.

T   F   **7.** Operating manuals are provided to the owner.

T   F   **8.** The heating contractor must coordinate work with the electrical and plumbing contractors.

T   F   **9.** The warranty period for HVAC work is one year.

T   F   **10.** The owner assumes no responsibility for expenses incurred in repairing the HVAC system while it is under warranty.

DIVISION 16—ELECTRICAL

True-False

T   F   **1.** All devices must be bonded to the conduit system.

T   F   **2.** Four copies of the materials and equipment list must be submitted to the architect for approval.

T   F   **3.** Use THHN cable for interior branch circuits.

T   F   **4.** Scotchlock Type R connects are used to splice smaller wires.

T   F   **5.** Register conduit cannot be shared with low-voltage conductors.

Completion

_____ **1.** All electrical work shall comply with the ___, state, and local codes.

_____ **2.** The ___ system must form a continuous path for ground.

_____ **3.** All electrical equipment must be ___ by Underwriters Laboratories.

_____ **4.** All disconnect switches shall be mounted in ___ enclosures.

_____ **5.** All feeder and branch circuits must be ___ during the electrical system test.

_____ **6.** Type ___ or better cable is required for service and panel feeder wiring.

_____ **7.** Electrical design is based on ___ conductors.

_____ **8.** All wiring must be run in ___.

_____ **9.** Wires #6 AWG and larger must be ___ with approved solderless connectors.

_____ **10.** No conduit larger than ___" is to be installed in the floor slab.

_____ **11.** Disconnect switches are required to be ___ from equipment vibration.

_____ **12.** The cash register system equipment ground conductor must be of ___ wire.

_____ **13.** The cash register system equipment ground conductor must not be used as a return or ___ conductor for any equipment.

_____ **14.** The ___ for the cash registers must be isolated from the mounting hardware.

_____ **15.** ___ for cash register equipment must not be used for any other equipment.

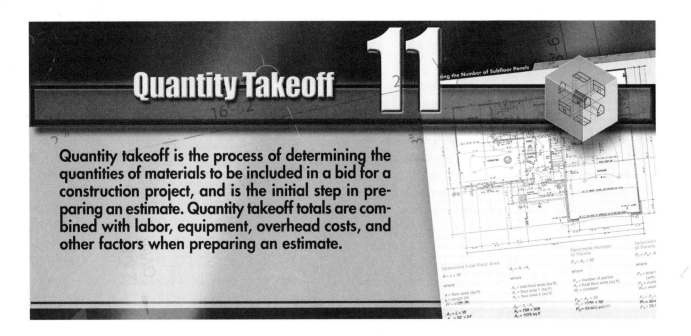

Quantity Takeoff

Quantity takeoff is the process of determining the quantities of materials to be included in a bid for a construction project, and is the initial step in preparing an estimate. Quantity takeoff totals are combined with labor, equipment, overhead costs, and other factors when preparing an estimate.

QUANTITY TAKEOFF

When a set of prints have been approved for construction by local building code officials, the amount of material required for construction must be taken off. *Takeoff* is the practice of reviewing contract documents, including the prints and specifications, to determine quantities of material to be included in a bid. General contractors, specialty contractors, and material suppliers employ estimators who read prints and specifications to determine material quantities required for proper construction. Prints and specifications are reviewed carefully before beginning quantity takeoff calculations. When the prints and specifications have been reviewed, a takeoff is prepared to develop an overall price for the construction of the building. Printreading and calculation skills are required to develop an accurate and comprehensive material list and takeoff that includes all materials and amounts of materials necessary for a construction project.

A takeoff includes determining the materials and calculating the amount of materials required for each major system of the building, including the structural, finish, mechanical, and electrical systems. The amounts are then totaled and priced to prepare an estimate.

STRUCTURAL SYSTEMS

Structural systems included in a quantity takeoff are site preparation, concrete formwork, concrete, structural and light-gauge steel, and structural wood members.

Earthwork

Earthwork quantities include the amount of excavation cutting and filling, final grading, and trenching required at a job site. The takeoff for excavation is commonly calculated in cubic yards, but can be calculated in cubic feet when the excavation requires the removal of only a few inches of soil.

Gridding. *Gridding* is the division of a plot plan for large areas to be excavated or graded into small squares or grids. Grids may be drawn as an overlay sheet of tracing paper directly from the plot plan. The site terrain is used to determine the size of the grids. Grids may represent squares with 100′ sides if the terrain is gradually sloped or squares with 25′ sides if the terrain is irregular. The approximate elevation at each corner of a grid is established using the nearest contour line. Interpolation between adjoining grids is required when the corners do not directly align with contour lines. Cut or fill averages are calculated for each grid, with the sum indicating the amount of fill or cut that must be accomplished at the site.

Excavation. *Excavation* is any construction cut, cavity, trench, or depression in the surface of the earth formed by equipment to create the engineering improvements. *Engineering improvements* are changes to a site that include footings, foundations, basements, and other belowground work. General excavation includes all excavation, other than rock and/or water removal, that is performed by earth-moving equipment or any type of mechanical equipment.

Calculating the volume of material to be excavated from a site is accomplished using the cross-section or average end area method. The cross-section method is used when the shape of the excavated area is roughly square or rectangular. The average end area method is used when the sides of the excavation area are irregularly shaped and not parallel.

When using the cross-section method, the volume of excavated earth is calculated by determining the average depth of excavation from various known points and multiplying by the total surface area of the excavation. The excavation volume for a grid square is calculated by determining the difference between the existing elevation and the proposed excavation at each corner of the grid.

For example, calculate the quantity of cut or fill using the cross-section method for a 100′ × 90′ grid with corners at elevations of 95.65′, 87.25′, 85.32′, and 80.03′ requiring excavation to 85′. See Figure 11-1. The planned elevation of 85′ is added or subtracted from each corner elevation to determine the difference between the existing elevation and planned elevation at each corner (95.65 − 85 = 10.65, 87.25 − 85 = 2.25, 85.32 − 85 = .32, 80.83 − 85 = −4.17). The four differences in depths are added (10.65 + 2.25 + .32 + (−4.17) = 9.05) and the sum is divided by 4 to obtain the average excavation cut depth or fill amount of 2.26′ at each corner. The average cut or fill excavation depth of 2.26′ is multiplied by the surface area of the square (100′ × 90′ = 9000 sq ft) to determine that 20,340 cubic feet of excavation (2.26′ × 9000 sq ft = 20,340 cu ft) is required. The total volume (in cubic feet) is divided by 27 to determine that 753.33 cu yd of earth must be excavated (20,340 cu ft ÷ 27 = 753.33 cu yd).

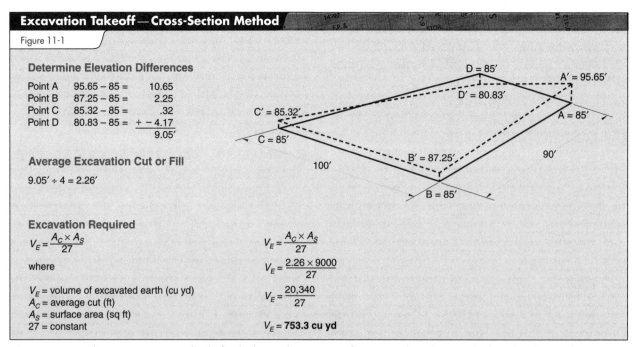

Figure 11-1. The cross-section method of calculating the amount of excavated earth is used when the shape of the excavation area is roughly square or rectangular.

When using the average end area method, the volume of excavated earth is calculated by the average cut area at each end of an excavation. The difference between the existing and planned elevation is determined in each corner of the excavation area. Imaginary planes are drawn representing the two ends of the excavation. The area of each plane is calculated in square feet. The two areas are added together and divided by 2 to determine the average end area. The average end area is multiplied by the length of the excavation to determine the total volume of the excavation in cubic feet. The total volume in cubic feet is divided by 27 to obtain the volume (in cubic yards) to be excavated.

For example, a 48′ long excavation area has a width of 24′ at one end and a width of 30′ at the other end. Both ends of the excavation area require 10′ of cut. The areas of the planes created by the ends of the excavation area are 240 sq ft (24′ × 10′ = 240 sq ft) and 300 sq ft (30′ × 10′ = 300 sq ft), respectively. The two values are added together (240 sq ft + 300 sq ft = 540 sq ft). The sum is divided by 2 to determine the average end area (540 sq ft ÷ 2 = 270 sq ft). The average end area is multiplied by the length of the excavation (48′) to determine that 12,960 cu ft of excavation is required (48′ × 270′ = 12,960 cu ft). The total volume (in cubic feet) is divided by 27 to determine that 480 cu yd of earth must be excavated (12,960 cu ft ÷ 27 = 480 cu yd). See Figure 11-2.

Grading. *Grading* is the process of lowering high spots and filling in low spots of earth at a construction site. Negative numbers are used to indicate fill-in areas where the planned elevation is above the existing elevation. A *zero line* is a line connecting points on a topographical map where existing and planned elevations are equal. Depending on the grid layout, some grids may require all cut or all fill while other grids require both cut and fill. Final grading quantities are taken off in square feet or in square yards of surface.

Dust and soil erosion control measures may be required around an excavation.

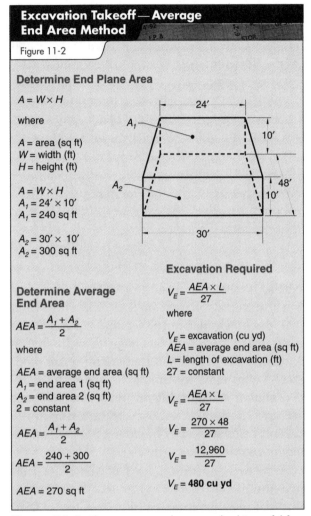

Figure 11-2. The average end area method is useful for calculating the amount of excavated earth from irregularly shaped excavations.

Concrete Formwork Materials

Information concerning the type and design of formwork is not typically provided on a set of prints. For large construction projects, a concrete form supplier provides a separate set of formwork drawings. Formwork design is based on concrete and foundation dimensions provided on foundation or floor plans and is developed by a formwork design specialist. Formwork drawings indicate the form identification numbers of the manufacturer, type of formwork, placement, shoring and bracing information, form fastening system, and the proper form ties to use. Concrete formwork design must take into account all forces to be placed on a form.

A formwork takeoff is performed when formwork drawings are not provided. A formwork quantity takeoff includes slab-on-grade forms and forms for footings and foundation walls. Formwork components for job-built forms include framing members and bracing materials such as 2×4s and 2×6s, and materials for the facing of the forms including Plyform® and other panel materials such as high density overlay (HDO). For patented forms, formwork components include the number, type, and size of various patented forms based on the materials available from the form manufacturer. Snap ties and other formwork inserts such as lift anchors and blockouts must also be listed in the formwork takeoff.

Walls. Information used in a takeoff for formwork materials of cast-in-place concrete walls includes elevations at the top and bottom of the wall, wall thickness, placement of wall surface features, any embedded items, and reinforcing steel. Length and width dimensions of the walls are shown on foundation plans, elevations, sections, and details. Concrete formwork uses takeoff calculations in linear feet or by square feet of contact area.

Snap tie quantities are calculated as a specified number of ties per square foot of wall area. Snap tie spacing is determined from the specifications, elevations, recommendations of the patented form manufacturer, or information provided by the snap tie manufacturer.

For example, information may state that snap ties are spaced 24″ OC for an 8″ thick wall. One snap tie for each 4 sq ft of wall area is typically recommended. The total area (in square feet) of a concrete wall is divided by 4 to determine the number of snap ties required. Each $4′ \times 8′$ (32 sq ft) section of concrete wall requires eight snap ties with allowances for adjoining forms (32 sq ft ÷ 4 = 8).

Job-Built Walls. The various materials used to construct job-built walls, such as facing material, framing members, plates, walers, and snap ties, are taken off individually. Like materials are then combined when totaling the materials. The amount of form facing material required for a concrete wall is calculated by multiplying wall length by wall height and then multiplying the total by 2. Dimensions are typically expressed in feet. The result provides the total area of the form facing (in square feet) required for both sides of a concrete wall. See Figure 11-3.

For example, the area of form facing material required for a wall 10″ thick by 38′-0″ long by 8′ high is determined by multiplying wall length by wall height by 2. The total area of form facing material required is 608 sq ft ($38′ \times 8′ \times 2 = 608$ sq ft). The number of $4′ \times 8′$ form facing panels required is determined by dividing the total area by 32. Nineteen $4′ \times 8′$ panels are required as form facing. Any fractional part of a sheet is rounded up to the next full sheet.

Lumber for formwork framing is calculated separately depending on the spacing of the studs. In addition, top and bottom plates are typically part of the form panel design. The number of studs for wall forms is calculated by dividing the wall length by the on-center spacing of the studs. The number of studs is doubled if there are two studs at each position or if studs are required for both sides of a wall.

For example, the number of studs required for a 38′-0″ long by 8′-0″ high wall with two studs placed 16″ OC is determined by multiplying the wall length by 2 (representing two studs at each position) and by .75. A total of 57 studs ($38′ \times 2 \times .75 = 57$ studs) are required for one side of the wall. A total of 114 studs ($57 \times 2 = 114$ studs) are required for both sides of the wall. Additional studs are added for each corner.

The linear feet (lf) of lumber for form plates is determined by multiplying the wall length by 2 for a single top and single bottom plate. The product is multiplied by 2 again to allow for both sides of the wall. The wall length is multiplied by 4 to allow for a form requiring double top and bottom plates. For example, a wall 38′-0″ long requiring single top and bottom plates contains 76 lf of lumber ($38′ \times 2 = 76$ lf). The wall requires a total of 152 lf ($76 \times 2 = 152$ lf) of lumber for plates on both sides of the wall.

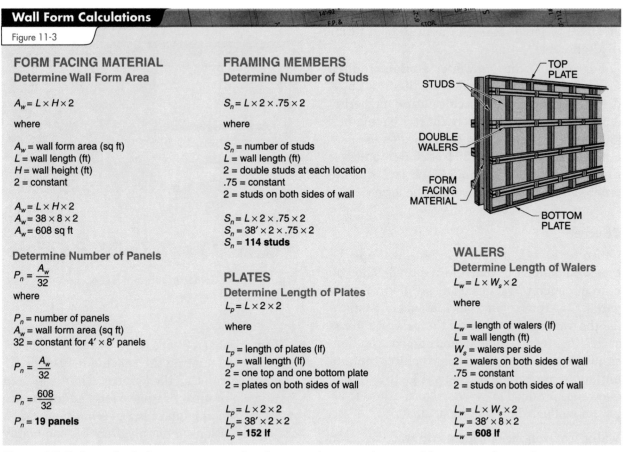

Figure 11-3. Several calculations are required to determine the materials required for concrete formwork.

A *waler* is a horizontal member used to align and reinforce concrete formwork. Wall walers are spaced at an on-center distance determined by the structural considerations of the formwork design. Lower waler rows are doubled because of greater hydrostatic pressure at the bottom of the form. The greater the height of a form, the greater the number of double rows of walers required. The number of walers required is calculated by dividing the overall form wall height by the on-center spacing to determine the number of rows of walers, then multiplying by the number of walers in each row (single or double).

For example, a 38′-0″ long by 8′-0″ high wall has double walers placed at a 2′ vertical spacing the entire wall height. The wall requires four rows of double walers (8′ ÷ 2 = 4 rows). The wall requires eight walers (4 rows × 2 walers = 8 walers). Continuous 2 × 4s are used in rows the entire length of the wall on both sides of the wall.

The total linear feet of 2 × 4 walers required is found by multiplying the length of the wall by the number of walers and then by 2 for both sides of the wall. A total of 608 lf of 2 × 4s is required for the walers (38′ × 8 × 2 = 608 lf). An allowance is typically made for overlap at all corners.

Patented Walls. Calculating the number of patented wall forms typically requires a wall elevation and a schedule of the forms required for each wall. A formwork schedule denotes the size and type of forms, quantity of each, amount of fastening hardware, type and number of snap ties, and number of walers required for the specific job.

Slab-on-Grade. Formwork for a slab-on-grade consists of an edge stop for concrete placement at the perimeter of the slab and necessary bracing. Calculating the linear feet around the perimeter of the slab area to be formed results in the linear feet of formwork required. Wood or metal bracing (stake) is used to hold forms in alignment.

For example, the formwork materials required for a 6″ thick concrete slab for a 30′-0″ × 28′-6″ detached garage requires calculating the perimeter of the structure. The perimeter equals 117′ (30′ + 30′ + 28′-6″ + 28′-6″ = 117′). To allow for overlap and material waste, 125 lf of 2 × 6s is added to the material list. Additional 2 × 4s or 1 × 4s are ordered if necessary for bracing the forms.

Concrete

Concrete takeoffs include reinforcement and the type and volume of concrete required. The volume of concrete required is specified in cubic yards. Concrete volume calculations must allow for the various variables in the concrete mixes such as aggregate, cement, and admixtures. Concrete volumes are reduced for structures containing large or numerous blockouts. A 1% to 2% waste allowance is added to concrete calculations to allow for spillage during placement.

Walls. The volume of concrete in walls is based on wall thickness, length, and height dimensions. For example, the volume of concrete for a wall 8″ thick by 30′ long by 6′ high is determined by multiplying wall thickness (in feet) by wall length by wall height for a total of 120 cu ft (.667′ × 30′ × 6′ = 120 cu ft), which equals 4.44 cu yd (120 cu ft ÷ 27 = 4.44 cu yd).

Rebar placement, spacing, and sizes are determined from details or sections. The amount of rebar (in linear feet) is determined by adding the length of the walls and multiplying by the number of rebar installed in each wall.

Slabs. The volume of concrete for slabs is determined by multiplying the surface area (in square feet) by the slab thickness (in feet). For example, the volume of concrete required for a 25′ × 48′ slab that is 16″ thick is calculated by multiplying 25′ × 48′ × 1.33′ to obtain 1596 cu ft (25′ × 48′ × 1.33′ = 1596 cu ft), which equals 59.11 cu yd (1596 cu ft ÷ 27 = 59.11 cu yd). Estimating software automatically calculates concrete volume when slab length, width, and thickness are entered. See Figure 11-4.

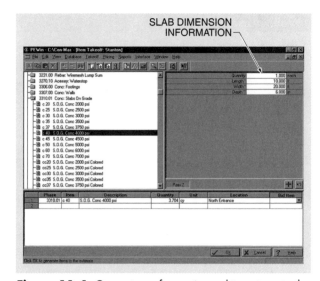

Figure 11-4. Computer software is used to automate the quantity takeoff process.

The number of each type of rebar is determined by calculating the spacing in each direction and calculating the number of bars required for a given number of square feet. Additions are made for the amount of bar overlap required in the specifications or details. Rebar is commonly priced at a cost per ton of steel. The cost per ton varies with the diameter of the rebar and type of steel.

The amount of welded wire reinforcement (WWR) required is based on the slab area (in square feet). WWR is available in rolls and sheets. Roll widths range from 5′ to 7′, and roll length is 150′ or 200′. Sheets are 5′ to 10′ wide and 10′, 20′, or 25′ long. Additions are made for overlap along the edges of the WWR.

Masonry

Masonry takeoff usually starts at the bottom of a structure and works upward, and from the outside of the structure moving inward. After calculating the amount of exterior masonry materials for foundations and walls, the amount of interior masonry materials for fireplaces, hearths, and interior walls is taken off. Materials for metal lintels over doors, windows, fireplaces, dampers, and cleanout doors are typically calculated last. The common waste factors are 2% to 5% for masonry and 10% to 20% for mortar.

The waste factor calculation is added to the area takeoff calculations.

Masonry takeoff is based on the area of masonry (in square feet) required. To calculate the number of brick in a building, the coverage area of the brick is calculated and areas not composed of brick, including any large openings, are subtracted. When calculating the quantity of face brick used as trim, the length of trim is measured and multiplied by the number of brick per linear foot.

Standard material tables are used to determine the number of masonry units required per square foot of wall. The material quantity is calculated by multiplying the area in square feet by the number of masonry units per square foot from a wall material table to determine the number of standard-size brick required for the job. See Figure 11-5.

> Mortar binds individual masonry units together. Standard mortar quantity tables are used to take off mortar quantities and ingredient amounts.

For example, to calculate the number of face brick laid in a running bond required for a brick-veneer wall that has dimensions of 24'-0" × 8'-6" and has two 3'-0" × 3'-6" window openings, the following procedure is used:

1. Calculate the area of the exterior wall. The area of the wall is 204 sq ft (24'-0" × 8'-6" = 204 sq ft).

2. Subtract the area of any openings. The area of the two openings is 21 sq ft (3'-0" × 3'-6" × 2 = 21 sq ft). The total area of the exterior wall after deducting the area of the window openings is 183 sq ft (204 sq ft − 21 sq ft = 183 sq ft).

3. Determine the number of brick required by multiplying 183 sq ft by the multiplier for an 8" brick-veneer wall or by referencing 200 sq ft on a masonry wall material table. Approximately 1232 brick are required for a 200 sq ft brick-veneer wall. Waste factors are added to the total, with other adjustments being made for mortar joint variations.

	MASONRY WALL STANDARD SIZE FACE AND BUILDING BRICK																
	Bonds																
	Running			**Common (Header Course Every 7th Course)**			**English and English Cross (Full Headers Every 6th Course)**			**Flemish (Full Headers Every 5th Course)**			**Double Headers (Alternating with Stretchers Every 5th Course)**			
Wall Area (sq ft)	**Face Brick**	**Building Brick**		**Face Brick**	**Building Brick**		**Face Brick**	**Building Brick**		**Face Brick**	**Building Brick**		**Face Brick**	**Building Brick**			
		8" Wall	**12" Wall**		**8" Wall**	**12" Wall**		**8" Wall**	**12" Wall**		**8" Wall**	**12" Wall**		**8" Wall**	**12" Wall**		
1	6.16	6.16	12.32	7.04	5.28	11.44	7.19	5.13	11.29	6.57	5.75	11.91	6.78	5.54	11.70		
5	31	31	62	36	27	58	36	26	57	33	29	60	34	28	59		
90	555	555	1110	634	476	1030	648	462	1017	592	518	1072	611	499	1053		
100	616	616	1232	704	528	1144	719	513	1129	657	575	1191	678	554	1170		
200	1232	1232	2464	1408	1056	2288	1438	1026	2258	1314	1150	2382	1356	1108	2340		
300	1848	1848	3696	2110	1584	3432	2157	1539	3387	1971	1725	3573	2034	1662	3510		
400	2464	2464	4928	2816	2112	4576	2876	2052	4516	2628	2300	4764	2712	2216	4680		
500	3080	3080	6160	3520	2640	5720	3595	2565	5645	3285	2875	5955	3390	2770	5850		

Figure 11-5. Standard tables for various masonry bonds and types of brick are used to estimate the number of brick required for a job.

The number of concrete masonry units (CMUs) required for a wall is determined by calculating the wall area (in square feet) and multiplying the answer by a standard multiplier based on the CMU used and the size of mortar joints.

The linear feet of rebar installed in masonry walls is based on the wall length and the spacing between the rebar. For example, a 20'-0" wall with two #4 rebar running horizontally and spaced 24" OC requires 40' of rebar ($20' \times 2 = 40'$).

Elevations, floor plans, and sections are used to determine the number and types of lintels over openings. Lintel quantities are calculated for each opening based on door and window schedules.

Structural and Light-Gauge Steel

Contractors work with steel fabrication shops for the manufacturing of structural steel members to ensure the proper size and shape of each member. Shop drawings are developed that indicate structural steel base plate requirements, bearing member sizes, types of welds to use, type of metals, hole locations, and other special elements necessary for a structural steel member.

Columns. To takeoff columns, each type of column is counted as an individual piece. Column locations are shown on erection plans according to a grid of letters and numbers that identify each column.

For example, a column located at the intersection of grid lines D and 2 is referred to as column D2. The design, size, and weight of each column is listed on the prints. A notation of $W12 \times 53$ indicates a column made of a wide-flange shape with a 12" web and weighing 53 lb per linear foot.

Round pipe columns have the nominal outside diameter and schedule number of the pipe indicated. For example, a round pipe column shown on a print as 8 SCH 60 indicates an 8" diameter (nominal) schedule 60 pipe column. The outside dimensions of a square tube column are indicated along with wall thickness. For example, a notation of $3 \times 3 \times ¼$ indicates a 3" square tube column with ¼" wall thickness.

Beams and Girders. Beam and girder sizes are shown on floor plans and elevations. Sizes are usually noted along the grid lines on floor plans with lengths obtained from the grid spacing dimensions. A letter and number system is used to identify each beam or girder. A schedule of beam sizes and types is provided in addition to the drawings. To perform a quantity takeoff for beams and girders, the number of structural steel beams of each type is counted.

Joists. The spacing and direction of joists is noted on floor plans. See Figure 11-6. An identification code number for a manufacturer or a fabrication shop code number is also used to identify the type of joist to be installed. A takeoff is completed by determining the type, length, and number required for all joists. Each portion of the floor or roof decking can have different types of joists, depending on the span and loads to be supported.

The takeoff of a drawing has the number of each individual type of joist listed on a spreadsheet for calculation. When performing a joist takeoff, it is common to utilize a colored marker or some other marking tool to mark on the drawing the joists that have previously been quantified, to avoid double counting or not counting a joist. Begin systematically across the building, bay by bay, to count the number of each type of joist.

Studs. Metal stud takeoff starts with a review of the prints for information concerning on-center spacing, length, gauge, and wall length (in linear feet). Multipliers for stud spacing are similar to multipliers for other framing members. For example, a 1' OC spacing requires 1 as a multiplier, a 16" OC spacing requires .75 as a multiplier, a 19.2" spacing requires .625 as a multiplier, and a 24" OC spacing requires .50 as a multiplier. Overall wall height determines stud length. Totals for each length of gauge classification must include an addition of approximately 3% to 5% for waste, depending on the overall size of the job.

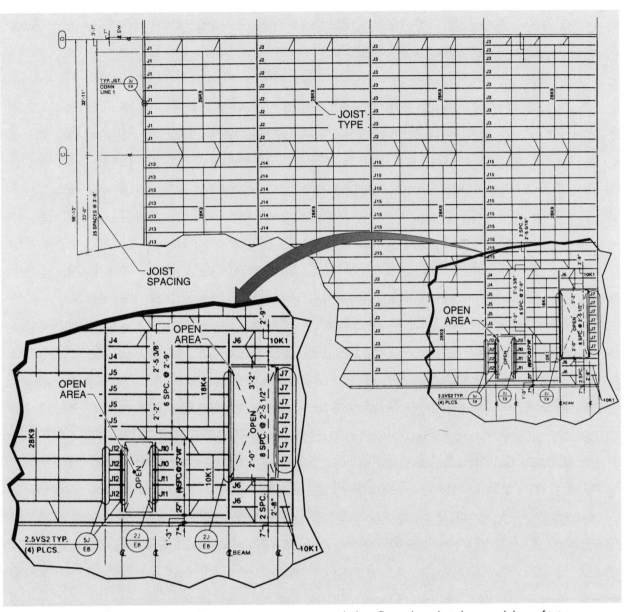

Figure 11-6. Metal bar joist type and span dimensions are provided on floor plans that show each bay of joist placement and floor or roof openings.

Metal Runners. Metal runner quantities are calculated in linear feet. The total length of metal-framed walls is multiplied by 2 to determine the linear feet of runner for the top and bottom track. Additional material is included for soffits and window, door, and frame openings.

Decking. A roof panel plan of a steel floor or roof deck is included in typical erection plans. See Figure 11-7. Takeoff for metal floor or roof decking is accomplished by counting the number of each type of decking piece used.

Structural Wood Members

Structural wood framing members are quantified for a takeoff by the individual number of pieces. Timber components are specified according to each piece and dimension. Sheathing materials are calculated according to the area (in square feet) to be covered.

Lumber dimensions are always specified as thickness, width, and length.

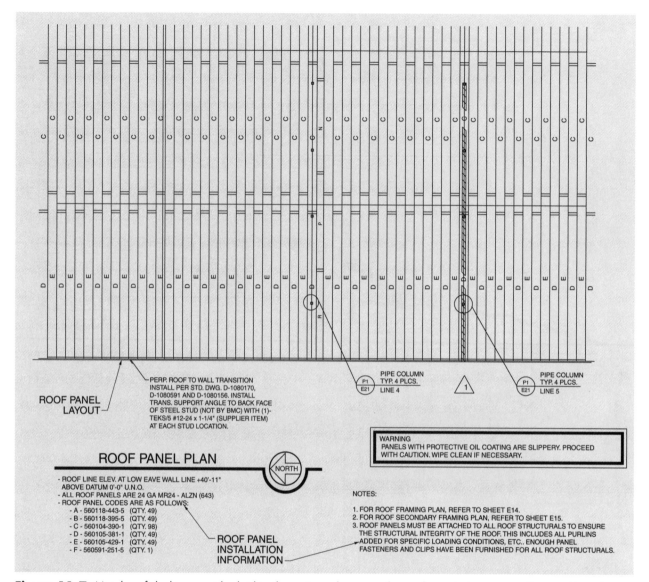

ROOF PANEL LAYOUT

PERP. ROOF TO WALL TRANSITION INSTALL PER STD. DWG. D-1080170, D-1080591 AND D-1080156. INSTALL TRANS. SUPPORT ANGLE TO BACK FACE OF STEEL STUD (NOT BY BMC) WITH (1)- TEKS/5 #12-24 x 1-1/4" (SUPPLIER ITEM) AT EACH STUD LOCATION.

PIPE COLUMN TYP. 4 PLCS.
P1 E21   LINE 4

PIPE COLUMN TYP. 4 PLCS.
P1 E21   LINE 5

ROOF PANEL PLAN NORTH

- ROOF LINE ELEV. AT LOW EAVE WALL LINE +40'-11" ABOVE DATUM 0'-0" U.N.O.
- ALL ROOF PANELS ARE 24 GA MR24 - ALZN (643)
- ROOF PANEL CODES ARE AS FOLLOWS:
  - A - 560118-443-5   (QTY. 49)
  - B - 560118-395-5   (QTY. 49)
  - C - 560104-390-1   (QTY. 98)
  - D - 560105-381-1   (QTY. 49)
  - E - 560105-429-1   (QTY. 49)
  - F - 560591-251-5   (QTY. 1)

ROOF PANEL INSTALLATION INFORMATION

WARNING
PANELS WITH PROTECTIVE OIL COATING ARE SLIPPERY. PROCEED WITH CAUTION. WIPE CLEAN IF NECESSARY.

NOTES:

1. FOR ROOF FRAMING PLAN, REFER TO SHEET E14.
2. FOR ROOF SECONDARY FRAMING PLAN, REFER TO SHEET E15.
3. ROOF PANELS MUST BE ATTACHED TO ALL ROOF STRUCTURALS TO ENSURE THE STRUCTURAL INTEGRITY OF THE ROOF. THIS INCLUDES ALL PURLINS ADDED FOR SPECIFIC LOADING CONDITIONS, ETC.. ENOUGH PANEL FASTENERS AND CLIPS HAVE BEEN FURNISHED FOR ALL ROOF STRUCTURALS.

Figure 11-7. Metal roof decking must be laid in the pattern shown on the roof panel plan to coordinate with roof panel quantities.

Structural wood members include sill plates, floor joists, floor and wall sheathing, top and bottom wall plates, studs, headers, bracing and blocking materials, ceiling joists, roof rafters, roof trusses, and roof sheathing. Timber framing members include glulam members, timbers, and planking.

The species, grade, stress rating, and moisture content of structural lumber is noted in the specifications. Structural lumber measurements are stated as thickness, width, and length. Standard lumber length is based on a multiple of 2', normally beginning at 8' in length and extending to 16' or 18'. Structural lumber length is always rounded up to the nearest 2' dimension for purchasing. Dimensions are taken from the architectural drawings and used to determine the number of each type of structural wood member.

Sill Plates. Sill plate quantities are calculated by determining the perimeter of the foundation walls (in linear feet) to be covered and the nominal size of the sill plates. The perimeter of foundation walls is determined based on dimensions on the foundation and floor plans. A notation on details or sections usually indicates the nominal size of sill plates. For example, a rectangular foundation measuring 48′ × 58′ requires 212 lf (48′ + 58′ + 48′ + 58′ = 212 lf) of lumber for the sill plates.

Floor Joists. The type and number of floor joists required is calculated by determining the nominal size, length, and on-center spacing of the joists from the floor plan, specifications, notations, or details. Floor joist length depends on the span between structural supporting members such as the sill plates and beams. Sufficient length is allowed for an adequate amount of joist overlap. For example, a 14′ floor joist is used when the distance between the outside of a sill plate and the center of the supporting beam is 13′-4″.

Similar to other framing members with on-center spacing, a multiplier is used to determine the actual number of joists required. A multiplier of 1 is used when joists are spaced 1′-0″ OC, .75 when joists are spaced 16″ OC, .625 when joists are spaced 19.2″ OC, and .5 when joists are spaced 2′-0″ OC. Additional floor joists are added and subtracted for stairwell openings, structure perimeter, and cantilevers.

Girders and Beams. Dimensions for wood girders and beams are determined from floor plans and details. The lumber and design of engineered or trussed components are shown on details and listed in the specifications. Girders, beams, engineered lumber, and trusses are counted as individual units for a takeoff.

Wall Framing Members. Wall framing members include plates, studs, headers, sills, blocking, and bracing. Each wall framing member requires a different method of calculation for the takeoff.

Plates, studs, sills, and blocking are usually the same width for an entire structure. In some cases, the exterior walls are framed with 2 × 6s and the interior partitions are framed with 2 × 4s. The number of linear feet of wall plates and lumber sizes are calculated from the wall length dimensions. The required length of plate material is calculated by adding the wall lengths

and multiplying by 2 for walls with single top plates or by 3 for walls with double top plates. For example, the exterior wall of a building shown on a floor plan has outside dimensions of 58′-0″ × 28′-0″ for a total of 172 lf of exterior walls (58′ + 28′ + 58′ + 28′ = 172 lf). See Figure 11-8. When single top plates are used, the total linear feet of plate material is 344′ (172′ × 2 = 344′). When double top plates are used, the total linear feet of plate material is 516′ (172′ × 3 = 516 lf).

Takeoff for headers over windows and doors is calculated by adding the opening width and enough room for the jamb and shim clearance on both sides. Approximately 2″ should be allowed for the jamb and shim clearance for common windows; 3″ is allowed for heavier windows and doors to provide room for an additional stud to allow for extra weight on each end of the header. The resulting value is multiplied by 2 for double headers. For example, a 2′-8″ wide swinging door has a 2′-10″ rough opening plus a 3″ jamb and shim allowance for a total of 3′-1″. A 3′-1″ single solid header is required for the opening (2′-10″ + 3″ = 3′-1″). The value is multiplied by 2 for a double header (3′-1″ × 2 = 6′-2″). An 8′ piece of header material is typically ordered for a double-header door opening.

The method for calculating the number of wall studs is similar to calculating the number of any structural member with an on-center spacing. For walls with studs 16″ OC, the wall length is multiplied by .75 to calculate the number of studs. For walls with studs 24″ OC, the wall length is multiplied by .5. Other elements to consider when determining the number of studs in a wall include additional studs required at intersecting walls and studs that may be omitted at door or window openings. One additional stud is added to the calculated number to complete wall framing at each corner.

Additional wall framing members are added for windowsills, cripple studs, blocking, header framing, intersecting wall framing, and bracing. The additional members are added based on the number of door and window openings and other framing requirements.

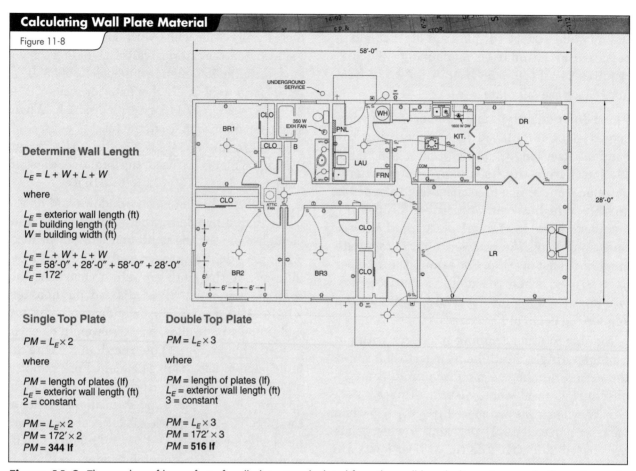

Calculating Wall Plate Material

Figure 11-8

Determine Wall Length

$L_E = L + W + L + W$

where

L_E = exterior wall length (ft)
L = building length (ft)
W = building width (ft)

$L_E = L + W + L + W$
$L_E = 58'\text{-}0'' + 28'\text{-}0'' + 58'\text{-}0'' + 28'\text{-}0''$
$L_E = 172'$

Single Top Plate

$PM = L_E \times 2$

where

PM = length of plates (lf)
L_E = exterior wall length (ft)
2 = constant

$PM = L_E \times 2$
$PM = 172' \times 2$
$PM = \textbf{344 lf}$

Double Top Plate

$PM = L_E \times 3$

where

PM = length of plates (lf)
L_E = exterior wall length (ft)
3 = constant

$PM = L_E \times 3$
$PM = 172' \times 3$
$PM = \textbf{516 lf}$

Figure 11-8. The number of linear feet of wall plates is calculated from the wall length dimensions on the floor plan and notations on details or specifications.

Ceiling Joists and Trusses. Ceiling joist length is determined based on the location of bearing walls on the floor plan. The quantity and type of material for ceiling joists is calculated depending on the on-center spacing (similar to floor joists and wall studs).

The number of roof trusses required is also calculated according to the on-center spacing of the trusses. For example, the number of roof trusses required for a structure that is 58′ long with roof trusses spaced 24″ OC is calculated by multiplying 58′ by .5 to obtain 29 trusses (58′ × .5 = 29 trusses). The number is rounded up to 30 trusses to allow for an additional truss at the end.

Wood Panels. The number of wood panels required for applications including floor decking, wall sheathing, and roof sheathing is determined based on area calculations. Each 4′ × 8′ panel

covers 32 sq ft. The number of panels required for an area is determined by dividing the total area (in square feet) to be covered by 32. Approximately 7% is added for waste material to determine the total number of panels required.

The number of subfloor or underlayment panels required for a floor is based on floor plan dimensions. For example, the floor area of a T-shaped structure is comprised of two basic rectangles of 32′ × 24′ and 22′ × 14′. The total floor area is 1076 sq ft ([32′ × 24′] + [22′ × 14′] = 1076 sq ft). The total floor area is divided by 32 to determine that 33.625 subfloor panels are required (1076 sq ft ÷ 32 = 33.625 panels). Approximately 7% is added for waste for a total of 35.98 panels (33.625 × 1.07 = 35.98 panels). The number is rounded up for a total of 36 panels. Deductions are made for large floor openings such as stairwells. See Figure 11-9.

Calculating the Number of Subfloor Panels

Figure 11-9

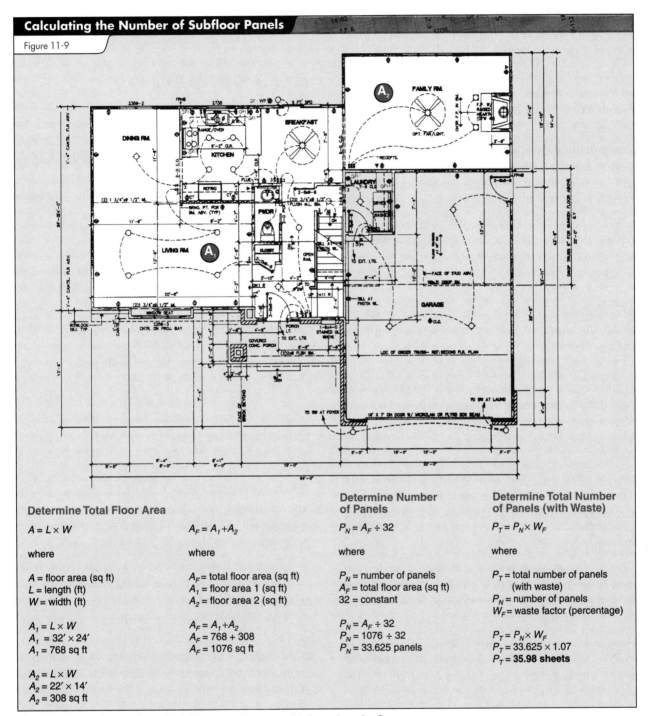

Determine Total Floor Area

$A = L \times W$

where

A = floor area (sq ft)
L = length (ft)
W = width (ft)

$A_1 = L \times W$
$A_1 = 32' \times 24'$
$A_1 = 768$ sq ft

$A_2 = L \times W$
$A_2 = 22' \times 14'$
$A_2 = 308$ sq ft

$A_F = A_1 + A_2$

where

A_F = total floor area (sq ft)
A_1 = floor area 1 (sq ft)
A_2 = floor area 2 (sq ft)

$A_F = A_1 + A_2$
$A_F = 768 + 308$
$A_F = 1076$ sq ft

Determine Number of Panels

$P_N = A_F \div 32$

where

P_N = number of panels
A_F = total floor area (sq ft)
32 = constant

$P_N = A_F \div 32$
$P_N = 1076 \div 32$
$P_N = 33.625$ panels

Determine Total Number of Panels (with Waste)

$P_T = P_N \times W_F$

where

P_T = total number of panels (with waste)
P_N = number of panels
W_F = waste factor (percentage)

$P_T = P_N \times W_F$
$P_T = 33.625 \times 1.07$
$P_T = \mathbf{35.98}$ **sheets**

Figure 11-9. The number of subfloor panels required is based on the floor area.

The number of panels needed to cover exterior walls is calculated using individual exterior wall lengths that are added to determine the total length of the walls (in linear feet). The total length is divided by 4 to estimate the number of $4' \times 8'$ sheets of wall sheathing for an 8' high wall.

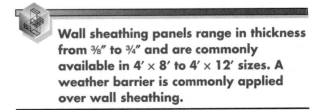

Wall sheathing panels range in thickness from ⅜" to ¾" and are commonly available in $4' \times 8'$ to $4' \times 12'$ sizes. A weather barrier is commonly applied over wall sheathing.

For example, the length of the exterior walls of a building is 227'-6". The exterior wall requires 56.875 panels (227.5' ÷ 4 = 56.875 panels) of 4' wide wall sheathing. The number is rounded up to 57 panels. The square foot method may also be used to determine the amount of wall sheathing required.

Roof sheathing calculations are based on rafter length and roof pitch. Rafter length is determined by the run of the roof shown on the floor plan and the pitch shown on exterior elevations. Steeply pitched roofs result in longer rafter lengths and require additional sheathing. The amount of sheathing required for a roof section is determined by multiplying rafter length by the length of the roof section. The roof area (in square feet) is divided by 32 to determine the number of 4' × 8' roof sheathing panels required.

For example, the number of roof sheathing panels required for a gable roof is determined by calculating the roof area and dividing by the area of the roof sheathing panels. See Figure 11-10. The dimensions of a rectangular light frame building with a gable roof are 53' × 41'. The rafters have a 4" in 12" pitch (12.65" run per foot). The rafter length for the roof is determined by multiplying the 12.65" run per foot by one-half of the main roof span of 41' (20.5') and dividing by 12 to obtain 21.61' ([12.65 × 20.5'] ÷ 12 = 21.61'). The roof length is multiplied by the rafter length and 2 to determine the total roof area (53' × 21.61' × 2 = 2290.66 sq ft). The total is divided by the coverage area of one roof sheathing panel (32 sq ft) to determine the number of panels required (2290.66 ÷ 32 = 71.58 panels). Five percent waste allowance is added for a total of 75.16 panels (71.58 panels × 1.05 = 75.16 panels). The number is rounded up to 76 roof sheathing panels.

FINISH MATERIALS

Takeoff for finish materials includes both exterior and interior finishes. Exterior finish materials include wall and roof coverings. Interior finish materials include walls, flooring, trim members, and fixtures such as cabinetry. Doors and windows are also taken off as finish materials. Each finish material is taken off in a different manner.

Exterior Walls and Siding

Exterior wall covering materials are calculated according to the area of coverage required (in square feet). Deductions are made for large wall openings such as doors and windows. Siding types and styles and other exterior wall finishes such as exterior insulation and finish systems (EIFS) appear on exterior elevations with various symbols and notations.

The areas of walls covered with siding are calculated in square feet. When taking off vinyl or wood siding, the total wall area is divided by 100 sq ft to determine the number of squares of vinyl or wood siding required. A *square* is a unit of measure equal to 100 sq ft.

For example, an exterior wall shown on an elevation is 48' long by 8' high. A chimney that is 5'-4" wide is subtracted from the overall wall length, resulting in 42.67' (48' − 5.33' = 42.67'). The total coverage area (in square feet) is determined to be 341.36' (42.67' × 8' = 341.36 sq ft). A waste factor of 5% is added for a total of 358.43 sq ft (341.36 sq ft × 1.05 = 358.43 sq ft). Approximately 3½ squares of siding are required to cover the wall (358.43 ÷ 100 = 3.58 squares). Four squares of siding are ordered for the job.

When applying EIFS, the total wall area to be covered is determined when calculating the number of square feet covered by expanded polystyrene, fiber reinforcing, or the number of gallons of finish coating material required based on manufacturer recommendations. The materials are added to a materials list with additional materials such as corners and edge materials calculated by the linear foot based on wall openings and perimeter conditions.

Panel Siding. Panel siding takeoff is based on the length of the wall to be covered. Panel siding is commonly manufactured in 4' × 8' and 4' × 9' sizes, and applied with the 4' dimension in a horizontal direction. The horizontal length of the exterior wall surface to be covered is divided by 4 to determine the number of panels required.

Quantity Takeoff **429**

Calculating the Number of Roof Sheathing Panels

Figure 11-10

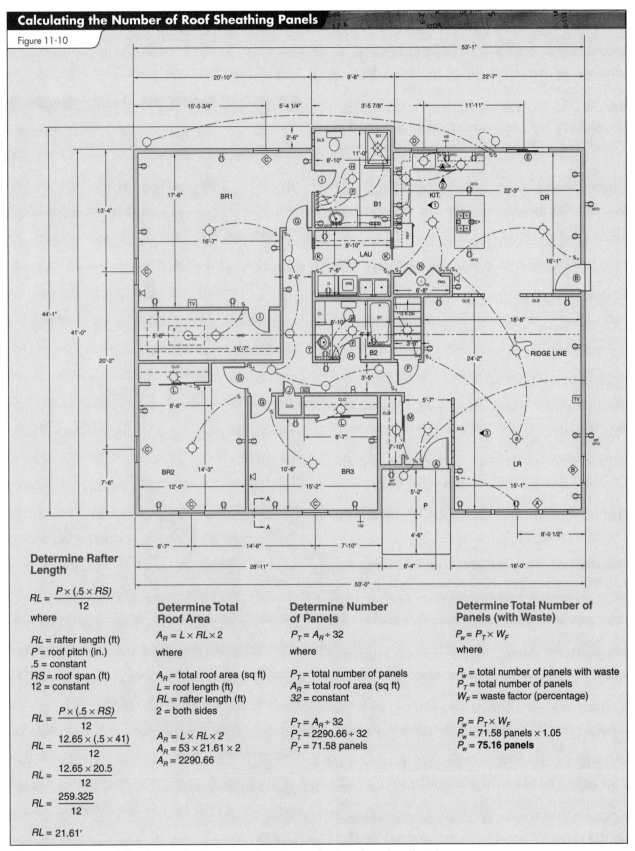

Determine Rafter Length

$$RL = \frac{P \times (.5 \times RS)}{12}$$

where

RL = rafter length (ft)
P = roof pitch (in.)
$.5$ = constant
RS = roof span (ft)
12 = constant

$$RL = \frac{P \times (.5 \times RS)}{12}$$

$$RL = \frac{12.65 \times (.5 \times 41)}{12}$$

$$RL = \frac{12.65 \times 20.5}{12}$$

$$RL = \frac{259.325}{12}$$

$$RL = 21.61'$$

Determine Total Roof Area

$$A_R = L \times RL \times 2$$

where

A_R = total roof area (sq ft)
L = roof length (ft)
RL = rafter length (ft)
2 = both sides

$$A_R = L \times RL \times 2$$
$$A_R = 53 \times 21.61 \times 2$$
$$A_R = 2290.66$$

Determine Number of Panels

$$P_T = A_R \div 32$$

where

P_T = total number of panels
A_R = total roof area (sq ft)
32 = constant

$$P_T = A_R \div 32$$
$$P_T = 2290.66 \div 32$$
$$P_T = 71.58 \text{ panels}$$

Determine Total Number of Panels (with Waste)

$$P_W = P_T \times W_F$$

where

P_W = total number of panels with waste
P_T = total number of panels
W_F = waste factor (percentage)

$$P_W = P_T \times W_F$$
$$P_W = 71.58 \text{ panels} \times 1.05$$
$$P_W = \textbf{75.16 panels}$$

Figure 11-10. Roof sheathing calculations are based on rafter length and roof pitch.

For example, a wall 38'-8" long would require ten 4' × 8' sheets of siding (38.67' ÷ 4 = 9.67 sheets). The plans are referred to in order to ensure the proper length of panel is added to the material list. Other trim members such as Z molding or other weatherstripping and edge treatments are also added to the material list after checking the specifications and elevations.

Metal. The length of vertical metal siding panels required for a building depends on the wall height. Wall length is divided by the width of each metal panel to determine the number of panels required. Metal trim members or anchor clips are required by some manufacturers. See Figure 11-11. Specifications and manufacturer notes are checked to verify that all items and components are included for installing vertical metal siding panels.

Roofing

The method of taking off for roofing materials depends on the roofing applied. Bituminous, elastomeric, composition shingles, wood shakes or shingles, and sheet metal each require slightly different calculations. Roofing material quantities are determined based on the total area of a roof (in square feet) or by the length of the roof (in linear feet).

Bituminous and Elastomeric. Bituminous or elastomeric roofing for flat or slightly pitched roofs is taken off according to the roof area to be covered. For example, the amount of elastomeric roofing material required can be calculated. See Figure 11-12. The elastomeric portion of the roof is 30' × 30' with ½" slope per foot. The small amount of slope is insignificant for the roof size so the roof area is calculated as 900 sq ft (30' × 30' = 900 sq ft). A stairway opening of 45 sq ft (15' × 3' = 45 sq ft) is present, which is subtracted from the roof area of 900 sq ft (900 sq ft – 45 sq ft = 855 sq ft) of elastomeric roofing required. Manufacturer specifications are consulted to adjust the roof area calculations for required overlaps. Additional roofing material is also added to allow for any wrap of the roofing such

as up onto a parapet surrounding the elastomeric roof section. If a parapet has a 120' perimeter, an additional 120 sq ft are added for each foot of height of the parapet.

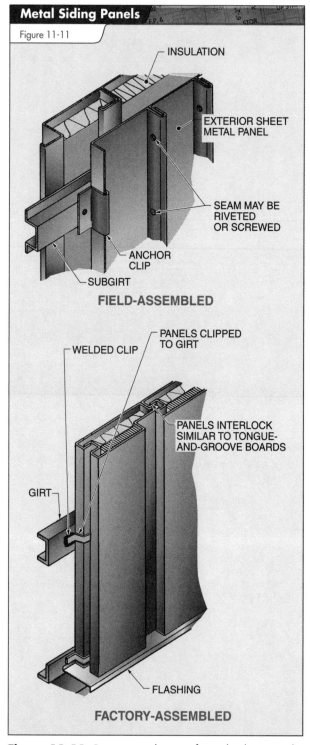

Figure 11-11. Proper attachment of metal siding panels to structural members requires proper clipping.

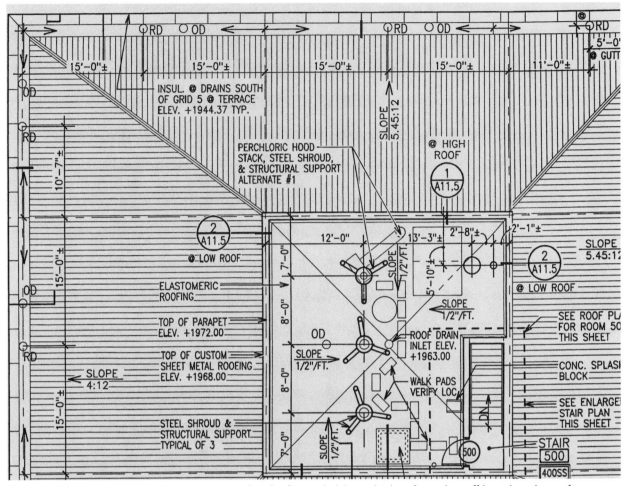

Figure 11-12. Bituminous and elastomeric roofing for flat or slightly pitched roofs is taken off based on the roof area to be covered.

Metal. Information necessary for taking off metal roofing includes the width of the metal sheets, the seams used at the edges, the sheets specified by the architect, and the square feet of coverage. The length of run of each piece of metal roofing is compared to the length of metal roofing materials available to determine the number of seams. The total length of the roof is divided by the width of a metal sheet to determine the number of sheets and the number of seams required.

For example, a building that has five sections of custom metal roofing has each section calculated individually, taking into account the roof length and slope. See Figure 11-13. The length of the rafters per foot of run must also be determined. For metal roof calculations for roof section 4A, the unit run of the roof section is a 4″ in

12″ slope or 12.65″. The length of a common rafter is calculated by multiplying the unit run by the required rafter run (12.65″ × 30′ = 31′-7½″). The area (in square feet) for the main rafter section is calculated by multiplying the length of the roof for section 4A (in linear feet) by the rafter length (30′ × 31′-7½″ = 948.75 sq ft). The area of a hip roof area (section 4B) is determined in a manner similar to that of a straight roof run, but the area is divided by 2 to allow for the triangular-shaped roof areas. The roof area for section 4A is divided by 2 for a result of 474.375 sq ft (948.75 ÷ 2 = 474.375 sq ft).

Metal roofing material that is 32′ long is utilized to avoid seams. As with other roofing products, manufacturer recommendations are useful when determining the amount to allow for waste, seams, and edge treatments.

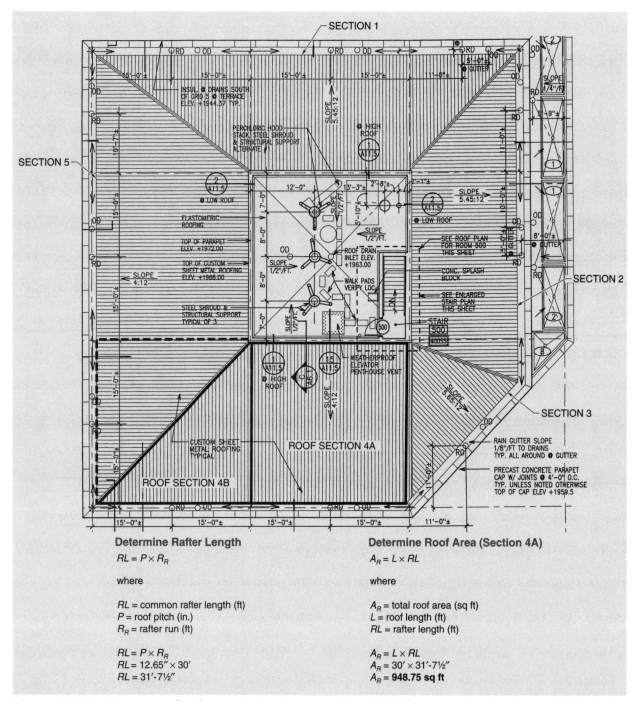

Figure 11-13. Various types of roof materials, dimensions, and slopes of roof sections are indicated on roof plans.

Determine Rafter Length

$RL = P \times R_R$

where

RL = common rafter length (ft)
P = roof pitch (in.)
R_R = rafter run (ft)

$RL = P \times R_R$
$RL = 12.65'' \times 30'$
$RL = 31'\text{-}7\frac{1}{2}''$

Determine Roof Area (Section 4A)

$A_R = L \times RL$

where

A_R = total roof area (sq ft)
L = roof length (ft)
RL = rafter length (ft)

$A_R = L \times RL$
$A_R = 30' \times 31'\text{-}7\frac{1}{2}''$
$A_R = \textbf{948.75 sq ft}$

Shingles and Tiles. Roof area takeoff for shingles and tile is determined by calculating the number of squares required for coverage. A square equals 100 sq ft of coverage. The total area of sloped roofs is determined by multiplying the roof width by the rafter length. Rafter length is determined from floor plan dimensions and slope information on exterior elevations. A waste factor of 10% is added for composition shingles, 20% for slate shingles, and 18% for roofing tiles. The total roof area is divided by 100 to determine the number of squares required for the roof. The area of any ridges, valleys, and hips covered is added to the total area.

For example, the number of shingle squares required for a gable roof of a structure must be calculated. The total roof area (2969.16 sq ft) is multiplied by a waste factor of 10% to obtain a total of 3266.08 sq ft (2969.16 sq ft × 1.10 = 3266.08 sq ft). The total area is divided by 100 to determine that 32.66 squares of shingles are required (2203.2 sq ft ÷ 100 = 32.66 squares). This number will be rounded to the next higher whole value, 33 squares. For composition shingles, additional bundles of shingles are added to the total to cover the ridge based on the type of shingle used and manufacturer recommendations. See Figure 11-14.

Interior Walls and Flooring

Many types of interior wall finishes can be applied depending on the durability and appearance desired. Gypsum board is one of the most common interior wall finish materials due to its economy, durability, and flexibility of appearance. Flooring materials are selected based on the same criteria as interior wall finishes. Carpet, tile, hardwood, and resilient flooring are the most common interior floor finish materials, and each is available in many grades, colors, and styles.

Southern Forest Products Association
A moisture meter is used to check the moisture content of strip flooring before it is installed.

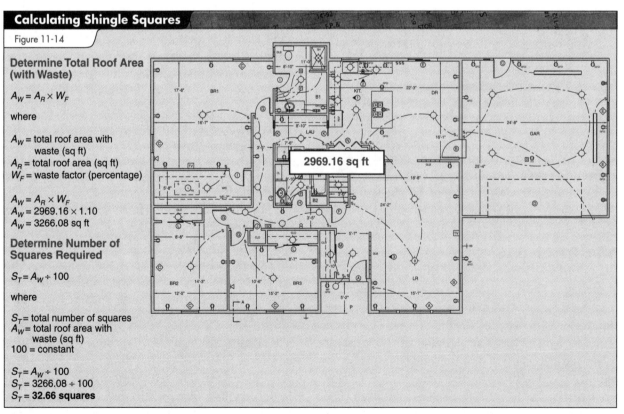

Figure 11-14. The total roof area with waste is based on the total roof area. Various waste factors are used for shingles and tiles such as 10% for composition shingles, 20% for slate shingles, and 18% for roof tiles.

Gypsum Board. The type of gypsum board and thickness are typically shown on details and room finish schedules. Takeoff is based on the area of interior wall coverage (in square feet). Prints and specifications are referred to in order to determine the number of gypsum board sheets required and the direction of application. In some areas, two or more layers of gypsum board can be specified. For some applications, gypsum board sheets are installed with the long dimension of the sheet running vertically, while other applications use horizontal installation. The orientation of the sheets determines the length of the sheets ordered. The length of the sheets also affects the coverage area of each gypsum board sheet. Gypsum board sheets are commonly 4′ wide, and are available in 8′, 12′, or 16′ lengths. Lengths are matched to room sizes to avoid an excessive number of joints between sheets.

For example, the number of sheets of gypsum board required for a bedroom is calculated using wall and ceiling areas. A bedroom with 8′ walls has dimensions of 17′ × 11′. Gypsum board sheets (4′ × 12′) are specified to be installed in the horizontal position. The total wall surface area is determined to be 448 sq ft (17′ + 11′ + 17′ + 11′ = 56 lf; 56 lf × 8′ height = 448 sq ft). Ten sheets of gypsum board are required for the walls (448 sq ft ÷ 48 sq ft = 9.33, rounded to 10). The ceiling area is 187 sq ft (17′ × 11′ = 187 sq ft) and is to be covered with 4′ × 12′ sheets of gypsum board. Four sheets of gypsum board are required to cover the ceiling (187 sq ft ÷ 48 sq ft = 3.89, rounded to 4). A total of 14 sheets of 4′ × 12′ gypsum board are required to cover the walls and ceiling of the bedroom (10 + 4 = 14 sheets).

Wood Paneling. A typical sheet of wood paneling measures 4′ × 8′, with the 8′ dimension running in the direction of the grain. To calculate the number of sheets of wall paneling required for walls 8′ or less in height, the wall length is divided by 4 if the 8′ dimension of the panel is oriented vertically. For example, the number of sheets of paneling required for a living room measuring 13′-0″ × 19′-6″ can be calculated. The paneling is installed with the short dimension running horizontally (grain vertical). The number of sheets of paneling is determined by calculating the wall length (13′ + 19′-6″ + 13′ + 19′-6″ = 65 lf) and dividing by 4, resulting in 16.25 sheets (65 lf ÷ 4 = 16.25 sheets) of paneling. Five percent waste is added, resulting in 17.06 sheets (16.25 sheets × 1.05 = 17.06 sheets) of paneling required. The total is rounded up to the next full sheet, making it necessary to purchase 18 sheets of paneling.

Flooring. Most rooms and areas on floor plans are named, numbered, or coded. The specifications or finish schedule identifies the floor finish materials to be installed. For large rooms or areas, the floor finish material is noted on the plans or on a specific detail that includes a note about the floor finish material. The amount of material required to finish a floor is determined by the total area to be covered in square feet or square yards, depending on the material specified. Quantity takeoffs for carpet and resilient flooring are calculated in square yards.

For example, carpet for a 10′-6″ × 9′-6″ bedroom is calculated by determining the floor area of 99.75 sq ft (10′-6″ × 9′-6″ = 99.75 sq ft) and dividing by 9 to determine the number of square yards of carpet required. Eleven square yards of carpet are required (99.75 sq ft ÷ 9 = 11.08 sq yd). Hardwood flooring and tile takeoffs are typically calculated in square feet. Any large openings such as stairwells are deducted during flooring takeoff calculations.

Trim Members

Finish materials and trim members are taken off in linear feet calculations or counted as individual pieces. Trim members include various moldings, cabinets, doors, windows, and other specialty items. Specifications and schedules are often required to accurately perform quantity takeoffs for trim materials.

Moldings. Moldings such as baseboard, casing, chair rail, and crown molding are taken off by the linear foot. The total linear feet of molding is determined from wall length dimensions on the floor plan. Tabulation is made for each type of molding required.

Baseboard molding is calculated in linear feet as a total length of the walls that create the perimeter of an area. Deductions are made for doors or large openings. The perimeters of all rooms are added and the total amount of baseboard required is determined. For example, the linear feet of baseboard molding required for a dining/living room area of a residence is based on the total linear feet of 54'-11" of walls (22'-9" + 6'-4" + 6'-4" + 9'-6" + 10' = 54'-11"). A minimum of 55' of baseboard is required for the rooms (with no allowances for doors or windows). Some additions may be necessary for fitting at the corners.

Casing length depends on the width and height of each door or window opening. For a 2'-6" × 6'-8" door, casing is installed on each side (6'-8" × 2 = 13'-4"). A 7'-0" length is required at each side to allow for mitering at each top corner. A 3'-0" piece of casing is required across the top of the door opening to allow for mitering (depending on the casing width). The total door casing required is 17 lf (7' + 7' + 3' = 17 lf).

Cabinets. Interior elevation drawings and related schedules provide location, dimension, and finish information for cabinets. See Figure 11-15. Notations and codes on interior elevations relate to a cabinet schedule. A cabinet schedule indicates width, height, and depth of each cabinet. A cabinet schedule or detail is provided to a cabinet shop for shop-built cabinets. Material takeoff calculations for job-built cabinets include materials used to construct the cabinets such as particleboard, plywood, and exterior finish material(s).

Doors. Door takeoff considerations include door type, height, width, thickness, material, hand (for swinging doors), transoms, hinge type and placement, lockset, fire rating, and door inserts such as louvers or lights. Doors are counted as individual units and similar doors are grouped together.

The number of doors and jambs can be individually counted and totaled from floor plans. A door schedule is another source of door information. See Figure 11-16.

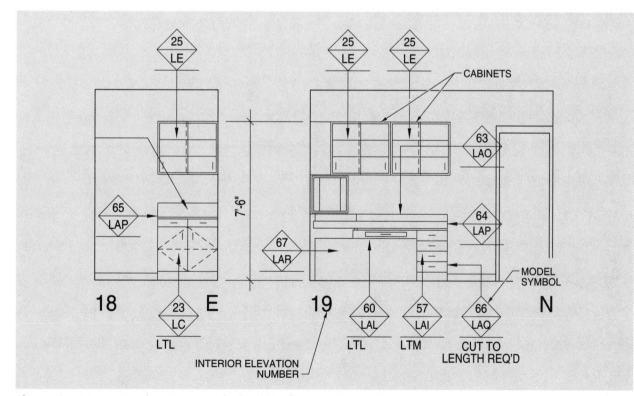

Figure 11-15. Interior elevations provide detailed information for cabinetry takeoff.

DOOR SCHEDULE ⬡

MARK	SIZE	TYPE	MAT'L	REMARKS
1	1¾" X 3'-0" X 6'-8"	FRONT EXT	INSUL MTL	W/12" SL
2	1¾" X 3'-0" X 6'-8"	FULL GLS	INSUL MTL	
3	1¾" X 3'-0" X 6'-8"	½ GLS	INSUL MTL	
4	1¾" X 3'-0" X 6'-8"	SC	INSUL MTL	
5	1⅜" X 3'-0" X 6'-8"	HC	BIRCH	6-PANEL
6	1⅜" X 2'-8" X 6'-8"	HC	BIRCH	6-PANEL
7	1⅜" X 2'-6" X 6'-8"	HC	BIRCH	6-PANEL
8	1⅜" X 2'-4" X 6'-8"	HC	BIRCH	6-PANEL
9	4'-0" X 6'-8"	POCKET	BIRCH	6-PANEL
10	4'-0" X 6'-8"	BYPASS	BIRCH	6-PANEL
11	2'-6" X 6'-8"	BYPASS	BIRCH	6-PANEL
12	1⅜" X 5'-0" X 4'-6"	HC	BIRCH	LOW HEADER
13	9'-0" X 7'-0"	OHD	HRDBD	FLUSH

WINDOW SCHEDULE ⬡

MARK	SIZE	TYPE	MFG	MFG#	REMARKS
A	2'-10 ¼" X 5'-0⅜"	CASEMENT	ANDERSEN	CR25	
B	4'-9" X 4'-0 ½"	CASEMENT	ANDERSEN	CW24	
C	2'-0 ⅝" X 5'-0⅜"	CASEMENT	ANDERSEN	C15	
D	7'-1⅞" X 5'-0⅜"	CASEMENT	ANDERSEN	CW15-3	
E	7'-1⅞" X 4'-0 ½"	CASEMENT	ANDERSEN	CW14-3	
F	4'-3¾" X 3'-0 ½"	CASEMENT	ANDERSEN	CR13-3	
G	4'-9" X 5'-0 ⅝"	CASEMENT	ANDERSEN	CW25	
H	6'-0⅜" X 3'-5⅝"	CASEMENT	ANDERSEN	C335	
J	4'-0 ½" X 3'-5⅜"	CASEMENT	ANDERSEN	C235	
K	3'-0" X 3'-0"	SKYLIGHT	VELUX	302	
L	21" X 46"	SKYLIGHT	VETTER	24FS	
M	3'-0" Ø	GLSS BLK			CUSTOM
N	4" X 32"	GLSS BLK			CUSTOM
O	7'-1⅞" X 5'-2⅝"	CIRCLE TOP	ANDERSEN	CTC3	

Figure 11-16. Door and window schedules indicate the sizes and types of doors and windows throughout a structure.

Windows. The number of windows and frames can also be individually counted and totaled from floor plans. A window schedule is usually provided that is related to the floor plans and elevations to further describe the number and types of windows required. Window schedules denote manufacturer identification codes that represent window frame and glass types.

MECHANICAL AND ELECTRICAL SYSTEMS

Mechanical system takeoffs include all piping, fittings, ductwork, equipment, and fixtures. Electrical takeoffs include interior and exterior wiring, electrical equipment, and electrical finish materials. See Figure 11-17. Specific dimensions for piping, ductwork, and electrical wiring are not typically provided. Location dimensions are obtained from architectural and structural plan views and elevations. For commercial buildings, mechanical and electrical information may be shown on specific mechanical or electrical plans.

Mechanical and electrical systems include equipment, piping, and wiring.

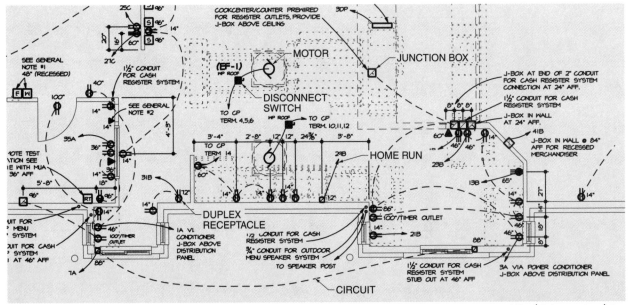

Wendy's International, Inc.

Figure 11-17. Detailed electrical plans are included on commercial prints to assist in electrical material takeoff.

Mechanical Systems

Heating, ventilating, and air conditioning (HVAC) systems provide temperature control and air circulation requirements for living areas, offices, meeting rooms, classrooms, and work areas. Floor plans and mechanical plans show the information required for quantity takeoffs for HVAC systems. Specifications, general notations, and schedules contain information concerning manufacturer designs and equipment codes. For example, an exhaust fan schedule notes that exhaust fan #6 is manufactured by Harrington Company, and is model number HPC 1050.

Piping. Mechanical system piping includes sanitary drainage and stormwater drainage piping, hot and cold supply water piping, natural gas piping, HVAC ductwork, and boiler piping if required. Isometric drawings are not typically provided with a set of prints for a small building. A plumbing contractor may be responsible for developing an isometric drawing. Isometric drawings may be provided on commercial buildings to help visualize the installation better. See Figure 11-18. Takeoff for piping and ductwork is performed in linear feet for each type of pipe or duct required.

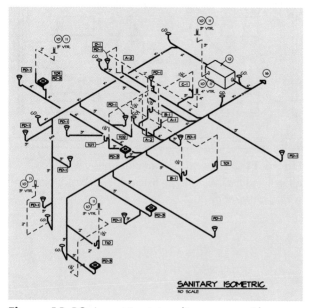

Figure 11-18. Isometric piping diagrams provide information regarding pipe diameter, type, purpose, and fittings for quantity takeoff.

For example, Room 109 ductwork is shown on a mechanical plan, which has a scale of ⅛″ = 1′-0″. Quantity takeoff begins by listing each individual type of duct required. Using an architect's scale, the linear feet of each type of pipe or duct can be calculated. The main portion of a 16″ × 15″ supply air duct is 14′ long, and the return duct is 2′ long. As with other portions of the drawings, each item is marked to note that it has been included in the takeoff to avoid double counting or possibly missing any item.

Equipment. Mechanical equipment such as furnaces, air conditioners, and hot water tanks are taken off of prints as individual pieces. Suppliers refer to the floor plans, notations, and specifications to ensure the proper loads are provided and manufacturer requirements are met.

For example, water heater #3 (WH-3), manufactured by A.O. Smith, holds 75 gal. of water. The water heater has an input rating of 120,000 Btu/hr and an outlet temperature of 140°F, and utilizes natural gas as a power source.

Electrical Systems

An electrical equipment circuit schedule may be included as part of the electrical plans. The electrical equipment circuit schedule lists each piece of equipment and indicates the amount of electric power necessary, as well as circuit assignments. See Figure 11-19. Knowledge of the National Electrical Code® is important when performing quantity takeoff for electrical work, as spacing of junction boxes, receptacles, fixtures, and other electrical apparatus must be performed so as to meet NEC® requirements. Electrical takeoff also requires that the appropriate length of cable and conductors of each type and size be provided for the job. Specifications and notes on the electrical plans commonly state the electrical equipment and requirements for installation.

Notations on the prints or in the specifications may specify minimum conduit sizes for routing conductors.

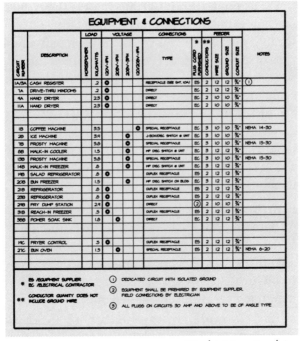

Wendy's International, Inc.

Figure 11-19. Information regarding electrical equipment and connections is commonly included in a schedule on the electrical plan.

Equipment. A wide variety of electrical equipment is required for most electrical installations, including junction and switch boxes, switches, receptacles, luminaires (lighting fixtures), panelboard(s), and other specialty items. Each item is quantified similar to other types of equipment by listing each individual type of electrical equipment shown on a plan, tabulating the quantity of each item, and marking them off on the plans to determine an accurate quantity.

For example, a light fixture plan showing Room 306 contains nine Type A luminaires, four Type K luminaires, and one Type Y luminaire. Five junction boxes are noted as J. In addition, five switches are shown near the entrance door. See Figure 11-20.

Wiring. Takeoff of wiring and cabling for electrical work is done in a manner similar to pipe and ductwork takeoff. An architect's scale or plan dimensions are utilized to determine the approximate length of each electrical run.

For example, Room 306 has luminaires spaced approximately 6′ apart in both directions around the five junction boxes. Allowing 4′ between a luminaire and the nearest junction box and an additional 1′ for each run between each luminaire and the junction box requires approximately 45′ (9 luminaires × 5′ = 45′) of cable to connect the luminaires to the junction boxes. Print notations indicate the type of each cable required.

Wiring calculations can become more complex when various circuits are made up and lengths of cable need to be determined for cable runs to panelboards. Locations of panelboards are determined and distances calculated to each circuit run. Allowances are also made for ceiling heights, especially in commercial and multistory buildings.

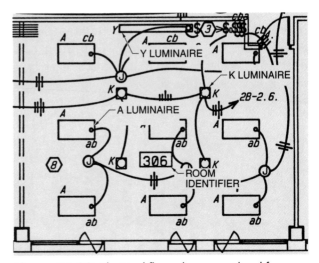

Figure 11-20. Electrical floor plans are utilized for quantifying luminaires (light fixtures), switches, boxes, and wiring for takeoff.

Name _____ Date _____

True-False

T   F   **1.** Standard lumber length is based on a multiple of 8′.

T   F   **2.** The volume of concrete for a slab (in cubic feet) is determined by multiplying the surface area (in square feet) by the slab thickness (in feet) and dividing by 27.

T   F   **3.** A round pipe column shown on a print as 8 SCH 60 indicates an 8″ diameter (nominal) schedule 60 pipe is used.

T   F   **4.** Approximately 4″ should be allowed for the jamb and shim clearance for common windows.

T   F   **5.** A 4′ × 8′ wall sheathing panel covers 36 sq ft.

T   F   **6.** A square of shingles covers 100 sq ft.

T   F   **7.** Junction boxes, receptacles, fixtures, and other electrical apparatus must be spaced in a manner that meets or exceeds the National Electrical Code® requirements.

T   F   **8.** Quantity takeoff for excavation is commonly calculated in square yards.

T   F   **9.** Information concerning the type and design of concrete formwork is not provided on a typical set of prints.

T   F   **10.** Items such as girders, beams, engineered lumber, and trusses are counted as individual units on a quantity takeoff.

Multiple Choice

_____ **1.** A ___ waste allowance is added to concrete calculations to allow for spillage during placement.
     A. 1% to 2%
     B. 3% to 5%
     C. 5% to 7%
     D. 10%

2. A(n) ___ is the practice of reviewing contract documents only to determine quantities of material to be included in a bid.

    A. engineering improvement
    B. estimate
    C. takeoff
    D. calculation

3. Snap tie quantities are calculated as a specified number of ties per ___ of wall area.

    A. foot
    B. square foot
    C. yard
    D. cubic yard

4. The cross-section method of calculating the volume of material to be excavated from a site is used when the shape of the excavated area is ___.

    A. irregularly shaped
    B. round
    C. rectangular
    D. triangular

5. ___ is the process of lowering high spots and filling in low spots of earth at a construction site.

    A. Excavating
    B. Trenching
    C. Shelling
    D. Grading

6. The amount of welded wire reinforcement required is based on the slab ___.

    A. volume
    B. area
    C. thickness
    D. length

7. Joist spacing and direction is noted on ___.

    A. details
    B. sections
    C. floor plans
    D. elevations

8. A(n) ___ line is a line connecting points on a topographical map where existing and planned elevations are equal.

    A. task
    B. zero
    C. apex
    D. contour

9. Hardwood flooring and tile quantity takeoffs are typically calculated in ___.
  A. linear feet
  B. square feet
  C. square yards
  D. none of the above

10. Trim moldings, such as baseboard, casing, chair rail, and crown molding, are taken off in ___.
  A. linear feet
  B. square feet
  C. square yards
  D. cubic yards

Completion

1. Structural lumber length is rounded up to the closest ___' dimension for purchasing.

2. Rebar placement, spacing, and sizing are determined from ___ or sections.

3. A multiplier of ___ is used to determine the actual number of joists required for a project when the joists are spaced 19.2" OC.

4. A typical sheet of wood paneling measures ___' perpendicular to the direction of the grain and ___' parallel to the direction of the grain.

5. A cabinet ___ indicates width, height, and depth of each cabinet used on a project.

6. ___ and door schedules are the primary sources of information about doors.

7. General contractors, specialty contractors, and material suppliers employ ___ who read prints and specifications to determine material quantities required for proper construction.

8. A(n) ___ scale or plan dimensions are utilized to determine the approximate lengths of electrical runs from prints.

9. ___ is the division of a plot plan for large areas to be excavated or graded into small squares.

10. ___ improvements are changes to a site that include footings, foundations, basements, and other below-grade work.

Name _____ Date _____

True-False

T   F   **1.** Rafters with a 4" in 12" pitch have a 12.65" run per foot.

T   F   **2.** To calculate the linear feet of lumber for single top and bottom form plates on both sides of a wall, multiply the linear feet of the wall by 4.

T   F   **3.** The amount of concrete required for a job site is specified in cubic feet measurements.

T   F   **4.** Estimating and quantity takeoff refer to the same process.

T   F   **5.** The approximate elevation at each corner of a grid is established by using the nearest contour line.

T   F   **6.** One snap tie for each 4 sq ft of wall area is typically recommended for cast-in-place concrete walls.

T   F   **7.** EIFS is a wood panel product that is fastened to wall framing members and painted.

T   F   **8.** Bituminous and elastomeric roofing are taken off using the same method.

T   F   **9.** The method for estimating the number of wall studs is the same as for any structural member with an on-center spacing.

T   F   **10.** Quantity takeoffs for carpet and resilient flooring are calculated in square feet.

Completion

_____ **1.** Structural lumber length is rounded up to the closest ___' for purchasing.

_____ **2.** When calculating the number of roof sheathing panels required for a building, the roof area is divided by ___ to determine the number of 4' × 8' panels required.

_____ **3.** A(n) ___ denotes the size and type of patented forms, quantity of each, amount of fastening hardware, type and number of snap ties, and number of walers required for the specific job.

_____ **4.** Rebar is commonly priced at a cost per ___ of steel.

_____ **5.** Concrete formwork uses takeoff calculations in linear feet or in square feet of ___ area.

443

_____ **6.** When calculating the number of metal studs required for a wall, a(n) ___ multiplier is used for 16" OC spacing.

_____ **7.** When calculating the number of linear feet of plate material for walls with double top plates, the sum of the wall lengths is multiplied by ___.

_____ **8.** A(n) ___ is a horizontal member used to align and reinforce concrete formwork.

_____ **9.** Sill plate quantities are calculated by determining the ___ of the foundation walls.

_____ **10.** Interior ___ and related schedules provide location, dimension, and finish information for cabinetry.

_____ **11.** A waste factor of ___% is added for composition shingles.

_____ **12.** ___ drawings indicate the form identification numbers of the manufacturer, type of formwork, placement, shoring and bracing information, form fastening system, and the proper form ties to use.

_____ **13.** Hardwood flooring and tile quantity takeoffs are typically calculated in ___.

_____ **14.** The common waste factor for mortar is ___.

_____ **15.** Quantity takeoff for piping and ductwork is performed in ___ for each type of pipe or duct required.

Math

_____ **1.** The roof of a building requires 33 TJI 55E joists cut to 35'-9" each. How many linear feet of joists are required?

_____ **2.** Two #12 THW copper conductors and one #12 grounding conductor are pulled in a 49'-9" run of ¾" conduit, which is available in 10' lengths. How many pieces of conduit are required?

3. A reflected ceiling plan for a room measuring 18'-0" × 32'-0" contains eight 2' × 4' recessed ceiling luminaires (light fixtures). How many 2' × 4' acousticalceiling tile are required for the ceiling?

4. Using the cross-section method, calculate the quantity of cut or fill (in cu yd) for a 120' × 80' grid with corners at elevations of 109.63', 96.31', 104.92', and 101.87' requiring excavation to 100'.

5. Using the average end area method, calculate the volume of excavation (in cu yd) of an 80' long excavation area that has a width of 35' at one end and 55' at the other end. Both ends require 15' of cut.

_____ **6.** Calculate the amount of concrete (in cu yd) required for a wall measuring 6″ thick by 50′ long by 8′ high.

_____ **7.** A 24′ × 50′ floor area with a 4′ × 7′ stairwell opening is to be covered with plywood subfloor. Calculate the number of 4′ × 8′ plywood panels required (allow 7% for waste allowance).

_____ **8.** A 45′ long by 8′ high wall requires double walers spaced 2′ apart on both sides. Calculate the amount of lumber (in linear feet) required for the walers (excluding overlap allowance).

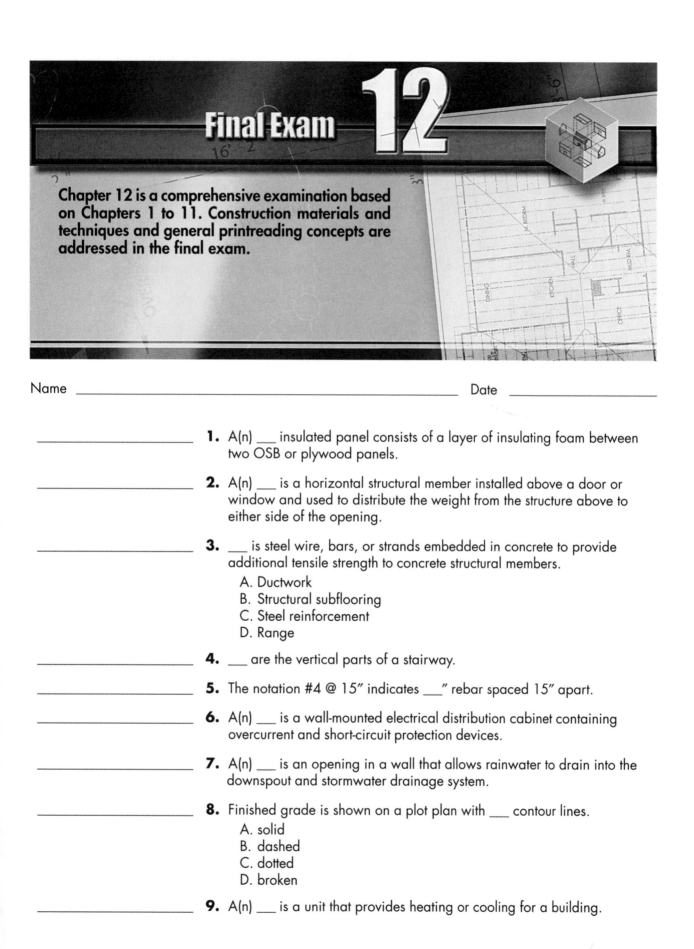

Final Exam 12

Chapter 12 is a comprehensive examination based on Chapters 1 to 11. Construction materials and techniques and general printreading concepts are addressed in the final exam.

Name _____ Date _____

_____ 1. A(n) ___ insulated panel consists of a layer of insulating foam between two OSB or plywood panels.

_____ 2. A(n) ___ is a horizontal structural member installed above a door or window and used to distribute the weight from the structure above to either side of the opening.

_____ 3. ___ is steel wire, bars, or strands embedded in concrete to provide additional tensile strength to concrete structural members.
     A. Ductwork
     B. Structural subflooring
     C. Steel reinforcement
     D. Range

_____ 4. ___ are the vertical parts of a stairway.

_____ 5. The notation #4 @ 15" indicates ___" rebar spaced 15" apart.

_____ 6. A(n) ___ is a wall-mounted electrical distribution cabinet containing overcurrent and short-circuit protection devices.

_____ 7. A(n) ___ is an opening in a wall that allows rainwater to drain into the downspout and stormwater drainage system.

_____ 8. Finished grade is shown on a plot plan with ___ contour lines.
     A. solid
     B. dashed
     C. dotted
     D. broken

_____ 9. A(n) ___ is a unit that provides heating or cooling for a building.

_____ **10.** Building ___ specify types of materials that must be used for particular aspects of construction.

T   F   **11.** Downspouts should always be run on the outside of exterior walls.

_____ **12.** A(n) ___ can be added to concrete as an admixture.
        A. accelerator
        B. superplasticizer
        C. retarder
        D. all of the above

_____ **13.** A raised earth embankment is a(n) ___.

T   F   **14.** Partitions are generally considered to be non-load-bearing.

_____ **15.** ___ are drawn to a larger scale to show the object more clearly.

_____ **16.** A(n) ___ plan shows the location of the house on a lot.

_____ **17.** ___ windows cannot be opened.

T   F   **18.** Door hand is the direction in which a door swings.

_____ **19.** ___ runs are electrical conductors that extend from the power source to the point of use.

_____ **20.** Building brick is also known as ___ brick.

_____ **21.** A(n) ___ is a brick ledge designed to support a load.

_____ **22.** ___ glass is nonshattering glass that has high impact resistance.

_____ **23.** Stormwater and sanitary sewer piping, and electrical, telephone, and natural gas service are shown on a(n) ___ plan.

_____ **24.** ___ is an engineered wood product comprised of layers of wood members that are joined together with adhesive to form larger members.
        A. Oriented strand board (OSB)
        B. Parallel strand lumber (PSL)
        C. Glued laminated timber (glulam)
        D. Plywood

T   F   **25.** A construction joint is a groove made in a concrete slab to create a weakened plane and control the location of cracking.

_____ **26.** A(n) ___ provides complete information on the type and size of doors specified.

T   F   **27.** Cavity walls are brick walls made of two wythes with an air space between the wythes.

T   F   **28.** When a standard set of prints is utilized on several similar projects, architects show a variety of options and features that may or may not be used on a particular project.

_____ **29.** A ___ waste allowance is added to concrete calculations to allow for concrete spillage during placement.
    A. 1% to 2%
    B. 3% to 5%
    C. 5% to 7%
    D. 10%

T   F   **30.** Interior doors generally require only two hinges.

_____ **31.** A typical sheet of wood paneling measures ___' perpendicular to the direction of the grain and ___' parallel to the direction of the grain.

T   F   **32.** Items such as girders, beams, engineered lumber, and trusses are counted as individual units on a quantity takeoff.

_____ **33.** A(n) ___ is a thin, moisture-resistant material placed over the ground or in walls to retard the passage of moisture into a building.

_____ **34.** ___ and door schedules are the primary sources of information about doors.

T   F   **35.** The arrow on a cutting plane reference indicates the direction of sight for the section.

_____ **36.** ___ ties are used to maintain spacing of form walls during concrete placement.

_____ **37.** A(n) ___ truss is a roof or floor truss that is supported by the top chord.
    A. top-loaded
    B. upper type
    C. underslung
    D. horizontal

T   F   **38.** Air supply registers may be located in floors or walls.

_____ **39.** Dimensions on a print show ___.
    A. size
    B. location
    C. size relationship of parts
    D. all of the above

_____ **40.** The survey drawing provides a means of determining elevations from datum points or ___.

T   F   **41.** Walls of metal-framed buildings are strengthened by diagonal straps or the use of plywood or OSB sheathing at the corners.

_____ **42.** The abbreviation "NIC" means ___.
    A. National Insulation Code
    B. not included in the contract
    C. notching in concrete
    D. near inside center

_____ **43.** ___ is the distribution system for forced-air systems.

_____ **44.** A(n) ___ is the practice of reviewing contract documents only to determine quantities of material to be included in a bid.

    A. engineering improvement
    B. estimate
    C. takeoff
    D. calculation

_____ **45.** A(n) ___ stud is placed at each side of the rough window opening to support the header.

T   F   **46.** Floor plans showing room size and layout are drawn with the line of sight parallel to the floor.

_____ **47.** A cabinet ___ indicates width, height, and depth of each cabinet used on a project.

_____ **48.** Cutting planes for sections are generally shown on ___.

    A. elevations
    B. floor plans
    C. details
    D. all of the above

_____ **49.** General contractors, specialty contractors, and material suppliers employ ___ who read prints and specifications to determine material quantities required for proper construction.

T   F   **50.** Exterior elevations show complete kitchen details.

_____ **51.** A cant strip is ___ in cross section.

    A. square
    B. rectangular
    C. triangular
    D. oval

_____ **52.** The ___ is a value used to indicate the ability of a material to resist heat flow.

_____ **53.** The ___ on doors and walls indicates the amount of time these building components can withstand fire without structural failure.

T   F   **54.** Elevations may be either interior or exterior.

_____ **55.** Trim moldings, such as baseboard, casing, chair rail, and crown molding, are taken off in ___.

    A. linear feet
    B. square feet
    C. square yards
    D. cubic yards

_____ **56.** Dimension lines are terminated by ___ lines.

T   F   **57.** A floor drain always requires the pumping action of a sump pump.

_____ **58.** The ___ is the highest point of a gable roof.

_____ **59.** When installed along the bottom edges of floor joists, resilient furring ___ reduce sound transmission between adjoining floors.

_____ **60.** The ___ size is the dimension of a piece of lumber before it is dried and surfaced.

_____ **61.** A(n) ___ door is a door that swings in two directions.

T   F **62.** Anchor bolts are used to secure gypsum board to wood or metal studs.

_____ **63.** A ___° angle is formed between the axes in isometric drawings.
  A. 60
  B. 90
  C. 120
  D. 180

_____ **64.** A surveyor's tape measure is divided into tenths and hundredths of a(n) ___.

_____ **65.** A brick- ___ building is essentially a frame building covered with brick.

_____ **66.** The cross-section method of calculating the volume of material to be excavated from a site is used when the shape of the excavated area is ___.
  A. irregularly shaped
  B. round
  C. rectangular
  D. triangular

_____ **67.** A double top ___ is the top member of an interior partition.

_____ **68.** ___ walls provide additional structural support to prevent building failures under unusual loading such as earthquakes or wind storms.

T   F **69.** Wall cabinets may have adjustable shelves.

T   F **70.** A square of shingles covers 100 sq ft.

_____ **71.** Orthographic projections are also referred to as ___ drawings.
  A. multiview
  B. pictorial
  C. isometric
  D. oblique

_____ **72.** A(n) ___ dimension locates a particular feature in relation to another feature.

T   F **73.** When there is a conflict between the information shown on the prints and the specifications, the specifications are to be followed.

T   F **74.** Acoustical ceilings must be suspended to prevent sound transmission.

_____ **75.** ___ is rough, irregular stone that is used as fill or to provide a rustic appearance.
    A. Ashlar
    B. Squared stone
    C. Rubble
    D. Cast stone

_____ **76.** Isolation joints are also known as ___ joints.

T   F **77.** Windows and doors are difficult to design into metal-framed buildings.

_____ **78.** Brick veneer is ___ wythe(s) thick.

_____ **79.** The amount of welded wire reinforcement required is based on the slab ___.
    A. volume
    B. area
    C. thickness
    D. length

_____ **80.** A(n) ___ mitre is a type of joint used at the outside corners of adjoining stone members in which the corners are trimmed flat at the ends to prevent the ends from splitting.

_____ **81.** A(n) ___ block is the logical place to begin reading a set of prints.

_____ **82.** Hardwood flooring and tile quantity takeoffs are typically calculated in ___.
    A. linear feet
    B. square feet
    C. square yards
    D. none of the above

T   F **83.** The _Description of Materials_ form is used mainly to provide information on which to base a mortgage loan.

T   F **84.** Polymer trim members are attached to a building using mastic and mechanical fasteners.

_____ **85.** A W14 × 34 steel beam weighs ___ pounds per running foot.

_____ **86.** A ___ tile is a clay masonry unit with one face colored and glazed, and is used for load-bearing applications.
    A. mosaic
    B. structural facing
    C. clay facing
    D. quarry

T   F **87.** The title block provides general information about the set of prints including the name of the architect.

T   F **88.** Complete specifications cover the ordering of specific materials, suitable options, and equivalent products.

_____ **89.** ___ cable is a single or multiconductor electrical assembly, with or without an overall jacket.

_____ **90.** Based on the National Electrical Code®, electrical wall outlets must be spaced no more than ___ apart, measured along the wall.

T   F   **91.** Outline specifications do not tell how material is to be applied.

_____ **92.** Snap tie quantities are calculated as a specified number of ties per ___ of wall area.
  A. foot
  B. square foot
  C. yard
  D. cubic yard

_____ **93.** Extension lines define size or ___.

_____ **94.** A(n) ___ line is an aligning mark on a print that is used when a drawing is too large to be contained on one sheet.
  A. dimension
  B. match
  C. section
  D. extension

T   F   **95.** Small remodeling jobs should have specifications.

T   F   **96.** The letter "E" in a title block on a set of prints denotes engineering drawings.

T   F   **97.** Medium density plywood (MDO) is used for concrete forming material.

_____ **98.** The actual size of a 2 × 4 stud is ___.

_____ **99.** The most commonly used scale for working drawings is ___.
  A. ⅛" = 1'-0"
  B. ¼" = 1'-0"
  C. 1'-0" = ⅛"
  D. 1'-0" = ¼"

_____ **100.** When referring to welded wire reinforcement, the letter "___" is used to designate smooth wire and the letter "___" is used to designate deformed wire.
  A. W; D
  B. W; S
  C. S; D
  D. D; S

Appendix

ABBREVIATIONS . . .

Term	Abbreviation	Term	Abbreviation	Term	Abbreviation
A		bench mark	BM	circumference	CRCMF
above	ABV	beveled	BVL or BEV	cleanout	CO
above finished floor	AFF	beveled wood siding	BWS	cleanout door	CODR
above surface of floor	ASF	bituminous	BIT	clear	CLR
access	ACS	blocking	BLKG	clear glass	CL GL
access panel	AP	board	BD	closed circuit television	CCTV
acoustic	AC or ACST	board foot	BF or BD FT	closet	C, CL, CLO, or
acoustical plaster ceiling	APC	boiler	BLR		CLOS
acoustical tile	AT. or ACT.	bookcase	BC	coaxial	COAX.
adjacent	ADJ	bookshelves	BK SH	cold air	CA
adjustable	ADJT or ADJ	boulevard	BLVD	cold-rolled	CR
aggregate	AGG or AGGR	boundary	BDRY	cold-rolled steel	CRS
air circulating	ACIRC	brass	BRS	cold water	CW
air conditioner	AIR COND	breaker	BRKR	collar beam	COL B
air conditioning	A/C or	brick	BRK	column	COL
	AIR COND	British thermal unit	Btu	color code	CC
alloy	ALY	bronze	BRZ	combination	COMB.
alloy steel	ALY STL	broom closet	BC	combustible	COMBL
alternate	ALTN	building	BLDG or BL	combustion	COMB.
alternating current	AC	building line	BL	common	COM
aluminum	AL	built-in	BLTIN	composition	COMP
ambient	AMB	built-up roofing	BUR	concrete	CONC
American National	AMER NATL			concrete block	CCB or
Standard	STD	**C**			CONC BLK
American National		cabinet	CAB.	concrete floor	CCF,
Standards Institute	ANSI	cable	CA		CONC FLR, or
American Steel Wire		canopy	CAN.		CONC FL
Gauge	ASWG	caulking	CK or CLKG	concrete masonry unit	CMU
American Wire Gauge	AWG	cantilever	CANV	concrete pipe	CP
ampere	A or AMP	cased opening	CO	concrete splash block	CSB
anchor	AHR	casing	CSG	condenser	COND
anchor bolt	AB	cast iron	CI	conductor	CNDCT
appearance	APP	cast iron pipe	CIP	conduit	CND
apartment	APT.	cast steel	CS	construction	CONSTR
approximate	APX or	cast stone	CST or CS	construction joint	CJ or
	APPROX	catch basin	CB		CONSTR JT
architectural	ARCH.	caulking	CK or CLKG	continuous	CONT
architecture	ARCH.	caulked joint	CLKJ	contour	CTR
area	A	cavity	CAV	contract	CONTR or
area drain	AD	ceiling	CLG		CONT
as drawn	AD	cellar	CEL	contraction joint	CJ or CLJ
asphalt	ASPH	cement	CEM	contractor	CONTR
asphalt roof shingles	ASPHRS	cement floor	CF	conventional	CVNTL
asphalt tile	AT.	cement mortar	CEM MORT	copper	CU
automatic	AUTO.	center	CTR	corner	COR
auxiliary	AUX	centerline	CL	cornice	COR
avenue	AVE	center matched	CM	corrugate	CORR
azimuth	AZ	center-to-center	C TO C	counter	CNTR
		central	CTL	county	CO
B		ceramic	CER	cubic	CU
barrier	BARR	ceramic tile	CT	cubic feet	CFT or CU FT
barrier, moisture		ceramic-tile base	CTB	cubic foot per minute	CFM
vapor-proof	BMVP	ceramic-to-metal (seal)	CERMET	cubic foot per second	CFS
barrier, waterproof	BWP	chamfer	CHAM or	cubic inch	CU IN.
basement	BSMT		CHMFR	cubic yard	CU YD
bathroom	B	channel	CHAN	current	CUR
bathtub	BT	check valve	CV	cutoff	CO
batten	BATT	chimney	CHM	cutoff valve	COV
beam	BM	chord	CHD	cut out	CO
bearing	BRG	cinder block	CINBL		
bearing plate	BPL or	circle	CIR	**D**	
	BRG PL	circuit	CKT	damper	DMPR
bedroom	BR	circuit breaker	CB or	datum	DAT
below	BLW		CIR BKR	decibel	DB
		circuit interrupter	CI	degree	DEG

... ABBREVIATIONS ...

Term	Abbreviation	Term	Abbreviation	Term	Abbreviation
degree	DEG	excavate	EXCA or EXC	general contractor	GEN CONT
depth	DP	exchange	EXCH	girder	G
design	DSGN	exhaust	EXH	glass	GL
detail	DTL or DET	exhaust vent	EXHV	glass block	GLB or GL BL
diagonal	DIAG	existing	EXST	glaze	GLZ
diagram	DIAG	expanded metal	EM	glued laminated	GLULAM
diameter	DIA or DIAM	expansion joint	EXP JT	grade	GR
dimension	DIM.	exterior	EXT	grade line	GL
dimmer	DIM. or DMR	exterior grade	EXT GR	gravel	GVL
dining room	DR or DNG RM			grille	G
		F		gross weight	GRWT
direct current	DC	face brick	FB	ground	GRD
direction	DIR	faceplate	FP	ground (outlet)	G
disconnect	DISC.	Fahrenheit	F	ground-fault circuit interrupter	GFCI
disconnect switch	DS	fiberboard, solid	FBDS	ground-fault interrupter	GFI
dishwasher	DW	finish	FIN. or FNSH	gypsum	GYP
distribution panel	DPNL	finish all over	FAO	gypsum board	GYP BD
divided	DIV	finish grade	FG	gypsum-plaster ceiling	GPC
door	DR	finish one side	FIS	gypsum-plaster wall	GPW
door stop	DST	finish two sides	F2S	gypsum sheathing board	GSB
door switch	DSW	finished floor	FIN. FLR, FIN. FL, or FNSH FL	gypsum wallboard	GWB
dormer	DRM				
double-acting	DA or DBL ACT	firebrick	FBRK or FBCK	**H**	
double-hung window	DHW	fireplace	FPL or FP	hardboard	HBD
double-pole double-throw	DPDT	fireproof	FP or FPRF	hardware	HDW
double-pole double-throw switch	DPDT SW	fire resistant	FRES	header	HDR
		fixed transom	FTR	heat	HT
double-pole single-throw	DPST	fixed window	FX WDW	heated	HTD
		fixture	FIX. or FXTR	heater	HTR
double-pole single-throw switch	DPST SW	flashing	FLG or FL	heating	HTG
		floor	FLR or FL	heating, ventilating, and air conditioning	HVAC
double-pole switch	DP SW	floor drain	FD		
double-strength glass	DSG	flooring	FLR or FLG	height	HGT
down	DN or D	fluorescent	FLUR or FLUOR	hexagon	HEX.
downspout	DS	flush	FL	high density overlay	HDO
dozen	DOZ	foot or feet	FT	high point	HPT
drain	D or DR	footing	FTG	highway	HWY
drain tile	DT	foundation	FND or FDN	hinge	HNG
drawer	DWR	frame	FR	hollow-core	HC
drawing	DWG	frostproof hose bibb	FPHB	hollow metal door	HMD
dressed and matched	D & M	full scale	FSC	honeycomb	HNYCMB
drip cap	DC	full size	FS	horizontal	HOR or HORZ
drop in pipe	D.I.P.	furnace	FURN	horsepower	HP
dryer	D	furred ceiling	FC	hose bibb	HB
drywall	DW	furring	FUR	hot air	HA
dwelling	DWEL	fuse	FU	hot water	HW
		fuse block	FB	hot water tank	HWT
E		fusebox	FUBX	humidity	HMD
each	EA	fuseholder	FUHLR		
east	E	fusible	FSBL	**I**	
elbow	ELB			illuminate	ILLUM
electric or electrical	ELEC	**G**		incandescent	INCAND
electrical metallic tubing	EMT	gallon	GAL.	inch	IN.
electric operator	ELECT. OPR	gallon per hour	GPH	inch per second	IPS
electric panel	EP	gallon per minute	GPM	inside diameter	ID
electromechanical	ELMCH	galvanized	GV or GALV	install	INSTL
elevation	ELEV or EL	galvanized iron	GI or GALVI	insulation	INS or INSUL
enamel	ENAM			interior	INT
end-to-end	E to E	galvanized steel	GS or GALVS	iron	I
entrance	ENTR or ENT				
equipment	EQPT	garage	GAR.	**J**	
equivalent	EQUIV	gas	G	jamb	JB or JMB
estimate	EST	gate valve	GTV	joint	JT
example	EX	gauge	GA	joist	J

...ABBREVIATIONS...

Term	Abbreviation	Term	Abbreviation	Term	Abbreviation
K		molding	MLD or MLDG	porch	P
kiln dried	KD	mortar	MOR	pound	LB
kitchen	K, KT, or KIT.	mullon	MULL.	power	PWR
				power supply	PWR SPLY
L		**N**		precast	PRCST
laminate	LAM	National Electrical		prefabricated	PFB or
laminated veneer lumber	LVL	Code	NEC		PREFAB
landing	LDG	National Electrical		prefinished	PFN
lateral	LATL	Safety Code	NESC	property	PROP
lath	LTH	natural grade	NG	property line	PL
laundry	LAU	negative	(–) or NEG	pull chain	PC
laundry tray	LT	noncombustible	NCOMBL	pull switch	PS
lavatory	LAV	north	N	pump	PMP
leader	L	nosing	NOS		
left hand	LH	not to scale	NTS	**Q**	
length	L, LG, or	number	NO.	quadrant	QDRNT
	LGTH			quarry tile	QT
length overall	LOA	**O**		quarry tile base	QTB
level	LVL	obscure glass	OBSC GL	quarry tile floor	QTF
library	LIB	octagon	OCT	quarter	QTR
living room	LR	on center	OC	quarter-round	¼RD
light	LT	one-pole	OP		
light switch	LT SW	opening	OPG or	**R**	
limestone	LMS or LS		OPNG	radiator	RAD or RDTR
linen closet	L CL	open web joist	OJ, OW J, or	radius	R or RAD
line	LN		OW JOIST	raised	RSD
lining	L	opposite	OPP	random	RDM
linoleum	LINO	optional	OPT	range	R
linoleum floor	LF or	ordinance	ORD	receptacle	RCPT
	LINO FLR	oriented strand board	OSB	recessed	REC
lintel	LNTL	outlet	OUT.	rectangle	RECT
living room	LR	outside diameter	OD	redwood	RWD
local	LCL	out-to-out	O TO O	reference	REF
long	LG	overall	OA	reference line	REFL
louver	LVR or LV	overcurrent	OC	reflected	REFLD
low point	LP	overcurrent relay	OCR	refrigerator	REF or REFR
lumber	LBR	overhead	OH or OVHD	register	REG or RGTR
				reinforce or reinforcing	RE or REINF
M		**P**		reinforced concrete	RC
main	MN	paint	PNT	reinforcing steel	RST
makeup	MKUP	panel	PNL	reinforcing steel bar	REBAR
manufactured	MFD	pantry	PAN.	required	REQD
marble	MRB or MR	parallel	PRL	retaining	RETG
masonry	MSNRY	parallel strand lumber	PSL	revision	REV
masonry opening	MO	partition	PTN	revolution per minute	RPM
material	MTL or MATL	passage	PASS.	revolution per second	RPS
maximum	MAX	penny (nails, etc.)	d	right hand	RH
median	MDN	perimeter	PERIM	riser	R
medicine cabinet	MC	perpendicular	PERP	road	RD
medium	MDM	per square inch	PSI	roof	RF
medium density overlay	MDO	phase	PH	roof drain	RD
meridian	MER	piping	PP	roofing	RFG
metal	MET. or M	plaster	PLAS or PL	room	RM or R
metal anchor	MA	plastered opening	PO	rough	RGH
metal door	METD	plate	PL	rough opening	RO or
metal flashing	METF	plate glass	PG, PL GL, or		RGH OPNG
metal threshold	MT		PLGL	rough-sawn	RS
mineral	MNRL	plate height	PL HT	round	RND
minimum	MIN	platform	PLAT	rubber	RBR
mirror	MIR	plumbing	PLBG	rubber tile	RBT or R TILE
miscellaneous	MISC	plywood	PLYWD	rustproof	RSTPF
miter	MIT	point	PT		
mixture	MIX.	point of beginning	POB	**S**	
modular	MOD	polyvinyl chloride	PVC	saddle	SDL or S

. . . ABBREVIATIONS

Term	Abbreviation	Term	Abbreviation	Term	Abbreviation
safety	SAF	square inch	SQ IN.	valley	VAL
sanitary	S	square yard	SQ YD or SY	valve	V
S-beam	S	stack	STK	variance	VAR
scale	SC	stained	STN	vent	V
schedule	SCH or SCHED	stainless steel	SST	vent hole	VH
		stairs	ST	ventilate	VEN
screen	SCN, SCR, or SCRN	stairway	STWY	ventilating equipment	VE
		standard	STD	vent pipe	VP
screen door	SCD	steel	ST or STL	vent stack	VS
screw	SCR	steel sash	SS	vertical	VERT
scuttle	S	stone	STN	vestibule	VEST.
section	SEC or SECT.	storage	STO or STG	vinyl tile	VT or V TILE
select	SEL	street	ST or STR	vitreous tile	VIT TILE
self cleaning	SLFCLN	structural	STRL	void	VD
self-closing	SELF CL	Structural Clay Products		volt	V
service	SERV or SVCE	Research Foundation	SCR	voltage	V
		structural clay tile	SCT	voltage drop	VD
sewer	SEW.	structural glass	SG	volt amp	VA
sheathing	SHTH or SHTHG	supply	SPLY	volume	VOL
		survey	SURV		
sheet	SHT or SH	suspended	SUSP		
sheeting	SH	switch	SW or S	**W**	
sheet metal	SM			wainscot	WSCT, WAIN., or WA
shelf and rod	SH&RD				
shelving	SH or SHELV	**T**		walk-in closet	WIC
shingle	SHGL	telephone	TEL	wall	W
shiplap	SHLP	television	TV	wallboard	WLB
shower	SH	temperature	TEMP	wall receptacle	WR
shower and toilet	SH & T	tempered plate glass	TEM PL GL	warm air	WA
shower drain	SD	terra cotta	TC	washing machine	WM
shutter	SHTR	terrazzo	TZ or TER	water	WTR or W
siding	SDG	thermostat	THERMO	water closet	WC
sidelight	SI LT	thick	THK or T	water heater	WH
sillcock	SC	threshold	TH	water line	WL
single-phase	1PH	tile base	TB	water meter	WM
single-pole	SP	tile drain	TD	waterproof	WTRPRF
single-pole double-throw	SPDT	tile floor	TF	water-resistant	WR
single-pole double throw switch	SPDT SW	timber	TMBR	watt	W
		toilet	T	weatherproof	WTHPRF or WP
single-pole single-throw	SPST	tongue-and-groove	T & G	weather-resistant	WR
single-pole single-throw switch	SPST SW	top of curb	TC	weatherstripping	WS
		township	T	weep hole	WH
single-pole switch	SP SW	tread	TR or T	welded wire reinforcement	WWR
single-strength glass	SSG	typical	TYP	west	W
single-throw	ST			white pine	WP
sink	SK or S			wide	W
skylight	SLT	**U**		wide-flange	W or WF
sliding door	SLD or SL DR	underground	UGND	window	WDO
slope	SLP	unexcavated	UNEXC	wire glass	WG or W GL
soffit	SF	unfinished	UNFIN or UNF	wood	WD
soil pipe	SP	unit heater	UH	wood frame	WF
soil stack	SSK	unless otherwise specified	UOS	wrought iron	WI
solid core	SC	untreated	UTRTD		
soundproof	SNDPRF	utility	U or UTIL	**Y**	
south	S	utility room	UR or U RM	yard	YD
specific	SP			yellow pine	YP
specification	SPEC				
splash block	SB	**V**		**Z**	
square	SQ			zone	Z
square feet	SQ FT	vacuum	VAC		

ARCHITECTURAL SYMBOLS . . .

Material	Elevation	Plan	Section
Earth			
Brick	WITH NOTE INDICATING TYPE OF BRICK (COMMON, FACE, ETC.)	COMMON OR FACE / FIREBRICK	SAME AS PLAN VIEWS
Concrete		LIGHTWEIGHT / STRUCTURAL	SAME AS PLAN VIEWS
Concrete Masonry Unit		OR	OR
Stone	CUT STONE RUBBLE	CUT STONE RUBBLE / CAST STONE (CONCRETE)	CUT STONE / CAST STONE (CONCRETE) RUBBLE OR CUT STONE
Wood	SIDING PANEL	WOOD STUD / REMODELING	ROUGH MEMBER TRIM MEMBER PLYWOOD
Plaster		METAL LATH AND PLASTER / SOLID PLASTER	LATH AND PLASTER
Roofing	SHINGLES	SAME AS ELEVATION	
Glass	OR / GLASS BLOCK	GLASS / GLASS BLOCK	SMALL SCALE LARGE SCALE

. . . ARCHITECTURAL SYMBOLS

Material	Elevation	Plan	Section
Facing Tile	CERAMIC TILE	FLOOR TILE	CERAMIC TILE LARGE SCALE / CERAMIC TILE SMALL SCALE
Structural Clay Tile			SAME AS PLAN VIEW
Insulation		LOOSE FILL OR BATTS / RIGID / SPRAY FOAM	SAME AS PLAN VIEWS
Sheet Metal Flashing		OCCASIONALLY INDICATED BY NOTE	
Metals Other Than Flashing	INDICATED BY NOTE OR DRAWN TO SCALE	SAME AS ELEVATION	SMALL SCALE / STEEL / CAST IRON / ALUMINUM / BRONZE OR BRASS
Structural Steel	INDICATED BY NOTE OR DRAWN TO SCALE	OR	REBAR / SMALL SCALE / LARGE SCALE

PLOT PLAN SYMBOLS

NORTH	FIRE HYDRANT	WALK	ELECTRIC SERVICE
POINT OF BEGINNING (POB)	MAILBOX	IMPROVED ROAD	NATURAL GAS LINE
UTILITY METER OR VALVE	MANHOLE	UNIMPROVED ROAD	WATER LINE
POWER POLE AND GUY	TREE	BUILDING LINE	TELEPHONE LINE
LIGHT STANDARD	BUSH	PROPERTY LINE	NATURAL GRADE
TRAFFIC SIGNAL	HEDGE ROW	PROPERTY LINE	FINISH GRADE
STREET SIGN	FENCE	TOWNSHIP LINE	EXISTING ELEVATION

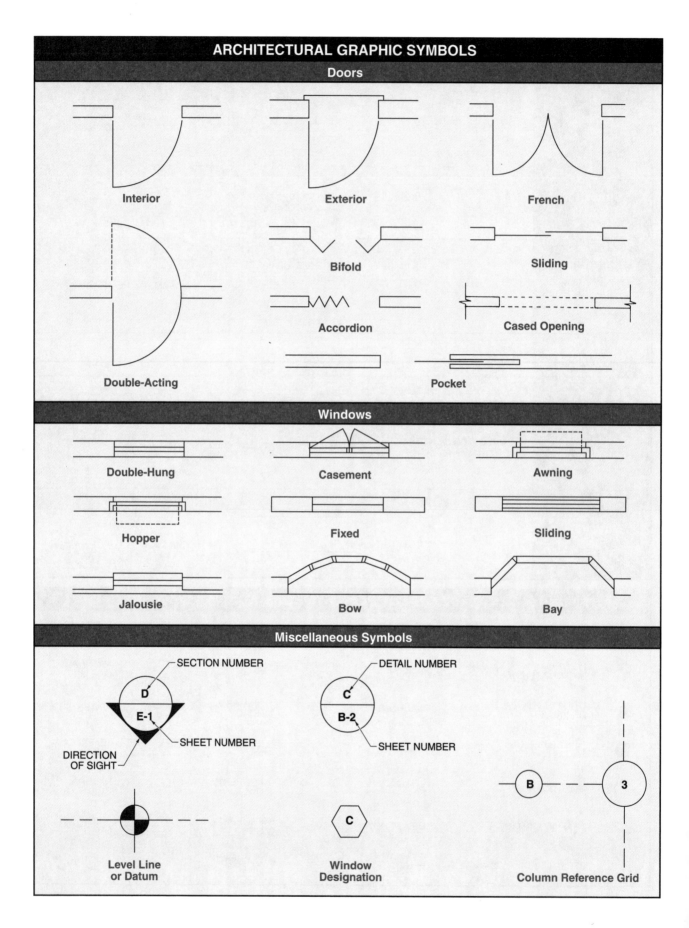

ARCHITECTURAL GRAPHIC SYMBOLS

Doors

Interior

Exterior

French

Double-Acting

Bifold

Accordion

Sliding

Cased Opening

Pocket

Windows

Double-Hung

Casement

Awning

Hopper

Fixed

Sliding

Jalousie

Bow

Bay

Miscellaneous Symbols

SECTION NUMBER

D

E-1

DIRECTION OF SIGHT

SHEET NUMBER

DETAIL NUMBER

C

B-2

SHEET NUMBER

B — — 3

Level Line or Datum

Window Designation

Column Reference Grid

ELECTRICAL SYMBOLS . . .

Lighting Outlets

OUTLET BOX AND INCANDESCENT LIGHTING FIXTURE	CEILING WALL
INCANDESCENT TRACK LIGHTING	
BLANKED OUTLET	B B
DROP CORD	D
EXIT LIGHT AND OUTLET BOX. SHADED AREAS DENOTE FACES.	
OUTDOOR POLE-MOUNTED FIXTURES	
JUNCTION BOX	J J
LAMPHOLDER WITH PULL SWITCH	L_{PS} L_{PS}
MULTIPLE FLOODLIGHT ASSEMBLY	
EMERGENCY BATTERY PACK WITH CHARGER	
INDIVIDUAL FLUORESCENT FIXTURE	
OUTLET BOX AND FLUORESCENT LIGHTING TRACK FIXTURE	
CONTINUOUS FLUORESCENT FIXTURE	
SURFACE-MOUNTED FLUORESCENT FIXTURE	

Panelboards

FLUSH-MOUNTED PANELBOARD AND CABINET	
SURFACE-MOUNTED PANELBOARD AND CABINET	

Convenience Outlets

SINGLE RECEPTACLE OUTLET	
DUPLEX RECEPTACLE OUTLET– 120 V	
TRIPLEX RECEPTACLE OUTLET– 240 V	
SPLIT-WIRED DUPLEX RECEPTACLE OUTLET	
SPLIT-WIRED TRIPLEX RECEPTACLE OUTLET	
SINGLE SPECIAL-PURPOSE RECEPTACLE OUTLET	
DUPLEX SPECIAL-PURPOSE RECEPTACLE OUTLET	
RANGE OUTLET	R
SPECIAL-PURPOSE CONNECTION	DW
CLOSED-CIRCUIT TELEVISION CAMERA	
CLOCK HANGER RECEPTACLE	C
FAN HANGER RECEPTACLE	F
FLOOR SINGLE RECEPTACLE OUTLET	
FLOOR DUPLEX RECEPTACLE OUTLET	
FLOOR SPECIAL-PURPOSE OUTLET	
UNDERFLOOR DUCT AND JUNCTION BOX FOR TRIPLE, DOUBLE, OR SINGLE DUCT SYSTEM AS INDICATED BY NUMBER OF PARALLEL LINES	

Busducts and Wireways

SERVICE, FEEDER, OR PLUG-IN BUSWAY	B B B
CABLE THROUGH LADDER OR CHANNEL	C C C
WIREWAY	W W W

Switch Outlets

SINGLE-POLE SWITCH	S
DOUBLE-POLE SWITCH	S_2
THREE-WAY SWITCH	S_3
FOUR-WAY SWITCH	S_4
AUTOMATIC DOOR SWITCH	S_D
KEY-OPERATED SWITCH	S_K
CIRCUIT BREAKER	S_{CB}
WEATHERPROOF CIRCUIT BREAKER	S_{WCB}
DIMMER	S_{DM}
REMOTE CONTROL SWITCH	S_{RC}
WEATHERPROOF SWITCH	S_{WP}
FUSED SWITCH	S_F
WEATHERPROOF FUSED SWITCH	S_{WF}
TIME SWITCH	S_T
CEILING PULL SWITCH	
SWITCH AND SINGLE RECEPTACLE	
SWITCH AND DOUBLE RECEPTACLE	
A STANDARD SYMBOL WITH AN ADDED LOWERCASE SUBSCRIPT LETTER IS USED TO DESIGNATE A VARIATION IN STANDARD EQUIPMENT	a,b a,b $S_{a,b}$

...ELECTRICAL SYMBOLS

Commercial and Industrial Systems

PAGING SYSTEM DEVICE

FIRE ALARM SYSTEM DEVICE

COMPUTER DATA SYSTEM DEVICE

PRIVATE TELEPHONE SYSTEM DEVICE

SOUND SYSTEM

FIRE ALARM CONTROL PANEL — FACP

Signaling System Outlets for Residential Systems

PUSHBUTTON

BUZZER

BELL

BELL AND BUZZER COMBINATION

COMPUTER DATA OUTLET

BELL RINGING TRANSFORMER — BT

ELECTRIC DOOR OPENER — D

CHIME — CH

TELEVISION OUTLET — TV

THERMOSTAT — T

Underground Electrical Distribution or Electrical Lighting Systems

MANHOLE — M

HANDHOLE — H

TRANSFORMER-MANHOLE OR VAULT — TM

TRANSFORMER PAD — TP

UNDERGROUND DIRECT BURIAL CABLE

UNDERGROUND DUCT LINE

STREET LIGHT STANDARD FED FROM UNDERGROUND CIRCUIT

Above-Ground Electrical Distribution or Lighting Systems

POLE

STREET LIGHT AND BRACKET

PRIMARY CIRCUIT

SECONDARY CIRCUIT

DOWN GUY

HEAD GUY

SIDEWALK GUY

SERVICE WEATHERHEAD

Panel Circuits and Miscellaneous

LIGHTING PANEL

POWER PANEL

WIRING—CONCEALED IN CEILING OR WALL

WIRING—CONCEALED IN FLOOR

WIRING EXPOSED

HOME RUN TO PANELBOARD
Indicate number of circuits by number of arrows. Any circuit without such designation indicates a two-wire circuit. For a greater number of wires indicate as follows: —///— (3 wires)
—////— (4 wires), etc.

FEEDERS
Use heavy lines and designate by number corresponding to listing in feeder schedule

WIRING TURNED UP

WIRING TURNED DOWN

GENERATOR — G

MOTOR — M

INSTRUMENT (SPECIFY) — I

TRANSFORMER — T

CONTROLLER

EXTERNALLY-OPERATED DISCONNECT SWITCH

PULL BOX

PLUMBING SYMBOLS. . .

Fixtures...

STANDARD BATHTUB	
OVAL BATHTUB	
WHIRLPOOL BATH	
SHOWER STALL	
SHOWER HEAD	
TANK-TYPE WATER CLOSET	
WALL-MOUNTED WATER CLOSET	
FLOOR-MOUNTED WATER CLOSET	
LOW-PROFILE WATER CLOSET	
BIDET	
WALL-MOUNTED URINAL	
FLOOR-MOUNTED URINAL	
TROUGH-TYPE URINAL	
WALL-MOUNTED LAVATORY	
PEDESTAL LAVATORY	
BUILT-IN LAVATORY	
WHEELCHAIR LAVATORY	
CORNER LAVATORY	
FLOOR DRAIN	
FLOOR SINK	

...Fixtures

LAUNDRY TRAY	
BUILT-IN SINK	
DOUBLE OR TRIPLE BUILT-IN SINK	
COMMERCIAL KITCHEN SINK	
SERVICE SINK	SS
CLINIC SERVICE SINK	
FLOOR-MOUNTED SERVICE SINK	
DRINKING FOUNTAIN	DF
WATER COOLER	
HOT WATER TANK	HWT
WATER HEATER	WH
METER	M
HOSE BIBB	HB
GAS OUTLET	G
GREASE SEPARATOR	G
GARAGE DRAIN	
FLOOR DRAIN WITH BACKWATER VALVE	

Piping...

SOIL, WASTE, OR LEADER—ABOVE GRADE	
SOIL, WASTE, OR LEADER—BELOW GRADE	
VENT	
COMBINATION WASTE AND VENT	SV
STORM DRAIN	SD
COLD WATER	

...Piping

CHILLED DRINKING WATER SUPPLY	DWS
CHILLED DRINKING WATER RETURN	DWR
HOT WATER	
HOT WATER RETURN	
SANITIZING HOT WATER SUPPLY (180° F)	
SANITIZING HOT WATER RETURN (180° F)	
DRY STANDPIPE	DSP
COMBINATION STANDPIPE	CSP
MAIN SUPPLIES SPRINKLER	S
BRANCH AND HEAD SPRINKLER	
GAS—LOW PRESSURE	G — G
GAS—MEDIUM PRESSURE	MG
GAS—HIGH PRESSURE	HG
COMPRESSED AIR	A
OXYGEN	O
NITROGEN	N
HYDROGEN	H
HELIUM	HE
ARGON	AR
LIQUID PETROLEUM GAS	LPG
INDUSTRIAL WASTE	INW
CAST IRON	CI
CULVERT PIPE	CP
CLAY TILE	CT
DUCTILE IRON	DI
REINFORCED CONCRETE	RCP
DRAIN—OPEN TILE OR AGRICULTURAL TILE	

. . .PLUMBING SYMBOLS

Pipe Fitting and Valve Symbols

	FLANGED	SCREWED	BELL & SPIGOT		FLANGED	SCREWED	BELL & SPIGOT		FLANGED	SCREWED	BELL & SPIGOT
BUSHING				REDUCING FLANGE				AUTOMATIC BYPASS VALVE			
CAP				BULL PLUG				AUTOMATIC REDUCING VALVE			
REDUCING CROSS				PIPE PLUG				STRAIGHT CHECK VALVE			
STRAIGHT-SIZE CROSS				CONCENTRIC REDUCER				COCK			
CROSSOVER				ECCENTRIC REDUCER				DIAPHRAGM VALVE			
45° ELBOW				SLEEVE				FLOAT VALVE			
90° ELBOW				STRAIGHT-SIZE TEE				GATE VALVE			
ELBOW—TURNED DOWN				TEE—OUTLET UP				MOTOR-OPERATED GATE VALVE			
ELBOW—TURNED UP				TEE—OUTLET DOWN				GLOBE VALVE			
BASE ELBOW				DOUBLE-SWEEP TEE				MOTOR-OPERATED GLOBE VALVE			
DOUBLE-BRANCH ELBOW				REDUCING TEE				ANGLE HOSE VALVE			
LONG-RADIUS ELBOW				SINGLE-SWEEP TEE				GATE HOSE VALVE			
REDUCING ELBOW				SIDE OUTLET TEE—OUTLET DOWN				GLOBE HOSE VALVE			
SIDE OUTLET ELBOW—OUTLET DOWN				SIDE OUTLET TEE—OUTLET UP				LOCKSHIELD VALVE			
SIDE OUTLET ELBOW—OUTLET UP				UNION				QUICK-OPENING VALVE			
STREET ELBOW				ANGLE CHECK VALVE				SAFETY VALVE			
CONNECTING PIPE JOINT				ANGLE GATE VALVE—ELEVATION				GOVERNOR-OPERATED AUTOMATIC VALVE			
EXPANSION JOINT				ANGLE GATE VALVE—PLAN							
LATERAL				ANGLE GLOBE VALVE—ELEVATION							
ORIFICE FLANGE				ANGLE GLOBE VALVE—PLAN							

HVAC SYMBOLS

Equipment Symbols	Ductwork	Heating Piping
EXPOSED RADIATOR	DUCT (1ST FIGURE, WIDTH; 2ND FIGURE, DEPTH) — 12 X 20	HIGH-PRESSURE STEAM — HPS —
RECESSED RADIATOR	DIRECTION OF FLOW	MEDIUM-PRESSURE STEAM — MPS —
FLUSH ENCLOSED RADIATOR	FLEXIBLE CONNECTION	LOW-PRESSURE STEAM — LPS —
PROJECTING ENCLOSED RADIATOR	DUCTWORK WITH ACOUSTICAL LINING	HIGH-PRESSURE RETURN — HPR —
UNIT HEATER (PROPELLER)—PLAN	FIRE DAMPER WITH ACCESS DOOR — FD / AD	MEDIUM-PRESSURE RETURN — MPR —
UNIT HEATER (CENTRIFUGAL)—PLAN	MANUAL VOLUME DAMPER — VD	LOW-PRESSURE RETURN — LPR —
UNIT VENTILATOR—PLAN	AUTOMATIC VOLUME DAMPER	BOILER BLOW OFF — BD —
STEAM	EXHAUST, RETURN OR OUTSIDE AIR DUCT—SECTION — 20 X 12	CONDENSATE OR VACUUM PUMP DISCHARGE — VPD —
DUPLEX STRAINER	SUPPLY DUCT—SECTION — 20 X 12	FEEDWATER PUMP DISCHARGE — PPD —
PRESSURE-REDUCING VALVE	CEILING DIFFUSER SUPPLY OUTLET — 20" DIA CD 1000 CFM	MAKEUP WATER — MU —
AIR LINE VALVE	CEILING DIFFUSER SUPPLY OUTLET — 20 X 12 CD 700 CFM	AIR RELIEF LINE — V —
STRAINER	LINEAR DIFFUSER — 96 X 6-LD 400 CFM	FUEL OIL SUCTION — FOS —
THERMOMETER	FLOOR REGISTER — 20 X 12 FR 700 CFM	FUEL OIL RETURN — FOR —
PRESSURE GAUGE AND COCK	TURNING VANES	FUEL OIL VENT — FOV —
RELIEF VALVE	FAN AND MOTOR WITH BELT GUARD	COMPRESSED AIR — A —
AUTOMATIC 3-WAY VALVE		HOT WATER HEATING SUPPLY — HW —
AUTOMATIC 2-WAY VALVE		HOT WATER HEATING RETURN — HWR —
SOLENOID VALVE	LOUVER OPENING — 20 X 12-L 700 CFM	

Air Conditioning Piping

REFRIGERANT LIQUID	— RL —
REFRIGERANT DISCHARGE	— RD —
REFRIGERANT SUCTION	— RS —
CONDENSER WATER SUPPLY	— CWS —
CONDENSER WATER RETURN	— CWR —
CHILLED WATER SUPPLY	— CHWS —
CHILLED WATER RETURN	— CHWR —
MAKEUP WATER	— MU —
HUMIDIFICATION LINE	— H —
DRAIN	— D —

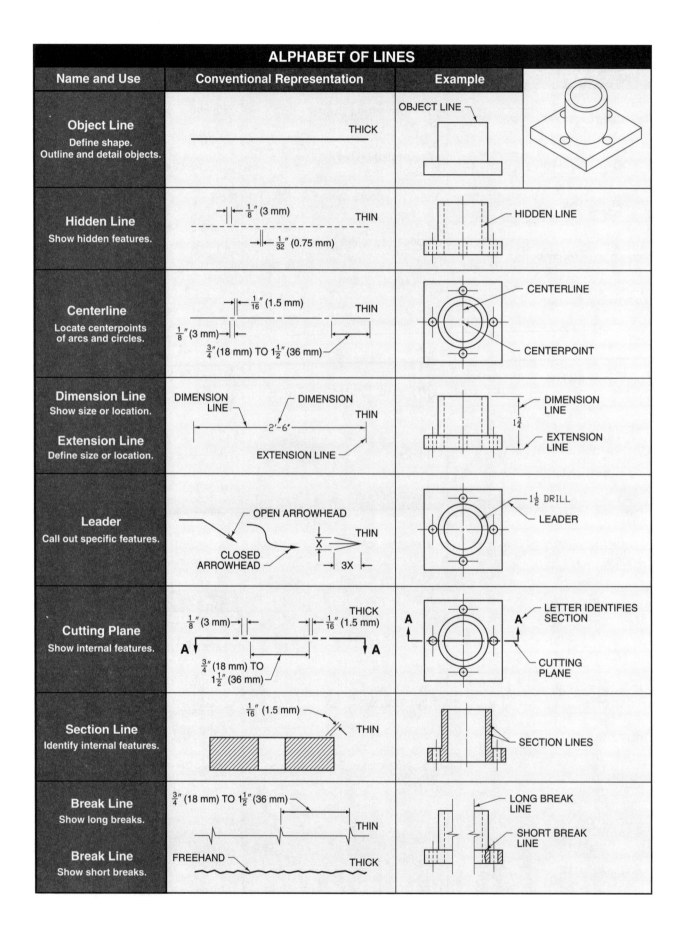

ALPHABET OF LINES

Name and Use	Conventional Representation	Example
Object Line — Define shape. Outline and detail objects.	THICK	OBJECT LINE
Hidden Line — Show hidden features.	$\frac{1}{8}''$ (3 mm) — THIN — $\frac{1}{32}''$ (0.75 mm)	HIDDEN LINE
Centerline — Locate centerpoints of arcs and circles.	$\frac{1}{16}''$ (1.5 mm) — THIN — $\frac{1}{8}''$ (3 mm) — $\frac{3}{4}''$ (18 mm) TO $1\frac{1}{2}''$ (36 mm)	CENTERLINE — CENTERPOINT
Dimension Line — Show size or location. **Extension Line** — Define size or location.	DIMENSION LINE — DIMENSION — THIN — 2'-6" — EXTENSION LINE	DIMENSION LINE — $1\frac{3}{4}$ — EXTENSION LINE
Leader — Call out specific features.	OPEN ARROWHEAD — THIN — X — CLOSED ARROWHEAD — 3X	$1\frac{1}{2}$ DRILL — LEADER
Cutting Plane — Show internal features.	$\frac{1}{8}''$ (3 mm) — THICK — $\frac{1}{16}''$ (1.5 mm) — A — A — $\frac{3}{4}''$ (18 mm) TO $1\frac{1}{2}''$ (36 mm)	A — A — LETTER IDENTIFIES SECTION — CUTTING PLANE
Section Line — Identify internal features.	$\frac{1}{16}''$ (1.5 mm) — THIN	SECTION LINES
Break Line — Show long breaks. **Break Line** — Show short breaks.	$\frac{3}{4}''$ (18 mm) TO $1\frac{1}{2}''$ (36 mm) — THIN — FREEHAND — THICK	LONG BREAK LINE — SHORT BREAK LINE

TRANSVERSAL SPACING (″)
LONGITUDINAL SPACING (″)

W = SMOOTH WIRE
D = DEFORMED WIRE

$6 \times 6 - W2.9 \times W2.9$

LONGITUDINAL
WIRE SIZE
(CROSS-SECTIONAL AREA)

TRANSVERSAL
WIRE SIZE
(CROSS-SECTIONAL AREA)

COMMON STOCK SIZES OF WELDED WIRE REINFORCEMENT

New Designation (W-Number)	Old Designation (Wire Gauge)	Diameter*		Steel Area†		Weight‡
				Longitudinal	Transverse	
$6 \times 6 - W1.4 \times W1.4$	$6 \times 6 - 10 \times 10$	.134	⅛	.028	.028	21
$6 \times 6 - W2.0 \times W2.0$	$6 \times 6 - 8 \times 8$	.160	5⁄32	.040	.040	29
$6 \times 6 - W2.9 \times W2.9$	$6 \times 6 - 6 \times 6$	.192	3⁄16	.058	.058	42
$6 \times 6 - W4.0 \times W4.0$	$6 \times 6 - 4 \times 4$	.226	¼	.080	.080	58
$4 \times 4 - W1.4 \times W1.4$	$4 \times 4 - 10 \times 10$	.134	⅛	.042	.042	31
$4 \times 4 - W2.0 \times W2.0$	$4 \times 4 - 8 \times 8$	.160	5⁄32	.060	.060	43
$4 \times 4 - W2.9 \times W2.9$	$4 \times 4 - 6 \times 6$	.192	3⁄16	.087	.087	62
$4 \times 4 - W4.0 \times W4.0$	$4 \times 4 - 4 \times 4$	.226	¼	.120	.120	85

* in In.
† in sq in./ft
‡ in lb per 100 sq ft

Wire Reinforcement Institute

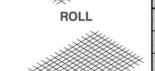

ROLL

SHEET

STANDARD REBAR SIZES

Bar Size Designation	Weight per Foot		Diameter		Cross-Sectional Area Squared	
	lb	kg	in.	cm	in.	cm
#3	0.376	0.171	0.375	0.953	0.11	0.71
#4	.0668	0.303	0.500	1.270	0.20	1.29
#5	1.043	0.473	0.625	1.588	0.31	2.00
#6	1.502	0.681	0.750	1.905	0.44	2.84
#7	2.044	0.927	0.875	2.223	0.60	3.87
#8	2.670	1.211	1.000	2.540	0.79	5.10
#9	3.400	1.542	1.128	2.865	1.00	6.45
#10	4.303	1.952	1.270	3.226	1.27	8.19
#11	5.313	2.410	1.410	3.581	1.56	10.07
#14	7.650	3.470	1.693	4.300	2.25	14.52
#18	13.600	6.169	2.257	5.733	4.00	25.81

MAIN RIB
INITIAL OF PRODUCING MILL
H
11 — BAR SIZE
S — STEEL TYPE (BILLET)
GRADE MARKS

LINE SYSTEM GRADE MARKS

MAIN RIB
INITIAL OF PRODUCING MILL
H
11 — BAR SIZE
S — STEEL TYPE (BILLET)
75
GRADE MARKS

NUMBER SYSTEM GRADE MARKS

ASTM

CONCRETE ESTIMATING TABLE*					
Thickness†	Coverage‡	Thickness†	Coverage‡	Thickness†	Coverage‡
1	324	5	65	9	36
1¼	259	5¼	62	9¼	35
1½	216	5½	59	9½	34
1¾	185	5¾	56	9¾	33
2	162	6	54	10	32.5
2¼	144	6¼	52	10¼	31.5
2½	130	6½	50	10½	31
2¾	118	6¾	48	10¾	30
3	108	7	46	11	29.5
3¼	100	7¼	45	11¼	29
3½	93	7½	43	11½	28
3¾	86	7¾	42	11¾	27.5
4	81	8	40	12	27
4¼	76	8¼	39	12¼	21.5
4½	72	8½	38	12½	18
4¾	68	8¾	37	12¾	13.5

* coverage and thickness based on 1 cu yd of concrete
† in in.
‡ in sq ft

ADMIXTURES		
Class	Function	Agent
Air-entraining	Improve durability Increase workability Reduce bleeding	Salts of wood resins Some synthetic detergents Salts of sulfonated lignin Salts of petroleum acids Fatty and resinous acids and salts Alkylbenzene sulfonates
Set-retarding	Delay setting time Offset adverse high-temperature weather conditions	Lignin Borax Sugars Tartaric acid and salts
Accelerating	Speed setting time Speed early-strength development Offset adverse low-temperature weather conditions	Calcium chloride Triethanolamine
Water-reducing	Reduce quantity of mix water needed for consistency Increase workability without decreasing strength Increase slump	Lignosulfonates Hydroxylated carboxylic acids
Superplasticizer (high-range water-reducing)	Greatly reduce quantity of mix water needed Increase workability without decreasing strength Increase slump	Sulfonated melamine formaldehyde condensates Sulfonated naphthalene formaldehyde condensates

Pozzolan	Improve workability
	Improve plasticity
		Natural materials:
		   Diatomaceous earth
		   Opaline cherts and shales
		   Tuffs and pumicites
		Artificial material:
		   Fly ash

Waterproofing and dampproofing	Decrease permeability Preserve design strength	Stearate of calcium, aluminum, ammonium, or butyl Petroleum greases or oils Soluble chlorides
Pigment	Add color	Pure mineral oxides
Fiber reinforcement	Reduce surface cracking Increase strength Decrease permeability	Plastic fiber Metal fiber

STANDARD LUMBER SIZES

Type	Nominal Size*		Actual Size*	
	Thickness	Width	Thickness	Width
Common Boards				
	1	2	¾	1½
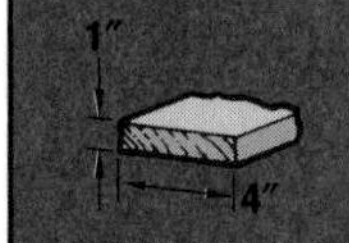	1	4	¾	3½
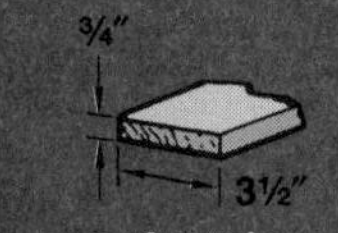	1	6	¾	5½
	1	8	¾	7¼
	1	10	¾	9¼
	1	12	¾	11¼
Dimension				
	2	2	1½	1½
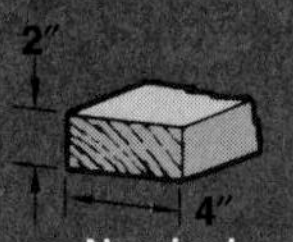	2	4	1½	3½
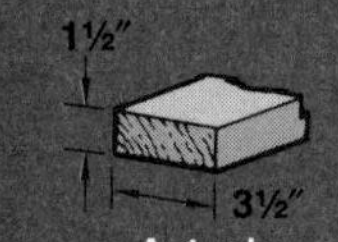	2	6	1½	5½
	2	8	1½	7¼
	2	10	1½	9¼
	2	12	1½	11¼
Timbers				
	5	5	4½	4½
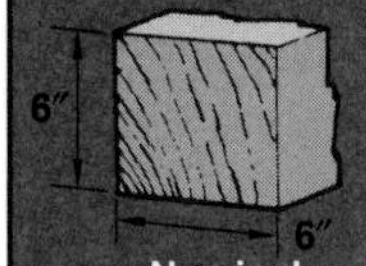	6	6	5½	5½
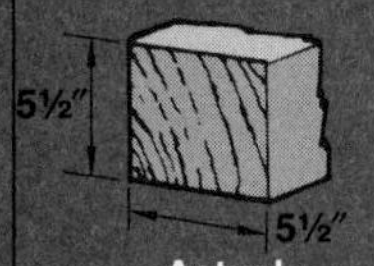	6	8	5½	7½
	6	10	5½	9½
	8	8	7½	7½
	8	10	7½	9½

* in in.

METRIC LUMBER AND PANEL SIZES

Lumber Sizes

Nominal*	Actual*	Metric†
2 x 4	1½ x 3½	38 x 89
2 x 6	1½ x 5½	38 x 140
2 x 8	1½ x 7¼	38 x 184
2 x 10	1½ x 9¼	38 x 235
2 x 12	1½ x 11¼	38 x 286

Panel Sizes

Nominal‡	Actual*	Metric†	
		Soft	Hard
4 x 8	48 x 96	1120 x 2440	1200 x 2400

* in in.
† in mm
‡ in ft

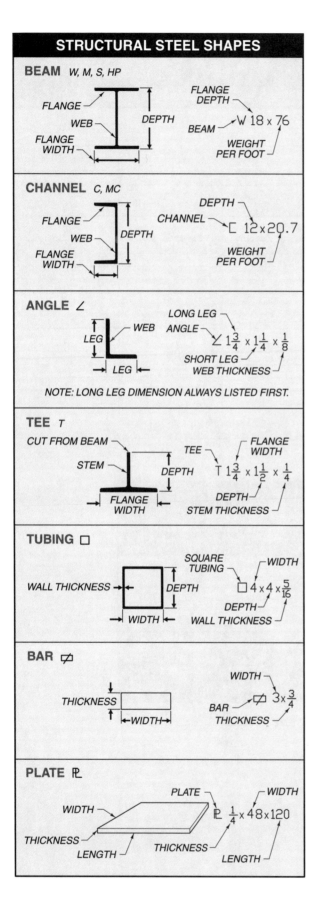

STRUCTURAL STEEL SHAPES

BEAM *W, M, S, HP*

FLANGE
WEB
FLANGE WIDTH
DEPTH
FLANGE DEPTH
BEAM — W 18 × 76
WEIGHT PER FOOT

CHANNEL *C, MC*

FLANGE
WEB
FLANGE WIDTH
DEPTH
DEPTH
CHANNEL — ⊏ 12 × 20.7
WEIGHT PER FOOT

ANGLE ∠

LEG
WEB
LEG
LONG LEG
ANGLE — ∠ 1¾ × 1¼ × ⅛
SHORT LEG
WEB THICKNESS

NOTE: LONG LEG DIMENSION ALWAYS LISTED FIRST.

TEE *T*

CUT FROM BEAM
STEM
FLANGE WIDTH
DEPTH
TEE — T 1¾ × 1½ × ¼
FLANGE WIDTH
DEPTH
STEM THICKNESS

TUBING ☐

WALL THICKNESS
WIDTH
DEPTH
SQUARE TUBING — WIDTH
☐ 4 × 4 × 5/16
DEPTH
WALL THICKNESS

BAR ▱

THICKNESS
WIDTH
WIDTH
BAR — ▱ 3 × ¾
THICKNESS

PLATE ℙ

WIDTH
THICKNESS
LENGTH
PLATE — WIDTH
ℙ ¼ × 48 × 120
THICKNESS
LENGTH

AMERICAN STANDARD CHANNELS

Designation	Depth d*	Flange Width b_f*	Flange Average Thickness t_f*	Web Thickness t_w*
C15 × 50	15	3¾	⅝	11/16
× 40	15	3½	⅝	½
× 33.9	15	3⅜	⅝	⅜
C12 × 30	12	3⅛	½	½
× 25	12	3	½	⅜
× 20.7	12	3	½	5/16
C10 × 30	10	3	7/16	11/16
× 25	10	2⅞	7/16	½
× 20	10	2¾	7/16	⅜
× 15.3	10	2⅝	7/16	¼
C 9 × 20	9	2⅝	7/16	7/16
× 15	9	2½	7/16	5/16
× 13.4	9	2⅜	7/16	¼
C 8 × 18.75	8	2½	⅜	½
× 13.75	8	2⅜	⅜	5/16
× 11.5	8	2¼	⅜	¼
C 7 × 14.75	7	2¼	⅜	7/16
× 12.25	7	2¼	⅜	5/16
× 9.8	7	2⅛	⅜	3/16
C 6 × 13	6	2⅛	5/16	7/16
× 10.5	6	2	5/16	5/16
× 8.2	6	1⅞	5/16	3/16
C 5 × 9	5	1⅞	5/16	5/16
× 6.7	5	1¾	5/16	3/16
C 4 × 7.25	4	1¾	5/16	5/16
× 5.4	4	1⅝	5/16	3/16
C 3 × 6	3	1⅝	¼	⅜
× 5	3	1½	¼	¼
× 4.1	3	1⅜	¼	3/16

* in in.

CHANNEL (C)

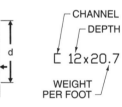

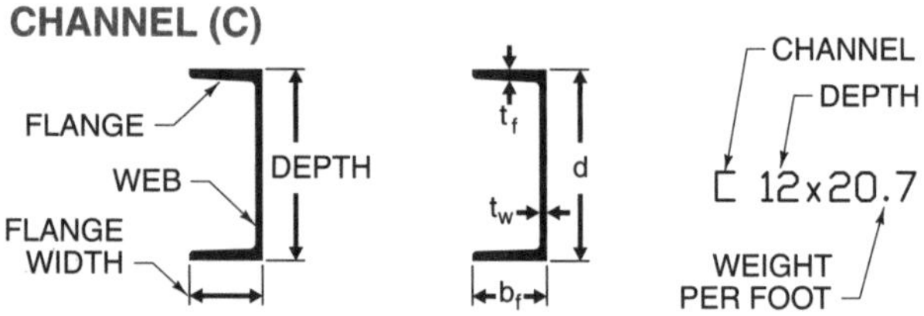

FLANGE
WEB
FLANGE WIDTH
DEPTH
t_f
t_w
d
b_f
CHANNEL
DEPTH
⊏ 12 × 20.7
WEIGHT PER FOOT

BEAM (W)

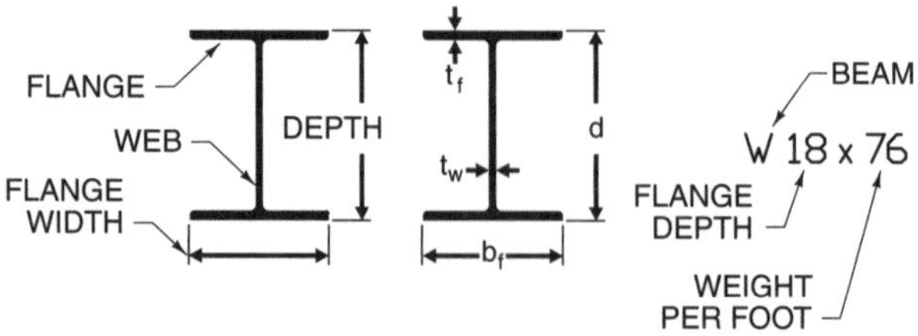

FLANGE
WEB
FLANGE WIDTH
DEPTH
t_f
t_w
d
b_f
BEAM
W 18 × 76
FLANGE DEPTH
WEIGHT PER FOOT

Note: See W Shapes – Dimensions for Detailing.

WIDE-FLANGE SHAPES—DIMENSIONS FOR DETAILING

Designation	Depth d^*	Flange Width b_f^*	Flange Thickness t_f^*	Web Thickness t_w^*	Designation	Depth d^*	Flange Width b_f^*	Flange Thickness t_f^*	Web Thickness t_w^*
W18 × 119	19	11¼	1 1/16	5/8	W12 × 336	16⅞	13⅜	2 15/16	1¾
× 106	18¾	11¼	15/16	9/16	× 305	16⅜	13¼	2 11/16	1⅝
× 97	18⅝	11⅛	7/8	9/16	× 279	15⅞	13⅛	2½	1½
× 86	18⅜	11⅛	3/4	1/2	× 252	15⅜	13	2¼	1⅜
× 76	18¼	11	11/16	7/16	× 230	15	12⅞	2 1/16	1 5/16
W18 × 71	18½	7⅝	13/16	1/2	× 210	14¾	12¾	1⅞	1 3/16
× 65	18⅜	7⅝	3/4	7/16	W12 × 190	14⅜	12⅝	1¾	1 1/16
× 60	18¼	7½	11/16	7/16	× 170	14	12⅝	1 9/16	15/16
× 55	18⅛	7½	5/8	3/8	× 152	13¾	12½	1⅜	7/8
× 50	18	7½	9/16	3/8	× 136	13⅜	12⅜	1¼	13/16
W18 × 46	18	6	5/8	3/8	× 120	13⅛	12⅜	1⅛	11/16
× 40	17⅞	6	1/2	5/16	× 106	12⅞	12¼	1	5/8
× 35	17¾	6	7/16	5/16	× 96	12¾	12⅛	7/8	9/16
W16 × 100	17	10⅜	1	9/16	× 87	12½	12⅛	13/16	1/2
× 89	16¾	10⅜	7/8	1/2	× 79	12⅜	12⅛	3/4	1/2
× 77	16½	10¼	3/4	7/16	× 72	12¼	12	11/16	7/16
× 67	16⅜	10¼	11/16	3/8	× 65	12⅛	12	5/8	3/8
W16 × 57	16⅜	7⅛	11/16	7/16	W12 × 58	12¼	10	5/8	3/8
× 50	15¼	7⅛	5/8	3/8	× 53	12	10	9/16	3/8
× 45	16⅛	7	9/16	3/8	W12 × 50	12¼	8⅛	3/8	5/8
× 40	16	7	1/2	5/16	× 45	12	8	5/16	9/16
× 36	15⅞	7	7/16	5/16	× 40	12	8	5/16	1/2
W16 × 31	15⅞	5½	7/16	1/4	W12 × 35	12½	6½	5/16	1/2
× 26	15¾	5½	3/8	1/4	× 30	12⅜	6½	1/4	7/16
W14 × 730	22⅜	17⅞	4 15/16	3 1/16	× 26	12¼	6½	1/4	3/8
× 665	21⅝	17⅝	4½	2 13/16	W12 × 22	12¼	4	1/4	7/16
× 605	20⅞	17⅜	4 3/8	2 5/8	× 19	12⅛	4	1/4	3/8
× 550	20¼	17¼	3 13/16	2 3/8	× 16	12	4	1/4	1/4
× 500	19⅝	17	3½	2 3/16	× 14	11⅞	4	3/16	1/4
× 455	19	16⅞	3 3/16	2	W10 × 112	11⅜	10⅜	1¼	3/4
W14 × 426	18⅝	16¾	3 1/16	1⅞	× 100	11⅛	10⅜	1⅛	11/16
× 398	18¼	16⅝	2⅞	1¾	× 88	10⅞	10¼	1	5/8
× 370	17⅞	16½	2 11/16	1⅝	× 77	10⅝	10¼	7/8	1/2
× 342	17½	16⅜	2½	1 9/16	× 68	10⅜	10⅛	3/4	1/2
× 311	17⅛	16¼	2¼	1 7/16	ö 60	10¼	10⅛	11/16	7/16
× 283	16¾	16⅛	2 1/16	1 5/16	× 54	10⅛	10	5/8	3/8
× 257	16⅜	16	8 7/8	1 3/16	× 49	10	10	9/16	5/16
× 233	16	15⅞	1¾	1 1/16	W10 × 45	10⅛	8	5/8	3/8
× 211	15¾	15¾	1 9/16	1	× 39	9⅞	8	1/2	5/16
× 193	15½	15¾	1 7/16	7/8	× 33	9¾	8	7/16	5/16
× 176	15¼	15⅝	1 5/16	13/16	W10 × 30	10½	5¾	1/2	5/16
× 159	15	15⅝	1 3/16	3/4	× 26	10⅜	5¾	7/16	1/4
× 145	14¾	15½	1 1/16	11/16	× 22	10⅛	5¾	3/8	1/4
W14 × 132	14⅝	14¾	1	5/8	W10 × 19	10¼	4	3/8	1/4
× 120	14½	14⅝	15/16	9/16	× 17	10⅛	4	5/16	1/4
× 109	14⅜	14⅝	7/8	1/2	× 15	10	4	1/4	1/4
× 99	14⅛	14⅝	3/4	1/2	× 12	9⅞	4	3/16	3/16
× 90	14	14½	11/16	7/16	W8 × 67	9	8¼	15/16	9/16
W14 × 82	14¼	10⅛	7/8	1/2	× 58	8¾	8¼	13/16	1/2
× 74	14⅛	10⅛	13/16	7/16	× 48	8½	8⅛	11/16	3/8
× 68	14	10	3/4	7/16	× 40	8¼	8⅛	9/16	3/8
× 61	13⅞	10	5/8	3/8	× 35	8⅛	8	1/2	5/16
W14 × 53	13⅞	8	11/16	3/8	× 31	8	8	7/16	5/16
× 48	13¾	8	5/8	5/16	W8 × 28	8	6½	7/16	5/16
× 43	13⅝	8	1/2	5/16	× 24	7⅞	6½	3/8	1/4
W14 × 38	14⅛	6¾	1/2	5/16	W8 × 21	8¼	5¼	3/8	1/4
× 34	14	6¾	7/16	5/16	× 18	8⅛	5¼	5/16	1/4
× 30	13⅞	6¾	3/8	1/4	W8 × 15	8⅛	4	5/16	1/4
W14 × 26	13⅞	5	7/16	1/4	× 13	8	4	1/4	1/4
× 22	13¾	5	5/16	1/4	× 10	7⅞	4	3/16	3/16

* in in.

ANGLES (EQUAL LEGS)—DIMENSIONS FOR DETAILING

Size and Thickness*	Size and Thickness*	Size and Thickness*
∠8 × 8 × 1⅛	∠4 × 4 × ¾	∠2 × 2 × ⅜
1	⅝	⁵⁄₁₆
⅞	½	¼
¾	⁷⁄₁₆	³⁄₁₆
⅝	⅜	⅛
⁹⁄₁₆	⁵⁄₁₆	∠1¾ × 1¾ × ¼
½	¼	³⁄₁₆
∠6 × 6 × 1	∠3½ × 3½ × ½	⅛
⅞	⁷⁄₁₆	∠1½ × 1½ × ¼
¾	⅜	³⁄₁₆
⅝	⁵⁄₁₆	⁵⁄₃₂
⁹⁄₁₆	¼	⅛
½	∠3 × 3 × ½	∠1¼ × 1¼ × ¼
⁷⁄₁₆	⁷⁄₁₆	³⁄₁₆
⅜	⅜	⅛
⁵⁄₁₆	⁵⁄₁₆	∠1 × 1 × ¼
∠5 × 5 × ⅞	¼	³⁄₁₆
¾	³⁄₁₆	⅛
⅝	∠2½ × 2½ × ½	
½	⅜	
⁷⁄₁₆	⁵⁄₁₆	
⅜	¼	
⁵⁄₁₆	³⁄₁₆	

* in in.

ANGLE ∠

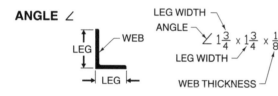

ANGLES (UNEQUAL LEGS)— DIMENSIONS FOR DETAILING

Size and Thickness*	Size and Thickness*	Size and Thickness*
∠9 × 4 × 1	∠6 × 3½ × ½	∠3½ × 2½ × ½
⅞	⅜	⁷⁄₁₆
¾	⁵⁄₁₆	⅜
⅝	¼	⁵⁄₁₆
⁹⁄₁₆	∠5 × 3½ × ¾	¼
½	⅝	∠3 × 2½ × ½
∠8 × 6 × 1	½	⁷⁄₁₆
⅞	⁷⁄₁₆	⅜
¾	⅜	⁵⁄₁₆
⅝	⁵⁄₁₆	¼
⁹⁄₁₆	¼	³⁄₁₆
½	∠5 × 3 × ½	∠3 × 2 × ½
⁷⁄₁₆	⁷⁄₁₆	⁷⁄₁₆
∠8 × 4 × 1	⅜	⅜
⅞	⁵⁄₁₆	⁵⁄₁₆
¾	¼	¼
⅝	∠4 × 3½ × ⅝	³⁄₁₆
⁹⁄₁₆	½	∠2½ × 2 × ⅜
½	⁷⁄₁₆	⁵⁄₁₆
⁷⁄₁₆	⅜	¼
∠7 × 4 × ⅞	⁵⁄₁₆	³⁄₁₆
¾	¼	∠2½ × 1½ × ⁵⁄₁₆
⅝	∠4 × 3 × ⅝	¼
⁹⁄₁₆	½	³⁄₁₆
½	⁷⁄₁₆	∠2 × 1½ × ¼
⁷⁄₁₆	⅜	³⁄₁₆
⅜	⁵⁄₁₆	⅛
∠6 × 4 × ⅞	¼	∠2 × 1¼ × ¼
¾	∠3½ × 3 × ½	³⁄₁₆
⅝	⁷⁄₁₆	⅛
⁹⁄₁₆	⅜	∠1¾ × 1¼ × ¼
½	⁵⁄₁₆	³⁄₁₆
⁷⁄₁₆	¼	⅛
⅜		
⁵⁄₁₆		
¼		

* in in.

ANGLE ∠

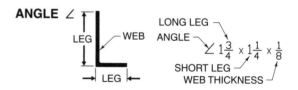

BRICK

Designation	Nominal Dimensions*			Joint Thickness*	Actual Dimensions*		
	t	h	l		t	h	l
STANDARD MODULAR	4	$2^2/_3$	8	$^3/_8$	$3^5/_8$	$2^1/_4$	$7^5/_8$
				$^1/_2$	$3^1/_2$	$2^3/_{16}$	$7^1/_2$
NORMAN	4	$2^2/_3$	12	$^3/_8$	$3^5/_8$	$2^1/_4$	$11^5/_8$
				$^1/_2$	$3^1/_2$	$2^3/_{16}$	$11^1/_2$
SCR	6	$2^2/_3$	12	$^3/_8$	$5^5/_8$	$2^1/_4$	$11^5/_8$
				$^1/_2$	$5^1/_2$	$2^1/_4$	$11^1/_2$
ENGINEER	4	$3^1/_5$	8	$^3/_8$	$3^5/_8$	$2^{13}/_{16}$	$7^5/_8$
				$^1/_2$	$3^1/_2$	$2^{11}/_{16}$	$7^1/_2$
ECONOMY	4	4	8	$^3/_8$	$3^5/_8$	$3^5/_8$	$7^5/_8$
				$^1/_2$	$3^1/_2$	$3^1/_2$	$7^1/_2$

CONCRETE MASONRY UNITS

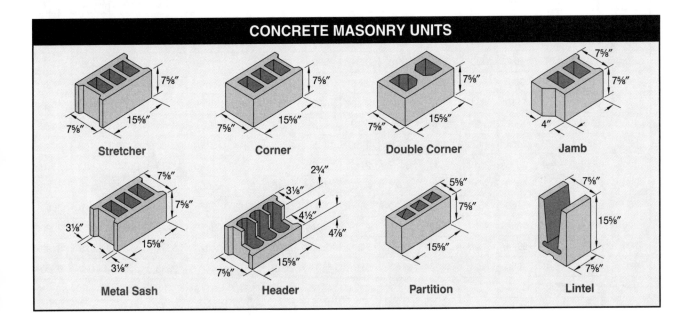

Stretcher   Corner   Double Corner   Jamb

Metal Sash   Header   Partition   Lintel

MASONRY WALL STANDARD SIZE FACE AND BUILDING BRICK*

Wall‡	Running			Common (Header Course Every 7th Course)			English and English Cross† (Full Headers Every 6th Course)			Flemish (Full Headers Every 5th Course)			Double Headers (Alternating with Stretchers Every 5th Course)		
	Face Brick	Building Brick		Face Brick	Building Brick		Face Brick	Building Brick		Face Brick	Building Brick		Face Brick	Building Brick	
		8″ Wall	12″ Wall		8″ Wall	12″ Wall		8″ Wall	12″ Wall		8″ Wall	12″ Wall		8″ Wall	12″ Wall
1	6.16	6.16	12.32	7.04	5.28	11.44	7.19	5.13	11.29	6.57	5.75	11.91	6.78	5.54	11.70
5	31	31	62	36	27	58	36	26	57	33	29	60	34	28	59
10	62	62	124	71	53	115	72	52	113	66	58	120	68	56	117
20	124	124	248	141	106	229	144	103	226	132	115	269	136	111	234
30	185	185	370	212	159	344	216	154	339	198	173	358	204	167	351
40	247	247	494	282	212	458	288	206	452	263	230	477	272	222	468
50	308	308	616	352	264	572	360	257	565	329	288	596	339	277	585
60	370	370	740	423	317	687	432	308	675	395	345	715	407	333	702
70	432	432	864	493	370	801	504	360	791	460	403	834	475	388	819
80	493	493	986	564	423	916	576	411	904	526	460	953	543	444	936
90	555	555	1110	634	476	1030	648	462	1017	592	518	1072	611	499	1053
100	616	616	1232	704	528	1144	719	513	1129	657	575	1191	678	554	1170
200	1232	1232	2464	1408	1056	2288	1438	1026	2258	1314	1150	2382	1356	1108	2340
300	1848	1848	3696	2110	1584	3432	2157	1539	3387	1971	1725	3573	2034	1662	3510
400	2464	2464	4928	2816	2112	4576	2876	2052	4516	2628	2300	4764	2712	2216	4680
500	3080	3080	6160	3520	2640	5720	3595	2565	5645	3285	2875	5955	3390	2770	5850
600	3696	3696	7392	4224	3168	6864	4314	3078	6774	3942	3450	7146	4068	3324	7020
700	4312	4312	8624	4928	3696	8010	5033	3591	7903	4599	4025	8337	4746	3878	8190
800	4928	4928	9856	5632	4224	9152	5752	4104	9032	5256	4600	9528	5424	4432	9360
900	5544	5544	11,088	6336	4752	10,296	6471	4617	10,161	5913	5175	10,719	6102	4986	10,530
1000	6160	6160	12,320	7040	5280	11,440	7190	5130	11,290	6570	5750	11,910	6780	5540	11,700

* For other than ½″ joints, add 21% for ⅛″ joint, 14% for ¼″ joint, 7% for ⅜″ joint. Subtract 5% for ⅝″ joint, 10% for ¾″ joint, 15% for ⅞″ joint, and 20% for 1″ joint
† Quantities also apply to common bond with headers in every sixth course
‡ in sq ft

POWER FORMULAS—1φ, 3φ

Phase	To Find	Use Formula	Example		
			Given	Find	Solution
1φ	I	$I = \dfrac{VA}{V}$	32,000 VA, 240 V	I	$I = \dfrac{VA}{V}$ $I = \dfrac{32,000\ VA}{240\ V}$ $I = \textbf{133 A}$
1φ	VA	$VA = I \times V$	100 A, 240 V	VA	$VA = I \times A$ $VA = 100\ A \times 240\ V$ $VA = \textbf{24,000 VA}$
1φ	V	$V = \dfrac{VA}{I}$	42,000 VA, 350 A	V	$V = \dfrac{VA}{I}$ $V = \dfrac{42,000\ VA}{350\ A}$ $V = \textbf{120 V}$
3φ	I	$I = \dfrac{VA}{V \times \sqrt{3}}$	72,000 VA, 208 V	I	$I = \dfrac{VA}{V \times \sqrt{3}}$ $I = \dfrac{72,000\ VA}{360\ V}$ $I = \textbf{200 A}$
3φ	VA	$VA = I \times V \times \sqrt{3}$	2 A, 240 V	VA	$VA = I \times V \times \sqrt{3}$ $VA = 2 \times 416$ $VA = \textbf{832 VA}$

VOLTAGE DROP FORMULAS—1φ, 3φ

Phase	To Find	Use Formula	Example		
			Given	Find	Solution
1φ	VD	$VD = \dfrac{2 \times R \times L \times I}{1000}$	240 V, 40 A, 60′ L, .764R	VD	$VD = \dfrac{2 \times R \times L \times I}{1000}$ $VD = \dfrac{2 \times .764 \times 60 \times 40}{1000}$ $VD = \textbf{3.67 V}$
3φ	VD	$VD = \dfrac{2 \times R \times L \times I}{1000} \times .866$	208 V, 110 A, 75′ L, .194 R, .866 multiplier	VD	$VD = \dfrac{2 \times R \times L \times I}{1000} \times .866$ $VD = \dfrac{2 \times .194 \times 75 \times 110}{1000} \times .866$ $VD = \textbf{2.77 V}$

RACEWAYS	
EMT	Electrical Metallic Tubing
ENT	Electrical Nonmetallic Tubing
FMC	Flexible Metal Conduit
FMT	Flexible Metallic Tubing
IMC	Intermediate Metal Conduit
LTFMC	Liquidtight Flexible Metal Conduit
LTFNMC	Liquidtight Flexible Nonmetallic Conduit
RMC	Rigid Metal Conduit
RNMC	Rigid Nonmetallic Conduit

CABLES	
AC	Armored Cable
BX	Tradename for AC
FCC	Flat Conductor Cable
IGS	Integrated Gas Spacer Cable
MC	Metal-Clad Cable
MI	Mineral-Insulated, Metal Sheathed Cable
MV	Medium Voltage
NM	Nonmetallic-Sheathed Cable (dry)
NMC	Nonmetallic-Sheathed Cable (dry or damp)
NMS	Nonmetallic-Sheathed Cable (dry)
SE	Service-Entrance Cable (dry)
TC	Tray Cable
UF	Underground Feeder Cable
USE	Underground Service-Entrance Cable

FUSES AND ITCBs	
Increase	Standard Ampere Ratings
5	15, 20, 25, 30, 35, 40, 45
10	50, 60, 70, 80, 90, 100, 110
25	125, 150, 175, 200, 225
50	250, 300, 350, 400, 450
100	500, 600, 700, 800
200	1000, 1200
400	1600, 2000
500	2500
1000	3000, 4000, 5000, 6000

1 A, 3 A, 6 A, 10 A, and 601 A are additional standard ratings for fuses.

COMMON ELECTRICAL INSULATIONS

60° C 140° F	75° C 167° F	90° C 194° F
TW	FEPW	TBS
UF	RH	SA
	RHW	SIS
	THHW	FEP
	THW	FEPB
	THWN	MI
	XHHW	RHH
	USE	RHW-2
	ZW	THHN
		THHW
		THW-2
		THWN-2
		USE-2
		XHH
		XHHW
		XHHW-2
		ZW-2

INSULATION — • TABLE 310-13

AMPACITY — • TABLE 310-16

COPPER, ALUMINUM, OR COPPER-CLAD ALUMINUM

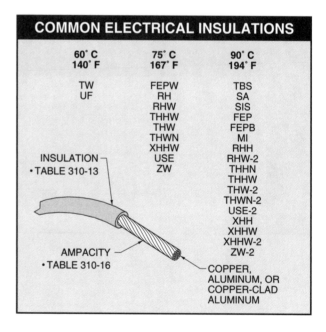

DECIMAL EQUIVALENTS OF AN INCH

Fraction	Decimal	Fraction	Decimal	Fraction	Decimal	Fraction	Decimal
1/64	0.015625	17/64	0.265625	33/64	0.515625	49/64	0.765625
1/32	0.03125	9/32	0.28125	17/32	0.53125	25/32	0.78125
3/64	0.046875	19/64	0.296875	35/64	0.546875	51/64	0.796875
1/16	0.0625	5/16	0.3125	9/16	0.5625	13/16	0.8125
5/64	0.078125	21/64	0.328125	37/64	0.578125	53/64	0.828125
3/32	0.09375	11/32	0.34375	19/32	0.59375	27/32	0.84375
7/64	0.109375	23/64	0.359375	39/64	0.609375	55/64	0.859375
1/8	0.125	3/8	0.375	5/8	0.625	7/8	0.875
9/64	0.140625	25/64	0.390625	41/64	0.640625	57/64	0.890625
5/32	0.15625	13/32	0.40625	21/32	0.65625	29/32	0.90625
11/64	0.171875	27/64	0.421875	43/64	0.671875	59/64	0.921875
3/16	0.1875	7/16	0.4375	11/16	0.6875	15/16	0.9375
13/64	0.203125	29/64	0.453125	45/64	0.703125	61/64	0.953125
7/32	0.21875	15/32	0.46875	23/32	0.71875	31/32	0.96875
15/64	0.234375	31/64	0.484375	47/64	0.734375	63/64	0.984375
1/4	0.250	1/2	0.500	3/4	0.750	1	1.000

DECIMAL AND METRIC EQUIVALENTS

Fractions	Decimal Inches	Millimeters
1/16	.0625	1.58
1/8	.125	3.18
3/16	.1875	4.76
1/4	.250	6.35
5/16	.3125	7.97
3/8	.375	9.52
7/16	.4375	11.11
1/2	.500	12.70
9/16	.5625	14.29
5/8	.625	15.88
11/16	.6875	17.46
3/4	.750	19.05
13/16	.8125	20.64
7/8	.875	22.22
1	1.00	25.40

DECIMAL EQUIVALENTS OF A FOOT

Inches	Decimal Foot Equivalent	Inches	Decimal Foot Equivalent	Inches	Decimal Foot Equivalent
1/16	0.0052	4 1/16	0.3385	8 1/16	0.6719
1/8	0.0104	4 1/8	0.3438	8 1/8	0.6771
3/16	0.0156	4 3/16	0.3490	8 3/16	0.6823
1/4	0.0208	4 1/4	0.3542	8 1/4	0.6875
5/16	0.0260	4 5/16	0.3594	8 5/16	0.6927
3/8	0.0313	4 3/8	0.3646	8 3/8	0.6979
7/16	0.0365	4 7/16	0.3698	8 7/16	0.7031
1/2	0.0417	4 1/2	0.3750	8 1/2	0.7083
9/16	0.0469	4 9/16	0.3802	8 9/16	0.7135
5/8	0.0521	4 5/8	0.3854	8 5/8	0.7188
11/16	0.0573	4 11/16	0.3906	8 11/16	0.7240
3/4	0.0625	4 3/4	0.3958	8 3/4	0.7292
13/16	0.0677	4 13/16	0.4010	8 13/16	0.7344
7/8	0.0729	4 7/8	0.4063	8 7/8	0.7396
15/16	0.0781	4 15/16	0.4115	8 15/16	0.7448
1	0.0833	5	0.4167	9	0.7500
1 1/16	0.0885	5 1/16	0.4219	9 1/16	0.7552
1 1/8	0.0938	5 1/8	0.4271	9 1/8	0.7604
1 3/16	0.0990	5 3/16	0.4323	9 3/16	0.7656
1 1/4	0.1042	5 1/4	0.4375	9 1/4	0.7708
1 5/16	0.1094	5 5/16	0.4427	9 5/16	0.7760
1 3/8	0.1146	5 3/8	0.4479	9 3/8	0.7813
1 7/16	0.1198	5 7/16	0.4531	9 7/16	0.7865
1 1/2	0.1250	5 1/2	0.4583	9 1/2	0.7917
1 9/16	0.1302	5 9/16	0.4635	9 9/16	0.7969
1 5/8	0.1354	5 5/8	0.4688	9 5/8	0.8021
1 11/16	0.1406	5 11/16	0.4740	9 11/16	0.8073
1 3/4	0.1458	5 3/4	0.4792	9 3/4	0.8125
1 13/16	0.1510	5 13/16	0.4844	9 13/16	0.8177
1 7/8	0.1563	5 7/8	0.4896	9 7/8	0.8229
1 15/16	0.1615	5 15/16	0.4948	9 15/16	0.8281
2	0.1667	6	0.5000	10	0.8333
2 1/16	0.1719	6 1/16	0.5052	10 1/16	0.8385
2 1/8	0.1771	6 1/8	0.5104	10 1/8	0.8438
2 3/16	0.1823	6 3/16	0.5156	10 3/16	0.8490
2 1/4	0.1875	6 1/4	0.5208	10 1/4	0.8542
2 5/16	0.1927	6 5/16	0.5260	10 5/16	0.8594
2 3/8	0.1979	6 3/8	0.5313	10 3/8	0.8646
2 7/16	0.2031	6 7/16	0.5365	10 7/16	0.8698
2 1/2	0.2083	6 1/2	0.5417	10 1/2	0.8750
2 9/16	0.2135	6 9/16	0.5469	10 9/16	0.8802
2 5/8	0.2188	6 5/8	0.5521	10 5/8	0.8854
2 11/16	0.2240	6 11/16	0.5573	10 11/16	0.8906
2 3/4	0.2292	6 3/4	0.5625	10 3/4	0.8958
2 13/16	0.2344	6 13/16	0.5677	10 13/16	0.9010
2 7/8	0.2396	6 7/8	0.5729	10 7/8	0.9063
2 15/16	0.2448	6 15/16	0.5781	10 15/16	0.9115
3	0.2500	7	0.5833	11	0.9167
3 1/16	0.2552	7 1/16	0.5885	11 1/16	0.9219
3 1/8	0.2604	7 1/8	0.5938	11 1/8	0.9271
3 3/16	0.2656	7 3/16	0.5990	11 3/16	0.9323
3 1/4	0.2708	7 1/4	0.6042	11 1/4	0.9375
3 5/16	0.2760	7 5/16	0.6094	11 5/16	0.9427
3 3/8	0.2813	7 3/8	0.6146	11 3/8	0.9479
3 7/16	0.2865	7 7/16	0.6198	11 7/16	0.9531
3 1/2	0.2917	7 1/2	0.6250	11 1/2	0.9583
3 9/16	0.2969	7 9/16	0.6302	11 9/16	0.9635
3 5/8	0.3021	7 5/8	0.6354	11 5/8	0.9688
3 11/16	0.3073	7 11/16	0.6406	11 11/16	0.9740
3 3/4	0.3125	7 3/4	0.6458	11 3/4	0.9792
3 13/16	0.3177	7 13/16	0.6510	11 13/16	0.9844
3 7/8	0.3229	7 7/8	0.6563	11 7/8	0.9896
3 15/16	0.3281	7 15/16	0.6615	11 15/16	0.9948
4	0.3333	7	0.6667	12	1.0000

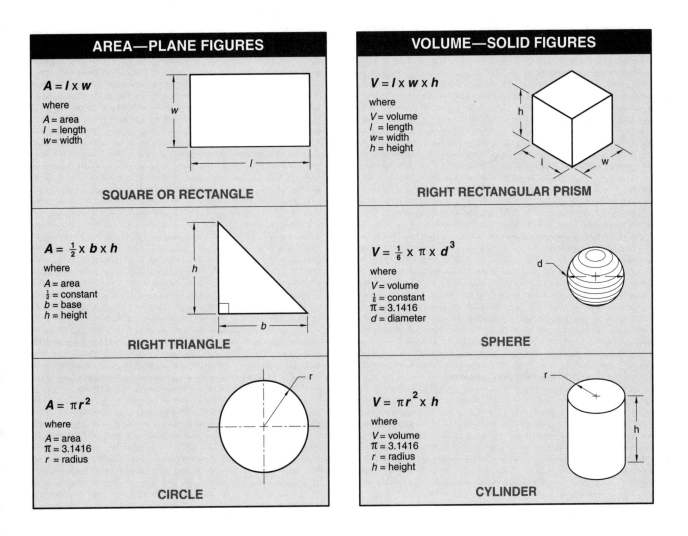

AREA—PLANE FIGURES

$A = l \times w$

where
A = area
l = length
w = width

SQUARE OR RECTANGLE

$A = \frac{1}{2} \times b \times h$

where
A = area
$\frac{1}{2}$ = constant
b = base
h = height

RIGHT TRIANGLE

$A = \pi r^2$

where
A = area
π = 3.1416
r = radius

CIRCLE

VOLUME—SOLID FIGURES

$V = l \times w \times h$

where
V = volume
l = length
w = width
h = height

RIGHT RECTANGULAR PRISM

$V = \frac{1}{6} \times \pi \times d^3$

where
V = volume
$\frac{1}{6}$ = constant
π = 3.1416
d = diameter

SPHERE

$V = \pi r^2 \times h$

where
V = volume
π = 3.1416
r = radius
h = height

CYLINDER

Sketching Isometric Drawings

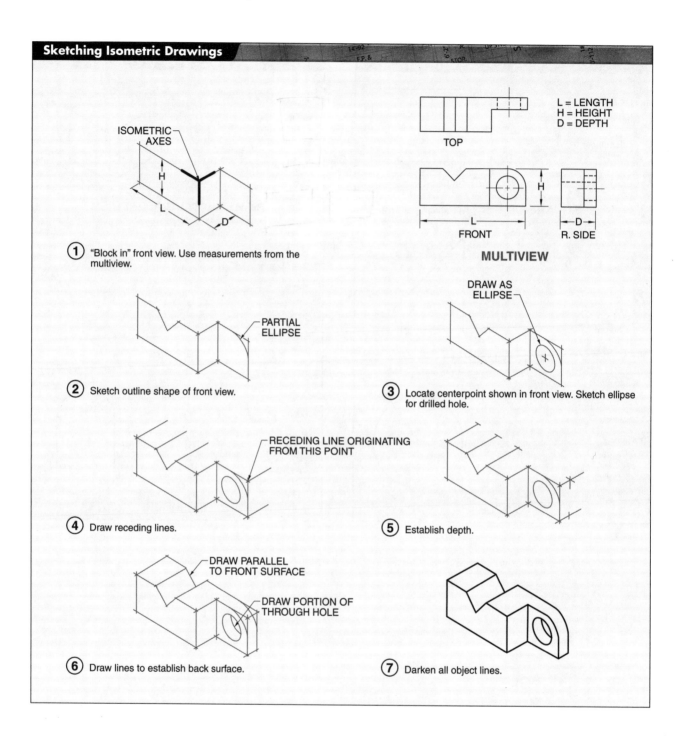

L = LENGTH
H = HEIGHT
D = DEPTH

TOP

FRONT

R. SIDE

MULTIVIEW

ISOMETRIC AXES

(1) "Block in" front view. Use measurements from the multiview.

PARTIAL ELLIPSE

(2) Sketch outline shape of front view.

DRAW AS ELLIPSE

(3) Locate centerpoint shown in front view. Sketch ellipse for drilled hole.

RECEDING LINE ORIGINATING FROM THIS POINT

(4) Draw receding lines.

(5) Establish depth.

DRAW PARALLEL TO FRONT SURFACE

DRAW PORTION OF THROUGH HOLE

(6) Draw lines to establish back surface.

(7) Darken all object lines.

Sketching Skewed Surfaces on Isometric Drawings

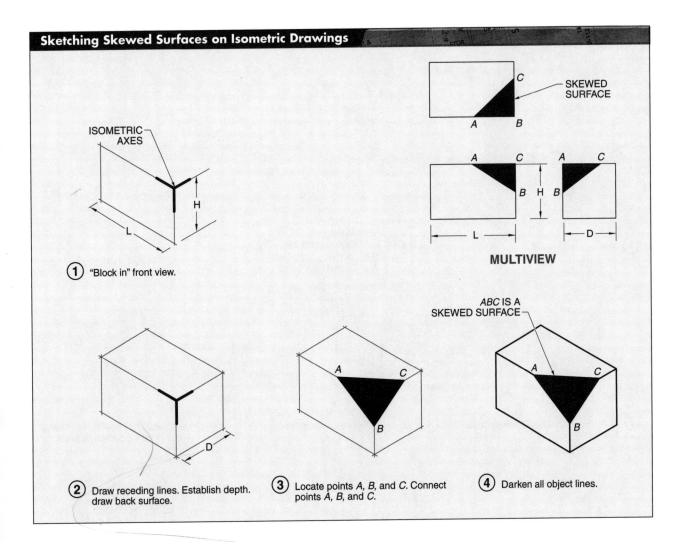

1. "Block in" front view.

2. Draw receding lines. Establish depth. draw back surface.

3. Locate points *A*, *B*, and *C*. Connect points *A*, *B*, and *C*.

4. Darken all object lines.

Sketching Isometric Circles

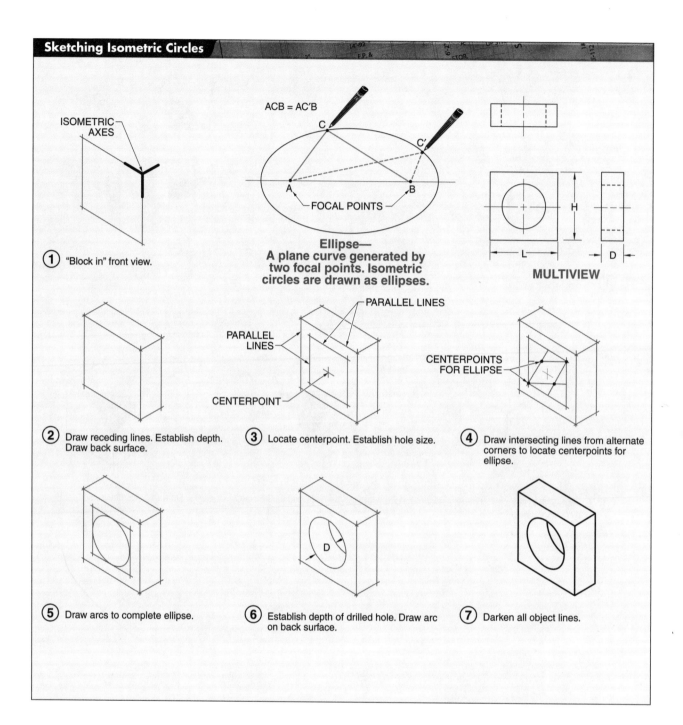

ACB = AC'B

FOCAL POINTS

Ellipse—
A plane curve generated by two focal points. Isometric circles are drawn as ellipses.

ISOMETRIC AXES

MULTIVIEW

H

L

D

(1) "Block in" front view.

(2) Draw receding lines. Establish depth. Draw back surface.

PARALLEL LINES

PARALLEL LINES

CENTERPOINT

(3) Locate centerpoint. Establish hole size.

CENTERPOINTS FOR ELLIPSE

(4) Draw intersecting lines from alternate corners to locate centerpoints for ellipse.

(5) Draw arcs to complete ellipse.

D

(6) Establish depth of drilled hole. Draw arc on back surface.

(7) Darken all object lines.

Sketching Prespective Drawings

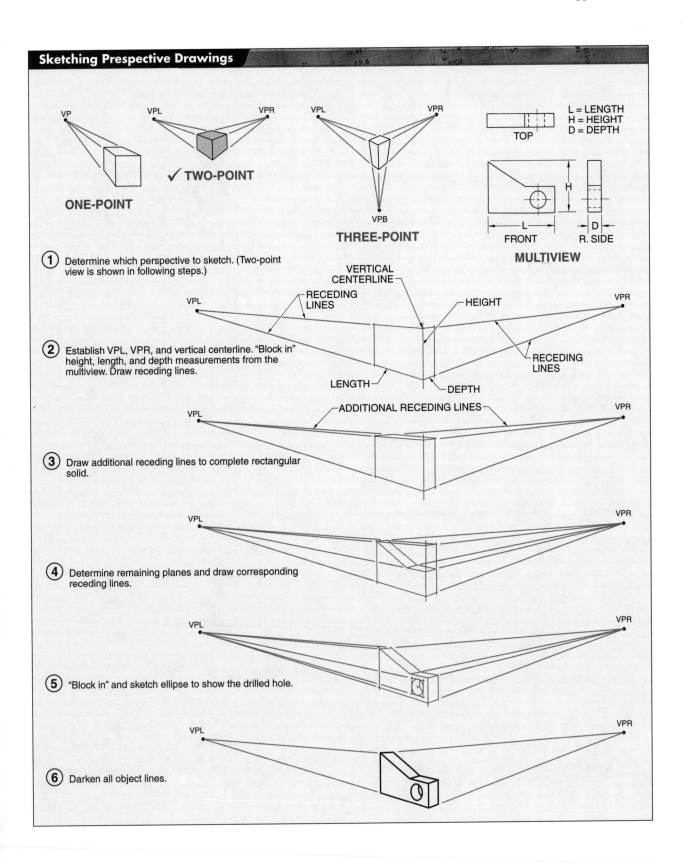

ONE-POINT

✓ **TWO-POINT**

THREE-POINT

MULTIVIEW

L = LENGTH
H = HEIGHT
D = DEPTH

TOP
FRONT
R. SIDE

① Determine which perspective to sketch. (Two-point view is shown in following steps.)

② Establish VPL, VPR, and vertical centerline. "Block in" height, length, and depth measurements from the multiview. Draw receding lines.

VERTICAL CENTERLINE
RECEDING LINES
HEIGHT
RECEDING LINES
LENGTH
DEPTH

③ Draw additional receding lines to complete rectangular solid.

ADDITIONAL RECEDING LINES

④ Determine remaining planes and draw corresponding receding lines.

⑤ "Block in" and sketch ellipse to show the drilled hole.

⑥ Darken all object lines.

Sketching Multiview Drawings

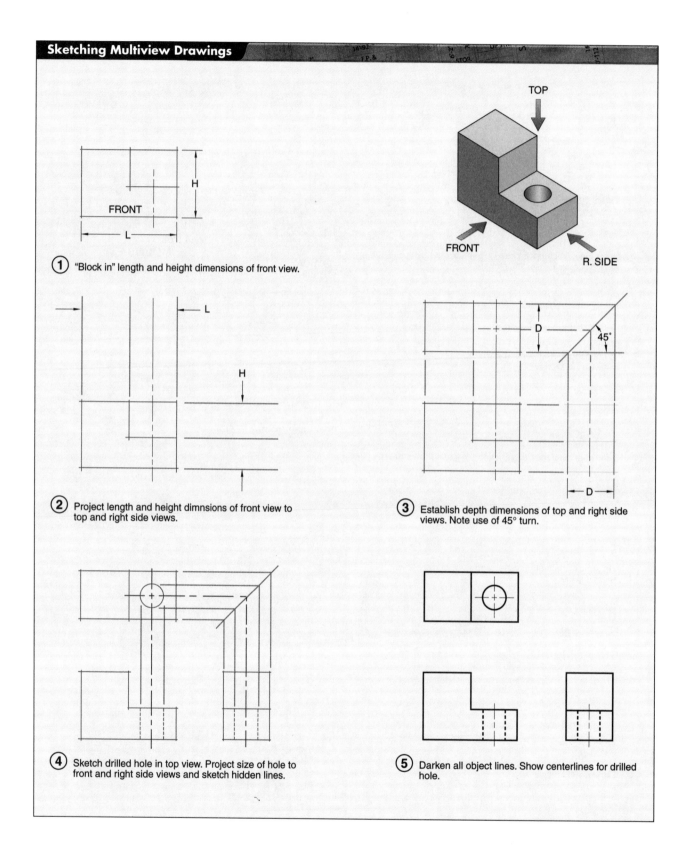

① "Block in" length and height dimensions of front view.

② Project length and height dimnsions of front view to top and right side views.

③ Establish depth dimensions of top and right side views. Note use of 45° turn.

④ Sketch drilled hole in top view. Project size of hole to front and right side views and sketch hidden lines.

⑤ Darken all object lines. Show centerlines for drilled hole.

abbreviation: Letter or series of letters denoting a complete word.

accelerator: Admixture that shortens the setting time and increases early strength of concrete.

acrylonitrile-butadiene-stryene (ABS) pipe and fittings: Black plastic pipe and fittings used for sanitary drainage and vent piping, and aboveground and underground stormwater drainage.

admixture: Substance other than water, aggregate, or cement added to concrete to modify its properties.

aggregate: Hard granular material, such as sand and gravel, that is mixed with cement and water to provide structure and strength in concrete.

air conditioner: Component in a forced-air air conditioning system that cools the air.

air diffuser: Air distribution outlet in a supply duct that is used to deflect and mix air.

air-entraining admixture: Admixture that provides greater resistance to freezing and high early strength properties.

annealed copper tube: Drawn copper tube that is heated to a specific temperature and cooled at a predetermined rate to impart the desired hardness and strength properties. Also called soft copper tube.

armored cable (AC): Assembly that contains one or more conductors wrapped in a flexible metallic covering.

ashlar: Stone cut to precise dimensions according to the prints.

awning window: Swinging-sash window that is hinged on the top rail of the sash with the lower rail swinging outward.

backflow preventer: Device used to protect the water supply from contaminated and undesirable substances entering the water supply system. Also called backflow prevention device.

balloon framing: A multistory framing method in which one-piece studs extend from the sill plate to the double top plate.

bearing partition: Interior partition capable of supporting heavy loads.

benchmark: Stable reference point marked with the elevation above mean sea level from which differences in elevation are measured. Also called datum point.

berm: Raised earth embankment.

boiler: Pressurized vessel that safely and efficiently transfers heat to water.

bond: Arrangement of masonry in a pattern to provide a desired architectural effect and/or additional structure.

box: Metallic or nonmetallic electrical enclosure for electrical equipment, devices, and pulling or terminating conductors.

box beam: Hollow horizontal member used for floor and roof supports or to span wide distances over openings.

brick: Individual rectangular unit made from clay or a clay mixture that is hardened by drying in a kiln.

brick veneer: Brick facing applied to the exterior wall surface of a frame structure or other type of structure.

cable assembly: Flexible assembly of two or more conductors with a protective outer sheathing. Also called cable.

carport: Covered shelter with one or more open sides.

cant strip: Triangular member, commonly wood, installed under the finish roofing material at the intersection of a parapet and roof.

casement window: Swinging-sash window with a vertically hinged sash that swings outward.

cathedral glass: Type of art glass available in a wide range of colors and with many surface treatments. Also called stained glass.

cavity wall: Masonry wall with at least a 2″ air space between adjacent faces.

cement: Mixture of shells, limestone, clay silica, marble, shale, sand, and other materials that are ground, blended, fused, and crushed to a powder.

change order: Formal, legal process authorizing any changes in location, layout, size, construction methods, or materials.

chase: Enclosure in a structure that allows for the placement of piping and wiring for plumbing, mechanical, and electrical systems.

chlorinated polyvinyl chloride (CPVC) pipe and fittings: Cream-colored thermoplastic materials specially formulated to withstand higher temperatures than other plastics.

circuit breaker: Overcurrent protection device with a mechanism that automatically opens a circuit when an overload condition or short circuit occurs.

clay facing tile: Masonry unit made of clay and fired (baked) in a kiln.

compressor: Mechanical device that compresses refrigerant.

concrete: Mixture of cement, fine and coarse aggregate, and water.

concrete masonry unit (CMU): Precast hollow or solid masonry unit composed of portland cement and fine aggregate and formed into modular or nonmodular dimensions.

condenser: Heat exchanger that removes heat from high-pressure refrigerant vapor.

conductor: Slender rod or wire that is used to control the flow of electrons in an electrical circuit.

contour line: Dashed or solid line on a plot plan that passes through points with the same elevation.

contraction joint: Groove made in a concrete surface to create a weakened plane and control the location of cracking.

corbel: Short projection from the face of a wall formed with successive courses of masonry to provide bearing space for the joists.

corner CMU: Concrete masonry unit used at square corners.

cross-linked polyethylene (PEX) tubing: Flexible thermosetting plastic used for water service piping and water distribution piping.

cul-de-sac: Street with only one outlet and a large circular area for turning around.

damper: Movable plate that controls and balances air flow in a forced-air system.

dead load: Weight of the permanent structure of a building and includes the materials that make up the wall, floor, ceiling, and roof units.

degree: Angular measurement equal to 1/360 of a circle.

detail: Scaled plan view, elevation, or section drawn at a larger scale to show special features.

door hand: Direction in which a door swings.

double-acting door: Door that swings in two directions.

double corner CMU: Concrete masonry unit used to make columns, piers, and pilasters.

double-hung window: Sliding-sash window in which the two sashes slide vertically past each other.

drain tile: Perforated pipe installed along the outer edge of foundation footings to collect stormwater and surface water and move it away from the foundation.

drawn copper tube: Copper tube that is manufactured by pulling copper through a die or series of dies to achieve a desired diameter. Also called hard copper tube.

ductwork: Distribution system for forced-air systems.

dwelling: One or more rooms for the use of one or more persons as a housekeeping unit with space for eating, living, and sleeping, and permanent provisions for cooking and sanitation.

electrical metallic tubing (EMT): Lightweight tubular steel raceway without threads on the ends. Also called thin wall or steel tube conduit.

elevation: Scaled view looking directly at a vertical surface.

engineering improvements: Changes to a site that include footings, foundations, basements, and other belowground work.

evaporator: Heat exchanger that absorbs heat from the surrounding air and adds the heat to low-pressure refrigerant liquid.

excavation: Any construction cut, cavity, trench, or depression in the surface of the earth formed by equipment to create engineering improvements.

expansion joint: Joint that separates sections of concrete to allow for movement caused by expansion and contraction of the concrete.

expansion valve: Device that reduces the pressure on liquid refrigerant by allowing the refrigerant to expand.

exterior insulation and finish system (EIFS): Exterior finish system consisting of exterior sheathing, insulation board, reinforcing mesh, a base coat of acrylic copolymers, and a finish of acrylic resins.

extreme fiber stress: Resistance to the shortening and lengthening of wood fibers when a wood member is placed in a position where it may bend under a load.

fireblock: Wood member nailed between studs, joists, or trusses to restrict air movement and reduce the spread of fire within walls.

fire door: Fire-resistant door and assembly, including the frame and hardware, commonly equipped with an automatic door closer.

fixed-sash window: Window in which the sash is inoperable.

fixture: Receptacle or device that is temporarily or permanently connected to a water distribution system, demands a supply of potable water, and discharges waste directly or indirectly into a sanitary drainage system.

flexible metal conduit (FMC): Raceway of metal strips that are formed into a circular cross-sectional raceway. Also called Greenfield.

float glass: Glass manufactured by floating liquid glass on a surface of liquid tin and slowly annealing it to produce a transparent, flat glass.

floor plan: Plan view of a building that shows the arrangement of walls and partitions as they appear in an imaginary horizontal section taken approximately 5'-0" above floor level.

flush door: Door with flat surfaces on each side; the stile and rails are concealed within the door.

foil, scrim, and kraft (FSK) insulation: Type of batt insulation that receives three facings to incorporate fireproofing characteristics, a reinforcing fabric, and a kraft paper face.

full-cut header: Special concrete masonry unit that is notched to receive the brick header course.

furnace: Self-contained heating unit that includes a blower, burner, and heat exchanger or electric heating elements, and controls.

fuse: Overcurrent protection device with a fusible link that melts and opens a circuit when an overload condition or short circuit occurs.

glass block: Hollow opaque or transparent block made of glass and used in non-load-bearing walls and partitions.

glued laminated timber (glulam): Engineered wood product comprised of layers of wood members (lams) that are joined together with adhesives to form larger members.

grading: Process of lowering high spots and filling in low spots of earth at a construction site.

gridding: Division of a plot plan for large areas to be excavated or graded into small squares or grids.

grille: Device that covers an opening of return ductwork.

grout: Fluid mortar mixture consisting of cement and water with or without aggregate.

gypsum: Soft mineral used as the core for gypsum board and gypsum lath, and may also be used as an ingredient in plaster.

gypsum lath: Gypsum product composed of an air-entrained gypsum core pressed between two sheets of absorbent paper.

haunch: Trim member installed at the termination of an arch.

header CMU: Concrete masonry unit with a portion of its shell removed to receive header courses of brick or stone to secure the wall together.

heat pump: Refrigeration system designed to carry heat to a transfer medium to provide cooling in the summer and to absorb heat for heating in the winter through a one-duct system.

high-pressure boiler: Boiler that has a maximum allowable working pressure above 15 pounds per square inch.

hollow-core door: Wood door with a core constructed of corrugated wood or fiber and covered with veneer plies.

hopper window: Swinging-sash window that is hinged along the bottom rail of the sash with the upper rail swinging inward.

horizontal shear: Resistance of wood fibers sliding past one another lengthwise when a wood member is placed in position where it may bend under a load.

horizontal sliding window: Sliding-sash window with sashes that slide horizontally past each other.

housewrap: Translucent spun-plastic sheet material that is tightly wrapped around a building to prevent water and air penetration into the building while allowing moisture vapor and gases from the building interior to move outward.

hydronic heating system: Heating system that uses water to convey heat from the source to the point of use.

indirect drain: Waste pipe that does not connect directly to the drainage system but conveys liquid waste by discharging it into a plumbing fixture, such as a floor drain or floor sink, that is directly connected to the drainage system.

in-line framing: Framing system in which all joists, studs, and roof rafters are in a direct vertical line with one another, allowing loads to be directly transferred to the foundation.

insulating concrete form: Specialized forming system that consists of a layer of concrete sandwiched between layers of insulating foam material on each side.

insulating glass: Window glass made of two pieces of sheet glass that are separated by a sealed air space.

insulation: Material used as a barrier to inhibit thermal and sound transmission.

isometric drawing: Drawing in which the three principal axes are 120° apart.

jamb CMU: Concrete masonry unit used with an extended ear to receive a window or door jamb.

Lally column: Steel post that is filled with concrete to provide additional support.

laminated glass: Specialty glass produced by placing a clear sheet of polyvinyl butyral (PVB) between two sheets of glass and subjecting the composite to intense heat and pressure.

latchset: Mechanical device used to hold a door shut when it is closed.

lintel: Horizontal structural member installed above a door or window and used to distribute the weight from the structure above to either side of the opening.

lintel CMU: Concrete masonry unit installed over openings to make bond beams.

live load: Moving or changing load that may be placed on different sections of a building.

location dimension: Dimension that locates a particular feature in relation to another feature.

lockset: Complete assembly of a bolt, knobs, escutcheon plates, and mechanical components for securing a door.

longitudinal section: Section created by passing a cutting plane through the long dimension of a building.

low-emittance (low-E) coating: Metal or metallic oxide coating that reduces the passage of heat and ultraviolet rays through windows.

low-pressure boiler: Boiler that has a maximum allowable working pressure of 15 pounds per square inch.

lumen: Measure of illumination.

luminaire (lighting fixture): Complete lighting unit including the components that distribute light, position and protect the lamps, and provide connection to the power supply.

MasterFormat™: Uniform system of numbers and titles for organizing information about construction requirements, products, and activities into a standard sequence.

match line: Aligning mark on a print that is used when a drawing is too large to be contained on one sheet.

metal-clad cable (MC): Assembly of one or more conductors, with or without fiber-optic members, and enclosed in an armor of interlocking metal sheath, or smooth or corrugated metal sheath.

metal sash CMU: Concrete masonry unit used to receive a metal window unit.

minute: Angular measurement equal to 1/60 of a degree.

modular brick: Brick in which the nominal dimensions are based on a 4″ unit.

modulus of elasticity: Relationship of unit stress to unit elongation.

mullion: Vertical member of the frame between the sashes.

nominal size: Dimensions of a piece of lumber before it is dried and surfaced.

nonmetallic-sheathed cable: Assembly of two or more insulated conductors with an outer sheathing of moisture-resistant, flame-retardant, nonmetallic material.

nonmodular brick: Brick in which the actual dimensions are used to express the size.

open web steel joist: Structural steel member constructed with steel angles and bars that are used as chords with steel angles or bars extending between the chords at an angle.

oriented strand board (OSB): Wood panel in which wood strands are mechanically oriented in particular directions and bonded with resin under heat and pressure.

orthographic projection: Drawing in which all the faces of an object are projected onto flat planes, generally at 90° to one another.

panelboard: Wall-mounted distribution cabinet containing overcurrent and short-circuit protection devices.

panel door: Door with individual panels between the stiles and rails.

parallel strand lumber (PSL): Engineered wood product manufactured from wood strands or flakes and waterproof adhesives and cured under intense heat and pressure.

parapet: Low protective wall at the edge of a balcony or roof.

parging: Thin coat of mortar on a vertical masonry surface that is used to provide additional waterproofing.

partition CMU: Concrete masonry unit used as a masonry backing or to form partitions.

patterned glass: Glass that has one side finished with a fine grid or an unpolished surface so the glass is translucent.

performance rated panel: Structural plywood panel that conforms to performance-based standards for dimensional stability, bond durability, and structural integrity.

perlite: Volcanic siliceous rock, crushed and heated at a high temperature, which expands it into lightweight glassy particles.

perspective drawing: Pictorial drawing showing an object as it appears when viewed from a given point.

platform framing: Framing method in which each story of a building is framed as a unit consisting of walls, joists, and a subfloor. Also called western framing.

plot plan: Scaled working drawing that shows the shape and size of a building.

plywood: Panel product made of plies (wood layers) that are glued and pressed together under intense heat and pressure.

point of beginning (POB): Fixed location on a building site used as a reference point for horizontal dimensions and vertical dimensions.

polyvinyl chloride (PVC) pipe and fittings: Plastic pipe and fittings used for sanitary drainage and vent piping, aboveground and underground stormwater drainage, water mains, and water service lines.

post-and-beam framing: Framing method in which the basic framework of the building consists of vertical posts and horizontal or sloping beams.

potable water: Water that is free from impurities that could cause disease or harmful physiological effects.

prehung door: Wood or metal door which is hung in the frame with hardware installed.

quirk mitre: Type of joint used at the outside corners of adjoining members in which the acute miter corners of adjoining members are trimmed flat at the ends to provide relief for the joint and prevent the ends from splitting.

raceway: Enclosed channel for conductors.

radiator: Type of terminal device used in a hydronic heating system.

range: Course of any thickness that extends across the face of a wall, but not all courses need to be the same thickness.

rebar: Steel reinforcing bar with deformations on the surface to allow the bar to interlock with concrete.

receptacle: Contact device installed at an outlet for the connection of equipment to an electrical system.

register: Device that covers the opening of air supply ductwork.

retarder: Admixture that delays the setting and hardening of concrete.

rigid metal conduit (RMC): Heavy conduit made of metal.

rigid nonmetallic conduit (RNMC): Conduit made of materials other than metal.

rubble: Rough, irregular stone that is used as fill or to provide a rustic appearance.

R value: Value that represents the ability of a material to resist heat flow.

scale: Relative size to which an object is drawn.

schedule: Detailed list on a print that provides information about building components such as windows, doors, and mechanical equipment.

SCR brick: Solid masonry unit with nominal dimensions of 6″ × 2⅔″ × 12″.

scupper: Opening in a wall that allows rainwater to drain into a downspout and stormwater drainage system.

second: Angular measurement equal to $\frac{1}{60}$ of a minute.

section: Scaled view created by passing a cutting plane either horizontally or vertically through a portion of a building.

service-entrance cable: Single- or multi-conductor assembly, with or without an overall jacket.

sheet glass: Glass manufactured by drawing it vertically or horizontally and slowly annealing (cooling) it to produce a high-gloss surface.

size dimension: Dimension that indicates the size of a particular feature or area.

sliding-sash window: Window in which the sashes slide vertically or horizontally past one another.

snap tie: Patented tie system with spreader cones to maintain form wall spacing and tie the walls together when concrete is placed.

solid-core door: Wood door with a core constructed of solid wood blocks or particleboard glued together and covered with veneer plies.

solid top CMU: Concrete masonry unit used to finish the top of a wall and provide a flat bearing surface for wood framing members or brick or stone masonry.

square: Unit of measure equal to 100 square feet.

squared stone: Rough stone made approximately square either at a quarry or at the job site.

stair ratio: Relationship between riser height (R) and tread width (T) in a stairway.

steel angle: Structural steel member with an L-shaped cross section with equal- or unequal-width legs.

steel reinforcement: Steel wire, bars, or strands embedded in concrete to provide additional tensile strength to concrete structural members.

stressed-skin panel: Structural unit used in floor, wall, and ceiling systems that consists of plywood panels nailed and glued to a wood frame.

stretcher CMU: Concrete masonry unit used for running walls.

structural facing tile: Clay masonry unit with one face colored and glazed; used for load-bearing applications.

structural insulated panel (SIP): Structural member consisting of a thick layer of rigid foam insulation pressed between two OSB or plywood panels.

superplasticizer: Admixture that significantly reduces the amount of water required in a concrete mixture and increases the workability of the concrete.

swinging-sash window: Window in which the sashes pivot to provide ventilation.

switch: Device with a current and voltage rating; used to open or close an electrical circuit.

symbol: Pictorial representation of a structural or material component used on a print.

takeoff: Practice of reviewing contract documents, including the prints and specifications, to determine quantities of material to be included in a bid.

tempered glass: Glass produced by heating a sheet of glass during the manufacturing process to near its softening point and then quickly cooling the glass under carefully controlled conditions.

terminal device: Device that transfers heat or coolness from the water in a piping system to the air in the living space.

terra cotta: Masonry building material produced by firing molded units of clay in a kiln.

terrazzo: Mixture of cement and water with colored stone, marble chips, or other decorative aggregate embedded in the surface.

throat: Opening at the top of a fire chamber extending into the smoke chamber where the damper is located.

total rise: In a stairway, the vertical distance from the surface of the lower floor to the surface of the floor above.

total run: In a stairway, the horizontal distance from the face of the bottom riser to the face of the top riser.

transverse section: Section created by passing a cutting plane through the short dimension of a building.

tray ceiling : Horizontal ceiling with angled sides around the perimeter so as to resemble an inverted tray.

underslung joist: Joist that is supported by its top chord.

underslung truss: Roof or floor truss that is supported by the top chord of the truss.

unit rise: Vertical distance from the top of one tread to the top of an adjoining tread in a stairway.

unit run: Width of the stair tread not including the nosing.

vapor barrier: Thin, moisture-resistant material placed over the ground or in walls to retard the passage of moisture into a building.

waler: Horizontal member used to align and reinforce concrete formwork.

welded wire reinforcement (WWR): Heavy-gauge wire joined in a grid and used to reinforce and increase the tensile strength of concrete.

wide-flange beam: Structural steel member with parallel flanges that are joined with a perpendicular web.

wire glass: Glass embedded with wire mesh to provide additional security.

wood I-joist: Load-bearing structural member that consists of an OSB or plywood web between two pieces of dimensional lumber, forming an I.

wythe: A single continuous vertical masonry wall that is one unit thick.

zero line: Line connecting points on a topographical map where existing and planned elevations are equal.

USING THE PRINTREADING FOR RESIDENTIAL AND LIGHT COMMERCIAL CONSTRUCTION— PART 2 CD-ROM

Before removing the CD-ROM, please note that the book cannot be returned for refund or credit if the CD-ROM sleeve seal is broken.

System Requirements

The *Printreading for Residential and Light Commercial Construction—Part 2* CD-ROM is designed to work best on a computer meeting the following hardware requirements:

- Intel® Pentium® processor
- Microsoft® Windows® 95, 98, 98 SE, Me, NT®, 2000, or XP® operating system
- 64 MB of free available system RAM (128 MB recommended)

- 90 MB of available disk space
- 800 × 600 16-bit (thousands of colors) color display or better
- Sound output capability and speakers
- CD-ROM drive

Adobe® Acrobat® Reader™ software is required for opening many resources provided on the CD-ROM. If necessary, Adobe® Acrobat® Reader™ can be installed from the CD-ROM. Microsoft® Windows® 2000, NT®, or XP™ users who are connected to a server-based network may be required to log on with administrative privileges to allow installation of this application. See your Information Systems group for further information. Additional information is available from the Adobe web site at www.adobe.com. The Internet links require Microsoft® Internet Explorer™ 3.0 or Netscape® 3.0 or later browser software and an Internet connection.

Opening Files

Insert the CD-ROM into the computer CD-ROM drive. Within a few seconds, the start screen will be displayed. Click on START to open the home screen. Information about the usage of the CD-ROM can be accessed by clicking on USING THIS CD-ROM. The Chapter Quick Quizzes™, Illustrated Glossary, Wendy's Restaurant, Printreading Tests, Master Math™ Problems, Media Clips, and Reference Material can be accessed by clicking on the appropriate button on the home screen. Clicking on the American Tech web site button (www.go2atp.com) or the American Tech logo accesses information on related educational products. Unauthorized reproduction of the material on this CD-ROM is strictly prohibited.

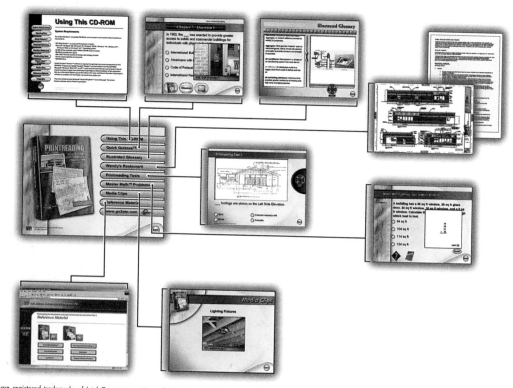